Including Students with Special Needs

A PRACTICAL GUIDE FOR CLASSROOM TEACHERS

Second Edition

Marilyn Friend
Indiana University–Purdue University
at Indianapolis

William D. Bursuck
Northern Illinois University

Allyn and Bacon
Boston • London • Toronto • Sydney • Tokyo • Singapore

Senior Editor: Ray Short
Senior Developmental Editor: Linda Bieze
Editorial Assistant: Karin Huang
Marketing Manager: Brad Parkins
Director of Education Programs: Ellen Mann-Dolberg
Editorial-Production Administrator: Donna Simons
Editorial-Production Service: Omegatype Typography, Inc.
Composition and Prepress Buyer: Linda Cox
Manufacturing Buyer: Megan Cochran
Cover Administrator: Linda Knowles
Cover Designer: Susan Paradise
Interior Designer: Carol Somberg/Omegatype Typography, Inc.
Illustrations: Omegatype Typography, Inc.
Electronic Composition: Omegatype Typography, Inc.

TO OUR FAMILIES

Mary Ellen Penovich
Bruce and Howard Brandon
Marian and Samuel Bursuck
Beth, Emily, and Daniel Bursuck

Between the time Website information is gathered and then published, it is not
unusual for some sites to have closed. Also, the transcription of URLs can result in
unintended typographical errors. The publisher would appreciate notification where
these occur so that they may be corrected in subsequent editions.

Library of Congress Cataloging-in-Publication Data

Friend, Marilyn Penovich
    Including students with special needs : a practical guide for
classroom teachers / Marilyn Friend, William D. Bursuck. — 2nd ed.
        p.   cm.
    Includes bibliographical references (p.   ) and index.
    ISBN 0-205-28085-4
    1. Inclusive education—United States.   2. Mainstreaming in
education—United States.   3. Special education—United States.
4. Handicapped children—Education—United States.   I. Bursuck,
William D.   II. Brandon, Marilyn Penovich Friend.   III. Title.
LC1201.F75   1999
371.9'046—dc21   97-51505
                                                      CIP

Text and photo credits appear on page 522, which constitutes an extension of the copyright page.

Printed in the United States of America
10 9 8 7 6 5 4 3 2 1   RRDW   03 02 01 00 99 98

Contents

chapter **4**   Analyzing Classroom and Student Needs   **106**

chapter 5

Students with Low-Incidence Disabilities 146

chapter 6

Students with High-Incidence Disabilities 186

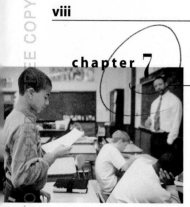

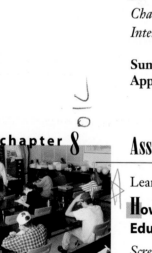

chapter 9

Instructional Adaptations   294

chapter **10** | ## Strategies for Independent Learning | **338**

chapter 11

Evaluating Student Learning

376

chapter 12

Responding to Student Behavior

414

chapter **13**

Approaches for Building Social Relationships   450

Features

Case in Practice

Professional Edge

Technology Notes

Preface

Over the past several years, the trend toward educating students with special needs in inclusive settings has, if anything, accelerated. Many students who might a decade ago have spent some, most, or all of their school days working in separate settings with special education teachers and other specialists now receive much or all of their instruction in general education classrooms. As a result, general education teachers need more than ever before to understand the nature of special education, the characteristics of students with special needs, strategies to work effectively with diverse student needs, and techniques for forming partnerships with special educators and parents.

The second edition of *Including Students with Special Needs: A Practical Guide for Classroom Teachers* reflects our continued strong commitment to inclusive practices. These practices are based on substantive administrative backing, support for general education teachers, and an understanding that sometimes, for a few students, not all needs can be met in a single physical location. We have brought to the project our own backgrounds as teachers in the field and as teacher educators. We also bring our own diversity: Marilyn with expertise in elementary education, especially in urban settings, and in collaboration; Bill with expertise in secondary education, especially in suburban and rural settings, and in instructional strategies.

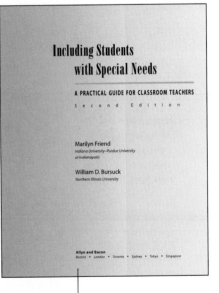

The areas of emphasis and organization of this book are a reflection of our beliefs about the most effective way to teach the often required "mainstreaming" course. This book is based on our experiences in teaching preservice and inservice general education teachers and our conversations with our colleagues across the country about the issues facing special education, as well as on the need to prepare classroom teachers for their roles in educating students with disabilities. Our efforts have also been heavily influenced by our observations, research, and professional development activities with practicing teachers who face the difficult task of being teachers during a time of ongoing reforms, increased expectations, and a widening range of student needs. We hope that the results of all our discussions, our interactions with others, and our individual struggles to "get it right" have resulted in a book that is reader friendly yet informative and responsive to the wide range of issues confronting teachers as they attempt to help all their students succeed.

Organization of the Book

The textbook is divided into three main sections. The **first section** provides fundamental background knowledge of the field of special education as well as current information on how students with disabilities are served within inclusive school environments. Chapter 1 presents a brief history of services to students with disabilities, culminating in the description of key federal legislation that provides the legal basis for serving students with disabilities in public schools. Information on the most recent federal special education legislation—the Individuals with Disabilities Education Act 1997—is included in this chapter.

Chapter 2 introduces the people who specialize in working with students with disabilities. Readers will learn about their role in working with other professionals and parents to determine student eligibility for special education, carrying out educational programs, and monitoring learning. As schools have moved toward creating more inclusive classroom arrangements, the working relationships among all the adults involved in the education of students with disabilities have become very important. In Chapter 3, the principles of collaboration and the school situations in which professionals are most likely to collaborate to meet the needs of students with disabilities are discussed. The special partnerships that are formed when teachers work with paraprofessionals and parents are also considered.

In the **second section** of the book, a framework for thinking about instructional accommodations is provided as an introduction for considering the characteristics of students with disabilities and other special needs. Chapter 4 introduces a step-by-step strategy for adapting instruction, called INCLUDE, that will help teachers accommodate students with special needs more effectively. This chapter also addresses the dimensions along which accommodations might occur. Chapters 5, 6, and 7 address student characteristics and needs. Although the various federal categories of exceptionality are addressed, the approach taken in the text is noncategorical; the emphasis is on major physical, psychological, learning, and behavior characteristics and the implications of these characteristics for instruction. In Chapter 5, readers will learn about the characteristics and educational needs of students with low-incidence disabilities, that is, moderate, severe, or multiple disabilities; sensory impairments; physical or health disabilities; and autism. Chapter 6 describes the characteristics and needs of students with high-incidence disabilities, that is, learning disabilities, speech or language disabilities, emotional disturbance, and mild cognitive disabilities. In Chapter 7, readers will be introduced to students who are not necessarily eligible for special education but who have special needs and often benefit from strategies similar to the ones that assist students with disabilities. The students addressed in this chapter include those protected by Section 504, including those with attention-deficit/hyperactivity disorder; those who are gifted and talented; those whose native language is not English and whose cultures are significantly different from those of most of their classmates; and students who are at risk because of special situations, including poverty, child abuse, and drug abuse.

The material in the **third section** of the text represents the crux of any course on inclusive practices: instructional approaches that emphasize teaching students effectively, regardless of disability or special need. Chapter 8 explores both formal and in-

Increased emphasis on working with parents and multicultural issues is reflected in new book features.

How Can You Work Effectively with Parents? | 97

Professional Edge

Working with Parents from Diverse Cultural Backgrounds

Parents from diverse racial and cultural groups often are less involved in their children's education than parents of children from majority-groups. Sometimes, this occurs because they are unfamiliar or uncomfortable with public school practices. For some long-term solutions to facilitating parent involvement, the school can provide the following:

1. Parent education programs that improve parents' formal education (e.g., English as a Second Language, basic reading, mathematics, reasoning skills) to
   - Increase parents' self-esteem and self-confidence
   - Facilitate positive interactions with school professionals
   - Broaden employment opportunities
   - Facilitate parent feelings of "being at home" in educational settings

2. Parent education programs to increase parents' influence on their children's education to
   - Ensure that schools are responsive to school and community values
   - Give parents the opportunity to participate in the school's decision-making process
   - Assure that educators observe and participate in community activities; listen to parents' wants, hopes, and concerns to develop mutual understanding; and encourage parents to define desired change and to develop an action plan.

3. Awareness training programs that provide opportunities for role playing and simulation to
   - Increase parent confidence levels for interacting with school personnel
   - Facilitate parents' understanding of and shared responsibility for children's education (e.g., training in the IEP process and for advocacy roles)
   - Teach new behaviors and skills needed to interact as educational team members (e.g., problem-solving, critical thinking, and communication skills such as active listening and self-disclosure)
   - Empower parents and extend leadership abilities in the educational community (e.g., school-community-based management, curriculum development committee).

4. Opportunities for parents to train and work as paraeducators in bilingual and bicultural programs to
   - Include language and customs as part of the curriculum
   - Learn instructional strategies that can be used to benefit their own children at home
   - Increase the likelihood that parents will choose to further their education.

SOURCE: From Sileo, T. W., Sileo, A. P., & Prater, M. A. (1996). "Parent and professional partnerships in special education: Multicultural considerations." *Intervention in School and Clinic, 31*, 145–153.

tors. For example, low-income Puerto Rican parents have been found to think of disability in terms of family identity and the school's failure to provide for the student, not as an inherent student problem (Harry, 1992a). African American parents sometimes distrust school professionals and the decisions made about their children because of past segregation and discriminatory special education practices (Harry,

formal assessment strategies that will help teachers contribute to the decision-making process for students with disabilities. Chapter 9 provides strategies for adapting curriculum materials, teacher instruction, and student practice activities for both basic-skills and content-area instruction. The emphasis is on adaptations that are relatively easy to make and that may also be helpful for students not identified as disabled. Chapter 10 focuses on ways to help students with and without special needs become more independent learners. Specific strategies are described, such as encouraging student self-awareness and self-advocacy skills, developing and teaching learning strategies directly in class, and instructing students on how to use these strategies on their own.

One of a teacher's major jobs is to evaluate students' educational progress, through traditional grading and testing as well as through performance-based assessments and portfolios. Teachers may need to adapt all of these evaluation practices for students with special needs. Chapter 11 provides effective options for adapting classroom evaluations to ensure that accurate information is gathered that is helpful in guiding instruction. In Chapter 12, readers will learn procedures for group behavior management, strategies for responding to individual student behaviors, and a problem-solving approach for changing student behavior. Together, these techniques will provide teachers with a foundation for effective classroom management that can positively influence the learning of students with and without disabilities. Finally, inclusive practices are most effective when students with special needs are carefully integrated into the classroom, both academically and socially. Chapter 13 explores several effective approaches for building positive relations among students with and without special needs, including cooperative learning, peer tutoring, and social-skills training.

Each chapter contains the URLs of websites that enable students to access relevant information.

Features in the Book

Many of the features from the first edition have been retained and enhanced in the second edition. These features have been designed to help readers learn more effectively:

- *Vignettes* that serve as introductory cases help readers think about how the content of chapters relates to teachers and students.
- *Key terms* throughout the text are clarified through the use of boldface type and easy-to-understand definitions provided both in context and in a glossary at the back of the book.
- *Chapter summaries* highlight key information covered in the chapter.
- *Application activities* at the end of each chapter are designed to encourage students to apply text content to real-life classroom situations.
- *Marginal annotations* are designed to stimulate higher-level thinking.
- *Case in Practice* features clarify key course principles by providing brief case studies of course content in action and teaching scripts as models.
- *Professional Edge* features provide many practical teaching ideas.
- *Technology Notes* features show the impact of the current technology explosion on key aspects of special and general education programming.

New Features of the Second Edition

Within these features students will find even more up-to-date information. For example, the book now includes information students can use to access information on the Internet. Every chapter includes, in its marginal annotations, the URLs of one or more websites containing information relevant to the chapter's focus. In addition, the Technology Notes have been updated to reflect the rapidly expanding options for using technology to address students' needs. Multicultural issues are addressed even more comprehensively, in marginal annotations, in Technology Notes, and in Case in Practice segments. Emphasis is placed on understanding others' perspectives, respecting those perspectives, and working with families in partnership to create instructional success for pupils.

Overall, we have worked to improve the book by keeping some of its components and refining others. Most notably, we have consolidated presentation of the INCLUDE strategy and methods for implementing accommodations in a new Chapter 4, "Analyzing Classroom and Student Needs." In addition, the book still offers many opportunities for application and practice, but it also stresses even more than before the crucial role that parents play in their children's education and emphasizes the increasingly multicultural world in which we live. The book's "user friendliness" has been enhanced by reducing the amount of information in the margins and adding questions to the end-of-chapter application exercises.

Each chapter ends with Applications in Teaching Practice, a feature designed to help students use their new knowledge and skills in realistic situations. Questions guide student understanding and encourage additional insights.

Supplements

This book comes with a rich supplement package for instructors, including an Instructor's Resource Manual and an Inclusion Video.

For each chapter, the updated Instructor's Resource Manual contains an overview, outline, activities, discussion questions, transparency masters, handout masters, and test items. The updated test item file, which is also available in computerized format for IBM and Macintosh, includes multiple choice, true-false, and case-based application items. Answer feedback and guidelines are provided.

The 23-minute Inclusion Video follows three students with special needs who are included in general education classrooms at the elementary, middle, and high school levels. In each case, parents, classroom teachers, special education teachers, and school administrators talk about the steps they have taken to help Josh, Eric, and Tonya succeed in inclusive settings.

Acknowledgments

A project as complex as writing a textbook can be completed successfully only with the help, encouragement, and wisdom of many, many people. First and most important, we would like to express our gratitude to our families. They have listened to us agonize about how to frame a particular topic and speak endlessly about the ins and outs of special education and general education teachers working with students with disabilities, and they have served many times as sounding boards for our thoughts and our struggles with both content and format. They have also patiently endured our need to disappear for long hours as we pursued the writing muse. This book would not exist without their support.

We would also like to thank the individuals who helped us with all the details that are part and parcel to writing a textbook. Deb Holderness gave us consistently high-quality work and displayed infinite patience in typing and formatting the many drafts of this manuscript. Marge Barrick took on the daunting responsibility of helping us obtain permission to reproduce various tables and figures found throughout the book.

The professionals at Allyn and Bacon have also supported this effort with both words and actions. Ray Short continues to provide support, guidance, and commitment to this textbook that has helped us now for several years. Linda Bieze, serving as our developmental editor, combined a careful reading of the second edition manuscript with clear and insightful suggestions for change; the book has matured significantly with her guidance.

We would also like to acknowledge the careful and insightful comments and feedback provided by our reviewers: Mary Banbury, University of New Orleans; Joanne Berryman, University of Kentucky; Sandra Cohen, University of Virginia; Harry Dangel, Georgia State University; Patricia Edwards, The University of Akron; Jean C. Faieta, Edinboro University of Pennsylvania; Pamela Fernstrom, University of North Alabama; Deborah Peters Goessling, University of Maine at Orono; Raymond Glass, University of Maine at Farmington; James A. Jacobs, Indiana State University–Terre Haute; Julie Jochum, Bemidji State University; Marie C. Keel, Georgia State University; Susan Klein, Indiana University–Bloomington; Earle Knowlton, University of Kansas; Elizabeth B. Kozleski, University of Colorado at Denver; Suzanne Lamorey, University of Missouri; Robert Lauson, Idaho State University; Barbara Mallette, SUNY Freedonia; James K. McAfee, Pennsylvania State University; Catherine McCartney, Bemidji State University; Thomas Mihail, Purdue University; Mark P. Mostert, Moorhead State University; Robert Reid, University of Nebraska; Diane Rivera, University of Texas; Sam Rust, Seattle University; Sandra K. Squires, University of Nebraska–Omaha; Kate Steffans, Bemidji State University; Carol Chase Thomas, University of North Carolina–Wilmington; Ellen Williams, Western Kentucky University. They sometimes gave us "ah-ha" experiences, sometimes annoyed us, but always helped us create a better text.

Finally, we continue to be grateful to all of our colleagues and students who influence our thinking about educating students with special needs in general education classrooms. Their comments on the first edition, their questions about best practices, their challenges to our thinking, and their suggestions on better communicating our message have been invaluable. We appreciate their input and hope they see themselves and their ideas accurately reflected in this edition.

chapter 1

The Foundation for Educating Students with Special Needs

Aaron has a learning disability that was identified when he was in second grade. Now in fifth grade, Aaron continues to learn how to compensate for the academic difficulties he experiences. Although he is a bright and personable young man, he reads at about a second-grade level and struggles to transfer his thoughts and ideas into written form. He doesn't like to talk about his learning disabilities (LD); he doesn't want other students to make fun of him or treat him differently because he's "LD." In his social studies class, he is most successful when his tests are read aloud; he understan the concepts even if he sometimes cannot read the test iter Since he doesn't like to be singled out, however, he sometimes refuses test-reading assistance. Aaron is an excellent soccer player, and on the field he feels equal to his friends; but his parents are concerned that his interest in sports is distracting him from his schoolwork. They are considering whether he should continue playing on the team. How like are you to teach a student like Aaron? What is a learning ability? What other disabilities might your students have?

Nicki is 17 years old and a junior in high school. She has a serious emotional disability that often manifests itself through aggressive, acting-out behavior. Last year, Nicki broke her wrist when she punched a wall after being reprimanded for using foul language. Nicki was hospitalized for 4 weeks earlier this semester after she assaulted a classmate. The hospital stay was for the purpose of helping her to understand her emotions and to learn to express them without hurting herself or others. Although Nicki is very intelligent, her grades in most classes are nearly failing. Why is Nicki considered disabled? What assistance does her school need to provide for her?

Ch. 1

The Foundation for Educating Students with Special Needs

From: Including students with special needs: A practical guide for classroom teachers. 1999 by Friend & Bursuck - Allyn & Bacon

Students like Aaron and Nicki are not unusual. They are among the nearly 5.5 million students in the United States who have disabilities that make them eligible for special education (U.S. Department of Education, 1996). But their disabilities do not tell you who they are: They are children or young adults and students first. Like all students, they have positive characteristics and negative ones, they have great days and some that are not so great, and they have likes and dislikes about school and learning.

As a teacher, you will probably instruct students like Aaron and Nicki along with other students with disabilities or other special needs. The purpose of this book is to help you understand students with disabilities and other special needs and to learn strategies for addressing those needs. You might be the teacher who can make a profound positive difference in a student's life. With the knowledge and skills you learn for teaching exceptional learners, you will be prepared for both the challenges and rewards of helping students with special needs achieve their potential.

What Basic Terms and Concepts Define Special Education?

Check Your Learning

What kinds of school services do students with disabilities receive?

When educators talk about students who need extra assistance, they may use several key terms. For example, when teachers refer to students with **disabilities,** they mean students who are eligible according to federal and state guidelines to receive special education services. **Special education** is the specially designed instruction provided by the school district or other local education agency that meets the unique needs of students identified as disabled. Special education may include instruction in a general education or special education classroom, education in the community for students who need life skills, and specialized assistance in physical education, speech/language, or vocational preparation. In addition, students with disabilities may receive **related services,** that is, assistance required to enable a student to benefit from special education. Examples of related services include transportation to and from school in a specialized van or school bus and physical therapy. All special education and related services are provided to students by public schools at no cost to parents.

Least Restrictive Environment

The basis for educating students with disabilities in classrooms comes from the concept of the **least restrictive environment (LRE),** a provision in the federal laws that have governed special education for more than the past two decades. LRE is a student's right to be educated in the setting most like the educational setting for nondisabled peers in which the student can be successful, with appropriate supports provided (D'Alonzo, Giordano, & Cross, 1995; McNulty, Connolly, Wilson, & Brewer, 1996). For many students, the least restrictive environment is a general education classroom. For example, when you met Aaron at the beginning of this chapter, you learned that he succeeds in his social studies class when tests are read aloud. His LRE is a general education classroom; the testing procedure is an appropriate support. In 1993–1994, approximately 43.4 percent of all students with disabilities received their education in general education classrooms (U.S. Department of Education, 1996).

For a student like Nicki, being in a general education classroom all day may be too academically and emotionally stressful. Nicki's LRE may be a general education classroom for most or part of the day and a special education classroom, sometimes called a resource room, for the remainder of the day. Appropriate supports for Nicki might include a highly structured behavior management plan implemented by all her teachers. Identifying an LRE other than a general education setting is a serious decision made only after intensive supports are provided in the general education classroom. Such supports can include alternative materials or curriculum, assistance from a paraprofessional or special education teacher, adaptive equipment such as a computer, or consultative assistance from a psychologist or counselor. During 1993–1994, approximately 29.5 percent of all students with disabilities were educated in combination general education and resource room placements (U.S. Department of Education, 1996).

For a few students, a general education classroom may not be the least restrictive setting. For example, a student with multiple disabilities who requires intensive medical care may receive education in a hospital setting. This setting clearly is very restrictive and used only in extraordinary circumstances. Two other settings that might be the least restrictive for some students are a separate special education classroom in an elementary or secondary school and a special school attended only by students with disabilities. A student with severe emotional problems who is clearly a danger to self or others might be educated in one of these settings. A total of 22.7 percent of students with disabilities received their education in separate classes during 1993–1994; 4.4 percent of students were educated in separate schools, home or hospital settings, or residential settings (U.S. Department of Education, 1996).

Mainstreaming

When the LRE concept became part of special education laws during the 1970s, the LRE for most students with disabilities was a part-time or full-time special education class. When such students were permitted to participate in general education, it was called mainstreaming. **Mainstreaming** is the term for placing students with disabilities in general education settings only when they can meet traditional academic expectations with minimal assistance, or when those expectations are not relevant (for example, participation in recess or school assemblies in order to have opportunities for social interactions). Originally, many authors' definitions of mainstreaming (for example, Corman & Gottlieb, 1978; Kaufman, Gottlieb, Agard, & Kukic, 1975) emphasized the importance of involving students with disabilities meaningfully in classroom activities. However, the implementation of mainstreaming now varies widely from place to place. In some schools, students are considered mainstreamed if they participate only in lunch and physical education with other students. In other schools, students are considered mainstreamed if they receive special education assistance for as little as 30 minutes a day. In both cases, placement depends on the kinds, amount, and intensity of special education services students need, and there is an assumption that special services can best be offered in a special class.

Inclusion

In recent years, many educators have seriously questioned the assumption that students who need more intensive services must receive them in a restrictive setting

Connections

Making decisions about placing students in special education programs is discussed in Chapter 2.

FYI

You might hear the phrase *Regular Education Initiative (REI)*. Popularized by Madeline Will, former Assistant Secretary of Education, the phrase emphasized that general education and special education personnel share the responsibility for educating students with mild or moderate disabilities.

■ **F Y I**

Inclusion is the integration of most students with disabilities into general education classes. *Full inclusion* is the integration of students with disabilities in the general education classrooms at all times regardless of the nature or severity of the disability.

■ **Do It!**

Talk to an experienced teacher in your community. How does he or she use the vocabulary in this section?

such as a special education room (for example, Sailor, 1991; Ferguson, 1995; McLeskey & Waldron, 1996). They stress that in the past many students with disabilities were only temporary guests in general education classrooms and that few efforts were made to provide assistance so they could be successfully educated with their nondisabled peers (Stainback & Stainback, 1992). These educators propose that all or most supports for students with disabilities can be provided in general education classrooms. They further maintain that if students cannot meet traditional academic expectations, then those expectations should be changed. They reject the mainstreaming assumption that settings dictate the type and intensity of services and propose instead the concept of inclusion. **Inclusion** represents the belief or philosophy that students with disabilities should be integrated into general education classrooms whether or not they can meet traditional curricular standards (Janney, Snell, Beers, & Raynes, 1995; Villa, Thousand, Meyers, & Nevin, 1996; York-Barr, Schultz, Doyle, Kronberg, & Crossett, 1996).

Advocates of inclusion believe that students should not be removed routinely from general education classrooms to receive assistance because doing so highlights their disabilities, disrupts their education, and teaches them to be dependent. Further, they maintain that specialized services often can be delivered in general education classrooms. For students with mild disabilities—such as learning disabilities—who typically can succeed in the general education curriculum, this might mean that a special education teacher or a paraprofessional assists them during instruction. It also might mean that adaptations such as simplified materials or alternative assignments are provided for the students. In some cases, it might be necessary for students to leave the classroom for particular instruction, but this is done only when classroom supports are insufficient and only for a limited period of time. For students with moderate or severe cognitive disabilities, inclusion might mean the provision of a paraprofessional in the general education classroom for a significant part of the day. It also might involve special education teachers preparing alternative activities for the students, or improvising ways in which the materials for instruction (for example, foil and wire for a science experiment) could be used by the students with disabilities for a related but much simpler task. As for students with more mild disabilities, inclusion does not suggest that it is always wrong to provide instruction in a separate setting. Occasionally this is necessary, but that decision should be made carefully and re-evaluated regularly.

Throughout this text, the term *inclusion* will refer to students' participation in general education settings as full members of the classroom learning community, with their special needs met there the vast majority of the time. We generally agree that inclusion maximizes the potential of most students, ensures their rights, and is the preferred option whenever possible.

Services for students with disabilities and other exceptional learners are changing rapidly. In your school, teachers might use the words *inclusion* and *mainstreaming* interchangeably, and they might have yet different terms to describe special education services. For example, teachers sometimes say *inclusion* only when referring to students with physical or cognitive disabilities and say *mainstreaming* for students with learning disabilities. To assist you with the vocabulary used in special education programs and instructional approaches, a glossary is provided in the back of this textbook. Although learning the terms used in special education is important, your most essential tasks will be to learn about special education services in your school and to define your role in teaching students with disabilities.

■ **Check Your Learning**

How do mainstreaming and inclusion differ?

How Did Special Education Services Come to Exist?

Special education as it exists today has been influenced by a number of different factors. Although people with disabilities have been identified and treated for centuries (Kanner, 1964), special education evolved rapidly only in the 20th century. As special education has grown, it has been shaped by federal law, the civil rights movement and related court cases, and changing social and political beliefs. Figure 1.1 illustrates some of the factors that have influenced the development of special education.

The Development of Education for Students with Disabilities

When compulsory public education began near the turn of this century, almost no school programs existed for students with disabilities (Scheerenberger, 1983). Students with disabilities that were relatively mild, that is, learning or behavior problems or minor physical impairments, were educated along with other students because their needs were not considered extraordinary. Many children with significant cognitive or physical disabilities did not attend school at all, whereas others were educated by private agencies and some lived in institutions.

Figure 1.1   Influences on Current Special Education Practices

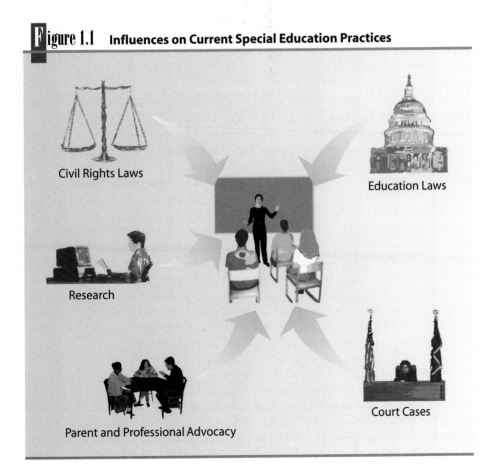

Civil Rights Laws

Education Laws

Research

Parent and Professional Advocacy

Court Cases

F Y I

The Council for Exceptional Children (CEC), founded in 1922 by Elizabeth Farrell, is a professional organization for teachers, administrators, parents, and other advocates for the rights of students with disabilities.

Special classes in public schools began as compulsory education became widespread. Schools were expected to be like efficient assembly lines, with each class of students moving from grade to grade and eventually graduating from high school as productive citizens prepared to enter the workforce (Patton, Payne, & Beirne-Smith, 1986; Scheerenberger, 1983). Special classes were developed as a place for students who could not keep up with their classmates. Because many students with disabilities were still not in school, most of the students sent to special classes probably had mild or moderate learning or cognitive disabilities. Educators at the time believed that such students would learn better in a protected setting and that the efficiency of the overall educational system would be preserved (Bennett, 1932; Pertsch, 1936).

By the 1950s, special education programs were available in many school districts, but some undesirable outcomes were becoming apparent. For example, students in special classes were often considered incapable of learning academic skills. They spent their school time practicing "manual skills" such as weaving and bead-stringing. Researchers began questioning this practice and conducted studies to explore the efficacy of special education. When they compared students with disabilities in special education classes to similar students who had remained in general education, they found the latter group often had learned more than the former (Blatt, 1958; Goldstein, Moss, & Jordan, 1965). Parents at this time also became active advocates for better educational opportunities for their children (Blatt, 1987). By the late 1960s, many authorities in the field agreed that segregated special classes were not the most appropriate educational setting for many students with disabilities (Blatt, 1958; Christopolos & Renz, 1969; Dunn, 1968; Hobbs, 1975; Lilly, 1971).

The Impact of the Civil Rights Movement on Special Education

Do It!

Invite a veteran teacher to your class to talk about special education prior to current laws. What questions will you ask your guest about the way students were educated and the responsibilities teachers had?

During the 1950s and 1960s, another force began contributing to the development of new approaches to special education. The civil rights movement, while initially addressing the rights of African Americans, expanded and began to influence thinking about people with disabilities (Chaffin, 1975; Rothstein, 1995). In the *Brown v. Board of Education* decision in 1954, the U.S. Supreme Court ruled that it was unlawful under the Fourteenth Amendment to arbitrarily discriminate against any group of people. The Court then applied this concept to the education of children, ruling that a separate education for African American students could not be an equal education. Soon, people with disabilities were recognized as another group whose rights often had been violated because of arbitrary discrimination. For children, the discrimination occurred when they were denied access to schools because of their disabilities. Beginning in the late 1960s and continuing through today, parents and others have used the court system to ensure that the civil and educational rights of children with disabilities are preserved. Figure 1.2 summarizes several of the court cases that have helped shape special education as it exists today.

Section 504.   One of the outcomes of the civil rights movement has been legislation designed to prevent discrimination against individuals with disabilities, whether they are children in schools or adults in the workforce. **Section 504** of the Vocational Rehabilitation Act of 1973 is a civil rights law that prevents discrimination against all individuals with disabilities in programs that receive federal funds, as do all public schools. For children of school age, Section 504 ensures equal opportunity

Figure 1.2   Court Cases Influencing Special Education

Matters relating to students with disabilities are addressed in federal and state laws. Issues concerning the interpretation of those laws often must be resolved through the courts. Since 1954, hundreds of legal decisions have clarified the rights of students with disabilities and the responsibilities of schools for educating them. In fact, in many instances court decisions have cleared the way for the passage of related legislation. As you review the landmark decisions listed here, you may recognize how each influenced P.L. 94-142, IDEA, and related legislation, which we discuss later in this chapter.

- **Brown v. Board of Education (1954).** This case established the principle that school segregation denies some students equal educational opportunity. Although the decision referred primarily to racial segregation, it has since become the cornerstone for ensuring equal rights for students with disabilities.

- **Diana v. State Board of Education (1970).** The state of California was required to correct bias in assessment practices used with Mexican American and Chinese American students. Students whose primary language was not English had to be tested in both English and their primary language; culturally biased items had to be eliminated from the tests, and appropriate alternative intelligence tests had to be developed to reflect Mexican American culture.

- **Pennsylvania Association for Retarded Children v. Commonwealth of Pennsylvania (1972).** In this suit, the court ruled that schools may not exclude students with mental retardation. The court ordered that a free public education was to be provided to all such students.

- **Mills v. Board of Education of District of Columbia (1972).** This case established several of the principles later reflected in P.L. 94-142, including the rights of students with disabilities to have access to a free public education, to be protected by due process before placement is changed, and to receive services even if schools claim funds are not available.

- **Board of Education of Hendrick Hudson School District v. Rowley (1982).** The court ruled that special education services must provide an appropriate education, but that students with disabilities may not be entitled to optimum services. The parents of a student with a hearing impairment were denied the services of an interpreter for their child in school because the child was achieving at grade level.

- **Larry P. v. Riles (1984).** In this ruling, IQ testing as a basis for placing African American students in special education programs as mentally retarded was found to be discriminatory. California schools were ordered to reduce the disproportionate numbers of African American students in such classes.

- **Honig v. Doe (1988).** This decision concerned the suspension or effective expulsion of students with disabilities from school. The court ruled that if a student is excluded from school for more than 10 days, it is considered a change in placement and all the procedures required to make a change in placement must be followed. In the same decision, it was clarified that brief removal from school may be permitted in emergency situations.

- **Daniel R.R. v. State Board of Education (1989).** This court decision established that two factors must be considered in determining the appropriate placement for a student with disabilities. The first factor is whether a student can be satisfactorily

(continued)

Figure 1.2 *(continued)*

educated in the general education setting with supplementary supports provided. The second factor is whether, in cases in which the general education setting is not successful, the student is mainstreamed to the maximum extent appropriate. For Daniel, a student with Down syndrome, the court ruled that the school district had not violated his rights when he was moved from general education after an unsuccessful attempt to include him.

- *Florence County School District No. 4 v. Carter* **(1993).** This case developed when a ninth-grade student with learning disabilities was removed from public school by her parents because they perceived her educational plan was not appropriate. They placed her at a private residential school specializing in learning disabilities that was not accredited by the state. The Supreme Court ruled that parents who place their children in a private school because of their disagreement with the education being provided by the public school are sometimes entitled to reimbursement for their expense even if the private school does not meet state special education standards.

- *Oberti v. Board of Education of Clementon School District* **(1993).** In this case concerning a student with Down syndrome, the district court ruled and the court of appeals upheld the ruling that school districts must make available a full range of supports and services in the general education setting to accommodate the needs of students with disabilities. The court further stipulated that just because a student learns differently from other students does not necessarily warrant exclusion from general education. This case is considered crucial in establishing the principles of inclusive practices.

- *Doe v. Withers* **(1993).** As Douglas Doe's history teacher, Michael Withers was responsible for making the oral testing accommodations needed by this student with learning disabilities. Although he was also a state legislator, Mr. Withers refused to provide the oral testing and Douglas failed this class, thus becoming athletically ineligible. The court awarded the family $5000 in compensatory damages and $30,000 in punitive damages. Although this case has limited applicability to other situations, it is widely cited as an example of the extent of general education teachers' responsibility to make good faith efforts to provide required accommodations for students with disabilities.

S O U R C E: Adapted from the following sources: Osborne, 1996; Rothstein, 1995; Yell, 1995; Zirkel, 1994.

for participation in the full range of school activities (National Information Center for Children and Youth with Disabilities, 1991). Through Section 504, some students not eligible for services through special education may be entitled to receive accommodations to help them in school. For example, Sondra is a student with a severe attentional problem. She cannot follow a lesson for more than a few minutes at a time; she is distracted by every noise in the hallway and every car that goes by her classroom window. Her teacher describes her as a student who acts first and thinks later. Sondra does not have a disability as established in special education law, but she does need extra assistance and is disabled according to Section 504 because her significant learning problem negatively affects her ability to function in school.

The professionals at her school are required to create and carry out a plan to help Sondra learn. Special education teachers may assist because they know techniques that will help Sondra, but Sondra is not a special education student. Other students who might receive assistance through Section 504 include those with health problems such as asthma or extreme allergies.

Americans with Disabilities Act.   In July 1990, President Bush signed into law the **Americans with Disabilities Act (ADA).** This civil rights law is based on the Vocational Rehabilitation Act of 1973, but it further extends the rights of individuals with disabilities. This law is the most significant disability legislation ever passed (Rothstein, 1995). It protects all individuals with disabilities from discrimination, and it requires most employers to make reasonable accommodations for them. Although ADA does not deal directly with the education of students with disabilities, it does clarify the civil rights of all individuals with disabilities and thus has an impact on special education. This law also ensures that buildings, transportation, and other public places are accessible to people with disabilities. As a teacher with a disability, you yourself might be influenced by ADA. For example, if your school is not accessible to wheelchairs and undergoes renovation, ramps, elevators, or wide entries with automatic doors might have to be installed. If you have a disability, this law also protects you from discrimination when you look for a teaching position. Some of the major provisions of ADA are summarized in Figure 1.3.

Check Your Learning

Why are Section 504 and the ADA called *civil rights* laws instead of *education* laws? What impact do they have on students, teachers, and schools?

Figure 1.3   **Key Provisions of the Americans with Disabilities Act of 1990**

- Employers may not discriminate against a person with a disability in hiring or promotion.

- Employers may not ask job applicants whether they have a disability.

- Employers must make "reasonable accommodations" in the workplace for persons with disabilities, as long as the accommodations do not cause undue hardship on others.

- New buses purchased by a community must be accessible to individuals with disabilities.

- In most cases, communities must provide transportation service to individuals who cannot access regular bus routes.

- Over the next 20 years, rail services, including stations and cars, must become accessible to individuals with disabilities.

- Public locations, including hotels, stores, and restaurants, may not discriminate against persons with disabilities and must be accessible to them.

- State and local governments may not discriminate against persons with disabilities, and government services must be accessible.

- Companies that provide telephone services must also provide adapted communication options for individuals who use telecommunication services for the deaf.

S O U R C E : Adapted from *Americans with Disabilities Act Requirements: Fact Sheet,* 1990, Washington, DC: U.S. Department of Justice.

The Legislative Basis for Least Restrictive Environment

Influenced by researchers' growing doubts about the effectiveness of special education classes and by civil rights court cases, by the early 1970s many states had begun to address special education issues by passing laws to guarantee that students with disabilities would receive an appropriate education. In 1975, Congress passed **P.L. 94-142,** the **Education for the Handicapped Act (EHA),** thereby setting federal guidelines for special education services. This law outlined the foundation on which current special education practice rests. It took into account many of the early court decisions that established the civil rights of students with disabilities, and it mandated the concept of least restrictive environment (LRE). For example, this law specifically described the categories of disabilities that make students eligible to receive special education. It clarified the related services to which students might be entitled. It also set out procedures for identifying a student as needing special education and outlined the rights of parents who disagree with the educational services offered to their children. The major provisions of P.L. 94-142 are outlined in Figure 1.4.

Public Law 101-476.   Passed in 1990, **P.L. 101-476** reauthorized P.L. 94-142. It also changed the name of P.L. 94-142 to the **Individuals with Disabilities Education Act (IDEA)** to reflect more contemporary "person-first" language. In addition, the term *handicapped* was removed from the law and the preferred term, *disability,* was substituted. This law continued to uphold the major provisions of P.L. 94-142, and it also added significantly to the provisions for very young children with disabilities and for students preparing to leave secondary school (Ysseldyke, Algozzine, & Thurlow, 1992). One other important change was the addition of two new categories of disability: autism and traumatic brain injury. Highlights of the additions P.L. 101-476 brought to special education law are included in Figure 1.5 on page 12.

Connections

The regulations and procedures for P.L. 105-17 are clarified further in Chapter 2.

Public Law 105-17.   In June, 1997, President Clinton signed into law the Individuals with Disabilities Education Act Amendments of 1997, **P.L. 105-17.** This law reauthorized P.L. 101-476 and added a number of new provisions. Perhaps most importantly for classroom teachers, this law recognized that most students with disabilities spend all or most of their school time in general education settings and so it included a provision that a classroom teacher become a member of the team that writes each student's Individualized Education Program. Another important change occurred regarding assessment. Acknowledging that students with disabilities were often excluded from local or state assessments, the law added a requirement that all students with disabilities be assessed as are other students, using either the same assessment tools used for typical learners, or some type of alternative tool. Additional details on the provisions of P.L. 105-17 are summarized in Figure 1.6 on page 13, and they are discussed further in Chapter 2.

Public Law 99-457.   In 1986, prior to the passage of P.L. 101-476, Congress enacted **P.L. 99-457.** This act extended the provisions of special education law to very young children, from birth through 5 years of age. The focus for services is on the entire family (Bailey, Buysse, Edmondson, & Smith, 1992). For example, the edu-

Figure 1.4   Key Provisions of P.L. 94-142

Free Appropriate Public Education

Students with disabilities are entitled to attend public schools and to receive the educational services they need. This education is provided at no cost to parents.

Least Restrictive Environment

Students with disabilities must be educated in the least restrictive environment in which they can succeed with support. For most students, this environment is the general education classroom.

Individualized Education

The instructional services and other assistance for students with disabilities must be tailored to meet their needs. This plan is accomplished by preparing an individualized education program (IEP) annually. The IEP includes a statement of the student's current level of functioning, a set of goals and short-term objectives for reaching those goals, and clear specification of who is responsible for delivering the student's services, how long they will last, where they will be provided, and how progress will be evaluated.

Nondiscriminatory Evaluation

Students should be assessed using instruments that do not discriminate on the basis of race, culture, or disability. In considering eligibility for special education services, students must be assessed by a multidisciplinary team in their native language using tests that are relevant to the area of concern. Eligibility cannot be decided on the basis of only one test.

Due Process

Students with disabilities and their parents are protected in all special education matters through due process procedures; that is, if a disagreement occurs concerning a student's eligibility for special education placement or services, no changes can be made until the issue has been resolved by an impartial hearing and, if necessary, the appropriate court. Likewise, if schools disagree with parents' requests for services for their children, they may also use due process procedures to resolve the dispute.

Zero Reject/Child Find

No student may be excluded from public education because of a disability. Further, each state must take action to locate children who may be entitled to special education services.

cation plan written for a very young child is called an **Individualized Family Service Plan (IFSP)** and may spell out assistance for parents. Parents typically have primary responsibility for teaching their babies and young children since they, not teachers, can take advantage of natural learning opportunities, such as teaching a child to grasp by holding a spoon at lunch. During 1994–1995, approximately 165,000 children from birth through age 2 and 524,000 children from 3 through 5 years old received special education through this program (U.S. Department of Education, 1996). For infants and toddlers, the discretionary services are often provided

> **F Y I**
>
> P.L. 99-457, which amended P.L. 94-142, established part H, which deals with programs and services for infants and toddlers with special needs and their families. This part of the law was revised again in 1997, and it is now included in IDEA-97 as Part C.

Figure 1.5   Additions to P.L. 94-142 Mandated in P.L. 101-476 (IDEA)

Transition Services

Individualized education programs for students who are 16 years of age or older (and those as young as 14 if appropriate) must include a description of transition services. This provision was designed to ensure that students receive assistance when preparing to leave school upon graduation, whether to find a job, attend a vocational school, or enter a university or college. The transition plan often includes connecting with professionals from other service agencies, including social services and vocational centers.

Early Childhood Education

This law provides funding for projects to improve services to infants, toddlers, and young children with disabilities. Areas of concern are the linkage between medical and early intervention services, assistive technology, parent education, and early identification of children with disabilities.

Severe Disabilities

For students with severe disabilities, this law funds projects that emphasize education in inclusive settings. The intent is to promote programs that include students with severe disabilities in general education settings.

Emotional Disturbance

The law supports projects aimed at improving services for students (like Nicki, whom you read about at the beginning of the chapter) with severe emotional disturbance. Topics of concern include coordination with mental health services, reduction of student placement in residential treatment facilities away from the students' home communities, collaboration among professionals, and the needs of minority-group children.

New Categories of Disability

Two new groups of students were specifically identified in this law as having disabilities that may entitle them to special education services: students who have traumatic brain injury and students who have autism.

S O U R C E : Adapted from *Critical Issues in Special Education* (2nd ed.) by J. E. Ysseldyke, B. Algozzine, and M. L. Thurlow, 1992, 30–64, Boston: Houghton Mifflin.

Check Your Learning

How do P.L. 94-142, P.L. 99-457, P.L. 101-476, and P.L. 105-17 relate to one another?

through home visits, sometimes for a fee; for preschoolers, services may occur in special classes in regular schools or in special schools. A growing trend is to provide education to preschoolers in private preschools and day-care centers that also serve young children without disabilities.

As you can see, special education has evolved on the basis of many factors. When special services began, essentially none of them was offered in public schools; today, comprehensive services in a wide variety of settings are supplied, and both very young children and young adults as well as students in elementary and secondary schools benefit from them. And as the rights and needs of students with disabilities have been better understood, classroom teachers have become increasingly involved in the education of students with disabilities, a trend that surely will continue.

Figure 1.6 Changes to P.L. 101-476 Mandated in P.L. 105-17 (IDEA-97)

General Education Teacher Roles and Responsibilities

At least one general education teacher must participate as a member of the team that writes a student's Individualized Education Program (IEP). In addition, the IEP must directly address student participation in general education and must justify placements that are not in general education.

Evaluation and Eligibility

IDEA-97 has several changes related to special education assessment. First, the law clarifies that when parents consent to have their child evaluated, they are not consenting to a possible future special education placement. Second, students cannot be eligible for special education because of poor math or reading instruction, or because of language differences. Third, for some students the former requirement that a complete re-assessment be completed every three years can be modified. That is, already existing information can be used in lieu of repeatedly administering standardized tests.

Assessment of Students

By July 1, 2000, states are required to measure the academic progress of students who have IEPs, either by including them in the standardized assessments other students take, or by using an alternative assessment process. Students are entitled to appropriate adaptations (for example, extended time, large print) during assessment.

 discrepant national data

Transition

Transition service needs must be addressed on IEPs for students beginning at age 14. These needs must be updated annually, and they must become increasingly detailed as students reach age 16 and beyond, even clarifying services the student will access outside of school (for example, a community vocational service).

why

Discipline

As needed, strategies for addressing student behavior must be included as part of the IEP. If a student is suspended or placed in an alternative interim placement, a behavior plan must be developed. In some cases (for example, when students bring weapons or drugs to school), schools may place students with disabilities in alternative interim placements for up to 45 days. They must continue to receive special education services during this time.

Paraprofessionals

Paraprofessionals, teaching assistants, and other similar personnel must be trained for their jobs and appropriately supervised.

Mediation

States must make mediation available to parents as an early and informal strategy for resolving disagreements about the identification of, placement of, or services for students with disabilities. The cost of mediation is borne by the State. Parents are not obligated to mediate, and mediation may not delay a possible hearing.

S O U R C E : Adapted from American School Board Association (1997). The New IDEA. *American School Board Journal, 184*(12), 20; Johns, B. (1997). Changes in IEP requirements based on the reauthorization of IDEA. *CCBD Newsletter, 11*(2), 1, 4; and Yell, M. L., & Shriner, J. G. (1997). The IDEA amendments of 1997: Implications for special and general education teachers, administrators, and teacher trainers. *Focus on Exceptional Children, 30*(1), 1–19.

Why Is Inclusion Controversial?

Few professionals would question the appropriateness of including students with disabilities in general education classes. However, considerable debate continues about which students should be part of general education classes and how much time they should spend there. On one side of the debate are those who contend that all students belong in general education classrooms nearly all the time (for example, Lenk, 1995; Lipsky & Gartner, 1992; McLeskey & Waldron, 1996; Skrtic, Sailor, & Gee, 1996). On the other side are those who believe that only students who can meet certain standards or maintain a certain rate of academic progress should be included (for example, Fuchs & Fuchs, 1995; Kauffman, 1995; Vaughn, Schumm, Jallad, Slusher, & Saumell, 1996). Most professionals' views fall somewhere between these two extremes. Many educators agree that students with disabilities too often have been educated in isolated settings that minimize instead of maximize their potential, but they recognize that for some students the general education setting is occasionally but not always the least restrictive environment (for example, Chalmers & Faliede, 1996; Sardo-Brown & Hinson, 1995).

Advocates of Inclusion

Those who advocate inclusion make the following points:

1. All students have a basic human right to attend school with other students who are their peers; this can occur only in a single school system in which all students are members of one learning community, in other words, in general education (Edgar, 1987; Ferguson, 1996; Gartner & Lipsky, 1989; McNulty et al., 1996; Sawyer, McLaughlin, & Winglee, 1994).

2. With support, all students benefit from education in inclusive settings. Students for whom traditional academic requirements are not relevant can still learn social skills by observing the appropriate behaviors of other students (Ferguson, 1996; Ryndak, Downing, Morrison, & Williams, 1996; Stainback & Stainback, 1988). They learn that they are full class members, not second-class citizens who are somehow inferior to others (Hahn, 1989). In addition, inclusion benefits students without disabilities by teaching acceptance. Students learn that having a disability is simply one type of diversity and that individuals with disabilities are people with whom they can learn and share (McLeskey & Waldron, 1996). For example, elementary school students who have a classmate with multiple disabilities learn that she is much like they are, an individual with certain likes and dislikes based on who she is inside, not on her outward appearance.

3. When students leave the general education classroom to go to a special education setting, they are stigmatized by their classmates and the labels associated with having disabilities (Lilly, 1992). Further, students who receive their education in a separate special education class often miss major topics covered in general education classrooms. For example, they sometimes receive little instruction in social studies or science because they are retaught language arts during that time. If students never leave the general education setting, they avoid both these problems (D'Alonzo et al., 1995; Simpson & Myles, 1990; Udvari-Solner & Thousand, 1996; Wang & Reynolds, 1996).

What particular challenges do students with "invisible disabilities"—such as learning disabilities—face in school? What is the role of public schools in preparing students with disabilities for adult life?

4. Some students with disabilities receive assistance from several professionals. If this means that the student leaves the classroom several times each day, often called a **pullout program,** the student loses many valuable instructional minutes in transitions. Pullout models also lead to fragmentation: Students have more difficulty generalizing what they have learned in a special education setting to the general education setting because the information is presented separately, not as an integral part of the student's school activities (Raynes, Snell, & Sailor, 1991; Sapon-Shevin, 1996).

5. The teaching approaches used in separate special education classes are in many cases not significantly different from those provided in general education classes, particularly for students with learning and emotional disabilities. Students sometimes receive more appropriate instruction in the general education setting (Carlberg & Kavale, 1980; Mercer, Lane, Jordan, Allsopp, & Eisele, 1996). For example, in a special education biology class, students might not have access to needed laboratory experiences readily available in the "real" biology class. When special education teachers' caseloads are not limited, special education classes may have 18 or 20 or even more students, making it extremely difficult to individualize.

Those Who Say, "It Depends . . . "

People who support inclusion only under certain conditions offer these arguments:

1. To say that all students should be in general education settings is to deny the unique characteristics of students with disabilities. Treating all students alike also denies those with disabilities the right to an individualized education and violates federal special education law (Council for Exceptional Children, 1993;

> **FYI**
>
> In *pullout programs,* students leave the general education classroom to receive specialized services. Special education teachers often offer pullout programs, but so do speech therapists, occupational and physical therapists, counselors, and even remedial reading teachers.

Fuchs & Fuchs, 1995; Kauffman, 1995). Alternatives must exist for those for whom the general education classroom is not appropriate.

2. In the past, many students, especially those with disabilities related to learning and behavior, too often have been relegated to special education classes when they could succeed in a general education setting. However, some students do need the specialized, structured environment and the highly individualized services that a special education class can provide (Roberts & Mather, 1995b; Vergason & Anderegg, 1992). In such settings, students learn more and at a faster rate than in general education.

3. The general education classroom is not always the least restrictive environment. Some of the services students with disabilities need (for example, speech therapy for articulation problems) often cannot be provided in the general education classroom without calling attention to student differences and disrupting the instructional flow (Brandel, 1992; Kauffman, Lloyd, Baker, & Riedel, 1995). Further, for some students, especially those approaching adulthood, an inclusive environment might be a workplace or other community setting, not a classroom (Brolin & Schatzman, 1989).

4. General education classrooms and the teachers who work there are not necessarily equipped to manage the learning needs of some students with disabilities (Taylor, Richards, Goldstein, & Schilit, 1997; Vaughn et al., 1996; Wigle & Wilcox, 1996). In some cases, teachers may lack skills for accommodating the needs of students with disabilities. In others, large class sizes and pressures to meet rigorous academic standards can prevent teachers from assisting students with disabilities. In yet others, the number of students with special needs, including those who are not identified as eligible for special education, is so great that more individualization is just not feasible. The learner diversity in many schools is already enormous; adding students with disabilities may become detrimental to the education of other students.

5. Students in inclusive situations and their classroom teachers should receive sufficient support services. With appropriate support, inclusion can often succeed. Without appropriate support, the risk of failure greatly increases (Vaughn & Schumm, 1995; Wolery, Werts, Caldwell, Snyder, & Lisowski, 1995). Supports may include materials, additional teacher training in instructional modifications, assistance from another professional (such as a special education teacher), or assistance from a paraprofessional. Unfortunately, too often inclusion is attempted without these needed supports in a misguided attempt to save money.

An Analysis of the Inclusion Debate

As you read more about inclusion, you may realize that professionals all share the same goal: providing the most appropriate education for students with disabilities. However, some individuals firmly believe that the major obstacles to including students are "yes, but" mindsets that focus attention on challenges to inclusion instead of opportunities. On the other hand, some individuals express concern that inclusion can mean the end of the protections and individualization that have been hard-won over the course of the past two decades or more. We believe that extreme positions are valuable in helping professionals examine their own beliefs about students and appropriate instructional practices but that in practice an optimistic moderation will prevail. That is, more and more students will continue to receive their

These two students with hearing impairments are included in a general education science classroom. What opportunities does this offer to these students, as well as to their classmate who does not have a hearing impairment?

education in less and less restrictive environments, often general education classrooms. For the few students for whom more structured settings are needed either occasionally or regularly—sometimes because of a lack of supports in a general education setting—options such as special education classrooms will continue to exist. Ultimately, what is most clear is that federal, state, and local education agencies must continue to commit financial and other resources to ensure that students with disabilities receive a high-quality education in the least restrictive environment. The Case in Practice on page 18 illustrates how general education teachers, special educators, and other school staff members can work toward successful inclusion through a collaborative effort.

Who Receives Special Education and Other Special Services?

Throughout this chapter, we have used the phrase *students with disabilities*. At this point, we will introduce you to the 12 specific types of disabilities that may entitle students to receive special education services, as well as other special needs that may lead to a need for specialized assistance.

Categories of Disability in Federal Law

When we say that students have "disabilities," we are referring to the specific categories of exceptionality prescribed by federal law. Each state has additional laws that clarify special education practices and procedures; the terms used to refer to disabilities in these state laws may differ from those found in federal law. Check with your instructor for the terms used in your state. According to P.L. 105-17, students with one of the following disabilities that negatively affects their educational performance are eligible for special education services:

Connections

More complete descriptions of the characteristics and needs of students with disabilities and other special needs are found in Chapters 5, 6, and 7.

Case in Practice

Problem Solving in Inclusive Schools: The Classroom Teacher's Role

At Highland Elementary School, staff members are meeting to discuss David, a third grader with autism. Ms. Dowley is David's teacher; Ms. Jackson is the special educator who provides needed support. Ms. Janes, the school psychologist, is also present.

Ms. Dowley: David is really a puzzle and a challenge. He is doing so much better at being in class than he was at the beginning of the year, but he can still disrupt the entire class when he throws tantrums. One of the parents called yesterday to complain about David taking time away from her daughter and the rest of the class. I'm starting to feel the same way. I hope we can come up with some ideas to improve the whole situation.

Ms. Jackson: What kinds of things seem to trigger the tantrums?

Ms. Dowley: That's part of the problem. I'm still pretty new at teaching, and I have my hands full with the whole class. I don't even have time to think carefully about what's happening with David. I just deal with him when a problem occurs.

Ms. Janes: The tantrums seem like a serious problem, but before we start addressing them, are there other things we should be discussing, too?

Ms. Dowley: No. Right now, it's the tantrums—and I want to be clear that I really can see all the other gains David has made. I *want* this to work for David. I know inclusion is right for him if we can just deal with this problem.

Ms. Janes: It seems as though we need more information. One question I have is this: What happens with you and the other students when David has a tantrum?

Ms. Dowley: Well, I try to ignore him, but that usually makes it worse. A few of the other students laugh, and that's not helping either.

Ms. Jackson: Maybe we should focus for a minute or two on when David doesn't tantrum. What are the times of the day or the activities that David does without having behavior problems?

Ms. Dowley: Let's see . . . He's usually fine and makes a good contribution when we're talking about science concepts. He loves science.

If math is activity-based, he's fine there, too.

Ms. Janes: Our meeting time is nearly up. I'd be happy to make time in my schedule to observe David, and perhaps Ms. Jackson could, too. I know you need answers right away, but I hope we can get a clearer sense of the pattern to David's behavior so we can find the right strategy for addressing it. If we can get in to observe this week, could we meet next Tuesday to try to generate some strategies?

Ms. Dowley: Sure. That would be great. Let's just work out the details on observing.

REFLECTIONS

Why was this meeting a positive example of teachers addressing a student problem in an inclusive school? What did they do that has set them up for success? If you were trying to understand David better, what other questions would you ask about him? What do you think will happen at the next meeting? On the basis of this case, how would you describe the role of classroom teachers in addressing the challenges of inclusion?

Learning disabilities (LD).   Students with **learning disabilities (LD)** have dysfunctions in processing information typically found in language-based activities. They have average or above average intelligence, but they often encounter significant problems learning how to read, write, and compute. They may not see letters and words in the way others do, they may not be able to pick out important features in a picture they are looking at, and they may take longer to process a question or comment directed to them. They may also have difficulty following directions, attending to tasks, organizing their assignments, and managing time. Sometimes these students appear to be unmotivated or lazy when, in fact, they are trying to the best of their ability. Aaron, whom you met at the beginning of this chapter, has a learning disability, but many types of learning disabilities exist, and no single description characterizes students who have one. Approximately half of all students receiving special education services in public schools in 1993–1994 had learning disabilities (U.S. Department of Education, 1996).

Speech or language impairments. When a student has extraordinary difficulties in communicating with others because of causes other than maturation, a **speech or language impairment** is involved. Students with this disability may have trouble with **articulation,** or the production of speech sounds. They may omit words when they speak, or mispronounce common words. They may also experience difficulty in fluency, as in a significant stuttering problem. Some students have far-reaching speech and language disorders in which they have extreme problems receiving and producing language. They may communicate through pictures or sign language. Some students have a speech or language disorder as their primary disability and receive services for this. For other students with disabilities, speech/language services supplement their education. For example, a student with a learning disability might also receive speech/language services, as might a student with autism or traumatic brain injury.

Mental retardation. Students with **mental retardation** have significant limitations in cognitive ability and adaptive behaviors. They learn at a far slower pace than do other students, and they may reach a point at which their learning levels off. Many states distinguish between students with mild mental retardation and those with moderate and severe mental retardation. Despite the degree of mental retardation, most individuals with this disability can lead independent or semi-independent lives as adults and can hold an appropriate job. The term **cognitive disability** is sometimes used instead of mental retardation. In this text, we use the two terms interchangeably.

Emotional disturbance. When a student has significant difficulty in the social/emotional domain, serious enough to interfere with the student's learning, an **emotional disturbance (ED)** exists. Students with this disability may have difficulty with interpersonal relationships and may respond inappropriately in emotional situations; that is, they may have trouble making and keeping friends, and they may get extremely angry when a peer teases or plays a joke on them, or show little or no emotion when the family pet dies. Some students with ED are depressed; others are aggressive. Students with ED display these impairments over a long period of time, across different settings, and to a degree significantly different from their peers. A student with an ED is not just a student who is difficult to manage in a classroom; like Nicki, whom you met at the beginning of the chapter, students with this disability have chronic and extremely serious emotional problems.

Autism. Students with **autism** usually lack social responsiveness from a very early age. They generally avoid physical contact (for example, cuddling and holding), and they may not make eye contact. Problems with social interactions persist as these

FYI

Depression is more common among children than previously thought. More information on this serious disorder can be found in Chapter 6.

Technology Notes

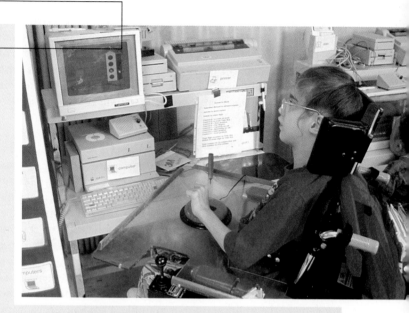

Students use assistive computer technology to attain a variety of learning goals.

Using Computers

Computers are one of the most readily available and helpful tools you will have for meeting the needs of students with disabilities in your classroom. Here are a few of the ways they can assist you.

1. Computers as instructional assistants. With the vast and ever-increasing array of computer software available for students of all ages, individualizing in classrooms and labs has become straightforward. You can provide a simpler math program to students not ready for your lesson on adding fractions; you can offer problem-solving practice at various levels. Computers can also enrich talented students' education and assist all students in maximizing their interests.

2. Computers as a motivational tool. For some students, opportunities to work on a computer can be tremendously rewarding. Students who have difficulty completing assignments might earn computer time as part of their instructional program.

3. Computers as a means for adaptive communication. Computers can help students communicate their ideas. Voice synthesizers can "read" for students with vision impairments, and specialized printers can translate braille into print or print into braille. For students with disabilities that prevent them from speaking, the computer offers a means to reach others. Computers fitted with picture boards help students with severe cognitive disabilities state their preferences and make their needs known.

4. Computers as a data collection tool. Using software that tracks the user's progress within the program, you can monitor students' learning. For example, most computer writing programs can easily count the number of words written at different intervals, which can provide you with a rough measure of students' writing fluency. Likewise, many programs

can track the number of math problems completed and the problem-solving level reached, which can give you a general sense of students' strengths and trouble spots.

5. Computers for teacher record keeping. Spending 5 or 10 minutes at the end of the school day entering attendance, permission forms returned, student scores, and student behavior data is a systematic and efficient way to keep professional records. Grading software can help you track student progress, as can spreadsheets. Simple files kept in word processing are appropriate for anecdotal records on students you are concerned about.

6. Computers for teacher communication. Teachers can also use computers to manage their many communication responsibilities. For example, you can prepare the class newsletter more easily on a computer than by hand. Letters sent to parents, schedules for and notes on meetings, and your news can all be stored on the computer for future reference. By keeping such files, you can maintain a chronology of your correspondence, and you can also create certain types of letters and notes just once and then copy them for future use.

children grow; they appear unaware of others' feelings and may not seek interactions with peers or adults. They may have unusual language patterns, including spoken language without intonation; echolalia, or repetition of others' speech; or little or no language. They may display repetitive body movements, such as rocking, and may need highly routinized behavior, such as a formalized procedure for putting on their clothes or eating their meals, to feel comfortable. The causes of autism are not well understood, and the best approaches for working with students with autism are still under considerable debate.

Hearing impairments.   Disabilities that concern the inability or limited ability to receive auditory signals are called **hearing impairments.** When students are **hard of hearing,** they have a significant hearing loss but are able to capitalize on residual hearing by using hearing aids and other amplifying systems. Students who are **deaf** have little or no residual hearing and therefore do not benefit from devices to aid hearing. Depending on the extent of the disability, students with hearing impairments may use sign language, speech reading, and other ways to help them communicate.

Visual impairments.   Disabilities that concern the inability or limited ability to receive information visually are called **visual impairments.** Some students are **partially sighted** and can learn successfully using magnification devices or other adaptive materials; students who are **blind** do not use vision as a means of learning and instead rely primarily on touch and hearing. Depending on need, students with visual impairments may use braille, specialized computers, and other aids to assist in learning. Some students need specialized training to help them learn to move around in their environment successfully.

Deaf–blindness.   Students who have both significant vision and hearing impairments are sometimes eligible for services as deaf–blind. These students are categorized separately because of the unique learning needs they have, particularly in the communication areas, and the highly specialized services they require. The severity of the vision or hearing loss may vary from moderate to severe and may be accompanied by other disabilities. Students in this category are likely to receive special education services beginning at birth or very soon thereafter.

Orthopedic impairments.   Students with **orthopedic impairments** have physical conditions that seriously impair their ability to move about or to complete motor activities. Students who have cerebral palsy are included in this group, as are those with other diseases that affect the skeleton or muscles. Students with physical limitations resulting from accidents may also be in this group. Some students with physical disabilities will be unable to move about without a wheelchair and may need special transportation to get to school and a ramp to enter the school building. Others may lack the fine motor skills needed to write and will require extra time or adapted equipment to complete assignments.

Traumatic brain injury (TBI).   Students with **traumatic brain injury (TBI)** have a wide range of characteristics and special needs, including limited strength or alertness, developmental delays, short-term memory problems, hearing or vision losses that may be temporary, irritability, and sudden mood swings. Their characteristics

FYI

Hearing and visual impairments are referred to as *sensory* impairments.

WWW Resources

Much information is available on the Internet about individuals with disabilities. One helpful source is the Internet Resources for Special Children (IRSC) website. It can be reached at <http://www.irsc.org>.

and needs depend on the specific injury they experienced, and their needs often change over time. Because TBI is a medical condition that affects education, diagnosis by a physician is required along with assessment of learning and adaptive behavior. Students who experience serious head trauma from automobile accidents, falls, and sports injuries might be eligible for services as TBI.

Other health impairments.   Some students have a disease or disorder so significant that it affects their ability to learn in school; the category of disability addressing these needs is called **other health impairments.** Students with severe asthma who require an adapted physical education program might be eligible for special education in this category, as might those who have chronic heart conditions necessitating frequent and prolonged absences from school. Students with diseases such as AIDS, sickle-cell anemia, and diabetes may be categorized as "other health impaired," depending on the impact of their illness on learning. Also, some students with severe attention deficit–hyperactive disorder (ADHD) receive special education services in this category.

Multiple disabilities.   The category used when students have two or more disabilities is **multiple disabilities.** Students in this group often have mental retardation as well as a physical disability, but this category may be used to describe any student with two or more disability areas. However, this classification is used only when the student's disabilities are so serious and so interrelated that none can be identified as a primary disability.

When you discuss students who have disabilities, keep in mind that their disabilities do not define them or tell you who they really are. To stay aware of this important consideration, as the Professional Edge explains, you should always use "person-first" language with and when referring to all students, regardless of what disability category pertains to them.

FYI

A *primary disability* is the one that most significantly influences the student's education. A *secondary disability* is an additional disability that affects education, but to a lesser degree.

Check Your Learning

What are the high-incidence disabilities? What are the low-incidence disabilities? Why are these terms sometimes used instead of the federal disability categories?

Cross-Categorical Approaches to Special Education

Federal and state education agencies and local school districts use the categories of disabilities just described for counting the number of students in special education and for allocating money to educate them. When you prepare to teach a student, however, you will probably find that the specific category of disability often does not guide you in devising appropriate teaching strategies. In some states, some of the categories are combined to permit more flexibility for planning educational services. Also, students in different categories often benefit from the same instructional adaptations. Throughout this book, students will sometimes be discussed in terms of only two categories: **High-incidence disabilities** are those that are most common, including learning disabilities, speech or language impairments, mild mental retardation, and emotional disturbance. Together, these disabilities account for over 90 percent of the disabilities reported in 1993–1994 (U.S. Department of Education, 1996). **Low-incidence disabilities** are those that are rare and include all the other categories: moderate to severe mental retardation, multiple disabilities, hearing impairments, orthopedic impairments, other health impairments, visual impairments, deaf–blindness, autism, and traumatic brain injury.

Consistent with a **cross-categorical approach,** when the characteristics of students with disabilities are discussed in more detail in Chapters 5 and 6, we pay more

Professional Edge

Finding the Right Words

Language *does* make a difference. "Person-first" language is the appropriate way to refer to anyone who has a disability. For example, you should say "a student who has a learning disability" or "my student with a cognitive disability" or "I teach four students who have learning disabilities" instead of "the LD student" or "my retarded student" or "I have four LDs." Actually, why not just call your students by their names?

As society's sensitivity to the rights of individuals with disabilities has grown, so too has an awareness of the subtleties of language. Although the term **handi-capped** used to be common (and still is used in some places and in some textbooks), it is not appropriate. In fact, the word *handicapped* comes from the time when people with disabilities were not able to earn any type of living and so resorted to begging on the street, often with their caps in their hands. They became known as "cap-in-handers," then "hand-in-cappers," and later "handicapped." Increasing awareness of this word's evolution has led to its disfavor.

Some professionals prefer to use the term *challenges* rather than *disabilities* when referring to students' special needs. For example, a student who uses a wheelchair might be referred to as "physically challenged"; another student might have "cognitive challenges." For some professionals, the word *challenge* seems to convey an obstacle that can be overcome and optimism that this will occur, whereas the word *disability* implies a problem that belongs only to the person and that is permanent.

---

attention to students' learning needs than to their labels. In addition, although some strategies specific to categorical groups (for example, the use of large-print books for students with vision impairments) are outlined in those chapters, most of the strategies presented throughout the text can be adapted for most students. If you adopt a cross-categorical approach in your own thinking about teaching students with disabilities, you will see that many options are available for helping students succeed.

Connections

Additional information on specific disabilities is included in Chapters 5 and 6.

Other Students with Special Needs

Not all students who have special learning and behavior needs are addressed in special education laws. Many of these other students, described in the following sections, benefit from the ideas presented throughout this book.

Students who are gifted or talented. Students who demonstrate ability far above average in one or several areas including overall intellectual ability, leadership, specific academic subjects, creativity, athletics, or the visual or performing arts are considered **gifted or talented.** Erin is included in this group; she seems to learn almost everything without effort, and she is also eager to learn about almost everything. Evan is also talented; still in elementary school, he has participated in state and national piano recitals, and his parents have requested that he have access to the music room during recess so he can practice. Students who are gifted or talented are not

Connections

Students with special needs who are not necessarily eligible for special education are addressed in more detail in Chapter 7.

addressed in federal special education law. In the majority of states, separate laws exist that provide guidelines for identifying and educating students with special talents. Funds are not always provided to implement these laws, however, and so the availability and scope of services for students with particular talents vary across the country and even within a particular state.

Students protected by Section 504.   Some students not eligible to receive special education services nonetheless will be entitled to protection through Section 504 and receive specialized assistance because of their functional disabilities, as described earlier in this chapter. Among those likely to be included in this group are students with **attention deficit–hyperactive disorder (ADHD).** Students with ADHD have a medical problem often characterized by an inability to attend to complex tasks for long periods of time, excessive motor activity, and impulsivity. The impact of this disorder on students' schoolwork can be significant. Identification of ADHD requires input from a physician. Students with ADHD may take medication, such as Ritalin, that helps them focus their attention.

Students at risk.   Often, the general term **at risk** refers to students who have characteristics, live in an environment, or have experiences that make them more likely than others to fail in school. Students whose primary language is not English are sometimes considered at risk, and they may need assistance in school learning. They may attend bilingual education programs or classes for English as a second language (ESL) for opportunities to learn English while also learning the standard curriculum. However, some students in this group may also have disabilities.

A second group of at-risk students are **slow learners,** whose educational progress is below average but who do not have a learning disability or mental retardation. These students are learning to the best of their ability, but they cannot keep up with the pace of instruction in most general education classrooms without assistance. They are sometimes referred to as "falling between the cracks" of the educational system because most professionals agree they need special assistance, but they

> **Cultural Awareness**
>
> Students whose language at home is not English are sometimes assigned to special education inappropriately because of academic difficulties that are actually caused by lack of proficiency in English.

What are the special needs of the student in this picture? Would knowing the label assigned to her help you know how to teach her? How are the lives of students with disabilities and those without disabilities changed because of their interactions with one another?

Professional Edge

Keeping Up to Date

Just as physicians and scientists keep abreast of the developments in their fields, so, too, do teachers keep up with the latest research in education. Listed below are some special and general education professional journals that might interest you as you work to include students with special needs in your class.

Special Education Journals

Beyond Behavior
Education and Training in Mental Retardation and Developmental Disabilities
Education and Treatment of Children
Exceptional Children
Focus on Exceptional Children
Intervention in School and Clinic
Journal of Learning Disabilities
Journal of Special Education

Learning Disabilities Research and Practice
Learning Disability Quarterly
Preventing School Failure
Remedial and Special Education
Teaching Exceptional Children

General Education Journals

Educational Leadership
Instructor
Journal of Educational Psychology
Journal of Kappa Delta Pi
Journal of Reading
Phi Delta Kappan
Reading Research Quarterly
Reading Teacher
Review of Educational Research

---

are not eligible for special education. They sometimes, however, receive assistance in remedial reading or tutorial programs.

Other students who might be considered at risk include those who are homeless or live in poverty, who are born to mothers abusing drugs or alcohol, who are drug or alcohol abusers themselves, or who are abused. Students in these groups are at risk for school failure because of the environments or circumstances in which they live.

You may find that students with special needs who do not have disabilities according to special education laws are particularly troubling because no single group of professionals is responsible for educating them. As students with disabilities spend increasing amounts of time in general education classes, special education teachers often informally assist teachers in planning and adapting educational activities for these students. Thus, other students with special needs often benefit from the trend toward inclusive education for students with disabilities.

Summary

Special education refers to the specialized services received by the millions of students in the United States who have disabilities and is based on the concept of the least restrictive environment (LRE). Current special education practices have evolved from a combination of factors, including the inception of compulsory public education early in the 20th century, research questioning instructional practices for students with disabilities, the civil rights movement and related court cases, and a series of federal civil rights and education laws.

The present trend in special education is toward inclusive practices. Some professionals fully support inclusion, whereas others caution that it might not be the best option for some students with disabilities. Federal law identifies 12 categories of disabilities that may entitle students to special education services: learning disabilities, speech or language impairments, mental retardation, emotional disturbance, autism, hearing impairments, visual impairments, deaf-blindness, orthopedic impairments, traumatic brain injury, other health impairments, and multiple disabilities. However, many other students with special needs also need assistance, including those who are gifted or talented; who have attention deficits; who are at risk, including non-native English speakers and slow learners. As a classroom teacher you often will be responsible for instructing students with disabilities and other special needs.

A p p l i c a t i o n s   i n   T e a c h i n g   P r a c t i c e

Understanding Contemporary Special Education Practices

It is a new school year—your first as a teacher in the Kenville School District. You learn that you will be responsible for these students:

- Cassie is a bright young woman who has a visual impairment. In order for her to read, she uses a computer that greatly magnifies her materials. She also needs to work in bright light, and she gets fatigued from the effort required to use what little vision she has.

- Ramon is a young man who has been identified as having a learning disability. His reading ability is at an early first-grade level. He also seems disorganized. He often forgets to bring materials and assignments to class, and he even forgets to return permission forms for field trips he wants to participate in.

- Tory lives in a foster home. He was removed from his mother's home because of several incidents of abuse. Tory is an angry child. He often refuses to work, he sometimes loses his temper and throws a book or crumples a paper, and he misses school frequently.

Questions

1. Why would Cassie, Ramon, and Tory be assigned to a general education classroom? What might be the goals you as a classroom teacher could accomplish with them?

2. If you spoke with a supporter of inclusive practices, what would that person say to explain your obligations to make accommodations that help these students succeed?

3. If you spoke with an opponent of inclusive practices, what would that person say about the appropriateness of each student being assigned to a general education classroom?

4. When you think about your responsibilities for educating students with disabilities and other special needs in your classroom—whether in kindergarten or in a senior-level, content-area class—what are your concerns and questions? In what ways do you see that you'll be able to make a contribution to your students' education? What types of supports might you need? If you write your responses to these questions, keep them with your text and use them as a basis for discussion as you learn more in later chapters.

Special Education Procedures and Services

Learner Objectives

After you read this chapter, you will be able to

1. Describe the professionals who may be involved in instructing students with disabilities and explain their responsibilities.

2. Explain the process through which a student becomes eligible to receive special education services.

3. Name the components of individualized education programs (IEP) and provide examples of them.

4. Describe the types of services that students with disabilities may receive and the settings in which they may receive them.

5. Discuss what occurs if parents and school district representatives disagree about a student's special education.

6. Outline the role of the general education teacher in the procedures and services of special education.

Ch. 2

Special Education Procedures and Services

Mr. Peterson is concerned. He teaches fifth grade, and one of his students, Leon, is having increasing difficulty mastering skills. Leon reads at about a second-grade level, has learned about half of the addition math facts, and reacts to other children's teasing by shouting and hitting. Mr. Peterson isn't sure what to do next; the strategies he has used in the past have not had an impact, and he fears Leon is giving up on learning. He has met with Leon's mother and stepfather. They report that they are having more and more difficulty getting Leon to mind them. Leon's parents are concerned that he doesn't seem to care about school and that he is spending much of his time hanging out with older boys. They are worried about gangs and drugs. What steps should Mr. Peterson take next? Whom might Mr. Peterson contact to help him decide whether Leon's difficulties are serious enough to consider assessing him for special education?

Tim, a junior in high school, has a learning disability. He is on schedule to graduate with his classmates. However, Tim is unsure about what he will do when he leaves school. He thinks he would like to go to college, but is concerned about whether he can succeed there. He has also considered enlisting in the army, but his parents are discouraging that. He knows he could get a job at the local paper factory, but that prospect seems, in his words, "too boring." What is the responsibility of school professionals in helping Tim decide on a suitable postgraduation activity? Who can help Tim make his decisions?

Ms. Turner teaches English to eighth graders. She just received a note in her box asking her to attend the annual review for Changyi, a seventh grader who has a severe physical disability. Ms. Turner gathers her grade book and a sample of Changyi's writing as dictated to her personal assistant. She then jots a few notes to herself to prepare for the meeting. She knows that the teachers on her middle school team take turns attending students' annual reviews to ensure that a general education point of view is represented. Ms. Turner also knows that Mr. Simpson, the assistant principal, and Mr. Tsai, the special education teacher on her team, will attend the meeting, along with Changyi's mother. What is an annual review? What is Ms. Turner's responsibility for participating in the annual review?

As a teacher, you will encounter students who are struggling. Some may appear to be doing everything they can *not* to learn. Others will be trying their best and still not be successful. You might even have students whom you suspect have a vision or hearing problem so serious that it prevents them from learning. You may find yourself wondering whether some of these students should be receiving special education services and who will provide them. This chapter introduces you to the people who specialize in working with students with disabilities and the procedures involved in deciding if a student is eligible for special education services. You will also learn how students' instructional programs are designed and monitored, and which services students with disabilities use. You will discover that when parents or students disagree with school professionals about special services, procedures exist to help them resolve these problems. Most important, you will learn about your role in working with other professionals and parents to determine student eligibility for special education, carrying out students' educational programs, and monitoring student learning.

Who Are the Professionals in Special Education?

Students with disabilities are entitled to a wide range of services. Not surprisingly, many different individuals can be involved in the delivery of these services. You will probably interact with some of the professionals, such as special education teachers, every day. Others might not be so available; they serve students indirectly, or work only with the few students with the most challenging disabilities.

General Education Teachers

Do It!

Talk to an experienced general education teacher about his or her range of responsibilities for students with exceptionalities. Compare findings with your classmates.

FYI

General education teachers' roles in relation to special education are especially critical given the changes occurring throughout education as part of school reform. Many professionals hope that we will soon have one integrated education system (NICHCY, 1993), not a special education system distinct and separate from general education.

You, the **general education teacher,** are the first professional included in this section because for many students with suspected or documented disabilities, you will be the person who has the most detailed knowledge of the students' day-to-day needs in your classroom. Your responsibilities span several areas. You are the person most likely to bring to the attention of other professionals a student whom you suspect may have a disability; that is, you may encounter a student who is reading significantly and persistently below grade level, a student whose behavior is so different from other students' that you suspect an emotional disorder, or a student who has extraordinary difficulty focusing on learning. When you suspect a disability, you will document the student's characteristics and behaviors that led to your concern, often by gathering samples of the student's work, compiling descriptions of the student's behavior, and keeping notes of how you have addressed the student's problem (Safran & Safran, 1996). You will work with special education colleagues to attempt accommodations in your classroom to further clarify whether the student's problems need further exploration. If the student is referred for assessment for special education, you will contribute information about the student's academic and social functioning in your classroom, and you will help identify the student's strengths, needs, and educational program components. For example, you might help others to understand the curricular expectations in your classroom and the types of adaptations that may be necessary for the student to succeed there. You might assist special services staff in updating parents on their child's yearly progress. Most important, you will be expected to work with special services staff to provide appropriate instruction within your classroom (Chalmers & Faliede, 1996; King-Sears

Figure 2.1   General Education Teacher Responsibilities in Special Education

Member of prereferral or
intervention assistance team

Provider of day-to-day
instruction

Identifier of students with possible
special needs

Communication link
with colleagues

Member of multidisciplinary team that
writes the IEP

Liaison to parents

& Cummings, 1996; Stainback, Stainback, & Stefanich, 1996). Responsibilities of a general education teacher are presented in Figure 2.1.

When all your responsibilities are listed, your role in planning and providing special services to students may appear overwhelming. However, studies of general education teachers' perceptions of their roles in working with students with disabilities generally report that the teachers are able and willing to contribute to students' education as long as some conditions are met. The most important conditions seem to be making time available for teacher planning and ensuring adequate funding for programs (Kruger, Struzziero, Watts, & Vacca, 1995; Taylor, Richards, Goldstein, & Schilit, 1997).

Special Education Teachers

The professionals with whom you are most likely to have ongoing contact in teaching students with disabilities are **special education teachers.** They are responsible for managing and coordinating the services a student receives, including the writing and implementation of the student's **individualized education program (IEP).** They also typically provide direct instruction to the students on their caseloads

What are this teacher's roles and responsibilities in helping identify students who may be entitled to special education and in assisting his students with disabilities and other exceptional learners in his class?

(Voltz & Elliott, 1990). In addition, they may consult with you regarding a student suspected of having a disability, working with you to determine whether a referral for assessment for possible special education is warranted.

Depending on the state in which you teach and the students in your classroom, you may work with different types of special education teachers. Sometimes, special education teachers are assigned to work with a specific category of students. For example, your school may have a teacher for students with learning disabilities or emotional disabilities. Likewise, a teacher for students with vision or hearing impairments may be your support for particular students. In states that do not use categorical labels, some teachers teach students with high-incidence disabilities (for example, learning disabilities) or low-incidence disabilities (for example, autism).

In other situations, though, special education teachers may be designated by the type of services they provide. For example, for some students with high-incidence disabilities in your class, you may work with a **consulting teacher** (DeBoer, 1995). This professional might meet with you regularly to monitor student progress and address your concerns about the students but might not directly teach them. You might also work with a **resource teacher** (Evans, Harris, Adeigbola, Houston, & Argott, 1993), who might divide time between directly instructing students and working with teachers.

A third type of special education teacher designated by type of services is an **inclusion specialist** or **support facilitator** (Janney, Snell, Beers, & Raynes, 1995). In inclusive schools, inclusion specialists are responsible for providing some student instruction, problem solving with teachers, and coordinating the services the student receives. Often, they focus on ensuring that the needs of students with moderate, severe, or multiple disabilities are being met.

If you work in a school district where each school has only a few students with disabilities, the special educator you interact with might be an **itinerant teacher.** Itinerant teachers travel between two or more school sites to provide services to students. Teachers for students with vision or hearing disabilities are sometimes itinerant. However, teachers who specialize in working with students with other disabilities may also deliver services this way, especially in districts with small enrollments.

One other type of special education teacher is a **transition specialist.** This professional typically works in a high school setting and helps prepare students to leave school for vocational training, employment, or postsecondary education. If you teach in business education, home economics, industrial or other vocational arts, or similar areas, you might work very closely with a transition specialist. However, this professional also spends time working directly with students to assess their skills and interests, arrange for them to explore vocational and educational opportunities, and assist them in finding and keeping jobs or locating an appropriate college or trade school. A transition specialist also works with community businesses to arrange student job sites and to resolve problems related to student workers (Cronin, 1996). He or she may also serve as a **job coach,** accompanying a student to a job site and helping the student master the skills needed to do the job successfully.

As the nature of special education services changes, so do the job responsibilities and titles of special educators. For example, you might find that the professionals in your school who used to be called special education teachers are now referred to as "support teachers." This change in title represents an effort to de-label teachers that parallels efforts to de-emphasize students' labels. As schools work to become more inclusive, the vocabulary related to teachers who work with students with special needs will probably continue to evolve.

Check Your Learning

What are the typical responsibilities of special education teachers? Why do they have different job titles?

Other Specialists and Related Service Providers

In addition to working with special education teachers, you will have contact with a variety of other service providers. They, too, play important roles in educating students with disabilities.

School psychologists.   These professionals offer at least two types of expertise related to educating students with disabilities. First, **school psychologists** often have a major responsibility for determining a student's cognitive, academic, social, emotional, and/or behavioral functioning. They typically contribute a detailed written analysis of the student's strengths and areas of need; in many school districts, this document is referred to as a "psych. report," that is, a psychological report. In a related role, school psychologists sometimes chair the multidisciplinary team that meets to decide whether a student has a disability, and if so, what types of services are needed.

A second major task for school psychologists is designing strategies to address students' academic and social behavior problems (Rosenfield & Gravois, 1996). Sometimes, school psychologists serve as behavior consultants. Occasionally, they assist a teacher by working with an entire class group on social skills. They might also provide individual assistance to students with emotional or behavioral problems who are not eligible for special education. Unfortunately, many school districts can employ only enough school psychologists to complete required assessment duties; when this occurs, school psychologists are seldom available to assist students or teachers directly.

Counselors.   Although **counselors** most often advise high school students, they also work at other school levels and contribute to the education of students with disabilities. For example, counselors in some school districts assess students' social and emotional functioning, including such areas as self-concept; motivation; attitude toward school, peers, and teachers; and social skills. Counselors also can provide services to both teachers and students. For teachers, they might suggest ways to draw out a student who is excessively shy, build into the curriculum activities designed to enhance students' self-concept, and create an emotionally safe classroom environment. For students, counselors might arrange group sessions with students from several classes who share specific needs, or they might work with an entire class on how to interact with a peer who has a disability.

Speech/language therapists.   Many students with disabilities have communication needs. Some have mild problems in pronouncing words or speaking clearly. Others have extremely limited vocabulary. Yet others can make only a few sounds and rely on alternative means of communication, such as communication boards. The professionals who specialize in meeting students' communication needs are **speech/language therapists.** They have a tremendously diverse range of school responsibilities. At the primary level, they might work with entire classes on language development or with individual students on pronouncing sounds. At the intermediate level, they might work on vocabulary with a group of students, but might also help a student with a moderate cognitive disability to pronounce some word more clearly or to combine words into sentences. At the high school level, they often focus on functional vocabulary and work mostly with students with low-incidence disabilities. For example, they might help a student with a cognitive disability learn to read common signs and complete tasks such as ordering in a restaurant or asking for assistance.

Check Your Learning

Based on the grade and subject area you plan to teach, which special educators are you most likely to work with?

FYI

Functional skills are those students need for adult independence. They include the ability to shop, ride a bus, ask for help, and so on. Functional vocabulary words are those that many adults need, words like *sale, restroom, exit,* and *stop.*

Social workers.   Social workers' expertise is similar to that of counselors in terms of being able to help teachers and students address social and emotional issues. Thus, they may serve as consultants to teachers and also may provide individual or group assistance to students. However, **social workers** have additional expertise. They often are the liaison between the school and the family. For example, they can create a family history by interviewing parents and visiting a student's home; this information may be critical in determining whether a student needs special education services. Similarly, they may help other school professionals work with families on matters such as gaining access to community health services. The school social worker often follows up on teacher reports about the suspected abuse or neglect of students. In some school districts, both counselors and social workers are available to meet student needs. In others, only one of these professional groups is employed.

Physical therapists and occupational therapists.   For some students to benefit from education, they require assistance for problems with gross and fine motor skills. Physical and occupational therapists are the professionals who have expertise in these areas.

Physical therapists assess students' needs and provide interventions related to gross motor skills. They might participate on a multidisciplinary team by assessing such areas as the obviously awkward gait of a student suspected of having a disability. They also interpret information about a student's physical needs that has been provided by a physician. For students with identified disabilities, physical therapists might provide direct training in large-muscle movement and control. They also might monitor student needs related to how they should be positioned, whether in a wheelchair, standing with assistance, or on the floor; how their physical needs are affecting their educational needs; and how classroom settings can be adapted to accommodate their needs.

Occupational therapists are concerned with fine motor skills; they often have the responsibility of assessing students' use of their hands and fingers and developing and implementing plans for improving related motor skills. For example, an occupational therapist may assess whether a student with a severe learning disability can appropriately grip and use a pencil. This professional might help younger students or those with more severe disabilities learn skills for feeding or dressing themselves. Occupational therapists are working increasingly with teachers to incorporate fine motor skills training into classroom routines.

Adaptive physical educators.   When students have significant gross or fine motor problems, typical physical education programs in schools may not be able to address their needs directly. **Adaptive physical educators** assess students' motor needs and work with teachers, physical educators, and others to meet them, or they work directly with students. These professionals are experts in adapting traditional physical education activities for students with disabilities. For example, they might create a simplified form of a basketball drill so that a student who has difficulty running can participate in the activity. They also might create activities that help students develop such skills as balancing, skipping, running, or throwing.

Nurses.   A link between students' medical and educational needs is provided by **nurses.** As needed, they develop student medical histories, and they may screen students for vision and hearing problems. They also provide the team information about specific medical conditions a student might have and the impact a student's medication might have on educational performance. Further, nurses assist other professionals in deciding whether a student's learning or behavior problem could have a medical basis and discussing such matters with parents. Day to day, nurses most often are responsible for ensuring that students with disabilities take required medication and for providing first aid or other emergency treatment. They also work with teachers and families to monitor student medical needs (for example, whether a change in medication is causing drowsiness or hyperactivity).

Administrators.   The school's principal, assistant principal, or sometimes a special education department chairperson or team leader are the **administrators** most likely to participate actively in the education of students with disabilities. Their role is to offer knowledge about the entire school community and provide perspective on school district policies regarding special education. Administrators assist the multidisciplinary team in determining students' eligibility for services and exploring strategies for meeting their needs. They also play an important role in addressing parent concerns. Every team that determines whether a student is eligible for special education must have administrative representation. For example, in one school, the mother of Marisha, a student with severe language delays, requested that her daughter receive speech/language therapy for 40 minutes daily. School professionals were in agreement that this amount of therapy was not appropriate. Dr. Wade, the principal, worked with the team and the parent to negotiate the amount of speech therapy needed to accomplish Marisha's goals.

In some locales, especially in large urban and suburban districts where it is difficult to ensure that all required special education procedures are followed, a **special services coordinator** is another administrator you will meet. Special services coordinators specialize in special education procedural information. They help alleviate the pressure on school administrators for accurately interpreting and following guidelines. They also explain services and options to parents, problem solve with teachers when issues arise, and assist in monitoring to ensure that students with disabilities receive needed supports.

Paraprofessionals.   Individuals who assist teachers and others in the provision of services to students with disabilities are called **paraprofessionals.** Although paraprofessionals may be certified teachers, they are considered noncertified staff according to the terms of their employment; that is, their responsibilities for decision making about students are limited. Paraprofessionals also might be called *instructional assistants, teaching assistants, aides,* or other titles, depending on local practices.

School districts use paraprofessionals in many different ways (Jones & Bender, 1993; Palma, 1994). These are two of the most common: First, some paraprofessionals are assigned to a specific student who needs ongoing individual assistance. For example, students with no ability to move their arms may have a paraprofessional who takes notes for them and completes other tasks such as feeding. A few students have medical conditions requiring that a specially trained paraprofessional be present to monitor their status. Paraprofessionals in this role may be referred to as **personal assistants.**

The second and more common type of paraprofessional is one who assists in the delivery of special services for many students. These paraprofessionals often work in both inclusive classrooms and special education classrooms as well as on the playground, at assemblies, and during bus duty. They have primary responsibility

FYI

Although research does not yet clearly support the effectiveness of paraprofessionals in delivering special education services, the move toward inclusion has led to a rapid rise in their use (Jones & Bender, 1993).

Connections

Additional information about working with paraprofessionals is included in Chapter 3.

What is the role of para-professionals in inclusive classrooms? How do itinerant and other special education teachers carry out their responsibilities toward students with disabilities?

for working with students with disabilities, but they sometimes also help other students and the teacher as the need arises and time permits.

Cultural Awareness

In schools with many students whose native language is not English, bilingual translators might be available to assist in communication with students and parents.

Other specialists. Depending on student needs and state and local practice, other professionals also may participate in the education of students with disabilities. For example, in some states a **psychometrist** completes much of the individual assessment of students potentially eligible for special education services and of those already receiving services. Sometimes, school districts have **consultants** who are used only when a need exists in their specific area of expertise (for example, severe behavior problems, autism, traumatic brain injury). If you work in a school district in which many students are non-native English speakers, you may also work with **bilingual teachers** or **bilingual special education teachers.** Bilingual teachers are not special educators, but they sometimes help in decision making related to students with disabilities who have limited English skills. Bilingual special education teachers are professionally trained both in special education and in bilingual education (Salend, Dorney, & Mazo, 1997). One other type of specialist is a **mobility specialist.** These professionals help students with vision impairments learn how to become familiar with their environments and how to travel from place to place safely. They consult with classroom teachers regarding students with vision impairments.

Another important service provider is a **sign language interpreter.** Interpreters are the communication link for students with significant hearing impairments. Interpreters listen to the instruction in a classroom and relay it to students with hearing impairments using sign language. Interpreters might accompany a student all day or might be needed only in academic subjects such as language arts. The Technology Notes feature explains another strategy, captioned television and video, that also helps bridge the communication gap for students with hearing impairments.

Professionals from agencies outside the school are also part of the specialist group. If a student has been receiving services through a hospital or residential program, a physician, nurse, social worker, or other representative from there may work with school personnel to ensure that the student has a smooth transition back to

Technology Notes

Teaching and Learning through Captioned Television

Captioning for television was developed primarily to assist individuals with hearing impairments. However, educators have discovered and research supports the fact that captioned television can be a powerful tool for helping many students, including those who are bilingual and those who have reading disabilities, learn reading and vocabulary skills. Many television programs, movies, and educational videos are available with closed captions. Beginning in 1993, new television sets were made with built-in caption display capabilities. For an older television, a set-top caption decoder can be purchased for approximately $160 and attached to the antennae connections. One source for caption decoders is Harris Communications (1-800-825-6758).

Here are some suggestions for using captioned television and other captioned video:

- Get to know your equipment. For new televisions with built-in caption display capabilities, switching on the captions usually requires using the remote control to change a setting in one of the on-screen setup menus. A set-top caption decoder is easy to attach to an older TV and has a button to switch on the captions.

- Select a high-interest captioned video. Many hours of captioned video are available each week. You can select programs appropriate for your students by reviewing a weekly television guide. One example of such a program is *Reading Rainbow*. This type of show has few viewing restrictions since it is intended for widespread educational use.

- Preview the video. You are unlikely to need to use an entire video. By previewing, you can select the most relevant segments and plan your lessons accordingly.

- Locate related texts. By gathering books and magazines that relate to the video, you create a supply of print materials for students to use that complement the programs you have selected.

- Introduce the video. Captioned video is no different from other teaching: It should be clearly in-

Closed-captioning can be used to develop reading skills.

troduced to students. Some students will need to become accustomed to reading the captions. Once they do, you can use the mute button on the television remote control to challenge students to read the screen. Likewise, you can have students read along with the video and retell the video after it has been watched and read.

- Create a video library. If you keep a record of the video activities you have used and enjoyed, you will be able to share them with your colleagues. You might also check to see if your school district has a video library. Remember that video materials are copyrighted and their use is restricted; your collection should not violate copyright laws.

If you would like more information on closed captioning, contact

The National Captioning Institute
1900 Gallows Road
Suite 3000
Vienna, VA 22182

S O U R C E : Adapted from "Captioned Video and Vocabulary Learning: An Innovative Practice in Literacy Instruction," by P. S. Koskinen, R. M. Wilson, L. B. Gambrell, and S. B. Neuman, 1993, *The Reading Teacher*, *47* (1), 36–43, by permission of the International Reading Association.

school. Individuals from the medical community also might be involved when students are being assessed for attentional problems or when they have been injured or ill. Professionals from agencies also might be included if a student is receiving assistance from a community agency or has contact with the juvenile justice system. In these instances, caseworkers may serve as liaisons to the school. Finally, if parents wish to obtain an expert opinion from a specialist not associated with the school, those individuals can attend team meetings or submit written reports for team consideration.

Parents, students, and advocates.   Whenever decisions are being made concerning a student with a suspected or documented disability, the best interests of the student and his or her family must be represented. Parents have the right to participate in virtually all aspects of their child's educational program (Osborne, 1996; Rothstein, 1995). Parent involvement spans the following areas:

Connections

Additional information on parent roles in working with teachers and other school professionals is included in Chapter 3.

1. Requesting assessment for special services.
2. Providing input on their child's strengths and needs.
3. Bringing to the team independent professionals' opinions about their child's needs.
4. Helping to decide if their child has a disability and if the child will receive special services.
5. Assisting in the writing of goals and objectives for their child's educational program.
6. Participating in delivering instruction to their child.
7. Monitoring their child's progress.
8. Seeking assistance in resolving disagreements with school professionals.

Often, parents are a strong ally for general education teachers. They can assist teachers by reviewing at home what is taught in school, rewarding their child for school accomplishments, and working with school professionals to resolve behavior and academic problems.

Whenever appropriate, students with disabilities are also active participants in their own education. Increasingly, educators are involving students so they can state directly their needs and goals and can learn to advocate for themselves. The extent of student participation on the team depends on the age of the student and the type and impact of the disability. The older the student and the greater his or her cognitive functioning, the greater the participation. Thus, if you teach first grade, your students with disabilities will not be expected to participate in very many decisions about their education. However, if you teach high school science, it is quite likely that your students with disabilities will attend and participate in team meetings that discuss them and request adaptations to help them learn. These students might also monitor their learning and behavior and assess their progress toward their educational goals.

Connections

The topics of student self-advocacy and student self-evaluation are addressed in depth in Chapter 10.

A final team member is an **advocate.** Sometimes, parents sense that they are not knowledgeable enough about the policies and procedures that govern special education to represent themselves. In other instances, they are not sure school district personnel are acting in the best interests of their children. In yet other situations, parents may be uncomfortable interacting with school personnel because of language or cultural differences, or for other reasons. Parents have the right to bring an advocate to team and other school meetings concerning their children. This person serves as their advisor and sometimes their spokesperson. Although advocates often do not have a direct role in implementing the education program for a student with a disability, they might assume responsibilities for the parent. Advocates are sometimes professionals who are compensated by parents for their services. Or they may be volunteers provided through a professional organization or parent support group, or friends or relatives.

F Y I

The National Resource Center on Family Based Services at the University of Iowa conducts research, provides technical assistance and training, and distributes information on family-centered approaches to serving students with exceptionalities.

How Can You Decide Whether a Student Need Might Be a Disability?

You will play a key role in deciding whether a student in your class should be evaluated for the presence of a disability. Although students with obvious cognitive, sensory, or physical impairments probably have been identified before reaching school age, learning, language, attention, and behavior disabilities often are not diagnosed until children start school. Because you are the professional in daily contact with the student, you are the person most likely to notice an unmet need. It is your judgment that often initiates a special education decision-making process.

Analyze the Unmet Needs

As you teach, you will sometimes discover that you have a nagging concern about a student. This concern might begin early in the school year, or it might take several months to emerge. When you review student records and your own impressions of the student and your concern, you decide that the student's achievement is not within your classroom's typical range, given the standards of your school district and community expectations. Should you ask other professionals to assess the student for eligibility for special education? Perhaps. But first, you need to ask yourself some questions. These questions are summarized in Figure 2.2 on page 40.

What are specific examples of the unmet needs?   Having a nebulous concern about a student is far different from stating specifically what your concerns are. For example, sensing that a student is unmotivated is not a clear concern. What does the student do that leads you to conclude that motivation is a problem? Is it that the student doesn't make eye contact when speaking to you, or that the rewards and consequences that affect other students seem to have no effect—positive or negative—on this student? Vague concerns and hunches should be supported by specific information. Phrases such as "slow learning," "poor attitude toward school," "doesn't pay attention," and "never gets work completed" might have very different meanings to different professionals. To prepare to share your concern with others, then, your first step is to ask yourself, "When I say the student . . . , what are examples that clarify what I mean?"

Is there a chronic pattern negatively affecting learning?   Nearly all students will go through periods in which they struggle to learn, behave inappropriately, or otherwise cause you concern. Sometimes, a situation outside of school may affect students.

Figure 2.2   **Teachers' Concerns about Student Needs**

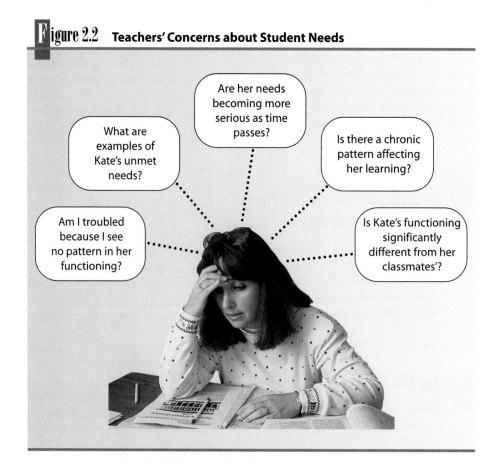

For example, parents divorcing, families being evicted from their apartments, elderly grandparents moving in with the family, or a family member being injured or arrested might all negatively affect student learning or behavior. However, the impact of these traumatic events should not be permanent, and the student should gradually return to previous levels of functioning.

Students with disabilities may also be affected by specific situations or events, but their learning and behavior needs form a chronic pattern. They struggle over a long period of time regardless of the circumstances. For example, Betsy, who has a learning disability, has difficulty learning sight words no matter what the level of the words or how creatively they are introduced. Jared, a high school student with an emotional disability, is withdrawn whether sitting in a large class or interacting in a small group. Julianna, an eighth grader who had a severe head injury last year, usually seems to grasp abstract concepts as they are taught, but she struggles to describe or apply them after instruction.

Is the unmet need becoming more serious as time passes?   Sometimes, a student's needs appear to become greater across time. For example, Ben, who seemed to see well at the beginning of the school year, now holds books closer and closer to his face, squints when he tries to read, and complains about headaches. In another example, Karen, who began the school year fairly close in achievement to her peers, is significantly behind by November. Indications that needs are increasing are a signal to ask for input from others.

Is the student's functioning significantly different from that of classmates?   As you think about your concerns about a student, you should ask yourself how the student compares to other students. For example, in urban settings it has been demonstrated that students at risk for special education referral are less involved in the classroom and receive less verbal feedback from their teachers (Bay & Bryan, 1992). If you have six students who are all struggling, it might be that the information or skills are beyond the reach of the entire group or that your teaching approach is not accomplishing what you had planned. Even though self-reflection is sometimes difficult, when many students are experiencing problems it is important to analyze how the curriculum or teaching might be contributing to the situation. In such instances, you should make changes in those two areas before seeking other assistance.

However, perhaps you are an elementary teacher who can't seem to find enough books at the right level for the one student in your fourth grade class who is almost a nonreader. Perhaps you are an eighth-grade industrial arts teacher who is worried about letting a student who gets extremely angry use equipment that could be dangerous, and this is the only student about whom you have this level of concern. Many students have needs that do not signal the presence of disabilities. Students with disabilities have needs that are significantly different from those of most other students.

Do you discover that you cannot find a pattern?   In some instances, the absence of a pattern to student needs is as much an indicator that you should request assistance as is a distinct pattern. Perhaps Curtis has tremendous mood swings, and you arrive at school each day wondering if it'll be a "good day" or a "bad day" for him. However, you can't find a way to predict which it will be. Or consider Becka, who learns science with ease but cannot seem to master even basic reading skills. You are not sure why her learning is so different in the two subjects. In a third example, in physical education, Tyrone some days seems to have average motor skills but on other days frequently stumbles and cannot participate fully in the learning stations you have created.

Communicate Your Observations and Try Your Own Interventions

Your analysis of your students' unmet needs is the basis for further action. Although your analysis can help you decide to seek assistance from special education professionals for one of your students, as part of your attempts to help the student you are responsible for gathering other information and trying to resolve the problem first.

Contact parents.   One of your first strategies should be to contact the family (Dyson, 1996). Parents or other family members often can inform you about changes in the student's life that could be affecting school performance. The Professional Edge on pages 42–43 provides some formats you can use to communicate effectively with students' families. Family members can also help you understand the student's activities outside of school that might influence his or her schoolwork, including clubs, gang involvement, employment, and responsibilities at home. Further,

Connections

In Chapter 8 you will learn more about evaluating student needs using curriculum-based assessment.

Check Your Learning

What questions should you explore to determine whether your concern about a student warrants referral for possible special education services?

Professional Edge

Communicating with Family Members

One of your most important responsibilities as a teacher working with parents of students with disabilities or other special needs is to maintain effective communication with them. The strategies you use to communicate with them are similar to those you would use to communicate with any parent; but you might also find that because this communication is so vital, you want to use some additional strategies.

Passport

One system of communication that can be valuable when daily communication is needed or when the student is not able to convey information to the parent is a passport (Runge, Walker, & Shea, 1975). A *passport* is a spiral notebook or paper-filled binder in which the teacher writes a few essential comments at the end of each school day. The passport goes home with the student so the parent can read the teacher's

Sample Page from a Passport

TO: Ms. Dolores   9:00 A.M.
Good day on the bus. Tom sat in his assigned seat and waited his turn to leave the bus. I praised his behavior and gave him two points.

Mr. Parker, Bus Driver

TO: Ms. Dolores   10:30 A.M.
During PE today the group played kickball. Tom was well-behaved but had difficulty participating effectively. I awarded him six points and praised his behavior. Can we meet to discuss some means of increasing his participation?

Ms. Minton, Physical Education

TO: Mr. and Mrs. Hogerty   2:30 P.M.
As you can see from the notes above, Tom had a good day at school.

    He received 89 percent on his reading test this morning. That's real progress. Please praise him for this accomplishment.

    This evening, Tom is to read pp. 1–5 in his new reading book.

    Even better news! Tom remembered to walk in the hallways today. He is very proud of himself.

    I shall talk to Ms. Minton today about increasing Tom's participation in PE. I'll let you know what we decide at tomorrow night's parent meeting.

Ms. Dolores

TO: Ms. Dolores   9:00 P.M.
We praised and rewarded Tom for his hard work on the reading test, the bus, and the hallways. You're right; he feels good about himself today.

    Tom read pp. 1–5 in the new book with his father. The words he had trouble with are underlined.

    We will see you at the parent meeting tomorrow night.

Mary Hogerty

S O U R C E : From *Parents and Teachers of Children with Exceptionalities: A Handbook for Collaboration* by T. M. Shea and A. M. Bauer, 1991, Copyright © 1991 by Allyn and Bacon. Reprinted by permission.

notes. The parent then either responds with additional notes or acknowledges having read the passport by signing the day's information. The first example shows what a page in a passport looks like.

Checklist

Another type of communication you can use when you and the parents are monitoring the behavior of a student who has several behavior problems is a *daily reporting system*. This reporting form is a brief list of critical behaviors and a check-mark assessment of the student's performance on these for the day. The parent signs the report and returns it to school. In some cases, an entire week's record can be kept on a single form, and the daily report is kept as a log of progress for the student. The second example shows a checklist report.

Class Updates or Newsletters

A third type of communication form to use with parents is an *informational sheet*. Typically, this one-page weekly update notifies parents about important class activities and identifies the types of supports you need from them for the upcoming week. It is most common at the elementary and middle school levels. For example, you might use such a newsletter to inform parents that the next science unit is on meteorology and includes a field trip to the planetarium. This advance notice enables you and the parents to work together to make any special necessary arrangements for the field trip. This type of communication form is particularly important if you have students with disabilities that affect their ability to communicate with their parents. Without an update from you, the parents of these children might not hear what's occurring in their children's class.

Sample Checklist Reporting System

Name _____Milton_____   Date _____2/6/96_____

	Great	Okay	With Prompt	Needs Work
Brought homework to class.				✓
Had all school supplies (pencils, paper, notebook).	✓			
Arrived in class on time.	✓			
Began assigned work promptly and without arguing.			✓	

Teacher comments:

All supplies brought today—homework is the next goal.

Parent comments:

I would like to meet with you to discuss homework issues. Next Monday when I pick Milton up? Please let me know if this is ok.

Parent signature _____Vivian Boerger_____

by contacting the family, you might learn that what you perceive as a problem is mostly a reflection of a cultural difference. For example, a student whose family emigrated from Thailand is extremely quiet because silence signals respect in her native culture, not because she is unable to participate.

Parents are also your partners in working to resolve some student learning problems. They can assist you in monitoring if homework is completed and returned to school, if behavior problems are occurring on the walk home, or if a physician is concerned about a child's medical condition. If you work with students whose homes do not have telephones and whose parents do not have transportation to come to school, your social worker or principal can help you make needed contact.

Contact colleagues.   Especially as a new teacher, you will want to discuss your concerns with other professionals to gain an additional perspective on the student's needs. In most schools, a special education teacher will arrange to observe the student in your class and then to discuss the observation. If your school psychologist is available, you might ask for consultation assistance. In schools where grade-level teams or other types of teams meet, you can raise your concerns in that context. One hallmark of today's schools is an array of professionals who have expertise in many areas. With a little exploration, you are likely to find that your school has an in-house resource you can access to check your perceptions against a broader perspective.

W W W Resources

An Internet source of information about a wide variety of special education issues is the Federal Resource Center for Special Education, <http://www. dssc.org/frc>. At this website you can learn about a federal project that provides supports to state and local education agencies on many matters related to providing services to individuals with disabilities.

Try interventions.   Part of your responsibility as a teacher is to create a classroom where students can succeed. To cultivate such a setting, you will make adaptations as part of your attempts to address students' unmet needs. For example, have you tried moving the student's seat? Have you removed distracting bulletin board items from the student's line of sight? Have you changed from writing your tests by hand to typing them on a computer to make them more legible? Do you give some students only part of their assignment at one time because they become overwhelmed otherwise? These are just a few alterations that many teachers make without even thinking of them as adaptations. Sometimes, these small accommodations will be sufficient to help a student learn. In any case, you should try common interventions before deciding a student might need special education. The Professional Edge suggests several strategies you can use to help you stay current on classroom interventions.

Document the unmet need.   If you anticipate requesting assistance for a student, you will need to demonstrate the seriousness of your concern and your attempts to help meet the student's needs. If you have implemented a behavior contract with the student, you can keep a record of how effective it has been. If you have contacted parents several times, you can keep a log of your conversations. If you have tried to decrease the number of times the student misses your first-hour class, you can summarize your attendance data. Strategies to document student needs serve two main purposes. First, they help you to do a "reality check" on whether the problem is as serious as you think it is. Especially if you gather data from other students as a comparison, you can judge whether the unmet needs of one student are significantly different from those of typical students. Second, the information you collect helps you communicate with other professionals. Special service providers cannot possibly meet every need in every classroom. Their work is reserved in large part for extraordinary student needs, and your documentation helps in the decision about providing the assistance you seek.

Professional Edge

Developing Alternative Interventions

Many teachers are constantly on the lookout for innovative ideas for helping students with exceptionalities in their classrooms succeed. Here are a few strategies for keeping your idea file up-to-date.

- Join a professional organization that provides journals to its members. Examples of these groups are the Council for Exceptional Children (CEC) and the Association for Supervision and Curriculum Development (ASCD). Most major disciplines also have professional organizations (for example, the National Council of Teachers of Mathematics and the National Council of Teachers of English). The publications distributed by such organizations often have many new and practical ideas for working with students with special needs. Some of these organizations have student chapters; most have discounted student membership fees.

- Attend state or national meetings of professional organizations. Most states have an annual special education conference and welcome participation by general education teachers and teachers-to-be. National organizations also have annual conventions. Participating in such meetings is a wonderful opportunity to build professional networks, find other professionals who share your interests, and learn what's "hot."

- Check on the availability of professional libraries in your local education agencies. In some parts of the country, some special education supports and services are provided through regional agencies that serve several school districts. These agencies have many different names. For example, in Wisconsin they are called the Cooperative Educational Service Agency, or CESA; in Illinois they are called joint agreements; and in Ohio they are called Special Education Regional Resource Centers, or SERRCs. Many such agencies keep professional libraries that you may be allowed to browse for information and ideas.

- Form a teacher support group. If you and three friends agree to meet once each month for a brown bag meal and to bring to your gathering one new idea to share, you will soon have lots of strategies in your repertoire.

- Visit your local teacher materials and supply store. Most urban and suburban areas have teacher supply stores that carry materials for helping students learn. These stores are particularly valuable for locating educational games and supplemental teaching materials.

How Do Students Obtain Special Services?

The majority of students who receive special education have high-incidence disabilities that you may be the first to recognize. If you teach at the elementary level, you will probably have students every year whom you refer for possible special services. If you teach in middle school, junior high, or high school, you will find that many students with disabilities already have been identified before they reach your class. However, there are exceptions; students may be found eligible for special education at any time during their school careers. As a teacher, you always have the option of asking a team of professionals to decide if special education is needed.

Having a serious and documented concern about a student is only the first step in considering whether a disability may be present. Your concern brings the student to the attention of other school professionals so that further information can be gathered and decisions made. The specific and formal procedures that must be followed to determine student eligibility for special education services are designed to ensure that only students who truly need these services receive them. These procedures are described in the following sections and summarized in Figure 2.3, which illustrates the flow of the procedures from beginning to end.

Initial Consideration of Student Problems

F Y I

Teams that meet to problem solve about students before consideration of special education might be called teacher assistance teams, intervention assistance teams, student–teacher assistance teams, or mainstream assistance teams. What are such teams called in your school district?

General education teachers, principals, special services personnel, parents, physicians, and social service agency personnel all may initiate the process of obtaining special education for a student. Most often, however, a student's classroom teacher will notice a pattern of academic underachievement, inconsistent learning, serious behavior problems, difficulties in social skills, or a persistent physical or sensory problem. When such problems occur, the teacher brings the student to the attention of others who will help decide whether special education is warranted.

Prereferral or instructional assistance teams.   A common way to begin the process of helping a student suspected of having a disability is to bring the problem to the attention of a team (Friend & Cook, 1997; Safran & Safran, 1996). This **prereferral** or **instructional assistance team** often includes general education teachers, special services personnel, and an administrator. Teachers wishing to "bring a student to the team" complete a referral form on which they describe the student's strengths and problems and describe efforts they have made to assist the student. The teacher then meets with the team to discuss the written information, consider alternative strategies for assisting the student, and determine if the student should have a detailed assessment for potential special education services (Elliott & Sheridan, 1992; Rankin & Aksamit, 1994). The unifying characteristic of this type of team is an emphasis on problem solving among all members. The Case in Practice on page 48 illustrates how this type of team operates.

Screening.   Not all schools have teams to help make decisions about the need for assessment for special education. In some schools, the school psychologist, counselor, principal, or other professional has the responsibility of **screening** the referral, meeting informally with a general education teacher about a student. This individual asks about the strategies the teacher has tried to assist the student and may make additional recommendations. If efforts remain unsuccessful and the presence of a disability is suspected, referral for a more comprehensive assessment will follow.

Diagnostic teaching is sometimes part of screening. A special education teacher or other special services professional may carry out sample lessons with the student, teaching different skills, using different teaching methods, and trying various ways of rewarding the student. By keeping detailed notes of what techniques were effective, this professional can make specific suggestions to teachers or recommend specific types of additional assessment.

Connections

Chapter 3 discusses professional collaboration, including how teams can work effectively.

When a team discusses or screens a student, it is not legally required that a parent be involved in the process. However, educators should notify parents of their

Figure 2.3 The Decision-Making Process for Special Education

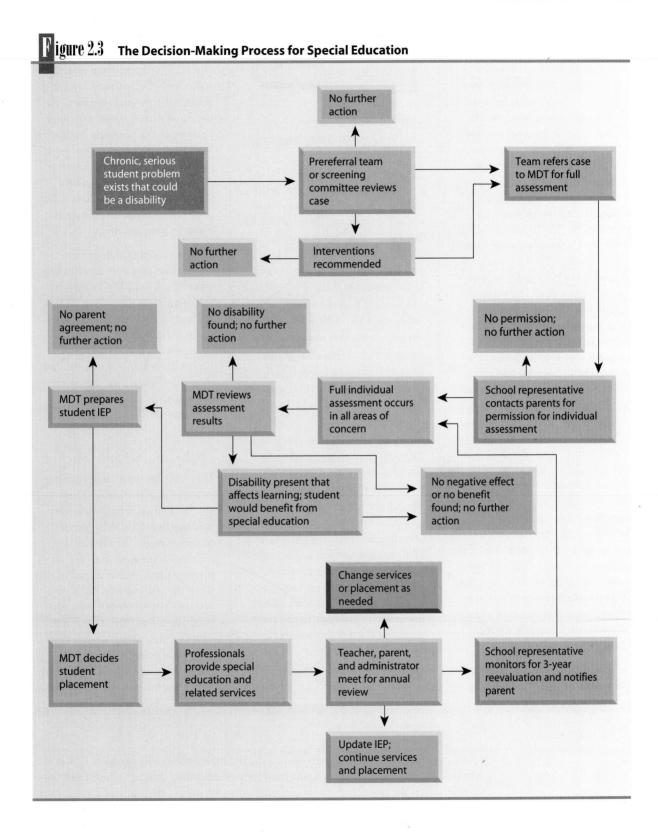

It is 3:15 P.M. and Ms. Jacob's last-hour students have just left. She gathers a stack of information from her desk and heads toward the conference room for an Intervention Assistance Team meeting. Ms. Jacobs is the sixth-grade representative on the team this year. Along with a seventh-grade and an eighth-grade representative, a special education teacher, and the assistant principal, Ms. Jacobs meets weekly to problem solve about students and to consider if any of their needs are so great that a referral for individual assessment should be made.

The first student to be discussed today is eighth grader Toby. Reviewing her information sheets, Ms. Jacobs sees that Toby is chronically late to school, has what his teacher describes as a sullen attitude, is failing in math and English, and has a D in science. Toby's teacher, Mr. Petrovich, is worried that Toby is headed toward failure, especially as he nears high school age. According to Mr. Petrovich, reward systems have not been successful; Toby's dad seems cooperative but tends to forget to follow through on homework monitoring and other requests; and other teachers on the eighth-grade team share concern about Toby's future.

As the meeting begins and preliminaries are completed, Ms. Jacobs asks Mr. Petrovich several questions.

Ms. Jacobs: Mr. Petrovich, you've spent a great deal of time working with Toby. If you were to summarize your greatest concern for him, what would it be?

Mr. Petrovich: Probably his "I don't care and you can't make me" attitude. It seems to be getting worse as the year goes by. Toby is really a good kid; I don't know what's causing his problems—unless it's peer pressure—and I really want to get to the bottom of this.

Ms. Jacobs: Of all the things you've tried with Toby, what seems to have the biggest positive impact on him?

Mr. Petrovich: Right now, what's keeping him going is sports and the computer lab. But if his grades don't improve, sports isn't going to last long.

Ms. Jacobs: If you think about Toby's strengths, what might we start with to try to come up with some ideas for him?

Mr. Petrovich: I'd really like to see us work on something that takes advantage of Toby's computer skills. I only see him in math and we have very limited computer time, but I've seen some of his projects, and he's really good. He seems to like the structure and logic of the computer and the fact that it doesn't "get in his face."

Ms. Jacobs: It sounds as though you have an idea in mind.

Mr. Petrovich: I do. I'm hoping all of you can work with me to design some kind of very structured program that combines getting work done and getting to use computer equipment as a privilege. I think we have all the necessary components, we just need to put them together . . . and I think that's a concrete area to work in. I don't think a direct confrontation on attitude is going to have any effect.

The meeting continues with all the team members contributing. After 30 minutes, Mr. Petrovich leaves with commitment from others to try a structured work-for-computer-privileges plan and an agreement to review its effectiveness in 3 weeks. Ms. Jacobs stays as the team discusses another student and recommends an individual assessment for this student.

REFLECTIONS

Why was this team meeting constructive and productive? How did Mr. Petrovich help make the meeting a success? What other strategies might the team try in addition to the work-for-computer-privileges idea? What might happen when the team reviews the intervention they planned? Given what you have learned about students with exceptionalities, do you think Toby is the type of student who might be referred for an individual assessment?

concerns and enlist parental assistance in trying to solve the problem. In some schools, parents are invited to team meetings. Remember, parents should never be surprised that the possibility of special education is raised—they should have known for quite some time that a serious problem existed.

The Special Education Referral and Assessment Process

If the decision as a result of team intervention or screening is that a full assessment for possible special education should occur, the parents are contacted. Their written permission for assessment must be obtained prior to any individual assessment (Rothstein, 1995). At this point, a **multidisciplinary team (MDT)** assumes responsibility for determining how to assess the student and for deciding if the student has a disability and is eligible for special education services.

Components of assessment. Assessment involves gathering information about the student's strengths and needs in all areas of concern. Typically, if the student has not had a vision and hearing screening and you have reason to suspect a sensory impairment, these tests will be completed before other assessments. If sensory screening raises concerns, parents are notified of the need for a more complete assessment by a physician or appropriate specialist.

Assessments completed by school professionals may address any aspect of a student's educational functioning (Taylor, 1993). Often, for example, students' cognitive ability is assessed. An individual intelligence test is administered and scored by a school psychologist or another qualified school professional. Academic achievement often is assessed, too. Students complete an individual achievement test administered by a psychologist, special education teacher, psychometrist, or other professional. A third area often evaluated is social/behavioral skills. This evaluation might involve a checklist that you and parents complete concerning student behavior, tests given by the school psychologist, or a series of questions asked of the student.

Another domain for assessment is the student's social and developmental history. Often, the social worker will meet with the parents to learn about the student's family life and major events in the student's development that could be affecting education. For example, parents might be asked about their child's friends in the neighborhood and favorite out-of-school activities, their expectations for their child as an adult, and their child's strengths. Parents might also be asked if their child has had any serious physical injuries, medical problems, or recurring social or behavioral problems.

As another assessment component, a psychologist, counselor, or special education teacher might observe the student in the classroom and other settings to learn how he or she responds to teachers and peers in various school settings. For example, a special education teacher may have observed Chris, who usually plays with younger students during recess and gets confused when playground games are too complex. Chris also watches other students carefully and often seems to take cues for how to act from how they are acting. These observations are all helpful for understanding Chris.

If a potential need exists for speech therapy or occupational or physical therapy, another component is added to the assessment. The professionals in those areas complete assessments in their respective areas of expertise. A speech/language therapist might use a screening instrument that includes having the student use certain words, tell stories, and identify objects. The therapist also might check for atypical use of the muscles of the mouth, tongue, and throat that permit speech and for unusual speech habits such as breathiness in speaking or noticeable voice strain. Similarly, occupational or physical therapists might assess a student's gait, strength and agility, range of motion, or ability to perform fine motor tasks such as buttoning and lacing.

What types of individually administered assessments are required to determine whether a student is eligible for special education services?

Cultural Awareness

Cultural sensitivity is an ongoing issue in the special education assessment process. For example, in one study it was found that assessment instruments used with Native American students generally were not sensitive to their cultures (Gritzmacher & Gritzmacher, 1995).

Throughout the entire assessment process, the general education teacher can provide details on the student's performance in class, patterns of behavior, and discrepancies between expectations and achievement. Your informal or formal observations play an important role in assessment.

Assessment procedures.   The exact procedures for assessing a student's needs vary according to the areas of concern that initiated the assessment process. What is important is that the assessment be completed by individuals trained to administer the tests and other assessment tools used, that the instruments be free of cultural bias, and that the student's performance be evaluated in a way that takes into account the potential disability. School professionals are responsible for ensuring that these obligations are met.

Parent rights.   Throughout the assessment process, parents' rights to participate in their child's education must be respected as established in IDEA and reinforced in virtually all subsequent legislation and litigation (Rothstein, 1995). Parents have the right to be informed in a meaningful way about the procedures and processes of special education and the right to give permission before any individual assessment is completed (Salend & Taylor, 1993). Parents also have the right to request information from a school district representative about how to get an independent evaluation for their child and the right to bring information from an independent evaluation to a meeting to discuss the educational needs of the student. In some cases, parents are entitled to be reimbursed for their expense in obtaining an independent evaluation. These and other parent rights ensured through federal special education laws are outlined in Figure 2.4. If you teach older students, you also might be interested in knowing that, beginning at least one year before reaching the age of majority, students must also be informed directly of their rights (Johns, 1997).

Decision Making for Special Services

After a comprehensive assessment of the student has been completed, the multidisciplinary team meets to discuss their results and make several decisions (Gritzmacher & Gritzmacher, 1995; Rodger, 1995; Zetlin, Padron, & Wilson, 1996). The first decision they must make is whether the student is eligible under the law to be categorized as having a disability. If the team decides that a disability exists, they then determine if the disability is affecting the student's education, and from that decide whether the student is eligible to receive services through special education. In most school districts, these decisions are made at a single meeting that includes the parents, other team members, and students as appropriate. As outlined in Figure 2.4, parents must agree with the decisions being made or the student cannot receive special education services. Most school districts have guidelines to guide team decision making, but the decisions ultimately belong to the team, and the team may decide that the guidelines do not exactly fit a particular case. For example, most states have guidelines specifying that students identified as having a mild cognitive disability have an IQ less than 70 as measured on an individual intelligence test such as a WISC-III and have serious limitations in adaptive behaviors. However, if a student's test scores were slightly above 70 and adaptive skills were particularly limited, a team could still decide that the student has a mild cognitive disability. Likewise, if this student had a measured IQ lower

Cultural Awareness

Over the past two decades, efforts have been made to reduce the racial and cultural bias in assessment instruments and procedures, especially for African American and Hispanic students (Figueroa, 1989; Henry, 1992).

FYI

The Weschler Intelligence Scale for Children–Revised (WISC-III) is an individual intelligence test often used to assess the intellectual ability of students referred for possible education services.

Figure 2.4 Summary of Parent Rights in Special Education

P.L. 94-142, now IDEA-97, established procedural safeguards to ensure that parents had the right to be active participants in their children's education. The following safeguards are some of the major ones provided to parents:

1. Parents are entitled to be members of any group that makes decisions about the educational placement of their child.

2. Parents are to be given written notice before the school initiates, changes, or refuses to initiate or change the identification or educational placement of a child.

3. Parents can participate directly in the development of the individualized educational program (IEP) and the periodic review, at least annually, of the IEP.

4. The school must obtain written, informed parental consent before conducting a formal evaluation and assessment and before initially placing a student in a program providing special education and related services. (*Note:* Written parental consent is required for initial evaluation and initial placement. Subsequent formal evaluation and placement actions require written notice, as described in item 1.)

5. Parents can inspect and review any educational records maintained by the school district or other agency providing service under IDEA. Access to educational records will be granted to parents without unnecessary delay and before any meeting regarding an IEP or before a hearing relating to identification, evaluation, or placement of the child, and in no case more than 45 days after the request has been made.

6. A parent may request, and the school district must provide, information on where independent educational evaluations may be obtained. A parent has the right to an independent educational evaluation at public expense if the parent disagrees with an evaluation obtained by the local school district or responsible public agency. However, the local school district or responsible public agency may initiate a due process hearing to show that the original evaluation is appropriate. If the final decision is that the evaluation is appropriate, the parent still has the right to an independent educational evaluation, but not at public expense. The results of an independent evaluation obtained by the parents at private expense will be considered by the local school district in any decisions about the provisions of a free appropriate public education to the child. Such results may also be presented as evidence at a due process hearing.

7. Parents have the right to request mediation as a means to resolving conflicts with school districts concerning their children with disabilities. Mediation must be available to parents prior to a due process hearing, but it may not delay a hearing. Information shared during mediation is confidential and may not be used as evidence at any subsequent due process hearing. The state bears the cost of mediation, not the parents.

8. Parents have the right to request a hearing by an impartial hearing officer in cases in which they disagree with school district decisions regarding their children's education. Hearings may relate to any aspect of special education, including the fairness of the evaluation procedures used to determine the presence of a disability, the appropriateness of the disability label given the child, the adequacy of the services provided, and the suitability of proposed changes of placement. If parents fail to win a due process hearing at the local level, they may appeal the results of the

(continued)

Figure 2.4   *(continued)*

hearing at the State Department of Education level. After this step, if parents are still dissatisfied with the outcome of the hearing, they may initiate court action.

9. Parents must be fully informed of their right and the procedural safeguards related to special education. They initially should receive this information in a readily understandable manner when their child is referred for evaluation. They should also receive it prior to each IEP meeting and re-evaluation, and when a complaint is registered.

SOURCE: Adapted from "Procedural Safeguards Insuring That Handicapped Children Receive a Free Appropriate Public Education," by M. Gerry, 1987, *National Information Center for Handicapped Children and Youth New Digest,* Number 7, Washington, DC: National Information Center for Handicapped Children and Youth and National Association of State Directors of Special Education, "Comparison of Key Issues: Current Law and 1997 IDEA Amendments." Alexandria, VA: Author.

than 70 but seemed to have many adaptive skills, the team might decide that the student does not have a disability.

If the multidisciplinary team determines that the student has a disability affecting his or her education and that the student is eligible for services according to federal, state, and local guidelines, the stage is set for detailed planning of the student's education and related services. This planning is recorded on the student's individualized education program (IEP). The IEP is the document that outlines all the special education services the student is to receive. Specific guidelines must be followed in developing an IEP. More details about IEPs and their preparation are provided later in this chapter.

The final decision made by the multidisciplinary team concerns the student's placement. **Placement** refers to the location in which the student's education will occur. For most students, the placement is the general education classroom, often with some type of supports offered. For a few, the placement is a special education setting. Later in this chapter, special education services are discussed and placement options are outlined in more detail.

In your school district, the spirit of the procedures outlined above will be followed, but the timelines used and the names for each part of the process will vary. However, all school districts' procedures are designed to ensure that students with disabilities are systematically assessed and that a deliberate and careful process is followed to provide for their education needs.

Monitoring Special Services

In addition to specifying the procedures that must be followed to identify a student as needing special education services, federal and state laws also establish guidelines for monitoring students' progress. The monitoring process is necessary to ensure that students' educational programs remain appropriate and that procedures exist for resolving disputes between school district personnel and parents.

Annual reviews.   The first strategy for monitoring special services is the **annual review.** At least once each year, the student's progress toward his or her annual goals

---

Do It!

Most communities have special education parent support and advocacy groups. Identify one in your area and attend a meeting. Whom did you meet? What did you learn?

must be reviewed, and the IEP changed or updated as needed. The purpose of this annual review is to see that the student's best interests are being protected. Not all multidisciplinary team members who participated in the initial decisions about the student's disability and educational needs are required to participate in annual reviews. However, a teacher instructing the student and an administrator or other professional representing the school district must meet with the student's parents to discuss whether goals and objectives are met and, if not, what to do next. In practical terms, if your school district completes all annual reviews during a given month, you will find that the special education staff with whom you work will be unavailable because of their other responsibilities, such as meeting with parents. Depending on local practices, you might be asked to attend annual reviews for some students. For many students, the general education teacher is the most knowledgeable about their day-to-day functioning. This concept was strengthened with the mandate in IDEA-97 that a general education teacher participate in the development of each student's IEP, not necessarily by writing it, but by contributing a classroom perspective.

Three-year reevaluations.   A second monitoring procedure required by law is the **three-year reevaluation.** At least every three years, and more often if deemed necessary by a multidisciplinary team, students receiving special education services must be reassessed to determine whether their needs have changed. This safeguard is designed to prevent students with disabilities from remaining in services or programs that may no longer be appropriate for them. In some cases, the reevaluation will include administering all the tests and other instruments that were used initially to identify the student as needing special education. However, IDEA-97 has streamlined the reevaluation process. It now permits existing information to be used for reevaluation instead of requiring new assessments. In fact, with parent agreement and team agreement, reevaluations may not involve any new assessment at all (Yell & Shriner, 1997). On the basis of the three-year reevaluation, the multidisciplinary team meets again to develop an appropriate IEP. According to current law, parents are informed that it is time for a three-year reevaluation, but school districts are not required to obtain written permission for this monitoring procedure. This practice enables school districts to continue providing high-quality services to students even if parents are no longer actively involved in their education.

Due process.   The third strategy for monitoring students receiving special education services is **due process,** the set of procedures outlined in the law for resolving disagreements between school district personnel and parents regarding students with disabilities. Due process rights begin when a student is first brought to the attention of a team as potentially having a disability. Both school districts and parents are entitled to protection through due process, but parents typically exercise their due process rights when they fear that school districts may not be acting in the best interests of the child (Rothstein, 1995). For example, if parents have their child independently evaluated because they believe the assessment for special education did not accurately portray their child's needs, and if the school district does not agree with the findings of the independent evaluator, the parents may request a due process hearing. Or, parents could request a hearing if they disagree with the goals and objectives listed on the IEP and how services are provided to meet those goals and objectives. A hearing is conducted by an independent and objective third party selected from a list provided by the state, but the school district bears the expense. If

Check Your Learning

How are annual reviews and three-year reevaluations similar and different?

either party disagrees with the outcome of a due process hearing, the decision can be appealed to a state-level review hearing officer. If disagreement still exists, either party can then take the matter to court. Due process hearings seldom address blatant errors on the part of schools or parents regarding special education; most often they reflect the fact that many decisions made about students with disabilities are judgment calls in which a best course of action is not always clear. For example, Mr. and Mrs. Schubat filed a due process complaint against their daughter's school district because they did not believe programs offered were addressing their daughter's needs. They wanted Judy to be more actively involved in general education activities despite her multiple disabilities. The school district personnel contended that the complexity of her needs prevented Judy from being reasonably accommodated in a classroom. They also indicated that she was part of a reverse tutoring program in which students without disabilities come to work in the special education setting. How do you think a hearing officer would decide this case?

In practice, most school districts and parents want to avoid due process hearings, which tend to be adversarial and can damage parent–school working relationships to the detriment of the student (Goldberg & Kuriloff, 1991). In order to foster a positive working relationship, IDEA-97 requires that all states have a system in place to offer **mediation** to parents at no cost as an initial means for resolving conflicts with schools (Yell & Shriner, 1997). In mediation, a neutral professional skilled in conflict resolution meets with both parties to help them resolve their differences informally. Mediation, however, cannot cause delay in parents' right to a due process hearing.

Although school districts work closely with parents to avoid due process hearings, if one occurs concerning a student you teach, you might be called to testify at the hearing. In such a case, you will be asked to describe the student's level of functioning in your classroom, the supports you provide, and your efforts with other special service providers to ensure the student is successful. An administrator and an attorney might help you prepare for the hearing, and they would answer any questions you might have about your role.

What Is an Individualized Education Program?

As mentioned earlier, the document that the multidisciplinary team uses to decide the best placement for a student with an identified disability and that serves as a blueprint for a student's education is called an individualized education program (IEP). The IEP addresses all areas of student need, including accommodations to be made in a general education class and the services and supports to be provided there; the IEP also documents that services are being provided (Rodger, 1995). Since the re-authorization of IDEA in 1997, classroom teachers must be involved as team participants in preparing IEPs if the student will have any participation in the general education setting (Johns, 1997). Whether or not you are the teacher who serves in this role for particular students, if you have students with disabilities in your classroom, you will have opportunities to examine their IEPs or to meet with special educators to go over highlights of this important plan. If you are not provided with opportunities to review and discuss student IEPs, you should ask for the information you need. A sample IEP is featured in Figure 2.5.

F Y I

A *due process hearing* (DPH) is the formal administrative procedure, outlined in IDEA, for resolving disputes between families and schools concerning special education. In a DPH, both parties present evidence.

Do It!

Obtain a copy of the IEP form used in your local school district. Compare it to Figure 2.5. How is it similar? Different? Does it include all the required components?

Figure 2.5   Sample Individualized Education Program

Quentinburg Public Schools—Special Education Department

Individualized Education Program

Student Name: Jillian Carol
School: Jefferson Elementary
Primary lang.: Home-English Student-English
Program start date: 8/28/97

Date of Birth: 4/2/87
Grade: 5
Date of meeting: 8/28/97
Review date: 8/28/98

Services required

General Education   Full-time participation with support from paraprofessional or special education teacher at least three hours weekly

Resources   Incidental as needed

Self-Contained   Speech/language therapy for language development

Related Services   40 minutes/week

Other

Justification for Placement (include justification for any time spent not in general education): Student's needs indicate that learning can appropriately take place in the general education classroom with appropriate supports provided. Supports will include adapted materials as well as adult assistance up to three hours per week. Incidental time noted in the resource room is intended to preserve the option of one-to-one assistance on specific goals and objectives as needed, as determined by the teachers.

Tests Used

Intellectual   WISC-III (Full Scale IQ = 64)

Educational   Woodcock Reading, Keymath

Behavioral   NA

Speech/language

Other

Vision   Within normal limits

Hearing   Within normal limits

Strengths (present level of functioning)

Jillian enjoys talking with peers and adults.

Jillian is polite and well-mannered.

Jillian generally responds appropriately to directions.

Jillian likes to tell stories she creates.

Weaknesses (present level of functioning)

1. Below grade level in word identification (3.1) and reading comprehension (3.2)

2. Below grade level in vocabulary usage (2.1)

3. Below grade level in math computation and problem solving (1.6)

(continued)

Figure 2.5 *(continued)*

Annual Goal: Jillian will improve her reading skills to approximately a 3.9 level.

STO 1: Jillian will read from a 3rd grade reader at 80 words per minute with fewer than 3 errors per minute.

STO 2: Jillian will answer with 80% accuracy comprehension questions about reading passages at a third-grade level.

Evaluation: Oral performance **Person(s):** Special education teacher

Annual Goal: Jillian will use vocabulary at approximately a 3.0 level

STO 1: Jillian will tell a story using vocabulary from third grade reading materials.

STO 2: Jillian will use 3rd grade vocabulary when talking about her out-of-school activities.

STO 3: Jillian will learn at least 40 vocabulary words by using a word bank.

Evaluation: Oral performance, checklist **Person(s):** Special education teacher
Classroom teacher

Annual Goal: Jillian will compute and problem solve at approximately a 2.5 level

STO 1: Jillian will write answers to basic addition and subtraction facts with 100% accuracy.

STO 2: Jillian will accurately compute two-digit addition and subtraction problems without regrouping with 90% accuracy.

STO 3: Jillian will correctly solve word problems written at her reading level and at approximately a 2.5 difficulty level with 90% accuracy.

Evaluation: Written performance **Person(s):** Special education teacher
Classroom teacher

Team Signatures

LEA Representative	Eva Kim
Parent	Julia Carol
Special Education Teacher	Vera Delaney
General Education Teacher	
Psychologist	Nadine Showalter
Counselor	
Speech/Language Therapist	Ed Briggs
Other	
Other	

Required Components of an IEP

The essential components of the IEP were established by P.L. 94-142, now IDEA. They were again modified in IDEA-97. The essential components are described in the following sections.

Present level of functioning.   Information about the student's current level of academic achievement, social skills, behavior, communication skills, and other areas of concern must be included on an IEP. Often, highlights of the information collected from the individual assessment of the student are recorded on the IEP to partially meet this requirement; that is, individual achievement test scores, teacher ratings, and summary assessments by specialists such as speech therapists or occupational therapists can be used to report the present level of functioning. Another component of this assessment is information about how the students' disabilities affect their involvement in the general education curriculum. Including information on the **present level of functioning** serves as a baseline and makes it possible to judge student progress from year to year.

Annual goals and short-term objectives.   The multidisciplinary team's estimate of what a student should be able to accomplish within a year, related to meeting the student's measured needs resulting from the disability, is referred to as **annual goals.** For some students, annual goals may refer primarily to academic areas and include growth in reading, math problem solving, and other curricular areas. A student with a learning disability might have an annual goal to read and comprehend books at a particular grade level or to demonstrate skills for finding and keeping a job. For other students, annual goals address desired changes in classroom behavior, social skills, or other adaptive skills. An annual goal for a student with a moderate intellectual disability, for example, may be to order a meal at a fast-food restaurant. A student with autism might have participating in a conversation as a goal. Annual goals may also encompass speech therapy, occupational and physical therapy, and other areas in which a student has specialized needs. There is no "right" number of annual goals. Some students will have as few as two or three, others as many as eight or ten (Epstein, Patton, Polloway, & Foley, 1992). With the reauthorization of IDEA in 1997, increased emphasis is placed on annual goals that enable a student to progress in the general education curriculum.

Short-term objectives are descriptions of the steps that will be followed to achieve an annual goal. For example, for a student to write a story that includes the elements of character, plot, and setting, the student will need to understand each of those elements, recognize them in others' stories, and be able to complete the tasks that go along with writing a story. Each of these smaller steps that leads to accomplishing the annual goal would be a short-term objective. For a student with a severe physical disability whose annual goal is to feed herself, short-term objectives might include grasping a spoon, picking up food with the spoon, and using the spoon to transport food from plate to mouth. The number of short-term objectives for each annual goal relates to the type and severity of the disability, its impact on student learning, and the complexity of the goal. For some students, only a few short-term objectives may be needed; for others, each annual goal may be divided into several smaller steps.

Date of initiation, frequency, and duration of service.   Each IEP must include specific dates on which specialized services will begin, the frequency of the services, and the period of time in which they will be offered. Because the law requires that students' progress in special education be monitored at least once each year, the most typical duration for a service is a maximum of one year. If during the year a multidisciplinary team member sees a need to reconsider the student's educational plan, additional IEP meetings can be convened.

Services needed.   The IEP contains a complete outline of the specialized services the student needs; that is, the document includes all the special education instruction to be provided and any other services needed to ensure instructional success. Thus, a student receiving adaptive physical education will have an IEP indicating that such a service is needed. A student's need for special transportation will be noted on the IEP, too. Finally, a student who is entitled to transition or vocational assistance will have an IEP that clarifies these services. Perhaps most importantly, the statement of services must include information about the modifications and supports to be provided so that the student can progress in the general education curriculum. If a student will not participate fulltime in general education, the IEP team must provide an explanation justifying this arrangement.

One additional part of this IEP component concerns assessment. IDEA-97 stipulates that if students need modifications on district or state assessments, these should be specified on the IEP. If a student is to be exempt from such assessments, the team must clarify why the assessment is not appropriate. By 2000, students who are exempt from district or state assessments must have some type of alternative assessment that takes into account their functioning levels and needs (National Association of State Directors of Special Education, 1997).

Part of identifying services is indicating who is responsible for providing them. Any of the professionals introduced earlier in this chapter could be listed on the IEP to deliver special services. As a general education teacher, you will be included, too. For some students, you will be the teacher who completes most of the required instruction; for others, you will assist but will not be primarily responsible. For example, your student with a mild cognitive disability will probably be able to complete many class tasks with minor modifications that you can make. However, if your student has significant cognitive and physical disabilities requiring an alternative curriculum, other professionals will undoubtedly help develop the materials you will use when the student is in your classroom.

Strategies for evaluation.   When a team develops an IEP, the members must clarify how to measure student progress toward achieving the annual goals and how to regularly inform parents about this progress. For each short-term objective, the team indicates the criteria that will be used to judge whether the objective has been met and the procedures that will be used to measure this. For the student learning to write a story, the criteria might include the actual production of a story, and a checklist might be used to judge whether the essential elements of plot, character, and setting are present. As with all aspects of special education, the evaluation criteria and procedures are individualized; they are as general or specific as needed to accomplish the student's educational goals.

Check Your Learning

When did transition become part of special education law? Why is transition a major concern for students with disabilities?

Transition plan. For all students who are 14 years of age and older, part of the IEP is a description of strategies and services for ensuring that the student is prepared to leave school for adult life, called a **transition plan.** Students with disabilities who are college bound might have transition plans that include improvement of their study skills, exploration of different universities and their services for students with disabilities, and preparation in life skills such as responsibly using credit cards and checking accounts. For students who will work after school, the transition plan might include skills such as reading employment ads and filling out job applications, and developing important job skills such as punctuality, pleasant manners, and respect toward people in authority and customers. As with IEPs, there is no single correct way to write a transition plan. It is tailored to meet the assessed strengths and needs of the particular student and it is updated annually.

In addition to their basic components, IEPs have several other requirements. For example, they are signed by the individuals who participate in their development, including the student's parent or guardian. They also list a justification for the placement recommended. For example, a decision that the student should receive some services in a pullout program might be justified on the basis of the student's need for one-to-one intensive instruction in order to succeed. Review the IEP in Figure 2.5 to find the components just discussed. In addition, if a student has specific types of needs these must be addressed in the IEP. Examples of such needs include behavior, communication, Braille (unless specifically excluded on the IEP), and assistive technology. In such cases, appropriate supports, services, and strategies must be specified (Johns, 1997).

To some educators, IEPs represent paperwork that mostly consumes time and energy (Smith, 1990). However, remember that IEPs guide the education of students with disabilities. The document helps you clarify your expectations for students and provides a means for you to understand the student's educational needs. An IEP also informs you about the types of services the student receives and when the student's educational plan will next be reviewed. Your job is to make a good-faith effort to accomplish the short-term objectives on the IEP. If you do that, you have carried out your responsibility; if you do not do that, you could be held accountable. For example, suppose an IEP indicates that a student should learn coins and make change for up to a dollar. If you can demonstrate that you are helping the student learn this by providing play money and opportunities to learn, you are carrying out your responsibility, even if the student does not master this skill. If you state that your students are no longer working on money skills and refuse to create opportunities for practice in this area, you are violating the IEP.

What Services Do Students with Disabilities Receive?

The services that students with disabilities can receive are comprehensive, limited only by the stipulation that they must be necessary as part of a student's education. These services are provided in a variety of placements. Both the services and placements are determined by the multidisciplinary team.

Special Education and Related Services

As noted in Chapter 1, the types of services students receive can be grouped into two categories: special education and related services. **Special education** refers to the specially designed instructional services students receive. These services may include adapted materials, alternative curriculum, access to a special education teacher qualified to teach students with a particular disability, and individualized instruction. When a student's special education teacher comes to the classroom and teaches with the general education teacher, that is special education. When a student leaves a classroom for 30 minutes three times each week for intensive tutoring, that is special education. When a middle school or high school offers a life skills class for students with disabilities, that is special education, too.

Related services refer to all the supports students may need in order to benefit from special education. Examples of related services are speech therapy, transportation, physical and occupational therapy, rehabilitation counseling, psychological services, and social work. A student's need to ride a special bus equipped with a wheelchair lift is a related service need. The student's need for assistance with personal care such as toileting is a related service need.

As you might guess, the range of possibilities for special education and related services is immense. Some students, particularly those with high-incidence disabilities, will receive a limited number of special education services and perhaps no related services. For example, Lucas, a high school student with a learning disability in math, attends a geometry class in which a special education teacher teams with a math teacher. Lucas's assignments are sometimes shortened, and he is allowed extra time to complete tests. He is already looking into colleges that are known to be supportive of students with his special needs. Students with more complex or severe disabilities may have a more highly specialized special education as well as numerous related services. For example, Changyi, whom you met at the beginning of this chapter, might have the services of a physical and occupational therapist, speech/language therapist, and inclusion specialist, as well as a special education teacher.

Student Placement

Until recently, any discussion of special education services typically began with a discussion of the least restrictive environment (LRE) and rapidly moved to a detailed discussion of the place in which the services would occur. This was because many students spent some, most, or all of the school day in a special education classroom where it was believed appropriate instruction could be delivered. Now, views about placements are changing rapidly (McLeskey & Waldron, 1996). It is true that many school districts still use special education classrooms, even for students with relatively mild disabilities, and that these are sometimes an appropriate LRE; however, the use of such classrooms is becoming more and more an exception as schools become more inclusive (U.S. Department of Education, 1996). In fact, with the passage of IDEA-97, students' placement in settings other than general education classes as the LRE must be specifically justified. As Figure 2.6 shows, the proportion of students with disabilities in various placements has changed over the past 5 years. The decision about placement is made by the multidisciplinary team

Figure 2.6   **Percentage of Students Ages 3–21 Served in Various Special Education Settings, 1988–1989 and 1993–1994**

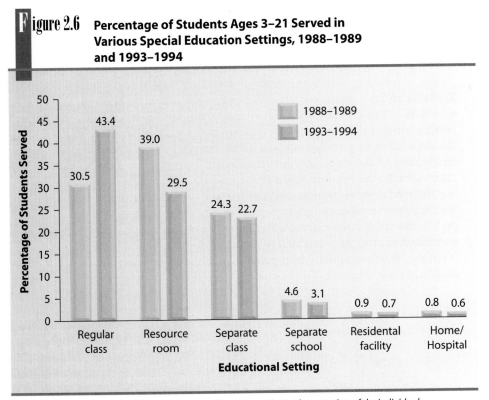

SOURCES: From *Thirteenth Annual Report to Congress on the Implementation of the Individuals with Disabilities Education Act,* 1991, and *Eighteenth Annual Report to Congress on the Implementation of the Individuals with Disabilities Education Act,* 1996, Washington, DC: U.S. Department of Education.

and reviewed at least annually along with the IEP. Placements can be changed as often as appropriate, with parental permission. Generally, if parents and school district representatives disagree about placement, the student remains in the current placement until the disagreement is resolved. Exceptions to this occur when discipline issues arise. Administrators may unilaterally change a student's placement to an alternative (e.g., suspension) for up to 10 days, provided such methods are used with other students, too. If students with disabilities bring a weapon or drugs to school, they can be placed in an alternative educational setting for up to 45 days while decisions are made concerning their long-term placement needs (Yell & Shriner, 1997).

Regular class.   Over 43 percent of students with disabilities receive their education in a **regular class,** a general education classroom, with direct or indirect assistance provided (U.S. Department of Education, 1996). For example, a student in kindergarten with a communication disorder might be served by a speech/language therapist who comes to the classroom and teaches language lessons with the general education teacher. For a student with cognitive and physical disabilities in middle school, an inclusion specialist might adapt a lesson on fractions by helping the student learn how to cut simple shapes into halves. For a student with a learning disability in high school biology, a paraprofessional might assist the student in carrying out lab directions and recording and completing assignments.

Resource room. Approximately 30 percent of students with disabilities attend school mostly in general education settings but also receive some assistance in a **resource room.** In elementary schools, resource rooms are sometimes organized by the skills being taught; that is, from 10 A.M. until 10:45 A.M., basic math skills are taught, and all the second-, third-, and fourth-grade students needing math assistance come to the resource room at that time. Alternatively, some resource rooms are arranged as same-aged groups. In these programs, all fifth graders with disabilities in resource room programs go to the resource room together. In another approach, special education teachers negotiate with general education teachers about specific times students attend. How a resource room program is organized depends on many factors, including the number of students to be served, the nature and intensity of their needs, and local policies.

WWW Resources

Would you like to obtain statistical information about individuals with disabilities? You can do so by contacting the Disability Statistics Center on the World Wide Web at <http://dsc.ucsf.edu>.

Separate class. Approximately 23 percent of students with disabilities attend **separate classes** for more than 50 percent of the school day. In this placement, a special education teacher has the primary instructional responsibility for the students, and the students probably spend a significant part of the day in that setting. However, a separate class placement does not mean that students do not interact with nondisabled peers; they may have an assigned classroom for part of the day, and they may also participate in fine arts and other school activities with peers. For example, although Kim is in a separate class most of the day at his high school, he takes a shop class with students without disabilities. A paraprofessional accompanies him because he has limited ability to understand directions and needs close guidance from an adult to operate equipment. At Kyle's elementary school, 45 minutes each day is called "Community Time," during which students read and write together, share important events from their lives, and learn about their neighborhood and community. For "Community Time," Kyle goes to Mr. Ballinger's fifth-grade class. The students are about Kyle's age and assist him with the community activities and learning. Kyle's special education teacher helps Mr. Ballinger plan appropriate activities for Kyle during that time.

Separate school. Approximately 3 percent of students with disabilities attend **separate schools.** Some separate schools exist for students with moderate and severe cognitive and physical disabilities, although such schools are rapidly becoming obsolete. Other separate schools serve students with multiple disabilities who need high levels of specialized services. For example, in a small community near Chicago, approximately 25 students are educated at a separate school. These students all need the services of a physical and occupational therapist, most have complex medical problems that must be closely monitored, and most cannot move unless someone assists them. These students have opportunities for contact with nondisabled peers through a special program that brings students to the separate school as "learning buddies."

Some students with serious emotional disabilities also attend separate schools. These students might harm themselves or others. They might not be able to cope with the complexity and social stress of a typical school.

Residential facility.   A few students have needs that cannot be met at a school that is in session only during the day. If students in separate classes have even higher needs, they might attend school as well as live in a **residential facility.** Fewer than 1 percent of students with disabilities are educated in this manner. The students for whom this placement is the LRE are often those with severe emotional problems or severe and multiple cognitive, sensory, and physical disabilities.

A somewhat different group of students also can be considered under the residential placement option. For the first time in IDEA-97, children and young adults who are imprisoned were directly addressed. Generally, if a child is convicted of a crime and incarcerated as an adult, that child is still entitled to special education services unless the IEP team determines there is a compelling reason to discontinue services (Education Week, 1997). Other provisions in the law address the cessation of services for individuals ages 18 through 21 incarcerated as adults and the requirement for services for youth who had IEPs or who had been identified as disabled prior to dropping out of school who were then incarcerated as adults.

Home or hospital.   For fewer than 1 percent of students with disabilities, education occurs in a home or hospital setting. This placement is often used for students who are medically fragile or who are undergoing surgeries or other medical treatments, or for students who have experienced an emotional crisis. For a few students with limited stamina, school comes to the home because the student does not have the strength to come to school.

If parents and school representatives disagree about an appropriate educational placement, students are sometimes educated at home pending the outcome of a due process hearing. When students are educated at home or in a hospital, the amount of actual instruction is often limited. Home services might be as little as 4 or 5 hours per week, delivered by an itinerant teacher. Hospital services range from a few hours of itinerant teaching to a full school program delivered by teachers at the hospital.

If needed according to the team's judgment, any of the services in any of the placements just described can be extended into school breaks and summer vacations through *extended school year* programs. The Professional Edge on page 64 discusses how and why this occurs.

As you can see, separate classes and schools for placement are rapidly becoming less important than supporting the education of students with disabilities in general education classrooms and schools. When placement includes a specialized setting, it often means that an alternative placement is appropriate for a specific skill or service, for a specific and limited period of time. However, "home" for most students with disabilities is the same classroom they would attend if they did not have a disability. As a general education teacher, you will play a major role in the education of students with disabilities, so it is important for you to understand the kinds of special services your students will receive.

Professional Edge

Understanding Extended School Year Services

Student placements sometimes involve more than considering the least restrictive environment during the school year. For some students, placement also relates to how they spend their summers. Most students forget some of what they have learned during school breaks and summer vacations, and teachers are accustomed to providing review to overcome this loss of learning. For students with disabilities, however, this forgetting may be so significant that the time spent reviewing would interfere with the overall effectiveness of students' education. To prevent such learning losses, some students with disabilities are entitled to *extended school year* (ESY) services. If most students in a school district attend school approximately 180 days each year, students receiving ESY services are entitled to additional days of services. The precedent for ESY comes from court cases in which judges have ruled that some students with disabilities are seriously harmed by long interruptions in their education, a violation of their right to an appropriate education, and that school districts must provide additional education for them (*Armstrong v. Kline*, 1979; *Battle v. Commonwealth of Pennsylvania*, 1980; *Holmes v. Sobol*, 1987–1988).

Although any student with a disability may be eligible for ESY, it is most often available to students with multiple disabilities, severe intellectual disabilities, or autism. Such students are most likely to meet the two criteria commonly used to make decisions about ESY services: (1) the severity of the *regression* a student will experience if schooling is interrupted; and (2) the amount of time and intensity of service needed to assist the student to *recoup* the lost learning. Typically, the special education team decides if a student needs ESY services. Because no single set of federal guidelines exists for addressing ESY, the number of students receiving ESY services varies greatly by state. For example, one recent study reported that Illinois provided ESY for 14.5 percent of its special education population, whereas Arkansas provided ESY for 0.8 percent of its students (Katsiyannis, 1990).

If you teach in a school district with a traditional school year, you may find that some students with disabilities receive special education services during the time other students attend summer school. If you teach on a year-round calendar, students with disabilities may have shorter or fewer breaks in their educational programs.

Summary

Many individuals work to ensure that students with disabilities receive an appropriate education. These people include general education teachers; special education teachers; other specialists and related service providers such as school psychologists, counselors, speech/language therapists, social workers, physical and occupational therapists, adaptive physical educators, nurses, administrators, paraprofessionals, and other specialists; and parents, students, and advocates. Depending on need, a student with a disability may receive instruction from just one or two of these professionals, or from many of them.

To determine whether special services are needed, general education teachers begin a process of deciding whether to request that a student be assessed for the presence of a disability. They carry out this process by analyzing the nature and extent of a student's unmet needs, clarifying those needs by describing them through examples, determining that the need is chronic and possibly worsening over time, comparing the student's needs to those of others in the class, recognizing that no pattern seems to exist for the student's performance, and intervening to address the unmet needs and documenting those efforts. Based on these early strategies, the student's needs may be assessed by an intervention team or screening team, and if warranted, special education referral and assessment steps are followed. This process includes completing an individualized assessment with parental permission, making decisions about the need for special education, developing an individualized education program (IEP), and monitoring the special education services.

When an IEP is developed, it includes the student's present level of functioning, goals and objectives, needed services, criteria for evaluation and the person(s) responsible for the services, and beginning and ending dates for service delivery. The IEP must be reviewed at least annually, and the student must be reevaluated at least every 3 years. The services students receive, as outlined by their IEPs, include special education and related services, and a designation of the placement for the student: a general education classroom, special education classroom, or separate special education setting. If parents and school personnel disagree on any aspect of a student's special education program or services and the disagreement cannot be resolved informally, due process procedures are used to ensure that the student receives the appropriate education.

General education teachers play an integral role in the education of students with disabilities. They are involved in the early identification of students who seem to have special needs, contribute during the assessment and identification process, and implement IEP goals and objectives as outlined by the multidisciplinary team.

Applications in Teaching Practice

A Visit to an MDT Meeting

Ms. Richards is a general education teacher working with a fourth-grade class. This year she will be working with Natasha, a student who is experiencing some difficulties with reading fluency and comprehension. To help set appropriate goals for the coming term, Ms. Richards is participating in a multidisciplinary team meeting to create an IEP for Natasha.

General education (fourth-grade) teacher: Ms. Richards
Special education teacher: Ms. Hill
Principal: Ms. Hubbert
Psychologist: Ms. Freund
Speech/language therapist: Mr. Colt
Parent: Ms. Wright

Ms. Hubbert: Our next task is to develop goals and objectives for Natasha. I'd like to suggest that we discuss academics first, then social areas, and wrap up with related services needed. Let's look at Natasha's strengths first.

Mr. Colt: Natasha has a very strong speaking vocabulary. She is considerably above average in that realm.

Ms. Freund: Along with that, Natasha's general knowledge is very good. She also is near grade level in basic math skills.

Ms. Richards: It's not really academics, but one strength Natasha has that I see is her willingness to help classmates. She really wants to help everyone in class learn.

Ms. Hill: As we write academic goals and objectives, then, we need to remember that Natasha has high vocabulary and common knowledge and that she does not need help in math. Perhaps we can use her social skills to help in the academic area. Ms. Wright, what strengths do you see in Natasha?

Ms. Wright: Hmmm. She minds me, that's for sure. And she helps out around the house with chores. She likes to help me watch her baby brother.

Ms. Hill: Helping really seems to be Natasha's thing—let's keep that in mind.

Ms. Hubbert: Let's focus for a minute on academic areas of need.

Ms. Freund: Reading comprehension is by far the area that needs the most work. Natasha's comprehension is just at a beginning first-grade level.

Ms. Wright: She says she doesn't like reading because the other kids make fun of her when she can't read the words and they tease her when Ms. Richards gives her a baby book.

Ms. Richards: I didn't realize that was a problem. Let's be sure that before we finish today we talk about that some more.

Ms. Freund: Ms. Richards and Ms. Hill, given what you know about Natasha, what might be an appropriate goal?

Ms. Hill: I agree that comprehension is the key. I think the goal should be for her to improve her comprehension on reading tasks that include stories, textbooks, and other materials such as children's magazines.

Ms. Richards: I agree. Natasha has a lot going for her, but we have to work on the comprehension.

Ms. Hubbert: Ms. Wright, how does that sound to you? [Ms. Wright nods.]

Ms. Hubbert: How about you, Mr. Colt?

Mr. Colt: That's fine.

Ms. Freund: What are the objectives we need to include?

Ms. Richards: We definitely need something about fluency. Natasha reads one word at a time.

The others agree. They write an objective that says Natasha will read aloud at a rate of 50 words per minute with fewer than three errors in a second-grade novel. Before the meeting ends, the MDT has generated these additional goals in reading comprehension using materials at her instructional level: Natasha will identify the main characters and the problem and solution in stories that she reads at a second-grade level. She will comprehend 80 percent on stories she reads aloud with the teachers; 80 percent on stories she reads aloud to herself; and 80 percent on stories she reads silently.

Questions

1. What are the responsibilities of the professionals represented at the meeting? Which of the professionals are required to attend? How would your response be different if this was an annual review?
2. What role was Ms. Richards taking at the meeting? Why was her presence so helpful in creating an educational program for Natasha?
3. What steps do you think had occurred prior to the point at which this vignette began? What had the general education teacher done? What other team responsibilities had been met?
4. What part of the IEP was the team addressing? What other parts have to be completed before the meeting ends? What must occur in order for the IEP to be valid?
5. If you were at this MDT meeting, what services would you recommend for Natasha? In what setting would they be likely to occur? Did you find any evidence that she needs related services?
6. What would happen if Natasha's mother asked the school district for a separate class as Natasha's placement and the school district disagreed with this?

Professional
Partnerships

Learner Objectives

Learner Objectives

After you read this chapter, you will be able to

1. Explain what the term *collaboration* means and describe the role of collaboration in providing services to students with disabilities, including your role in making it effective.

2. Describe inclusive programs and services in which collaboration is important, including shared problem solving, co-teaching, teaming, and consulting.

3. Identify ways in which you can work effectively with parents to educate students with special needs successfully.

4. Outline your responsibilities in working with paraprofessionals and ways in which you can enhance collaboration with them.

In Ms. Godina's biology class, 5 of her 42 students have IEPs. April, who has a mild learning disability, does not need assistance in the course. Enrico and Austen, both receiving services for emotional disabilities, are capable of completing the work but need a great deal of structure and support to do so. Carl, a student with a mild cognitive disability, does part of the course work, but he is not expected to master the extensive vocabulary nor to write lengthy lab reports. Janet, who has a physical disability that makes it necessary for her to use a motorized wheelchair and who has limited stamina, often needs encouragement to keep up with the work. Twice each week, Ms. Godina is joined during biology by Mr. MacLean, a special education teacher. During these class periods, the two teachers share teaching responsibilities and group the students for instruction in a variety of ways—by skill needs, by interest, and by random assignment, among others. On two of the days that Mr. MacLean is not in class, Ms. Hugo, a teaching assistant, is available to help Ms. Godina and individual students. What happens when two teachers share instructional responsibilities in a classroom? What topics might Ms. Godina and Mr. MacLean need to discuss to ensure that their shared teaching is effective?

The three fourth-grade teachers are having a grade-level team meeting; Ms. Chiang, the special education teacher, is also present. They have discussed a curriculum issue related to social studies, and now the conversation has turned to a common problem. Mr. Balen states that the students with disabilities are taking a disproportionate amount of his time, especially in the morning. He explains that this group of students does not seem to be able to come into the classroom, put away their belongings, and settle into work without his close and constant supervision. Mrs. Dyer agrees but adds that many students without disabilities are having the same problem. After a few minutes of general conversation about this problem, the teachers begin generating ideas for dealing with it. Included in the list of ideas is letting students choose their own morning work, assigning all students a "morning study buddy," and reviewing expectations with all the classes. Even though Ms. Chiang does not teach fourth grade, she is in the classrooms to assist students, observe, or take part in lessons so often that she has several excellent ideas to contribute to the discussion. What is Ms. Chiang's role on the team? How can the team ensure that all the members feel committed to the team and valued as team members?

■ Chris's parents, Mr. and Mrs. Werner, arrived promptly for their after-school meeting with Ms. MacDougal, the middle school inclusion facilitator, and Mr. Saunders, the seventh-grade team leader. Mrs. Werner began by declaring that the school was discriminating against Chris because of her learning disability. Mr. Werner asserted that Chris was not to be singled out in any way because of her special needs and that he had learned that she was receiving tutoring during a lunch-period study hall. He strongly expressed that the family provides tutoring for Chris so that this type of discrimination does not occur at school. Further, Mr. and Mrs. Werner showed the teachers examples of modified assignment sheets, another example of discrimination. When Mr. Saunders started to explain that he was modifying Chris's work so she could learn more in his class, Mr. Werner cut him off, stating that a teacher's poor instructional practice was no excuse to destroy a child's self-concept through public humiliation. If you were Mr. Saunders, what type of assistance would you want from Ms. MacDougal during this difficult interaction? How can you prevent miscommunication in your work with parents of students with disabilities?

In the past, becoming a teacher—whether in general education or in special education—meant entering a profession frequently characterized by isolation and sometimes loneliness (Little, 1982; Lortie, 1975). Teachers typically spent most of the day alone in a classroom with students. They learned that they were expected to have all the skills to manage student learning and discipline issues, and they rarely had opportunities to discuss their questions, concerns, and misgivings with anyone, but especially not their colleagues at school.

That atmosphere of isolation is changing. Elementary school teachers are meeting on grade-level teams to share ideas and problem solve, and middle school and high school teachers are creating interdisciplinary teams to redesign curriculum and share instructional responsibility for smaller groups of students. School reform efforts are also characterized by partnerships. For example, professional development schools in which teacher trainees work with experienced educators and university instructors emphasize team approaches (Dixon & Ishler, 1992). Likewise, entire schools are stressing the need to build a collaborative learning community (Pugach & Johnson, 1995). As Barth (1990) comments, "The success of a school, I believe, depends above all on the quality of interactions between teacher and teacher, and teacher and administrator" (p. 15).

As the scenes that open this chapter illustrate, these emerging partnerships extend to special education and other support staff as well. Particularly as schools move toward increased inclusion, the working relationships among all the adults involved in the education of students with disabilities have become critical. For example, as a classroom teacher, you may find that you have questions about a student's behavior in class. A consultant might come to your class, observe the student and the overall classroom setting, and then meet with you to discuss how to address your concerns. Similarly, you might find that some of your students cannot complete the grade-level work you are accustomed to assigning. To assist you, a special education teacher might meet with you to design the necessary modifications.

At first glance, these interactions seem like logical and straightforward approaches to optimizing education. However, because of the strong tradition in education of professionals working alone and the limited availability of preparation for teachers in how to work effectively with other adults, problems sometimes occur (Cook & Friend, 1993). In some instances, support personnel are reluctant to make suggestions for fear that they will sound as if they are interfering with the classroom teacher's instruction. In other cases, the classroom teacher insists that no change in classroom activities is possible, even though a special education teacher is available for co-teaching. And often, when professionals in schools disagree, they are very uncomfortable discussing the issues.

Many school personnel in inclusive schools assert that collaboration is the key to their success in meeting the needs of all students (Bardak, 1995; Friend & Cook, 1996). The purpose of this chapter is to introduce you to the principles of collaboration and the school situations in which professionals are most likely to collaborate to meet the needs of students with disabilities. You also will learn how to develop strong working relationships with parents, an essential part of every teacher's responsibilities, and an especially important one when educating students with special needs. Finally, the special partnerships that are formed when teachers work with paraprofessionals also are considered.

What Are the Basics of Collaboration?

As a teacher, you will hear colleagues refer to many of their activities as *collaboration*. Sometimes they will be referring to a team meeting to propose ideas to help a student; sometimes they will mean sharing a classroom to teach a particular subject; and sometimes they will even use the term as a synonym for inclusion. How can all these things be collaboration? Actually, they are not. Collaboration is *how* people work together, not *what* they do. As Cook and Friend (1993) have clarified, **collaboration** is a style professionals choose to use in order to accomplish a goal they share. Professionals often use the term *collaboration* to describe any activity in which they work with someone else. But just the fact of working in the same room with another person does not ensure that collaboration will occur. For example, in some team meetings, one or two members tend to monopolize the conversation and insist that others agree with their points of view. Although the team is in proximity, it is not collaborative. Only on teams where all members feel their contributions are valued and the goal is clear, where they share decision making, and where they sense they are respected, does true collaboration exist.

Connections

Students experience many of the elements of adult collaboration through co-operative learning, a topic discussed in Chapter 13. This chapter's focus is adult interactions.

Characteristics of Collaboration

Collaboration for schools has a number of defining characteristics that clarify its requirements. Friend and Cook (1996) have outlined these key attributes, which are summarized in Figure 3.1.

Check Your Learning

If you are *required* to work with special education teachers and other colleagues, how can collaboration be voluntary?

Collaboration is voluntary.   Teachers may be assigned to work in close proximity, but they cannot be required to collaborate. They must make a personal choice to work collaboratively in such situations. You and another teacher could be told that you are expected to be part of a prereferral intervention team. You could choose to keep your ideas to yourself instead of readily participating. On the other hand, you could conclude that even though you had not planned on volunteering for this activity, as long as you are a team member, you will contribute like a team player and collaborate. Your principal assigned the activity; you decided to collaborate. Because collaboration is voluntary, teachers often form close but informal collaborative partnerships with colleagues whether or not collaboration is a school-wide ethic.

Collaboration is based on parity.   Teachers who collaborate must believe that all individuals' contributions are valued equally. The amount and nature of particular teachers' contributions may vary greatly, but teachers need to recognize that what they offer is integral to the collaborative effort. If you are at a meeting concerning highly complex student needs, you might feel you have nothing to offer. However, you have important information about how the student responds in your class and the progress the student has made in developing peer relationships. The technical

Figure 3.1   **Characteristics of Collaboration**

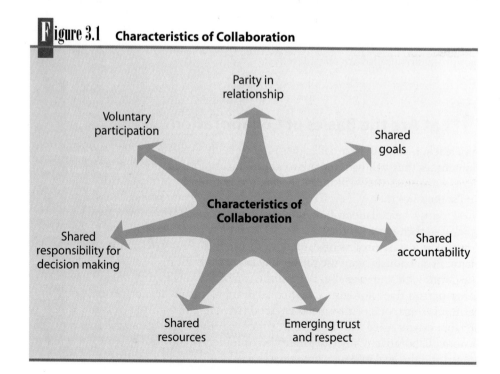

discussion of the student's disabilities is not your area of expertise, nor should it be; your ideas are valued because of your expertise in your classroom.

Collaboration requires a shared goal.   Teachers collaborate only when they share a goal. For example, if two third-grade teachers want to plan an integrated unit on the environment, their goal is clear. They will pool their knowledge and resources and jointly plan the instruction. However, if one wants to work on an environmental unit whereas the other prefers to stress weather, they will not develop their units collaboratively. Teachers sometimes perceive that they share a goal when in fact their goals differ. For example, if the two third-grade teachers agree to work on an environmental unit but one means global issues whereas the other means the pragmatics of recycling, either the content of the unit will have to be negotiated or the collaborative planning might not be possible.

Collaboration includes shared responsibility for key decisions.   Although teachers may divide the work necessary to complete a collaborative teaching or teaming project, they should share as equal partners the fundamental decision making about the activities they are undertaking. This shared responsibility reinforces the sense of parity that exists among the teachers. In the environmental unit example, the teachers share decisions about the topics to address within the unit, perhaps the order of them, the learning objectives for students, and accommodations for students with special needs. However, they are likely to assign many tasks to just one person. One will contact the local zoo for information on tropical rain forests and arrange for a videotape on recycling. The other will duplicate the logs students will use to record information they find in the newspaper about the environment and will contact the local nature preserve to arrange for a guest speaker.

Collaboration includes shared accountability for outcomes.   This characteristic follows directly from shared responsibility; that is, if teachers share key decisions, they must also share accountability for the results of the decisions, whether those results are positive or negative. If both the third-grade teachers carry out their assigned tasks, their unit will have a high probability of success. If one fails to contact a guest speaker, their shared unit is less effective. If something happens that is just wonderful (the classes begin a school recycling project that receives local and then national press attention), the teachers share the success. If something happens that is not so wonderful (the experiment to measure the impact of pollutants on climate fizzles and students become bored with it), they share the need to change their plans.

Collaboration is based on shared resources.   Each teacher participating in a collaborative effort contributes some type of resource. This contribution increases commitment and reinforces each professional's sense of parity. Resources may include time, expertise, space, equipment, or other assets. The teachers working on the environmental unit contribute the time needed to make necessary plans, but they also pool their knowledge on teaching about the environment, share information on local resources to access for the unit, and share the equipment needed to show the recycling video.

Check Your Learning

What is an example of each of the defining characteristics of collaboration?

Collaboration is emergent.   Collaboration is based on belief in the value of shared decision making, trust, and respect among participants. However, although these qualities are needed to some degree at the outset of collaborative activities, they are not mature in a new collaborative relationship. As teachers become more experienced at collaboration, their relationships will be characterized by the trust and respect that grow within successful collaborative relationships. If our third-grade teachers have worked together for several years, they may share freely, including offering constructive criticism to each other. If this is their first collaborative effort, they are much more likely to be a bit guarded and polite, hesitant about sounding critical, because they are unsure how the other person would respond.

Prerequisites for Collaboration

Cultural Awareness

How might cultural differences affect collaboration? When people from very different cultures collaborate, what could you do to ensure that their collaboration is successful?

Creating collaborative relationships requires effort on everyone's part. Most professionals who have close collaborative working relationships note that it is hard work to collaborate—but worth every minute of the effort. They also emphasize that collaboration gets better with experience; when colleagues are novices at co-teaching or working on teams, their work seems to take longer and everyone has to be especially careful to respect others' points of view. However, with additional collaboration, everyone's comfort level increases, honesty and trust grow, and a sense of community develops. Here are some essential ingredients that foster the growth of collaboration.

Reflecting on your personal belief system.   The first ingredient for collaboration is your personal beliefs. How much do you value sharing ideas with others? Would you prefer to work with someone to complete a project, even if it takes more time that way, or do you prefer to work alone? If your professor in this course offered the option of a small-group exam, would you be willing to receive a shared grade with your classmates? If your responses to these questions suggest that you prefer working with others, you will probably find professional collaboration exciting and rewarding. If your responses are just the opposite, you might find that you would "rather do it myself" and find collaboration somewhat frustrating. For collaboration to occur, all those participating need to feel that their shared effort will result in an outcome that is better than could be accomplished by any one participant (DeBoer, 1995). They must also believe that a shared effort has value, even if the result is somewhat different from what each person envisioned at the outset (Phillips & McCullough, 1990).

Do It!

Write a statement of your beliefs about working with school colleagues and about collaborating on behalf of students with special needs. Compare your views with those of classmates.

   Part of examining your belief system also concerns your understanding of and respect for others' belief systems. This tolerance is especially important for your collaborative efforts with special educators in inclusive programs. For example, what are your beliefs about changing the standards in your classroom in order to help a student succeed? You might at first say that changing your standards is no problem, but when you reflect on the consequence of that belief, you might have second thoughts. For example, it means that you will give alternative assignments to students needing them, that you will teach *students* not *subject matter*, and that you will grade on the basis of student effort and progress instead of according to a single standard. The special educators with whom you work are likely to believe strongly that alternative standards are not only helpful in inclusive settings, but that they are a requirement. How will you respond if you meet a colleague with this belief? Similarly, what if three of the teachers in your department are strongly opposed to alternative standards for students with disabilities? Will you debate the matter with them and hold your beliefs, or will you feel pressured to compromise? Teachers have faced these issues in the past. However, in schools in which collaboration is stressed, issues such as these tend to become more apparent and the need to resolve them more intense. Further, as collaboration becomes more integral to public schools, learning to value others' opinions and to disagree respectfully with them while maintaining a positive working relationship becomes more and more essential.

Refining your interaction skills.   The second ingredient you can contribute to school collaboration is effective skills for interacting. In many ways, interaction skills are the fundamental building blocks on which collaboration is based since it is through our interactions with others that collaboration occurs. There are two major types of interaction skills. The first are communication skills, some of which you may have already learned about in a speech or communication course. These skills include listening, attending to nonverbal signals, and asking questions and making statements in clear and nonthreatening ways. They also include paralanguage, for example, your tone of voice and your use of comments like "Uh-huh" and "okay." Examples of these communication skills are included in the Professional Edge on page 76.

The other type of interaction skill describes the steps that make interactions productive. Have you ever been in a meeting and felt that the same topic was being discussed repeatedly? Perhaps you wished someone would say, "I think we've covered this; let's move on." Or have you ever been trying to problem solve with classmates or friends only to realize that every time someone generated an idea, someone else began explaining why the idea could not work? In both instances, the frustration occurred because of a problem in the interaction process, that is, the steps that characterize an interaction. The most needed interaction process for you as a teacher is shared problem solving. Other interaction-process skills include conducting effective meetings, responding to resistance, resolving conflict, and persuading others.

You need both types of interaction skills for collaboration to occur. If you are highly skilled in communicating effectively but cannot help to get an interaction from its beginning to its end, others will be frustrated. Likewise, even though you know the steps in shared problem solving, if you speak to others as though you know all the answers, others will withdraw from the interaction.

Contributing to a supportive environment.   The third ingredient for successful collaboration is a supportive environment (Pugach & Johnson, 1995). As a teacher, you will contribute to this atmosphere by your personal belief system and interaction skills, but this ingredient includes other items as well. For example, most professionals working in schools that value collaboration comment on the importance of administrative support. Principals play an important role in fostering collaboration (Johnson & Pajares, 1996). They can raise staff awareness of collaboration by making it a school goal and distributing information on it to staff. They can reward teachers for their collaborative efforts. They can urge teachers who are uncomfortable with collaboration to learn more about it and to experiment in small-scale collaborative projects, and they can include collaboration as part of staff evaluation procedures. When principals do not actively nurture collaboration among staff, collaborative activities are more limited, more informal, and less a part of the school

FYI

Communication skills are the words, paralanguage, and nonverbal signals you use to convey meaning to others. *Interaction processes* are the steps for using communication skills to accomplish a goal.

FYI

As constraints on collaboration, general education teachers mention time, financial resources for needed supplies, the perceptions of other teachers, fears about sharing traditionally isolated classrooms, and the difficulty of maintaining communication.

Professional Edge

Communication for Effective Collaboration

Strong interaction skills are the basis of effective collaboration. Your recognition of your own frame of reference, your willingness to consider others' points of view, and your being a good listener are among the communication skills described here that foster successful interactions.

1. Use knowledge of frame of reference to foster effective collaboration. You have a frame of reference that influences your interactions. Others might have a frame of reference that is very different from yours. Whereas you view a student's use of "bad" language as very inappropriate, the special education teachers are delighted that the student has transferred his expressions of anger from physical to verbal aggression. They see this change as progress. By recognizing such differences, you can strive for better communication by looking first for a true understanding of others' words and only later for ways to present your point of view.

2. Recognize that shared problem solving begins with the understanding that there are many "right" answers for addressing student learning and behavior. Someone else's view that a student would be best served by spending more time in your class for the social interactions and modeling is as valid as your conviction that the student would best learn social skills by participating in an intensive, separate program.

3. Develop effective strategies for listening. You can make sure you have accurately heard others' messages by paraphrasing the information and requesting confirmation that you have correctly received it. A colleague says, "I feel pulled in 20 directions at once. I don't know if I can keep up with this new inclusive education!" If you respond by commenting that you agree that the teacher is being given too much responsibility in the new program, you may have just made a huge error in listening. Perhaps the teacher is just tired after a hectic day; you should have checked your selective listening and interpretation for accuracy.

4. When someone shares a concern with you, avoid the temptation to offer advice immediately. Perhaps that person just wanted to vent a frustration or to share a new idea. When a colleague says, "I have a student who just won't work alone. I have to help her every minute," it is tempting to respond by saying something like, "When I had a student like that last year, it helped if I assigned another student to assist." Although this comment may be appropriate later in the interaction, you should first find out more information about what the teacher is saying.

5. As much as possible, focus your interactions on observable information. The more you rely on opinions or inferences, the more likely is miscommunication. Noting that a student threw a book on the floor and left a classroom is more accurate than discussing a student's "tantrum" and "serious attitude problem."

6. Use collaborative language; that is, ask questions that encourage others to speak (for example, "What are the goals for Marcus in math this year?" instead of "Does Marcus need to learn long division in my classroom?") and avoid comments that guide (for example, "I'd like Marcus's math worksheets adapted. How can we accomplish that?" instead of "You should give me adapted worksheets for Marcus for math").

7. Monitor how much you talk. If you tend to monopolize, invite others to speak. If you tend not to contribute, offer some comments.

8. If you have a disagreement with a colleague, address it as soon as possible and in a straightforward manner. Avoid discussing the issue with others, especially if you have not shared your concern with the colleague. For example, if you are co-teaching and your partner is, in your opinion, spending too much time on drilling basic information, you should discuss this issue with your partner, not with your best teacher friend from another school district.

culture. If you work in this type of school, you may find that you collaborate with specific teachers but that your efforts are considered a luxury or frill and are not rewarded or otherwise fostered.

Another component of a supportive environment is the availability of time for collaboration (Raywid, 1993). It is not enough that each teacher has a preparation period; shared planning time also needs to be arranged. In many middle schools, shared planning occurs as part of the middle school team planning period. In other schools, substitute teachers are employed periodically so that classroom teachers and special services staff can meet. In an increasing number of school districts, "early release" days are used. Once each week or month, students are dismissed in the early afternoon. Teachers use the time created to plan instructional units, confer about student problems, and attend professional development activities.

As a teacher, you will find that time is an important issue (Cole & McLeskey, 1997; Stump & Wilson, 1996). The number of tasks you need to complete during your preparation period will be greater than the number of minutes available. The time before and after school will be filled with faculty meetings, meetings with parents, preparation, and other assignments. You can help yourself maximize time for collaboration if you keep these things in mind: First, it may be tempting to spend the beginning of a shared planning time discussing the day's events or comparing notes on some school activity. But if you engage in lengthy socializing, you are taking away time from your planning. A trick discovered by teachers in collaborative schools is to finish the business at hand first and then to "chat" if time is left. Second, since you will never truly have enough time to accomplish all that you would like to as a teacher, you must learn to prioritize. You will have to choose whether collaborating about a certain student or teaching a certain lesson is justified based on the needs of students and the time available. Not everything can be collaborative, but when collaboration seems appropriate, time should be made available for it.

What Are Effective Applications of Collaboration in Inclusive Schools?

The basic principles of collaboration are your guides to many types of partnerships in schools. These partnerships may involve other classroom teachers, special education teachers, support staff such as speech therapists or counselors, paraprofessionals, parents, and others. Four of the most common activities concerning students with disabilities in which educators value and seek collaboration are shared problem solving, co-teaching, teaming, and consultation.

Shared Problem Solving

Shared problem solving is the basis for many of the collaborative activities school professionals undertake on behalf of students with disabilities (Jayanthi & Friend, 1992). Although shared problem solving sometimes occurs when a classroom teacher and a special education teacher meet to decide on appropriate modifications or other interventions for a student, it occurs in many other contexts, too. For example, as you read the applications that follow this one, you will find that some variation of shared problem solving exists in each. This happens because one way of

FYI

In our fieldwork with thousands of experienced teachers each year, lack of time is consistently noted as the most serious obstacle to collaboration.

WWW Resources

Sometimes your problem solving can be facilitated by obtaining more information. If you would like to explore the resources available on the Internet related to disabilities, try the Comprehensive List of Disability-Related Web Sites at <http://www.icdi.wvu.edu/Others.htm>.

thinking about co-teaching, teaming, and consultation is as specialized problem-solving approaches.

You might be wondering why problem solving is such a critical topic for professional partnerships. You may consider yourself adept at problem solving already since it is an ongoing responsibility of educators. Because most professionals learn problem solving in isolation, the topic is critical. However, as many authors have noted (for example, Friend & Cook, 1996; Pugach & Johnson, 1995), when professionals problem solve together the process is much more complex because the needs, expectations, and ideas of each participant must be blended into shared understandings and mutually agreed-upon solutions. This is not a simple task!

Discover a shared need.   As shown in Figure 3.2, the starting point for problem solving is discovering a shared need, which demonstrates the point about the complexity of shared problem solving. If you face a problem that concerns only you, you try to resolve it by yourself. When you problem solve with colleagues and parents, all participants need to perceive that a problem exists. Further, it is important that all participants believe that they can have an impact on the problem, that they feel

Figure 3.2   **A Model for Shared Problem Solving**

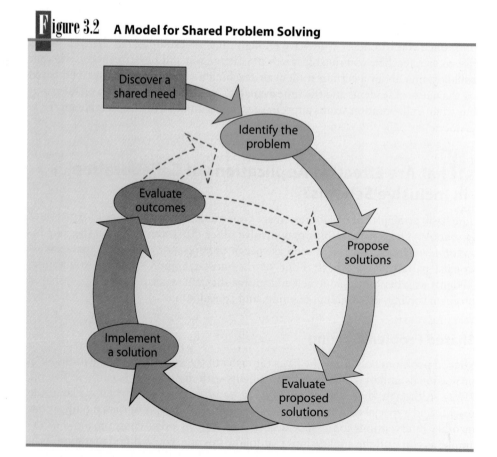

accountable for the results of problem solving, and that they can contribute constructively to resolving the problem. When these conditions exist, shared problem solving results in a high level of commitment. When these conditions do not exist, "shared" problem solving is not shared at all and may appear one-sided, with some participants trying to convince others to contribute. For example, many teachers report that they have been unable to enlist parents' help in resolving discipline problems. They then go on to describe meetings with parents in which school personnel describe the problem and the parents respond that they do not see such behavior occurring at home. Too often, instead of working to come to a shared understanding of the problem behavior, this type of meeting ends with the parents superficially agreeing to assist in a problem they do not believe exists and the school professionals perceiving the parents as only marginally supportive. The dilemma can be avoided if more effort is made to identify a shared need to problem solve.

Identify the problem. Research on problem solving suggests that the most critical step in the process is problem identification (Rodgers-Rhyme & Volpiansky, 1991). However, when educators meet to share problem solving, they often feel pressured because of time constraints to resolve the problem; hence, they rush through this essential stage. Problem-solving experts suggest that up to half of the time available for problem solving should be devoted to this step (Bergan & Tombari, 1975). Problem identification includes gathering information, compiling it, analyzing it, and reaching consensus about the nature of a student's problem.

In a shared problem-solving situation, you can help emphasize the importance of problem identification by asking whether everyone has agreed on the problem, by asking someone else to restate the problem to check your understanding of it, and by encouraging participants who have not spoken to share their opinions. Consider the following situation, which shows what can happen when problem identification is not done correctly. A teacher in a shared problem-solving session says to the parent of a student whose attendance is irregular and who consistently comes to school without assignments or basic supplies, "We really need your help in making sure Rickie gets up when his alarm goes off so he can catch the bus. And we'd like to establish a system in which you sign off on his written assignments." The parent replies, "It's so hard. I work until midnight and I don't get up when it's time for the kids to go to school. I don't think he sees any point in the homework he's getting— that's why he doesn't bring it back." In this situation, the educator has identified the problem before the meeting has even started: Rickie needs to assume responsibility, and his parents need to provide more guidance for school activities. The teacher is further proposing a solution to the problem and not exploring the problem itself. The parent's response suggests that the parent does not see the same problem; in fact, the parent is implying that perhaps the problem does not belong to Rickie at all, but to the school staff!

As an alternative, consider how this interaction could have been handled: The teacher says to the parent, "Ms. Trenton, thanks so much for taking time off work to meet with us. We appreciate your concern for Rickie. Lately, we've seen a problem with Rickie's attendance. We asked you to come to school so we can learn about your perspective on this situation and to let Rickie know that we're working together to help him." When the parent replies with the comment about her working hours and Rickie's perception of the homework, the teacher replies, "That's

Do It!

Practice problem identification by participating in a mock prereferral team meeting with classmates. Who in the group helps keep others focused on problem identification? Who keeps offering solutions instead of focusing on understanding the problem?

important information for us. We're hoping we can find ways to motivate Rickie to come to school—and that includes assignments that he sees as valuable." In this situation, the school professionals are working *with* the parent to identify the problem, not against her.

Propose solutions.   Once a problem has been clearly identified, the next step is to create a wide range of options that might be tried to solve the problem. One of the most common ways to come up with solutions is to **brainstorm.** VanGundy (1988) clarifies brainstorming as being based on two important principles. First, judgment is deferred; that is, in order to free the mind to be creative, we must suspend our predisposition to judge ideas. Second, quantity leads to quality; that is, the more ideas that are generated for solving a problem, the more likely it is that novel and effective solutions will be found. Brainstorming requires openness and creativity. The fourth-grade team you met at the beginning of this chapter was engaged in proposing solutions. What other solutions might they have generated if they had stressed brainstorming principles?

Evaluate ideas.   With a list of ideas, the next step in shared problem solving is to evaluate the ideas by considering whether they seem likely to resolve the problem and whether they are feasible. One way to evaluate ideas is to use a decision sheet as illustrated in Figure 3.3. On this decision sheet, the participants have listed the problem—helping Angela to work independently on classroom tasks—and generated ideas for achieving this goal. They then selected criteria by which to judge the merits of each idea. They considered (1) how well the idea will do for increasing the amount of time Angela works on her independent assignments; (2) the extent to which the idea has a low time cost; and (3) the extent to which the idea preserves classroom routines. Ideas not seriously considered were crossed out, and the criteria for decision making were applied to those remaining, with each idea being rated against each criterion. In Figure 3.3, the two ideas with the highest rating were assigning a study buddy and using picture directions.

Plan specifics.   Once one or two ideas are decided upon using a process such as the one just described, more detailed planning needs to occur. For example, if you and others have decided that you would like to try having a high school service club provide volunteer tutoring in an after-school program, some of the tasks to assign include asking the club about their interests, arranging a place for the program, ensuring that needed supplies are available, obtaining permission to operate the program, establishing a schedule for students, determining who will provide adult supervision and scheduling it, advertising the program, and creating training sessions for the tutors and delivering them.

Typically, at this step of shared problem solving, participants not only list the major tasks that need to be completed to implement the solution, but they also decide who will take responsibility for each task. They also specify a timeline for completing all the tasks and usually decide how long to implement the solution before meeting to evaluate its effectiveness.

Implement the solution.   If all the steps in the shared problem-solving process have been carefully followed, implementing the idea(s) decided upon may be the most straightforward part of the process. When problem solving occurs concerning

Figure 3.3   **A Sample Decision-Making Chart for Problem Solving**

Problem Statement: How can we help Angela to work independently on assigned classroom tasks?

Ideas:

Tape-record instructions

Have an assigned "study buddy"

Make the work easier

Use pictures for directions

Ask a parent volunteer to help

~~Don't give independent work~~

Let her choose the assignment

~~Make her stay in from recess to~~

~~complete~~

Decision Making: (3 = high, 2 = medium, 1 = low)

Criteria

Idea	Angela will work for at least 5 min.	Low time commitment for teacher	Doesn't disrupt class routine	Total	Rank
1. Taped instructions	3	1	2	6	
2. Study buddy	3	3	3	9	1
3. Easier work	2	2	2	6	
4. Picture directions	3	2	3	8	2
5. Parent volunteer	1	3	2	6	
6. Choose assignment	1	2	1	4	

a student with a disability in an inclusive school, each team member may have some responsibility for implementing the solution. Occasionally, you will have much of the immediate responsibility. In other cases, parents will have a major role to play. What is critical is that each person involved does his or her part so that the solution has a high probability of success. During implementation, it is helpful to keep some type of record documenting your efforts and the impact of the intervention on the student.

Evaluate outcomes. After a period of time—anywhere from just a few days to two or more weeks—the professionals who are implementing the solution meet to

Do It!

Role-play a shared problem-solving interaction in class. Complete all the steps up to implementation and then discuss what occurred.

Check Your Learning

What are the steps in problem solving? As you observe others problem solving, can you recognize each step?

evaluate its effectiveness. At this time, three possibilities exist. First, if the solution has been especially effective, it may be judged a success. It will then either be continued in order to maintain the results, discontinued if no longer needed, or gradually phased out. Second, if the solution seems to be having a positive effect but is not ideal for some other reason, it may be modified. For example, a behavior management plan may be helping a student attend class rather than skip it, but the classroom teacher notes that the system is too time-consuming. The problem-solving group may then try to streamline the plan to make it more feasible. Finally, even when the steps in problem solving are carefully completed, a solution is occasionally judged ineffective. The team then must decide what to do next: Should a different solution be selected from the list already generated? Should additional solutions be proposed? Is the problem accurately identified? The team needs to consider all these possibilities before additional problem solving occurs.

Professionals who regularly employ the strategies of shared problem solving are quick to acknowledge that the steps do not automatically lead to simple solutions that always work. What they report, however, is that when they problem solve in this fashion, they feel that their professional time is well spent and that the problem-solving process is truly a collaborative endeavor.

Co-Teaching

Co-teaching occurs when two or more teachers share the instruction for a single group of students, typically in a single classroom setting (Bauwens & Hourcade, 1995). Although any two teachers can co-teach, we focus here on the co-teaching that occurs between a classroom teacher and special education support staff.

Co-teaching is becoming a very popular strategy for achieving inclusion (Walther-Thomas, Bryant, & Land, 1996). In a classroom with several students with disabilities, combining the strengths of the general education teacher and a special educator can create options for all students (Cook & Friend, 1995). Co-teaching typically occurs for a set period of time either every day (for example, every morning from 9:30 until 10:15) or on certain days of the week (for example, on Mondays and Wednesdays during third hour). Occasionally, especially in middle and high schools, a group of students with disabilities who used to attend a separate class for a specific subject will join a general education class permanently. In such cases, the special education teacher may be available every day. For example, if a school used to have general science for students with disabilities, the group of eight students from that class and their teacher may become members of a general education biology class of 25 students. The burden of extra students is more than offset by the advantage of two teachers being assigned to the class full-time. One other strategy for co-teaching is to have a special education teacher and a classroom teacher share instruction for a particular unit, often one that many students find difficult (for example, changing decimals to fractions). After the unit is completed, the co-teaching is stopped until another specific need arises.

Effective as it is, co-teaching is not the answer for every inclusion situation. Co-teaching is only one option for meeting the needs of students in inclusive schools (Reinhiller, 1996). Further, it is relatively expensive (that is, the cost of two teachers with one group of students) and should be reserved for situations in which the number of students with disabilities in a class justifies the presence of two teach-

FYI

Co-teaching is an instructional arrangement in which two or more teachers share responsibility for a group of students. In an inclusive setting, one of the co-teachers is a special education teacher or other special service provider.

ers, or the class is one in which all students with disabilities enroll (for example, in high school, it may be U.S. history).

Many approaches are available to teachers who decide to co-teach (Bauwens & Hourcade, 1995; Walther-Thomas et al., 1996). Cook and Friend (1995) have outlined some of the common ones, which are depicted in Figure 3.4.

One teach, one support.   In this approach, one teacher leads the lesson and the other takes an assisting role. For example, while the special education teacher leads a lesson on listening strategies or a test review, the classroom teacher gathers observational data on target students. Alternatively, while the classroom teacher leads a lesson on the causes of the Civil War, the special education teacher helps keep students on task, checks written work as it is being completed, and responds quietly to student questions. The key to using this approach successfully is to make it only one out of many approaches you use. With overuse, one of the teachers, often the special educator, may feel that he or she has no legitimate role in the class.

Figure 3.4   **Co-Teaching Approaches**

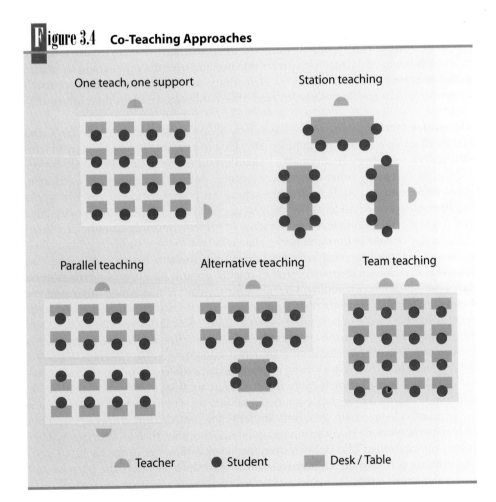

Station teaching.   This approach is similar to the concept of stations found in many kindergarten classes. In **station teaching**, curricular content is divided into two parts. One teacher teaches half of the content to half of the students while the other teaches the other part to the rest. The groups then switch and each teacher repeats his or her part of the lesson. With classes of students able to work independently, a third group may be formed with "learning buddies" who tutor each other on a review assignment. Alternatively, a parent volunteer may provide instruction at a third station. In elementary schools, an entire lesson based on stations may be completed in a single day; in secondary schools, a station may take an entire class period or more. For example, in a ninth-grade math class, some of the students are working with the general education teacher on a new concept. A second group is meeting with the special education teacher to apply information taught last week to day-to-day situations. A third group of students is working on an assignment in pairs. Each station lasts the entire class period.

Parallel teaching.   Sometimes when two teachers are present, they find it advantageous simply to divide a heterogeneous class group in half and have each teacher instruct half the class separately. In this **parallel-teaching** format, every student would have twice as many opportunities to participate in a discussion or respond to teacher questions. A teacher particularly skilled in presenting information through pictures could use this approach, while the other teacher could emphasize learning through listening. Students who prefer one method over the other could be placed with the appropriate teacher. In an elementary school classroom, this approach might be used to enable students to read different books based on their interests.

Alternative teaching.   In most classrooms, dividing the class into one large and one small group is sometimes appropriate. This co-teaching option is referred to as **alternative teaching**. Traditionally, a small group has been used primarily for remediation, but many other options are possible and recommended. For example, some students may benefit from preteaching. In preteaching, one teacher works with a small group of students who may struggle to learn (whether or not they have IEPs), are shy, or need to feel a strong sense of success. Information to be presented the next day or later in the same day or class is taught to these students so that when questions are asked or vocabulary introduced, the students have a "jump start" on learning. Enrichment also works well in smaller groups. As a unit of instruction on space exploration is concluding, several students might have a strong interest in the topic. As the other students review and complete assigned tasks, this group might meet to discuss career opportunities related to the space industry or to write letters to obtain more information on current U.S. space efforts. The members in this group could include high-achieving students, students who have average academic achievement but who have a strong interest in space topics, a student with a behavior disorder who will benefit more from this activity than from the assigned work, and a student with a moderate cognitive disability for whom the written work is not appropriate. Occasionally, grouping students for remediation is appropriate, but only if it is one among many grouping options. Otherwise, such an arrangement becomes the equivalent of running a special education program in the back of a general education classroom, an arrangement that completely belies the purpose and principles of inclusion.

Teachers experienced in collaboration say it is well worth the effort. What does it take to make collaboration work? How might you approach co-teaching if it becomes an option for you?

Team teaching. In the co-teaching option of **team teaching,** the teachers share leadership in the classroom; both are equally engaged in the instructional activities. For example, one teacher may begin a lesson by introducing vocabulary while the other provides examples to place the words in context. Two teachers may role-play an important event from history or a science concept. Two teachers may model how to address conflict by staging a debate about a current event. One teacher may lecture while the other models note-taking strategies on the chalkboard. You reach the limits of team teaching only when you run out of exciting ideas for creating instruction with two teachers instead of one.

Co-teaching pragmatics. As you consider these co-teaching approaches, you might notice that many considerations need to be taken into account (Cook & Friend, 1995; Reinhiller, 1996; Walther-Thomas et al., 1996). First, in a co-taught class, students are heterogeneously grouped so students with disabilities are appropriately integrated with their peers without disabilities. Thus, in a station teaching arrangement, students with special needs are in each of the three station groups, and when alternative teaching occurs, the smaller group may or may not contain students with disabilities. Second, both teachers take on teaching and supportive roles. This principle is critical if students are to view both teachers as credible; without using it, the special education teacher may be seen as a helper who does not have teacher status. Third, which approach is best depends on student needs, the subject being taught, the teachers' experience, and practical considerations such as space and time for planning. Novice co-teachers may prefer station teaching or parallel teaching over team teaching, especially in a class that includes several students with attention problems who would benefit from a smaller group structure. We make this recommendation because those approaches require less minute-to-minute coordination with another teacher. Sometimes, the type of curriculum dictates the approach. Curriculum that is hierarchical obviously cannot be taught in stations,

Do It!

Review lesson plans you have made in other classes. How could you adapt them for co-teaching? Create an example for each co-teaching approach.

Professional Edge

Tips for Successful Co-Teaching

Co-teaching is one approach that facilitates the inclusion of students who have disabilities in general education classrooms. The two teachers involved, often a general education teacher and a special educator, can together offer instructional options for all students. Keep in mind the following tips to make your co-teaching efforts successful.

1. Planning is the key. Make time to plan lessons and to discuss exactly how you will work together throughout your co-teaching experience.

2. Discuss your views on teaching and learning with your co-teacher. Experienced co-teachers agree that both teachers should share basic beliefs about instruction.

3. Attend to details. Clarify classroom rules and procedures, such as class routines for leaving the room, using free time, discipline, grading, and so on.

4. Prepare parents. If parents have questions, explain to them that having two teachers in the class gives every child the opportunity to receive more attention than before; it does not change the curriculum except to enrich it.

5. Avoid the "paraprofessional trap." The most common concern about co-teaching is that the special education teacher becomes a classroom helper, which quickly becomes boring for the special education teacher and awkward for the general education teacher. Using a variety of co-teaching approaches can help teachers avoid this predicament.

6. When disagreements occur, talk them out. To have some disagreements in co-teaching is normal. But be sure to raise your concerns while they are still minor and to recognize that both of you may have to compromise to resolve your differences.

7. Go slowly. If you begin with co-teaching approaches that require less reliance on one another, you have a chance to learn each other's styles. As your comfort level increases, you can try more complex co-teaching approaches.

SOURCE: Adapted from "The New Mainstreaming" by M. Friend and L. Cook, 1992b, *Instructor, 101*(7), 30–32, 34, 36. Reprinted by permission of Scholastic, Inc.

especially in a cramped classroom; it might be best presented in a format of one teach, one support, followed by parallel-taught study groups. The Professional Edge provides some additional guidelines for successful co-teaching.

Teaming

In Chapter 2, you learned that you have responsibility as a member of an intervention assistance team to problem solve about students before they are considered for special education. You also learned that you may be a member of the multidisciplinary team that determines whether a student is eligible to receive special education services and that writes the student's IEP. Now you need to understand the concepts and procedures that make those teams and other school teams effective.

When you think about highly successful teams, what comes to mind? Your favorite athletic team? A surgical team? An orchestra? What is it about these teams that makes them noteworthy? **Teams** are formal work groups that have certain characteristics. They have clear goals, active and committed members, and leaders; they practice to achieve their results; and they do not let personal issues interfere with the accomplishment of their goals. Can you think of other characteristics of effective teams?

The teams you will be part of at school have many of the same characteristics as other teams (Friend & Cook, 1997). Their success depends on the commitment of every member and the clarity of their goals (Safran & Safran, 1996). On effective school teams, members keep in mind why they are a team, setting aside personal differences in order to reach a goal, often designing the best educational strategies possible for students with disabilities or other special needs. Figure 3.5 summarizes team characteristics typically associated with effectiveness.

Team participant roles.   Team members must assume multiple roles (Harris, 1995; Rankin & Aksamit, 1994). First, you have a **professional role.** In your role as a classroom teacher, you bring a particular perspective to a team interaction, as do the special education teacher, counselor, adaptive physical educator, principal, and other team members. You contribute an understanding of what students without disabilities are accomplishing in your grade or course, knowledge of curriculum and its pace, and a sense of the prerequisites of what you are teaching and the expectations likely to follow the next segment of instruction.

The second contribution you make is through your **personal role.** The characteristics that define you as a person shape this role. For example, are you an eternal optimist, a person who sees the positive aspects of almost any situation? You will probably be the person who keeps up the team's morale. Are you a detail person who

> **Do It!**
>
> Think about a team that is unrelated to education (for example, a professional sports team). List the strategies that help the team succeed. How would these strategies help a school team?

Figure 3.5   Characteristics of Effective Teams

1. All participants understand, agree to, and identify the primary goal for the team.

2. The team is characterized by open communication that includes ideas, opinions, and feelings.

3. Team members trust one another, that is, they know that no team member will deliberately take advantage of another.

4. Team members support each other by demonstrating care and concern.

5. Team members manage their human differences. They clarify how they are different from one another and use these differences as strengths for creative problem solving rather than as hindrances to problem resolution.

6. Teams meet and work together only when necessary.

7. Team members have fundamental team skills, including those for communication, those for addressing task goals, and those for maintaining effective team functioning.

8. Teams have leaders but recognize that leadership is shared by all team members.

S O U R C E : Adapted with permission from NTL Institute, "Characteristics of Effective Teams," by W. W. Burke, 3–14, in *Team Building: Blueprints for Productivity and Satisfaction,* edited by W. Brendan Reddy and Kaleel Jamison, copyright 1988.

Check Your Learning

What are the differences among professional, personal, and team roles? What team roles are you most likely to take?

is skilled at organizing? You will probably be the team member who ensures that all the tasks get completed and all the paperwork is filed.

Third, you have a **team role** to fulfill as well. You may be the individual who makes sure the agenda is being followed or who watches the time so that team meetings do not last too long. Or, you may have the role of summarizing and clarifying others' comments or suggesting ways to combine what seem to be contradictory points of view into integrated solutions to student problems. As an effective member, you will recognize your strengths and offer them to the team; you will also be vigilant so that your weaknesses do not interfere with the team accomplishing its tasks. Common formal team roles include team facilitator, recorder, and timekeeper. These roles might rotate so that every team member has the opportunity to experience each one. Informal team roles include being a compromiser, an information seeker, and a reality checker. These informal roles are not usually assigned, but team members ensure that they are being fulfilled as the need arises.

Team goals.   One of the keys to effective teams is attention to goals (Friend & Cook, 1997). Being clear and explicit about goals is particularly important in educational settings since team goals are often assumed or too limited. For example, on some intervention assistance teams, teachers perceive the team goal to be to document interventions so that the special education assessment and identification procedures can begin. Others believe the team functions to help teachers problem solve so that the entire referral process can be avoided. Note how crucial this difference is! With the former, a team may function as a sort of "confirmation hearing" process for students with learning and behavior problems. In the latter, it may be a resource and idea support group. Without clear and specific goals, teams often flounder.

Another aspect of team goals is especially important. The goals just discussed are commonly referred to as **task goals;** that is, they are the business of the team. But teams have another set of goals as well, called maintenance goals. **Maintenance**

What types of teams might you find at your school? How do teams use shared problem solving to meet student needs?

goals refer to the team's status and functioning as a team. Maintenance goals may include beginning and ending meetings on time, finishing all agenda items during a single meeting, taking time to check on team members' perceptions of team effectiveness, improving team communication both during meetings and outside of them, and so on. These and other maintenance goals enable effective teams to accomplish the task goals they set.

One maintenance goal many teams struggle with concerns how their meetings are scheduled, structured, and operated. Complaints frequently heard include some members' failure to arrive on time, the tendency of the group to wander off topic, some members' habit of monopolizing the conversation while others seldom say anything, and the pattern of hurrying to finish meetings and in the process making hasty decisions. All of these problems can be addressed and often alleviated through team attention to them.

The following example from an elementary school problem-solving meeting shows how each team member plays a vital role. The team included the principal, two general education teachers, a special education teacher, a speech/language therapist, a reading teacher, and a social worker. The reading teacher often spoke a great deal more than other team members, talking until others simply nodded their heads in agreement with whatever she wanted. At one team meeting, the reading teacher left early, just after the team had decided to assess a student for possible special education services. No sooner had the teacher left than the team members confronted the principal, explaining that they did not believe the referral for assessment was appropriate and asking the principal to make the reading teacher stop pushing through ideas other team members did not want. The principal made a wise reply. He said, "Wait a minute. If there's a problem it's a team problem. If a poor decision was made, it was a team decision. It's not what am *I* going to do, it's what are *we* going to do." In the conversation that followed, team members recognized that each of them had a responsibility to speak out if they disagreed with an idea that was presented. They also acknowledged that they were uncomfortable confronting the reading teacher about her interactions during team meetings. However, with the help of the principal, the team spent part of their next meeting talking about each team member's verbal contributions and establishing procedures for checking all team members' perceptions prior to making a decision. Although their actions did not completely change the reading teacher's style, they did bring the team closer together and dramatically increased the team's effectiveness.

The Case in Practice on page 90 lets you listen in on another team meeting, this time an annual review that includes a parent. Notice how each team member collaborates to make the meeting successful.

Consulting

In some cases, you may find that you do not have direct support for a student in your classroom. Perhaps the student does not have an identified disability, or perhaps the student's needs can be met with occasional supports. For example, you might have an outgoing student who suddenly begins acting very withdrawn. Or you may learn that for the next school year you will have a student who has a significant hearing impairment; you would like to know how to assist the student and whether you should enroll in a sign language class. If you have a student with autism in your class, you might find that both you and the special education teacher need assistance

F Y I

Although special education teachers sometimes act as consultants, school psychologists, counselors, and specialists in areas such as student behavior management more often function in this role.

Case in Practice

Collaboration at an Annual Review Team Meeting

At Hyman's annual review, his mother, Ms. Matthis, is present, along with Ms. Otipoby, Hyman's special education teacher; Mr. Dirk, his first-grade teacher; and Ms. Goldman, the principal. Here is how the meeting begins.

Ms. Otipoby: Thanks for joining us, Ms. Matthis. How are you doing? I saw you at the community center the other day, but you were too far away to say "Hi" to.

Ms. Matthis: Oh. I'm usually there every Wednesday. You should've come over.

Ms. Otipoby: As usual, I was in a hurry. And unfortunately, I'm going to have to hurry us now. I know you have to be back at work in less than an hour.

Ms. Matthis: Yeah, I do.

Ms. Otipoby: Did you receive the annual review planning form I sent home with Hyman?

Ms. Matthis: Yeah.

Ms. Otipoby: We sent that home to give you a chance to think a little bit about what you've seen happen with Hyman this year and what you would like to see happen at school for him next year. Before we get too far into this, is there anything from the form or anything else about Hyman's schooling this year that you have questions about?

Ms. Matthis: No, I don't think so. Except that I wondered what happened after he had that fight with that other little girl.

Ms. Otipoby: There really hasn't been anything else that happened. Hyman spent part of his recess for a week in the time-out box on the playground thinking about what he had done. He hasn't fought again.

Ms. Matthis: Okay. I was just worried about that. Him hitting a girl and all.

Ms. Goldman: I'm glad you thought to ask. Maybe we could have Mr. Dirk talk a little bit about Hyman's learning this year.

Mr. Dirk: Well, Hyman's actually doing fairly well in language arts....

REFLECTIONS

What occurred at the beginning of this annual review that promotes positive interactions with parents and helps them feel part of the team? What strategy was Ms. Otipoby using in how she addressed Ms. Matthis? Why do you think Ms. Goldman waited to refocus the meeting on Hyman's learning? What does this interaction demonstrate about the importance of the early part of team meetings setting the tone for the entire meeting?

FYI

The detail of the information you provide for a consultant is important. If you are sketchy in describing the student's needs, the consultant will have to spend valuable time backtracking to learn necessary basic information.

from someone else to help the student transition from activity to activity. These are the types of situations in which you might seek support through consultation.

Consultation is a specialized problem-solving process in which one professional who has particular expertise assists another professional (or parent) who needs the benefit of that expertise (DeBoer, 1995; Sheridan, Welch, & Orme, 1996). You may contact a behavior consultant for assistance when a student in your class is aggressive. You might meet with a vision or hearing consultant when students with those disabilities are included in your class. If you have a student who has received medical or other services outside of school, you may consult with someone from the agency that has been providing those services.

Although consultation is most effective when it is based on the principles of collaboration presented earlier in this chapter, it has a different purpose than collaboration. Even though the consultant working with you may learn from you and benefit from the interaction, the goal of the interaction is to help *you* resolve a problem or deal with a concern, not to foster shared problem solving, in which both or all participants share the problem. In consulting, the assumption is that you are experiencing a problem and that the consultant's expertise will enable you to solve the problem more effectively.

The process of consulting generally begins when you complete a request form or otherwise indicate that you have a concern about a student (Witt, Gresham, & Noell, 1996). The consultant then contacts you to arrange an initial meeting. At that meeting, the problem is further clarified, the teacher's expectations are discussed, and often, arrangements are made for the consultant to observe in the teacher's room. Once the observation phase has been completed, the consultant and teacher meet again to finalize their understanding of the problem, generate and select options for addressing it, and plan how to implement whatever strategies seem needed. A timeline for putting the strategies into effect is also established. Typically, the teacher then carries out the strategies. Following this phase, the consultant and teacher meet once again to determine whether the problem has been resolved. If it has, the strategy either will be continued to maintain the success or eliminated as no longer needed. If a problem continues to exist, the consultant and teacher may begin a new consulting process, or they may decide that some other action is needed. When appropriate, the consultant "closes" the case.

For consulting to be effective, both the consultant and the consultee (that is, you as the teacher) need to participate responsibly. Your role includes preparing for meetings, being open to the consultant's suggestions, using the consultant's strategies systematically, and documenting the effectiveness of ideas you try. The Professional Edge on page 92 includes specific ideas for preparing for and collaborating successfully with consultants.

Check Your Learning

What are the steps in consultation? How are they similar to the steps in shared problem solving? What are some differences between these two collaborative activities?

How Can You Work Effectively with Parents?

The partnerships presented thus far in this chapter have focused primarily on your interactions with special education teachers and other professionals who will support you in meeting the needs of students with disabilities in your classroom. In this section, we will emphasize your working relationship with parents.

The quality of your interactions with the parents of all your students is important, but it is vital for your students with disabilities (Sileo, Sileo, & Prater, 1996). Parents may be able to help you better understand the strengths and needs of their child in your classroom. They also act as advocates for their children, so they can help you ensure that adequate supports are provided for the child's needs. Parents often see their child's experiences in your classroom in a way that you cannot; when they share this information, it helps both you and the student achieve more success. Finally, parents are your allies in educating students; when you enlist their assistance to practice skills at home, to reward a student for accomplishments at school, to communicate to the child messages consistent with yours, you and the parents are multiplying the student's educational opportunities and providing a consistency that is essential to maximize student learning.

Understanding the Perspective of Family Members

You might be tempted to assume that because you work with a student with a disability in your classroom on a daily basis you understand what it would be like to be

Professional Edge

Working with a Consultant

Some teachers have a cynical view of consultants. They roll their eyes and discuss experiences in which consultants' suggestions were not appropriate or ideas for addressing a problem were not realistic. Although these types of issues may arise because some consultants might be lacking in skills to assist teachers, they can also occur because the consultant did not understand the information the teacher provided and the expectations for the specific classroom and teacher. Here are some suggestions for ensuring that you get the maximum benefit from your interactions with consultants.

1. **Do your homework.** Working with a consultant should be an intervention you seek only after you have attempted to identify and resolve the problem by analyzing the situation yourself, talking about it with parents, presenting it at a grade-level meeting, and so on. By asking others for input, you will clarify your own thinking about the problem and your expectations for its resolution.

2. **Demonstrate your concern with documentation.** At your initial meeting with a consultant, bring samples of student work, notes recounting specific incidents in the classroom, records of correspondence with parents, and other concrete information. Chapter 12 includes strategies for collecting information about students having difficulty.

3. **Participate actively.** If you clearly describe the problem, contribute specific information about your expectations for how the situation should change, offer your ideas on how best to intervene to resolve the problem, implement the selected strategy carefully, and provide your perception of the effectiveness of the strategy, you will find consultation very helpful. If you expect the consultant to assume your responsibilities by asking you all the right questions, you are likely to be disappointed.

4. **Carry out the consultant's suggestions carefully and systematically.** Consultants often lament that teachers do not implement their suggestions but then complain about ineffective consultation. If you are asked to record certain behaviors for a student every day, then skipping a day here and there may reduce the effectiveness of the strategy. Likewise, if you agree to send a communication home each afternoon with the student, postponing the communication with the intent of just calling the parents some evening is not adequate. If you carry out a suggestion faithfully and it is not effective, you will be better prepared to discuss the matter with the consultant.

5. **Contact the consultant if problems occur.** Because the consultant is unlikely to have direct contact with the student and will be able to spend only a very limited amount of time in your classroom, you will need to monitor carefully the effect of the strategies you are implementing. If you find they are not effective or the student's problem is worsening, you should contact the consultant rather than wait for your next scheduled meeting.

---

the student's parent. This assumption could not be further from the truth. For example, the parent of a high school student with a moderate cognitive disability as well as multiple physical disorders made this comment at a meeting of parents and teachers:

> You see my child in a wheelchair and worry about getting her around the building and keeping her changed. But remember, before you ever see her in the morning, I have gotten her out of bed, bathed her, cleaned her, washed

her hair and fixed it, fed her, and dressed her. I have made sure that extra clothes are packed in case she has an accident, and I have written notes to teachers about her upcoming surgery. When she's at school I worry about whether she is safe, about whether kids fighting in the hall will care for her or injure her, and whether they are kind. And when she comes home, I clean up the soiled clothes, work with her on all the skills she is still learning, make sure that she has companionship and things to do, and then help her get ready for bed. And I wonder what will be the best option for her when she graduates in three years. You can't possibly know what it's like to be the parent of a child like my daughter.

As a teacher, you need to realize what this parent so eloquently demonstrated: that you do not understand what it is like to be the parent of a child with a disability unless you are the parent of one. That means that you should strive to recognize that the range of interactions you have with parents will be influenced in part by the stresses they are experiencing, their prior dealings with school personnel, and their own beliefs about their child's future. Apply this concept to Chris's parents, Mr. and Mrs. Werner, whom you met at the beginning of the chapter. What might be influencing their interactions with the school professionals? How would knowing about their reluctance to have Chris identified as needing special education and their concerns about the stigma of the "learning disability" label help the teachers to respond appropriately to them?

Parent Reactions to Their Child's Disability

Parents of children with disabilities have many reactions to their children. Some parents go through several emotions roughly in a sequence, whereas others may experience only one or several discrete reactions. For some, the reactions may be minor and their approach pragmatic. For others, the child's disability might affect their entire family structure and life. Part of your work with parents includes recognizing that how parents respond to you may be influenced by these responses to their children's disabilities.

1. Grief. Some parents feel grief about their child's disability. Sometimes this is a sorrow for the pain or discomfort that their child may have to experience; sometimes it is sadness for themselves because of the added stress on the family when a child has a disability; and sometimes it is a sense of loss for what the child may not be able to become. Parents have a right to grieve about their child, a right educators should respect.

2. Ambivalence. Another reaction parents may have toward their child is ambivalence. This feeling may occur as parents attempt to confirm that the child's disability is not temporary or "fixable," as they try to determine what the best educational options are for their child, and as they ponder how their child will live as an adult. The decisions that parents of children with disabilities have to make are often difficult, and these decisions continue throughout childhood and adolescence, and sometimes through adulthood. Parents often attend meetings at which tremendous amounts of information are shared with little time for explanations, and they often meet with representatives from many different disciplines. It is no wonder that they may feel ambivalent!

Do It!

Talk to the parents of a child with a disability. What would they like you to do to educate their child? What do they wish all teachers knew about working with their child?

3. Optimism. One of our students was once interviewing the parent of a student with a mild cognitive disability. When asked what it was like having a child with a cognitive disability in the family, the parent replied, "Mary is my child. Just like any other child. I love her as my child. She is sometimes funny and sometimes clever and sometimes naughty. She can really get into trouble. She's just like my other children, except she's Mary." For this parent, her child's special needs are just part of the configuration of needs that the children in any family may have. In this family, the emphasis is on the person, not the disability. There are many families like this one. In these families, the special needs of the child are met without extraordinary reactions. Parents may work diligently to optimize their child's education, but they are hopeful about their child's future. They work closely with educators and others to ensure that the child's life, whatever it may be, is the best one possible.

How parents respond when they have a child with a disability depends on many factors. One is the intensity and complexity of the disability. The reaction of a parent of a child with a learning disability diagnosed in third grade is likely to be somewhat different from that of parents who learned 2 months after their child was born that she could not see.

Another factor affecting how parents respond is how the information about the disability is shared with them. When such information is presented in a coldly clinical manner, without adequate sensitivity to the parents' emotions, their response can be quite negative. This is true even for mild disabilities. When a parent was told about her son's learning disability, the parent said, "Wait a minute. Stop and let me think. Do you realize what you've just said? You've just unraveled my whole way of thinking about my son. What do you mean a learning disability? What does that mean? Will it ever change? How can you sit there and keep talking as though it's no big thing?" A father told of learning about his daughter's moderate cognitive disability from a physician who simply said, "She's retarded. There's nothing we can do." The father left the office crying, partly because of the information and partly because of the insensitive way in which it had been communicated.

One other factor that affects parent response concerns resources, including financial support. If parents have the resources necessary to provide what they believe is the best set of support services for their child, they are less likely to experience negative emotions. However, when parents know that their child would benefit from some intervention, whether it is surgery, a piece of computer equipment, or tutoring, they are invariably frustrated when they cannot provide the needed support and have difficulty accessing it from school and community resources. The other type of resource is personal. In large families, families with many supportive relatives living in the same community, or families with a strong network of neighbors and friends, the stresses of having a child with a disability are greatly reduced. When parents are isolated or when friends and family are uncomfortable with the child, it is far more likely that the parents will experience difficulties.

Collaborating with Parents

Your working relationship with parents will depend on the student's particular needs, the parents' desire to be actively involved in their child's education, and your efforts to make parents feel as though your partnership with them is important. In some cases, collaboration may be too ambitious a goal. For example, if you are going to interact with a parent only three or four times during the school year, you may simply not have adequate opportunity for collaboration to occur. Similarly, some parents may have so many other obligations and stressors that collaboration is not a realistic goal for them. Still, for others collaboration is not only appropriate, but recommended. Your first goal in working with parents, however, is to help them to participate in meetings, conferences, and other interactions. In this way, you will have the opportunity to learn whether collaboration is an appropriate next step.

One of the most important factors that will influence whether you can develop strong working relationships with parents and families is your sensitivity to the parents' point of view (Grossman, 1995). For example, some parents find school an unpleasant or intimidating place. They may have had negative experiences when they were students, or, if they are from another country they may be unfamiliar with expectations for involvement in American public schools. If parents' primary language is not English, they may be uncomfortable because of the need for an interpreter, or they may misunderstand information communicated by school personnel, whether in face-to-face interactions or in writing. Some parents may consider the frequent written communication that comes from schools to be a nuisance (Harry, Torguson, Katkavich, & Guerrero, 1993).

Some parents may not be as involved as you would like because of pragmatic barriers. If a parent works at a job that is far from school, he or she may not be able to take time off to participate in activities at school and may not be able to afford the lost work time. For some parents, involvement is largely a matter of economics: The costs of child care and transportation may prevent them from being able to work with you.

In general, your attitude toward parents and their perceptions of their children will greatly affect how you interact with them. If you telegraph through your choice of words, your question-asking skills, and your body posture that the parents are limited participants in their children's education, you will probably find that parents do not communicate with you and may, in fact, perceive you as an ineffective teacher. However, if you make parents feel welcome in your classroom, listen carefully to their perceptions and concerns, treat them as important, and work with them to address student needs, you will find many benefits for the student, for the family, and for you. With a positive approach, students learn more and your time is spent in creating options and opportunities, not responding to parent complaints.

Parent Conferences

In addition to various types of communication systems, you will also collaborate with parents through conferences. Preparing effectively for parent conferences will help ensure successful conferences with the parents of all your students, including students with disabilities.

Prior to a conference.   Before parent conferences, you should take several steps to prepare. First, you should clarify the purpose of the conference, both for yourself and for parents. If the purpose is to explain briefly a class or course and parents understand this, they will be less likely to be disappointed when you do not share

Cultural Awareness

In schools with many bilingual students, parents are sometimes enlisted to work as paraprofessionals. In this way, the students' language is present in the classroom. At the same time, the parents gain a better understanding of the expectations for their children.

Do It!

Starting at the library, find resources for communicating with parents. What suggestions do they make on how you can nurture a strong communication link with parents?

specific information about their child. If the purpose is to spend a specific amount of time discussing a child's progress and parents know this, they can come to school prepared for such a discussion. You can help parents prepare for a conference by sending home in advance a list of questions and suggestions. A sample of this type of conference-preparation flier is presented in Figure 3.6.

You should also prepare for conferences by arranging details to maximize the time available and create a comfortable atmosphere for both the parents and yourself. Specifically, you should plan to meet with parents at a conference table, not your desk, since your desk may be perceived as a symbol of power. If your classroom is equipped for young children, you should also arrange to have adult-sized furniture available for the meeting. A box of tissues should be within easy reach, and you should make sure that the conference will be private, perhaps by posting a sign at your door that instructs parents to knock to indicate they have arrived and then to wait until you come to the door to greet them. Another part of planning a conference is preparing the questions and topics you wish to discuss with parents. These might include specific questions regarding how a student behaves at home and how rewards are given, or they might be a list of academic strengths and concerns. Having samples of student work, your grade and plan books, and other pertinent student records easily available is also important.

During a conference.   During the conference, your goal is to create a two-way exchange of information. To do this, greet parents positively, set a purpose for the conference, and actively involve parents in discussions. You should use all the collaboration skills you employ with colleagues in working with parents. In addition, you should use language respectful of the parents, their child, and their culture. Parents should be addressed as "Mr." or "Ms.," not as "Dad" or "Mom." Students should be referred to by name. Jargon should be avoided. In addition, teachers should work to understand that parents might interpret the meaning of *disability* and educators' response to it in ways different from the meanings given by educators. For example, low-income Puerto Rican parents have been found to think of

Figure 3.6   **Sample Set of Questions to Help Parents Prepare for Conferences**

1. What is your child's favorite class activity?
2. Does your child have worries about any class activities? If so, what are they?
3. What are your priorities for your child's education this year?
4. What questions do you have about your child's education in my class this year?
5. How could we at school help make this the most successful year ever for your child?
6. Are there any topics you want to discuss at the conference that I might need to prepare for? If so, please let me know.
7. Would you like other individuals to participate in the conference? If so, please give me a list of their names.
8. Is there particular school information you would like me to have available? If so, please let me know.

Professional Edge

Working with Parents from Diverse Cultural Backgrounds

Parents from diverse racial and cultural groups often are less involved in their children's education than parents of children from majority groups. Sometimes, this occurs because they are unfamiliar or uncomfortable with public school practices. For some long-term solutions to facilitating parent involvement, the school can provide the following:

1. Parent education programs that improve parents' formal education (e.g., English as a Second Language, basic reading, mathematics, reasoning skills) to
   - Increase parents' self-esteem and self-confidence
   - Facilitate positive interactions with school professionals
   - Broaden employment opportunities
   - Facilitate parent feelings of "being at home" in educational settings.

2. Parent education programs to increase parents' influence on their children's education to
   - Ensure that schools are responsive to school and community values
   - Give parents the opportunity to participate in the school's decision-making process
   - Assure that educators observe and participate in community activities; listen to parents' wants, hopes, and concerns to develop mutual understanding; and encourage parents to define desired change and to develop an action plan.

3. Awareness training programs that provide opportunities for role playing and simulation to
   - Increase parent confidence levels for interacting with school personnel
   - Facilitate parents' understanding of and shared responsibility for children's education (e.g., training in the IEP process and for advocacy roles)
   - Teach new behaviors and skills needed to interact as educational team members (e.g., problem-solving, critical thinking, and communication skills such as active listening and self-disclosure)
   - Empower parents and extend leadership abilities in the educational community (e.g., school–community-based management, curriculum development committee).

4. Opportunities for parents to train and work as para-educators in bilingual and bicultural programs to
   - Include language and customs as part of the curriculum
   - Learn instructional strategies that can be used to benefit their own children at home
   - Increase the likelihood that parents will choose to further their education.

S O U R C E : From Sileo, T. W., Sileo, A. P., & Prater, M. A. (1996). "Parent and professional partnerships in special education: Multicultural considerations." *Intervention in School and Clinic, 31,* 145–153. Copyright 1996 by PRO-ED, Inc. Reprinted by permission.

disability in terms of family identity and the school's failure to provide for the student, not as an inherent student problem (Harry, 1992a). African American parents sometimes distrust school professionals and the decisions made about their children because of past segregation and discriminatory special education practices (Harry, 1992b). The Professional Edge suggests several strategies that a school or district

Technology Notes

Enhancing Communication

Readily available and simple-to-use technology can enhance your communication with parents and your colleagues. Here are some examples.

Videotape

If parents are unable to attend school meetings or have questions about their children's behavior or developing skills, or if special educators want to get a better understanding of a student's functioning in your class, videotape may provide a tool for communication. Because most households now have videocassette recorders, you could tape students' plays, reports, or projects and make copies for parents who request them. You could focus the camera on a student who acts out frequently and record the occurrences for a behavior consultant. Keep these tips in mind if you want to use videotape to communicate with parents or other teachers:

1. Check local policies on videotaping students. You may need to obtain parents' permission.
2. If you are taping behaviors, you might need a day or two for students to become accustomed to the camera before you get "realistic" results.

Students can tape-record themselves reading or giving a report. These tapes can then be shared with parents.

3. Consider asking a parent volunteer or older student to help operate the camera; even with help, a tripod is essential.
4. If you are taping a school event, check to see whether your school district has equipment to copy tapes easily.

Audiotape

Audiotapes offer many of the advantages of videotapes but with less need for expensive equipment and less

could use to facilitate the involvement at conferences by parents unfamiliar with or uncomfortable with public schools.

During a conference, you might be meeting both with parents and a special education teacher. As teachers, you share the responsibility for creating a collaborative environment as well as for ensuring that all critical information is presented to parents, that parents have ample opportunities to share information with you, and that any needed strategies are developed and follow-ups planned.

After a conference. After a parent conference, you have several additional responsibilities to complete. First, you should write a few notes to remind yourself of the important points discussed. These notes will help you to be accurate in your rec-

intrusion into your classroom. Audiotapes can be used to record student reports and to share with parents how their children read in school. For the latter use, students can use a reading station to record their own tapes. Audiotapes can also be used as a sort of "audio passport" if you prefer that approach to the written one presented in Chapter 2. They can also be used as verbal running conversations between busy teachers who simply keep a small tape recorder nearby for those rare moments available for such communication.

Telephone

The telephone is a powerful communication tool, and not just for periodic phone calls to let parents know how their child is doing in your class. For example, you may be able to simplify the task of arranging meetings by having a conference call. You would contact a parent at his or her job, connect with the speech/language therapist who is at another school, and arrange for the special educator and you to share a speakerphone.

If you have a phone in your classroom or can access one for evening calls, you could set up a weekly hot line by connecting an answering machine. You record highlights of the week's activities and let parents know which night and which phone number to call. If you do not want parents to leave messages, set the answering machine function to "announce." If you want parents to have the opportunity to leave a message, invite them to leave a brief one. If you live in a community in which many families have fax machines, you can send a monthly newsletter by pro-

gramming the multiple number function on your fax machine. If faxes are not available, you might try a telephone tree with parents: You make three phone calls, and each parent you call relays information by calling three other parents. Obviously, this strategy requires conscientious parents who listen carefully.

Computer

Depending on your school and community technology use level, you might be able to communicate within your school on a local area network and with parents through an on-line service. E-mail enables educators to communicate with each other, with parents, and with others in the community easily and quickly. Messages from someone can be forwarded to others as needed, and messages can be sent to an entire group of individuals with little effort. E-mail can even take the place of written notes between teachers and parents.

If your school district has a website, you may also be able to create your own home page. You can prepare announcements, scan and display student work, and share information about topics of interest, and all of this material becomes available to anyone who logs on. Of course, using this approach requires that you periodically update the information you provide.

If parents have access to computers, you can send messages, announcements, newsletters, interesting information, and many, many other items of interest home on disk. Parents can also reply. Of course, equipment compatibility is a concern, but it is less of a problem than in earlier generations of computers.

ollections. Second, if you have made any major decisions regarding strategies that you and the parents will be implementing, you might want to write a brief note to the parents to confirm the decisions you made. Third, if you agreed to any action (for example, sending information to parents, asking a counselor to call parents), it is best to carry it out as soon as possible. Finally, if the special education teacher did not attend the conference, he or she may appreciate a brief note from you with an update on the conference outcomes.

Of course, you will communicate with parents on many occasions besides conferences, using strategies such as those introduced in Chapter 2. The Technology Notes feature describes some additional ways to communicate effectively with parents.

How Can You Work Effectively with Paraprofessionals?

Throughout this chapter, in our discussion of forming partnerships with others in schools an assumption has been made that everyone involved has equal status; that is, a general education teacher has approximately the same level of authority and equivalent responsibilities as a special education teacher, speech/language therapist, school psychologist, reading teacher, and so on. In many school districts, individuals in these types of positions are referred to as *certified staff.*

One other partnership you may form involves another type of staff. As mentioned in Chapter 2, paraprofessionals are noncertified staff members who are employed to assist certified staff in carrying out the educational programs and otherwise helping in the instruction of students with disabilities. (Although some school districts also employ other types of paraprofessionals, for our discussion, we are referring only to paraprofessionals who are part of special education services.) When students with disabilities are members of your class, a special educator may not have adequate time or opportunity to assist them frequently, or the student might not need the direct services of that professional. Instead, a paraprofessional might be assigned to you for a class period or subject, or, depending on the intensity of student needs, for much of the school day (Jones & Bender, 1993).

Understanding Your Working Relationship with Paraprofessionals

The partnerships you form with paraprofessionals are slightly different from those with certified staff since you have some supervisory responsibility for the paraprofessional's work, a situation that would not exist in your work with colleagues (Wadsworth & Knight, 1996). For example, you may be expected to prepare materials the paraprofessional will use to work with a group of students, you may have the responsibility of assigning tasks to this person on a daily basis, and you may need to provide informal training to the paraprofessional regarding your classroom expectations.

Many classroom teachers have never been supervisors, and they worry about what types of tasks to assign to a paraprofessional and how to set expectations. Adding to the complexity is the fact that some paraprofessionals have extensive professional preparation, a teaching license, and years of classroom experience, which makes them want to do nearly everything you do, whereas others have a high school diploma and little training or experience in working with students (Morehouse & Albright, 1991). Figure 3.7 outlines some typical paraprofessional responsibilities. If you will be working with a paraprofessional, you will probably receive a written description of that person's job responsibilities that specifies the activities that individual is to complete. You can also arrange to meet with the special education teacher or other professional who has overall responsibility for the paraprofessional's job performance. The general guidelines for working effectively with paraprofessionals are these: First, paraprofessionals generally enjoy working with students and want to participate actively in that process, and they should have the

Figure 3.7   **Sample Responsibilities for Paraprofessionals in General Education Classrooms**

Instructional Responsibilities

1. Review skills that already have been presented by the teacher.

2. Read to groups of students.

3. Help students carry out lab instructions.

4. Read tests to students.

5. Adapt materials under the teacher's direction.

6. Assist a teacher in presenting a lesson by running a VCR, filmstrip projector, or overhead projector.

7. Facilitate the interactions of a student cooperative learning group.

8. Lead a group of students practicing a skill presented by the teacher.

9. Take notes for identified students.

10. Take dictation from a student responding to a test or "writing" an assignment.

Noninstructional Responsibilities

1. Assist the teacher in setting up classroom activities (for example, materials and equipment).

2. Grade papers based on a model provided by the teacher.

3. Duplicate materials needed for classroom instruction.

4. Supervise students at lunch or on the playground, as specified.

5. Assist specific students with bathrooming and other personal hygiene matters.

6. Move students who need such assistance from one location to another.

7. Assist in feeding students as needed.

8. Put up bulletin boards or other classroom displays.

9. Record grades or behavior data, or complete other record-keeping duties.

10. Attend professional development meetings or team meetings as appropriate.

opportunity to do so. However, they are also appropriately expected to help teachers accomplish some of the "chores" of teaching, such as record keeping and instructional preparation tasks. Second, paraprofessionals always complete their assignments under the direction of a teacher who has either already taught the information or decided what basic work needs to be completed; that is, paraprofessionals should not do initial teaching, nor should they make instructional decisions without input from a certified staff member.

You have a key role in setting the expectations for paraprofessionals who work in your classroom, for ensuring that you and the paraprofessional are satisfied with your working relationship, and for resolving any problems that arise. At the beginning of the school year, you can orient the paraprofessional to your classroom by providing a place for the paraprofessional to leave personal belongings and instructional materials, explaining essential rules and policies for your classrooms, clarifying where you want the paraprofessional to work, and asking the paraprofessional for his or her questions and concerns. It is particularly important to touch base with the paraprofessional frequently early in the school year to be certain that expectations are clear. The paraprofessional may be working in several classrooms and trying to remember several sets of directions from different teachers, all with their own styles.

To continue nurturing the working relationship you have with a paraprofessional, you should communicate clearly and directly all activities that you would like the paraprofessional to complete. Some paraprofessionals report that they enter teachers' classrooms only to find that the teacher is working with students and expects the paraprofessional to know what lesson to review with the students with special needs, assuming that the special education teacher has provided this direction. The special educator is assuming that the general education teacher is guiding the paraprofessional. Unfortunately, the paraprofessional may be left wondering how to proceed.

Although most paraprofessionals work diligently, have a tremendous commitment to working with students with disabilities, and manage their roles superbly, occasionally problems arise. If you teach older students, you might find that the paraprofessional does not have enough knowledge of the information being presented to reinforce it with students. A few paraprofessionals violate principles of confidentiality by discussing classroom or student matters away from school. Some paraprofessionals are disruptive in classrooms, their speech too loud or their movements too noticeable. If problems such as these occur and cannot be resolved directly between you and the paraprofessional, you should request that the special educator with whom you work meet with you and the paraprofessional to problem solve. If further action is needed, an administrator such as a principal or special education coordinator can assist.

Collaborating with Paraprofessionals

An often-asked teacher question regarding paraprofessionals is, "Given the supervisory nature of teacher–paraprofessional work, is it possible to collaborate with this group of staff members?" The answer is "Yes!" Paraprofessionals can collaboratively participate in shared problem solving about student needs, in planning field trip details, and in making decisions regarding how to best adapt information for a specific student. Your responsibility as a teacher is to encourage this type of collaboration. At the same time, you should clearly inform the paraprofessional when a matter being discussed is *not* one in which the principles of collaboration are appropriate.

To help get your work with paraprofessionals off to a positive start, it might be helpful to arrange a meeting that includes you, the special education teacher under whom the paraprofessional works, and the paraprofessional. At this meeting, some of the important topics to address might include these: Is the paraprofessional's role in the classroom to assist only a targeted student or group of students, or is it permissible for the paraprofessional to support the students by assisting throughout the class? Who is the individual specifically responsible for evaluating the paraprofessional's job performance? What limits exist regarding the types of tasks the paraprofessional may be assigned to do? What are the paraprofessional's expectations for working in the classroom? What are the other job components for the paraprofessional (for example, other duties, times for breaks)? What type of communication should be used to ensure that small matters are resolved before they become serious problems and that all parties feel valued and informed? The time this type of meeting takes at the beginning of the school year is well worth the payoff of a strong, year-long partnership. Both you and the paraprofessional will be more informed about expectations and more comfortable with your roles and responsibilities (Palma, 1994).

Do It!

Think about working with a paraprofessional. List the questions you as a new teacher would ask an experienced teacher about working with paraprofessionals. If possible, invite a paraprofessional to your class to learn more about the paraprofessional's role.

Summary

Collaboration has become an important job responsibility for all educators and is especially important in educating students with special needs. Collaboration is the style professionals use in interacting with others, and it includes key characteristics such as voluntary participation, parity, shared goals, shared responsibility for key decisions, shared accountability for outcomes, shared resources, and the emergence of a collaborative belief system, trust, and respect. You help make your school's collaborative efforts more successful by identifying and clarifying your personal beliefs about collaboration, refining your interaction skills, and contributing to a supportive environment.

The collaboration you participate in can occur in many applications, but for students with special needs its most common ones include shared problem solving, co-teaching, teaming, and consulting. Each of these applications has its own set of guidelines and its own use in educating students.

Yet another collaborative responsibility teachers have relates to parents. You need to understand parents' perspectives on having a child with a disability, to work collaboratively with parents on the basis of your respect for their perspective, to communicate effectively with parents in conferences and in other ways, and to respond professionally to parents in team meetings, annual reviews, and other interactions at which you and they might be present.

A final group with whom general education teachers collaborate is paraprofessionals. Understanding your roles and responsibilities and those of the paraprofessional and basing your collaboration on these will lead to positive working relationships with these individuals.

Applications in Teaching Practice

Collaboration Comes to Lawrence Elementary School

Although the 23 teachers at Lawrence Elementary School have always worked together informally, when they began emphasizing inclusive programs for students with disabilities, they realized that they needed more than ever to work collaboratively. Dr. Tompkins, the principal, strongly agreed. Last spring, the teachers met on committees to decide what it would mean for them to be collaborative, what their collaborative priorities would be, and who would be involved in their first-year efforts.

First, the teachers reviewed their school mission statement as a starting point for discussions of their beliefs about how students learn, how teachers teach, and how schools can be learning communities. They quickly realized that their mission statement, although not bad, did not explicitly say that teachers in the school are expected to work together to meet the needs of all their students. With another after-school meeting, the mission statement was revised.

Next, the teachers began to discuss forms their collaboration might take. Carole, a first-grade teacher anticipating a class group with many special needs, argued strongly for co-teaching. She stated that she needed someone to help her for at least a couple of hours each day. Peggy reminded her that with only two special education teachers and one paraprofessional for everyone, kindergarten through fifth grade, she was asking for far too much, especially since they also have other responsibilities. Jim, the special education teacher who works with students with moderate and severe disabilities, agreed. He noted that he had to reserve time to work individually with some of his students in a special education setting. Carole's reply to these comments was that she knew that when it really got down to it, there would not be enough resources to make their collaborative approach to meeting student needs work. She said little during the rest of the meeting.

For the first year, the teachers agreed that co-teaching should occur in four classrooms with particularly high needs. Jim would co-teach with a fourth-grade teacher and a fifth-grade teacher since most of his assigned students were in those grade levels. Marta, the teacher for students with high-incidence disabilities, would co-teach in first grade and third grade because of the needs of her assigned students and other students in those grade levels. Kindergarten would not have co-teaching since parent volunteers seemed to provide all the assistance needed. Second grade would have the services of Stu, the paraprofessional, for an hour four times each week.

The teachers also decided to begin one more collaborative approach. They agreed to meet in grade-level teams at least once every other week. These separate teams would function as prereferral intervention teams for each grade level. They negotiated a schedule so that some grade levels met before school and others after school, and they staggered the meeting days so that Jim or Marta could attend all the team meetings. The teachers' goal for these teams was to renew their efforts to meet students' needs without relying on special education services, except when students clearly needed that extra assistance.

With much excitement and a little anxiety, the teachers finished their detailed planning. For example, they were a little concerned because fourth grade would have two new teachers who have not had the opportunity to participate in the planning. In the meantime, Dr. Tompkins lobbied for a few extra resources for the school's innovative plan so that the school could release the teachers for half a school day twice during the next year for evaluation of their efforts and problem solving.

Questions

1. Which characteristics of collaboration can you identify from the teachers' interactions and plans? Which are not evident?
2. How were the teachers working to ensure that their collaborative efforts would be successful? What was Dr. Tompkins's role?
3. How would you respond to Carole? What do you recommend that she do? What do you recommend that her colleagues do in their interactions with her?
4. What forms of collaboration did the teachers plan to try? What are key concepts the teachers should keep in mind related to each form?
5. How could the teachers communicate with parents about their plans? What reactions might they expect from parents? Why? How could they involve parents in their programs?
6. How should the second-grade teachers plan for the year with Stu? What are some responsibilities Stu should have? What are some responsibilities that should not be given to Stu?

chapter 4

Analyzing Classroom and Student Needs

After you read this chapter, you will be able to

1. Explain what it means to make "reasonable" accommodations for students with special needs.

2. Describe the steps of a decision-making process for accommodating students with special needs in your classroom.

3. Identify and describe the key elements of an instructional environment.

4. Describe the major components of classroom organization and explain how they can be adapted for students with special needs.

5. Explain various ways that students can be grouped for instruction in an inclusive classroom.

6. Explain how the use of effective classroom materials and instructional methods can benefit students with special needs.

Mr. Rodriguez teaches world history at a large urban high school. When he introduces new content to his students, he teaches to the whole class at once. First, he reviews material that has already been covered, pointing out how that material relates to the new content being presented. Next, he provides any additional background information that he feels will help his students understand the new material better. Before Mr. Rodriguez actually presents the new material, he hands out a partially completed outline of the major points he will make. This outline helps his students identify the most important information. Every 10 minutes or so, he stops his lecture and allows his students to discuss and modify their outlines and ask questions. When Mr. Rodriguez completes his lecture, he has his students answer a series of questions on the lecture in cooperative learning groups of four. Manuel is a student with a learning disability who is included in Mr. Rodriguez's class. Manuel has a history of difficulty staying on task during lectures and figuring out what information to write down. He also has trouble remembering information from one day to the next. How well do you think Manuel will perform in Mr. Rodriguez's class? What changes in the classroom environment might help Manuel to succeed?

Josh has cerebral palsy. His scores on intelligence tests are in the normal range. However, he has lots of trouble with muscle movements; he has little use of his lower body and legs and also has problems with his fine muscle coordination. As a result, Josh uses a wheelchair, has trouble with his speech (he speaks haltingly and is difficult to understand), and struggles to write letters and numbers correctly. Josh is included in Ms. Stewart's second-grade class. What aspects of the classroom environment do you think Ms. Stewart will need to adapt for Josh? How do you think she could use technology to facilitate Josh's inclusion?

isabilities and other special needs arise when there is an interaction between the characteristics of individual students and the various features of the students' home and school environments. Effective teachers analyze their classroom environment in relation to students' academic and social needs and make accommodations to ensure student success in the classroom. For example, Manuel has difficulty staying on task and retaining new information. However, features of Mr. Rodriguez's class make it easier for Manuel to function. The partially completed lecture outlines help Manuel focus his attention on specific information as he tries to listen and stay on task; the pauses help him catch any lecture information he might have missed. The review sessions should help Manuel retain information by giving him a mechanism for rehearsing newly learned material. Josh has some serious motor problems, but he may be able to function quite independently if Ms. Stewart makes her classroom accessible to a wheelchair and works with special educators to use assistive technology to meet Josh's needs in handwriting and oral communication.

This chapter introduces you to a systematic approach to adapting instruction for students with special needs, called INCLUDE. The rest of the text—especially Chapters 8 through 13, where specific strategies are presented—expands and elaborates on this approach. Later chapters also present a more in-depth look at the relationship between your classroom environment and the diverse needs of learners. An important assumption throughout the text is that the more effective your classroom structure is, the greater the diversity you will be able to accommodate and the fewer the individualized adaptations you will need to make.

How Can the INCLUDE Strategy Help You Make Reasonable Accommodations for Students with Special Needs?

At a recent conference presentation that included both classroom teachers and special education teachers, one of the authors asked the audience how many of those present worked with students with disabilities. A music teacher at the back of the room called out, "*Everyone* in schools works with students with disabilities!" He is right. Although the professionals who have specialized in meeting the needs of students with disabilities are valuable and provide critical instructional and support systems for students, you and your peers will be the primary teachers for many students with disabilities and other special needs, and you will form partnerships with special educators to meet the needs of others. That makes it critical for you to feel comfortable making accommodations for students.

The INCLUDE strategy is based on two key assumptions. First, student performance in school is the result of an interaction between the student and the instructional environment (Lilly, 1979; Ysseldyke & Christensen, 1987). In other words, students do have problems, but sometimes the task or the setting causes or magnifies the problems. Second, by carefully analyzing students' learning needs and the specific demands of the classroom environment, teachers can *reasonably* accommodate most students with special needs in their classrooms. You can maximize student success without taking a disproportionate amount of teacher time or diminishing the education of the other students in the class. For example, Mr. Chavez provided Royce, a student with a mild hearing impairment, an outline of lecture notes to help him keep up with the lesson. Soon, other students who struggled to recognize the important lecture points were also requesting and benefiting from the outlines. Such a reasonable accommodation assists many students in the class.

The **INCLUDE** strategy for accommodating students with special needs in the general education classroom has the following seven steps:

Step 1 **I**dentify classroom environmental, curricular, and instructional demands.
Step 2 **N**ote student learning strengths and needs.
Step 3 **C**heck for potential areas of student success.
Step 4 **L**ook for potential problem areas.
Step 5 **U**se information gathered to brainstorm instructional adaptations.
Step 6 **D**ecide which adaptations to implement.
Step 7 **E**valuate student progress.

These steps are designed to apply to a broad range of special needs and classroom environments.

Step 1: Identify Classroom Demands

Because the classroom environment significantly influences what students learn, analyzing classroom requirements allows teachers to anticipate or explain problems a student might experience. Then, by modifying the environment, teachers can solve or lessen the impact of these learning problems. Common classroom demands may relate to classroom organization, classroom grouping, instructional materials, and instructional methods.

Classroom organization. The ways in which a teacher establishes and maintains order in a classroom are referred to as **classroom organization** (Doyle, 1986). Classroom organization includes a number of factors: physical organization, such as the use of wall and floor space and lighting; classroom routines for academic and nonacademic activities; classroom climate, or attitudes toward individual differences; behavior management, such as classroom rules and reward systems; and the use of time for instructional and noninstructional activities. LaVerna is a student who needs adaptations in physical organization; she uses a wheelchair and requires wide aisles in the classroom and a ramp for the step leading to her classroom. DeShawn would benefit from a behavior management system; he might move from class to class prior to the end of each period to eliminate many potential opportunities to fight with classmates. He would also benefit from an efficient use of time; minimizing transition times or the amount of time between activities would eliminate further opportunities to engage in inappropriate interactions with his classmates.

Classroom grouping. Teachers use a variety of **classroom grouping** arrangements. Sometimes they teach the whole class at once, as when they lecture in a content area such as social studies. Other times teachers may employ small-group instruction. For example, they may teach a small group of students who have similar instructional needs, such as a group of students who all require extra help on multiplication facts. They may also group students of differing interests and abilities in an effort to foster cooperative problem solving and/or peer tutoring. Finally, classroom groups may be either teacher centered, in which the teacher is primarily responsible for instruction, or peer mediated, in which much of the instruction is carried out by students. Mike needs adaptations in classroom grouping to succeed; for example, he might do better in a small group in which other students read assignments aloud so that he can participate in responding to them.

Instructional materials.   The types of **instructional materials** teachers use can have a major impact on the academic success of students with special needs. Although many teachers are choosing to develop or collect their own materials, prepublished textbooks are used most commonly. Prepublished textbooks include basic-skills texts called *basals* and texts that stress academic content in areas such as history and science. Other materials commonly used by teachers include concrete representational items, such as manipulative devices and technological devices, including audiovisual aids, telecommunications systems, and computers. Roberta's use of large-print materials to assist her in seeing her work and Carmen's use of a study guide to help her identify important information in her history text are both examples of adaptations in instructional materials.

Instructional methods.   The ways in which teachers teach content or skills to students and evaluate whether learning has occurred are the essence of teaching and are crucial for accommodating students with special needs. Teachers use a number of different approaches to teach content or skills. Sometimes they teach skills directly, whereas other times they assume the role of a facilitator and encourage students to learn on their own. Instructional methods also involve student practice that occurs in class, through independent seatwork activities, or out of class, through homework. Ms. Correli's decision to use the overhead projector and then give Lon a copy of the transparency to help his learning is an example of an adaptation in presentation of subject matter. A paraprofessional who writes a student's words is an example of an adaptation in student practice.

Finally, **student evaluation,** or determining the extent to which students have mastered academic skills or instructional content, is an important aspect of instructional methods. Grades are frequently used to communicate student evaluation. When evaluating students with disabilities, teachers must focus on measuring what a student knows rather than the extent of his or her disability. For example, Alex, who has a severe learning disability in writing, may need to speak the answers to a test aloud to convey all he knows; if he writes the answers, you may only be measuring his writing disability. For some students, grading is an appropriate evaluation strategy. But for others, such as Anita, a student who has a moderate cognitive disability and is learning to recognize her name in her fifth-grade class, a narrative report might be a better evaluation tool.

Step 2: Note Student Learning Strengths and Needs

Once instructional demands are specified, the *N* step of INCLUDE calls for identifying student strengths and needs. Remember that students with disabilities are a very heterogeneous group; a label cannot communicate a student's learning profile. For example, some students with cognitive disabilities will learn many life skills and live independently, whereas others will always need daily assistance. Also keep in mind that students with disabilities are more like their peers without disabilities than different. Like their nondisabled peers, they have patterns of learning strengths and weaknesses. Focusing on strengths is essential (Aune, 1991; Bursuck & Jayanthi, 1993; Epstein & Sharma, 1997).

Three areas describe student learning strengths and needs: academics, social-emotional development, and physical development. Problems in any one of these areas may prevent students from meeting classroom requirements.

Academics. The first part of academics is basic skills, including reading, math, and oral and written language. Although these skills might sometimes be bypassed (for example, through the use of a calculator in math), their importance in both elementary and secondary education suggests you should consider them carefully. For example, a student with a severe reading problem is likely to have trouble in any subject area that requires reading, including math, social studies, and science, and on any assignment with written directions.

Cognitive and learning strategies make up the second part of academics. These strategies involve "learning how to learn" skills such as memorization, textbook reading, note-taking, test-taking, and general problem solving. Such skills give students independence that will help them in adult life. Students with problems in these areas will experience increasing difficulty as they proceed through the grades. For example, students who have difficulty memorizing basic facts will have trouble learning to multiply fractions, and students who cannot take notes will probably fall behind in a history course based on a lecture format.

What classroom demands might this student have difficulty meeting? What bypass strategies or adaptations might help him demonstrate that he has learned his assignment as well as his classmates have?

Survival skills, the third area of academics, are skills practiced by successful students, such as attending school regularly, being organized, completing tasks in and out of school, being independent, taking an interest in school, and displaying positive interpersonal skills (Brown, Kerr, Zigmond, & Harris, 1984). Students lacking in these areas usually have difficulty at school. For example, disorganized students are not likely to have work done on time, nor are they likely to get parent permission forms for field trips taken home or returned to school. Survival skills also help some students compensate for their other problems. For example, given two students with identical reading problems, teachers sometimes offer more help to the student who always attends school and tries hard.

Social-emotional development. Students' social-emotional development involves classroom conduct, interpersonal skills, and personal/psychological adjustment. Classroom conduct problems include a number of aggressive or disruptive behaviors, such as hitting, fighting, teasing, hyperactivity, yelling, refusing to comply with requests, crying, and destructiveness. Although most of these behaviors may be exhibited by all children at one time or another, students with special needs may engage in them more frequently and with greater intensity. Conduct problems seriously interfere with student learning and can lead to problems in interpersonal relations and personal psychological adjustment. For example, students who are disruptive in class are less likely to learn academic skills and content; their outbursts also may be resented by their peers and lead to peer rejection, social isolation, and a poor self-image.

Interpersonal skills include but are not limited to initiating and carrying on conversations, coping with conflict, and establishing and maintaining friendships. Although these skills are not ordinarily part of the explicit school curriculum, their overall impact on school adjustment makes them important. For example, students lacking in peer support may have difficulty completing group projects (an example of student practice) or finding someone to help with a difficult assignment (an example of homework).

Personal/psychological adjustment involves the key motivational areas of self-image, frustration tolerance, and proactive learning. For example, students with poor self-image and low tolerance for frustration may do poorly on tests (an example of student evaluation); students who are inactive learners may have difficulty pursuing an independent science project (an example of student practice).

Physical development. Physical development includes vision and hearing levels, motor skills, and neurological functioning. Students with vision problems will need adapted educational materials. Students with poor fine motor skills may need a computer to do their homework, an adaptation for student practice. Finally, students with attention deficits may need a wider range of approaches for presenting instruction, including lecture, discussion, small group work, and independent work.

Step 3: Check Potential Areas of Student Success

The next INCLUDE step is *C*, analyzing student strengths in view of the instructional demands identified in Step 1 and checking for activities or tasks students can do successfully. Success enhances student self-image and motivation. For example, Jerry doesn't read but can draw skillfully. In social studies, his teacher asks him to be the class cartographer, drawing maps for each region of the world as it is studied. Kurt has a moderate cognitive disability and learns very slowly, but he always comes to school on time. His second-grade teacher appoints him attendance monitor.

Step 4: Look for Potential Problem Areas

In the *L* step of the INCLUDE strategy, student learning needs are reviewed within a particular instructional context, and potential mismatches are identified. For example, Susan has a learning need in the area of expressive writing; she is unable to identify spelling errors in her work. She has an academic learning need. When evaluating students' work her history teacher deducts one letter grade from papers that contain one or more spelling errors. For Susan to succeed in writing, this mismatch needs to be addressed. Similarly, Sam has a severe problem in speaking fluently, a physical problem that is a learning need. His fourth-grade teacher requires that students present book reports to the class, a demand for student practice. Again, a potential mismatch exists that could prevent Sam from succeeding.

Step 5: Use Information to Brainstorm Adaptations

Once potential mismatches have been identified, the *U* step of INCLUDE is to use this information to identify possible ways to eliminate or minimize the effects of them. Adaptations could include bypassing the student's learning need by allowing the student to employ compensatory learning strategies, making a modification in classroom teaching or organization, and teaching the student basic or independent learning skills. The Professional Edge summarizes points to keep in mind when making instructional adaptations for students.

Professional Edge

Selecting Appropriate Instructional Adaptations

Here are some general guidelines to help you make reasonable accommodations in instruction.

- Employ an adaptation only when a mismatch occurs. Your time and energy as a teacher are limited; make changes only when necessary.

- Be certain that the student's problems are not physical in origin before you make any adaptations. This concern relates particularly to students with no obvious physical or sensory needs. Prior to adapting your class for a student with an attentional problem, be sure that the problem is not the result of a hearing loss, seizure disorder, or other physical problem.

- Determine whether you are dealing with a "can't" or a "won't" problem. Blankenship and Lilly (1981) describe a "can't" problem as one in which the student, no matter how highly motivated, is unable to do what is expected. A "won't" problem implies that the student could do what is expected but is not motivated to do so. Each type of problem may require a different adaptation. A student unable to do what is expected might need a bypass strategy; a student unwilling to do the work might need a behavior management strategy. This distinction can also save you time. For example, if a student failed a test because she didn't feel like working on the day of the test, a teacher's attempt to provide extra tutorial assistance would likely be wasted effort. The "can't" and "won't" problems are particularly relevant for adolescents, who are often less likely than younger students to work to please their teachers.

- Keep the changes as simple as possible. A good rule of thumb is to try the intervention that requires the least time and effort on your part that is likely to positively affect the student. Try a more involved adaptation only if needed.

Bypass strategies.   Bypass strategies allow students to gain access to or demonstrate mastery of the school curriculum in alternative ways. For example, a bypass strategy for Claire, who has a serious problem with spelling, would be a computerized spell checker. Alternatively, a peer could help her proofread her work. However, bypassing cannot be used on a primary area of instruction: Susan cannot spell check her spelling test. Also, bypassing a skill does not necessarily mean that the skill should not be remediated. Susan may need spelling instruction as part of her English class. Finally, bypass strategies should encourage student independence. For example, Susan might be better off learning to use a spell checker rather than relying on a peer proofreader.

Classroom teaching and organization.   Teachers can make adaptations in their classroom organization, grouping, materials, and instruction to help students succeed. For example, if Ramos has attention problems, he might be seated near the front of the room, and he might benefit from a special system of rewards and consequences and a classroom in which "busy" bulletin board displays are removed. All of these are classroom organization adaptations. A change in classroom instruction would be to call on Ramos frequently during class discussions and to allow him to earn points toward his grade for appropriate participation.

FYI

Bypass strategies are techniques students with special needs use to learn or demonstrate mastery of curriculum in a way that minimizes the impact of their disability.

Intensive instruction on basic skills and learning strategies.   A third option for including students with special needs is to provide intensive instruction designed to address basic skills or learning strategies in which the student is deficient. Often a special education teacher carries out this instruction in a resource room. This approach assumes that basic skills and learning strategies are prerequisites for successful general education experiences. Unfortunately, the results of research on whether or not skills taught in pullout programs transfer to the general education class are mixed; some studies show positive results (Marston, 1996; Snider, 1997), while other show minimal effects (Wang, Reynolds, & Walberg, 1988).

An alternative is to provide this type of instruction yourself. This option is feasible when many students have similar instructional needs and when you can easily monitor skill development. For example, Mr. Higgins, a seventh-grade science teacher, lectures frequently. As a result, students need to be proficient note-takers. At the beginning of the school year, Mr. Higgins noticed during a routine check of student notebooks that many students were not taking adequate notes. With assistance from the special education teacher, he taught note-taking as part of science. Three students for whom note-taking was especially difficult handed in their notes each day so Mr. Higgins could monitor their progress.

Step 6: Decide Which Accommodations to Implement

After you have brainstormed possible bypass strategies or instructional adaptations, you will implement the *D* step in INCLUDE, which involves selecting strategies to try. A number of guidelines are suggested here to help you decide which accommodations best suit your students' needs.

Check Your Learning

What are three examples of age-appropriate interventions? Why is age-appropriateness a key concept for thinking about students with special needs in general education classes?

Select age-appropriate adaptations.   Students' adaptations should match their age. For example, using a third-grade book as a supplement for an eighth-grade science student reading at the third-grade level would embarrass the student. In such a situation, a bypass strategy such as a taped textbook would be preferable if the student has the necessary background and cognitive skills to listen to the book with understanding. A good rule of thumb is to remember that *no* students, whether in first grade or twelfth and regardless of their special needs, want to use what they perceive as "baby" books or materials.

Select the easiest accommodations first.   Accommodations need to be feasible. Although making adaptations often will mean some additional work for you, they should not require so much time and effort that they interfere with teaching the entire class. It is easier to circle the 6 out of 12 math problems you want Maria to complete than to create a separate worksheet just for her.

Select adaptations you agree with.   You are more likely to implement an approach successfully if you believe in it (Polloway, Bursuck, Jayanthi, Epstein, & Nelson, 1996), especially in the area of behavior management. For example, in selecting rewards for students, if you are uncomfortable with candy, try activities such as time on the computer. However, adaptations should not be considered only in light of teacher beliefs. IDEA-97 is clear that the unique needs of students take precedence over the convenience of schools. With imagination and some input from special educators, you will undoubtedly find strategies that match your teaching approach while maximizing your students' learning.

Select adaptations with demonstrated effectiveness. Over the past 25 years, a massive body of professional literature on effective teaching practices has accumulated. This research will help you avoid fads and other unvalidated practices. The strategies suggested throughout this text are based on research and form a starting point for your understanding of validated practices. Another means of staying professionally current is to read relevant professional journals.

Step 7: Evaluate Student Progress

Although many effective teaching practices exist, it is impossible to predict which will be effective for a given student. As a result, once an adaptation is implemented, the *E* step of INCLUDE is essential: evaluate strategy effectiveness. You can track effectiveness through grades; observations; analysis of student work; portfolios; performance assessments; and teacher, parent, and student ratings. Gathering this information will let you know whether to continue, to change, or to discontinue an intervention.

In the next section, the relationship between your classroom and the diverse needs of learners will be examined. As we have said, the use of effective practices allows teachers to accommodate more diversity in their classrooms while at the same time lessening the need for making more individualized adaptations. The key aspects of classroom environments are shown in Figure 4.1 on page 116. These features include classroom organization, classroom grouping, instructional materials, and instructional methods.

How Is an Inclusive Classroom Organized?

Your classroom organization involves physical organization, routines for classroom business, classroom climate, behavior management systems, and the use of time. You may need to use the INCLUDE strategy to make reasonable accommodations for students with special needs in all of these areas.

Physical Organization

Although the direct effects of physical organization on student academic performance are open to interpretation (Doyle, 1986), how a classroom is physically organized can affect student learning and behavior in a number of areas. For example, carefully arranged classrooms can decrease noise and disruption, improve the level and quality of student interactions, and increase the percentage of time that students spend on academic tasks (Paine, Radicchi, Rosellini, Deutchman, & Darch, 1983). Classroom organization influences learning conditions for all students and the accessibility of instructional presentations and materials for students with sensory and physical disabilities. Physical organization includes the appearance of the classroom and the use of space, including wall areas, lighting, floor space, and storage.

Connections

A list of general education and special education publications appeared in Chapter 1.

Check Your Learning

What are all the steps in INCLUDE? What is an example of each?

FYI

The rest of this chapter aims to help you answer two questions: How can I teach my whole class so that students' individual difficulties are minimized? and, What adaptations of the instructional environment might I still need to make to meet individual students' special needs?

Figure 4.1   **Overview of Classroom Environments**

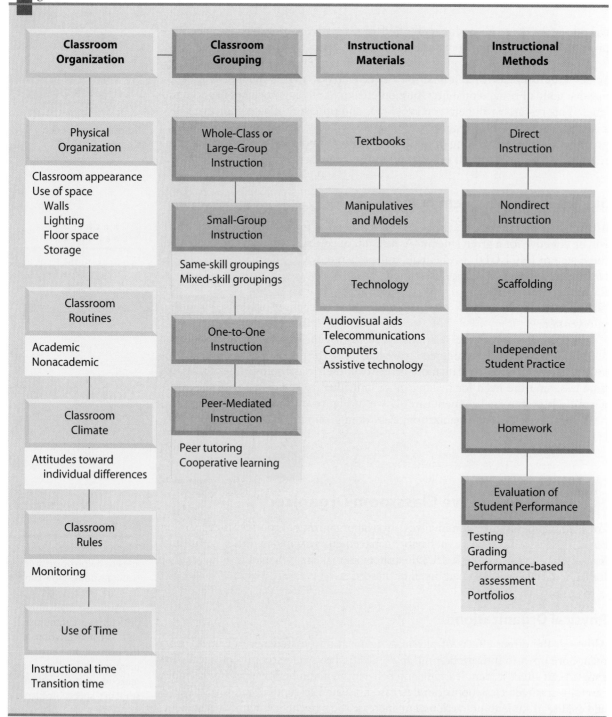

Wall areas can be used for decorating, posting rules, displaying student work, and reinforcing class content, sometimes through the use of bulletin boards. For example, one teacher taught a note-taking strategy and posted the steps on a bulletin board to help her students remember them. In using wall space, keep in mind two possible problems. First, wall displays may divert students with attention problems from concentrating on your instruction. Place these students where they are least likely to be distracted by displays. Second, students may not notice that important information appears on a display, and you may need to direct their attention to it. For example, Ms. Huerta posted a display showing graphic representations of the basic fractions. She reminded her students to look at these fractions while they were doing their independent math work.

Lighting, either from windows or ceiling lights, also can be problematic for students with special needs. Students with hearing impairments might need adequate light to speech read; they also are likely to have problems with glare in areas where the light source comes from behind the speaker. Students with visual impairments also have difficulty working in areas that are not glare-free and well lighted. Occasionally, students with learning disabilities or emotional disturbances may be sensitive to and respond negatively to certain types of light. In most cases, problems with lighting can be remedied easily by seating students away from glare caused by sunshine coming through the classroom windows.

The way in which floor space is organized and the kinds and placement of furniture used also need to be considered. For example, floors that do not have a non-slip surface can make wheelchair travel difficult. Furniture that is placed in lanes that provide access to the chalkboard or materials such as computers can make mobility difficult for students in wheelchairs or students with visual impairments. Tables, pencil sharpeners, and chalkboards that are too high may prevent access for students who use wheelchairs. Desks that are too low can interfere with students who have prostheses (artificial limbs). Special equipment in science labs, computer centers, and vocational areas also can present access problems for students with special needs. For example, the lathe in the woodworking room might be positioned too high for a person in a wheelchair to operate; the space between work areas in the science lab might not be wide enough for a wheelchair to get through. Finally, the arrangement of your class should be predictable. This means that you should not make major changes without first considering their impact on students with special needs and then informing these students so they have time to adapt. For example, Mr. Tate decided to move one of the bookshelves in his classroom. He noticed, however, that the new location blocked the passageway from the door to the desk of a student in his class who was blind. Mr. Tate informed the student of the move in advance and together they worked out an alternative route to the student's desk.

The arrangement of student desks, whether in rows, circles, or small groups, can have considerable impact on students with special needs. For example, traditional row configurations, which provide students with an immediate, unobstructed view of the teacher, have been shown to help students with attention disorders focus better when the teacher is instructing the whole group at one time. On the other hand, the placement of desks into clusters of four works better when you are using mixed-ability, cooperative learning groups to help integrate a student who is socially withdrawn. Another important consideration about floor space concerns student monitoring: Teachers should be able to see all parts of the classroom at all times, whether they are teaching large or small groups, or are working at their desks. Designing such visual access means that all specially designated areas in the classroom, such as learning/interest centers, computer stations, small-group instructional areas, or study carrels, need to be positioned so they can be monitored.

This is a teacher-centered grouping arrangement for small-group instruction. What are some advantages and disadvantages of this strategy for students with special needs? What other ways of grouping students should be part of a teacher's instructional repertoire?

An additional area of physical organization is storage. For example, students with visual disabilities may need to store equipment such as tape recorders, large-print books, braille books, and magnifying devices. For students with severe disabilities, space might be needed to store book holders, paper holders, page turners, braces, crutches, and communication boards.

Routines for Classroom Business

Establishing clear routines in both academic and nonacademic areas is important for two reasons. First, routines that are carefully structured (that is, clear to students and used consistently) reduce nonacademic time and increase learning time. Second, you can prevent many discipline problems by having predictability in your classroom routines.

Most students, especially those with special needs, find stability in knowing that classroom activities will be similar each day. In the absence of this stability, misbehavior often follows. You can find many examples of breaks in school routines. On the day of a field trip, elementary school students are more likely to hit or push, to delay beginning assignments, and to do poor work. In middle schools and high schools, teachers often dread shortened schedules for assemblies and other school programs because of increased student behavior problems.

You can create daily classroom routines that help students learn. For example, you might expect fourth graders to enter your classroom each morning, to begin their morning work, and to read quietly if they finish before instruction begins. Having routines for sharing time, setting up science experiments, preparing to go to physical education, moving to the computer lab, and so on will help students meet your expectations. Routines are especially helpful to students who need a strong sense of structure in classroom life. In secondary schools, routines might include having specific lab procedures, starting each class with a 5-minute review, or scheduling a particular activity on the same day every week. For example, in a geometry class, students who complete their assignments might choose to begin the day's homework, complete a Math Challenger worksheet from the activity file, or work on research papers or other long-term projects.

Classroom Climate

A number of authors have noted that classroom climate contributes significantly to the number and seriousness of classroom behavior problems (Jones & Jones, 1990; Morse, 1987). The **classroom climate** concerns the overall atmosphere in the classroom—whether it is friendly or unfriendly, pleasant or unpleasant, and so on. Climate is influenced by the attitudes of the teacher and students toward individual differences: Is the classroom characterized by a cooperative or a competitive atmosphere? Is the classroom a safe place for all students to take risks? Are skills for interacting positively with children and adults actively supported in the classroom?

Teachers who communicate respect and trust to their students are more successful in creating positive classroom environments in which fewer behavior problems occur (Deluke & Knoblock, 1987). For example, Mr. Elliott reprimanded a student who talked out of turn by saying, "I know you have a question about your work, and I'm glad you care enough to ask for help; but I need to have you raise your hand because I can only help people one at a time." Mr. Elliott showed respect for the student and built the student's trust by not putting her down. Yet, Mr. Elliott stuck to his rule about not speaking before being called on and explained why it was important. Similarly, Harriet's teacher, Ms. Belson, asked Harriet to define the word *diffident*. Harriet gave an incorrect definition, saying it meant "being bored." Ms. Belson said, "Harriet, I can see how you might think the meaning is *bored* because *diffident* looks a lot like *indifferent*. The word actually means 'lacking in confidence.'"

You build the overall quality of your communication with your students in many small ways. For example, finding the time each week to speak privately with students lets them know that you care about them as individuals. Asking older students sincere questions about their friends, out-of-school activities, or part-time jobs also conveys your interest in them. Taking the time to write positive comments on papers lets students know that you appreciate their strengths and do not focus only on their needs. When you encourage each student to achieve his or her own potential, without continually comparing students to one another, you are communicating the idea that each class member has a valuable contribution to make. Teachers who fail to take these small steps toward positive communication with students, or who publicly embarrass a student or punish a group for the behavior of a few, soon may create a negative classroom climate that thwarts appropriate and effective learning.

Classroom Rules

What rules do you intend to establish in your classroom? Rules help create a sense of order and expectations for a classroom, and they form a significant first step in setting up a learning environment based on preventive classroom management.

FYI

Classrooms in which instruction is relevant, interesting, and active are classrooms with fewer behavior problems. Strategies to design instruction effectively to maximize student learning are covered in Chapters 9 and 10.

FYI

Research suggests that the most effective classroom rules are ones that students develop themselves and express with teacher guidance (Bullara, 1993).

Teachers who are effective classroom managers have well-defined rules for their classrooms (for example, Bullara, 1993; Smith & Mirsa, 1992).

Effective classroom rules share three key characteristics: they are brief and specific, positively worded, and clearly understood by students (Doyle, 1990). First, rules should be few in number but as specific as possible. For example, a list of 10 or 12 rules that urge students to be fair, kind, and respectful are not as useful as 3 or 5 rules such as "Speak one at a time," "Keep your hands to yourself," and "Be prepared to start class when the bell rings by having all your learning materials ready."

Second, rules should be worded in a positive way (Bullara, 1993). In some classrooms, rules sound punitive because they are so negative. Consider the difference between a rule that states "Don't call out answers" and one that says "Raise your hand to speak." If students assist in making classroom rules, you can encourage positive wording by rephrasing rules that students suggest if they are inappropriately worded. Keep in mind that students who participate in rule making might be more motivated to obey rules.

Cultural Awareness

If your classroom includes students who are not native English speakers, you need to make sure that these students understand classroom expectations.

Third, rules should be explained carefully to your students. Post rules during the first weeks of school, explain and discuss them, and model them for students. Violations of the rules should be pointed out and corrected immediately. For example, after you and your students have established and reviewed classroom rules, explain their use, congratulate students for following them, and ask students whom you reprimand to explain why their behavior violated the rules. Younger students could draw pictures about their classroom rules and procedures. Older students could write about the necessity for rules. This early attention to setting your classroom expectations has a year-long payoff. By rehearsing and focusing student attention on them, you will make the rules part of students' understanding of their classroom. If you do not take this time to teach the rules, too often they become merely a bulletin board display, ignored by teachers and students alike.

Finally, you will need to be sure that your rules accommodate students from different cultures. For example, rules about respecting other students' property may be puzzling for Hispanic students, for whom sharing one's belongings is a highly valued activity. Similarly, rules related to aggressive behavior may need to be enforced with care for African American males, for whom some degree of aggression and assertiveness toward their peers is expected (Grossman, 1995). It is important to note that taking cultural differences into account does not necessarily mean that the rules need to be changed, only that the rules may need to be more carefully explained and enforced.

Monitoring

Connections

Strategies for effective classroom management programs are presented in more detail in Chapter 12.

In addition to having clear expectations, you also need to monitor student classroom behaviors frequently. For example, scan the room to check that students are following the rules. To do this, you always need to have a clear view of the entire class, regardless of the activity in which you or the class are engaged. If student behavior is not carefully monitored, students choose not to follow the rules consistently. For example, Charmaine is a student with behavior problems who is included in Ms. Patrick's fifth-grade class. Ms. Patrick has a rule that students need to complete all of their independent work before they can go to the computer station to play a problem-solving game. Ms. Patrick did not have time to monitor Charmaine's behavior. One day, she saw Charmaine at the computer station and asked her if she had completed her assignments. Not only had Charmaine not completed her assignments on that day, but she hadn't done any work for the past three days. Thereafter, Ms. Patrick was careful to monitor the work completion behavior of all her students.

Use of Time

How teachers use time in the classroom is one of the most important aspects of classroom organization. Use of instructional time and managing transition time constitute two particularly important areas.

Use of instructional time. The amount of time that students are meaningfully and successfully engaged in academic activities in school is referred to as **academic learning time** (Arends, 1991). Research has shown that the greater the academic learning time in a classroom, the more students learn (Fisher et al., 1980). Time usage is particularly important for students with special needs, who may need more time to learn than their peers.

Paine and colleagues (1983) suggest several ways in which teachers can maximize instructional time. One way is to minimize the time spent on organizational activities such as lunch counts, opening activities, getting drinks, sharpening pencils, cleaning out desks, and going to the bathroom. Another way is to select activities with the greatest teaching potential and that contribute most to students achieving the core school curriculum. While learning activities can be fun, they should ultimately be selected for the purpose of teaching students something important. Finally, the strategies described in this chapter and throughout this book for organizing your classroom, grouping your students, and adapting your methods and materials will also help ensure the productive use of your students' time.

Another way to increase the academic learning time of your students is described in the Professional Edge on pages 122–123.

Managing transition time. Just as important as the amount of time spent in academic activities is the management of transition time. **Transition time** is the time it takes to change from one activity to another. Transition time can occur when students remain at their seats and change from one subject to another, move from their seats to an activity in another part of the classroom, move from somewhere else in the classroom back to their seats, leave the classroom to go outside or to another part of the school building, or come back into the classroom from outside or another part of the building (Paine et al., 1983, p. 84).

Research studies show that teachers sometimes waste instructional time by not managing transitions carefully (Ornstein, 1990). Paine and colleagues (1983) suggest that you have rules devoted specifically to transitions and that you teach these rules directly to students. Among the rules they suggest are these:

1. Move quietly.
2. Put your books away and get what you need for the next activity. (You may need to state what that activity will be and what materials students need for it.)
3. Move your chairs quietly. (In some classes with small-group instruction, students carry their desk chairs to the group for seating there.)
4. Keep your hands and feet to yourself. (p. 85)

D o   I t !

Interview teachers about the role of classroom organization in behavior management. For example, how can seating arrangements and activity transitions support or undermine behavior conducive to learning?

Professional Edge

Using "Sponges" to Increase Academic Learning Time

You almost always have times during the day when you have a minute or two before a scheduled academic activity or before the class goes to lunch, an assembly, or recess. You can fill that extra time with productive activities by using "sponges." Sponges are activities that fit into brief periods of time and that give students practice or review on skills and content you have already covered in class. The following lists of sponges will help you "soak up" that extra classroom time.

Lower Grade Sponges

1. Be ready to tell one playground rule.
2. Be ready to tell me the names of the children in our class that begin with *J* or *M*, and so on.
3. Be ready to draw something that is drawn only with circles.
4. Be ready to tell a good health habit.
5. Flash fingers—have children tell how many fingers you held up.
6. Say numbers, days of the week, months—and have children tell what comes next.
7. What number comes between these two numbers: 31–33, 45–47, and so forth.
8. What number comes before/after 46, 52, 13, and so on?
9. Write a word on the board. Have children make a list of words that rhyme with it.
10. Count to 100 by 2s, 5s, 10s, and so on, either orally or in writing.
11. Think of animals that live on a farm, in the jungle, in water, and so forth.
12. Name fruits, vegetables, meats, and the like.
13. List things you can touch, things you can smell, and so on.

Dismissal Sponges

1. "I Spy"—Who can find something in the room that starts with *M*, *P*, and so on?
2. Who can find something in the room that has the sound of short *a*, long *a*, and so forth?
3. Number rows or tables. The teacher signals the number of the table with fingers, and children leave accordingly.
4. Count in order or by 2s, 5s, and so on.
5. Say the days of the week, the months of the year.

As with all rules, those for transitions need to be consistently monitored and reinforced.

How you organize classroom materials also can affect the management of transitions. For example, you need to have all materials ready for each subject and activity. In addition, materials should be organized so that they are easily accessible. No matter how well organized your transitions, you still may need to adapt them for some students with special needs. Students with physical disabilities may need more time to take out or put away their books. Students with physical and visual disabilities may have mobility problems that cause them to take more time with such transitional activities as getting into instructional groups or moving from room to room.

6. What day is it? What month is it? What is the date? What year is it? How many months in a year? How many days in a week? and so on.

7. Reward activity: "We have had a good day! Who helped it be a good day for all of us? Betty, you brought flowers to brighten our room. You may leave. John, you remembered to rinse your hands, good for you. You may leave. Ellen showed us that she could be quiet coming into the room today. You may leave, Ellen. Bob remembered his library book all by himself. Dawn walked all the way to the playground—she remembered our safety rules. Lori brought things to share with us. Tom surprised us with a perfect paper—he must have practiced. . . ." Some students can be grouped together for good deeds to speed things up. The teacher can finish with, "You're all learning to be very thoughtful. I'm very proud of all of you and you should be very proud of yourselves."

8. Use flashcards. A first correct answer earns dismissal.

9. To review the four basic shapes, each child names an object in the room either in the shape of a triangle, circle, square, or rectangle.

Upper Grade Sponges

1. List the continents.

2. Name as many gems or precious stones as you can.

3. List as many states as you can.

4. Write an abbreviation; a Roman numeral; a trademark; a proper name (biological); a proper name (geographical).

5. How many countries and their capitals can you name?

6. List five parts of the body *above the neck* that have three letters.

7. List one manufactured item for each letter of the alphabet.

8. List as many nouns in the room as you can.

9. List one proper noun for each letter of the alphabet.

10. How many parts of an auto can you list?

11. List as many kinds of trees as you can.

12. List as many personal pronouns as you can.

13. Name as many politicians as you can.

How many sponges can you think of for your grade or subject area?

SOURCE: From "Effective Teaching for Higher Achievement" by D. Sparks and G. M. Sparks, 1984, *Educational Leadership, 49*(7), Reprinted with permission of the Association for Supervision and Curriculum Development. Copyright © 1984 by ASCD. All rights reserved.

You may need an individualized system of rewards or other consequences to guide students with ADHD or behavior disorders through transition times.

How Can You Group All Your Students for Instruction in Inclusive Classrooms?

Students with special needs benefit from a variety of classroom grouping arrangements, including large- or small-group instruction, mixed- and same-skill groupings,

F Y I

An advantage of co-teaching (see Chapter 3) is that it gives teachers more grouping options and students more time with the teacher.

and teacher-centered or peer-mediated group instruction. It is important to remember that the particular arrangement you choose depends on your instructional objectives as well as your students' particular needs.

Whole-Class or Large-Group Instruction

Students with special needs benefit from both whole-class and small-group instruction. One advantage of whole-class instruction is that students spend the entire time with the teacher. In small-group instruction, on the other hand, students spend part of the time with the teacher and also spend time working independently while the teacher works with the other small groups. Research shows that the more time students spend with the teacher, the more they learn (Rosenshine & Stevens, 1986). This increase in learning may be because students are more likely to go off task when they are working on their own, particularly if they have learning or behavior problems. Whatever grouping arrangements you use, try to make sure that students spend as much time as possible working with you. Another advantage of whole-group instruction is that it does not single out students with special needs as being different from their peers. However, you may need to adapt whole-group instruction for students with special needs. For example, students in a fourth-grade class were reading *Charlotte's Web* as a large-group instructional activity. One student in the class read more slowly than the rest of the class. To help her keep up, the teacher made a list of hard words for each chapter on which a peer tutor drilled the student before she read. The teacher also gave the student more time to answer comprehension questions about the story in class because it took her longer to look up some of the answers. In another example, a high school science teacher identified technical words he was going to use in a lecture ahead of time and worked on them with a small group of students with vocabulary problems before school.

Small-Group Instruction

F Y I

Forming same-skill groupings across grade levels, sometimes referred to as the *Joplin Plan*, gives teachers more options for meeting the specific skill needs of their students.

You may encounter situations in which small-group instruction is more appropriate for students with special needs. You can use either same-skill groupings or mixed-skill groupings in setting up your small groups.

Same-skill groupings are helpful when some but not all students are having trouble mastering a particular skill and need more instruction and practice. For example, a teacher was showing her students how to divide fractions that have a common denominator. She gave her class a mini quiz to see who had learned how to do the problems. She found that all but five students had mastered the skill. The next day, the teacher worked with these five students while the rest of the class did an application activity. It is important to recognize that small-group instruction is not only for special education or remedial students; most students benefit from extra help in a small group at one time or another. In fact, many times your students with special needs will not need extra instruction.

Small, same-skill groups have also been proven effective in basic skill areas when students are performing well below most of the class (Mosteller, Light, & Sachs, 1996). For example, Lori is in Ms. Hubbard's fourth-grade class and is reading at the second-grade level. Lori is learning decoding and vocabulary skills in a small group with other students who are at her level. Because the group is small and homogeneous, Ms. Hubbard is able to proceed in small steps, present many examples, and allow students to master skills before they move on. Lori is making progress and feels good about herself because she is becoming a better reader. But keep in mind that small, same-skill groups should be used only when attempts to adapt instruction in the large group have been unsuccessful. Same-skill groups tend to become permanent and take on a life of their own, and students are more likely to become stigmatized when they are entrenched in low groups. Although some students do require instruction that is more individualized and intensive than can be provided in the large group, the ultimate goal of any small group should be its eventual dissolution. Also, on many days, students can benefit from instruction with the rest of the class. For example, Lori's group participates in large-group reading when the teacher is reading a story and working on listening comprehension. Another potential problem in using same-skill groupings is the danger that students who are in a low-achieving group in one area will be placed in low groups in other areas even though their skill levels do not justify it. For example, just because Lori is in the lowest group in reading does not automatically mean she needs to be in low groups in other areas such as math.

The major advantage of **mixed-skill groupings** is that they provide students with special needs a range of positive models of both academic and social behavior. In mixed-skill groupings, students often help each other, so such groups can also be a vehicle for providing direct instruction to individual students, something for which classroom teachers often do not have time. In addition, mixed-skill groups, like large groups, tend not to single out students with special needs.

One-to-One Instruction

Providing **one-to-one instruction** for students with special needs can be very effective under some circumstances. In this grouping arrangement, students work with either a teacher or a computer in well-sequenced materials that are geared to their specific level and proceed through the materials at their own pace. For example, Waldo is having trouble with addition and subtraction facts. For 15 minutes each day, he works at the classroom computer station on an individualized drill-and-practice program. Right now he is working on addition facts through 10. When he masters these, the machine will automatically place him into more difficult problems. Although one-to-one instruction may be appropriate in some circumstances, it is not necessarily the grouping arrangement of choice. First, it is inefficient; when it is carried out by the classroom teacher, the extensive use of one-to-one instruction will result in less instructional time for everyone. Second, the logistics of one-to-one instruction sometimes require that students complete much independent work while the teacher moves from student to student. This can lead to high levels of off-task behavior, a problem many students with special needs experience (Hardman, Drew, Egan, & Wolf, 1996; Mercer, 1997). Third, the lack of peer models in one-to-one instruction makes it more difficult to motivate students, a problem particularly relevant at the high school level (Ellis & Sabornie, 1990). Sometimes, its exclusive use can exclude students from critical social interactions. Finally, if a student requires one-to-one instruction for extended periods of time, further analysis of his or her needs and instructional setting is needed.

Cultural Awareness

Research suggests that students can sometimes benefit from working in same-sex groups. The achievement scores of girls grouped together for science instruction are generally higher than for girls grouped with boys (Moody & Gifford, 1990).

Do It!

Observe student groupings in action. Based on your observations, what factors contribute to effective grouping procedures, group characteristics, and group dynamics?

Connections

The grouping strategies in this chapter are all teacher-centered. Strategies for using groupings that are peer-mediated, such as peer tutoring and cooperative grouping, are covered in Chapter 13.

How Can You Evaluate Instructional Materials for Inclusive Classrooms?

The nature of the instructional materials you use is another very important consideration in accommodating students with special needs in your classroom. Classroom instructional materials include textbooks, manipulatives and models, and technology.

Textbooks

F Y I

Workbooks are commonly used to practice skills taught in basal materials. The material on practice activities in this chapter and in Chapter 9 applies to workbooks as well.

Basal textbooks (often called **basals**) are books used for instruction in any subject area that contain all the key components of the curriculum being taught for that subject. The careful evaluation of basals is vital because the selection of well-designed textbooks can save you much time and energy since better books require fewer adaptations for students with special needs. For example, a math basal that contains enough practice activities will not need to be adapted for students who require lots of practice to master a skill. Similarly, a history textbook that highlights critical vocabulary and includes clear context cues to help students figure the words out on their own may make it unnecessary for teachers to prepare extensive vocabulary study guides.

Fortunately, over the past 20 years, guidelines for distinguishing well-designed texts have been developed (Armbruster & Anderson, 1988; Kameenui & Simmons, 1991). A set of questions to help you evaluate basals and other basic-skills materials is included in the Professional Edge on pages 128–129.

Carefully evaluating basals helps alert you to any adaptations you will need to make. For example, a spelling basal with little provision for review can be troublesome for students who have problems retaining information. You may want to develop review activities for every three lessons rather than every five as is done in the book.

Many teachers are choosing to develop or collect their own materials rather than depending on prepublished basal series. For example, some teachers have their students read trade books instead of traditional reading books; others have their students engage in the actual writing process rather than or in addition to answering questions in a book. Still others involve their students in real-life math problem solving rather than basal math books. Even if you choose not to use basals, however, the guidelines for teaching basic skills discussed here apply.

Connections

Ways to adapt content-area texts are described in Chapter 9. Student strategies for reading texts are covered in Chapter 10.

If you use **content-area textbooks,** which are books used for instruction in content areas such as science or social studies, they also need to be evaluated. In secondary schools, students are expected to access curriculum content, often by reading their textbooks (Armbruster & Anderson, 1988; Deshler, Putnam, & Bulgren, 1985). Because students are required to read and understand their texts, often without previous instruction, the texts should be written at a level at which students can easily understand them. Armbruster and Anderson (1988) refer to readable textbooks as "considerate." Considerate textbooks are easier for students to use independently and require fewer teacher adaptations. The guidelines here refer to features involving content, organization, and quality of writing:

Check the content covered in the text to see whether it stresses "big ideas" rather than facts in isolation. "Big ideas" are important principles that enable learners to understand the connections among facts and concepts they learn (Carnine, Caros,

Crawford, Harniss, & Hollenbeck, 1996). For example, in a text that stressed facts in isolation, students learned that Rosa Parks was an important figure because she led the Montgomery bus boycott in 1955. In a text that stressed "big ideas," students learned that the bus boycott, led by Rosa Parks in 1955, was carried out in response to a problem of segregation in the South in the early 1950s and that the boycott was the first in a series of civil rights protests eventually leading to the Civil Rights Act of 1965.

Check to see whether support is provided for student comprehension. Support for student comprehension can be detected in the following ways:

1. Check the organization of the headings and subheadings. Make an outline of the headings and subheadings in a few chapters. How reasonable is the structure revealed? Is it consistent with your knowledge of the subject matter?

2. Check the consistency of organization in discussions of similar topics. For example, in a science chapter on vertebrates, information about the different groups of vertebrates should be similarly organized; that is, if the section on amphibians discusses structure, body covering, subgroups, and reproduction, the section on reptiles should discuss the same topics, in the same order.

3. Look for clear signaling of the structure. A well-designed text includes information headings and subheadings. The most helpful headings are those that are the most specific about the content in the upcoming section. For example, "Chemical Weathering" is a more helpful content clue than "Another Kind of Weathering." A well-signaled text also includes format clues to organization. Page layouts, paragraphing, marginal notations, graphic aids, and the use of boldface, italics, or underlining can all serve to highlight or reinforce the structure. For example, a discussion of the four stages in the life cycle of butterflies could be signaled by using a separate, numbered paragraph for each state (that is, 1. egg; 2. larva; 3. pupa; 4. adult) and by including a picture for each stage. Finally, look for signal words and phrases that designate particular patterns of organization. For example, the phrases "in contrast" and "on the other hand" signal a compare and contrast organization, whereas "First, . . . ; second, . . . ; third, . . . " indicate an enumeration or list pattern.

Check to see that important background knowledge is activated. Despite its importance for comprehension (McKeown, Beck, Sinatra, & Loxterman, 1992), many textbooks assume unrealistic levels of students' background knowledge (McKeown & Beck, 1990). A failure to activate important background knowledge may be especially problematic for students with special needs, who are more likely to be lacking in this information (Lenz & Alley, 1983). A number of textbook features indicate adequate attention to background knowledge. For example, in social studies texts background knowledge is often activated by providing definitions for important vocabulary content, showing students geographical information on maps, and demonstrating when in time key events took place (Harniss, 1996).

Check for quality of writing. The quality and clarity of writing can also affect student comprehension. Quality of writing can be evaluated in a number of ways.

1. Look for explicit or obvious connectives, or conjunctions. The absence of connectives can be particularly troublesome when the connective is a causal one (for

FYI

Taped textbooks can be helpful for students with reading problems. Ellis (1996) suggests that you tape only key sections of texts and that you highlight the main points in the text to help students focus on the most critical information.

Professional Edge

Guidelines for Evaluating Basals or Other Basic-Skills Curricula

Before evaluating any material, read the evaluative questions here and place an asterisk next to those that are critical for the type of material you are examining. Answer each question with a "yes" or "no." Examine all your responses in a single area, paying special attention to the questions you designated as critical. Rate each area inadequate (1), adequate (2), or excellent (3). If the area is inadequate, designate if the features could be easily modified (M).

Rating Scale:	Inadequate	Adequate	Excellent	Easily modified
	1	2	3	M

1 2 3 M   Effectiveness of Material

Yes No   Is information that indicates successful field testing or class testing of the material provided?

Yes No   Has the material been successfully field tested with students similar to the target population?

Yes No   Are testimonials and publisher claims clearly differentiated from research findings?

1 2 3 M   Prerequisite Skills

Yes No   Are the prerequisite student skills and abilities needed to work with ease in the material specified?

Yes No   Are the prerequisite student skills and abilities compatible with the objectives of the material?

Yes No   Are the prerequisite student skills and abilities compatible with the target population?

1 2 3 M   Content

Yes No   Are students provided with specific strategies rather than a series of skills in isolation?

Yes No   Does the selection of subject matter, facts, and skills adequately represent the content area?

Yes No   Is the content consistent with the stated objectives?

Yes No   Is the information presented in the material accurate?

Yes No   Is the information presented in the material current?

Yes No   Are various points of view, including treatment of cultural diversity, individuals with disabilities, ideologies, social values, gender roles, and socioeconomic status, represented objectively?

Yes No   Are the content and the topic of the material relevant to the needs of students with disabilities?

1 2 3 M   Sequence of Instruction

Yes No   Are the scope and sequence of the material clearly specified?

Yes No   Are facts, concepts, and skills ordered logically?

Yes No   Does the sequence of instruction proceed from simple to complex?

Yes No   Does the sequence proceed in small, easily attainable steps?

Rating Scale: Inadequate Adequate Excellent Easily modified
                         1   2   3   M

1 2 3 M   **Behavioral Objectives**

Yes No   Are objectives or outcomes for the material clearly stated?
Yes No   Are the objectives or outcomes consistent with the goals for the target population?
Yes No   Are the objectives or outcomes stated in behavioral terms, including the desired behavior, the conditions for measurement of the behavior, and the desired standard of performance?

1 2 3 M   **Initial Assessment and Placement**

Yes No   Does the material provide a method to determine initial student placement in the curriculum?
Yes No   Does the initial assessment for placement contain enough items to place the learner accurately?

1 2 3 M   **Ongoing Assessment and Evaluation**

Yes No   Does the material provide evaluation procedures for measuring progress and mastery of objectives?
Yes No   Are there enough evaluative items to measure learner progress accurately?
Yes No   Are procedures and/or materials for ongoing record keeping provided?

1 2 3 M   **Instructional Input (Teaching procedures)**

Yes No   Are instructional procedures for each lesson either clearly specified or self-evident?
Yes No   Does the instruction provide for active student involvement and responses?
Yes No   Are the lessons adaptable to small-group and individualized instruction?
Yes No   Are a variety of cueing and prompting techniques used to gain correct student responses?
Yes No   When using verbal instruction, does the instruction proceed clearly and logically?
Yes No   Does the material use teacher modeling and demonstration when appropriate to the skills being taught?
Yes No   Does the material specify correction and feedback procedures for use during instruction?

1 2 3 M   **Practice and Review**

Yes No   Does the material contain appropriate practice activities that contribute to mastery of the skills and concepts?
Yes No   Do practice activities relate directly to the desired outcome behaviors?
Yes No   Does the material provide enough practice for students with learning problems?
Yes No   Are skills systematically and cumulatively reviewed throughout the curriculum?

S O U R C E : From *Instructional Materials for the Mildly Handicapped: Selection, Utilization, and Modification* by A. Archer, 1977, Eugene, OR: Northwest Learning Resources System, University of Oregon. Used by permission of the author.

example, *because, since, therefore*), which is frequently the case in content-area textbooks. Therefore, look especially for causal connectives. For example, "Because the guard cells relax, the openings close" is a better explanation than "The guard cells relax. The openings close."

2. Check for clear references. One problem to watch for is confusing pronoun references when more than one noun could be used. For example, "Both the stem of the plant and the leaf produce chloroform, but in different ways. For one, the sun hits it, and then . . . ." Here, the pronouns *one* and *it* could be referring either to *the stem* or *the leaf*. Also look out for vague quantifiers, those that do not indicate the noun being quantified (for example, *some, many, few*). For example, "Some whales have become extinct" is clearer than "Some have become extinct." In addition, check for definite pronoun phrases without a clear referent (for example, "She saw the man," in which the identity of the man is unclear).

3. Look for transition statements. These transitions help the reader move easily from idea to idea. Given that a text will be covering many topics, make sure that the topic shifts are smooth.

4. Make sure the chronological sequences are easy to follow. In a discussion of a sequence of events, the order of presentation in the text should generally proceed from first to last; any alteration of the order could cause confusion if not clearly signaled.

5. Make sure graphic aids are clearly related to the text. Graphic aids should be important for understanding the material rather than simply providing decoration or filling space, clearly referenced in the text so the reader knows when to look at them, easy to read and interpret, and clearly titled and labeled.

Manipulatives and Models

Manipulatives and models can help students make connections between the abstractions often presented in school and the real-life products and situations these abstractions represent. **Manipulatives** are concrete objects or representational items, such as blocks and counters (for example, base-10 blocks for math), used as part of instruction. **Models** are also tangible objects; they provide a physical representation of an abstraction (for example, a scale model of the solar system). Strategies to help students make these connections have great potential benefit for students with special needs, who may lack the background knowledge and reasoning skills to understand abstractions (Hutchinson, 1993). Still, manipulatives and models should be used carefully (Clements & McMillen, 1996). When using these valuable tools, consider these guidelines (Marzola, 1987; Ross & Kurtz, 1993):

1. Select materials that suit the concept and the developmental stage of the student. When you are first introducing a concept, materials should be easy to comprehend. Generally, the order in which you introduce materials should follow the same order as students' understanding: from the concrete to the pictorial to the abstract. However, not all students need to start at the same level. For example, in a biology lesson on the heart, many students will benefit from viewing a three-dimensional model of a human heart, whereas other students will be able to understand how a heart works just by seeing a picture of one.

2. Use a variety of materials. Students with special needs may have trouble transferring their understanding of a concept from one form to another. For example, Wally's teacher always demonstrated place value using base-10 blocks. When Wally was given a place-value problem using coffee stirrers, he was unable to do it. Wally's teacher could have prevented this problem by demonstrating place value in the first place using a range of manipulative materials such as coffee stirrers, paper clips, and so on.

3. Use verbal explanations whenever possible to accompany object manipulation. Models and manipulative demonstrations should be preceded and accompanied by verbal explanations of the concept or skill being demonstrated. Verbal explanations are important because students may not be able to identify the important features of the model on their own. For example, Ms. Balou put a model of a two-digit by two-digit multiplication problem on the board. She verbally explained all the steps in computing the problem to her students and wrote each step on the chalkboard as it was completed.

4. Encourage active interaction. It is not enough just to have the teacher demonstrate with manipulatives or models and students observe. Allow your students to interact actively with models and manipulatives. This hands-on experience will help them construct their own meaning from the materials.

5. Elicit student explanations of their manipulations or use of models. Encourage your students to verbalize what they are doing as they work with models and manipulatives. This is a good way for you to assess whether they really understand the concept or skill. For example, Ms. Conway had her students name the main parts of the human heart using a model. Mr. Abeles had his students explain out loud how they would subtract 43 from 52 using base-10 blocks. Although explanations can help you evaluate how your students process information, students with special needs may not be able to articulate concepts right away because of language problems or a lack of reasoning skills. These students may require more frequent demonstrations of how to articulate what they are doing.

6. Move your students beyond the concrete level when they are ready. Some students with special needs may have trouble moving from one learning stage to another. One effective way to help students make the transition from the concrete to the abstract is to pair concrete tasks with paper-and-pencil tasks. For example, Ms. Washington had her students label a picture of a human heart after they had observed and discussed a physical model. Mr. Parks had his second graders solve subtraction problems using manipulatives and then record their answers on a traditional worksheet. However, Marsh & Cooke (1996) found that students with learning disabilities who were taught to solve story problems using manipulatives were able to solve similar problems at an abstract level without having to go through the representational stage.

Technology

Teachers today have available to them a broad array of technology to enhance the presentation of material to their students. These technologies range from more traditional audiovisual aids, such as audiotape, videotape, and overhead projectors, to the more advanced technologies of computers, videodiscs, and telecommunications and electronic networks.

Professional Edge

Features of Effective Drill-and-Practice Software

The introduction of technology in the classroom has given teachers a new array of tools to use in presenting material to students. Students with special needs can especially benefit from using drill-and-practice software, which allows them to learn at their own pace. Keep in mind the following guidelines when choosing an effective drill-and-practice program for your students who have special needs.

What to Look for	What to Avoid	Rationale
Programs that provide high rates of responding relevant to the skill being learned	Programs that take too much time to load and run or that contain too many activities unrelated to the skill being learned	The more time students spend on task, the more they learn.
Programs in which animation and graphics support the skill or concept being practiced	Programs with animation or graphics that are unrelated to the program's instructional objective	Although animation and graphics may facilitate student interest in an activity, they may also distract students, interfere with skill mastery, and reduce practice time.
Programs in which reinforcement is clearly related to task completion or mastery	Programs in which the events that occur when students are incorrect (for example, an explosion) are more reinforcing than the events that occur when the student is correct (for example, a smiling face)	Some programs may inadvertently encourage students to practice the incorrect response in order to view the event that they find more interesting.

Cultural Awareness

Research suggests that teachers can reduce classroom gender bias by providing boys and girls equal access to all hands-on instructional materials, including computer time (Sadker, Sadker, & Klein, 1991).

A number of guidelines for using all types of technology in your classroom have been suggested (Schuller, 1982). First, you should have clearly defined objectives for why you are using the technology. You should also know the content of the film, software, or other materials you are using. Being familiar with the content will make it easier to decide which technologies will work for you and how you can best use them. You should also guide learners on what to look for. This guidance is especially relevant for students with disabilities, who often have trouble focusing on the essential information. Finally, evaluate the results to see if the technology has helped students meet your instructional objectives.

One common use of computers in inclusive classrooms is to provide instruction to students through drill-and-practice programs, tutorials, and simulations. In general, drill-and-practice programs are used most often with students with special needs. Drill-and-practice programs have been shown to be effective for students with special needs largely because they allow students to learn in small steps, provide systematic feedback, and allow for lots of practice to mastery. Still, not all drill-

What to Look for	What to Avoid	Rationale
Programs in which feedback helps students locate and correct their mistakes	Programs in which students are merely told if they are right or wrong or instructed to "try again"	Without feedback that informs them of the correct answer after a reasonable number of attempts, students may become frustrated and make random guesses.
Programs that store information about student performance or progress that can be accessed later by the teacher	Programs without record-keeping features	Students may encounter difficulties with the skills covered by a program that requires teacher intervention. However, teachers often find it difficult to monitor students as they work at the computer. Access to records of student performance enables the teacher to determine if a program is benefiting a student and whether the student needs additional assistance.
Programs with options for controlling features such as speed of problem presentation, type of feedback, problem difficulty, and number of practice trials	Programs that must be used in the same way with every student	Options are cost-effective; they enable the same program to be used with a broad range of students. Furthermore, they permit a teacher to provide more appropriately individualized instruction.

S O U R C E : From "Computers and Individuals with Mild Disabilities" by C. M. Okolo, 1993, in *Computers and Exceptional Individuals*, edited by J. Lindsey. Austin, TX: PRO-ED. Copyright © 1993 by PRO-ED, Inc. Reprinted by permission.

and-practice programs are created equal (Okolo, 1993). Some guidelines for what to look for and what to avoid in these programs are given in the Professional Edge.

Computers can also provide initial, sequenced instruction for students, using **tutorials,** as well as instruction in problem solving, decision making, and risk taking, using **simulations.** Each of these forms of computer-assisted instruction has potential advantages and disadvantages (Roblyer, Edwards, & Havriluk, 1997). For example, tutorials can present instruction to mastery in small, sequential steps, an instructional approach shown to be effective with students with special needs. Tutorials can also provide one-to-one instruction at varying levels of difficulty, something teachers usually do not have time to do. On the other hand, you need to check to be sure that students have the necessary prerequisite skills to benefit from the tutorials. In addition, tutorials may not provide sufficient review for students, and students may not be motivated enough to work through them independently (Roblyer et al., 1997). Simulations are of great potential benefit in teaching students to be active learners by confronting real-life situations. However, simulations may be dif-

WWW Resources

Learn about ways to improve your teaching through technology by contacting the Instructional Technology Resource Center (ITRC) at <http://www.itrc.ucf.edu>.

Computer technology, telecommunications networks, and assistive technology for students with disabilities promise to revolutionize education in U.S. schools. In what ways might technology serve as a "great equalizer" in inclusive classrooms?

Do It!

Interview teachers to find out how they use assistive technology with their students who have special needs.

ficult to integrate with academic curriculum, may require much teacher assistance, and can be time consuming (Roblyer et al., 1997).

Computer technology is an important part of an inclusive classroom. A great variety of **assistive technology** is available to enable students with both low- and high-incidence disabilities to communicate or have access to information by allowing them to bypass their disability. Students with physical disabilities such as Josh, whom you met at the beginning of the chapter, can operate computers with a single key or switch rather than through a regular keyboard. Students with physical disabilities can use voice command systems to enter information into a computer verbally. Students who are deaf can communicate with hearing students or other deaf students using computer-assisted telecommunication devices such as those described in Chapter 5. Computer-generated large print, braille translations, and synthesized speech can assist students with visual disabilities in communicating. Students with communication problems can benefit from augmentative communication devices, which are computers equipped with speech synthesizers that can type text and produce speech heard by everyone. These devices can also be programmed with words and phrases for particular situations. Students with learning disabilities can compensate for poor handwriting, spelling, and grammatical skills using word processing equipment. Uses of telecommunications technology for teaching literacy skills are presented in the Technology Notes feature on pages 136–137 of this chapter.

How Can You Analyze Instructional Methods in Relation to Student Needs?

Teachers use a number of instructional methods in class, including direct instruction, nondirect methods of instruction, scaffolding, independent student practice, and evaluation of student performance. Each of these methods should be analyzed in relation to student needs and then used and/or adapted as needed.

Elements of Direct Instruction

Several decades of research in teaching effectiveness have shown that many students learn skills and subject matter more readily when it is presented very explicitly, often referred to as **direct instruction** (Aber, Bachman, Campbell, & O'Malley, 1994; Christenson, Ysseldyke, & Thurlow, 1989; Rosenshine & Stevens, 1986). Direct instruction consists of six key elements:

1. Review and check the previous day's work (and reteach if necessary). This aspect of direct instruction may include having established routines for checking homework and reviewing relevant past learning and prerequisite skills. All these procedures are important because students with special needs might not retain past learning and/or know how to apply it to new material. For example, on Thursday, Ms. Guzik taught her students how to round to the nearest whole number. On Friday, she gave her class a story problem to solve that required rounding. Before the students solved the problem, she pointed to a chart in the front of the room that showed a model of how to round numbers and suggested that they refer to this chart when they got to the end of solving the problem.

2. Present new content or skills. When content or skills are presented, teachers begin the lesson with a short statement of the objectives and a brief overview of what they are going to present and why. Material is presented in small steps, using careful demonstrations that incorporate illustrations and concrete examples to highlight key points. Included within the demonstrations are periodic questions to check for understanding.

3. Provide guided student practice (and check for understanding). At first, student practice takes place under the direct guidance of the teacher, who frequently questions *all* students on material directly related to the new content or skill. You can involve all students in questioning by using unison oral responses or by having students answer questions by holding up answer cards, raising their hands if they think an answer is correct, or holding up a number to show which answer they think is right. For example, when asking a yes or no question, tell your students to hold up a 1 if they think the answer is yes and a 2 if they think the answer is no. This approach can be used with spelling, too. Have your students spell words onto an index card and then hold up their answers. Unison responses not only give students more practice, but they also allow you to monitor student learning more readily. Prompts and additional explanations or demonstrations are provided during guided practice where appropriate. Effective guided practice continues until students meet the lesson objective. For example, Mr. Hayes was teaching his students how to add *es* to words that end in *y*. After modeling two examples at the board, he did several more examples *with* the students, guiding them as they applied the rule to change the *y* to *i* before they added *es*. Next, Mr. Hayes had them do a word on their own. Students put their answers on an index card and held the card in the air when directed by the teacher. Mr. Hayes noticed that five students did not apply the rule correctly. He called these students up to his desk for additional instruction and had the rest of the students add *es* to a list of words on a worksheet independently.

Connections

Presenting new content also involves using strategies for activating students' prior knowledge. These strategies are explored further in Chapter 9.

Technology Notes

Teaching Writing Skills through Telecommunications

Telecommunications systems are ideal for fostering the literacy skills of all your students, including those who have special needs. They allow students to retrieve information in a variety of content areas through access to the World Wide Web. For example, students can develop a search strategy to locate information that supplements a topic presented in class. They can then scan a number of sources on the World Wide Web and identify sources that are credible, relevant, and merit a more in-depth look. Finally, students can synthesize information across all sources, and develop and implement a plan for how they will communicate what they have found.

Telecommunications systems also allow students to communicate in writing from one computer to another using a modem. Students can write and receive messages using electronic bulletin boards or mail boxes. For example, they can write letters to get acquainted; write formal reports on different topics; write poetry to share thoughts, feelings, and images of the world; do electronic journalism; and have dialogues on social issues. They can share questions, answers, research, and creative writing with students all over the world. Male (1997) and Mike (1996) suggest a number of important benefits in using

How is technology enhancing the instruction and learning in this classroom?

telecommunication systems to build your students' literacy skills:

1. **Risk-free self-expression.** In most cases, students do not know the students they are communicating with. Therefore, they feel comfortable expressing themselves freely.
2. **Focus on content rather than personality and physical attributes.** In telecommunications, people communicate invisibly. They can interact free of barriers that often isolate them, such as wheelchairs, appearance, and race.
3. **Cross-cultural respect and curiosity.** Using telecommunications, students can communicate

FYI

Anita Archer (1992) has summarized the direct instruction steps as: "I do it. We do it. You do it" (p. 17).

4. **Provide feedback and correction (and reteach if necessary).** When students answer quickly and confidently, the teacher asks another question or provides a short acknowledgment of correctness (for example, "That's right"). Hesitant but correct responses might be followed by process feedback (for example, "Yes, Yolanda, that's right because . . . "). When students respond incorrectly, the teacher uses corrections to draw out an improved student response. Corrections can include sustaining feedback (that is, simplifying the question, giving clues), explaining or reviewing steps, giving process feedback ("The reason we need to regroup in this subtraction problem is because the top number is smaller than the bottom

readily across state and national boundaries. Such access can motivate students to find out more about other cultures and promote respect for these cultures. In one California school, students coproduced a newsletter with a school in Alaska.

4. **Self-worth.** Students feel important when they receive electronic mail and have their work acknowledged by people from all over the world.

5. **Elimination of time pressure from communication.** Students receive messages and can work on them off-line, which gives them a chance to get input and feedback from peers or teachers and to revise.

6. **Literacy development involving higher-order thinking.** Students involved in a search for information on the Internet must exercise and coordinate a number of higher-order literacy strategies including setting a purpose for reading, regulating reading rate, making evaluative judgments, and synthesizing textual information.

7. **Promotion of a sense of audience in reading and writing.** When students communicate on the Internet, or read e-mail or news group messages, they are writing to and are members of a real audience. Sensitivity to audience has been identified as important to the development of literacy skills.

8. **Literacy for authentic purposes.** When students explore the Internet, they are, in effect, exploring the real world. Such activity is less likely to be seen as contrived by students than, for example, the reading of assigned textbook chapters (Mike, 1996; p. 8).

Here are some activities that you might want to try with your students to get them started using a telecommunications system:

1. Students generate their own World Wide Web home pages for their schools, including student and staff profiles, special activities underway, or links to students' favorite websites.

2. Students create a monthly newsletter about events in their school, community, state, or country.

3. Students collaborate with other classes in the publication of electronic journals and literary magazines.

4. Students write the beginning of a story, and students at a sister school complete the story.

5. Students compete in Internet search contests. For example, the first group to answer a given question correctly wins (for example, "In what city and year was Martin Luther King assassinated?" Answer: Memphis, 1968).

6. Students compare their own perspectives of historical events with those of other students in different geographical regions or countries.

7. Students describe favorite meals and include instructions for preparing them, allowing the receiving students to experience something new and different to eat from a different region or culture.

S O U R C E S : From *Technology for Inclusion: Meeting the Special Needs of All Students* by M. Male, 129–131. Copyright © 1997 by Allyn and Bacon. Reprinted by permission. Mike, D. G. (1996). "Internet in the schools: A literacy perspective." *Journal of Adolescent and Adult Literacy, 40*(1), 4–13.

---

number"), or reteaching last steps ("Remember, at the end of this experiment you need to tell whether the hypothesis was accepted or rejected. Let me show you what I mean"). Corrections continue until students have met the lesson objective, with praise used in moderation. Specific praise ("I'm impressed at how you drew a picture of that story problem!") is more effective than general praise ("Good boy, Leon").

5. Provide independent student practice. Students practice independently on tasks directly related to the skills taught until they achieve a high correct rate.

Practice activities are actively supervised and students are held accountable for their work.

6. Review frequently. Systematic review of previously learned material is provided, including the incorporation of review into homework and tests. Material missed in homework or tests is retaught. (Rosenshine & Stevens, 1986)

Rosenshine and Stevens (1986) are careful to note that for older students or for those who have more subject-matter knowledge or skills, these six steps can be modified, such as by presenting more material at one time or spending less time on guided practice. For example, when a second-grade teacher presented a unit on nutrition, she spent a whole week defining and showing examples of complex carbohydrates, fats, sugar, and protein. In an eighth-grade health class, this material was covered in one day, largely because students already had much background information on this topic. Although each of the direct-instruction steps is not required for every lesson you teach, they are particularly helpful to students with learning and behavior problems, who have been shown to benefit greatly from a high level of classroom structure (Algozzine, Ysseldyke, & Campbell, 1994; Christenson et al., 1989).

The Case in Practice presents an example of a direct-instruction lesson.

Nondirect Methods of Instruction

Nondirect instruction is based on the belief that children are naturally active learners and that given the appropriate instructional environment, they will actively con-

With the appropriate support, nondirect instruction can be effective for students with special needs. What steps should this teacher take to ensure effective instruction using scaffolding?

Case in Practice

A Direct-Instruction Lesson

This direct-instruction lesson is designed to teach two-digit subtraction problems that involve renaming. Notice that the teacher first reviews the preskills of knowing when to rename. Then she guides students through several problems.

Teacher: Yesterday we learned a rule about renaming with subtraction problems. What is that rule?

Students: When we take away more than we start with, we must rename.

Teacher: Great! Now tell me whether we need to rename in doing this problem. [Teacher writes on the board.]

$$42$$
$$-37$$

Students: Yes, we need to rename.

Teacher: Why is that?

Students: Because we're taking away more than we start with. We start with 2 and take away 7. Seven is more, so we have to rename.

Teacher: Okay. Today we're going to learn how to rename in subtraction. [Teacher writes on the board.] Read this problem.

$$53$$
$$-26$$

Students: 53 take away 26.

Teacher: The 1s column tells us to start with 3 and take away 6. What does the 1s column tell us to do?

Students: Start with 3 and take away 6.

Teacher: Do we have to rename?

Students: Yes.

Teacher: Right! We start with 3 and have to take away more than 3. Here's how we rename: First we borrow a 10 from the five 10s. What do we do first?

Students: Borrow a 10 from the five 10s.

Teacher: How many 10s will be left?

Students: Four 10s.

Teacher: So I cross out the 5 and write 4 to show that the four 10s are left. [Teacher crosses out 5 and writes 4.]

Teacher: We borrowed a 10. What do we do next?

Students: Put the 10 with the three 1s.

Teacher: Right. Put 10 with the three 1s. [Teacher writes 1 in front of 3.] Now we have 13 in the 1s column. Figure out what 13 minus 6 is. [Pause] What's 13 minus 6?

Students: Seven.

Teacher: We write 7 in the 1s column. [Teacher writes 7 under the 1s column.]

Teacher: The 10s column says four 10s minus two 10s. How many is four 10s minus two 10s?

Students: Two 10s.

Teacher: What is 53 minus 26?

Students: 27.

[Teacher repeats with two more problems.]

REFLECTIONS

What direct-instruction steps did the teacher use here? Why do you think direct instruction is particularly effective for students with learning and behavior needs? Can you think of some situations in which you would not want to use direct instruction?

struct knowledge and solve problems in developmentally appropriate ways (Harris & Graham, 1996). This type of teaching is often referred to as being *constructivistic* because of the belief that students are capable of constructing meaning on their own, in most cases without explicit instruction from the teacher (Hallahan, Kauffman, & Lloyd, 1996; Poplin, 1988). Nondirect instruction is used by classroom teachers in both basic skills and content areas.

F Y I

Both whole language and the standards of the National Council on Teaching Mathematics (NCTM) represent nondirect, constructivistic approaches.

A common nondirect method is called **inquiry,** or **discovery learning** (Hoover & Hollingsworth, 1982; Jarolimek & Foster, 1993; Putnam & Wesson, 1990). Unlike direct instruction, which is very teacher-centered, in the inquiry approach, the teacher's role is "that of a guide-stimulator, a facilitator who challenges learners by helping them identify questions and problems and who guides their inquiry" (Jarolimek & Foster, 1993, pp. 142–143). The learners, then, are placed "in a role that requires considerable initiative in finding things out for themselves. They must be actively engaged in their own learning" (Jarolimek & Foster, 1993, p. 143). The teacher guides the students through five steps: (1) defining a problem, (2) proposing hypotheses, (3) collecting data, (4) evaluating evidence, and (5) making a conclusion.

Scaffolding

Connections

Ways to use scaffolding to teach students study skills are described in the discussion of learning strategies in Chapter 10.

Nondirect methods of instruction have great potential for use with students with disabilities, many of whom are characterized as being passive learners who lack skills in these areas. Still, in order to succeed in a discovery format, students with special needs need support from the teacher. An approach that has been used successfully to support students as they develop problem-solving skills is called **scaffolding** (Pearson, 1996). Scaffolds are "forms of support provided by the teacher (or another student) to help students bridge the gap between their current abilities and the intended goal" (Rosenshine & Meister, 1992, p. 26).

Before using scaffolding, you need to find out whether students have the necessary background ability to learn a cognitive strategy (Rosenshine & Meister, 1992). For example, a strategy for helping a student read a physics textbook would not be useful if the student lacked a basic knowledge of mathematics and physical properties. Similarly, teaching a strategy for solving math word problems would not be successful for a student who did not have basic math computation skills. Using scaffolding to teach higher-order cognitive strategies consists of the following six steps:

1. Present the new cognitive strategy. In this step, the teacher introduces the steps in the strategy concretely, using a list of strategy steps. The teacher then models the strategy, including all *thinking* and *doing* steps. For example, Mr. Bridges is teaching his history class how geographic features and natural resources affect the growth and location of cities. First, he introduces the problem-solving strategy to his students: (1) define the problem, (2) propose hypotheses to explain the problem, (3) collect data to evaluate your hypotheses, (4) evaluate the evidence, and (5) make a conclusion. These steps are posted on the chalkboard for easy reference. Mr. Bridges then models the strategy steps by showing students a map of the state of Illinois and saying the following:

> The problem here is finding out why Chicago came to be located where it is and not anywhere else in Illinois. Some possible factors that might affect where big cities are located might include the presence of water (rivers and lakes), mountains, valleys or other land forms, climate, access to other cities, and whether or not there are mineral or oil deposits nearby. Next, I'm going to collect some data or information to see which of these factors had an influence on the development of Chicago. Chicago is on a large lake, Lake Michigan. This makes it easier for people and goods to travel in and out. It is also

centrally located; it is in the middle of the country; people from other cities can get to it easily. There are also no mountains around it so this also makes it easy to get to. There are no major mineral deposits nearby, so that doesn't seem to be important here. The climate is cold, so I don't think people came to Chicago for the weather. The evidence leads me to conclude that Chicago is where it is because of Lake Michigan and because it is easy to get to from a lot of places.

2. Regulate difficulty during guided practice. Students begin practicing the new strategy using simplified materials so they can concentrate on learning the strategy. At first, the strategy is introduced one step at a time. Students are guided carefully through the steps, with the teacher anticipating particularly difficult steps and completing these difficult parts of the task as necessary. For example, before tackling more difficult examples, such as the geography example above, Mr. Bridges first has his students use the problem-solving steps to solve simpler problems on topics familiar to them. For example, he had them solve problems such as why the cookies someone made were dry, why a hypothetical student was late for school every day, or why the school lunches tasted awful. He also helped students brainstorm ideas for how to collect data, a step that can be difficult. Mr. Bridges did this by compiling an initial list of data collection procedures for each problem. For the problem of why the cookies were dry, Mr. Bridges gave his students a list of possible data collection procedures such as identifying the ingredients, finding out how long the cookies were baked, and figuring out how old the cookies were.

3. Provide varying contexts for student practice. Students practice the strategy on actual classroom tasks under the teacher's direction. The teacher starts out leading the practice, but the students eventually carry out the practice sessions in small cooperative groups. In Mr. Bridges's class, students practiced the problem-solving strategy using examples from their history textbooks.

4. Provide feedback. The teacher provides corrective feedback to students using evaluative checklists based on models of expert problem solving carefully explained to the students. Students are encouraged to evaluate their performance using these checklists. For example, each time Mr. Bridges's students used the problem-solving strategy, they evaluated their performance by asking themselves questions such as, Did we clearly state the problem? Did we state a complete list of hypotheses? How thorough were our data collection procedures? Did the information collected allow us to evaluate all the hypotheses? Did we interpret the results accurately? Were our conclusions consistent with our results?

5. Increase student responsibility. Next, the teacher begins to require students to practice putting all the steps together on their own. Student independence is encouraged by removing elements of the scaffold. For example, prompts and models are diminished, the complexity and difficulty of the materials are increased, and peer support is decreased. The teacher checks for student mastery before going to the last step, independent practice.

6. Provide independent practice. Finally, the teacher provides the students with extensive practice and helps them apply what they have learned to new situations. For example, Mr. Bridges showed his students how problem solving could be used in their other subjects, such as science. (Rosenshine & Meister, 1992)

Check Your Learning

How can scaffolding be used to make nondirect instruction more effective for students with special needs?

Independent Student Practice

The major purpose of practice is to help students refine or strengthen their skills in various areas. Consider these guidelines for using practice activities effectively in your classroom:

1. **Students should practice only skills or content they have already learned.** This guideline is particularly important if students are to be able to perform practice activities independently. Tasks that are too difficult can lead to high levels of off-task behavior.

2. **Practice is more effective if students have a desire to learn what they are practicing.** Whenever possible, point out to students situations in which they can use the skill in other phases of learning. For example, "If you learn to read more quickly, it will take you less time to finish your homework."

3. **Practice should be individualized.** Exercises should be organized so that each student can work independently.

4. **Practice should be specific and systematic.** Practice should be directly related to skills and objectives you are working on in class. This guideline is particularly important for students with special needs, who need more practice in order to master academic skills.

5. **Students should have much practice on a few skills rather than a little practice on many skills.** Focusing on one or two skills at a time is less confusing and gives students more practice on each skill.

6. **Practice should be organized so that students achieve high levels of success.** Correct answers are reinforcing to students and encourage them to do more. Most students need at least 90 percent accuracy when doing practice activities, though higher-achieving students can tolerate a 70 percent rate as long as the teacher is present to give them needed assistance (Good & Brophy, 1988).

7. **Practice should be organized so that students and the teacher have immediate feedback.** You need to know how students do so you can decide whether to move to the next skill. Students need to know how they are doing so they can make meaningful corrections of their work. (Ornstein, 1990)

For your students with special needs, consider these additional questions. First, what are the response demands of the activity? Do students have to answer orally or in writing? How extensive a response is required? Do the students have enough time to finish the activity? Response demands are important because students who are unable to meet them will not be able to do the practice activity independently. For example, Mr. Edwards is having his class practice weekly vocabulary words orally in class by giving their definitions. Ross stutters and is unable to give his answer out loud. Mr. Edwards allows him to submit a written list of definitions. Ms. Osborne is having her students answer short-answer questions in their history books. Clarice has a physical disability and is unable to write her answers independently. She uses an adapted classroom computer to prepare her answers. Mr. Nusbaum asked his students to write a paragraph summarizing the reasons for the stock market crash of 1929. Maurice cannot write a coherent paragraph but can answer orally into a tape recorder. Amanda writes very slowly, so Mr. Nusbaum gave her more time to complete the activity.

Homework

Perhaps the most common form of practice used by teachers is **homework.** Research shows that homework can have a positive effect on student achievement if it is assigned properly (Cooper, 1989; Cooper & Nye, 1994).

Homework is often a challenge for students with special needs. For example, most teachers expect homework to be completed independently, and students must have the sensory, academic, and organizational skills to do so. A student with a severe reading disability might be unable to read a chapter in a history book and answer the questions without some form of adaptation such as a peer-reader or taped text. Similarly, a student with fine motor difficulties might be unable to answer the written questions unless allowed to do so orally or with an adapted word processor. In addition, you may need to provide this same student more time or to assign fewer problems. Therefore, it is important that you carefully examine your own particular homework requirements and adapt them to ensure full participation by all your students.

▌Connections

Strategies for adapting seatwork, independent practice activities, and homework for students with special needs are presented in Chapter 9.

Evaluation of Student Performance

The major purpose of student evaluation is to determine the extent to which students have mastered academic skills or instructional content. The results of student evaluations often are communicated through grades, which are determined in a number of ways, including tests and assignments. Because student evaluation is so important, you need to consider how classroom tests and assignments may interact with student learning needs. Most critical is that the method of evaluation measures skill or content mastery, not the student's disability. For example, Carson, a student who has an attention deficit, should be given tests in small segments to ensure that the test measures his knowledge, not his attention span. Similarly, Riesa, a student with a severe learning disability in writing, needs to be given an essay test in history orally if the test is to be a valid measure of her history knowledge, not her writing disability. The type of report-card grade used as well as the system used to arrive at that grade might also need to be adapted for some students. For example, Hal was discouraged about always getting a C in English no matter how hard he tried. His teacher decided to supplement his grade with an A for effort to encourage Hal to keep trying. Mr. Henning encouraged his students to come to class on time by giving them credit for punctuality.

▌Connections

Chapter 11 explores strategies for adapting classroom tests and report-card grades for students with special needs. It also covers potentially valuable additions to testing and grading, such as performance-based assessments and portfolios.

ummary

Various aspects of classroom environments can affect the learning of all students, including those with special needs. Fewer individualized accommodations for students with special needs will be required in classrooms that are well structured and organized. However, even in the best situations, some adaptations will be needed.

The INCLUDE strategy is a decision-making process to help teachers make "reasonable" accommodations for students with special needs. "Reasonable" accommodations are those that maximize student success without taking a disproportionate amount of time or diminishing the education of the other students in the class. The steps in INCLUDE are: *I*dentify classroom, environmental, curricular, and instructional demands; *N*ote student learning strengths and needs; *C*heck for potential areas of student success; *L*ook for potential problem areas; *U*se information gathered to brainstorm instructional adaptations; *D*ecide which adaptations to implement; and *E*valuate student progress.

An important part of the INCLUDE strategy is analyzing classroom demands. Demands covering four major areas should be analyzed: classroom organization, classroom grouping, instructional materials, and instructional methods. Classroom organization includes physical organization, classroom routines, classroom climate, classroom rules, monitoring, and the use of time. Key aspects of classroom grouping involve the use of whole-class and small instructional groups, same-skill and mixed-skill groups, and one-to-one instruction. Instructional materials that need to be considered are basic skills materials, content-area textbooks, manipulatives and models, and instructional and assistive technology. With regard to teaching demands, two common instructional models used in schools are direct and nondirect instruction. Sometimes students with special needs may require support or scaffolds when participating in nondirect teaching. Finally, consider the demands of your practice activities and follow guidelines for using practice effectively.

Applications in Teaching Practice

Planning Adaptations in the Instructional Environment

Consider these two scenarios:

- Verna is a student with a learning disability who is included in Ms. Chang's fourth-grade class. Ms. Chang uses whole-group instruction in math. This method is sometimes hard for Verna, who is behind her peers in math; Verna is slow to answer math facts, has trouble keeping numbers straight in columns, and sometimes forgets a step or two when she is computing a problem that requires several steps.

- Mr. Howard want to teach the following textbook reading strategy to his freshman history students:

R	*Review* headings and subheadings.
E	*Examine* boldface words.
A	*Ask*, "What do I expect to learn?"
D	*Do* it: Read!
S	*Summarize* in your own words (Battlett, Marchio, & Reynolds, 1994).

Questions

1. What can Ms. Chang do to help Verna succeed in the large group?
2. How can Ms. Chang use direct instruction to teach students to round numbers to the nearest 10? Design such a lesson.
3. How can Mr. Howard use scaffolding to teach his history students the READS strategy?
4. Find a drill-and-practice computer program for elementary or high school students and evaluate it. Does it meet the criteria discussed in this chapter?

chapter 5

Students with Low-Incidence Disabilities

Learner Objectives

After you read this chapter, you will be able to

1. Describe what it means to say that a student has a low-incidence disability.

2. Outline the characteristics of students with moderate, severe, or multiple disabilities and the accommodations general education teachers can make for them.

3. Explain the characteristics of students with sensory impairments and the accommodations general education teachers can make for them.

4. Describe the characteristics of students with physical or health impairments and the accommodations general education teachers can make for them.

5. Outline the characteristics of students with autism and the accommodations general education teachers can make for them.

■ Jesse is a ~~kindergartner~~ with multiple disabilities. He has a moderate cognitive disability and mild cerebral palsy. He is learning some basic colors and shapes but has not yet learned letters and sounds. He especially likes the simplified color-matching game he plays with classmates and the furry puppets sometimes used for storytelling. Jesse uses a wheelchair; he also needs help feeding himself and using the bathroom. His personal assistant makes sure he is moved whenever needed and also attends to his personal care. Jesse's limited speech is difficult to understand, especially when he is excited, and sometimes the other children in the class explain to the teacher, Ms. Cutter, what he is saying since they seem to understand it easily. In fact, the other students have welcomed Jesse and interact with him as with any other classmate, especially after Ms. Cutter explained that Jesse can do many things for himself and does not always need help. When the class is working at learning stations, Jesse participates as much as possible. His puzzles have larger and simpler pieces than those other children use, and sometimes he is matching shapes instead of learning words; but those and many other adaptations are just part of Jesse being in class. What are the learning characteristics and needs of students like Jesse? What adaptations does Jesse need to succeed in kindergarten? If Ms. Cutter has a question about Jesse, how can she find an answer?

■ Donisha is a fourth-grade student. She seldom volunteers any type of answer in class, and she is extremely meticulous in her class work. In fact, Donisha will do an assignment again and again instead of erasing any mistakes she might have made. Donisha is fascinated by anything related to astronomy. She not only knows the names of the planets and many constellations, but she also knows the sizes of the planets, their distances from Earth, the number of moons each has, and the makeup of their atmospheres. She can also recite the history of the names of the constellations, the major stars in each, the distances of each from Earth, and how to locate them in the sky. Donisha gets high grades in science, but she barely passes her other subjects. Donisha doesn't have any real friends among her classmates; they sometimes call her names. She seems happiest when left alone, and in social situations, her teachers comment that she doesn't quite know what to do. Donisha has been diagnosed as having a mild form of autism. What is autism? What should Donisha's teacher do to help her learn? What accommodations might Donisha need?

■ Timothy has a moderate cognitive disability. He can read stories written at a first-grade level and recognizes many words he sees daily (for example, *exit, men, ladies, sale*); socially, he wants to be friends and interact with his peers, but he often does not understand their conversations. In his eighth-grade science class, he is responsible for only a very small part of the vocabulary and concepts taught. For example, in the unit on chemistry, he learned what oxygen is. His other goal for that unit was related to fire safety: stopping fires by depriving them of oxygen and rules to follow in case of a fire. He did not learn the chemical formulas other students learned, nor did he write the chemical equations. Although he listens to some of the presentations on topics meaningful to him, since one of his IEP goals is to sit quietly during explanations, he works with a paraprofessional on his objectives for at least part of the class. When other students are completing assignments, he does, too, but his assignments have been specially prepared for him by his special education teacher with input from his science teacher. How are decisions made about what Timothy should be learning in each of his classes? What can Timothy's teacher do to include Timothy in classroom activities?

■ Martina is a senior this year. She plans to become a special education teacher someday, and she is studying hard to improve her chances of succeeding at college. Martina has had a profound hearing loss since she was 3 months old. At that time, she had an extremely high fever that the doctor believes caused her hearing problem. Martina's speaking voice is a little difficult to understand, and she receives speech therapy, as she has since she was two. Martina did not learn sign language until she began high school. She now prefers signing as a communication approach, and she has an interpreter who accompanies her to core academic classes. Martina's most difficult subject is English. She has problems writing down her ideas logically and elaborating on them. She becomes frustrated and occasionally says maybe she won't try to go to college after all. Her special education teacher is working with her on developing work habits and attitudes that will assist her in college. How do hearing impairments affect learning for students like Martina? What are Martina's responsibilities for self-advocacy? What can her teachers do to help her prepare for college?

Students like Jesse, Donisha, Timothy, and Martina have the same rights as other students to be part of the classroom community with nondisabled peers. For Jesse, attending kindergarten with peers prepares him for the demands of school and also of the real world. For Martina, success in college depends on her receiving the strong academic background available in general education classes. Because of their disabilities, however, these and other students in inclusive schools might need specialized equipment or assistance.

In this chapter, you will learn about the characteristics and needs of students with low-incidence disabilities, that is, moderate, severe, or multiple disabilities; sensory impairments; physical or health disabilities; and autism. The federal terms for these disabilities and the proportion of students with low incidence served through IDEA are summarized in Table 5.1. You also will learn about accommodations general education teachers can make that enable students with these disabilities to learn.

Connections

In Chapter 1, all the categories of disabilities are listed and the concept of high- and low-incidence disabilities is explained.

Table 5.1 School-Age Students with Low-Incidence Disabilities Receiving Special Education Services in 1994–1995[a]

Federal Disability Category	Defining Characteristics	Total Number of Students	Percentage of All Students Receiving IDEA Services
Mental retardation	Significant below-average general intellectual functioning with deficits in adaptive behavior	570,855	11.6[b]
	Identified between birth and 18 years of age		
	Adversely affects educational performance		
Multiple disabilities	Two or more disabilities so interwoven that none can be identified as the primary disability	89,646	1.8
	Adversely affects educational performance		
Hearing impairments	Hearing loss is permanent or fluctuating, mild to profound in nature, in one or both ears	65,568	1.3
	Loss may be referred to as "hard of hearing" or "deaf"		
	Adversely affects educational performance		
Orthopedic impairments	Physically disabling conditions that affect locomotion or motor functions	60,604	1.2
	May be the result of a congenital anomaly, a disease, an accident, or other causes		
	Adversely affects educational performance		

(continued)

149

Table 5.1 *(continued)*

Federal Disability Category	Defining Characteristics	Total Number of Students	Percentage of All Students Receiving IDEA Services
Other health impairments	Condition resulting in limited strength, vitality, or alertness and caused by chronic or acute health problems Adversely affects educational performance	106,509	2.2
Visual impairments	Vision loss in which student cannot successfully use vision as a primary channel for learning or has such reduced acuity or visual field that processing information visually is significantly inhibited and specialized materials or modifications are needed Adversely affects educational performance	24,877	0.5
Deaf–blindness	Presence of both a vision and a hearing disability that causes severe communication and related problems Adversely affects educational performance	1,331	0.0
Autism	Developmental disability characterized by impairments in communication, learning, and reciprocal social interactions Usually identified in infancy or early childhood Adversely affects educational performance	22,780	0.5
Traumatic brain injury	Impairments manifested by limited strength, vitality, alertness, or other impaired development resulting from a traumatic brain injury Adversely affects educational performance	7,188	0.1

[a] Students age 6–21 receiving services through IDEA, Part B (U.S. Department of Education, 1996). Additional students receive services under Part H of the same law, and under Chapter 1.

[b] Because federal categories of disability do not distinguish among students with various degrees of mental retardation, it is difficult to provide a precise estimate of the number of students with moderate or severe cognitive disabilities. However, approximately one-third of the students in this category have moderate or severe cognitive disabilities.

S O U R C E : From *Eighteenth Annual Report to Congress on the Implementation of the Education of the Handicapped Act,* 1996, Washington, DC: U.S. Department of Education.

What Are Low-Incidence Disabilities?

When you work with students with low-incidence disabilities, you will be struck by the diversity of their needs, the range of educational services they access, and the variety of specialists who ensure they receive an appropriate education. Typically, individuals within any of the categories of disability do not exhibit all the characteristics of that disability, but they display them much more than other students do. The following points can help you keep students' needs and your role in their education in perspective.

First, students with low-incidence disabilities together make up only about 10 percent of all the students with disabilities in schools. That means that you probably will teach students with these needs some years but not others and will make the accommodations described in this chapter for a small number of students. An exception to this situation could occur if your school district operates **cluster programs,** in which students with low-incidence disabilities from throughout the district are bussed to a single school. In such cases, you might find that your school has a "class" of students with low-incidence disabilities, making it likely that you will teach more students with such needs.

Second, students with low-incidence disabilities often have received some type of special education services from birth or shortly thereafter. They might come to kindergarten already having been in an infant-stimulation program or a preschool program in which their special needs were addressed in a day-care, inclusive preschool, or special education setting. You will find that many supports and extensive technical assistance are available for students with low-incidence disabilities.

Third, students with low-incidence disabilities need the same basic attention from you that other students do. If you are unsure about a student need, it is nearly always best to rely on the same professional judgment you would use in working with other students. If you encounter difficulty, you can access the technical support that special education professionals offer. Students with some disabilities, especially severe or complex ones, often are accompanied by a paraprofessional or personal assistant who might be able to offer insight about responding to the student.

If you learn you will have a student with a low-incidence disability in your classroom, you might have many concerns about meeting that student's needs. The Professional Edge on page 152 features questions you can use to prepare for a student with a low-incidence disability to join your class. The questions address the student's strengths and potential, learning and social needs, and physical or health needs. They also cover domains in which accommodations might be needed, including the physical arrangement of the classroom. What other questions would you add to these lists?

You might have noticed that students with cognitive disabilities are addressed in both the high-incidence and low-incidence disability groups. This dual consideration occurs because the federal category of mental retardation is used for all students with this disability, whether the disability is mild or severe. In this chapter, only students with moderate or severe cognitive disabilities are addressed. Students with mild cognitive disabilities have characteristics and needs similar to those of students with learning and behavior disabilities, and they are discussed with those groups in Chapter 6.

> **F Y I**
>
> One valuable source of information about students with disabilities and related topics is the federally funded National Information Center for Children and Youth with Disabilities (NICHCY). You can request information from NICHCY by writing to P.O. Box 1492, Washington, D.C. 20013-1492.

> **Connections**
>
> The INCLUDE strategy (see Chapter 4) can also guide you through the process of providing appropriate instruction for students with moderate or severe disabilities.

What Accommodations Can You Make for Students with Moderate, Severe, or Multiple Disabilities?

Students with moderate, severe, or multiple disabilities include those with cognitive disabilities whose cognitive impairments and adaptive behavior deficits are so significant and pervasive that considerable support is needed for them to learn. This group

Professional Edge

Questions to Ask When Working with Students with Low-Incidence Disabilities

If you will be teaching a student with a low-incidence disability, you will probably have questions about the student's needs and your responsibilities for helping the student succeed. Here are some key questions you might ask in your conversation with a special education teacher or administrator to help both you and the student feel more comfortable.

Student Needs

1. What is the student's greatest strength?

2. What activities or rewards does the student most enjoy?

3. What is the student's level of functioning academically, socially, emotionally, behaviorally, and in other domains?

4. Does the student have physical or health needs that require my attention? For example, does the student need to take medication? Is the student likely to have a reaction to medication? Does the student tire easily? Does the student need assistance in moving from place to place?

Student Goals

1. What are the three or four most important instructional goals for this student in my class? What are the academic, social, emotional, or other goals?

2. What are the goals for this student in each subject (for elementary teachers)?

3. What are the goals that this student is working on all day long?

Student Supports and Accommodations

1. If I have a question about the student, who is my primary contact person? How do I reach that person?

2. Does the student have an assistant or interpreter? If there is an assistant, what are his or her major responsibilities? Can that person help other students in the class as well?

3. What other services (for example, speech/language services) will the student access? How often? Who will be in touch about arranging these services? Will they be delivered in the classroom or in another location?

4. Do I need to adapt the physical environment for this student? How?

5. Do I need to adapt my expectations for this student because of physical or health needs? How? Are there restrictions on this student's participation in any class activities?

6. How can I adapt my teaching approach to accommodate the student's needs?

also includes students with multiple disabilities, that is, students who have more than one disabling condition. These students typically have a curriculum significantly different from that of other students in your class, but many of them can still learn in a general education setting and benefit from the social interactions with classmates that occur there.

Students with Moderate to Severe Cognitive Disabilities

Students with moderate to severe cognitive disabilities have ongoing needs for intensive supports during their school years and into adult life. Most states use scores on intelligence tests and adaptive behavior scales to determine the presence of this disability, but leaders in the field argue that a more appropriate strategy is to define the disability on the basis of its impact on daily life activities and student needs for services (Beirne-Smith, Patton, & Ittenbach, 1994).

Generally, students with moderate or severe cognitive disabilities have several noticeable characteristics (Alper & Ryndak, 1992). First, their rate of learning may be quite slow. Because these students are limited in the amount of information they can learn, the need to emphasize skills that will help them live independently as adults is crucial. Such skills include those related to living and working in the community and to choosing appropriate recreational activities. Second, students with moderate and severe cognitive disabilities may have difficulty maintaining their skills; without ongoing practice, they are likely to forget what they once learned. To ensure that these students continue to practice necessary skills, teachers should stress skills they will use both in and outside of school. Third, students in this group may have difficulty generalizing skills learned in one setting or situation to another setting or situation. It is thus critical that they learn as many skills as possible in context. For example, rather than have these students practice buttoning and unbuttoning out of context as part of a segregated classroom exercise, have them apply this skill in the morning and afternoon as they enter and leave school wearing coats or sweaters. An additional challenge facing students with moderate to severe cognitive disabilities is combining small skills into a larger one. For example, a student may be taught each step involved in making a sandwich, but unless the steps are taught in an integrated way, the student is probably going to have difficulty carrying them all out in a logical sequence.

Helen is a young woman with **Down syndrome,** a condition that often includes a moderate cognitive disability. She attended elementary school with her peers even though she did not always learn the same things they were learning. Her teachers expected her to behave appropriately, and her peers helped her when she got confused by classroom directions or otherwise needed support in the classroom. As she moved to middle school, she participated with peers in co-taught science and social studies and in elective classes such as foods and computers, and she received some of her reading and math instruction in a special education classroom. In high school, she took several classes, including choir, U.S. history, home economics, career exploration, and family living. She also entered a vocational preparation program so she would be ready to get a job after high school. At 21, Helen graduated from high school. She now works in a local medical office. Her job includes duplicating medical records, doing simple filing tasks, running errands, and helping get mail ready to send. Helen's success as an adult is in large part a result of learning many skills fostered in inclusive schools.

Two principles usually guide instruction for students with moderate or severe cognitive disabilities (Ford, Davern, & Schnorr, 1990). The first is the principle of a **functional curriculum.** In a functional curriculum, the goals for students, whether they attend a general education classroom or receive supports elsewhere, are based on real-life skills they need to succeed. For example, such a student might benefit more from learning to make purchases than learning to write a story, since most adults make purchases regularly. Some of the most important job skills Helen learned during her school career were punctuality, following multiple-step directions, and keeping her voice appropriately low. Timothy, whom you met at the beginning of the chapter, was taught fire safety as a functional skill within the context of a much broader science curriculum.

FYI

Another term you may hear in conversations about students with moderate or severe disabilities is *developmentally delayed.* This term is broad, including students with cognitive disabilities, multiple disabilities, and autism.

Cultural Awareness

In rural areas, parents of children with severe or multiple disabilities face the problem of isolation. They are likely to be the only parents in the area with a child with complex needs, and they may not have a network to provide support and information. Advances in telecommunications can help alleviate this dilemma.

Do It!

With a classmate, generate ideas for making an elementary or secondary curriculum area more functional and community based. Share your ideas with others in class.

The second principle is that education should be **community based;** that is, it should relate what is learned in school to what occurs in the community. Many students, both those with and those without disabilities, benefit from applying skills learned in school to real-life settings and activities. For some, systematic instruction in the community is necessary to teach skills needed to live, work, recreate, and continue to learn there. Lessons on the local community might include going to the bank, visiting people who live in a retirement center, and exploring job possibilities in local restaurants, hotels, and other businesses. Part of Helen's community-based instruction included learning how to ride the bus from her home to her job.

Instructional Adaptations for Students with Moderate to Severe Cognitive Disabilities

Experience shows that teachers in many school districts are looking for a single strategy that will make including students with moderate and severe disabilities in their classrooms clear and simple. Unfortunately, such a strategy does not exist. Most successful inclusive programs use many strategies and many variations of them (Janney, Snell, Beers, & Raynes, 1995), as you can see in the Case in Practice. In fact, many of the adaptations and general school conditions needed by students with moderate and severe disabilities are the same ones that make learning more successful for all students.

WWW Resources

Many groups dedicated to specific disabilities have their own websites. Examples are The ARC, an organization on mental retardation at <http://TheArc.org/welcome.html> and the Down Syndrome WWW Page at <http://www.nas.com.downsyn/>.

Clarify expectations and use instructional approaches that match those expectations. As a teacher, you should know what a student is expected to learn, whether or not that student has a disability. For example, in a social studies class, the goal for a student with a moderate cognitive disability might be to locate states where relatives live on a map, while the goal for other students might be to understand detailed topographical maps. For a student with a severe disability, a pertinent activity might be to identify photos of local community businesses. A fundamental ingredient for adaptation is to make learning standards appropriate for the student as well as a natural part of the instructional environment. You should work with a special educator to arrange learning activities suitable for reaching those standards using age-appropriate materials (Giangreco, Dennis, Cloninger, Edelman, & Schattman, 1993; Williams & Fox, 1996). One detailed system designed to accomplish this planning examines the overall goals for the student and clarifies expectations that should exist all day (for example, approaching adults and peers in an age-appropriate fashion) as well as those for specific subject areas (for example, making choices between two items during math) (Forest & Lusthaus, 1990).

Check Your Learning

How does meeting the needs of students with moderate or severe disabilities in your class help you meet the needs of your other students?

Use heterogeneous classroom groups. Most professionals who write about adapting general education classrooms to include students with moderate and severe disabilities stress the importance of strategies such as peer tutoring, cooperative learning, and friend support systems in classrooms with a heterogeneous group of learners, including a few students with disabilities (Wisniewski & Alper, 1994). By structuring your teaching so that students work with each other, you foster a sense of classroom community and help students learn to value and respect their classmates with disabilities as individuals (York, Vandercook, MacDonald, Heise-Neff, & Caughey, 1992).

Case in Practice

Teaching a Student with a Moderate Cognitive Disability

Gabriel is a first grader with a moderate cognitive disability. He is a member of Ms. Biernat's class for about three-fourths of the school day. During the late morning, he receives intensive instruction from a special education teacher or speech therapist. Gabriel is functioning at about a 3-year-old level. He knows his name, color words, and some functional words like *exit* and *boys*. Gabriel's speech is indistinct. For the word *big*, he says "bi-i-"; for the word *orange*, he says, "o-onge." However, Gabriel is also learning sign language and knows many words in sign. Gabriel thoroughly enjoys being in first grade with other students and enthusiastically participates in activities with them. He has a tendency, though, to shout instead of using words or signs as a means of interacting, and when he gets excited, as sometimes happens climbing the monkey bars at recess, he occasionally wets his pants.

Ms. Biernat has this to say about Gabriel: "He's a real charmer. When I first met him, he looked so scared and little. I realized that even though I was worried about Gabriel being in my class, he was nearly terrified about joining a large class group. I've learned that there are some things about Gabriel that I have to attend to. For example, he doesn't like changes in anything. On days that we have a school program in the auditorium, I have to tell him several times what is going to happen and remind other students to help Gabe as we go to and from the

program. I still need to stay close in case he panics. At least he gives me clear cues. If he sits down on the floor and yells "No!" I know I've pushed him past the limits of his ability to change. But Gabe also makes a real contribution. He is a friend to everyone, and he is always enthusiastic about lessons.

"In class, one problem I've had to deal with is his tendency to yell. When he wants to tell someone something, he tends to get louder and louder. The students and I know that saying 'Sign it, Gabe' is the right way to respond. During show-and-tell, the same problem can occur. When it was bear day, Gabe brought a bear to share. As he tried to tell about its name, he began shouting. I started asking him questions he could answer with one word or a sign. That helped.

"Gabe can be as mischievous as any other student. In the cafeteria, he tries to get attention by eating with his mouth wide open. The other day in math he was supposed to be finding all the fives on the page while the other students were computing answers to the addition problems. Instead, Gabe began systematically dropping his crayons in the space between the desks. When I stopped him, he grinned. It was definitely just to get attention.

"I've learned a lot from Gabe and I know the other students have, too. There are definitely days when I can't think of the right adaptations for him, but the special education teacher or paraprofessional always has an idea. It helps when the speech therapist comes to class, too. She has been very helpful in showing me how to encourage Gabe to use both signs and speech and to do it without making a big deal. Gabe knows his name and address, he matches color words and a few functional words, and he can count to five and match objects to numbers. He is interested in everything that we do in social studies and science. With support from the special educators, Gabe is having a successful first-grade experience, and I'm learning a lot about meeting student needs."

REFLECTIONS

What are the strengths and needs that Gabriel brings to his first-grade classroom? If you were Gabriel's teacher, what questions would you ask about his educational program? What other situations might cause Gabriel to panic, as sometimes happens during school programs without careful advance planning and intervention? How is Ms. Biernat ensuring that Gabriel is a full member of first grade? How is Ms. Biernat drawing on special education professionals as resources to support Gabriel's instructional program in first grade?

Identify optimal times for specialized instruction. Students with moderate or severe disabilities sometimes need to learn skills that are unlikely to arise as part of the traditional school curriculum. For example, a fifth grader who needs to learn how to tell time on a digital clock may not have enough opportunities to practice in class. However, if a peer works with her as classmates are entering the room during the morning or for a few minutes between lunch and the beginning of afternoon activities, critical instruction can occur without the need for teaching telling time out of context in an isolated setting. Timothy, whom you met at the beginning of this chapter, has some specialized needs that are met in this way.

Enlist natural support systems. Peers, older students, parent volunteers, student teachers, interns, and other individuals at school can all assist a student with a moderate or severe disability (Fulton, LeRoy, Pinckney, & Weekley, 1994). Peers can often answer simple questions or respond to basic requests without adult intervention. In some cases, they understand their classmate with a disability better than adults do (Hendrickson, Shokoohi-Yekta, Hamre-Nietupski, & Gable, 1996). Older students can serve as peer tutors or special buddies, both for instruction and for the development of appropriate social skills. Parents, student teachers, interns, and others can all assume part of the responsibility for supporting students. For example, an administrative intern who reads a story to the class releases the classroom teacher to observe the student with a moderate or severe cognitive disability or to work briefly with that student.

> **Connections**
>
> In Chapter 2, you learned about strategies for communicating with parents of students with disabilities. Such strategies can foster a positive educational experience for students with moderate or severe disabilities.

Create a collaborative effort with families. When you teach a student with a moderate or severe disability, you should communicate regularly with the student's parents. Families know their children better than school professionals, and parents can provide valuable information about teaching them. They might also have questions about how to reinforce skills learned at school at home. Occasionally, you will encounter a family that does not want to be actively involved in the education of their child. In these cases, it is your responsibility to accept their decision without judging it.

Take advantage of assistive technology. Consider, for example, the many low-tech and high-tech means for enhancing learning. Many students who cannot use language to communicate use various forms of **augmentative communication**, that is, alternative communication forms that enable students to convey their message. Other students use technology to aid movement. Assistive technology can be either simple or complex, as shown in the Technology Notes feature.

Multiple Disabilities

Because their needs can be extraordinary, students with multiple disabilities are considered a separate group in IDEA. Most students with multiple disabilities have a cognitive disability and a physical or sensory impairment. Jesse, the kindergartner you met at the beginning of this chapter, has a cognitive disability and a physical disability. The needs of these students and the adaptations that will help them succeed can be similar to those for students with moderate and severe cognitive disabilities, differences being a matter of degree and complexity. For example, in one school in-

Technology Notes

Assistive Technology

Many students with disabilities use assistive technology to help them learn. Assistive technology devices can include adaptive clothing and toys, seating systems, communication devices, and many other items. In your classroom, students might use a wide variety of computer devices and systems, special tables or chairs, and alternative communication systems such as communication boards. A student's needs for assistive technology support are written into the IEP. School districts are responsible for providing such equipment or devices if a student needs them, unless insurance or some other funding source is available. Here are two examples of assistive technology.

Gait Trainers

A gait trainer is a wide-based steel frame with four casters and optional wheels whose purpose is to help students learning to walk. A student is supported in the middle of the device in a slightly forward-leaning position that encourages walking movements. Unlike walkers that assist people with poor balance or strength, gait trainers can help students ambulate even if they have very little control of their bodies. The independence a gait trainer can give to students and families can be a major milestone for them.

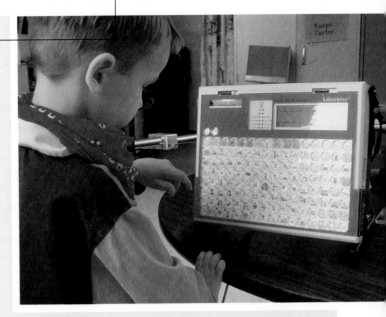

This student uses a communication board to interact with his peers.

Computer Access Devices

For some students, computers are a critical learning and communication tool, but they need assistance in accessing the computer. A student with paralysis might use a joy stick controlled by the chin in order to move the cursor. Another possibility is to use a head pointer. The latter device permits the student to point to items on the computer screen using the head rather than a computer mouse. It can be used in combination with an on-screen keyboard to make computing accessible. If a student's voice is relatively clear, voice recognition equipment, which can take the student's spoken word and convert it into written language, is a possibility.

tegrating students with multiple disabilities into general education classes, the primary challenges teachers faced included the following:

- Providing a functional curriculum within the context of the general education class
- Providing community-based instruction for all students
- Scheduling staff coverage
- Promoting social integration between students with multiple disabilities and other students (Hamre-Nietupski, McDonald, & Nietupski, 1992)

Because many students with multiple disabilities have limited speech and do not easily convey their preferences and needs, communicating with them can be a challenge. One strategy for communication includes the use of augmentative communication systems, the same systems that are sometimes used by students with moderate or severe cognitive disabilities.

As a teacher, you can expect that some but probably not all students with multiple disabilities will participate in general education activities in your school. They are likely to receive considerable support from a special education teacher or a paraprofessional who thus becomes available for co-teaching and other classwide integration activities (Jones-Carter, 1995). These professionals and other members of the multidisciplinary team can assist you in setting expectations for students, planning appropriate educational experiences, monitoring their performance, and problem solving when concerns arise (Williams & Fox, 1996). In an elementary school, a student with multiple disabilities might attend your class for morning activities, remain in the room for language arts, and participate in art and music with other students. That student might also receive some services in other building locations (for example, the library, gym, learning center, special education classroom, or home economics laboratory). In a secondary school, a student with multiple disabilities might attend some core classes with peers and spend part of the school day learning to function in the broader community and to perform job-specific skills.

Deaf–Blindness

Although students with dual sensory impairments typically are not totally blind or deaf, they do have extraordinary needs related to staying in touch with the environment, making sense of events that most teachers and students take for granted, and learning with limited access to vision and hearing (Giangreco, Edelman, MacFarland, & Luiselli, 1997). These students sometimes have average or above average intelligence (as did Helen Keller), but they often have cognitive or other disabilities. Although a student with **deaf–blindness** might attend the school where you teach, he or she is likely to be a member of your class for academic instruction only with extensive supports. What is more typical is that you might include this student, along with a special education teacher or personal assistant, on some field trips, at assemblies, in selected class activities, or for particular school programs. The specialists working with the student can prepare both you and your students, letting you know how to approach and greet the student, telling you what to expect in terms of behavior, and explaining why inclusive activities are important for the student and what learning or social objectives are being addressed.

What Accommodations Can You Make for Students with Sensory Impairments?

Students with **sensory impairments** have vision or hearing disabilities so significant that their education is affected. Their specialized needs can range from slight to complex. Because school learning relies so heavily on seeing and hearing, students with these disabilities often experience academic problems and need both

Professional Edge

The Vocabulary of Sensory Impairments

To be effective in making adaptations for your students with sensory impairments, you need to understand the terminology used to describe these disabilities. The following terms are some you will encounter in your dealings with students who have sensory impairments and the special educators who work with them.

Impairment	Description
Visual	
Refractive disorders	The way the eye focuses light is impaired, as in myopia (near-sightedness), hyperopia (far-sightedness), and astigmatism (blurred vision).
Muscle disorders	The ability to control eye movements is impaired, as in strabismus (crossed eyes).
Receptive disorders	The ability to receive and process signals from light is impaired, as in retinal detachment caused by glaucoma or a blow to the eye.
Hearing	
Conductive disorders	The way the ear transmits sound is impaired; these disorders are generally correctible through surgery or medication.
Sensorineural disorders	The auditory nerve, by which we receive and process signals from sound, is impaired; these disorders are generally not correctible through amplification or hearing aids.
Mixed losses	A combination of conductive and sensorineural impairments.

teacher accommodations and adaptive equipment. Some of the vocabulary used to describe sensory disabilities is included in the Professional Edge.

Students with **visual impairments** cannot see well enough to use vision as a primary channel for learning without significant assistance. Some students are considered **legally blind,** which means that the vision in their best eye, with correction, is 20/200 or less, or their visual field is 20 degrees or less. What a person with normal vision could see at 200 feet, these students can see only at 20 feet. Students legally blind because of a limited visual field can see just a 20 percent or less "slice" of what a person with normal vision would see within his or her range of vision.

Although the concept of legal blindness is an important one that helps students access special services throughout their lives, a different set of terms is used in schools. For educators, the term **blind** is generally reserved to describe the few students who have little useful vision. They use touch and hearing for most learning. Most students with visual impairments are **partially sighted,** meaning that they have some useful vision; their vision is between 20/70 and 20/200, or they have another vision problem that has a serious negative effect on their learning.

Do It!

Ask a student who has a visual impairment to visit your class to discuss his or her experiences at your college or university. Prepare questions you would like to ask.

Students with **hearing impairments** cannot hear well enough to use hearing as a primary channel for learning without significant assistance. Because a huge proportion of formal and incidental learning occurs through conversations, formal presentations, and overheard information, and relies on understanding language, many consider hearing impairments primarily language or communication impairments. A small number of students with hearing impairments are **deaf.** They cannot process linguistic information through hearing, with or without hearing aids. Most students, however, are **hard of hearing,** meaning that they have some residual hearing that lets them process linguistic information through hearing, usually by using hearing aids or other assistive devices.

Do It!

What services are available in your community to assist individuals with hearing impairments? Compile a list of these resources.

To determine the severity of a hearing loss, professionals check the loudness of sounds as measured in **decibels** (dB) and the pitch or tone of the sound as measured in **hertz** (Hz). Normal speech is usually in the 55–60 dB range at 500–2000 Hz. In contrast, a whisper is about 15–25 dB, and a rock band plays at about 110 dB. Students with a hearing loss of 25–40 dB are considered to have a mild loss; they might not hear every word in a conversation or might not distinguish between words with similar sounds (*breathing, breeding*). Those with a loss of 40–60 dB have a moderate loss; they typically cannot hear enough of a conversation to follow it auditorily. Those with 60–80 dB have a severe loss, and those with more than 80 dB have a profound loss. Students with severe and profound hearing losses typically cannot process speech, even when amplification is used. They rely on sight as an alternative means of learning.

Another factor professionals consider in judging the seriousness of a student's hearing loss is when the loss occurred. Students who have been hearing impaired since birth are often at a disadvantage for language learning because they did not go through the natural process of acquiring language. These students can speak, but because they learned to talk without hearing how they sounded, their speech may be difficult to understand. They might prefer sign language and an interpreter for communicating with you and others. Students who lose their hearing after they learn language, after about age 5, sometimes experience fewer language and speech difficulties.

Accommodations for Students with Visual Impairments

Although students with visual impairments have the same range of cognitive ability as other students, they typically have had fewer opportunities to acquire information usually learned visually. For example, students generally learn about maps by looking at them. Although students who are blind can feel a raised map to learn, this method is not as efficient as using vision. The same problem can occur with academics. Students with visual impairments often experience learning difficulties simply because they cannot easily use vision to process information. Think about how you read this text: You probably scan the pages, focus on words and phrases in boldface print, and visually jump between reading the type and looking at a figure or photo. If you could read this book only by magnifying it 15 times, or by listening to it on audiotape, or by reading it in braille, you would find it much more tedious to scan, select important words and phrases, and go back and forth between elements. If you multiply this dilemma across all the visual learning tasks students face, you can begin to understand the difficulty of learning with a visual impairment.

As is true for all individuals, students with visual impairments vary in their social and emotional development. Some students encounter little difficulty making friends, interacting appropriately with peers and adults, and developing a positive self-concept. Other students need support in these areas. For example, it is important to teach some students who cannot see to adhere to social norms such as facing a person when talking, taking turns, and keeping an appropriate social distance. Conversely, teachers should keep in mind that some students might miss another student's or a teacher's puzzled expression about something they had said and continue to interact as if they understood. They should also help other students to understand that a student with a visual impairment cannot help a wiggling eye, or that they stand a little too close during interactions because they have difficulty judging distance.

Adaptations needed by students with visual impairments depend on many factors. First, take into account students' overall ability level, use of learning strategies and other learning skills, and attentional and motivational levels, just as you would for any other student. Then make accommodations depending on the amount of students' residual vision and the nature of their vision problems. Some specific adaptations you can make and unique needs you must consider for students with visual impairments are covered in the following paragraphs.

One important area of need for students with visual impairments is orientation and mobility, that is, the sense of where they are in relation to other objects and people in the environment and the ability to move about within a space. For example, in a classroom, students with visual impairments need to understand where furniture, doorways, bookshelves, and the teacher's desk are in relation to their location. In addition, they need to be able to move from the classroom to the auditorium to the cafeteria and out to the bus in a timely manner. Your first task in preparing for a student with a visual impairment might be to arrange your classroom carefully, leaving adequate space for all students to move about. Depending on the amount of sight the student has, you might need to keep furniture and supplies in the same places, and make sure the student has an opportunity to learn where everything is. If you decide to rearrange the room or move your supplies, alert your student with a visual impairment to the changes and allow opportunities to adapt to them. Another orientation and mobility issue is safety. Half-open doors or trash cans inadvertently left in aisles can be serious hazards for students with visual impairments. For fire drills or emergencies, pair all students with buddies to assist each other so as to avoid singling out any individual student.

You might also be asked to modify your teaching slightly to accommodate a student with a visual impairment. For example, you might need to identify the novels you plan to use in class prior to the start of the school year so they can be ordered in **braille,** large-print, or audiotape format. The braille alphabet is shown in Figure 5.1 on page 162. For visual clarity, you might need to use a whiteboard with a black felt-tipped marker instead of a traditional chalkboard, or to provide the student paper that has heavy black lines instead of the traditional light blue ones. In addition, you should be sure to recite what is written on the chalkboard; call students by name so the student with a visual impairment can learn the sounds of everyone's voices and where they are seated; allow the student to move close to demonstrations and displays; give specific directions instead of using general words such as "here" or "there"; and seat the student so as to optimize visual learning (for example, away from bright light, or near the front of the room). Usually, an itinerant vision specialist or other

FYI

Although a few students have guide dogs, more adults use them because of the training and expense involved.

Check Your Learning

What common classroom arrangements and items might prove hazardous for a student with a visual impairment?

WWW Resources

You can learn more about sensory impairments by accessing Deaf World at <http://deafworldweb.org/dww/> and the American Foundation for the Blind at <http://afb.org/afb/index.html>.

Figure 5.1   The Braille Alphabet

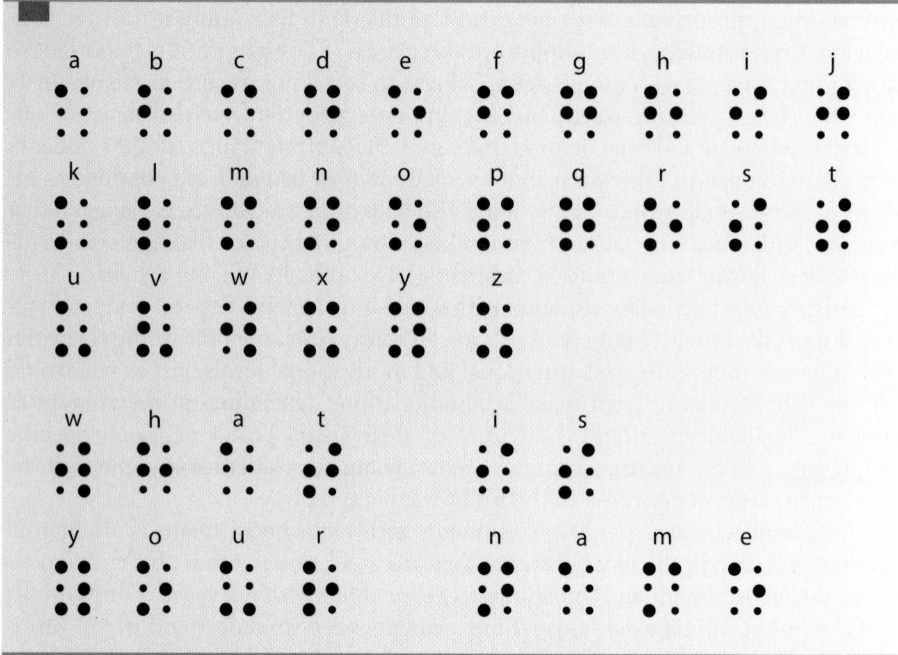

special educator will alert you to these types of accommodations and arrange for any classroom modification.

Some general modifications will also help a student with a visual impairment in your classroom. Meet with the itinerant vision specialist or other resource persons to discuss the student's needs and the extent of assistance required, including the important matter of problems related to storing students' specialized equipment. Based on that information, some or many of these accommodations might be appropriate: Assign a buddy to assist a new student at the beginning of the school year, especially in dealing with the cafeteria, moving from room to room, and locating supplies. This assistance might be discontinued later in the school year to avoid creating unneeded dependence. Some students with visual impairments need additional time to complete assignments, either during class or as homework. Monitor closely to ensure that the student is not spending too much time on a single task; this might be a signal that the task needs to be shortened or otherwise modified. Be alert for a student's need for a change-of-pace activity. A student who is fidgeting or refusing to work might be fatigued, a common problem for students who have to make extraordinary efforts to learn using vision. Letting the student take a break or substitute an alternative activity both helps the student and prevents discipline problems. Also keep in mind how to plan alternative learning opportunities for students. If you are talking about history and using a timeline, if you use white glue or some other means of marking points on the timeline, a student with a visual impairment can participate meaningfully in the discussion by touching the points in time and feeling the distance between them. A vision specialist will help you develop such alternative learning opportunities. Finally, teachers sometimes worry about the impact of words and phrases such as "Do you see my point?" or "That's quite a sight" on a student with a visual impairment. Generally, you should just use the vocabulary you normally would; avoiding words related to seeing is not necessary.

Learning Tools for Students with Visual Impairments

Students with visual impairments use a wide variety of equipment or devices to facilitate their learning. If they have some residual vision, they can use devices to help them acquire information visually. Some use simple devices such as magnifying lenses or bright light in order to read or do other school work. Others might hold their books close to their eyes or at an unusual angle in order to see the print. Many students with visual impairments use computers. For example, if students use a speech synthesizer or text enlarger with a standard word processing program, they may be able to type their assignments exactly like their peers. For students who read braille, assignments can be printed on a braille printer as well as a standard printer so that both the teacher and student can read them. A further sample of the learning tools available for students with visual impairments is included in the Professional Edge on page 164.

Accommodations for Students with Hearing Impairments

Students with hearing losses have the same range of cognitive ability as other students. However, if intelligence is assessed using a test based on language, they might have depressed scores. Academically, many students struggle because their hearing loss has affected their ability to understand language and this affects their learning. Martina, the student with a hearing impairment introduced at the beginning of the chapter, finds this problem especially frustrating. Students might have difficulty learning vocabulary and as a result understanding the materials they read and the lessons you present. For example, students with hearing impairments often miss subtle meanings of words, which can affect both their learning and their social interactions. One simple example can illustrate the complexity of learning language. Think of all the meanings you know for the word *can*. As a noun, it refers to a container made of metal for storing food, for example, a can of peas. But it also means a container with a lid—as in the type of can that tennis balls are packaged in. *Can* also has slang meanings, as a synonym for *bathroom* and *prison*. As a verb, it means "to be physically able," as in "I can do that by Tuesday." It also refers to preserving produce from the garden, as in "I plan to can green beans this year"; to losing a job, as in "I just got canned"; and to the state of being likely, as in "Can that be true?" If you think about all the words in the English language that have multiple and sometimes contradictory meanings, it becomes easier to understand the difficulties faced by students with hearing impairments.

Socially and emotionally, students with hearing impairments are sometimes immature. This lack of maturity occurs for two reasons. First, much of the etiquette children acquire comes from listening to others and modeling what they say and do. This learning is not available to many students with hearing impairments. Second, these students can become confused in interactions that involve many people and multiple conversations. Because these types of situations are often uncomfortable for them, they sometimes avoid them and fail to develop social skills needed in group interactions. For example, Jim is a seventh-grade student with a moderate

FYI

Some students with vision impairments use a Perkins braillewriter, a specialized mechanical device that works similarly to a typewriter but types in braille.

Cultural Awareness

Some people who are deaf consider deafness its own culture, and ASL its language. They discourage students from using oral language and encourage them to communicate through sign language.

Professional Edge

Learning Tools for Students with Visual Impairments

Students with visual impairments can benefit from a variety of learning tools and technology. The following list describes some of these items:

- **Large print materials.** Books or other materials printed somewhat larger than typical print, which is 14- to 18-point for children's books.

- **Low vision devices.** Specially designed optical devices that enable students to read print and to see distant objects such as writing on the chalkboard.

- **Braillewriter.** A mechanical device developed in the 1950s for efficient writing of braille. It has six keys, a spacebar, a carriage return, and a paper advance. To produce braille, the student simultaneously presses down various key combinations.

- **Slate and stylus.** The oldest method for producing braille. The slate is a frame of two metal strips containing braille cells composed of a rectangle with six notches in the four corners and two sides. The stylus is positioned to press raised dots in the braille paper, which is held in place by the slate.

- **Closed circuit television.** System used by students to enlarge print information. A television camera is mounted on a stand to input the print, and the student reads the enlarged print from a monitor.

- **Portable notetaker.** A small device equipped with six keys and a spacebar, but also a speech synthesizer. It is used to take notes or to compose written information and to print it in braille or print.

- **Specialized computers.** Computers equipped with (a) screenreading software and a speech synthesizer enabling the student to listen to the information presented on the screen, (b) braille translation software enabling the teacher or student to convert information on the screen to braille and to print it using a braille printer, or (c) screen enlargement software enabling a student with significant sight to read information directly from the screen.

hearing impairment in Mr. George's science class. When students work in lab groups, Jim tends to "tune out" because he cannot follow what everyone is saying. Sometimes he tries to participate in the activity, but he often does so by making an exaggerated face or drawing a cartoon to show others. He does this even when the other students are working intently, and they become annoyed with his antics. When Jim realizes his attempts to participate are not being successful, he withdraws from the group and becomes passive. Mr. George and the hearing specialist are working to address this problem. Mr. George makes sure that he monitors the group's work, and he sometimes intervenes by asking Jim a question that will help him participate. Mr. George reminds his students that unless every group member understands a science experiment, the group is not finished. Jim also receives help on his social interactions in a support group led by a social worker that he attends with several other students twice each week.

A student with a visual impairment uses specialized books and equipment.

Accommodations for students with hearing impairments emphasize helping them use whatever residual hearing they may have and accessing language to promote formal and informal learning. Although the specific types of accommodations needed by a student you teach will be determined by the multidisciplinary team that writes the student's IEP, these are some common adaptations.

Because many students with hearing impairments get some information through **speech reading,** or watching others' lips, mouth, and expressions, teachers should always face the class when presenting information and stand where no glare or shadow would make it difficult for a student to see. They should also stand in one location instead of moving around the room. The student should sit near them. These adjustments facilitate speech reading but are also necessary if an interpreter is present. Teachers should avoid exaggerating sounds or words; doing this makes it more difficult for the student, not easier. Because some students with

FYI

Even the best speech readers get only about 25 percent of a spoken communication. Most individuals receive only 5–10 percent of spoken communication using this strategy.

hearing impairments do not use speech reading, and even those who do will get only part of the message that way, teachers should use as many visual aids as possible. Important directions can be written on the chalkboard, either with words or, for younger students, pictures. Major points in a lecture for older students can be written on an overhead projector or on the chalkboard. With an overhead projector, the teacher can face students while writing, thus enabling students with hearing impairments to speech read. If teachers talk and write on a chalkboard at the same time, students with hearing impairments can become confused because they cannot see the teacher's lips or facial expression if the teacher is facing the board to write.

If a student with a hearing impairment speaks to you and you do not understand what has been said, ask the student to repeat the information. If you still do not understand or the student becomes frustrated, a switch to paper and pencil is sometimes appropriate. When a student appears confused following directions or answering a question you have asked, the difficulty might be vocabulary. Try using a simpler word as a substitute or offering a word you think the student might be trying to convey. Above all else, be patient when communicating with students who have hearing impairments.

As with students with visual impairments, safety also needs to be kept in mind. Assigning a buddy to assist the student during a fire, tornado, or earthquake drill is a simple strategy for addressing this issue. For other specific adaptations regarding safety, a hearing specialist will assist you.

If a student with a hearing impairment uses sign language, you might consider enrolling in a sign class yourself and inviting a deaf education teacher to your class to teach some signs to the entire group. Students generally enjoy this experience, and both you and they will be better able to communicate with the student who cannot hear. In the Case in Practice, you can learn a little more about what it is like to teach a student with a hearing impairment.

This student with a hearing impairment and teacher are using American Sign Language. In what other ways might they communicate? What technologies might they use to receive instruction? What would be the advantage of using an FM amplification system?

Case in Practice

Including Students with Hearing Impairments

Ms. Skinner is a fifth-grade teacher at Lunar Elementary School. This year in her class of 31 she has two students with hearing impairments. The girls, who are twins, have profound hearing losses present since birth. Since they use sign language as their primary means of communication, they are accompanied by Ms. Mohammed, their interpreter.

Ms. Skinner discussed what it is like to teach in this class: "When I first heard I was going to get Jenna and Janice this year, I was worried. I knew they'd been in fourth grade and done well, but there's so much more curriculum at this level. I didn't know how I was going to teach everything and also do all the work necessary for Jenna and Janice. As it turned out, it hasn't been much of an adjustment at all. Ms.

Mohammed interprets for the girls, and she adds explanations if they need it. The hardest part for me was learning to stay in one place when I talk—for a teacher like me, who is constantly moving around the room, that has been very difficult. Ms. Mohammed has taught all of us some basic signs—that puts us all in touch. Jenna and Janice have some serious academic problems mostly related to vocabulary, but the other kids just think of them as classmates. I've learned a lot this year. I'm a lot more confident that I really can teach any student who comes through my door!"

Adaptive Devices for Students with Hearing Impairments

Students with some residual hearing are likely to use amplification devices such as hearing aids. If you have a student who wears hearing aids, you should be alert for signs of inattention that might signal the hearing aid is not turned on or the battery needs to be replaced. Other students might use an FM system consisting of a microphone worn by the teacher and a receiver worn by the student. When the teacher talks, the sound is converted into electrical energy carried on a specific radio frequency through the air. The receiver converts the electrical energy back to sound, amplifies it, and sends it to the student's ear.

Keep in mind that both hearing aids and FM systems amplify sounds, but they do not discriminate important sounds like the teacher's voice from other sounds. Thus, a student wearing hearing aids can be distracted by the amplified noise of someone typing on the computer keyboard, a door slamming, or chairs scraping on the floor. A student using an FM device will also receive the sounds of a teacher's jewelry hitting the microphone or the static from a teacher's fingering the microphone. Any of these extraneous noises can interfere with the student's understanding of spoken information and can be distracting to learning. Amplification clearly assists some students with hearing impairments, but it also has limits.

Students who have a severe or profound hearing impairment often use sign language. Sometimes they use **American Sign Language (ASL)**, a separate language not based on standard English grammar and structures. Learning ASL is a little bit like learning Spanish, French, or another language. Other students will use **signed exact English (SEE)**, that is, spoken English converted to a set of signs. Students will sometimes use **finger spelling,** in which every letter of a word is spelled out. For example, finger spelling is needed for names or technical terms for which no signs exist. The manual alphabet used for finger spelling is presented in Figure 5.2.

Students who use sign language often are accompanied by an interpreter who translates your words and those of classmates into sign language (Jones, Clark, & Soltz, 1997). The interpreter needs to sit facing the student and near you so that the student can both watch you and follow the interpreter. Some older students also use

Figure 5.2　**Finger Spelling**

The manual alphabet as the receiver sees it:

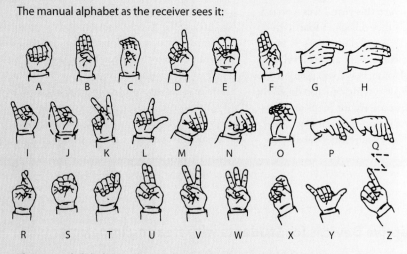

The manual alphabet as the sender sees it:

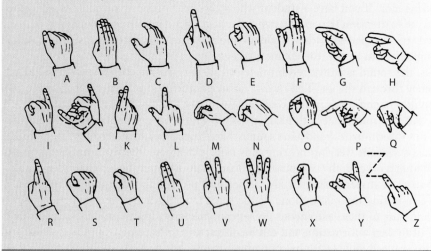

a note-taker (who could be a classmate) since they cannot both watch an interpreter and a teacher and take notes. Even if a student uses an interpreter, however, you should speak directly to the student when asking questions, giving directions, or otherwise conversing. Do not speak to the interpreter instead of the student. The interpreter will make sure the student understands what you said. For example, you should say to Paige, a student with a profound hearing loss, "Do the first five examples on the page." You should not direct your remarks to the interpreter, as in, "Tell Paige to do the first five examples on the page." Also keep in mind that interpreters need breaks; you might be asked to make small changes in your instructional pattern to ensure that the interpreter can take a break without negatively affecting student learning.

What Accommodations Can You Make for Students with Physical or Health Disabilities?

Some students receive special education and related services because they have physical disorders, chronic or acute medical problems, or health impairments that interfere with their learning. In IDEA, three categories of disabilities can be loosely grouped in this area: orthopedic impairments, other health impairments, and traumatic brain injury. **Orthopedic impairments** are diseases or disorders related to the bones, joints, or muscles. **Other health impairments** include medical or health conditions such as AIDS, seizure disorders, and asthma. **Traumatic brain injury** is any insult to the brain caused by an external force and includes injuries sustained in auto accidents and during play. Because students in these groups have disabilities because of physical or health problems resulting from a wide variety of causes, they have many different levels of innate ability and academic achievement and can have needs that range from mild to severe.

Orthopedic Impairments

The largest group of students with orthopedic impairments in public schools are those who have **cerebral palsy** (CP) (Sirvis, 1988). Some 5000 infants and babies and 1500 preschoolers are diagnosed each year as having this condition (United Cerebral Palsy Associations, n.d.). Cerebral palsy occurs because of injury to the brain before or during birth and results in poor motor coordination and abnormal motor patterns. These problems can occur in just the arms or legs, in both the arms and legs, or in a combination of limbs. A brief explanation of the terms used to describe these specific conditions, which can also affect other students with orthopedic impairments, is included in Table 5.2 on page 170. For some students, CP also affects other muscle groups, such as those controlling the head and neck. Thus, some students with cerebral palsy walk on their toes with their knees close together. They might also hold their arms with their elbows bent and their hands near shoulder height. Other students with CP need braces or a walker to move about. Yet others use wheelchairs. For some students, head supports keep their heads from lolling side to side. Cognitively and academically, students with CP can be gifted, average, or below average, or they might have a cognitive disability. Don is a student with CP. His arms and hands are drawn up close to his body and he does not control their

FYI

Cerebral palsy is the most frequently occurring orthopedic disability among children and youth. Students with cerebral palsy often have cognitive disabilities as well.

Table 5.2   **Types of Paralysis**

Classification	Affected Area
Monoplegia	One limb
Paraplegia	Lower body and both legs
Meiplegia	One side of the body
Triplegia	Three appendages or limbs, usually both legs and one arm
Quadriplegia	All four extremities and usually the trunk
Diplegia	Legs are more involved than arms
Double hemiplegia	Both halves of the body, with one side more involved than the other

S O U R C E : From *Human Exceptionality: Society, School, and Family,* 5th ed., by M. L. Hardman, C. J. Drew, M. W. Egan, and B. Wolf, 1996. Copyright © 1996 by Allyn and Bacon. Reprinted by permission.

movement. He moves around school in a motorized wheelchair and Mike, his personal assistant, helps with personal care (going to the bathroom, eating) and tasks such as writing. Don has low average ability, but his physical disabilities sometimes cause others to think he has a cognitive disability as well, especially since most of his speech is difficult to understand. Don's teacher has learned to engage him in class activities by asking yes or no questions to which he can respond fairly easily. If she asks a question requiring a longer answer, she gives Don time to form the words needed and does not let other students speak for him.

> **Do It!**
>
> Rent a wheelchair and try completing many of your daily tasks. What did you learn from this experience?

Another orthopedic impairment is **muscular dystrophy,** a disease that weakens muscles. Students have increasing difficulty walking and otherwise moving actively about. Gradually, they lose their ability to stand and they require a wheelchair. They also fatigue more and more easily. Students with muscular dystrophy usually die during their late teens (Sirvis, 1988). Frank was a student with muscular dystrophy. When he began elementary school, he seemed no different from any other student. However, when he began middle school, he returned to school with a wheelchair that he used when he was tired. By the end of that year, he used the wheelchair all the time. By late in his sophomore year, Frank was too weak to attend school and received instruction from an itinerant teacher at his home. He died in late September of his junior year of high school.

A third orthopedic impairment is **spinal cord injury.** As the term implies, these injuries exist when the spinal cord is severely damaged or severed, usually resulting in partial or extensive paralysis (Kirk, Gallagher, & Anastasiow, 1997). Spinal cord injuries are most often the result of automobile or other vehicle accidents. The characteristics and needs of students with this type of injury are often similar to those of students with cerebral palsy. Judy suffered a spinal cord injury in a car accident. She was hospitalized for nearly half the school year, and when she returned to school she could not walk and had the use of only one arm. She is as bright and articulate as ever and still gets in trouble when she challenges teachers' authority. What has changed is how she moves from place to place.

Cerebral palsy, muscular dystrophy, and spinal cord injuries are just a sample of the range of orthopedic impairments students can have. You are likely to teach students who have physical disabilities caused by amputations or birth defects that resulted in the absence of all or part of a limb. Likewise, you might have a student with **spina bifida,** a birth defect in which an abnormal opening in the spinal column results in some degree of paralysis. Whatever the orthopedic impairment a student has, your responsibility is to learn about the student's needs and work with special education professionals to ensure those needs are met through various adaptations.

The adaptations you make for students with orthopedic impairments will depend on the nature and severity of the disability and on the students' physical status. For example, you need to be alert to changes you might need to make in the physical environment so that students can comfortably move into, out of, and around the classroom. Such changes include rearranging classroom furniture and adding supports such as handrails to walls. Other physical adaptations, such as creating adapted work spaces with large tables and lowering chalkboards, can facilitate student learning. These and similar accommodations are outlined in the Professional Edge on page 172.

A second area of adaptation to consider for students with orthopedic impairments involves their personal needs (Kirk et al., 1997). Many students become fatigued and might have difficulty attending to learning activities late in the school day. A few take naps or otherwise rest. Other students need to stop during the school day to take medication. Some students need assistance with personal care such as using the bathroom and eating. Students who use wheelchairs might need to reposition themselves because of circulation problems. This repositioning can be done readily for young children, who can be moved to sit or lie on the classroom floor during stories or other activities. Paraprofessionals typically assume personal-care responsibilities and those related to moving students. If you have questions about these areas, a special educator can assist, or the student's parent can explain what is needed.

Academically and socially, it is not possible to generalize about student needs. Some students with orthopedic impairments enjoy school and excel in traditional academic areas. Others experience problems in learning. Some are charming and gregarious students who are class leaders; others have a low self-concept and are likely to have problems interacting with peers. If you think about a student like Judy, the student with a spinal cord injury introduced earlier, you can imagine that her reaction to her accident and her need to use a wheelchair is influenced by many factors, including her family support system, her self-concept, and her peers' reactions. The suggestions included throughout this text for working with students to help them learn and succeed socially are as applicable to this group of students as to any other.

Other Health Impairments

Students with health impairments often are not immediately apparent to a casual observer. For example, one common group of health impairments is seizure disorders, or **epilepsy,** a physical condition in which the brain experiences sudden but brief changes in functioning. The result is often a lapse of attention or consciousness and uncontrolled motor movements. About 75,000 new cases of epilepsy occur for children each year, and for most cases no specific cause is ever determined (Epilepsy Foundation of America, 1986).

Epilepsy can result in different types of seizures. **Generalized tonic-clonic seizures** involve the entire body. A student experiencing a generalized tonic-clonic

Check Your Learning

What accommodations is a student with orthopedic impairments likely to need? Who is responsible for ensuring that these are made?

FYI

Nationwide, some 500,000 individuals have epilepsy. It can occur in anyone of any age, sometimes for no apparent reason, but also as a result of illness or injury.

Professional Edge

Classroom Accommodations for Students with Physical Disabilities

Basic changes in the environment can help students with physical disabilities move around and learn more effectively at school. If you teach students with physical disabilities, your school might need to make these accommodations:

1. Handrails for students who use crutches or braces. Handrails can make it possible for a student to move around the classroom and nearby hallways more easily.

2. Desks or worktables adapted for student needs. Some students in wheelchairs will have a built-in work space in the form of a lap desk. Others, though, will need to have tables or desks high enough to allow them to position themselves so they can work comfortably.

3. Wide aisles and walkways. Students with mobility needs, whether braces or a wheelchair, often need extra space in order to move around. Instead of arranging student desks in traditional rows, put groups of desks together to form worktables, saving space for aisles. Pay particular attention to space around supply shelves or students will not be able to access needed materials.

4. Chalkboards and bulletin boards. If you expect students to write at the chalkboard, an accommodation might be needed for a student in a wheelchair. You might lower the boards or provide a slate for the student. If you create activities that are displayed on bulletin boards, students in wheelchairs need to be able to access these as other students do.

5. Safety issues. Plans should be in place for emergency drills. In addition, if students with poor fine motor control participate in high school lab classes or shop activities, adapted equipment can be requested or changes in procedures made to eliminate safety concerns. For example, a student might need a beaker with a handle for a surer grip, or a lab partner might be reminded to handle the chemicals. In shop, adaptations might include teaching specific safety procedures or adapting assignments so that they require less or simplified use of equipment. Special educators provide assistance when these types of modifications are needed.

---

seizure falls to the ground unconscious; the body stiffens and then begins jerking. Breathing may become shallow, and the student might lose bladder or bowel control. After a minute or two, the movements stop and the student regains consciousness. Steps you should take if a student has a generalized tonic-clonic seizure are summarized in the Professional Edge on page 173.

Other seizures do not involve the entire body. **Absence seizures** occur when students appear to temporarily "blank out" for just a few seconds. If they are walking or running, they might stumble because of their momentary lapse of awareness. If you observe a student with these symptoms, alert the school nurse or another professional who can further assess the student. It is not unheard of for students to attend school for several years before someone realizes that their inability to pay attention is actually the result of a seizure disorder.

Most students who have seizures take medication to control their disorder. If their medication is carefully monitored and their status is not changing, you might

FYI

Previously, generalized tonic-clonic seizures were referred to as *grand mal* seizures. Absence (pronounced "ob-sonce") seizures were referred to as *petit mal* seizures.

Professional Edge

What to Do If a Student Has a Seizure

As a teacher in an inclusive school and as a responsible citizen, you should know how to respond if someone has a seizure. Here are the recommended steps from the American Epilepsy Foundation:

1. Keep calm and reassure other people who may be nearby.
2. Clear the area around the student of anything hard or sharp.
3. Loosen ties or anything around the neck that may make breathing difficult.
4. Put something flat and soft, like a folded jacket, under the head.
5. Turn the student gently onto his or her side. This will help keep the airway clear. Do *not* try to force his or her mouth open with any hard implement or with your fingers. It is not true that a person having a seizure can swallow his or her tongue, and efforts to hold the tongue down can injure the teeth or jaw.
6. Do not hold the student down or try to stop his or her movements.
7. Do not attempt artificial respiration except in the unlikely event that a student does not start breathing again after the seizure has stopped.
8. Stay with the student until the seizure ends naturally.
9. Be friendly and reassuring as consciousness returns.
10. Follow whatever procedures have been established for notifying parents that a seizure has occurred.

SOURCE: From *Epilepsy: Questions and Answers about Seizure Disorders*, 1986, Landover, MD: Epilepsy Foundation of America.

---

not even be aware of the student's disability. However, when children are growing rapidly and gaining weight, and when they approach puberty and undergo many physical and hormonal changes, seizures may occur as the student's body changes.

Another health impairment is **sickle-cell anemia.** This disorder is inherited and occurs most often in African American students. It is characterized by abnormally shaped and weakened red blood cells and results in fatigue and reduced stamina. Individuals with sickle-cell anemia often experience severe and chronic pain in their abdomen, arms, or legs. In children, sickle-cell anemia can affect growth. Students with sickle-cell anemia experience crises in which their symptoms are acute and include high fevers, joint swelling, and extreme fatigue; they are likely to miss school during these times.

A third health impairment is **acquired immune deficiency syndrome (AIDS).** AIDS results when students are infected with the **human immuno–deficiency virus (HIV)** and their bodies lose the ability to fight off infection (Shea & Bauer, 1994). Students with AIDS can often attend school with little assistance until their illness progresses to the point that they lack the stamina to complete school work or that the risk of catching an infection or illness from a classmate becomes too great. As you probably know, no medical cure currently exists for AIDS. Studies of the impact of AIDS on children are just beginning.

Check Your Learning

Review the steps for treating a person having a seizure. Can you name each one?

Do It!

What is your local school district's policy on educating students with AIDS? If possible, obtain a written copy of the information to share with classmates.

Orthopedic disabilities and other health impairments can include a great variety of conditions, injuries, and chronic illnesses, including spina bifida, diabetes, asthma, cystic fibrosis, hemophilia, absence or loss of limbs, cancer, and AIDS. What are some specific strategies for working with students with physical disabilities and health impairments?

Connections

Students with mild forms of health impairments in which there is not an ongoing adverse effect on education might receive services through Section 504. Such cases are explained further in Chapter 7.

There are many other health impairments students may have. For example, you might teach a student who has been badly burned and is undergoing medical treatment and physical or occupational therapy to restore range of movement in affected limbs. You might also teach students with **asthma,** a physical condition in which students experience difficulty breathing, especially during physically or psychologically stressful activities. Other health impairments your students might have include **hemophilia,** a genetically transmitted disease in which blood does not coagulate properly; **diabetes,** a condition in which the body does not produce enough insulin to process the carbohydrates eaten; and **cystic fibrosis,** a genetically transmitted disease in which the body produces excessive mucus that eventually damages the lungs and causes heart failure.

The adaptations you make for students with health impairments often relate to helping them make up for work missed because of an absence or hospitalization and recognizing their social and emotional needs and responding to them (Lynch, Lewis, & Murphy, 1993b). In one study of parents' and educators' perceptions of problems faced by children with chronic illness, parents reported that their children's most frequent problems were "feeling different," undergoing constant medical procedures, pain, and facing death. Educators listed absences, falling behind in school, the lack of interaction with peers, school's inability to meet the student's needs, and social adjustment as the most serious problems (Lynch et al., 1993a).

Specific strategies for working with students with health impairments include these:

1. Find out students' most difficult problems and help them work these through. Strategies include having students write or draw about their concerns or referring a student to the school counselor or social worker as you see a need.

2. Provide materials for the students about others who have a similar disease or disorder. Books, videotapes, movies, and informational materials can help students with health impairments understand how others have successfully coped with their illnesses, and they can be useful for explaining the needs of these students to peers without disabilities.

3. Consider including death education in your curriculum if you have a student with a life-threatening condition such as cancer (Peckham, 1993). A special educator, counselor, or social worker can probably prepare a unit and help you present it.

4. Work closely with families. Parents can often be the most valuable source of information concerning their child's status and needs. They can also alert you to upcoming changes in medications and emotional problems occurring at home, and they can help their children work on missed school assignments. (Lynch et al., 1993b)

In terms of academic and curricular adaptations, you should respond to students with health impairments as you would to other students with disabilities. Using the INCLUDE strategy, you can identify their needs. If modifications in the environment, curriculum, or instruction are needed, you can carry them out using the suggestions made throughout the remainder of this text.

Traumatic Brain Injury

Traumatic brain injury (TBI) occurs when a student experiences a trauma to the head from an external physical force that results in an injury to the brain, often including a temporary loss of consciousness. TBI has many causes, including child abuse and gunshot wounds (Savage & Wolcott, 1994). The most common causes of TBI, however, accounting for 89 percent of the 200,000 cases reported annually, are falls and bicycle, motor vehicle, and sporting accidents. Whether TBI is the result of a severe injury or a mild one, it can have a pervasive and significant impact on the student's educational performance (Lord-Maes & Obrzut, 1996).

One of the most perplexing aspects of teaching students with TBI is that they can appear just as they did prior to their injuries and yet have significant learning and social problems. They can also seem to be "back to normal" one day only to seem lethargic and incapable of learning the next day. Because of the extreme variability in needs of students with TBI, the information presented in this section should be considered illustrative; if you teach a student with TBI, seeking input from a specialist is essential.

Cognitively, students with TBI might have the same abilities they had before, or they might experience a loss of capacity. For example, Michael, a high school honor student who used to be a class leader, was left after an automobile accident struggling to remaster basic math facts. His injury affected his school learning. Students might experience difficulty initiating and organizing their learning tasks, remembering what they have learned, and reasoning or problem solving. They might also have difficulty processing verbal information and producing spoken and written language.

Students with TBI also have physical needs. Depending on the severity of the injury and the extent of recovery, some students have limited use of their arms and legs. Others have problems in fine motor movements such as those needed to grasp a pencil or turn the pages of a book. Yet others have limited strength and stamina. Students with these needs sometimes attend school only part of the day.

Check Your Learning

What adaptations are students with health impairments likely to need?

FYI

Working with students with TBI has become an important topic because of many recent medical advances. Many students who used to die from their injuries now survive and return to school.

Socially and emotionally, students with TBI experience many difficulties. One comment made about students with TBI is that they sometimes have changes in their personalities, that they are not who they used to be (Kehle, Clark, & Jenson, 1996). For example, they often remember what they were able to do prior to their injuries and sometimes become depressed as they recognize their current limitations (Prigatano, 1992). Because they often need a high degree of structure and do not respond well to change, they can display behavior problems when a sudden change in schedule occurs, as when an assembly interrupts an accustomed routine. Some students lose their ability to interpret and respond appropriately to social cues. As a result, they might laugh at inappropriate times, speak loudly when everyone else has realized a whisper is needed, or wander off when distracted by something. Their behaviors can be puzzling or frustrating unless you understand how to respond to them. Some of the most common characteristics and related behaviors of students with TBI, along with potential responses teachers can make, are included in Table 5.3.

It is especially important to mention families as part of considerations about TBI. Often, parents or siblings have witnessed the student in a totally unresponsive state, and they have psychologically prepared for the possibility of death. They might be tremendously relieved that the student survived, but at the same time traumatized at the amount of physical care the student needs and the drain on financial and psychological family resources. Depending on the amount of uncertainty about the extent to which the student will eventually recover, the impact of the TBI on the student's intellect and personality, and the family's ability to provide for the student's needs, families can experience a range of emotions, including shock, denial, sorrow, and anger (Wade, Taylor, Drotar, Stancin, & Yeates, 1996). Eventually, many adapt. You need to be sensitive to the family's stress and their changing capacity to follow up on schoolwork at home or otherwise to support your efforts.

If you teach a student with TBI, you might attend at least one planning meeting to discuss the details of the student's abilities and needs and to prepare you for helping the student in the classroom. This transition planning, which typically occurs when a student is moving from the hospital or rehabilitation center back to school, is essential to ensure that appropriate expectations are set for the student, procedures are established for responding to changes in the student's condition, and coordination of all services occurs (Clark, 1996).

In your classroom, adaptations include those related to physical needs, instructional and organizational routines, academic content, and the social environment. Because students with TBI need structure and routine, you should follow the same pattern in classroom activities, expect the same types of student responses, and keep supplies and materials in the same place in the classroom. If a break in routine is necessary, you can prepare the student by alerting him or her, assigning a buddy, and staying in close proximity.

You will probably need to make changes in the academic expectations for a student with TBI. Since students might know information one day but forget it the next, and sometimes learn easily whereas at other times struggle, the need for flexibility is ongoing. Students are also likely to become frustrated with their inability to learn the way they did in the past, and so your patience in reteaching information, providing additional examples and exercises, and using strategies to help them focus attention can be essential.

Socially, emotionally, and behaviorally, students with TBI rely on you to set clear expectations but to be supportive and responsive to their changing needs. One

Table 5.3   **Classroom Behaviors of Students with Traumatic Brain Injury**

Characteristics	Behavior	Solutions
Overestimates abilities	Student brags to friends that he or she is still the fastest runner or will win the spelling bee.	Do not challenge the student. Reassure him or her that individuals change after a head injury.
Lowered social inhibition and judgment	Student tries to touch and hug everyone.	Redirect student's attention to an appropriate behavior. Model correct or alternative behavior for student.
Lowered impulse control	Student interrupts teachers and peers at inappropriate times.	Verbally remind student of rules. Provide alternative ways to have his or her needs met (raises hand or other private signal).
Faulty reasoning	Student confronts peers and teachers with unfair accusations.	Do not feel obligated to respond immediately. Reassure student and move on. Return later to resolve the problem.
Lowered initiative	Student will not begin a task without a reminder or assistance.	Be proactive and impose organization before assigning tasks. Cognitive behavior modification techniques may be beneficial.
Depression	Student appears uninterested and passive, even in activities once considered highly enjoyable. The emotional stress of the injury may be prolonged and can be overwhelming.	Involve the student directly in the activity. Assign a specific role to hook the student's interest. Individual counseling or support group participation can be beneficial.
Fatigue	Student may be fatigued as a result of both the injury and the medication. Sleep disorders are common.	Review medical information regarding physical limitations. Provide variety by changing tasks often and giving frequent breaks. Consider a shortened school day.
Acting-out behavior	Student may yell or curse about being asked to do a task he or she does not want to do. He or she may walk out of class or knock over a desk.	First protect other students and yourself from physical injury. The student may need to be removed to another location (with adult supervision) in the school.
Impulsivity	Student may be unable to wait his or her turn at a drinking fountain or in the cafeteria. He or she may talk out during a test or speak before being called on.	Restate the classroom rules or limits. Reassure the student that there is plenty of time for the activity.
Rigidity	Student may be unable to adapt to changes in schedule or routine. Student may be unwilling to go to an assembly if it is scheduled during regular academic subjects.	Alert the student in advance to anticipated changes in each day's accustomed routine.
Flat affect	Student seems to have no voice inflections. Face seems expressionless; eyes seem vacant; he or she does not laugh or smile appropriately.	Try to remember that this behavior is characteristic of a person with a head injury and not necessarily a demonstration of low motivation or apathy. Use novel or stimulating learning activities that are relevant to the student's interests and goals.
Low motivation	What appears as low motivation may actually be confusion and inability to conceptualize and plan how to do the task.	Ask the student to verbalize the first step toward completing the task. Ask for succeeding steps if necessary.
Agitation and irritability	Varying degrees of agitation and irritability may manifest. Student may become annoyed over picky things or become aggressive toward self or teachers.	Try to redirect the student's attention away from the source of agitation, offer an alternative activity, or move him or her to another area or room where it is quiet and he or she can regain control.

S O U R C E :   From "Traumatic Brain Injury: An Overview of School Re-entry" by B. F. Tucker and S. E. Colson, 1992, *Intervention in School and Clinic,* 27(4), 198–206. Copyright © 1992 by PRO-ED, Inc. Reprinted by permission.

student, Gary, had been in a coma but gradually regained enough ability to function to return to his middle school, at first for only an hour or two each day and eventually for the entire day. However, he continued to forget common words and would grow increasingly frustrated when he could not convey his message. His teachers began providing the words he needed. Because many students with TBI seem unable to form a realistic picture of how they are functioning, you might need to confront them gently about socially inappropriate behavior. Frustrated with his language skills, Gary would yell at friends but still be unclear in his sentences. Teachers intervened to help him learn to control his anger and to assist friends to understand him. Students with TBI might also overestimate their abilities. Informally, you can assist in this area by discussing realistic options for the near future and, with older students, for career choices.

In general, the adaptations needed by students with TBI are much the same as those needed by students with physical or health disabilities, learning disabilities, and emotional disabilities (Adams et al., 1991). The uniqueness of students with TBI and the reason they are grouped as a separate category in IDEA is that their needs are difficult to predict, change either slowly or rapidly, and vary in intensity. With patience and a willingness by teachers to meet the student wherever he or she is and work forward from there, students with TBI can achieve school success.

What Accommodations Can You Make for Students with Autism?

Autism was first identified as a disorder in 1943 by Dr. Leo Kanner. Since then, it has been the source of much research and ongoing professional debate. Autism has been considered part of various emotional disabilities, including schizophrenia, and has been addressed as a form of mental retardation. Currently, however, autism is considered a unique disorder that affects boys more than girls in a ratio of approximately 4:1. Autism frequently occurs with other disorders. In particular, it is estimated that 70 percent of individuals with autism also have mental retardation; but that number could be an overestimate because of the communication difficulties that accompany the disability and the resulting problems in obtaining accurate estimates of ability (Freeman, 1994).

Although autism is like most of the other low-incidence disabilities in that it can exist in many forms, from mild to severe, and cannot be treated as a single disorder with a single set of adaptations, it does have specific characteristics. First, students with autism have seriously impaired social relationships. Many students with autism resist human contact and social interactions from a very early age, and they have difficulty learning the subtleties of social interactions (Ratey, Grandin, & Miller, 1992). They often do not make eye contact with others, and they can seem uninterested in developing social relationships. For example, young children often ask teachers to watch them do something ("Look at me!"), and they bring interesting items to share with the teacher and their classmates. A young child with autism would not seek out such opportunities for social interactions. Albert, a 13-year-old with autism, discussed his problems in the social domain. He maintained that others view him as extremely ugly, but he did not understand why he does not have friends. When an interviewer asked him what he talked about with others, the two topics he mentioned were wind and smells in the environment (Cesaroni & Garber, 1991). He did not take on the perspective of others, and he did not understand that others' interests, which are very different from his own, are also part of social interaction. Ideas for teaching social skills to students with autism are included in the Professional Edge on pages 180–181.

Students with autism also experience problems in both verbal and nonverbal communication. They often have significantly delayed language development, and if they have language skills, they struggle to maintain a conversation with another person. In writing about her experiences of being autistic, Temple Grandin provides a clear example of her communication problems (Grandin, 1984). She explains that once when her mother wanted her to wear a hat while riding in the car, she didn't have the words to refuse. Instead, she screamed and threw the hat out the window, causing her mother to hit another car. Unlike Temple Grandin, many students with autism cannot write or otherwise clearly communicate about their experiences, although some can communicate by typing their thoughts. Often, however, students with autism use inappropriate behaviors instead of words to convey many needs. Unless taught alternative behaviors, they might hit a peer as a way of saying hello, or run from a classroom instead of saying they do not like the assignment just given. Some students with autism have **echolalic speech.** They repeat what others have said instead of producing original communication.

Another characteristic of students with autism is a very limited range of interest, such as a student who is fascinated with radios to the exclusion of nearly everything else. When they have such an interest, students with autism can spend literally hours and hours absorbed in a private world of exploration. They might act bored with every topic and every activity unless it relates to their special interest. Such a narrow range of interest often has a negative impact on social relationships with peers and adults since the student does not discern that others are not as interested in the preferred topic.

Students with autism have a low threshold for and difficulty in dealing with stress (Grandin, 1984). A change in a class schedule could be difficult for a student with autism, as could be the introduction of a new route from the classroom to a bus or an alternative order for the day's activities. Particular noises or odors or a noisy environment also can be stressful. Many students with autism respond to stress with **stereotypic behaviors.** They complete the same action or motion again and again. For example, they may rock rapidly in their chairs, spin an object repeatedly, or twirl themselves or their arms. In other situations, students might develop a ritual to complete a task. For example, they might need 10 minutes to prepare to complete an assignment because they need to arrange paper and pencil on the desk in a precise pattern, check that all books in the desk are also stored in a specific order, and make sure their desk is aligned precisely at the intersection of tiles on the classroom floor. In your classroom, you should be aware of potentially stressful situations for a student with autism. You can either allow time for the student to prepare for the situation, talk about the situation well in advance, assign a peer partner to assist the student, or enlist the assistance of a special educator or paraprofessional. If a student's response to stress is demonstrated with aggressive or extremely disruptive behavior, you should work closely with a special educator, behavior consultant, or other specialist to address the problem. In some instances, the student might need to spend part of the school day in a more structured, less stressful environment such as the school library or learning center.

WWW Resources

The National Rehabilitation Information Center (NARIC) collects and disseminates information from federally funded research projects about disabilities, including autism. Their website is located at <http://www.naric.com/naric>.

Professional Edge

Teaching Social Skills to Students with Autism

Students with autism have a great need to develop appropriate social skills that will serve them well in school and throughout their lives. These are some useful skills and ideas for addressing them.

Behavior	Examples	Strategies for Teaching
Waiting	Waiting in line	Establish clear rules, such as "Stand up when the teacher calls your name."
	Waiting for someone else to answer	Teach the student to occupy wait time doing a favorite activity of choice.
	Waiting for a program to start	Try to keep wait time as short as possible at first; reward the student for successfully waiting.
Taking turns being first	Being first in line	Create a chart to show who is to be first in line each day and put marks on the floor as a guide if needed.
	Being first to answer	Set rules about answering questions; for example, the student can be the first to answer every sixth time only.
Transitioning before completing something	Stopping before a workbook page is completed	Try to avoid this problem by allowing enough time for the student to finish a game or activity.
	Leaving the computer in the middle of a game	Give the student warnings when time is about to run out. For example, alert the student 5 minutes before the end of the time period, and again at 2 minutes and 1 minute before the end using visual cues.
Changing topics	Asking endless questions about what is going to happen	Set a time limit on the amount of time a student can talk about a topic. Use a visual timer.
	Talking endlessly about favorite topics	Give the student three or four picture cards of alternative topics.
	Repeating that others do not like him or her	Create a rule about the number of times you will respond to the same questions. For example, after two times, say, "You know the answer to that." Write the answer for the student.
		Write a story or script to give specific information.

In the past, nearly all students identified as autistic had noticeable behaviors and serious problems in social relationships and communication. Recently, however, professional attention has turned to students with milder forms of autism, including **Asperger's syndrome.** These students sometimes seem like "perfect students" (Coppola, 1987), somewhat like Donisha, the fourth grader described at the beginning of the chapter. These students usually develop speech at a normal age, but they sometimes have problems knowing whether to use a first-person, second-person, or third-person pronoun. They have limited facial expression, seem inept at interpreting others' nonverbal communication, and are awkward in social situations, as though they do not quite understand the unspoken rules for social interactions.

Behavior	Examples	Strategies for Teaching
Finishing	Finishing lunch Finishing an assignment	Define "finished" in concrete terms. For example, finishing a paper might be defined as putting an answer in every space or filling a specific amount of the page with writing.
	Finishing a game or activity	Finishing games or activities might be cued by all the cards being drawn, everyone having had a turn, or a bell or buzzer.
Being flexible	Teacher absence Art class canceled because of an assembly Field trip delayed because of rain	Use pictures to show the expected routine, and cross out the part of the routine that is changing. If possible, prepare the student for the change by describing it verbally and visually and asking the student to explain it to you.
Being quiet	Being quiet while working Being quiet when others are being quiet Being quiet while others are talking	Teach a specific and concrete strategy for being quiet, either by setting a time limit or setting rules such as, "When someone else speaks, keep completely quiet."
Monitoring behavior when excited	Learning to stop clapping or laughing when others have done so Learning when it is okay to run and talk loudly and when it is not okay	Teach a student to watch others and stop clapping or laughing as soon as they do. Set rules for when and where loud talking and running is okay. Use visual cues to remind the student.

S O U R C E : From *Some Social Behaviors That Students with Autism Need Help to Learn and Apply in Everyday Situations* by N. Dalrymple, 1990, Bloomington, IN: Indiana Resource Center for Autism, Institute for the Study of Developmental Disabilities. Used by permission of the author.

They sometimes have problems in gross motor coordination but are highly intelligent, with intense interest in one or two topics (Atwood, 1993). These students may be quiet since they do not seek out interactions with others, and they often have trouble forming friendships because of this.

Supporting Appropriate Behavior

Students with autism often have behaviors that are unusual and can be disturbing to teachers and students who do not understand this disorder. However, many of the behaviors can be corrected with highly structured behavior support programs, and some can be ignored. Many students with autism can receive some or all of their education in a general education classroom, provided that needed supports are in place for them (Pratt & Moreno, 1994; Simpson, 1995).

Generally, the adaptations you make for students with autism involve creating a structured and predictable environment and encouraging appropriate social interactions (Connor, 1990). To create a positive learning environment, establish clear procedures and routines for classroom tasks and follow them consistently. For example, in an elementary classroom, you can create procedures for students to retrieve their coats to leave for lunch, or begin each day with the same activities in the same order. For secondary students, you can set a clear pattern in your instruction by beginning each class with a 3-minute review followed by a 20-minute lecture followed by a 15-minute individual or small-group work session.

In addition to having structure, students with autism may need opportunities during the day to work alone and be alone (Christof & Kane, 1991). This time serves as a break from the stresses of the classroom and the social and communication demands of that setting. A special education teacher can probably advise you about whether this is necessary for a particular student and assist in making arrangements for a quiet place for the student to work.

To help students with social interactions and communication, you can observe student behavior to understand its purpose from the student's perspective (Christof & Kane, 1991). For example, if a student with autism withdraws from classroom activities and begins rocking every day at about 11:00 A.M., it could be a signal that the student is too hungry to work until a 12:15 P.M. lunchtime. Providing a snack in a quiet corner of the classroom could reduce the problem. If a student has been working in a small group but suddenly leaves the group and runs to the room next door, it could be a signal that the student has reached the limits of his or her tolerance for social interactions. It might be appropriate to work with another teacher to provide a safe and isolated location where the student can take a break from the classroom social demands. With these understandings, you can communicate to a special educator or paraprofessional the behaviors of concern and possible explanations for them, thus setting up a positive approach for problem solving. Other social areas in which general education teachers can accommodate students with autism include teaching them to wait, to take turns, to stop an activity before it is complete, to negotiate, to change topics, to finish an activity, to be more flexible, to be quiet, and to monitor their behavior.

Communicating with Students with Autism

Communication with students with autism is accomplished through a wide variety of strategies (Brown, 1994). A few students with autism can communicate adequately with speech, especially if they do not feel pressured. Others learn to communicate through sign language, just as many students with hearing impairments do. For some students, the motor activity of signing seems to help successfully convey their needs and preferences. For yet other students, communication boards are useful tools: By simply touching pictures, students can communicate with others even when they cannot speak the appropriate words. Other communication devices that help students with limited speech, including those with autism, were described earlier in this chapter.

Check Your Learning

How can you determine the function of a student's behavior?

Some students now use a widely publicized and controversial technique called **facilitated communication** (Biklen, 1993; Graley, 1994). Facilitated communication involves a person trained in the technique sitting next to the student with autism and providing touch support to the wrist, elbow, or shoulder as the student types responses or other information on a typewriter, computer, adapted keyboard, or communication board. The purpose of the touching is not to guide the student's hand, but instead to provide steadiness and support for it. Some professionals and parents have found this technique helpful in enabling students with autism to communicate, often for the first time in their lives. They report many examples of students who previously had been thought to have significant cognitive disabilities who through facilitated communication now can type (sometimes independently) and share their thoughts, feelings, and needs (Beirne-Smith et al., 1994). Others question whether the written work produced represents the student's thinking or that of the facilitator. The best communication strategies for a student with autism are generally determined by the multidisciplinary team. A special educator or paraprofessional will inform you about a student's communication needs and strategies and will help you develop an effective communication system.

$\mathbb{S}$ummary

Students with low-incidence disabilities comprise only about 10 percent of all students with disabilities, but they account for eight of the federal categories of disabilities and part of the mental retardation category. Together, these students have tremendously diverse abilities, challenges, and needs. Many of them can succeed in your classroom if you take into account that you will teach only one or two students with these disabilities at any single time and that they are students first and have disabilities second. Many of the teaching strategies you have already learned will be effective in teaching them, and other professionals and parents will be available to assist you in creating successful learning experiences for them.

One group of students with low-incidence disabilities is composed of those with moderate or severe cognitive disabilities, multiple disabilities, and deaf-blindness. These students learn slowly, and they usually need assistance to maintain and generalize their skills, and to combine skills in order to complete complex activities. They need a functional and community-based education that can be accomplished in general education settings with appropriate supports and a commitment to effective teaching and learning practices such as multiple levels of instruction occurring in one classroom, heterogeneous student grouping, the use of natural support systems, and the development of partnerships with families.

Students with sensory impairments are those with visual and hearing impairments. The impact of these students' disabilities on their education can be slight or significant. They often have needs related to academic learning, social and emotional skills, and skills for living in their environments. They also use adaptive equipment or materials to help them learn.

Some students have orthopedic impairments or other health impairments, including traumatic brain injury. Their special supports and services are determined by their needs. Students in these groups often have medical needs that directly or

Check Your Learning

What alternative communication approaches have you learned about in this chapter that students with autism might use? What augmentative communication devices might they use?

indirectly affect their learning. Their cognitive levels can include an entire range. Most students in this group have social and emotional needs because of their illnesses, and accommodations in these areas are likely to be necessary.

Autism is another low-incidence disability. Students with autism have impairments in their social relationships, communication, range of interests, and ability to respond to stressful events. They need highly structured learning environments with clear procedures and routines. Recently, more attention is being paid to students with mild forms of autism, including Asperger's syndrome.

Applications in Teaching Practice

Planning Adaptations for Students with Low-Incidence Disabilities

Mr. Guidroz teaches English to ninth graders. This year he has several students with learning disabilities and emotional disabilities in his class, but his primary concern is Viral, a young man who is quadriplegic. Mr. Guidroz has been told that Viral has average intelligence and is capable of learning. He is meeting with Ms. Bickel from the special education department to answer his questions about Viral.

Mr. Guidroz: I need more information about Viral. Can he really do the work? How is he going to take tests? What is his assistant supposed to be doing? Am I accountable if Viral has a medical problem during class?

Ms. Bickel: It sounds like you haven't gotten the information I thought you had. Let me try to help clarify. Viral is quite a good student. He usually gets A's and B's in his core academic classes, and he is eager to learn. Because he can't use his voice, he "talks" using his communication board. I'll be working with you to be sure the board includes all the key words you want it to contain. All Viral has to do is point his head toward the answer he wants and the laser pointer activates the board, which "says" the answer out loud. Probably one adaptation Viral will need is extra time to answer; he really wants to participate but might need a moment to get the laser beam focused on the answer he wants to give.

Mr. Guidroz: I'll have to see how that works. What does his assistant do?

Ms. Bickel: Mr. Owen is responsible for Viral's personal care and for making sure he gets from class to class. He also takes notes for Viral, and records answers Viral gives on his communication board. He can help you out in class if there's a chance, but Viral needs his attention much of the time.

Mr. Guidroz: Oh, I wasn't trying to get more help. I just need a picture of what this will be like. I need an extra place for Mr. Owen in class, don't I?

Ms. Bickel: Yes, he'll need to sit right next to Viral.

The teachers continued talking for another 45 minutes. The next week, Ms. Bickel asked Mr. Guidroz how it was going with Viral. Mr. Guidroz commented that he was surprised how smoothly and easily things were going. Viral "spoke" in class on the first day, and the other students asked a few questions about the equipment, but that was all. He asked if Ms. Bickel could help him deal with two other students who already seemed to have behavior problems.

Questions

1. What type of disability does Viral have? Why is he included in Mr. Guidroz's English class?
2. What adaptations should Mr. Guidroz make in his classroom and his instruction to accommodate Viral's special needs?
3. If you were meeting with Ms. Bickel, what additional questions would you ask? About Viral? About needed accommodations? About Mr. Owen?
4. What assistance would you need from Ms. Bickel in order to feel comfortable teaching Viral?

Students with High-Incidence Disabilities

Learner Objectives

After you read this chapter, you will be able to

1. Explain what is meant by high-incidence disabilities, including their prevalence and the key elements of the federal definitions for each of the high-incidence categories.

2. Describe the characteristics and needs of students with communication disorders and explain how you can make classroom adaptations for them using the INCLUDE strategy.

3. Describe the characteristics and needs of students with cognitive, learning, and emotional disabilities and the adaptations you can make for them using the INCLUDE strategy.

Malcolm is in the fourth grade and has difficulty communicating in class. Whether he is having a conversation or trying to answer a question, Malcolm can't seem to find the right words to express himself. The other day, his teacher asked him about the different kinds of dinosaurs he had seen on a TV show. Malcolm responded, "Well, uh, there was this one big uh, I mean it really was a big one. It had a funny uh thing on its back and it uh looked like it uh was like funny." This problem he has with finding the right word makes it hard for Malcolm to make friends. The other day, Malcolm started to ask a classmate to come to his house after school, but the classmate walked away before Malcolm could get the words out to invite him. What kind of a language problem does Malcolm have? How will this problem affect his academic and social adjustment in school? What can Malcolm's teachers do to help him with this problem?

Clarissa is a student with a mild cognitive disability who is included in Ms. London's second-grade class. Clarissa's intellectual, language, and motor skills developed much more slowly than her brother's. When she entered kindergarten, Clarissa's language skills were much lower than those of her classmates. She does not understand many of the words her teachers and classmates use, and she has trouble expressing herself when she wants something or when she is conversing with a classmate. She cannot identify letters or numbers, nor can she throw or catch a ball. Clarissa recently was given standardized achievement and intelligence tests by the school psychologist. Her IQ was well below average. Her reading, math, and written language skills were at about the kindergarten level. Clarissa seems to get along well with her peers, but she withdraws when play activities require more advanced language or motor skills. What high-incidence disability does Clarissa have? What can her teacher do to include her in classroom academic and social activities?

Seth is an eighth-grade student at King Middle School. Most people who know Seth outside of school would never guess that he has a learning disability. He converses easily with children and adults, has a great sense of humor, and is renowned among his peers for his "street smarts." Things don't go as well for Seth in school; basic academic skills are particularly problematic. He reads slowly, struggling with each word, and as a result, he often cannot tell you what he has read. Seth's written language is also a problem. His handwriting is illegible, his spelling is inconsistent, and his written essays lack organization. In math, Seth still doesn't know the basic math facts, and when faced with answering word problems, he simply gives up. What disability does Seth have? What factors do you think may have contributed to Seth's academic problems? What kinds of adaptations should Seth's teacher make for him? What other kinds of support do Seth and his teacher need?

■ Rick is heading toward his 15th birthday and major trouble in and out of school. Rick's behavior in school has never been easy to manage. In the primary grades, he was disruptive in class but responded well to rewards given him at home by his parents for good behavior in school. When Rick was in fifth grade, his parents divorced. It was at this time that his behavior problems in school began to worsen. Rick began to talk abusively to peers in class and to refuse loudly to do any work. He began to bully other students, particularly those least likely to be able to defend themselves. In seventh and eighth grades, Rick attended an alternative school. Although his school behavior improved somewhat, he became involved in gang activities when he was in the eighth grade. This year, Rick is a freshman in high school and is attending all general education classes in addition to seeing a special education teacher once a day in the resource room. His school and class attendance has been spotty, and he occasionally engages in disruptive behavior in his classes. What is Rick's disability? How do you think his general education teacher can accommodate his behavior? What kinds of support do Rick and his teacher need?

Students like Malcolm, Clarissa, Seth, and Rick have high-incidence disabilities. These students' disabilities affect their language, learning, and behavior. You probably will teach students with high-incidence disabilities in your classroom. All of these students can benefit from being in a general education setting, but they require support from general and special education professionals. For example, Malcolm's teacher gives him the questions she will ask him ahead of time so he has the opportunity to rehearse his answers with his parents the night before. Clarissa has a peer tutor work with her on high-frequency sight words in reading and on math facts. She also works on oral language skills by listening daily to stories read by her teacher and answering questions. Seth is learning word processing skills to help him overcome his problems with spelling and handwriting. He is also using texts on tape in his science and social studies classes, which are sometimes co-taught. Rick and his teachers have developed an individualized behavior contract in which Rick is allowed extra access to the auto mechanics shop for attending class and complying with teachers' requests. In this chapter, you will learn about the characteristics and needs of students with high-incidence disabilities and about classroom accommodations that enable these students to learn.

What Are High-Incidence Disabilities?

Students with **high-incidence disabilities** have speech or language disabilities, learning disabilities, emotional disturbance, or mild cognitive disabilities. The federal terms for high-incidence disabilities and the proportion of students with these disabilities served through IDEA are summarized in Table 6.1 on page 190. Students with high-incidence disabilities share a number of important characteristics. They are often hard to distinguish from their peers without disabilities, particularly in nonschool settings. In addition, students with high-incidence disabilities often exhibit a combination of behavioral, social, and academic problems. Finally, students with high-incidence disabilities benefit from systematic, highly structured instructional interventions such as those discussed in this chapter and throughout the remainder of this book.

What Accommodations Can You Make for Students with Communication Disorders?

Malcolm and Clarissa are part of a large group of students who have communication disorders. Communication is the exchange of ideas, opinions, or facts between people. Effective communication requires that a sender send a message that a receiver can decipher and understand (Bernstein, 1985). Students with communication disorders have problems with speech and/or language that interfere with communication.

Understanding Speech Problems

Speech is the behavior of forming and sequencing the sounds of oral language (Hallahan & Kauffman, 1997). One common speech problem is **speech articulation,** or the inability to pronounce sounds correctly at and after the developmentally appropriate age. For example, Stacey is in second grade but cannot pronounce the *s* sound, a sound most students master by the age of 5. Other speech difficulties involve voice and fluency. Examples of these speech problems are shown in Figure 6.1 on page 191.

Because communication is social, students with speech disorders, such as **stuttering,** often experience social problems. Although students who communicate clearly draw positive attention from peer relationships, students whose speech is unclear often are avoided by their peers and sometimes ridiculed. The experience of peer rejection can be devastating, leading to lack of confidence, poor self-image, social withdrawal, and emotional problems later in life (Cowen, Pederson, Babijian,

Connections

Compare Table 6.1 with Table 5.1 on page 149. How do these tables support the concept of high-incidence and low-incidence disabilities? How do the concepts of mild, moderate, and severe disabilities also contribute to a cross-categorical view of students with special needs?

FYI

Students with mild cognitive disabilities comprise two-thirds of the federal category of mental retardation. The federal definition of mental retardation is in Table 5.1 on page 149.

FYI

Stuttering is the most common kind of speech problem involving fluency. *Stuttering* is a speech impairment in which an individual involuntarily repeats a sound or word, resulting in a loss of speech fluency.

Table 6.1 **Proportion of Students with High-Incidence Disabilities Receiving Special Education Services in 1994–1995[a]**

Federal Disability Category	Defining Characteristics	Total Number of Students	Percentage of All Students Receiving IDEA Services
Learning disabilities	General intellectual functioning within the normal range	2,513,977	51.1
	Significant difference between ability and school achievement		
	Difference in ability/achievement *not* due to (a) a visual, hearing, or motor handicap; (b) mental retardation; (c) emotional disturbance; and (d) environmental, cultural, or economic disadvantage		
Emotional disturbance	Inability to learn that cannot be explained by intellectual, sensory, or health factors	428,168	8.7
	Inability to build or maintain satisfactory interpersonal relationships with peers and teachers		
	Inappropriate types of behavior or feelings under normal circumstances		
	General pervasive mood of unhappiness or depression; or tendency to develop physical symptoms or fears associated with personal or school problems		
Speech[b] or language[c] impairments	Speech is disordered when it deviates so far from the speech of other people that it calls attention to itself, interferes with communication, or causes the speaker or listeners distress.	1,023,665	20.8
	Three kinds of speech disorders are articulation (abnormal production of speech sounds), voice (absence of or abnormal production of voice quality, pitch, loudness, resonance and/or duration), and fluency (impaired rate and rhythm of speech, for example, stuttering).		
	Language is disordered when comprehension and/or use of a spoken, written, and/or other symbol system is impaired or does not develop normally.		
	Language disorders may involve form (word order, word parts, word usage), content (word meaning), and function (words that communicate meaningfully).		

[a] Students age 6–21 receiving services through IDEA, Part B (U.S. Department of Education, 1996). Additional students receive services under Part H of the same law, and under Chapter 1.

[b] From definitions developed by Van Riper and Emerick (1984).

[c] From definitions developed by the American Speech-Language-Hearing Association (1982).

SOURCE: From *Eighteenth Annual Report to Congress on the Implementation of the Education of the Handicapped Act,* 1996, Washington, DC: U.S. Department of Education.

Figure 6.1 Speech Problems

Articulation

1. Difficulty pronouncing sounds correctly (at and after the developmentally appropriate age). Frequent articulation errors include *f, v, k, g, r, l, s, z, sh, ch,* and *j.* Sounds may be distorted or omitted, or one sound may be inappropriately substituted for another.

2. Speech may be slurred.

Voice

1. Speech is excessively hoarse.

2. May use excessive volume or too little volume.

3. Speech has too much nasality.

4. Speech lacks inflection.

Fluency

1. Stutters when speaking.

2. May have excessively slow rate of speech.

3. May exhibit uneven, jerky rate of speech.

S O U R C E : *Adapting Instruction in General Education for Students with Communication Disorders* by D. Barad, 1985, unpublished manuscript, DeKalb, IL: Northern Illinois University.

Izzo, & Trost, 1973). For example, a freshman in high school stutters. After years of being ridiculed by his peers, he speaks infrequently and has no friends. He would like to ask a girl in his math class to a dance but is petrified that he will not be able to do so without stuttering.

Understanding Language Problems

Language is a system of symbols that represents parts of our lives such as objects, feelings, and actions. Language is the message contained in speech. It is possible to have language without speech, such as sign language for people who are deaf, and speech without language, such as birds that are trained to talk (Hardman, Drew, Egan, & Wolf, 1996). Students who have language problems have trouble with the two key parts of language: receptive language and expressive language. **Receptive language** involves understanding what people mean when they speak to you. **Expressive language** concerns speaking in such a way that others understand you. Receptive language problems occur when students are unable to understand what their teachers and peers are saying. For example, students with receptive language difficulties may not understand questions, have trouble following directions, and cannot retain information presented verbally. Students with expressive language problems are unable to communicate clearly; their spoken language may include incorrect grammar, a limited use of vocabulary, and frequent hesitations. Some common receptive and expressive language problems are listed in Figure 6.2 on page 192.

Cultural Awareness

Learning English is particularly challenging for students with learning disabilities whose native language is not English (Lerner, 1997). For these students, teachers need to draw upon instructional methods from both bilingual education and special education.

FYI

In remembering the distinction between receptive and expressive communication disorders, think of the root words *to receive* and *to express.*

Figure 6.2 Language Problems

Expressive Language Problems

1. Uses incorrect grammar or syntax ("They walk down together the hill"; "I go not to school").

2. Lacks specificity ("It's over there by the place over there").

3. Frequently hesitates ("You know, uhm, I would, uhm, well, er, like a, er, Coke").

4. Jumps from topic to topic ("What are feathers? Well, I like to go hunting with my uncle.").

5. Has limited use of vocabulary.

6. Has trouble finding the right word to communicate meaning (word finding).

7. Uses social language poorly (inability to change communication style to fit specific situations, to repair communication breakdowns, and to maintain the topic during a conversation).

8. Is afraid to ask questions, does not know what questions to ask, or does not know how to ask a question.

9. Repeats same information again and again in a conversation.

10. Has difficulty discussing abstract, temporal, or spatial concepts.

11. Often does not provide enough information to the listener (saying, "*We* had a big fight with *them*," when *we* and *them* were not explained).

Receptive Language Problems

1. Does not respond to questions appropriately.

2. Cannot think abstractly or comprehend abstractions as idioms ("mind sharp as a tack"; "eyes dancing in the dark").

3. Cannot retain information presented verbally.

4. Has difficulty following oral directions.

5. Cannot detect breakdowns in communication.

6. Misses parts of material presented verbally, particularly less concrete words such as articles (*the* book; *a* book) and auxiliary verbs and tense markers (He *was* going; She *is* going).

7. Cannot recall sequences of ideas presented orally.

8. May confuse the sounds of letters that are similar (*b, d; m, n*) or reverse the order of sounds and syllables in words (*was, saw*).

9. Has difficulty understanding humor or figurative language.

10. Has difficulty comprehending concepts showing quantity, function, comparative size, and temporal and spatial relationships.

11. Has difficulty comprehending compound and complex sentences.

S o u r c e s: *Adapting Instruction in General Education for Students with Communication Disorders* by D. Barad, 1985, unpublished manuscript, DeKalb, IL: Northern Illinois University; and *Strategies for Teaching Students with Learning and Behavior Problems* (3rd ed.) by C. S. Bos and S. Vaughn, 1994. Copyright © 1994 by Allyn and Bacon. Reprinted by permission.

Students with language problems may also have difficulty using language in social situations. For example, they may be unable to vary their language to match the person they are talking with or the context in which it is occurring, maintain a topic during conversation, take turns during a conversation, recognize when a listener is not understanding and take action to clarify, and be a considerate speaker and listener (Bos & Vaughn, 1994). As with problems in communicating clearly, problems in using language appropriately can seriously impede students' social development and peer relationships. General education teachers can intervene in the classroom to help such students socially.

Early language development forms the underpinning for much of the academic learning that comes when students go to school. It is not surprising, then, that students with speech and language disorders are likely to have trouble with academics as well. Problems with sounds can result in students having difficulties acquiring word-analysis and spelling skills. Receptive language problems can make reading for comprehension very difficult and can result in trouble understanding mathematical terms such as *minus, regroup,* and *addend* and confusion sorting out words with multiple meanings, such as *carry* and *times* (Mercer, 1997). Language disabilities can seriously impede the content-area learning stressed in middle, junior high, and high school. In these settings, much information is provided orally using lecture formats, the vocabulary and concepts covered are much more abstract, and students are expected to learn with less support from the teacher. These task demands are difficult for students with language disorders.

Another part of learning independently is solving problems. Students with language disorders may have difficulty verbalizing the steps to solve a problem. For example, when a language-proficient student solves story problems, she talks to herself as follows: "First I need to find the key words. Okay, here they are. Now, do these key words tell me to add or subtract? I think they tell me to subtract because the problem asks me how many are left." A student with language problems cannot talk herself through problems.

Accommodations for Students with Communication Disorders

As discussed in Chapter 4, the INCLUDE strategy suggests that before you make adaptations, you should carefully consider potential student problems in view of your instructional demands. For students with speech and language problems, note especially any areas in which students are required to understand oral language (for example, listening to a lecture or a set of verbal directions) or to communicate orally (for example, responding to teacher questions or interacting with classmates when working in cooperative groups). Here are some specific suggestions for working with students with speech and language disorders.

Create an atmosphere of acceptance.   You need to help students believe they can communicate without worrying about making mistakes. You can foster this nonjudgmental atmosphere in several ways. First, when students make an error, model the correct form instead of correcting their mistake directly:

Teacher: Kareem, what did Jules do with the frog?

Kareem: Put pocket.

Do It!

Students in Ms. Kelly's class were asked to respond orally to the following question about a book read to them in class: "In *Bedtime for Frances,* what did Frances do to delay going to bed?" Explain why students with language disorders might have difficulty responding.

Cultural Awareness

It is incorrect to view students as having communication disorders when they use ethnic or regional dialects, speak a form of nonstandard English learned at home, or are native speakers of languages other than English and have limited English proficiency.

Teacher: Oh. He put it in his pocket?

Kareem: Yes.

Second, try to allow students who stutter or have other fluency problems more time to speak, and do not interrupt them or supply words that are difficult for them to pronounce. Offering praise or other reinforcement for successful efforts to communicate, as you would for your other students, is also helpful. Sometimes, you should praise even an attempt.

Teacher: Anthony, what did you do when you went home yesterday?

Anthony: Television.

Teacher: Great, you told me one thing you did. You watched television.

Finally, try to minimize peer pressure. One effective way to do this is to model and reinforce tolerance of individual differences in your classroom.

Encourage listening and teach listening skills. Even though students spend more time listening than doing any other school activity, very little time is devoted to teaching listening skills (Mandlebaum & Wilson, 1989). First, listen carefully yourself and praise listening among your students. For example, when Ms. Hernandez listens to a student speak, she leans forward and nods. Many of her students copy these listening actions. Second, be sure to engage your students' attention before you begin speaking by increasing your proximity to the listeners, giving direct instruction (such as, "Listen to what I'm going to say"), and reducing competing stimuli (have only one activity going on at once, or have only one person speak at a time). You can also use verbal, pictorial, or written advance organizers to cue students when to listen ("When we get to number 3 on this list, I want you to listen extra carefully for an error I am going to make") (Lenz, Alley, & Schumaker, 1987; Robinson & Smith, 1981). Third, make oral material easier to understand and remember by simplifying vocabulary, simplifying syntax, using high-frequency words, repeating important information, giving information in short segments using visual aids for emphasis, having students rehearse and summarize information, and using cues that signal when you are going to say something important (Mandlebaum & Wilson, 1989). Finally, teach listening skills directly. Provide practice on skills such as predicting what might be heard, following directions, appreciating language, identifying main ideas and supporting details, drawing inferences, differentiating fact from fiction, and analyzing information critically (Brent & Anderson, 1993).

When you speak, you can also enhance your students' listening skills by stressing words that are important to meaning. For example, use "He *hit* the *ball*" or "*He* hit the ball," depending on what you want to emphasize. Stressing inflectional patterns, such as using an upward inflection when asking a question, also helps students better understand what you are saying.

Use modeling to expand students' language. You can expand students' language by adding relevant information to student statements:

Student: John is nice.

Teacher: Yes, he is very nice, and polite, too.

You can also expand language by broadening a minimal statement:

Student: My shoe.

Teacher: Your shoe is pretty.

■ Connections

Using modeling, providing meaningful learning contexts, and developing other instructional methods are discussed in greater detail in Chapters 9–11.

Modeling to expand students' language is most effective when it is done as an on-going part of your everyday communications with your students.

Provide many meaningful contexts for practicing speech and language skills.
The goal of successful language programs is to teach students to use appropriate language in a variety of social and academic situations both in and out of school. You can help students meet that goal by providing them with as many opportunities as possible to practice their language skills within meaningful contexts (Hardman et al., 1996). Practice helps students refine their language skills and make them more natural and automatic. When students practice in many different contexts, they can apply what they have learned more readily. For example, Ms. Crum just taught her class the meaning of the word *ironic*. During health class, the class discussed the irony of the government warning people against fat consumption and then funding school lunches that are high in fat. During a trip to the museum, Ms. Crum pointed out the irony of the guard telling them to be quiet when he was wearing shoes that squeaked loudly when he walked.

It is also helpful to encourage students with communication disorders to talk about events and things in their environment, describing their experiences in as much detail as possible (Hardman et al., 1996). For example, Ms. Cusak, a first-grade teacher, starts every day by having two students tell about something they did over the weekend. Mr. Drake, a sixth-grade teacher, uses a *Saturday Night Live* format whereby students in his class act out something funny that happened to them over the weekend.

Finally, whenever possible, instruction should be embedded in the context of functional areas. For example, in Ms. Taylor's consumer math class, she has students go out to appliance stores, talk to salespeople about service contracts, and then describe and compare the various service contracts that are available. In Ms. Ellen's second-grade class, students invite and converse with classroom visitors.

Cultural Awareness

Teaching language in meaningful contexts is also an effective strategy for students with limited English proficiency. Strategies for building background information help all students comprehend what they read.

Check Your Learning

What are the differences between language disorders and speech disorders? How can you modify instruction to promote success among students with communication disorders?

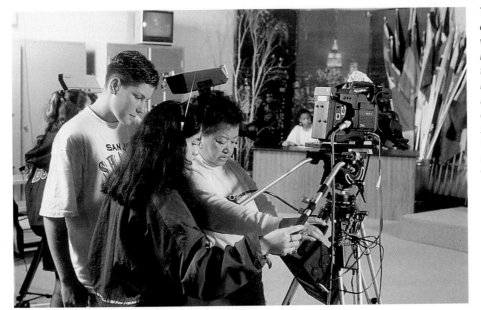

To help students develop communication skills, provide many "safe" and meaningful contexts for students to learn and practice listening skills, speaking skills, interaction skills, and self-expression skills. What are some specific strategies for teaching students with communication disorders?

FYI

Students with emotional disturbance often are referred to as **behavior disordered (BD).** Another term for students with mild cognitive disabilities is **educable mentally handicapped (EMH).**

FYI

Some advocacy groups prefer the term *specific learning disability* because it emphasizes that only certain learning processes are affected.

Cultural Awareness

African American students, especially those in urban middle schools, are at risk of being over-identified for behavior disorders; children from Hispanic or Asian American families are at risk of under-identification (Peterson & Ishi-Jordan, 1994). Why do you think this is so?

What Are the Learning Needs of Students with Learning and Behavior Disabilities?

Students with learning and behavior disabilities have learning disabilities, emotional disturbance, and mild cognitive disabilities. These are the students who are most likely to be included in your classroom, since they comprise more than 80 percent of all students with disabilities in the United States (U.S. Department of Education, 1996). Students with **learning disabilities** are students who achieve less academically because they have trouble with the process of taking in, organizing, and applying academic information. Students with learning disabilities are of normal intelligence, have presumably received adequate instruction, and have not been shown to be sensory impaired, emotionally disturbed, or environmentally disadvantaged. Students with **mild cognitive disabilities** are students who have some difficulty meeting the academic and social demands of general education classrooms, due in large part to below average intellectual functioning (55–70 on an IQ test). Students with mild cognitive disabilities can meet at least some of the academic and social demands of general education classrooms. Students with **emotional disturbance** are of average intelligence but have problems learning primarily because of external (acting out; poor interpersonal skills) and/or internal (anxiety; depression) behavioral adjustment problems.

Students with learning disabilities, mild cognitive disabilities, and emotional disturbance differ in a number of ways. (Hallahan & Kauffman, 1997). The behavior problems of students with emotional disturbance are more severe, and students with mild cognitive disabilities have lower levels of measured intelligence. Students with learning disabilities may have more pronounced learning strengths and weaknesses than students with mild cognitive disabilities, who are likely to show lower performance in all areas. Still, the academic and social characteristics of students with these disabilities overlap considerably. All three groups may experience significant problems in academic achievement, classroom behavior, and peer relations.

The causes of these disabilities are largely unknown because learning and behavior result from a complex interaction between students' individual characteristics, the various settings in which they learn, and the tasks or other demands they face in those settings (Ysseldyke & Algozzine, 1995). It is often difficult to identify the primary cause of a learning or behavior problem. For example, Thomas is lagging behind his classmates in acquiring a sight-word vocabulary in reading. Learning disabilities tend to run in his family, but Thomas's school district also changed from a basal to a literature-based reading program last year. In addition, Thomas's parents separated in the middle of the school year and divorced several months later. Why was Thomas behind in reading? Was it heredity? Was it the new reading program? Was it his parents' marital problems? All of these factors may have contributed to Thomas's problem.

The most important reason students with high-incidence disabilities are grouped together for discussion is that whatever behaviors they exhibit and whatever the possible causes of these behaviors, the students benefit from the same instructional practices (Algozzine, Ysseldyke, & Campbell, 1994; Christenson, Ysseldyke, & Thurlow, 1989). These practices are introduced in this chapter and covered in considerable depth throughout the rest of this book. For example, Raeanna has a mild cognitive disability. She has difficulty reading her classmates' social cues. As a result, she does not recognize when she is acting too aggressively with her classmates and often is rejected by many of them. Del is a student with learning disabilities. He also has trouble reading the social cues of his peers. Although Raeanna and Del may learn new social skills at different rates, both can benefit from social-skills training that provides considerable guided practice and feedback on how to read social cues. The point to remember is that categorical labels are not particularly useful in describing specific students or developing instructional programs for them (Hardman et al., 1996). For example, both Damon and Aretha have learning disabilities, yet their areas of difficulty differ. Damon has a severe reading problem, but excels in mathematics and various computer applications. Aretha, on the other hand, is reading at grade level, but has significant problems with math. Though both students are categorized as having learning disabilities, they have very different needs. You must analyze each individual student's needs and then make adaptations as necessary. This individualization is at the heart of the INCLUDE strategy introduced in Chapter 4.

Students with learning and behavior disabilities have many learning needs. They have difficulty acquiring basic skills in the areas of reading, math, and written language. They may also lack skills necessary for efficient learning, such as attending to task, memory, independent learning skills, language skills, reasoning, conceptualization and generalization, motor, and school survival skills.

Reading Skills

Students with learning and behavior disabilities have two major types of reading problems: **decoding** and **comprehension.** Decoding problems involve the skills of identifying words accurately and fluently. They are most readily observed in students' oral reading, when they mispronounce words, substitute one word for another, or omit words (Lerner, 1997). Students with reading fluency problems can read words accurately but do not recognize them quickly enough. They read slowly, in a word-by-word fashion, without grouping words together meaningfully (Lerner, 1997). Many of these reading decoding problems are shown in this oral reading sample of a student with a learning disability.

Here is what the student said:

> Then Ford had uh other i . . . a better idea. Take the worrrk to the men. He deee . . . A long rope was hooked onto the car . . . wheels . . . There's no rope on there. The rope pulled the car . . . auto . . . the white wheels along . . . pulled the car all along the way. Men stood still. Putting on car parts. Everybody man . . . put on, on, a few parts. Down the assembly line went the car. The assembly line saved . . . time. Cars costed still less to buh . . . bull . . . d . . . build. Ford cuts their prices on the Model T again. (Hallahan, Kauffman, & Lloyd, 1985, p. 203)

Here is the actual passage the student was to read:

> Then Ford had another idea. Take the work to the men, he decided. A long rope was hooked onto a car axle and wheels. The rope pulled the axle and wheels along. All along the way, men stood still putting on car parts. Down the assembly line went the car. The assembly line saved more time. Cars cost still less to build. Ford cut the price on the Model T again. (Hallahan et al., 1985, p. 203)

Students who have serious difficulties decoding written words are sometimes referred to as having *dyslexia*. The Professional Edge on page 198 discusses the meaning of this often-controversial term and suggests instructional approaches.

WWW Resources

The Learning Disabilities Association (LDA) is a helpful support group for parents of students with learning disabilities. Valuable information on parental rights and tips for parenting are available on their website: <http://www.ldonline.org>.

Professional Edge

Understanding Dyslexia

The term *dyslexia* is used a lot these days. You hear that a friend's child has dyslexia, or you see a "dyslexic" on television, or you read that Albert Einstein and Thomas Edison had dyslexia. The word *dyslexia*, which means developmental word blindness, has a medical sound to it, so you may automatically assume that it is medically based. Yet we really do not know what dyslexia is. Some people believe dyslexia is a brain disorder, that people with dyslexia have a different brain structure that leads to difficulties in processing oral and visual linguistic information and that this faulty brain structure is genetically based (Flowers, 1993). Others think it is a severe reading disorder that cannot be distinguished from other reading disorders caused by a lack of appropriate teaching or cultural disadvantage (Shaywitz, Escobar, Shaywitz, Fletcher, & Makuch, 1992). Although research using more sophisticated technology provides some support for a genetic, neurological basis for reading problems (Filipek, 1995; Pennington, 1995), the evidence is still largely circumstantial. In any case, knowing the cause of severe reading problems is one thing; knowing what to do to help students who have these problems is another altogether. Perhaps the best way to describe dyslexia at this point is to say that it is a term used to describe any serious reading difficulty.

Although the cause of dyslexia is unknown, its characteristics are well known. Put very simply, students with dyslexia have serious problems learning to read despite normal intelligence, normal opportunities to learn to read, and an adequate home environment. Students with dyslexia have trouble learning the components of words and sentences (Mercer, 1997). For example, they have difficulty discriminating and writing letters (*b, d; p, b*), numbers (39, 93; 15, 51), and words (*was, saw*) that look and/or sound alike. They may also have trouble differentiating letters from words, words from sentences, and sentences from paragraphs. As a result, the oral reading of students with dyslexia is marked by slow, word-by-word reading.

Students with dyslexia also have trouble with the basic elements of written language, such as spelling and sentence and paragraph construction. Finally, students with dyslexia may have difficulty understanding representational systems, such as telling time, directions, and seasons (Bryan & Bryan, 1986). Dyslexia commonly is considered a type of learning disability, and students with dyslexia are served under the learning disability classification of IDEA.

It is important to identify students with dyslexia or other severe reading disabilities early, before they fall far behind their peers in word-recognition reading skills. Students who appear to be learning letter names, sounds, and sight words at a significantly slower rate than their classmates are at risk for developing later reading problems. Research shows that these students benefit from a beginning reading program that includes the following elements:

1. **Direct instruction in language analysis.** For example, students need to be taught skills in sound segmentation or in orally breaking words down into their component sounds.

2. **A highly structured phonics program.** This program should teach the alphabetic code directly and systematically using a simple-to-complex sequence of skills, teaching regularity before irregularity, and discouraging guessing.

3. **Writing and reading instruction in combination.** Students need to be writing the words they are reading.

4. **Intensive instruction.** Reading instruction for at-risk students should include large amounts of practice in materials that contain words they are able to decode.

5. **Teaching for automaticity.** Students must be given enough practice so that they are able to read both accurately and fluently (Felton, 1993; Hallahan et al., 1996).

Students with learning and behavior disabilities have problems comprehending stories in the elementary grades and content-area textbooks and advanced literature in the upper grades. Although these difficulties result in part from poor decoding skills, they may also occur because these students lack strategies for identifying the key elements of stories and content-area texts. For example, Todd's teacher asked him questions about a book he had just read as part of his classroom literature program. Todd was unable to tell her where the story took place (setting) or the lesson of the story (moral) because the answers to these questions were not directly stated in the story and Todd lacked the necessary inference strategies to figure them out. Patsy was unable to answer a study question comparing the causes of World Wars I and II because she could not locate key words, such as *differences* and *similarities*. In addition, students may not be able to adjust their reading rate to allow for skimming a section of text for key information or reading more slowly and intensively to answer specific questions. For example, it takes Dennis a lot of time to locate key dates in his history book because he thinks he needs to read every word in the chapter while he is looking for the dates.

Written Language Skills

The **written language difficulties** of students with learning and behavior disabilities include handwriting, spelling, and written expression. Handwriting problems can be caused by a lack of fine motor coordination, failure to attend to task, the inability to perceive and/or remember visual images accurately (Smith, 1994), and inadequate handwriting instruction in the classroom (Graham & Miller, 1980). Students may have problems in the areas of formation (Is the letter recognizable?), size, alignment, slant, line quality (heaviness or lightness of lines), straightness, and spacing (too little or too much between letters, words, and lines). As shown in Figure 6.3 on page 200, students with learning and behavior disabilities may have trouble writing both manuscript and cursive letters.

Students with learning and behavior disabilities also have trouble with spelling. The English language consists largely of three types of words: those that can be spelled phonetically, those that can be spelled by following certain linguistic rules, and those that are irregular. For example, words like *cats, construction,* and *retell* can be spelled correctly by applying phonics generalizations related to consonants, consonant blends (*str*), vowels, root words (*tell*), prefixes (*re*), and suffixes (*ion, s*). Words like *babies* can be spelled by applying the linguistic rule of changing *y* to *i* and adding *es*. Words such as *said, where,* and *through* are irregular and can be spelled only by remembering what they look like. Students with learning and behavior disabilities may have trouble with all three types of words. Some common types of spelling errors students with learning and behavior disabilities make are shown in Table 6.2 on page 201.

Students with learning and behavior disabilities have two major types of written expression problems: product problems and process problems (Isaacson, 1987). Their written products are often verb–object sentences, characterized by few words, incomplete sentences, overuse of simple subject–verb constructions, repetitious use of high-frequency words, a disregard for audience, poor organization and structure, and many mechanical errors such as misspellings, incorrect use of punctuation and capital letters, and faulty subject–verb agreements and choice of pronouns (Isaacson, 1987).

FYI

Teachers often mistake natural stages of child and adolescent development for signs of the presence of learning disabilities or emotional problems. Reversing letters or confusing *b* and *d*, for example, is common among children first learning to write.

Connections

Specific strategies for teaching written language skills are given in Chapter 10.

Figure 6.3 Handwriting Problems

Third-Grade Student with Learning Disabilities

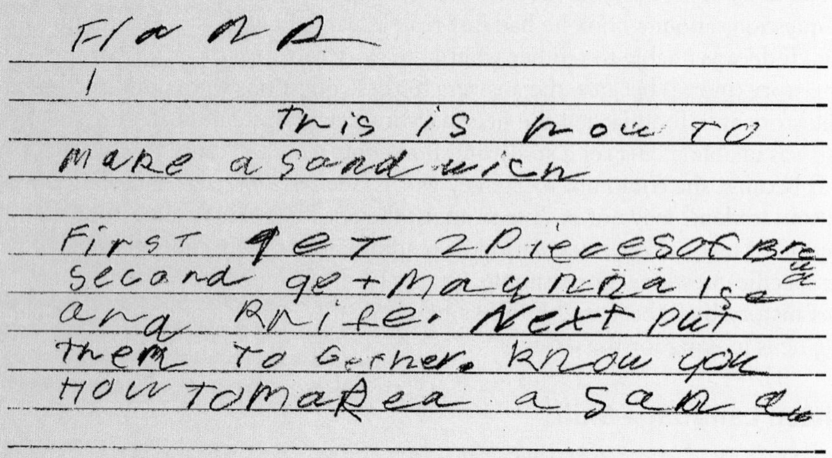

14-Year-Old Student with a Learning Disability

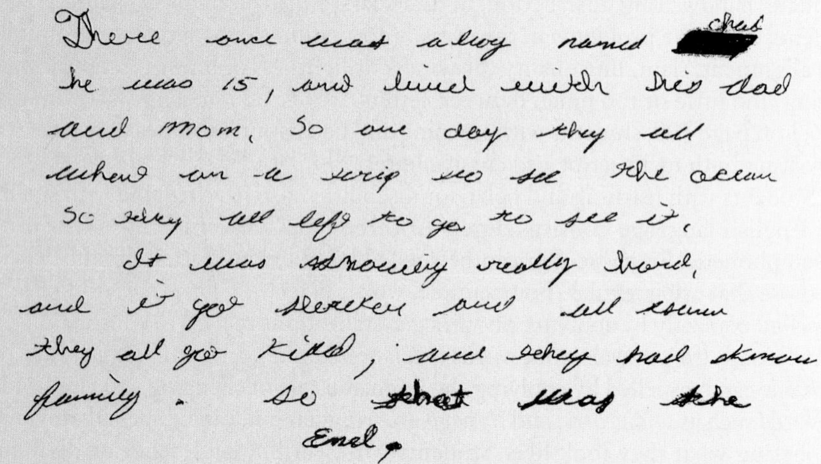

These students also have trouble with the overall process of written communication. Their approach to writing shows little systematic planning, great difficulty putting ideas on paper because of a preoccupation with mechanics, failure to stop to monitor writing, and little useful revising (Isaacson, 1987). A writing sample from a student who has a disability is shown in Figure 6.4. What types of product problems do you see in this sample? What process problems do you think might have led to these problems?

Table 6.2 Common Spelling Errors of Students with Learning and Behavior Disabilities

Error	Example
Addition of unneeded letters	*dressses*
Omissions of needed letters	*hom* for *home*
Reflections of a child's mispronunciations	*pin* for *pen*
Reflections of dialectical speech patterns	*Cuber* for *Cuba*
Reversals of whole words	*eno* for *one*
Reversals of vowels	*braed* for *bread*
Reversals of consonant order	*lback* for *black*
Reversals of consonant or vowel directionality	*brithday* for *birthday*
Reversals of syllables	*telho* for *hotel*
Phonetic spelling of nonphonetic words or parts thereof	*cawt* for *caught*
Wrong association of a sound with a given set of letters	*u* has been learned as *ou* in *you*
Neographisms, such as letters put in that bear no discernible relationship with the word dictated	*fest* for *fought*
Varying degrees and combinations of all these or other possible patterns	

S O U R C E : "But He Spelled It Right This Morning" by R. Edgington, 1968, in J. I. Arena (Ed.), *Building Spelling Skills in Dyslexic Children* (pp. 23–24), San Rafael, CA: Academic Therapy Publications.

Figure 6.4 Sample of One 9-Year-Old's Written Expression

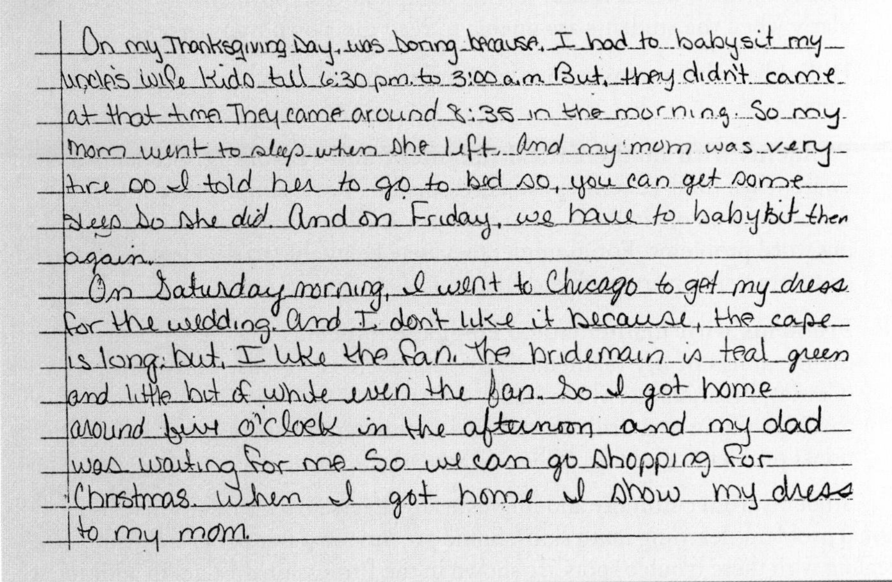

On my Thanksgiving Day, was boring because. I had to babysit my uncle's wife kids till 6:30 p.m. to 3:00 a.m. But, they didn't came at that time. They came around 8:35 in the morning. So my mom went to sleep when she left. And my mom was very tire so I told her to go to bed so, you can get some sleep. So she did. And on Friday, we have to babysit then again.

On Saturday morning, I went to Chicago to get my dress for the wedding. And I don't like it because, the cape is long. but, I like the fan. The bridesmaid is teal green and little bit of white even the fan. So I got home around five o'clock in the afternoon and my dad was waiting for me. So we can go shopping for Christmas. When I got home I show my dress to my mom.

Math Skills

Math can also be problematic for students with learning and behavior disabilities. Their problems tend to occur in eight key areas (Smith, 1994; Strang & Rourke, 1985).

1. **Spatial organization.** Students may be unable to align numbers in columns, may reverse numbers (write a 9 backwards; read 52 as 25), or may subtract the top number from the bottom number in a subtraction problem such as

$$\begin{array}{r} 75 \\ -39 \\ \hline 44 \end{array}$$

2. **Alertness to visual detail.** Students misread mathematical signs or may forget to use dollar signs and decimals when necessary.

3. **Procedural errors.** Students may miss a step in solving a problem. For example, they may forget to add the carried number in an addition problem or subtract from the regrouped number in a subtraction problem:

$$\begin{array}{r} 29 \\ +53 \\ \hline 72 \end{array} \qquad \begin{array}{r} 41 \\ -28 \\ \hline 23 \end{array}$$

4. **Failure to shift mind set from one problem type to another.** Students solve problems of one type but when required to solve another type of problem, inappropriately solve them in the way they did the first type. For example, Kristy just completed several word problems that required addition. The next problem required subtraction, but she continued to use addition.

5. **Difficulty forming numbers correctly.** Students' numbers are too large or poorly formed, which makes solving computational problems awkward, particularly when the students are unable to read their own numbers.

6. **Difficulty with memory.** Students are frequently unable to recall basic math facts.

7. **Problems with mathematical judgment and reasoning.** Students are unaware when their responses are unreasonable. For example, they might not see the obvious errors in $9 - 6 = 15$ or $4 + 3 = 43$. They may also have trouble solving word problems. For example, they may be unable to decide whether to add or subtract in a story problem.

8. **Problems with mathematical language.** Students may have difficulty with the meanings of key mathematical terms such as *regroup*, *place value*, or *minus* (Cawley, Fitzmaurice, Shaw, Kahn, & Bates, 1979). They may also have trouble participating in oral drills or verbalizing the steps in solving word or computational problems (Cawley, Miller, & School, 1987).

Students from culturally and linguistically diverse backgrounds may have additional problems learning math skills. Some potential trouble spots and strategies for dealing with these trouble spots are shown in the Professional Edge. In addition, the Technology Notes feature on pages 204–205 presents uses of hypermedia to teach math problem-solving skills to students from all backgrounds.

FYI

Adaptations of materials and formats in math instruction include keeping models on the board, providing graph paper to align problems, and using visual cues, such as color-coded or boldfaced signs and arrows, as reminders of direction, and line boxes to set off problems and answers.

Professional Edge

Adapting Math Instruction for Students Who Are Linguistically and Culturally Different

Math can be a challenging subject for all students, including students with learning and behavioral difficulties. Students from linguistically and culturally diverse backgrounds may face additional challenges when learning math. Scott and Raborn (1996) present some potential trouble spots and suggested strategies for teaching math to students from linguistically and culturally diverse backgrounds.

Trouble Spot	Recommendation
Learning a new language	• Determine the student's level of proficiency in both English and the native language. • Assess math abilities in both languages. • If a student is stronger in math than in English, provide math instruction in the primary language. • Listen to the words you most frequently use in teaching math. Work together with the ESL teacher to help the student learn these words or to help you learn them in the student's language. • Use a variety of ways to communicate such as gesturing, drawing sketches, writing basic vocabulary and procedures, rewording, and providing more details. • Provide time and activities that will allow students to practice the English language and the language of math.
Cultural differences	• Use story problem situations that are relevant to students' personal cultural identity (e.g., ethnicity, gender, geographical region, age). • Share examples of the mathematical heritage of students' cultures (e.g., folk art, African and Native American probability games, measurement systems). • Involve family and community members in multicultural math.
Tricky vocabulary	• Use concrete activities to teach new vocabulary and the language of math. • Use only as many technical words as are necessary to ensure understanding. • Give more information in a variety of ways to help students understand new vocabulary. • Develop a picture file; purchase or have students make a picture dictionary of math terms and frequently used vocabulary.
Symbolic language	• Allow students to draw pictures, diagrams, or graphic organizers to represent story problems. • Make clear the meaning and function of symbols. • Point out the interchangeable nature of operations. • In algebra, teach students to translate phrases to mathematical expressions.
Level of abstraction and memory	• Allow students to develop mathematical relationships using concrete representations accompanied by verbal descriptions. • Develop mathematical understanding from concrete to abstract form. • Use visual and kinesthetic cues to strengthen memory. • Keep distractions to a minimum.

SOURCE: From "Realizing the gifts of diversity among students with learning disabilities" by P. Scott and D. Raborn (1996), *LD Forum, 21*(2), 10–18. Reprinted by permission of the Council for Learning Disabilities.

Technology Notes

Using Hypermedia to Teach Math Problem-Solving Skills

Hypermedia is multimedia information linked and accessed by a computer (Lynch, 1991). Hypermedia programs go beyond texts and traditional computer-assisted instruction because they incorporate sound, animation, photographic images, and video clips. Hypermedia programs can benefit students with special needs in a number of ways. They present information in many different formats, a feature that can help students retain and use information more effectively. Hypermedia programs also allow students instant access to a range of instructional supports such as synthesized speech, definitions of terms, and concept maps. Finally, hypermedia programs are interactive, a critical feature of effective instruction for students with special needs.

Babbitt (1993; 1996) has described a hypermedia program designed to teach students with special needs the following six-step math problem-solving strategy:

1. Read the problem.
2. Understand the problem situation.
3. Choose a solution strategy and solve the problem.
4. Check to make sure that the question is answered.

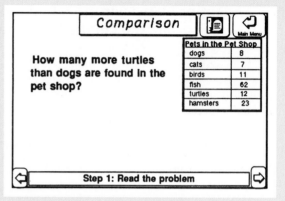

5. Check the reasonableness of the answer.
6. Consider applications and extensions of the problem.

Each screen of the program prompts students to use the appropriate strategy step. For example, in the screen for Step 1 shown above, students are reminded to use the first step in the problem-solving strategy: Read the problem.

Students who need help reading the problem simply have to click on the speech button and the problem is read to them using synthesized speech. Students can also highlight individual words, phrases, sentences, or the entire problem.

Learning Skills

Connections

Approaches to adapting instruction for students with ADHD, which are covered in Chapter 7, are also applicable here.

Students with learning and behavior disabilities have difficulty performing skills that could help them learn more readily. One such skill is attention. Students may have difficulty coming to attention or understanding task requirements (Hallahan et al., 1996). For example, Janice frequently fails essay tests; she is unable to focus on key words in the questions to help her organize a response. As a result, she loses valuable writing time just staring at the question and not knowing how to begin. Benito misses important information at the beginning of science lectures because it takes him 5 minutes to get into the teacher's presentation. Students may also have trouble focusing on the important aspects of tasks. For example, Anita can tell you the color of her teacher's tie or the kind of belt he is wearing, but nothing about the information he is presenting. When Arman tries to solve word problems in math, he is unable to tell the difference between information that is needed and not needed

Step 2 of the strategy, understand the problem situation, is divided into three parts: What do you want to know? (Step 2a); What do you know already? (Step 2b); and What else do you know? (Step 2c). These parts are shown below.

Students are guided through the steps with graphics, animation, and sound. Note that the relevant problem text is identified through highlighting or changing the typeface. Students can also click on the Pictures button to have the "object" pictured, or the Letters/Numbers button to have the words and numbers placed on the screen. Of course strategy prompts can be faded over time as students become proficient in their use.

S O U R C E : From "Hypermedia: Making the mathematics connection" by B. C. Babbitt, 1993, *Intervention in School and Clinic,* 28(5), pp. 294–301. Copyright 1993 by PRO-ED, Inc. Reprinted with permission.

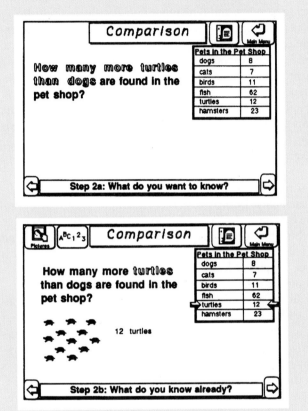

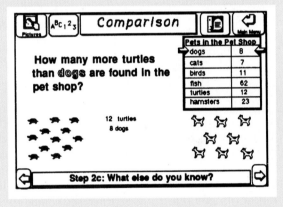

to solve the problem. Finally, students with learning and behavior disabilities may have trouble sticking to a task once they have started it.

Memory problems may also make learning difficult for students (Wong, 1996). Some problems occur when information is first learned. For example, Carla cannot remember information when it is presented just once. Sal has practiced math facts many times but still cannot remember some of them. Students may also fail to retain what they learn. For example, Abby had learned addition facts in the fall but remembered only about 50 percent of them when tested in the spring. Finally, students sometimes learn something but do not remember to use the information to solve problems or learn other information. For example, a student who learned a note-taking strategy in a resource room failed to use the strategy in her content-area classes.

Students with learning and behavior disabilities may have trouble organizing and interpreting oral and visual information despite adequate hearing and visual

Connections

Specific strategies for helping students remember information are described in Chapter 11.

skills (Lerner, 1997). For example, Rodney is a student with a learning disability who has trouble with visual tasks. He frequently loses his place while reading and copying; has trouble reading and copying from the chalkboard; does not notice details on pictures, maps, and photographs; is confused by worksheets containing a great deal of visual information; and often cannot remember what he has seen. LaTonya, on the other hand, has trouble with auditory tasks. She has difficulty following oral directions, differentiating between fine differences in sounds (*e/i; bean/been*), taking notes during lectures, and remembering what she has heard.

Students may also lack **reasoning** skills necessary for success in school. Important reasoning skills include reading comprehension, generalization (the ability to recognize similarities across objects, events, or vocabulary), adequate background and vocabulary knowledge, induction (figuring out a rule or principle based on a series of situations), and sequencing (detecting relationships among stimuli) (Salvia & Ysseldyke, 1995). For example, Stu has difficulty understanding a lecture on the civil rights movement because he lacks the necessary background information; he is unsure what a "civil right" is. Tamara has trouble recognizing a relationship on her own, even after repeated examples; her teacher presented five examples of how to add *s* to words that end in *y*, but Tamara still could not figure out the rule.

Some students with learning and behavior disabilities may have motor coordination and fine motor impairments (Lerner, 1997). For example, Denise is a first-grade student who has some fine motor and coordination problems. She has trouble using scissors, coloring within the lines, tying her shoes, and printing letters and numbers. Cal is in third grade. His handwriting is often illegible and messy. Cal is also uncoordinated at sports, which has lessened his opportunities for social interaction on the playground since he is never selected to play on a team.

Check Your Learning

What learning needs might students with learning and behavior disabilities share? How might you modify instruction in the basic academic skills for these students?

Independent learning can also be a challenge for students with learning and behavior disabilities. They have been referred to as **passive learners,** meaning that they do not believe in their own abilities; have limited knowledge of problem-solving strategies; and even when they know a strategy, cannot tell when it is supposed to be used (Hallahan et al., 1996; Lerner, 1997). Being a passive learner is particularly problematic in the upper grades, where more student independence is expected. For example, when LaVerne reads her science textbook, she does not realize when she comes across information that she does not understand. So instead of employing a strategy to solve this problem, such as rereading, checking the chapter summary, or asking for help, she never learns the information and as a result is doing poorly in the class. When Darrell studies for tests, he reads quickly through his text and notes but does not use any strategies for remembering information, such as asking himself questions, saying the information to himself, or grouping the information he needs to learn into meaningful pieces.

Students with learning and behavior disabilities may also have problems in the area of **academic survival skills** such as attending school regularly, being organized, completing tasks in and out of school, being independent, taking an interest in school, and displaying positive interpersonal skills with peers and adults (Brown, Kerr, Zigmond, & Haus, 1984). For example, Duane is failing in school because he rarely shows up for class; when he does attend class, he sits in the back of the room and displays an obvious lack of interest. Nicole is always late for class and never completes her homework. Her teachers think she does not care about school at all.

As you can see, students with learning and behavior disabilities have problems in a number of academic and learning areas. Some parents and teachers have tried unproven interventions in search of quick fixes for such students. The issue of using unproven controversial therapies is discussed in the Professional Edge on pages 208–209.

What Are the Social and Emotional Needs of Students with Learning and Behavior Disabilities?

Students' social needs are crucial to consider because students who have social adjustment problems in school are at risk for academic problems (Epstein, Kinder, & Bursuck, 1989; Rock, Fessler, & Church, 1996) as well as serious adjustment problems when they leave school (Cowen et al., 1973). Students with learning and behavior disabilities may have needs in several social areas, including classroom conduct, interpersonal skills, and personal and psychological adjustment.

FYI

Estimates of the number of students with learning disabilities who are at risk for social problems range from 34 to 59 percent (Bryan, 1997).

Classroom Conduct

Students with learning and behavior disabilities may engage in a number of aggressive or disruptive behaviors in class, including hitting, fighting, teasing, hyperactivity, yelling, refusing to comply with requests, crying, destructiveness, vandalism, and extortion (Deitz & Ormsby, 1992; Hallahan & Kauffman, 1997). Although many of these behaviors may be exhibited by all children at one time or another, the classroom conduct of students with behavior disorders is viewed by teachers as abnormal, and their behavior has a negative impact on the other students in class (Cullinan, Epstein, & Lloyd, 1983). For example, Kenneth is an adolescent with learning and behavior problems. His father died last year, and his mother has been working two jobs just to make ends meet. Kenneth has begun to hang out with a rougher crowd and has been getting into fights in school. He has also been talking back to his teachers frequently and refusing to comply with their demands. Kenneth's behavior has gotten so bad that other students and their parents are complaining about it to the teacher. Some cautions involved in disciplining students like Kenneth are presented in the Professional Edge on pages 210–211.

Connections

The use of strategies for responding to student behavior, including punishment, is the topic of Chapter 12.

Interpersonal Skills

Students with learning and behavior disabilities are likely to have difficulty in social relations with their peers. Evidence for these problems comes from over 20 years of research showing that these students have fewer friends, are more likely to be rejected or neglected by their peers (Bryan, 1997), and are frequently rated as socially troubled by their teachers and parents (Smith, 1994). Many of these problems can be traced to the failure of students to engage in socially appropriate behaviors or social skills in areas such as making friends, carrying on conversations, and dealing with conflict.

There are a number of explanations for why students have social-skills problems. Some students may simply not know what to do in social situations. This lack of knowledge could be because they do not learn from naturally occurring models of social behavior at home or in school. Students also may have trouble reading **social cues** and may misinterpret the feelings of others (Bryan & Bryan, 1986). For example, a story was told recently about five boys sitting on the floor of the principal's office, waiting to be disciplined. Four of the boys were discussing their failing

Cultural Awareness

Social skills are learned in cultural contexts. Teach your students about the variance in social behavior within all cultures and emphasize the notion that families and individuals experience their cultures in personal ways.

Professional Edge

Controversial Therapies in Learning and Behavior Disabilities

It is not easy being the parent or teacher of a student with learning disabilities. Students with learning disabilities often do not respond favorably to the first approach tried—or, for that matter, to the first several. Failure and frustration can lead to the search for miracle cures. This problem is compounded by the fact that journals that publish research about the effectiveness of various treatments are not normally read by parents and teachers. Unfortunately, this void is readily filled by a steady stream of information, much of it not substantiated by research, from popular books, lay magazines, or television talk shows (Silver, 1995).

As a teacher, you need to be well informed about these therapies so you can give parents reliable, up-to-date information when they come to you for advice. The best way to get this information is to read professional journals. Any treatment may work for a few students, but this is not the same as demonstrating effectiveness in a controlled research study. If you

or a student's parents decide to use a controversial therapy, you must monitor its effectiveness carefully and discontinue it if necessary. Several controversial therapies are summarized here.

Neurophysiological Retraining

In this group of approaches, learning difficulties are seen as the result of dysfunctions in the central nervous system that can be remediated by having students engage in specific sensory or motor activities. One common example of this approach is patterning (Doman & Delacato, 1968), in which students are taken back through earlier stages of development (creeping and crawling). Another approach is optometric visual training, in which students do eye exercises designed to improve their visual perception and hence their reading skills. No research evidence suggests that either patterning or optometric visual training improves students' cognitive functioning or reading ability (Silver, 1987).

FYI

Social cues are verbal or nonverbal signals people give that communicate a social message.

or near-failing grades and the trouble they were going to be in when the fifth boy, a student with a learning disability, chimed in to say that his grandparents were coming to visit the next week. Other students may know what to do—but not do it. For example, some students with learning and behavior disabilities are **impulsive;** they act before they think. In Del's sessions with the school social worker, he is able to explain how he would act in various social situations, but in an actual social setting he gets nervous and acts without thinking. Other students may choose not to act on their knowledge because their attempts at socially appropriate behavior may have gone unrecognized and they would rather have negative recognition than no recognition at all. For example, James was rebuffed by one group of students so often that he began to say nasty things to them just to provoke them. He also began to hang out with other students who chronically misbehaved because, according to James, "at least they appreciate me!" Finally, still other students may know what to do socially but lack the confidence to act on their knowledge in social situations, particularly if they have had a history of social rejection or have lacked opportunities for social interactions. Consider Holly, a student who is socially withdrawn. Holly worked for a year with her school counselor to learn how to initiate a social activity with a friend but is afraid to try it out for fear of being rejected.

Diet Control Therapies

A number of therapies involve using diet to control hyperactivity and other learning disorders. One of these (Feingold, 1975) claimed to decrease student hyperactivity by eliminating various artificial flavors, colors, and preservatives from the student's diet. Most research studies have shown that the Feingold Diet is not effective in controlling hyperactivity (Smith, 1994). Others have suggested that refined sugars in the diet lead to hyperactivity. Again, these claims have not been proven by research (Barkley, 1995; Connors & Blouin, 1982/1983). Another diet therapy for learning disorders involves using mega-vitamins to treat emotional or cognitive disorders (Cott, 1977; 1985). This therapy has not been verified by research (American Academy of Pediatrics, 1976). Another theory purports that deficiencies in trace elements such as copper, zinc, magnesium, manganese, and chromium along with the more common elements of calcium, sodium, and iron cause learning disorders; but these claims remain unsubstantiated (Silver, 1987). Finally, there is a theory that hypoglycemia (low blood sugar levels) is a cause of learning disabilities. Clinical studies on this theory have been inconclusive (Rappaport, 1982/1983).

Scotopic Sensitivity Syndrome

This syndrome has been defined as a difficulty in processing light efficiently that causes a reading disorder (Irlen, 1991; Lerner, 1997). Symptoms include abnormal sensitivity to light, blinking and squinting, red and watery eyes, frequent headaches, word blurriness, print instability, slow reading, skipping and rereading lines, and difficulty reading at length because of general eye strain and fatigue (Irlen, 1991). Following a screening test, students identified as having scotopic sensitivity are treated with plastic overlays or colored lenses, which can be expensive. Although many people treated with tinted lenses claim that the lenses eliminate their symptoms and help them read better, research shows that tests for scotopic sensitivity are flawed (Silver, 1995), and the effects of the lenses have not been verified (Fletcher & Martinez, 1994). Caution is advised.

Personal and Psychological Adjustment

Students with little success at academics and/or social relationships may have personal and psychological problems as well (Kerschner, 1990; Torgeson, 1991). One common personal problem is **self-image.** Students with learning and behavior disabilities often have a poor self-concept; they have little confidence in their own abilities (Licht, Kistner, Ozkaragoz, Shapiro, & Clausen, 1985). Poor self-image, in turn, can lead to **learned helplessness.** Students with learned helplessness see little relationship between their efforts and school or social success. When these students succeed, they attribute their success to luck; when they fail, they blame their failure on a lack of ability. When confronted with difficult situations, students who have learned helplessness are likely to say or think, "What's the use? I never do anything right anyway." For example, Denny is 15 years old and a sophomore in high school. He has been in special education since the second grade. He has never received a grade better than a C, and has received quite a few D's and F's. Last quarter, Denny started to skip classes because he felt that even when he went to class he did not do well. Denny is looking forward to dropping out of school on his 16th birthday and going to work for a fast food chain, where at least he is able to do the work.

> **Check Your Learning**
>
> What social-emotional needs might students with learning and behavior disabilities share? Why is it important to address students' social and emotional needs?

Disciplining Students with Emotional Disturbance

Students with emotional disturbance some-times behave in ways that disrupt the education of other students in the class or threaten their safety. When this happens, you may need to punish the student both to defuse the situation and to deter the student from acting out again. Punishment involves decreasing inappropriate behavior by either presenting something negative or taking away something positive. Although the courts have held that it is permissible to punish students with emotional disturbance, they have also held that the punishment must be delivered according to the following principles (Yell, 1990; Yell, Clyde, & Puyallup, 1995):

1. Teachers must be careful not to violate the due process rights of their students. This means that you will need to communicate clearly to parents and students the behaviors you expect and the specific consequences for inappropriate behaviors. As needed, these items should be written in the student's IEP.

2. When using punishment, do not violate the educational rights of students with emotional disturbance. Punishments such as expulsion, serial suspensions (successive, consecutive suspensions), prolonged in-school suspensions, and prolonged periods of time-out (removing students from classroom activities; see Chapter 12) constitute a change of placement and therefore cannot be done without due process. Temporary suspensions of 10 days or fewer are permissible; possession of a weapon or illegal drug, or other extraordinary situations, can result in a suspension of up to 45 days. To expel a student for more than 10 days, a committee, in-cluding the student's parents, must determine that the misconduct had nothing to do with the disability. Finally, in the case of any suspension, students must be presented with the evidence against them and given the opportunity to present their side of the story.

3. The punishment of students with emotional disturbance must serve a legitimate purpose. Its use must serve an educational purpose, and clearly written guidelines for its use must exist. For example, Calvin is told that his verbal outbursts in class are preventing him and his classmates from learning. He is handed a written contract indicating that if he engages in more than one verbal outburst in class he will be required to sit in the back of the room and not participate in any classroom activities for 3 minutes.

4. The punishment procedure used must be reasonable according to these guidelines:

   a. Was the rule being enforced reasonable?

   b. Did the punishment match the offense?

   c. Was the punishment reasonable in light of the student's age and physical condition?

   d. Did the teacher deal out the punishment without malice or personal ill to the student?

5. More intrusive punishments should be used only after more positive procedures have been tried. For example, Calvin's teacher had tried giving Calvin 5 minutes of free time for *not* having a verbal outburst first. When this approach did not work, he tried a different reward. When this con-

Students with learning and behavior problems may also have severe **anxiety** or **depression** (Cullinan & Epstein, 1994; Wright-Strawderman, Lindsey, Navarette, & Flippo, 1996). Depressed or anxious students may refuse to speak up when in class, may be pessimistic or uninterested in key aspects of their lives, may be visibly nervous when given an assignment, may become ill when it is time to go to school, or may show a lack of self-confidence when performing common school and social tasks. For example, Barrett is a 9-year-old boy with a consistent history of school

sequence did not work, Calvin's teacher resorted to sitting him by himself for a period of time.

6. When you use punishment, keep records of all the procedures you tried. Write down the behavior that precipitates the punishment, the procedures used, the length of time they were used, and the results. This information can help you make informed decisions about a student's behavior management program. It can also help clarify for parents why you used a particular procedure.

7. Punishment procedures for students with emotional disturbance should be carried out in conjunction with the special education teacher as agreed upon in the student's IEP. Any major changes in punishment should be decided on only in collaboration with these same people. For example, each time Calvin's teacher changed to a different punishment procedure, he did it in consultation with Calvin's special education teacher and parents.

8. Remember that punishment should always be used in conjunction with positive consequences for appropriate behavior. The use of positive consequences can greatly reduce the need for using punishment in the future and can help build positive behaviors that benefit students throughout their lives.

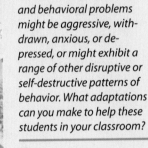

Students with emotional and behavioral problems might be aggressive, withdrawn, anxious, or depressed, or might exhibit a range of other disruptive or self-destructive patterns of behavior. What adaptations can you make to help these students in your classroom?

failure. Barrett is sick just about every morning before he goes to school. At first his mother let him stay home, but now she makes him go anyway. When at school, Barrett is very withdrawn. He has few friends and rarely speaks in class. Barrett's teachers tend not to notice him because he is quiet and does not cause problems. If you have a student in your class who exhibits the signs of depression shown in Figure 6.5 on page 212, get help for him or her by contacting your school counselor, psychologist, or social worker.

Figure 6.5 **Diagnostic Criteria for Major Depression**

Depression is a dysphoric mood (unhappy; depressed affect), a loss of interest or pleasure in all or almost all usual activities. At least four of the following symptoms also must have been present consistently *for at least two weeks.*

a. change in appetite or weight
b. sleep disturbance
c. psychomotor agitation or retardation
d. loss of energy
e. feelings of worthlessness
f. complaints of difficulty to concentrate
g. thoughts of death or suicide

S O U R C E : *Diagnostic and Statistical Manual of Mental Disorders* (4th ed.), 1994, Washington, DC: American Psychiatric Association. Reprinted by permission.

What Accommodations Can You Make for Students with Learning and Behavior Disabilities?

As you have just read, students with learning and behavior disabilities have a range of learning and social-emotional needs. Although these needs may make learning and socializing difficult for them, students with learning and behavior disabilities can succeed in your classroom if given support. Some initial ideas about how you can accommodate students with learning and behavior disabilities in your classroom are discussed here. You will find much more in-depth treatment of such accommodations in Chapters 8–13.

Addressing Academic Needs

Do It!

Interview classroom teachers about their experiences with students who have learning and behavior disabilities. What approaches work best for teaching these students in inclusive settings?

As we have already discussed, you can find out whether students with learning and behavior disabilities need adaptations by using the INCLUDE strategy to analyze their learning needs and the particular demands of your classroom. You can try three different types of adaptations: bypassing the student's need by allowing the student to employ compensatory learning strategies; making an adaptation in classroom organization, grouping, materials, and methods; and providing the student with direct instruction on basic or independent learning skills. For example, Jessica is a student with learning disabilities who is included in Mr. Gresh's high school general science class. Mr. Gresh uses a teaching format in which the students first read the text, then hear a lecture, and finally conduct and write up a lab activity (demands). Jessica has severe reading and writing problems. She is reading at about a sixth-grade level and has difficulty writing a legible, coherent paragraph (student learning needs). However, she does have good listening skills and is an adequate note-taker (student strength). In Mr. Gresh's class, Jessica will have difficulty reading the textbook and meeting the lab writing requirements independently (problem). She will be able to get the lecture information she needs because of her good listening skills (success). Mr. Gresh, with help from Jessica's special education teacher, brainstormed a number of possible adaptations for Jessica and then agreed to implement three of them. He developed a study guide to help Jessica identify key points in the text (adaptation). He also set up small groups in class to review the study guides (adaptation) and assigned Jessica a buddy to help her with the writing demands of the lab activity (bypass). Finally, Mr. Gresh and the special education teacher set up a schedule to monitor Jessica's progress in writing lab reports and reading the textbook. Several more examples of how the INCLUDE strategy can be applied are provided in Table 6.3 on pages 214–215.

Addressing Social and Emotional Needs

One of the most important reasons given to explain the trend toward inclusive education is the social benefits for students with and without disabilities (Schaps & Solomon, 1990; Stainback & Stainback, 1988). Unfortunately, experience shows that many students with learning and behavior problems will not acquire important social skills just from their physical presence in general education classes (Sale & Carey, 1995). Although much of the emphasis in your training as a teacher concerns academics, your responsibilities as a teacher also include helping all students develop socially, whether or not they have special needs. As with academics, the support students need will depend largely on the specific social problem each student has.

Students who have significant conduct problems benefit from a classroom with a clear, consistent behavior management system. In classrooms that are effectively managed, the rules are communicated clearly and the consequences for following or not following those rules are clearly stated and consistently applied. Conduct problems can also be minimized if students are engaged in academic tasks that are meaningful and can be completed successfully. Still, conduct problems may be so significant that they require a more intensive, individualized approach. For example, Rick, whom you met at the beginning of this chapter, talked out repeatedly and loudly refused to carry out any requests his teachers made of him. His school attendance was also spotty. Rick's general education teachers got together with Rick's special education teacher to develop a **behavior contract.** According to the contract, each teacher was to keep track of Rick's attendance, talk-outs, and refusals to comply

■ **Connections**

Review all the steps of the INCLUDE strategy (see Chapter 4). What are they? How can you use them for students with high-incidence disabilities?

■ **Connections**

Detailed information on how to write a behavior contract is presented in Chapter 12.

In what ways might students with cognitive, emotional, and behavioral disorders have difficulty learning? How can teachers address each of these areas of difficulty?

Table 6.3 Making Adaptations for Students with Learning and Behavior Disabilities Using Steps in the INCLUDE Strategy

Identify Classroom Demands	Note Student Strengths and Needs	Check for Potential Successes / Look for Potential Problems	Decide on Adaptations
Student desks in clusters of four	*Strengths* Good vocabulary skills *Needs* Difficulty attending to task	*Success* Student understands instruction if on task *Problem* Student off task—does not face instructor as she teaches	Change seating so student faces instructor
Small-group work with peers	*Strengths* Good handwriting *Needs* Oral expressive language—problem with word finding	*Success* Student acts as secretary for cooperative group *Problem* Student has difficulty expressing self in peer learning groups	Assign as secretary of group Place into compatible small group. Develop social-skills instruction for all students
Expect students to attend class and be on time	*Strengths* Good drawing skills *Needs* Poor time management	*Success* Student uses artistic talent in class *Problem* Student is late for class and frequently does not attend at all	Use individualized student contract for attendance and punctuality—if goals met, give student artistic responsibility in class
Textbook difficult to read	*Strengths* Good oral communication skills *Needs* Poor reading accuracy Lacks systematic strategy for reading text	*Success* Student participates well in class Good candidate for class dramatizations *Problem* Student is unable to read text for information	Provide taped textbooks Highlight student text
Lecture on women's suffrage movement to whole class	*Strengths* Very motivated and interested in class *Needs* Lack of background knowledge	*Success* Student earns points for class attendance and effort *Problem* Student lacks background knowledge to understand important information in lecture	Give student video to view before lecture Build points for attendance and working hard into grading system
Whole class instruction on telling time to the quarter hour	*Strengths* Good coloring skills *Needs* Cannot identify numbers 7–12 Cannot count by fives	*Success* Student is able to color clock faces used in instruction *Problem* Student is unable to acquire telling time skills	Provide extra instruction on number identification and counting by fives

(continued)

Table 6.3 *(continued)*

Identify Classroom Demands	Note Student Strengths and Needs	Check for Potential Successes Look for Potential Problems	Decide on Adaptations
Math test involving solving word problems using addition	*Strengths* Good reasoning skills	*Success* Student is good at solving problems	Allow use of calculator
	Needs Problems mastering math facts, sums of 10–18	*Problem* Student misses problems due to math fact errors	
Multiple choice and fill-in-the-blanks test	*Strengths* Memory—good memory for details	*Success* Student does well on fill-in-the-blank questions that require memorization	Use bold type for key words in multiple choice questions
	Needs Attention—cannot identify key words in test questions Weak comprehension skills	*Problem* Student is doing poorly on multiple choice parts of history tests	Teach strategy for taking multiple choice tests

in class. The contract specified that when Rick talked out or refused to comply once, he would be given a warning. If he engaged in these behaviors again, he would be required to serve 5 minutes of detention for each violation. The contract also specified that for each class Rick attended without incident, he would receive points that his parents would allow him to trade for coupons to buy gasoline for his car.

Adaptations will depend on the types of interpersonal problems your students have. You can use **social-skills training** for students who do not know how to interact with peers and adults (Goldstein, Sprafkin, Gershaw, & Klein, 1980). For example, Tammy is very withdrawn and has few friends. One day her teacher took her aside and suggested that she ask one of the other girls in class home some day after school. Tammy told her that she would never do that because she just would not know what to say. Tammy's teacher decided to spend several social studies classes working with the class on that skill and other skills such as carrying on a conversation and using the correct words and demeanor when asking another student whether he or she would like to play a game. She felt that many of the students in class besides Tammy would benefit from these lessons. First, Tammy's teacher posted the steps involved in performing these skills on a chart in front of the classroom. Then, she and several students in the class demonstrated the social skills for the class. She then broke the class into small groups, and each group role-played the various skills and were given feedback by their classmates and peers. To make sure that Tammy felt comfortable, the teacher put her in a group of students who had a positive attitude and liked Tammy. An example of how to carry out social-skills training is presented in the Case in Practice on page 216.

For students who know what to do in social situations but lack the self-control to behave appropriately, **self-control training** can be used (Kauffman, 1997). In

Connections

Ways of teaching students self-control are covered in Chapters 10 and 12.

Case in Practice

A Social-Skills Training Session

Ms. Perez and her fourth-grade class are working on a unit on social skills in social studies. They are learning the skill of listening to someone you are talking with by doing the following:

1. Look at the person who is talking.
2. Remember to sit quietly.
3. Think about what is being said.
4. Say "Yes," or nod your head.
5. Ask a question about the topic to find out more.

Jeanine, a student in the class, has just practiced these listening skills in front of the class by role-playing the part of a student who is talking to her teacher about an assignment. In the role-play, Ms. Perez played herself. The class is now giving Jeanine feedback on her performance.

Ms. Perez: Let's go through each of the listening steps and give Jeanine some feedback on how she did. First, did Jeanine look at me when I was talking? Before you answer, can someone tell me why it's important to look at the person who is talking?

Lorna: Well, it's important because like you don't want the other person to think you're not listening even though you are. So you really have to *show* them you are listening.

Ms. Perez: That's right, Lorna. Well, how did Jeanine do on this one?

Charles: Well, she looked at you at first but while you were explaining the assignment she looked down at her feet. It kind of looked like she wasn't listening.

Jeanine: I was listening, but I guess I should have kept good eye contact all the way through.

Ms. Perez: Yes, Jeanine. To be honest, if I didn't know you better, I would have thought that you didn't care about what I was saying. You need to work harder on that step. Okay. Let's talk about the next step, which is to remember to sit quietly. How did Jeanine do with this one?

Milton: I think she did well on this step. She just sat there and remembered not to laugh, fidget, or play with anything while you were talking.

Ms. Perez: I agree, Milton. Jeanine did well on that step. Nice work, Jeanine. Now, can someone tell me what the next listening step is?

Kyrie: It's to think about what the person is saying.

Ms. Perez: Right, Kyrie. Let's let Jeanine evaluate herself on this one.

Jeanine: Well, I tried to think about what you were saying. Once I felt my mind start to wander but I followed your suggestion and started thinking about a question that I could ask you.

Ms. Perez: Good, Jeanine. Trying to think of something specific like a question to ask can be very helpful. How did you think you did on the next step? Did you nod your head or say "Yes" to show you were following me?

Jeanine: I think I did; at least I wanted to.

Ms. Perez: What do the rest of you think? Did Jeanine nod her head or say "Yes"?

Tara: Well, I saw her nod a little but it was hard to tell. Maybe she needs to nod more clearly.

Ms. Perez: I agree, Tara. Jeanine, you need to nod more strongly or the teacher won't realize you are doing it.

REFLECTIONS

What teaching procedures is Ms. Perez using to teach her students listening skills? Do you think they are effective? What do you think she could do to make sure that her students actually use this skill in their classes? For what settings outside of school would the teaching of this and other social skills be important?

self-control training, students are taught to redirect their actions by talking to themselves. For example, Dominic does not handle conflict very well. When his friends tease him, he is quick to lose his temper and lash out verbally at them. His outbursts only encourage the students, and they continue teasing and taunting him any chance they get. Dominic's teacher taught him a self-control strategy to help him ignore his friends' teasing. Whenever he was teased, Dominic first counted to 5 to himself to get beyond his initial anger. He then told himself that what they were saying wasn't true and that the best way to get them to stop was to ignore them and walk away. When he walked away, Dominic told himself he did a good job and later reported his efforts to his teacher.

Some students may know what to do socially but lack opportunities for using their social skills. For example, students who are newly included in your classroom and/or new to the school will need opportunities to interact with their classmates to get to know them better. One way to create opportunities for social interaction is to allow students to work in small groups with a shared learning goal. For example, Thomas is a student with a mild cognitive disability who is included in Mr. Jeffreys's sixth-grade class. This is Thomas's first year in general education; until this year, he had been in a self-contained special education classroom. Mr. Jeffreys decided to use peer learning groups in science because he thought it would be a good way for Thomas to get to know his classmates and make some friends. Every two weeks, Thomas has the opportunity to complete various lab activities with a different group.

Students who exhibit learned helplessness can benefit from **attribution retraining** (Ellis, Lenz, & Sabornie, 1987). The idea behind attribution retraining is that if you can convince students that their failures are due to lack of effort rather than ability, they will be more persistent and improve their performance in the face of difficulty (Schunk, 1989). Some ideas for how to carry out attribution retraining are shown in Figure 6.6 on page 218.

You can enhance student self-image by using the following strategies suggested by Mercer (1997):

1. **Set reasonable goals.** When setting goals for students, make sure that they are not too easy or too hard. Self-worth is improved when students reach their goals through considerable effort. Goals that are too ambitious perpetuate failure. Goals that are too easy can give students the idea that you think they are not capable of doing anything difficult.

2. **Provide specific feedback contingent upon student behavior.** Feedback should be largely positive, but it should also be contingent upon student completion of tasks. Otherwise, students are likely to perceive your feedback as patronizing and just another indication that you think they are unable to do real academic work. Do not be afraid to correct students when they are wrong. Providing corrective feedback communicates to students that you think they can succeed if they keep trying and that you care about them.

3. **Give the student responsibility.** Assigning a responsibility demonstrates to students that you trust them and believe they can act maturely. Some examples include taking the class pet home on weekends, taking the lunch count, being a line leader, taking messages to the office, and taking attendance.

4. **Teach students to reinforce themselves.** Students with poor self-images say negative things about themselves. You can help students by reminding them of their strengths, encouraging them to make more positive statements about themselves, and then reinforcing them for making these statements.

5. **Give students a chance to show their strengths.** Part of the INCLUDE strategy is to identify student strengths and then help students achieve success by finding or creating classroom situations in which they can employ their

igure 6.6   **Teaching Positive Attributions**

Students attribute their successes and failures to various causes. Negative attributions result when students cite causes that reflect negatively on themselves and are beyond their control. To help students use positive attributions when they talk about their performance in your classroom, try this strategy:

1. Identify the negative attributions you most often hear a student making. Examples include "I got it right. I must have been lucky," "I never do this kind of assignment right," "I'm not smart enough to do this," and "I can't learn this—it's too hard."

2. Create a positive alternative to the negative attribution. Here are some examples based on the attributions given above:

"I must have been lucky."	"And I worked hard to learn the material."
"I never do this . . . right."	"But this time I'll figure out what I need help on and ask for it."
"It's too hard."	"But I know I can learn it."

3. When you hear a student use a negative attribution, take a moment to introduce your alternative, and discuss with the student how to use it. Model the use of a positive attribution.

4. Create opportunities for the student to use the positive attributions and praise their use.

5. Monitor for students' spontaneous use of positive attributions. Call these to the students' attention and praise them.

strengths. For example, Cara cannot read very well but has an excellent speaking voice. After her group wrote a report on the 1960 presidential election, Cara was given the task of presenting the report to the whole class.

Summary

Students with high-incidence disabilities are students who have speech and language disabilities, learning disabilities, emotional disturbance, or mild cognitive disabilities. Students with high-incidence disabilities make up about 90 percent of all students who have disabilities. They are often hard to distinguish from their peers; exhibit a combination of behavioral, social, and academic problems; and are likely to benefit from systematic, highly structured interventions.

Students with communications disorders have a number of learning, social, and emotional needs. Their language problems can affect their performance in all academic areas, including reading, math, written expression, and content-area instruction. Socially, they can be withdrawn, rejected by their peers, and have considerable difficulty using language in social situations. The academic and social performance of students with speech and language problems can be enhanced through a number of adaptations, including creating an atmosphere of acceptance, actively encouraging listening skills, stressing words that are important to meaning, presenting many examples of vocabulary and concepts being taught and presenting them several times, using modeling to teach students to expand their language, and teaching within a context that is meaningful for students.

Students with learning and behavior disabilities receive special education services within the categories of learning disabilities, emotional disturbance, and mental retardation (mild). Students with learning and behavior disabilities have many learning needs. They have difficulty acquiring basic skills in the areas of reading, math, and written language. They may also lack skills necessary for efficient learning, such as attending to task, memory, independent learning skills, language skills, reasoning, conceptualization and generalization, motor, and school survival skills. You can make adaptations for these students in academic areas using the INCLUDE strategy.

Students with learning and behavior disabilities have social and emotional difficulties in classroom conduct, interpersonal skills, and personal and psychological adjustment. Their classroom conduct may be characterized by disruptive behaviors in class, including hitting, fighting, teasing, refusing to comply with requests, crying, destructiveness, and vandalism. Students with learning and behavior disabilities also are likely to have interpersonal problems. They are at risk for being rejected or neglected by classmates, and they may have a number of social skills deficits. The personal/psychological adjustment of students with learning and behavior disabilities may also be problematic. They sometimes have a poor self-image, are not proactive in academic and social situations, and may experience bouts of depression or anxiety. Adaptations for students with learning and behavior disabilities in social areas include individualized behavior management, social-skills training, self-control training, and attribution retraining.

Applications in Teaching Practice

Using the INCLUDE Strategy with Students with High-Incidence Disabilities

Tell how you would apply the INCLUDE strategy to accommodate the students described in the vignettes at the beginning of Chapter 6 by answering the following questions.

Questions

1. What communication, academic, behavior, and social and emotional needs does each student have?
2. Keeping in mind the major aspects of the classroom environment including classroom organization, classroom grouping, instructional materials, and instructional methods, what kinds of problems are these students likely to have?
3. What types of adaptations would you make for each of these problems?
4. Are these adaptations "reasonable" in terms of teacher time and ease of implementation? What support (if any) would you need to carry them out?
5. How will you monitor the effectiveness of your adaptations? What will you do next if your first adaptation is ineffective?

To help you with this application, refer to Table 6.3 on pages 214–215 and to the section on the INCLUDE strategy in Chapter 4.

chapter 7

Other Students with Special Needs

Learner Objectives

After you read this chapter, you will be able to

1. Describe students protected through Section 504 and the accommodations general education teachers can make for them.

2. Explain accommodations general education teachers can make for students with attention deficit–hyperactive disorder.

3. Outline the adaptations students who are gifted and talented may need in general education classrooms.

4. Explain how general education teachers can address the needs of students from diverse cultural backgrounds.

5. Describe how general education teachers can make adaptations for students at risk for school failure, including students who live in poverty, those who are abused or neglected, and those who live in homes in which drugs, including alcohol, are abused.

Victor is a student in Mr. Steinberg's seventh-grade computer class. Mr. Steinberg says Victor just cannot attend to the work at hand, even though students usually enjoy the computer class and all the specialized technology they have access to there. Victor is constantly looking around, distracted by almost anything, including computers operating, students conversing, changes in the light when a cloud momentarily blocks the sun, or a passerby outside the classroom door. Instead of raising his hand during class discussions, Victor just blurts out what is on his mind, and he is as likely to make a comment about his visit with his aunt last weekend as he is to contribute a comment relevant to the topic being presented. Victor also has a habit of acting first and thinking later. It almost seems that he is incapable of reversing this process. For example, in class the other day, as Mr. Steinberg cautioned students not to remove a disk from the floppy drive while the drive light was on, Victor was already in action. He ruined the disk he was using and didn't seem to understand how he had caused this to happen. Mr. Steinberg is convinced that Victor is likely to do this again since he doesn't seem to learn from experience. Victor's parents report that he is "all boy," much like his father. They readily admit, however, that keeping up with him can be an exhausting task. Does Victor have a disability? What are Victor's special needs? What is the responsibility of school personnel for meeting those needs?

Kham's family has always struggled to make ends meet, but their situation is particularly stressful now. Kham's father left the family 2 months ago, leaving his mother to care for four children under the age of 11. The family was evicted from their apartment, and they have been living either in a shelter or in the family car—a 1982 Cutlass. Kham is characterized by his teachers as an "average" student, but lately his fourth-grade teacher has been expressing concerns. Kham's homework is not completed, he seems distracted during class, and he has been in two playground fights in the past week. The music teacher has noticed that Kham, who in the past has been an eager student with a genuine talent for music, is becoming uninterested. When she called on him to choose a song for the class, he said he didn't care. He is also starting to make friends with older students, many of whom have a reputation for gang activity. Kham says these boys are his friends, but his teachers have the sinking feeling that they are "losing" Kham to the life of the streets. How common are problems like Kham's? What other characteristics and behaviors might Kham display in school? What should his teachers do to help Kham stay interested in school?

■ Lydia is a fourth-grade student who is gifted and talented. She has been reading since she was 3, and she frequently borrows her sister's high school literature anthology as a source of reading material. She knew most of the math concepts introduced in fourth grade before the school year began, and she also has a strong interest in learning Spanish, playing flute and piano, and volunteering to read to residents of a local nursing home. Lydia's idea of a perfect afternoon is to have a quiet place to hide, a couple of wonderful books, and no one to bother her. Lydia's teacher, Mr. Judd, enjoys having her in class because she is so enthusiastic about learning, but he admits that Lydia's abilities are a little intimidating. He has also noticed that Lydia doesn't seem to have much in common with other students in class. She is a class leader but does not appear to have any close friends as other students do. Is Lydia entitled to receive special services because of her giftedness? Is Lydia typical of students who are gifted or talented? What can Mr. Judd do to help Lydia reach her full potential? What social problems do students like Lydia encounter?

Connections

Review the information about IDEA and the procedures for serving students through special education in Chapters 1 and 2.

Most educators agree that many students in U.S. schools have special needs but that only a small percentage of them receive assistance through special education. In fact, teachers comment that they have students in their classes not eligible for special education services whose needs are greater than those of students protected by IDEA. For example, even though Victor has a significant attention problem, he does not qualify for special education. Likewise, Kham's teachers worry about his future and are frustrated that they cannot make his life better and help him reach his potential. They sometimes feel powerless to influence students, like Kham, who have so many difficulties in their young lives. Lydia's teacher is concerned that he cannot possibly make time to provide the advanced instruction that would benefit her.

This chapter is about students who are not necessarily eligible for special education but who have special needs and often require special attention from general education teachers. In fact, you may find that you have characteristics similar to those of the students described in this chapter or that you have had similar experiences. If that is the case, you bring to your teacher preparation program knowledge other teachers may not have, and you may have a perspective on student diversity that you can draw on in understanding student needs. The students examined in this chapter include those who have functional disabilities addressed by Section 504 but not IDEA, including those with attention deficit–hyperactive disorder; those who are gifted and talented; those whose native language is not English and whose cultures differ significantly from that of most of their classmates; and those who are at risk because of special situations including poverty, child abuse, and drug abuse.

The rationale for discussing Victor, Kham, and Lydia, and other students like them in this text has three parts. First, students with special needs often benefit greatly from the same strategies that are successful for students with disabilities. Thus, one purpose is to remind you that the techniques explained throughout this text are applicable to many of your students, not just those who have IEPs. Second, it is important for you to understand that you will teach many students with a tremendous diversity of needs resulting from many different factors, disability being just one potential factor. Creating appropriate educational opportunities for all your students is your responsibility. Third, although many special educators are committed to helping you meet the needs of all your students, they cannot take primary responsibility for teaching students like Victor, Kham, and Lydia. These are not students who "should be" in special education. They represent instead the increasingly diverse range of students that all teachers now instruct, and they highlight the importance of creating classrooms that respect this diversity and foster student learning, regardless of students' special needs.

This chapter also highlights how complex student needs have become (Reynolds & Heistad, 1997). For example, you probably realize that students with disabilities can also have the special needs described here. A student with a physical disability might also be academically gifted. A student with a cognitive disability might also live in poverty. A student with a learning disability might speak a language other than English at home. You probably also recognize that the student groups emphasized in this chapter are not necessarily distinct, even though it is convenient to discuss them as if they are. Students who live in poverty can also be gifted and from a cultural minority. An abused student can be at risk from drug abuse. Keep in mind as you read this chapter that your responsibility as a teacher for all students, regardless of their disabilities or other special needs, is to identify strengths and needs, arrange a supportive instructional environment, provide high-quality instruction, and foster student independence. When students have multiple special needs, these tasks can be especially challenging; that is when you should seek assistance from professional colleagues, parents, and other resources.

> **Connections**
>
> Section 504 was defined in Chapter 1. It is civil rights legislation protecting students with functional disabilities.

> **Do It!**
>
> With classmates, discuss the types of diversity found in the schools where you plan to teach. How are you effectively preparing to teach students from diverse backgrounds?

Which Students Are Protected by Section 504?

In Chapter 1, you learned that some students with special needs do not meet the eligibility criteria for receiving services through IDEA, but they are considered functionally disabled as defined through Section 504 of the Vocational Rehabilitation Act of 1973. Students in this group are entitled to receive reasonable accommodations that help them benefit from school. These accommodations can include many of the same types of services and supports that students eligible through IDEA receive, but there are crucial differences (Roberts & Mather, 1995a). First, the definition of a disability in Section 504 is considerably broader than it is in IDEA. Any condition that substantially limits a major life activity, such as learning in school, is defined as a disability (Katisiyannis & Conderman, 1994). This definition means

Do It!

Ask a local school administrator to speak to your class about the guidelines and policies that govern Section 504. What questions will you ask about differences between the services provided by IDEA and Section 504?

that students with a wide range of needs are eligible for assistance through Section 504. For example, a student who is photophobic might receive services through Section 504, but so also might students with significant attention problems, drug addiction, or chronic health problems. Second, unlike IDEA, no funds are provided to school districts to carry out the requirements of Section 504. Third, the responsibility for making accommodations for students qualifying as disabled through Section 504 belongs to general education personnel, not special education personnel. Special educators might provide some assistance, but their aid is not mandated as it is in IDEA. The types of accommodations required vary based on student needs but could include alterations in the physical environment, such as providing a quiet work space or a room with specialized lighting; modifications in instruction, such as decreasing an assignment or allotting additional time to complete it; and changes in the student's schedule, such as allowing a rest period. Individual school districts establish policies for meeting the requirements of Section 504.

For students to receive assistance through Section 504, their needs must be assessed and a decision made concerning their eligibility. These assessment procedures can be similar to those used for IDEA. Students determined eligible have a Section 504 plan developed by a team. The plan outlines the accommodations needed, who is to implement them, and how they will be monitored.

Although many students can qualify for assistance through Section 504, two common groups will be addressed in this chapter: students with medical or health needs and students with attention deficit–hyperactive disorder (ADHD). (The first group is discussed here; students with ADHD are covered in the following major section.)

Students with chronic health or medical problems who are not eligible for IDEA services according to established criteria and as determined by a multidisciplinary team comprise one of the major groups that can qualify for assistance through Section 504. For example, a student who has asthma might have a Section 504 plan. The plan could address accommodations related to the student's need for occasional rest periods, opportunities to take medication, exemption from certain physical activities, and provisions to make up assignments and tests after absences. A student with severe allergies might have a plan that addresses materials in school that cannot be used (for example, paints, chalk), guidelines for participation in physical education, and requirements for providing assignments that can be completed at home if necessary. A student who is photophobic (that is, highly sensitive to bright light) might have a Section 504 plan that calls for darkening shades on classroom windows and a shaded area in which the student can work. A student with diabetes might need a Section 504 plan that spells out procedures to be followed in case of an insulin reaction or other illness.

As you can tell, some of the responsibility for implementing Section 504 plans belongs to administrators, who authorize physical modifications to classrooms and make arrangements for students to have rest periods or take medications. Your responsibility is to implement instructional adaptations outlined in the plan, such as providing assignments in advance and allowing extra time for work completion. Your interactions with students protected by Section 504 differ from your interactions with other students only in your responsibility to make the accommodations required. However, you will find that some students with Section 504 plans have learning and behavior problems. These students benefit from the many strategies presented in this text.

How Can You Accommodate Students with Attention Deficit–Hyperactive Disorder (ADHD)?

Students with attention problems have long been a concern of teachers, especially at the elementary school level. In recent years, this concern seems to have escalated. One special education clearinghouse reported that it is receiving thousands of requests each year for information about attention problems (Fowler, 1994). Even popular magazines are tackling the topic of children who cannot pay attention (for example, Wallis, 1994). A few students with significant attentional problems as described in this section are eligible for services through IDEA, but others receive assistance through Section 504 (Reid & Katsiyannis, 1995).

The term for severe attention problems is **attention deficit–hyperactive disorder (ADHD),** a condition defined in the *Diagnostic and Statistical Manual of Mental Disorders* (DSM-IV) (American Psychiatric Association, 1994). ADHD is characterized by chronic and serious inattentiveness, hyperactivity, and/or impulsivity. You might also hear the term **attention deficit disorder (ADD)** used to label the condition. ADD is an earlier term for describing attention problems, and some professionals use the terms ADHD and ADD interchangeably. Some authors use ADD as a general term to describe all serious attention problems and ADHD only for students who display symptoms of hyperactivity.

Estimates of the prevalence of ADHD range from less than 1 percent to over 20 percent of the student population (Armstrong, 1996), but experts seem to agree that it affects no more than 3 to 5 percent of students (Barkley, 1990). The causes of the disorder are not clear, although many professionals suspect it has a neurological basis (Hynd, Voeller, Hern, & Marshall, 1991). A few authors have suggested that ADHD is the result of food additives or food allergies, inner ear problems, vitamin deficiencies, or bacterial infections, but none of these causes has been demonstrated (Lerner, Lowenthal, & Lerner, 1995). Usually, a diagnosis of ADHD is the result of individualized testing for cognitive ability and achievement, a medical screening, and behavior ratings completed by family members and school professionals (Maag & Reid, 1994).

Characteristics and Needs of Students with ADHD

The characteristics and needs of students with ADHD can vary considerably. For example, some students with ADHD have primarily an **attention disorder.** They have difficulty sustaining attention to schoolwork or play activities, they often lose things, and they appear forgetful. Other students with ADHD have a **hyperactive-impulsive disorder.** They tend to fidget constantly, need to move around a room even when other students can stay seated, and frequently interrupt others. A third group of students with ADHD have a **combination disorder,** with both the inattentive and hyperactive-impulsive characteristics.

Although all students might occasionally demonstrate some symptoms of ADHD, students diagnosed with this disorder display many of them prior to 7 years of age. Further, their symptoms are chronic and extraordinary. For example, Joyce, the mother of 8-year-old Matt, who has been diagnosed with ADHD, described one memorable morning like this: Matt was 4 years old. He had spilled an entire box of breakfast cereal on the kitchen floor and then had a screaming tantrum when Joyce

FYI

Research suggests that 25 percent of students with ADHD also have a learning disability. Although the connection between ADHD and emotional disabilities is not clear, students with ADHD are likely to have serious behavior problems, including oppositional behaviors, conduct problems, disruptive behaviors, or depression (Lerner, Lowenthal, & Lerner, 1995).

FYI

Parents and teachers often misuse the term *hyperactive* to refer to any students whose high activity levels and easy distractibility make them challenging to teach.

instructed him to help her pick it up. He then knocked over a vase of flowers and announced sincerely that he didn't do it. Joyce believed he meant what he said even though she saw him do it. Part of the reason Matt was home that day was because his preschool had asked Joyce not to bring him back. He was too disruptive in class and the parents of other students were complaining that he often hit, kicked, or bit their children. The final straw that morning came when Matt ran upstairs after being asked to sit down. He slammed the bathroom door, locking himself in; in his haste to shut the door, he broke the lock mechanism. After an hour of trying to dismantle the lock to open the door, while Matt opened drawers and cabinets, taking apart the bathroom, Joyce declared defeat and called the fire department. The firefighters extricated Matt by entering the bathroom through a window and bringing him down the ladder. Joyce called this just one more day that made her question her own parenting skills and even her sanity. She said that there were far too many days like that. Matt's home behavior is somewhat like the behavior of Victor, whom you met at the beginning of this chapter. Both Matt and Victor seem incapable of controlling their actions, and they seem not to learn from past experiences.

Cognitively, students with ADHD can function at any level, although the disorder is usually diagnosed for students who do not have cognitive disabilities. Students who are below average in ability and achievement, students who are average learners, and students who are gifted and talented can all have ADHD. Some students with the disorder experience very serious learning problems. They sometimes receive special services under the "learning disabled" category, or they might be classified as having "other health impairments." Other students experience low achievement apparently because of extremely low self-esteem or other emotional or behavior problems. In some cases, students with ADHD receive services as emotionally disturbed. Some authors assert that nearly half of all students with ADHD already receive services through special education (Reeve, 1990). The remaining students may or may not have serious learning problems. Problems can occur in reading, especially with long passages in which comprehension demands are high; spelling, which requires careful attention to detail; listening, especially when the information presented is highly detailed; and math, which often requires faster computational skills than students with ADHD can handle (Zentall, 1993). All of these learning problems can be related to students' inability to focus on schoolwork for extended periods of time and their difficulty in attending selectively only to important aspects of information.

Socially and emotionally, students with ADHD are at risk for a variety of problems. For example, they are more likely to be depressed or to have extremely low confidence or self-esteem. They are often unpopular with peers and have difficulty making friends.

The frequency of behavior problems of students with ADHD varies. Students whose disorder is inattention might not act out in class, but they can be disruptive when they try to find lost items or constantly ask classmates for assistance in finding their place in a book or carrying out directions. Students with hyperactive-impulsive disorder often come to teachers' attention immediately because they have so many behavior problems. Their constant motion, refusal to work, and other behaviors can be problematic in even the most tolerant environments.

ADHD also has a physical component. Recent research suggests that brain dysfunction might contribute to the disorder (Riccio, Hynd, Cohen, & Gonzalez, 1993). First, a neuroanatomical perspective proposes that ADHD is caused by a dys-

Check Your Learning

What characteristics of ADHD does Matt display?

FYI

Behavior rating scales are frequently used in determining if a student has ADHD. Commonly used rating scales include the *Achenbach Behavior Checklist for Parents*, the *Connors Rating Scale*, and the *Behavior Problems Checklist*.

function in part of the brain, especially the frontal lobe, possibly because this area is developing more slowly or abnormally. Second, a neurochemical perspective suggests that a chemical imbalance exists that affects neurotransmitters, the chemicals that regulate how the brain controls behavior. Because of the imbalance, students with ADHD are not capable of rapidly monitoring and controlling their behavior, and hence they are impulsive and inattentive.

Interventions for Students with ADHD

Academic Interventions: To assist students with ADHD academically, you can emphasize key features of their learning and eliminate unnecessary information (Zentall, 1993). For example, keep oral instructions as brief as possible. Rather than giving directions, providing multiple examples, and then recapping what you have said, instead list directions by number using very clear language (for example, "First, put your name on the paper; second, write one sentence for each spelling word; third, put your paper in your spelling folder"). When reading for comprehension, students with ADHD tend to perform better on short passages than on long ones. Thus, it would be better to ask a student with ADHD to read just a small part of a long story and check comprehension at that point, then have him or her read another part, and so on rather than read an entire story or chapter. In spelling, using color cues to highlight words to be learned can be helpful, but only after students have practiced the words without the color cues. In math, students should be given extended periods of time to complete computational work since their attentional problems interfere with their efficiency in this type of task.

In addition to the types of interventions just outlined, most recommendations for helping students with ADHD academically are similar to those used for students with learning and emotional disabilities, and for other students who need highly structured and especially clear instruction. In the following chapters, you will find many instructional approaches that will meet the needs of students with ADHD.

Behavior interventions.   For responding to behavior, professionals generally recommend interventions that emphasize structure and rewards, with limited use of reprimands (Abramowitz & O'Leary, 1991). As the INCLUDE strategy outlines, you should first consider environmental demands and address these as a means of preventing behavior problems. For example, students with ADHD exhibit less acting-out behavior when they sit near the front of the room, and they often benefit from working in an area with few visual distractions (for example, away from bulletin board displays). In addition, students often respond well to a systematic use of rewards. You might tell Tamatha, a student with ADHD, that she will earn a sticker for each five math problems she completes. The stickers can later be redeemed for time working on the computer. With older students, contracts for appropriate behavior can be used.

If a student needs to be corrected, provide a clear and direct but calm reprimand. If you say, "Tamatha, I know you are trying hard, but you have to try harder to raise your hand before speaking," Tamatha might not even realize that you are correcting her. A preferred response would be to say quietly to her, "Tamatha, do not call out answers. Raise your hand." This message is much clearer.

Both to address behavior issues and to teach social skills, some professionals recommend that students with ADHD learn strategies for monitoring their own

F Y I

Because interest in ADHD is so high, parents may ask if you think their child has this disorder. It is essential for you to remember *not* to offer a diagnostic opinion. Refer parents to their family doctor or pediatrician for this information.

Check Your Learning

What cognitive, academic, social and emotional, and behavior characteristics of students with ADHD does Victor, the student you met at the beginning of the chapter, display? What types of interventions might help Victor learn?

behavior through self-talk. Whether these types of strategies are actually effective, however, has been questioned, especially for younger students (Abikoff, 1991). One area in which self-talk strategies are generally recommended is anger control. Students with ADHD often need to learn to control their anger because they experience much frustration that can lead to angry outbursts. If you teach a student who needs to learn anger management, a special education teacher, counselor, or social worker would probably design a program to meet this need; your responsibility would be to provide follow-through in your classroom.

Use of medication.   The most common intervention for students with ADHD is the prescription of psychostimulant medications. Approximately 750,000 students, 2 percent of the school age population, take such medication each year (DuPaul, Barkley, & McMurray, 1991). Stimulant medications, including drugs such as **Ritalin,** have been demonstrated to be effective in approximately 80 percent of cases in decreasing students' activity level and increasing their compliance (Swanson et al., 1992). The most common medications prescribed for ADHD are described in Table 7.1.

Despite the apparent effectiveness of stimulant medications in treating ADHD, their use remains somewhat controversial. For example, teachers often encounter the problem of students not consistently taking their medication, or sharing their medication. This situation can endanger other students, or at least result in a loss of learning (Howell, Evans, & Gardner, 1997). Another issue concerns the proper dosage. Some researchers contend that dosages high enough to cause an improvement in behavior can negatively affect students' academic learning and performance (Swanson et al., 1992). A third area of concern pertains to side effects. For example, approximately 30 percent of students have a **rebound effect** from their medication (DuPaul et al., 1991). As the medication wears off, the student displays behaviors that may be worse than those that existed before the medication was administered. Some students can also experience a loss of appetite accompanied by suppressed weight and height gain (Reeve, 1990). However, once the medication is discontinued, students catch up in height and weight.

Ultimately, a student's physician decides whether to prescribe medication. However, you are likely to be asked to provide educational input into this decision. These are some guidelines to consider when you are thinking about whether medication is likely to have a positive effect:

1. The student's attention is extremely limited, and his or her behavior is extremely disruptive.

2. Other interventions, in both academic and behavior domains, have been systematically attempted and have failed.

3. The student does not display symptoms of emotional problems such as anxiety.

4. The parents are supportive of trying medication.

5. The student can be adequately supervised so that medication is taken consistently.

6. The student understands the purpose of the medication and does not have a strong negative opinion about taking it. (DuPaul et al., 1991)

WWW Resources

You can access the website for CHADD (Children and Adults with Attention Deficit Disorder) at <http://www.chadd.org>. CHADD is a nonprofit organization dedicated to bettering the lives of those with ADD and their families.

Table 7.1 Overview of Medications Commonly Used for ADHD

Brand Name [Generic Name]	Type of Medication	Positives	Negatives	Comments
Ritalin (tablets) [Methylphenidate]	Psychostimulant	Excellent safety record. Easy to use and evaluate. Works in 15–20 minutes.	Lasts only 4 hours. Must be administered frequently.	The most frequently prescribed medication. Watch for tics or Tourette's syndrome.
Ritalin SR20 (sustained release) [Methylphenidate]	Psychostimulant	Excellent safety record. Easy to use and evaluate. Longer lasting (6–8 hours).	Does not work as well as Ritalin tablets.	Can be used along with regular Ritalin.
Dexedrine (tablets) [Dextroamphetamine]	Psychostimulant	Excellent safety record. Rapid onset (20–30 minutes).	Lasts only 4 hours. Must be administered frequently.	Some patients do well on Dexedrine tablets.
Dexedrine (spansules) [Dextroamphetamine]	Psychostimulant	Excellent safety record. Longer lasting (6–8 hours).	Slower onset (takes 1–2 hours).	Can be used along with Dexedrine tablets. Some patients do well.
Cylert (tablets) [Pemoline]	Psychostimulant	Long lasting (6–8 hours).	Slower onset (several hours).	Not as safe as the other stimulants. Requires liver function blood test every 6 months.
Tofranil and Norpramin (tablets) [Imipramine and desipramine]	Antidepressant	Long lasting (12–24 hours). Can be administered at night. Often works when stimulants do not.	Has possible side effects. May take 1–3 weeks for full effects. Should not be started and stopped abruptly.	High doses may improve depression symptoms and mood swings.
Catapress (patches or tablets) [Clonidine]	Antihypertensive medication	Patches long lasting (5–6 days). Can be used with Tourette's syndrome.	Tablets are shorter lasting (4 hours). Patches are expensive.	Tablets cost less. Often has positive effect on defiant behavior.

S O U R C E : From *Attention Deficit Disorders: Assessment and Teaching* by J. W. Lerner, B. Lowenthal, and S. R. Lerner. Copyright © 1995 Brooks/Cole Publishing Company, a division of International Thomson Publishing Inc., Pacific Grove, CA 93950. By permission of the publisher.

Before we close this discussion of ADHD, it is important to mention that this disorder still spurs heated discussions. Although most educators and physicians acknowledge the existence of ADHD (for example, Adams, 1994; Epstein, Shaywitz, Shaywitz, & Woolston, 1991), others question whether ADHD is a distinct condition (for example, Reid et al., 1994). Questions about the existence of ADHD usually center on the widely different prevalence rates reported, the difficulty in distinguishing ADHD from disabilities such as learning and emotional disabilities, and the absence of a consistent or unique approach for intervening for students with ADHD. Further, some professionals fear that medication has become too easy an intervention for students with attention problems. They comment that

FYI

The three medications most frequently administered to students with ADHD are Ritalin (methylphenidate), Dexedrine (dextroamphetamine), and Cylert (pemoline).

giving a pill can be perceived as more efficient than teaching students behavioral or cognitive strategies to monitor their own actions (Swanson et al., 1992), and that even though best practice demands that medication be accompanied by other interventions, too often this does not occur.

How Can You Accommodate Students Who Are Gifted and Talented?

In addition to students who are not able to meet typical curricular expectations, you will also have in your classroom students who have extraordinary abilities and skills. The term used to describe these students is **gifted and talented.** The federal definition for this group of students is stated in the 1988 Gifted and Talented Students Education Act (P.L. 100-297), which pertains to students who possess demonstrated or potential high-performance capability in intellectual, creative, specific academic and leadership areas, or the performing and visual arts. The federal definition further clarifies that these students need services in school that other students do not. However, unlike services offered through IDEA, federal legislation does not require specific services for gifted and talented students, and so the extent to which programs exist is largely determined by state and local policies.

An ongoing discussion in defining giftedness and serving these students concerns prevalence. As you have learned about several other groups of students with special needs, the reported prevalence of giftedness varies considerably from location to location. For example, the state of New Jersey identifies 9.9 percent of its students as gifted, whereas North Dakota identifies only 0.7 percent (Shriner, Ysseldyke, Gorney, & Franklin, 1993). This variability is probably due to many factors, including funding, variations in state definitions of giftedness, and the procedures used to identify students for gifted services.

Prevalence of giftedness is also greatly affected by two other factors. First, researchers and writers have recently begun questioning traditional concepts of intelligence (Armstrong, 1994; Gardner, 1993). They argue that measured IQ is far too narrow a concept of intelligence and that a person's ability to problem solve, especially when in a new situation, is a more useful way of thinking about intelligence. Gardner (1993) has proposed that there are **multiple intelligences** that describe the broad array of talents that students possess. These intelligences are outlined in Table 7.2. Because they range from the ability to use words and language effectively through the ability to produce and appreciate music, this concept of intelligence suggests that many individuals can be gifted and that their talents need to be developed in schools.

The second factor that affects the number of students identified as gifted is the notion of potential. Although some students who are gifted can be easily identified because they use their special abilities and are willing to be recognized for them, it is widely acknowledged that some gifted students go unnoticed. These students mask their skills from peers and teachers because low expectations are set for them or their unique needs are not nurtured. Groups at risk for being underidentified include young boys, adolescent girls, students who are highly gifted or talented who might be considered geniuses, students from minority groups, and students with disabilities.

Connections

The use of performance-based assessments, often helpful in identifying students who are gifted and talented, is discussed in more depth in Chapter 11.

Table 7.2   Summary of Multiple Intelligences

Type of Intelligence	Core Components
Linguistic	Sensitivity to the sounds, structure, meanings, and functions of words and language
Logical–Mathematical	Sensitivity to, and capacity to discern, logical or numerical patterns; ability to handle long chains of reasoning
Spatial	Capacity to perceive the visual–spatial world accurately and to perform transformations on one's initial perceptions
Bodily–Kinesthetic	Ability to control one's body movements and to handle objects skillfully
Musical	Ability to produce and appreciate rhythm, pitch, and timbre; appreciation of the forms of musical expressiveness
Interpersonal	Capacity to discern and respond appropriately to the moods, temperaments, motivations, and desires of other people
Intrapersonal	Access to one's own feeling life and the ability to discriminate among one's emotions; knowledge of one's own strengths and weaknesses

S O U R C E : From *Multiple Intelligences in the Classroom* by Thomas Armstrong, 1994, 6. Alexandria, VA: Association for Supervision and Curriculum Development. Copyright by ASCD. Reprinted with permission. All rights reserved.

Characteristics and Needs of Students Who Are Gifted and Talented

Students who are gifted and talented have a wide range of characteristics, and any one student considered gifted and talented can have just a few or many of these characteristics. Although early studies presented a limited number of descriptors, the studies were frequently completed with high achievers from privileged backgrounds and did not take into account the diverse nature of today's society (Terman, 1925). More recently, especially with the increasingly recognized need to address gifted-ness among the entire population, including students from diverse cultural groups, deciding whom to identify as gifted or talented and how to describe them has become complex. For example, as noted in the preceding section, some students with gifts or talents have gone unrecognized (Gallagher & Gallagher, 1994). Some of these students have avoided identification because of low self-esteem leading to avoidance of academic tasks (Davis & Rimm, 1994). These students sometimes have very poor academic test scores and may have poor relationships with peers. Other students have not been identified because of cultural bias in assessment and other identification procedures (Davis & Rimm, 1994). The following information about student characteristics is intended to provide an overview of students who are gifted and talented and should be viewed as a sample of what is known, not as a comprehensive summary.

Cognitive abilities and academic skills.   The area of cognitive functioning and academic skills is the most delineated aspect of gifted education. Students who are gifted and talented in the area of cognitive functioning generally have an extraordi-

Students who are gifted and talented are often difficult to identify and challenging to teach. What kinds of intelligence will you recognize in your students? Within your inclusive classroom, how will you address the academic and social-emotional needs of students who are gifted and talented?

nary amount of information, which they retain easily; a wide variety of interests; and high levels of language development and verbal ability. They also have advanced ability to comprehend information using accelerated and flexible thought processes, a heightened ability to recognize relationships between diverse ideas, a strong capacity to form and use conceptual frameworks, and an exceptional degree of persistent, goal-directed behavior (Clark, 1992). These students tend to be skilled problem solvers because they are better able than other students to pick out important information that will help them solve the problem and are more likely to monitor their problem-solving efforts (Rogers, 1986).

The cognitive abilities of students who are gifted and talented sometimes lead them to high academic achievement, but not always. Consider these two students who are gifted and talented: Belinda was identified as gifted and talented in second grade. She has been reading since the age of 3, seems as comfortable interacting with adults as with her peers, and invariably becomes the leader of the groups of children with whom she plays, even if they are older. She enjoys school immensely and wants to be a university professor when she grows up. Omar is also identified as gifted and talented. He has been taking violin and piano lessons since the age of 5, and his first music teacher recommended him to a local university program. In the sixth grade, Tomas is a veteran pianist, and he already plans to major in music theory when he goes to college. He has an unusual grasp of the subtleties of music, and he already offers his own interpretations of both classical and contemporary music. In his academic studies, however, Tomas is just slightly below average in achievement. He is also somewhat shy; he appears more comfortable with his musical instruments than with his peers.

Social and emotional needs.   Socially and emotionally, gifted and talented students can be well liked and emotionally healthy, or they can be unpopular and at risk for serious emotional problems. Affectively, they tend to have unusual sensitivity to others' feelings as well as highly developed personal emotional depth and intensity, a keen sense of humor that can be either supportive or hostile, and a sense of justice (Clark,

1992). They often set high expectations for themselves and others, which can lead to frustration when those expectations cannot be met (Mendaglio & Pyryt, 1995).

Because some gifted students have a superior ability to recognize and respond to others' feelings, they can be extremely popular with classmates and often sought after as helpmates. However, if they tend to "show off" their talents or repeatedly challenge adult authority, they may be perceived negatively by peers and teachers and have problems developing appropriate social relationships (Clark, 1992). For example, Ms. Ogden is concerned about eighth grader Esteban. On some days, Esteban seems to have just a four-word vocabulary: "I already know that." He says this to teachers, to peers, and to his parents about nearly any topic under discussion. Although it is often true that Esteban does know about the subjects that are being discussed, Ms. Ogden finds herself becoming annoyed at Esteban's style of interacting, and she knows the other students don't want to be grouped with Esteban because of it.

Another student who experiences social difficulties is Willis. He tends to think of himself as being different from his peers and so does not readily talk with others or join in class activities. When Willis does work in a group activity in class, he usually ends up criticizing the other students because they do not do their share of the work, know enough about the topic, write fast enough, or make the project look good enough. Willis tends to express his frustration through cynicism and cruel jokes. He states loudly and repeatedly that working in groups is a waste of his time. This attitude does not endear him to classmates.

Students' emotional status is one factor that contributes to their social skills. Some gifted and talented students are self-confident, have a strong positive self-concept, and are generally happy (Hoge & Renzulli, 1993). Others, however, feel isolated or alienated and can experience depression, low self-concept, and other emotional problems. If they find school boring and have difficulty forming friendships, students who are gifted and talented can also have poor attitudes toward learning and school activities in general. These students are at risk for dropping out of school (Davis & Rimm, 1994).

Behavior patterns. Students who are gifted and talented display the entire range of behaviors that other students do. They can be model students who participate and seldom cause problems, often serving as class leaders. In this capacity, students are sensitive to others' feelings and moderate their behavior based on others' needs (Winebrenner, 1992). However, because students who are gifted and talented often have an above-average capacity to understand people and situations, their negative behavior can sometimes be magnified compared with that of other students. This behavior can be displayed through an intense interest in a topic and refusal to change when requested by a teacher (Smith & Luckasson, 1995). Other behavior problems some students who are gifted and talented display include being bossy in group situations, purposely failing, and valuing and participating in counterculture activities (Van Tassel-Baska, Patton, & Prillaman, 1991; Winebrenner, 1992).

Interventions for Students Who Are Gifted and Talented

Although some school districts operate separate classes and programs for students who are gifted and talented, you will likely be responsible for meeting some or all of the needs of these students in your classroom (Sapon-Shevin, 1994). Four strategies most often used to challenge gifted and talented students are *enrichment,*

FYI

Students with disabilities have been underrepresented in gifted and talented programs. It is essential that students with learning disabilities, emotional disabilities, communication disorders, orthopedic impairments, sensory impairments, and other disabilities not be overlooked in nurturing giftedness.

Figure 7.1 **Eight Great Gripes of Gifted Kids**

1. No one explains what being gifted is all about—it's kept a big secret.
2. The stuff we do in school is too easy and it's boring.
3. Parents, teachers, and friends expect us to be perfect, to "do our best" all the time.
4. Kids often tease us about being smart.
5. Friends who really understand us are few and far between.
6. We feel too different and wish people would accept us for what we are.
7. We feel overwhelmed by the number of things we can do in life.
8. We worry a lot about world problems and feel helpless to do anything about them.

S O U R C E : From "The Eight Great Gripes of Gifted Kids: Responding to Special Needs" by Judy Galbraith, 1985, *Roeper Review, 8*(1), 16. Reprinted with permission of *Roeper Review,* P.O. Box 329, Bloomfield Hills, MI 48303-0329.

acceleration, sophistication, and *novelty* (Gallagher & Gallagher, 1994). These approaches should help you overcome the major complaints that gifted and talented students make about school, which are listed in Figure 7.1.

Enrichment is an instructional approach that provides students with information, materials, and assignments that enable them to elaborate on concepts being presented as part of the regular curriculum (Gallagher & Gallagher, 1994). This option requires you to find related information, prepare it for the students who need it, and create relevant activities for them. One teacher provided enrichment to her students in math (Winebrenner, 1992). She gave a pretest for each unit to the students who are gifted and talented, and if they had already mastered all the concepts, they were given a choice of alternative activities and assignments. If any concepts had not yet been mastered, the students were required to participate in the lesson on the days those concepts were taught. Students excused from lessons were expected to take a unit test with the rest of the class. The expectations for student work, options for enrichment, lessons to attend, and testing requirements were all summarized on a student learning contract. For enrichment to be effective, you need to ensure that students have opportunities to complete alternative assignments designed to encourage advanced thinking and product development, that they do such assignments in lieu of other work instead of as additional work, and that many learning resources are available to them both in and out of the classroom (Maker, 1993).

Acceleration is providing students with curriculum that takes them from their current level of learning and moves them forward (Feldhusen, Winkle, & Ehle, 1996). For example, Stephen is a student who is gifted in math. In middle school, he worked in an individualized and independent program to advance his skills. In high school, he completed the available curriculum during his freshman year and then began taking math courses at a local university. Stephen's program is based on acceleration. Acceleration can occur in one area, as is the case with Stephen, or can be total. For a few students, acceleration includes entering kindergarten early, skipping grades, taking correspondence courses, and attending residential high schools designed to enable students to work at their own rate through an advanced curriculum (Davis & Rimm, 1994).

Sophistication is a strategy in which teachers help students to see the principles or systems that underlie the content being learned by the rest of the class (Gallagher & Gallagher, 1994). For example, in an elementary school classroom, as students are reading stories and answering questions about vocabulary or the main idea, a student who is gifted might analyze how character, plot, and setting are intertwined in the story. In a music class, a student who is talented might be assigned to add harmony to a basic melody other students are learning.

Novelty is an approach in which teachers give students opportunities to explore traditional curricular content in alternative and unusual ways (Gallagher & Gallagher, 1994). For example, students might develop interviews with historical figures to gain their perspectives on world events of the past instead of simply reading about them. They might likewise be asked to create multimedia presentations that capture concepts being taught in a science class. Working with a mentor, using problem-based learning, and creating learning materials that other students can use are examples of novelty approaches for teaching students who are gifted and talented (Savoie & Hughes, 1994; Winebrenner, 1992).

Further examples of these four approaches to intervening with students who are gifted and talented are summarized in Table 7.3. The Case in Practice on page 236 illustrates a teacher using some of these strategies.

Some professionals contend that strategies for instructing students who are gifted or talented are appropriate for most students (Culross, 1997; Sapon-Shevin, 1995). They suggest that your job as a general education teacher is to design effective instruction for all students, and that this instruction will also meet the needs of students who are gifted and talented. To reach all your students, you will need to offer activities that address several ability levels at one time, that accommodate a variety of interest areas, and that enable students to integrate their learning. You must also have an overall plan for your instruction (Maker, 1993).

F Y I

Two variations on the instructional approaches presented here include *accelerated integrated learning* and *curriculum compacting*, in which students study the same themes and topics as the rest of the class but in greater detail or depth and with enhanced opportunities for application.

Table 7.3 **Sample Content Modification for Gifted Students**

| Modification | SUBJECT | | | |
	Math	Science	Language Arts	Social Studies
Acceleration	Algebra in fifth grade	Early chemistry and physics	Learning grammatical structure early	Early introduction to world history
Enrichment	Changing bases in number systems	Experimentation and data collecting	Short story and poetry writing	Reading biographies for historical insight
Sophistication	Mastering the laws of arithmetic	Learning the laws of physics	Mastering the structural properties of plays, sonnets, and so on	Learning and applying the principles of economics
Novelty	Probability and statistics	Science and its impact on society	Rewriting Shakespeare's tragedies with happy endings	Creating future societies and telling how they are governed

SOURCE: From James J. Gallagher and Shelagh A. Gallagher, *Teaching the Gifted Child* (4th ed.), 100. Copyright © 1994 by Allyn and Bacon. Reprinted by permission.

Case in Practice

Meeting the Needs of a Gifted Student

It is Wednesday morning and Ms. Ollendorf is preparing for the school day. She is thinking about what to do with Mary Jo, a student in her class who is clearly gifted in a number of areas. Yesterday afternoon in a conference with Mary Jo's mother, Ms. Ollendorf explained that she was concerned that Mary Jo was not doing as well in science as she had the potential to do. Mary Jo's mother offered this explanation:

Mary Jo has said probably 20 times during the past month that science is boring. She thinks the book is too simple and doesn't explain "interesting" things. She says she could finish her reports on the experiments before doing them because they are not complex enough to challenge her. She also said that she doesn't do the extra-credit work that you give students as an option because she can get perfect scores on everything anyway. Why would she want to do extra work?

In thinking about Mary Jo, Ms. Ollendorf has to admit that the child has made a few good points. Mary Jo is truly far beyond the science text in her understanding of most of the concepts addressed, and she does not seem pleased, as the other students do, when the day's activities include a science experiment. What concerns Ms. Ollendorf most, though, is the possibility of Mary Jo becoming uninterested in science when she so clearly has the potential to pursue a science-related career if she so chooses.

A week later, Ms. Ollendorf introduces a different sort of science to Mary Jo. She has gathered advanced supplemental science textbooks and has contacted several friends who work in local businesses to be mentors for Mary Jo. She has also spoken with a friend who is a science education professor about how to challenge Mary Jo. She offers Mary Jo these options:

1. She will take unit tests prior to instruction.
2. If she scores at least 80 percent on a unit test, she can work 4 days per week in the alternative science materials. If she does not achieve 80 percent, she will participate in the lessons on the parts of the unit she has not mastered.
3. For each unit of instruction completed in this manner, Mary Jo is to select and create a product that will demonstrate the science concepts she has explored. For example, during the unit on matter, she may choose to explore the gas laws and create and present an experiment demonstrating her knowledge.
4. Mary Jo will have a once-per-month visit with a mentor. Mentors might include a high school student, one of the local businesspeople, or another teacher.

REFLECTIONS

What type of gifted student is Mary Jo? If you had to make a prediction, how do you think she behaves in other subject areas? What did Ms. Ollendorf do to make science a more challenging subject for Mary Jo? Which of the four approaches to providing appropriate instruction to gifted and talented students did Ms. Ollendorf use? What other strategies could Ms. Ollendorf implement to expand Mary Jo's science instruction further?

What Are the Needs of Students from Culturally Diverse Backgrounds?

The racial, cultural, and linguistic diversity of U.S. classrooms has been growing steadily, and all indications are that it will continue to do so. For example, between 1984 and 1991, elementary school enrollment rose by 11 percent. However, the enrollment of Anglo European American students rose by just 5 percent, whereas Hispanic American enrollment increased by 45 percent; African American enrollment increased by 17 percent; and enrollment by Asian Americans, Pacific Islanders, and Native Americans rose by 28 percent. Approximately 31 percent of all elementary school students are members of racial and ethnic minority groups (Snyder, 1993).

Evidence suggests that students from cultures other than Anglo European sometimes experience an extraordinarily high failure rate in school. For example, although the dropout rate for all students is approximately 25 percent, approximately 40 percent of Hispanic American students and 48 percent of Native American students do not graduate from high school (Wyman, 1993). The reasons for these students' failure to complete school are complex and interrelated, but involve several identifiable factors (Stephen, Varble, & Taitt, 1993). First, students from racial and ethnic minority groups often lack role models since most teachers are from the majority Anglo European culture. Second, societal expectations and realities for these students are often contradictory. Although they are told that they can meet high educational standards, they may be discriminated against in assessment for and access to advanced programs. Third, instructional practices can negatively affect students. In particular, textbooks with cultural biases can promote stereotypes and omit culturally important information. Teaching practices that do not allow for opportunities for student-centered learning also can put students from different cultures at a disadvantage, because students' background and experiences may lead them to learn more effectively from small-group peer interactions. A mix of teaching approaches is needed. Finally, school policies and organization can penalize students. For example, few schools operate mentor programs specifically designed to connect students from diverse cultures with leaders in business, industry, and education. These contacts can be essential for helping students succeed.

The relationship among school failure, special education, and diverse student needs is not a comfortable one (Grossman, 1995). Historically, students from racial or cultural minorities were sometimes inappropriately placed in special education programs based on discriminatory assessment practices (Drew, Logan, & Hardman, 1992). Concern about this issue continues today (Carter & Goodwin, 1994; Ford, 1992). This practice can be attributed at least partly to an inappropriate school perspective that students with non-Anglo European values or those who speak languages other than English need to be remediated in some way (Grossman, 1995). Current programs that emphasize multicultural education for both teachers and students are designed to increase sensitivity to cultural and linguistic diversity, which should counteract this bias.

Cultural Awareness

Understanding the characteristics of students who are members of racially and culturally diverse groups involves recognizing that the contradictions between some of these students' home and community experiences and the expectations placed on them at school can lead to learning and behavior problems. It also includes acknowledging that teachers sometimes misunderstand students and their parents, which can lead to miscommunication, distrust, and negative school experiences.

The make-up of today's general education classrooms reflects the racial, linguistic, and cultural diversity of the communities they serve. The Technology Notes feature on pages 238–239 describes how computers can be used to foster students'

Check Your Learning

Why are students with culturally and linguistically diverse backgrounds given special attention in a textbook about students with special needs?

Cultural Awareness

By the year 2020 it is estimated that 28 percent of the population under the age of 18 will be Hispanic, up from the current 11 percent. Some 40 percent of Hispanic children live in poverty, and in at least some cases, the children and mothers may be homesick for their family, language, and customs (Holman, 1997).

Cultural Awareness

Cultural awareness includes understanding that individuals and families experience various degrees of assimilation and that the United States has been a culturally diverse society for hundreds of years. Teachers should not assume cultural traits on the basis of ethnic identity alone.

Technology Notes

Using Computer Technology to Foster Cultural Awareness

Technology can be used effectively to build a greater understanding of world politics and cultural differences. In the following lesson plan developed by Roblyer, Edwards, and Havriluk (1997), the teacher assists students in using a variety of technologies as they develop a multicultural resource center for the employees of an international business.

Computers with access to the World Wide Web offer a wealth of multicultural learning opportunities.

Activity:	Training for Cultural Awareness
Level:	Grades 9–12
Purpose of Activity:	To familiarize students with the intricacies of other cultures through the development of a project
Instructional Activity:	**Setting the Stage: The Training Department Dilemma.** Over the past 2 years your company, NUTECH, has experienced a surge in overseas business. This has resulted in a tremendous increase in the amount of foreign travel for NUTECH employees, who have conducted business in locales where they knew very little about the local cultures. The employees report that they believe that this has put them at a distinct disadvantage, and they would like to get training on how to relate more effectively to indigenous populations when traveling abroad.
	Your training team has been assigned the task of putting together a multicultural center that will provide the employees with an easy-to-access compilation of resources. At a team meeting, a brainstorming session identified several ideas for potentially valuable resources.

cultural awareness. However, as the preceding discussion of cultural bias suggests, such awareness and sensitivity also must be cultivated among general and special education teachers.

If you live in an area in which many different cultures are represented in a single classroom, the thought of learning about all of them can be intimidating. It is probably not possible, nor necessary, to learn many details about all the cultures of your students (Wallis, 1993). However, it is your responsibility to learn fundamental characteristics students might have because of their backgrounds. For example, some students might keep their questions to themselves instead of asking you because of concern about interacting with the teacher, who is perceived as an authority figure.

Ideas for Multicultural Resource Center

- **Brochure.** The brochure should include a brief description of the history of the country along with relevant geographic and cultural data. It would be helpful to stress any cultural difference that visitors should recognize; for example, in Thailand it is considered very rude to sit with one leg crossed over the other with a foot pointing at another person. Students should use a desktop publishing or word processing program to develop the brochure. Graphics should enhance the layout.

- **Videotape.** Create a videotape that provides useful information to a traveler in a specific country. The information should enable that person to function more effectively in the local culture by stressing customs, values, and historical perspectives.

- **Bar-coded videodisc presentation.** Develop a bar-code-driven program that accesses relevant segments of a videodisc that pertain to a specific culture. Students should use a bar-code generator and a word processor for the project materials, which they should mount on tagboard and laminate.

- **Multimedia display.** Create a multimedia display that provides suggestions for travelers in a particular country. Video segments would enhance the program, either imported into the program or through interaction with a videodisc player.

- **Database.** Develop a database of resources for each country to which employees might travel. This should include magazine and newspaper articles, videos, books, etc. Students could access much of this information via the Internet.

Suggestions for Teacher: For this activity, students will need to choose a country on which to focus. They must understand the purpose of the product—to provide a resource for someone who needs help functioning in another country's culture. To develop a quality product, students will need to strive to truly understand the culture of the chosen country. Encourage students to use telecommunications resources to locate information. The Internet may offer them an opportunity to actually converse with citizens of the chosen country. They may also have access to foreign nationals living nearby.

SOURCE: Roblyer, M. D., Edwards, J., & Havriluk, M. A. (1997). *Integrating educational technology into teaching*. Columbus, OH: Merrill.

If you understand this reticence, you can make a special effort to initiate interactions with those students. Further, when a student displays behavior that you find troublesome, you should determine if a cultural reason prompted the behavior before responding to it or assuming that it represents misbehavior. This information can be learned by talking with students, their families, or teachers experienced in working with students from the culture, or by consulting your district's print or video resources on cultural diversity. Of course, you should also keep in mind that not all students from diverse backgrounds will encounter these problems, nor will all families from racial or ethnic minority groups use discipline practices different from those schools use.

Connections

The role of cultural awareness in teacher–parent communication and in professional collaboration is introduced in Chapters 2 and 3.

The INCLUDE strategy can be a valuable tool for making decisions about instruction for students from culturally and linguistically diverse groups. First, you should consider the demands of the classroom setting, and then identify strengths and interests that students bring to the learning environment. Next, you should look for potential problem areas across your entire instructional program and use that information to brainstorm ideas for ameliorating the problems and select those with the most potential for success. As you go through this process, it is essential to monitor student progress and make adjustments as needed.

The impact of cultural and linguistic diversity in educational settings can be examined from three perspectives: how cultural factors affect student behavior, how teaching approaches can be tailored to culturally diverse groups, and how communication with non-native English speakers can be enhanced. We examine each perspective briefly.

Cultural values and student behavior.   Varying cultural values have an impact on students' behaviors and the way educators interpret these behaviors. For example, for some Native American students, time is a fluid concept not necessarily bound by clocks. A student might come to school "late" by Anglo European culture standards that measure time precisely, but "on time" according to events happening at the student's home. Another example of the differences between Anglo European standards and some students' cultures concerns school participation. Hispanic American students sometimes are more likely to participate when they have established a close relationship with their teachers and peers (Wallis, 1993). Contrast this fact with the common high school structure in which one teacher sees as many as 180 students each day and often uses an instructional format that minimizes interactions. In such settings, Hispanic American students can be at a great disadvantage. Similarly, recent research suggests that some African American students learn better in cooperative situations (Wallis, 1993). If these small-group learning experiences are not offered in the classroom, some students are being denied access to a potentially powerful learning opportunity. Table 7.4 summarizes traditional values from three different cultures. What impact might these values have on students' learning characteristics and instructional needs?

Informed instructional decision making.   Decisions about teaching approaches occur by matching the needs of students from culturally diverse backgrounds to instructional approaches (Banks, 1993). For example, not only many African American, but also many Hispanic American and Asian American students respond well to cooperative rather than competitive learning environments (Guild, 1994). Such approaches should become integral to your teaching. Likewise, since traditional Native American students dislike responding individually and out loud in a large-group situation, you may need to create opportunities for individual contacts and quiet participation.

Cross-cultural communication.   For students who do not speak English as their native language, school can be a frustrating experience. These are examples of common problems: Students who do not use English proficiently can easily be discriminated against when they are assessed. As noted earlier, students could be identified as needing special education just because their English skills are limited; particular care must be taken to ensure that non-native speakers are not mistakenly labeled. Another example concerns the perceptions of teachers and classmates. Students

Check Your Learning

What types of communication problems can occur between school professionals and parents of students from racially and ethnically diverse groups?

Table 7.4 **Examples of Differences in Traditional Values**

Polynesian/ Native American	Asian	Western
1. Individual valued as part of family	1. Individual valued as part of family	1. Individual valued apart from family
2. Self-control, humility	2. Self-control, humility	2. Self-expression, pride
3. Reciprocate within family system	3. Submit to family rule	3. Negotiate within family
4. Spiritual harmony	4. Spiritual balance	4. Spiritual duality
5. Reverence/respect for life	5. Partnership with nature	5. Mastery over nature
6. Cooperation, mutual help	6. Cooperation, mutual help	6. Competition, self-reliance
7. Loyalty, obedience, shared responsibility	7. Obedience, duty, honor	7. Self-pride, honor, duty
8. Do what is necessary, play more	8. Work hard, play less	8. Work hard, then play

SOURCE: Reprinted with the permission of Prentice-Hall, Inc. from *Exceptional Children in Focus* (5th ed.) by James R. Patton, James S. Payne, James M. Kauffman, Gwenth B. Brown, and Ruth Ann Payne. Copyright © 1991 by Macmillan College Publishing Company.

with limited English skills are sometimes considered deficient; teachers might have difficulty understanding students and might assume they have limited ability, and peers may exclude students from social activities because of language differences. These language-related issues sometimes lead to a third problem, namely, a belief that for students to learn when English is not their primary language, they must be segregated from other students. Suggestions for helping students with limited English proficiency are included in the Professional Edge on pages 242–243.

For students from culturally and linguistically diverse backgrounds, home–school communication is critical. You might have difficulty in even basic communication, though, because of language differences and the lack of availability of an interpreter. Another problem you may face concerns cultural values and parent responses to school personnel (Dennis & Giangreco, 1996). For example, in traditional Asian American families, pride and shame are often emphasized, and indirectness is valued. Imagine a parent conference in which an insensitive teacher describes in detail the academic and learning problems an Asian American child is having and directly asks the parents whether they can assist in carrying out a home–school behavior change program. If they follow traditional Asian values, the parents might be humiliated by the public accounting of their child's failures and embarrassed at the teacher's direct and unnecessary request for their assistance.

A third example of the importance of communication relates to the parents' perceptions of school and how they should interact with school personnel contrasted to school staff expectations for parent involvement. For example, the parents of some students might find school foreign and intimidating, and they might believe that their role is to listen passively to what school personnel say. For students from diverse

Professional Edge

Helping Students with Limited English Proficiency

As our society continues to become more diverse, you will be likely to have students with limited English proficiency (LEP) in your class. The fact that these students have LEP does not mean that they cannot participate actively in and benefit from verbal instruction in your classroom. In fact, active participation will maximize the language benefits they will accrue from your instruction. The following suggestions will help you include students with LEP in verbal instruction in your classroom (Simich-Dudgeon, McCreedy, & Schleppegrell, 1988–1989).

1. Students with LEP may not know the right words to use when they are answering teachers' questions. Before teaching each lesson, identify new and important vocabulary. You can help students understand the meanings of words by using them in relevant contexts. Here is an example of how a teacher effectively defines a word:

Teacher: The first question says, "Name the properties used to describe the powders." We didn't call them properties, but what words did we use to describe the powders? Eric?

Student: Color, shape, smell . . . [The teacher writes these words on the board.]

Teacher: These things are the properties of the powders . . .

Here is an example of how to guide a student in using the right words:

Student: . . . because the soap makes the water heavy?

Teacher: Is *heavy* a good word to use for that? When something flattens that way, what kind of power do we say it has?

Student: Adhesive force?

Teacher: Good.

2. Sometimes students know the answer but express it in a way that is hard for the teacher to understand. When you realize that a student is having difficulty expressing a correct answer cohesively, let him or her know that the answer is basically correct. Then, rephrase the response and redirect the question to another student:

Teacher: What is the most important thing to remember?

Student: Put the zero, . . . you times . . .

Teacher: [To the whole class] That's correct—who can say it in another way?

3. Make explicit your expectations for a good verbal response. Here are some features of a good verbal response you may want to stress:

a. Using appropriate words (relevant vocabulary)

b. Including details and description; being specific

c. Giving a complete, well-organized answer

d. Giving an on-topic, thoughtful answer, not just guessing; showing you know what you are talking about

e. Giving the correct answer

cultural backgrounds who have disabilities, it is particularly important to be sure that adequate information is communicated to parents about the student's instructional program and the procedures used in special education (Sontag & Schacht, 1994). You will share this responsibility with special education professionals.

Another example of potential home–school misunderstanding related to cultural diversity concerns discipline. Some discipline practices Anglo European educators

Make a list of these features on the chalkboard. As students answer, tell them good qualities about their answers as well as areas they can improve.

4. If you cannot understand a student's English, try these two techniques:

a. Repeat what the student says, with question intonation, to check your comprehension of the answer.

Student: Forty-seven

Teacher: Forty-seven? Right . . .

b. Tell the student you do not understand. ("Sorry, I don't understand; please say it again.")

To be most effective, these techniques should be explained to all students in the class so that everyone expects them and feels comfortable using them.

5. Rephrase your questions and the answers other children give so that students with LEP have more than one opportunity to understand what is said. For example, when you see a child is having trouble understanding, change questions that require full content answers into questions that give students a simpler choice:

Teacher: What happened when you added the drops to the powder? . . . [no answer] . . . Did the powder change color when you added the drops?

6. When students' grammar is incorrect, focus on the content of what the child says and respond to the meaning, while modeling the correct form. One strategy is to repeat what the student said, supplying the correct grammatical form:

Student: Did the kids went outside already?

Teacher: Did the kids go outside already? Yes, they did.

Student: Some them low.

Teacher: Yes, some of the books are on the low shelf.

Writing the correct version of students' responses on the board is a good way to model good grammar without embarrassing the student with an overt correction:

Teacher: Okay, what did this prove? Juan?

Student: If it purple, it's with starch.

Teacher: [Writes on board] What did this prove?

"If it turned purple, it had starch in it. If it didn't turn purple, there was no starch in it."

7. For students who do not actively participate in class discussions, check to see if different cultural conventions for classroom participation might be the cause. Some cultures do not value children who volunteer answers or speak out. Remember also that students with LEP can understand before they can speak. Their seemingly passive behavior may mask their active role in attending to and learning from the interaction.

Ask students who have recently immigrated to the United States to share with you and their classmates how schools are organized in their native countries, how their teachers teach, how teachers signal their expectations, and what behaviors are expected from students. Parents of these students might be invited to talk to the class and share their experiences. Parents and children with limited English proficiency need to feel proud of their heritage to be motivated to learn and be proud of their new country.

might consider abusive are widely accepted in some cultures (McIntyre & Silva, 1992). In some low-income Hispanic American families from the Caribbean Islands, children kneel on uncooked rice as a punishment for misbehavior. In some unassimilated Asian American families, children are locked out of the house as punishment if they are perceived as forgetting their own cultural values. In some Vietnamese American families, children have pierced ears. When they misbehave, they

Cultural diversity offers rich opportunities for learning but is also a source of misunderstandings that can lead to school failure. What steps will you take to ensure that you are responding appropriately to all your students as individual members of diverse cultural groups? How will you promote student acceptance of cultural differences in your classroom?

are tied by their ear to a doorknob (McIntyre & Silva, 1992). Practices such as these are not typical in Anglo European American culture, and teachers might consider them a reason to report the family for abuse or neglect. Further, teachers' perceptions can easily be telegraphed to parents, leading to less than ideal home–school interactions. Of course, discipline practices such as these are not common in all families from cultural and ethnic minority groups. Through clear communication and a willingness to understand your students' backgrounds, you can avoid stereotyping.

Multicultural and Bilingual Education

Do It!

Find out whether your state offers a separate credential for bilingual special education teachers. If possible, visit a bilingual special education program in a local school district.

Creating a classroom in which students' cultures are acknowledged and valued is a fundamental characteristic of **multicultural education,** that is, curriculum and instruction that reflects the diversity of our society. Multicultural education begins with examining how you decorate your classroom and how you select learning materials (Banks, 1993). Do your bulletin board displays include students from ethnic and cultural minority groups? When you portray historical events, are members of several cultural groups included? Does your classroom contain stories or literature about successful individuals from a variety of cultures? Is respect for diversity infused throughout your curriculum? Two points are especially noteworthy regarding multicultural education. First, professionals agree that multicultural education should not be an event that occurs for one week out of each school year. It is better addressed through ongoing inclusion of multicultural information in students' education activities. Second, multicultural education is not a topic that is confined to social studies, as some educators believe. It should pervade all subject areas, being reflected in the stories or literature addressed in language arts or English, in

Professional Edge

Assessing Your Effectiveness as a Teacher in a Culturally Diverse Classroom

As a teacher, it is your responsibility to respond positively to the cultural and linguistic diversity in your classroom. These questions can help you focus on making your teaching culturally sensitive:

- Do I have an understanding of the cultures that are represented in my classroom?

- Am I aware of culture-based learning styles?

- Are my expectations as high for students of color as for Anglo students?

- Do I make conscious efforts to engage all students in learning activities?

- Do I make conscious efforts to give equivalent attention and encouragement to all students?

- Do I participate in staff development programs that help teachers better understand student diversity?

- Do the staff development programs for my school and district address multicultural and bilingual education issues?

- Am I open to identifying racial and cultural biases in myself, my students, and my curriculum materials?

- Do I use methodology that fosters integration (for example, cooperative learning)?

- Do my instruction and methodology conflict with the cultural beliefs of any students in my classroom?

- Do I use a variety of tasks, measures, and materials in assessing student competencies to avoid inadvertent bias in assessment?

SOURCE: Adapted from *How to Respond to Your Culturally Diverse Student Population* by Sarah LaBrec Wyman, 1993, Alexandria, VA: Association for Supervision and Curriculum Development. Copyright © 1993 by ASCD. Reprinted with permission. All rights reserved.

assignments given in science and math classes, and in the community contacts students make in vocational classes.

The school in which you teach might also offer **bilingual education programs.** Bilingual education programs are based on the assumption that students need to learn English by being immersed in the language environment, but that until a level of proficiency in English is achieved, many students do not learn concepts and skills from English language instruction (Bennett, 1995). In bilingual programs, students spend part of the school day receiving instruction in core academic areas in their native language and the remainder of the day with English-speaking students. For students receiving special education services, a **bilingual special education program** staffed by a bilingual special education teacher may be provided in which students receive individualized services designed to strengthen their learning and demonstrate respect for their language and culture (Díaz-Rico & Weed, 1995).

If you develop curiosity about your students' cultures and languages, you will be sensitive to their learning needs and responsive to them. To guide you in looking at the curriculum and instruction you will use, the Professional Edge provides a list of questions for successful teaching in a diverse classroom.

WWW Resources

You may wish to locate more resources related to multicultural education. One good site that has many listed resources, including information about African American and Native American children, is <http://curry.edschool.virginia.edu/go/multicultural/teachers.html>.

How Can You Meet the Needs of Students Who Are At Risk?

In addition to all the other special needs you will find among your students, you are likely to encounter one that is found in virtually every public school classroom in the country. That special need is being at risk for school failure. Students who are at risk are students who have been exposed to some condition that negatively affects their learning. Stevens and Price (1992) include the following groups in their list of students at risk:

- Newborns who have been prenatally exposed to drugs, including alcohol
- Over 300,000 school-age children who are homeless each year
- More than 3 million children who have been exposed to toxic levels of lead
- Between 1 million and 2 million children annually who are abused or neglected
- Approximately 37,000 babies born annually weighing less than 3.5 pounds who survive because of medical interventions

Many other students are also considered at risk. Students who are bullies and those who are victims are included on the list as well as those who have recently experienced the death of someone close to them. Students who are school phobic are at risk, as are those considering suicide, those who are considered physically unattractive, and those who are socially underdeveloped. Slow learners, children who live in poverty, teenage mothers, and school dropouts are also at risk. It is difficult to understand the range of problems students face and the tremendous impact these problems have on their lives. One school district committee, formed to identify the district's at-risk learners and to create options for helping them succeed, became overwhelmed at the enormity of their task. One teacher finally suggested that at-risk students were all students who were not achieving in the way teachers thought they could. Another conceptualization of at-risk learners is included in the Professional Edge.

You might be wondering why students who are at risk are discussed in a text about students with disabilities. The reasons include these: First, with a well-designed education, many students who are at risk for school failure succeed in school. The strategies for accommodating the needs of students with disabilities are usually effective for students at risk, strategies that are discussed in the remaining chapters of this text. Second, it is well known that effective early school experiences for students who are at risk can establish a pattern of success in school learning (Bowman, 1994). Without such experiences, students at risk are more likely to be identified as having learning or emotional disabilities. Third, many students with disabilities also are students at risk. Increasing your understanding of risk factors and approaches for working with students at risk benefits all your students at risk for school failure.

Characteristics and Needs of Students At Risk

Cognitively, socially and emotionally, behaviorally, and physically, students considered at risk are as diverse as students in the general school population. What

Professional Edge

Identifying Students At Risk

Many authors have addressed the topic of students at risk for school failure and failure in later life. In an effort to better understand issues related to at-risk students, the professional education organization Phi Delta Kappa completed a national study of the topic. As part of their work, they conducted a literature search and identified 45 factors associated with being at risk, and educators ranked these factors according to their importance.

1. Attempted suicide during the past year
2. Used drugs or engaged in substance abuse
3. Has been a drug "pusher" during the past year
4. Has a negative sense of self-esteem
5. Was involved in a pregnancy during the past year
6. Was expelled from school during the past year
7. Consumes alcohol regularly
8. Was arrested for illegal activity
9. Parents have negative attitudes toward education
10. Has several brothers or sisters who dropped out
11. Was sexually or physically abused last year
12. Failed two courses last school year
13. Was suspended from school twice last year
14. Was absent more than 20 days last year
15. Parent drinks excessively and is an alcoholic
16. Was retained (held back) in grade
17. One parent attempted suicide last year
18. Scored below 20th percentile on a standardized test
19. Other family members used drugs during the past year
20. Attended three or more schools during the past 5 years
21. Average grades were below C last school year
22. Was arrested for driving while intoxicated
23. Has an IQ score below 90
24. Parents divorced or separated last year
25. Father is an unskilled laborer who is unemployed
26. Father or mother died during the past year
27. Diagnosed as being in special education
28. English is not the language used most often in the home
29. Mother is an unskilled laborer who is unemployed
30. Lives in an inner-city, urban area
31. Mother is only parent living in the home
32. Is a year older than other students in the same grade
33. Mother did not graduate from high school
34. Father lost his job during the past year
35. Was dropped from an athletic team during the past year
36. Experienced a serious illness or accident
37. Does not participate in extracurricular activities
38. Parent had a major change in health status
39. Had a close friend who died during the past year
40. Had a brother or sister who died during the past year
41. Father did not graduate from high school
42. Changed schools during the year
43. Changed place of residence during the past year
44. Has three or more brothers and sisters
45. Is the youngest child in the family

SOURCE: From "Special Education and Students At Risk: Findings from a National Study" by T. P. Lombardi, K. S. Odell, and D. E. Novotny, 1990, *Remedial and Special Education*, *12*(1), 56–62. Copyright © 1990 by PRO-ED, Inc. Reprinted by permission.

distinguishes them from other students is the high likelihood that they will drop out of school prior to earning a high school diploma and that they will experience difficulty throughout their lives. Some also share other characteristics and needs, including a tendency to be noncompliant, problems in monitoring their learning and behavior, language delays, difficulties with social relationships, and problems understanding the consequences of their behaviors (Stevens & Price, 1992). To illustrate further the needs these students have, three representative groups of at-risk students will be discussed briefly: children living in poverty, including those who are homeless; children who have been abused or neglected; and children who live in homes in which substance abuse occurs. Keep in mind that although this discussion treats each group as distinct for the sake of clarity, any single student could be in all three groups.

Students who live in poverty. Students who live in poverty often come to school tired and preoccupied from the stresses they experience in their lives away from school (Kirst, 1991). They might not have nutritious meals, a safe and warm place to play and sleep, or needed supplies to complete homework. They are sometimes worried about their family's circumstances, and older students might be expected to work evenings and weekends to help support the family or to miss school in order to babysit for younger siblings. Students living in poverty also are more likely than advantaged students to experience parental neglect, witness violence, and change schools and residences frequently.

Like Kham, whom you met at the beginning of this chapter, some poor families are homeless; it has been estimated that anywhere from 68,000 to 500,000 children are homeless on any single night (Linehan, 1992). Further, many more families are in temporary living arrangements with relatives or friends. Homelessness results in many educational problems. Students sometimes leave their neighborhood school when they move to a shelter or stay with family or friends. This can leave gaps in their learning. Other students are placed in foster care when the family is homeless, and this arrangement affects their social and emotional adjustment. In addition to learning problems, students who live in poverty or who are homeless sometimes (although not always) display acting-out, restless, or aggressive behavior; depression; regressive behaviors; and anxiety (Linehan, 1992).

Students who are abused or neglected. A second group of students at risk are the approximately one million who are abused and neglected each year. Although the precise meaning of the term varies from state to state, **child abuse** generally refers to situations in which a parent or other caregiver inflicts or allows others to inflict injury on a child, or permits a substantial risk of injury to exist (Bear, Schenk, & Buckner, 1992/1993; Tower, 1989). **Child neglect** is used to describe situations in which a parent or other caregiver fails to provide the necessary supports for a child's well-being, whether these are basic food and shelter, education, medical care, or other items. Figure 7.2 summarizes the demographic characteristics of students who are abused and of the individuals who abuse them.

Some students who have been abused or neglected will have visible signs such as bruises, burns, or other untreated physical problems. They might also complain

Figure 7.2 **Child Abuse: A National Profile**

In 1995, over 3 million children were reported to child protective services because of abuse or neglect. 996,000 of these cases were substantiated. Between 1986 and 1995, child abuse reporting levels increased 49%.

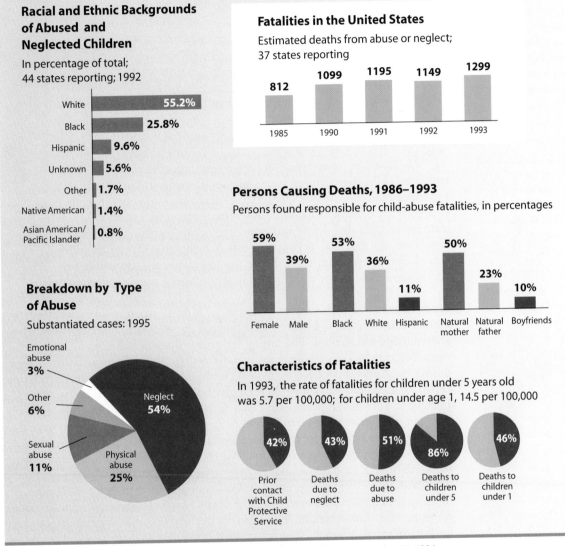

Racial and Ethnic Backgrounds of Abused and Neglected Children

In percentage of total; 44 states reporting; 1992

- White: 55.2%
- Black: 25.8%
- Hispanic: 9.6%
- Unknown: 5.6%
- Other: 1.7%
- Native American: 1.4%
- Asian American/Pacific Islander: 0.8%

Breakdown by Type of Abuse

Substantiated cases: 1995

- Emotional abuse 3%
- Other 6%
- Sexual abuse 11%
- Physical abuse 25%
- Neglect 54%

Fatalities in the United States

Estimated deaths from abuse or neglect; 37 states reporting

- 1985: 812
- 1990: 1099
- 1991: 1195
- 1992: 1149
- 1993: 1299

Persons Causing Deaths, 1986–1993

Persons found responsible for child-abuse fatalities, in percentages

- Female: 59%
- Male: 39%
- Black: 53%
- White: 36%
- Hispanic: 11%
- Natural mother: 50%
- Natural father: 23%
- Boyfriends: 10%

Characteristics of Fatalities

In 1993, the rate of fatalities for children under 5 years old was 5.7 per 100,000; for children under age 1, 14.5 per 100,000

- Prior contact with Child Protective Service: 42%
- Deaths due to neglect: 43%
- Deaths due to abuse: 51%
- Deaths to children under 5: 86%
- Deaths to children under 1: 46%

SOURCE: From "Teaching Parents Not to Abuse" by M. A. Lev and K. Brandon, September 18, 1994, *Indianapolis Star,* D1. Reprinted with permission of Knight-Ridder/ Tribune Information Services. *Child abuse and neglect statistics* at <http://www.childabuse.org/rsrch2.html>.

of hunger. Germinario, Cervalli, and Ogden (1992) also note the following student behaviors that might signal to school professionals the presence of abuse or neglect:

- Is fearful of contacting parents
- Reports injury by parents

F Y I

In addition to the general terms *abuse* and *neglect*, the following terms are frequently used to describe maltreatment of children: physical abuse, sexual abuse, emotional abuse, physical neglect, educational neglect, and emotional neglect.

- Displays aggression
- Appears withdrawn
- Asks for or steals food
- Arrives early to or departs late from school
- Reports no supervision at home
- Is fatigued, falls asleep
- Is reluctant to change for gym or participate
- Exhibits regressive, infantile behavior
- Runs away or displays other delinquent behavior
- Lags developmentally
- Shows precocious or bizarre sexual behavior (pp. 134–135)

You should be aware that you have a legal and ethical obligation to report any suspected child abuse among your students (Pearson, 1996). Although the specific reporting requirements for teachers vary from state to state, federal law requires that every state maintain a hotline and other systems for reporting abuse, and every state has statutes that define abuse and neglect and establish reporting procedures. If you suspect that one of your students is being abused, you should follow your school district's procedures for reporting it. If you are unsure about those procedures, you should notify your principal, school social worker, or school nurse.

Students who live with substance abuse.   A third group of students at risk for school failure are those involved in substance abuse. Some students' parents have abused drugs and alcohol. The impact on students begins before they are born and often affects them throughout their lives. Babies born to mothers who drink heavily during pregnancy may have a medical condition called **fetal alcohol syndrome (FAS)**, or a milder form known as **fetal alcohol effects (FAE)**. Babies with FAS or FAE are smaller than expected, may have facial and other slight physical abnormalities, and often experience learning and behavior problems when they go to school. The prevalence estimate for these disorders is 1 in 500 to 600 children born for FAS and 1 in 300 to 350 children born for FAE (Burgess & Streissguth, 1992). Students with FAS or FAE tend to use poor judgment, leaving a situation when things do not go as planned or failing to predict the consequences of their behavior (Burgess & Streissguth, 1992). Babies born to mothers who have been abusing cocaine or other drugs are often low in weight. They also are likely to become overstimulated, which leads to an array of irritable behaviors (Griffith, 1992). When these children reach school age, they are likely to experience a wide variety of learning and behavior problems. Some are low achievers, and others may become eligible for special education services. They may be inattentive, hyperactive, and impulsive.

Researchers estimate that some 12 million children grow up in homes where alcohol or drugs are abused (Germinario et al., 1992). They are at risk because of a number of factors. For example, they are at risk for being neglected or abused. In homes in which drugs are abused, these students may be passive recipients of drugs that can be inhaled or may accidentally ingest other drugs (Griffith, 1992). Students who live in homes in which alcohol or drugs are abused display at least several of the following characteristics at school:

- Poor or erratic attendance
- Frequent physical complaints and visits to the nurse
- Morning tardiness, especially on Mondays
- Inappropriate fear about the possibility of parents being contacted
- Equating any drinking with being drunk or being alcoholic
- Perfectionistic and/or compulsive behavior
- Difficulty concentrating, hyperactivity
- Sudden emotional outbursts, crying, temper tantrums
- Regression (for example, thumb sucking)
- Friendlessness, isolation, withdrawn behavior
- Passivity but becoming active or focused during drug/alcohol awareness lessons
- Lingering after drug/alcohol awareness lessons to ask unrelated questions
- Signs of abuse or neglect (Germinario et al., 1992, p. 106)

A third group of students affected by substance abuse includes students who themselves abuse drugs or alcohol. It is estimated that 18 percent of students have used illicit drugs by the time they are 17 years old, and half of the young adults aged 18 to 25 have done so (Drugs & Drug Abuse Education, 1994). Approximately 90 percent of high school seniors report having used alcohol sometime in their lives, and 60 percent report having used it in the past 30 days (Morgan, 1993). Students with emotional disabilities are at particularly high risk for alcohol and drug abuse. Students who are substance abusers often have poor diets, sleep disturbances, feel a great deal of stress, and are at risk for depression and suicide. In school, they typically recall only information taught while they are sober, interact poorly with peers and teachers, and display excessive risk-taking behavior.

As you can see, students who live in poverty, who are abused or neglected, or who live with substance abuse, as well as other at-risk students, collectively have many characteristics and needs that affect their learning. Although some of them are resilient and will not suffer long-term consequences because of their stressful lives, the majority will not thrive without the support of an understanding school system and knowledgeable and committed teachers.

Interventions for Students At Risk

As a classroom teacher, you will be faced with the sometimes frustrating situation of not being able to take away from your students the stresses that often prevent them from learning to their potential. However, you can offer them a safe environment, with clear expectations and instructional support, that might become an important place in their lives.

Generally, recommendations for intervening to teach students at risk include four areas, none of which is completely unique to these students: set high but realistic expectations, establish peers as teaching partners, seek assistance from other professionals, and work closely with parents or other caregivers. Each recommendation is discussed briefly here.

Set high but realistic expectations. When you are teaching students who are at risk, it is tempting to make assumptions about how much they are capable of learning. For example, you might think that since the student does not have books at home and the parent is either unable or unwilling to read with the student, the student will not be a successful learner. The result of such thinking is often inappropriately low expectations—which students might "live down" to (Ramirez-Smith, 1995). Low expectations can also lead to your overusing teaching strategies that emphasize drilling students on lower-level academic skills. Although drill activities have a place in educating at-risk students, they must be balanced with other approaches as well. For example, students need to learn thinking processes along with basic skills, and they need to learn to construct their own knowledge along with receiving it from you (Knapp, Turnbull, & Shields, 1990). This more balanced approach is illustrated in Project Achievement (Mercure, 1993), an after-school program designed to provide students with an enriching and challenging learning environment. Activities included in the project occur mainly in heterogeneous groups and involve photography, television production, and even the creation of a pond ecosystem. This project demonstrates that when students have challenging tasks that are interesting and provide them with opportunities to make decisions, they can be successful and motivated learners.

One other strategy for setting high expectations should be mentioned. Many professionals now believe that the still-common practice of **tracking,** that is, grouping students for instruction by perceived ability (O'Neil, 1992), can discriminate against students at risk. Tracking leads to a sense of failure among some students, and it tends to lead to lowered expectations for at-risk students. Grouping students heterogeneously generally does not place high-achieving students at a disadvantage, but it may help raise the achievement of at-risk learners (Wheelock, 1992). Although teachers appropriately group students by their need for instruction in specific skills as part of their overall instructional plan, and some secondary schools

High expectations and family involvement contribute to the greater academic success of some students at risk. In your classroom, how will you identify students who are at risk? What other interventions and instructional strategies will you use to help them succeed in school?

offer advanced classes that lead to a limited amount of tracking, you should be aware of the potential negative effects of tracking. As a teacher, you can ensure that you do not overuse this type of grouping in your classroom, and you can work with your colleagues to create a school in which students of many different abilities learn together.

One word of caution about setting standards is necessary. Some students who are at risk have such high stresses outside school that they might not have much support from their parents and other family members for school assignments and work. Two examples from teachers help to illustrate this point. One talked about a student who was not returning homework. The teacher was penalizing the student by giving her lower grades and making her complete the work during recess. She later found out that the family was penniless and had a single light bulb in their tiny apartment. When the bulb burned out, there was no light after sunset, and homework was not the priority. Another teacher described a high school student who always slept in class. Detention did not help, nor did attempts to contact parents. The teacher later learned that this student left school each day, cooked dinner for her younger siblings, and then worked at a fast food restaurant until midnight. Thus, high expectations are important, but they need to be tempered with understanding of the circumstances in the student's life outside school.

Effective instruction for students at risk includes the same strategies you would use for other students, with particular attention to the physical and social-emotional challenges these students often face. Students at risk need a structured learning environment, systematic instruction in basic skill areas, and strategies for learning independence.

Establish peers as teaching partners. Peers learning from one another is a strategy recommended earlier for students from diverse cultural and linguistic backgrounds; it is also useful for at-risk students. For example, in the Success for All Program (Slavin et al., 1994), an intensive early reading program designed to help at-risk learners acquire foundational learning that will help them throughout their school careers, a key ingredient is a cooperative learning approach. Students work with each other in structured groups to learn vocabulary, writing, comprehension, and other reading skills. This program appears to have great potential for helping students achieve school success.

Another example of a peer partner program comes from the Touchstones Project (Comber, Zeiderman, & Maistrellis, 1989). This middle school program emphasizes restructuring middle school classes to reduce overreliance on teacher-directed, lecture-based instruction. The program instead emphasizes class discussions and active student participation during lessons; the outcome is better learning and enhanced social interactions for students. Students also gain independence as they learn to self-direct their learning and learn from one another instead of relying just on the teacher (Landfried, 1989).

Collaborate with other professionals. A third strategy for teaching at-risk students involves increasing your problem-solving capability by adding the skills and resources of your colleagues. In a survey of teachers' and principals' preferences for providing support to students at risk, these individuals were mentioned as potential resources: special education teachers, other special education professionals, psychologists, social workers, reading teachers, and paraprofessionals (Lombardi et al.,

Connections

Peer teaching and other forms of peer-mediated instruction are discussed in Chapter 13.

Professional Edge

Best Practices for Including All Students

These are considered the best practices for creating schools that include all students, whether they have low-incidence or high-incidence disabilities or other special needs:

1. **School climate and structure** includes a mission statement that reflects the school's commitment to inclusive education and an instructional support system for all students and staff.

2. **Collaborative planning** creates opportunities for teachers and others to meet during the school day to develop support systems for students and staff.

3. **Social responsibility** is fostered by creating opportunities for students to demonstrate self-reliance through peer tutoring, participation in school decision making, and the like.

4. **Curriculum planning** ensures that the school curriculum includes age-appropriate content and process-oriented goals and objectives that set high standards of excellence for all students.

5. **Delivery of instructional support services** occurs as part of ongoing school and community activities.

6. **Individualized instruction** takes place for all students using a wide range of materials and methods, with instruction delivered by peers and others as well as by teachers.

7. **Transition planning** so that students move smoothly from one educational setting to another and from school to postschool activities is deliberately and carefully addressed.

8. **Family–school collaboration** is valued and fostered.

9. **Planning for continued best-practice improvement** is addressed by arranging to develop a revised plan every 3 to 5 years.

SOURCE: Adapted from "Strategies for Educating Learners with Severe Disabilities within Their Local Home Schools and Communities" by J. S. Thousand and R. A. Villa, 1990, *Focus on Exceptional Children, 23*(3), 1–24.

1990). Other programs for at-risk students enlist the assistance of volunteers, counselors, and administrators.

The purpose of problem solving with your colleagues about at-risk students is that you can check your own perspectives against theirs, gain access to their expertise, and coordinate your efforts. For example, if you are teaching Shaneal, a student whom you suspect has been abused, you can first ask the counselor or social worker if there is any past documentation of abuse, and you can request that one of these professionals speak with the student. If you are teaching Jack, a student who is missing quite a few school days and increasingly refuses to complete assignments, you might want to consult with colleagues about the causes of Jack's behavior and how to address them.

Support family and community involvement. As with all students, it is essential that you maintain positive contact with parents or other caregivers of your at-risk students. However, the level of participation you can expect will vary considerably. Some parents will be anxious to ensure that their children have all the advantages a positive education can give them, and they will do all they can to assist you in teaching. Other parents are themselves not functioning well (Germinario et al., 1992), and they probably cannot be expected to participate actively in their children's education. Stevens and Price (1992) recommend several strategies for improving the involvement of families and communities in their children's education. For example, sometimes it might be more appropriate for a student to bring to school something important from home and to base an assignment on that, rather than being assigned more traditional homework. It can also be helpful to assist parents in connecting with community resources such as health clinics and social service agencies. One school district, struggling because of the rapidly increasing number of at-risk students, worked with local church leaders to connect families with resources and improve the communication between school personnel and families.

When you think about the diversity of students you will teach, it is easy to become overwhelmed by the challenge of meeting all your students' instructional needs. Keep in mind that classrooms structured to celebrate diversity rather than treat it as a deficiency or an exception are classrooms with many options for learning and a blend of structure and flexibility. In the Professional Edge, you will find recommendations for making classrooms and schools inclusive for all students.

FYI

Effective prevention and intervention programs exist for all grade levels. Programs for students at risk are most effective when family and community support are present.

Summary

In addition to students with disabilities, you will teach many other students who have extraordinary learning needs. Some students receive specialized services through Section 504, federal legislation requiring that accommodations be provided by general educators to students who have functional disabilities that might limit their access to an education.

One major group of students who receive Section 504 assistance is students with attention deficit–hyperactive disorder (ADHD), a medically diagnosed problem characterized by chronic and severe inattention and/or hyperactivity-impulsivity. Students with ADHD are served through a variety of academic and behavior interventions, and they often are helped by medication. Most other students protected through Section 504 have physical conditions or medical problems, and their plans outline needed academic, behavioral, and physical or medical accommodations.

Students who are gifted and talented comprise a second group with special needs. Students who are gifted and talented include those with generally high intellectual ability as well as those with specific talents in areas such as music. The interventions most often used to help them achieve school success are enrichment, acceleration, sophistication, and novelty.

A third group with special needs includes students from culturally and linguistically diverse backgrounds. These students and their families sometimes have values that differ from those of schools. Teachers need to learn about students' cultures, teach in a manner that is responsive to the cultures, and acknowledge and value diverse cultures in the classroom in order to teach students from diverse cultural backgrounds effectively.

Finally, students at risk for school failure because of environmental influences such as poverty, child abuse, and drug addiction also have special needs. Because students at risk often live in unpredictable and stressful environments, strategies for teaching them include setting appropriate expectations, understanding the often fluctuating range of their needs, and stressing structure and accomplishment in their classroom instruction.

Applications in Teaching Practice

Developing Strategies to Reach All of Your Students

Marta Collings is a second-grade teacher in a suburban school district. Although it is only the fourth week of school, she is concerned. She is confident of her teaching skills and has a strong commitment to teaching all of the students assigned to her, but she is worried that she won't be able to meet the diverse needs represented in her class this year. She is well aware that student needs in school are becoming increasingly diverse, and her current class group clearly demonstrates that fact. For example, Thuan, who just emigrated to the United States from Vietnam, speaks very little English and seems overwhelmed by nearly everything at school. Ms. Collings can't recall ever seeing Thuan smile. Then there is Sonny. Sonny is supposed to be taking medication for ADHD, but it doesn't seem to be having any effect on him. At the after-school meeting where Ms. Collings, the school psychologist, the counselor, and the principal discussed the matter, it was noted that Sonny recently had a growth spurt and that perhaps the dosage needed to be changed. The counselor is supposed to follow up on this issue and let Ms. Collings know what is happening. In the meantime, while everyone is sympathetic, Sonny is in her classroom and, as Ms. Collings puts it, "bouncing off the walls." Jenny is a concern as well. She and her twin sister, Jenna, who is in the other second-grade class, are struggling academically despite lots of individual attention and supportive parents. Neither girl is reading at grade level; last year's teacher had questioned whether they were ready to go to second grade, but the school discourages retention except in extraordinary circumstances. Ms. Collings knows that the twins' father has been out of work for nearly a year and that the family is barely getting by on donations from friends and their church. She wonders how much of the twins' learning problems are related to their home situation. She also teaches Kimberly, who is so far ahead of other students that Ms. Collings wishes she had a complete set of sixth-grade materials to use as resources for her. Two other students—Lisa and Paul—are from families that have very little; they come to school without supplies and seem reluctant to interact with the other children. In thinking about her class, Ms. Collings realizes that at least half of her students have special needs of one sort or another. She wants to reach them all. She is unsure whether she can accomplish her goal.

Questions

1. How typical is the type of class group Ms. Collings has? What other types of diverse needs might you expect to have represented in a class you are responsible for teaching?

2. What general strategies might Ms. Collings use in her class that would benefit many students with special needs and harm none?

3. For each student with special needs Ms. Collings has identified, consider what strategies she might use by making a chart specifying at least one strategy in each pertinent domain. It should include these parts:

Intervention Area	Thuan	Sonny	Jenny	Kimberly	Lisa and Paul
Academic					
Social/Emotional					
Behavioral					
Medical/Physical					

4. There is a special education teacher in Ms. Collings's school. What is that teacher's role in assisting Ms. Collings and other teachers in the school to meet the diverse needs of students, including those who do not have IEPs?

5. How might Ms. Collings work with the parents of her students to help ensure their needs are addressed?

6. What realistic expectations can Ms. Collings set for herself as a teacher for this school year? How can she reach her goal of meeting the needs of all her students?

chapter 8

Assessing Student Needs

Learner Objectives

After you read this chapter, you will be able to

1. Explain how general education teachers can contribute significantly to the assessment process.

2. Describe the uses of standardized achievement and psychological tests in making educational decisions for students with special needs.

3. Define curriculum-based assessment and explain how it can help general education teachers.

4. Construct and use probes of basic academic skills, content-area prerequisite skills, and independent learning skills.

5. Use curriculum-based assessments to make special education decisions.

■ Ms. Lyons is concerned that Rob, a student in her second-grade class, is not keeping up with the rest of the class in math. Mr. Blair, the special education teacher, suggests that Ms. Lyons do some informal assessment herself before going through the special education referral process. What kind of assessments can Ms. Lyons use to clarify Rob's problems in math? How might these assessments help Ms. Lyons make adaptations for Rob in math? Under what circumstances should she refer Rob for special education?

■ Mr. Blount teaches a high school American history class. He has learned that three special education students will be included in his class next fall. Mr. Blount was told that these students have some reading problems and that they may have trouble reading the textbook. Mr. Blount decided to make up a test to give at the beginning of the year to see how well the students were able to use the textbook. Using a section of a chapter from the text, Mr. Blount wrote questions to test how well students could figure out the meaning of key vocabulary words, use parts of the book (for example, the table of contents, glossary, or index), read maps, and read for information (for example, note main ideas, draw conclusions). When Mr. Blount gave the test in the fall, he found that the three identified students had trouble reading the text, but that many other students also had difficulty. What decision might Mr. Blount make on the basis of the assessment?

■ Roberto is a student with moderate to severe disabilities who is included in Ms. Benis's sixth-grade social studies class. As a result of Roberto's cerebral palsy, he has significant cognitive, language, and motor deficits. Roberto can read his name, as well as some high-frequency sight words. He uses a wheelchair, and he has trouble with fine motor movements such as cutting and handwriting. Roberto speaks with the aid of a communication board. Ms. Benis is doing a unit on recycling with her class. The students are working in small, mixed-skill groups, with each group constructing a graphic of the recycling process for either paper products, plastic, or metal. What assessment process can Ms. Benis carry out to help her develop a plan for including Roberto in this unit?

As more and more students with disabilities are served in general education classes, teachers will need to make many important decisions that can greatly affect these students' success. For example, in the vignettes above, Ms. Lyons was trying to find out whether Rob needed intensive math instruction from a special education teacher or whether his needs could be met through adaptations in her regular math program. Mr. Blount wanted to find out whether his students with disabilities could read the textbook for his history class to help him decide whether he would need to adapt the book. Ms. Benis wants to include Roberto, who has moderate to severe disabilities, in her social studies class. To answer questions such as these, teachers need accurate, relevant information. Thus, they need to develop informal measures to help them make a number of instructional decisions as well as participate in special education decision making. This chapter explores assessment strategies that help general education teachers contribute to the process of decision making for students with special needs. This decision making involves, for example, determining if a student needs special education services, when a student is ready to learn in inclusive settings, and what classroom accommodations to try, continue, or change.

How Do Your Student Assessments Contribute to Special Education Decisions?

Connections

The assessment types and procedures described in this chapter are an integral part of the INCLUDE model presented in Chapter 4.

As a classroom teacher, you make an important contribution to the process of identifying and meeting the needs of students with special needs. A major part of that contribution involves assessing student needs. **Assessment** has been defined as the process of gathering information to monitor progress and make educational decisions if necessary (Overton, 1996). The two most common ways of collecting information are through standardized, commercially produced tests and informal tests devised by the teacher. Much of the information in this chapter is about ways in which these measures can be used to make decisions about students with special needs.

General education teachers contribute assessment information for six important decisions about students with special needs: screening, diagnosis, program placement, curriculum placement, instructional evaluation, and program evaluation.

Screening

Check Your Learning

What questions are involved in making a screening decision?

The major **screening** decision is whether or not a student's performance is different enough from that of his or her peers to merit further, more in-depth assessments to determine the presence of a disability. For example, to clarify Rob's problems in math, Ms. Lyons, whom you met at the beginning of this chapter, examined the most recent group achievement test scores for her class in math and found that Rob's total math score was 1 to 2 years below grade level. Ms. Lyons then gave Rob and his classmates some minitests on various math computation skills she had taught to see whether Rob was behind his peers on these skills. Using this information, Ms. Lyons found that a number of students were performing similarly to Rob. She therefore decided not to refer Rob for a more comprehensive evaluation until she tried some adaptations in the classroom first, with Rob and several other students.

Diagnosis

The major decision related to **diagnosis** is eligibility for special education services. Does the student meet established federal guidelines for being classified as having a disability? If so, what is the nature and extent of the student's disability? For example, Ms. Clark referred Paula for a case-study evaluation because she suspected that Paula had a learning disability. The school psychologist administered an individual intelligence test and found that Paula's performance was in the above-normal range. The school psychologist also gave Paula a test of cognitive functioning, including a test of memory, attention, and organization, and an individual achievement test. She found that Paula was slow in processing visual information (letters, numbers, shapes) and that her achievement in reading was significantly lower than that of other students her age. Her achievement in math was at grade level. Ms. Clark evaluated Paula's classroom reading performance by having her and five "average" students read orally and answer questions from a grade-level trade book that was part of the classroom literature program. Paula read slower and with less accuracy than her peers, and she was able to answer only 40 percent of the comprehension questions. Because Paula showed problems processing visual information quickly enough, and because her potential as measured by the intelligence test and her achievement as measured by both a standardized achievement test and informal classroom reading tests differed significantly, Paula was declared eligible to receive services for learning disabilities.

Program Placement

The major **program-placement** decision involves where a student's special education services will take place (for example, in a general education classroom, resource room, or full-time special education classroom). The IEP team must make this decision with great care. In the past, the tendency was to pull students out of general education classrooms without carefully considering whether they could be supported within the general education program instead. In this book, the emphasis is on doing all that you can within the general education class first. Still, students have different needs, and some may require instruction in an area at a level of intensity that cannot be delivered in the general education classroom. That is why it is important to make placement decisions based on measures that accurately reflect student performance in class. For example, Carlos has been shown to be eligible for receiving services for learning disabilities in math. His IEP team is trying to decide whether his learning needs can be met by adapting the math methods and materials in the general education classroom or whether he should be provided more intensive instruction in a resource room setting. Carlos's classroom teacher gave Carlos and his classmates a series of informal math tests. She found that Carlos was significantly behind his peers on some but not all of the tests; his math problem solving was very deficient compared to that of his classmates, but his math computational skills were fine. The IEP team decided to keep Carlos in his general education class and support his instruction in problem solving by providing him extra teacher-guided practice whenever a new problem-solving skill was introduced. The team also decided that they would carefully monitor Carlos's problem-solving skills; if those skills showed little improvement, they would consider other options.

Check Your Learning

What questions are involved in diagnosing a student?

Check Your Learning

What questions are involved in making a program placement?

FYI

Program-placement decisions for students with moderate to severe cognitive disabilities should be based on the supports needed to meet the curricular goals outlined in their IEPs.

Curriculum Placement

Check Your Learning

What questions are involved in placing students into the classroom curriculum?

Curriculum-placement decisions involve where to begin instruction for students. For an elementary school teacher, such a decision may mean choosing a reading or math book. For example, Ms. Tolhurst has her students read orally and answer questions to find the appropriate trade books in which to place them (that is, the level of difficulty at which the books are neither too easy nor too hard in her literature-based reading program). At the secondary level, curriculum-placement decisions are likely to involve which class in a sequence of classes a student should take. For example, Mr. Nowicki, Scott's math teacher, is trying to decide whether to place Scott in his Algebra 1 class. Mr. Nowicki identifies basic math skills that he feels all students entering algebra should have. He constructs a test based on those skills and gives it to Scott as well as other incoming freshmen.

Instructional Evaluation

Decisions in **instructional evaluation** involve whether to continue or change instructional procedures that have been initiated with students. For example, Ms. Bridgewater is starting a peer tutoring program to help Cecily, a student with severe cognitive disabilities, read her name and the names of her family members. Each week, Ms. Bridgewater tests Cecily to see how many of the names she has learned. Mr. Jackson decides to accompany each of his history lectures with a graphic organizer of the material. He gives weekly quizzes to find out whether his students' performance is improving.

Program Evaluation

Program-evaluation decisions involve whether the special education program should be terminated, continued as is, or modified. A key consideration is whether

Students' needs can be identified, addressed, and monitored through assessments based on observation, screening, diagnostic testing, program placement and evaluation, curriculum placement, and instructional evaluation. What role do general education teachers play in assessing students' special needs?

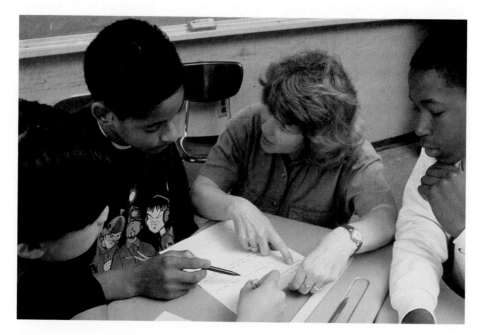

or not students are meeting their IEP goals. For example, Amanda is receiving social work services twice per week. Her IEP goal is to decrease the number of times she has a verbal confrontation with Mr. Alvarez, her teacher. Mr. Alvarez is keeping track of the number of times daily that Amanda refuses to comply with his requests to see whether sessions with the social worker are improving Amanda's behavior.

Check Your Learning

What questions are involved in evaluating the program of a student with special needs?

What Information Sources Are Used in Programming for Students with Special Needs?

A number of information sources are used in programming for students with special needs. The use of multiple assessment sources is consistent with the principle of nondiscriminatory testing, discussed in Chapter 2, which says that no single measure should be used to establish eligibility for special education services. The measures described in this section include standardized achievement tests, reports of psychological tests, the environmental inventory process, and curriculum-based assessments.

Standardized Achievement Tests

A common source of information for making educational decisions is the **standardized achievement test.** These tests are designed to measure academic progress, or what students have retained in the curriculum. Standardized achievement tests are norm-referenced. In a norm-referenced test, the performance of one student is compared to the average performance of other students in the country who are the same age or grade level. Student performance is often summarized using grade equivalents and/or percentile ranks. Grade equivalents simply indicate the grade level, in years and months, for which a given score was the average, or middle, score in the norm group. For example, a score of 25 with the grade equivalent of 4.6 means that in the norm group, 25 was the average score of pupils in the sixth month of fourth grade. Percentile ranks represent the percentage of students who scored at or below a given student's score. A percentile score of 75 percent, then, means that the student scored higher than 75 percent of all students in his or her age group that took the test. Keep in mind that grade-level equivalencies and percentiles look at student performance only from the standpoint of how different they are from average, *not* according to how well they performed a skill from the standpoint of mastery. For example, a grade equivalent score of 3.2 in reading comprehension means that the student achieved the same score as the average of all students in the third grade, second month, who were in the normative sample; it does not say anything about how well the student is able to answer the various kinds of comprehension questions that may be in the third-grade reading curriculum.

Group-administered tests. There are two major types of standardized achievement tests: group-administered and individually administered diagnostic tests. As the name implies, group-administered standardized achievement tests are completed by large groups of students at one time; this usually means that the general education teacher gives the test to the entire class. These tests assess skills across many areas of the curriculum, none in much depth. For this reason, they are intended to be used solely as screening measures. Nonetheless, information obtained from group-administered achievement tests may be inappropriate for making some decisions, even in screening, for the following reasons:

1. Administration in a group environment does not allow students to ask the teacher questions about directions or to clarify test questions (Overton, 1996). For example, Alicia has a learning disability in reading and has problems comprehending written directions. When Alicia obtained a low score on a social studies subtest, it was hard to determine whether her low score was due to a lack of knowledge or her inability to follow the directions.

2. Many group tests are timed, which may limit the responses of students with disabilities. For example, Carmen has a problem with eye-hand coordination and makes errors in transferring her answers to a computer-scored answer sheet. Corrine has an attention deficit and is unable to complete a reading subtest in one 45-minute sitting.

3. National or even local norms might not match actual distribution of classroom achievement (Deno, 1985; Marston, 1989; Salvia & Ysseldyke, 1995). For example, Darryl is in fourth grade and scored at the second-grade level on a standardized achievement test in reading, a score that was at least 6 months below the rest of his classmates. However, the results of an informal reading probe based on his classroom literature-based program revealed that four other students in class were reading at a level roughly equivalent to Darryl's. The teacher decided to form an instructional group made up of these students to help them with their literature books and did not refer Darryl for special services.

4. The results of standardized tests provide little useful data to guide instruction (Bursuck & Lessen, 1987; Deno, 1985; Marston, 1989; Salvia & Ysseldyke, 1995; Shinn, Collins, & Gallagher, 1997). For example, Ellen's math achievement scores showed that she was one year below grade level in math computation. However, the test contained too few items to find out the particular kind of errors she was making.

Check Your Learning

What are the drawbacks in using group-administered standardized achievement tests to make educational decisions for students?

5. Standardized achievement tests might be culturally biased, and they can lead to the overrepresentation of minorities in special education classes (Garcia & Pearson, 1994; Oakland, 1981). For example, Bill comes from a single-parent home in a high-rise apartment building in the city. When he read a story on a standardized achievement test about an affluent two-parent family in the suburbs, he had difficulty predicting the outcome.

6. The content of a standardized achievement test might not match what is taught in a particular classroom (Deno, 1985; Deno & Fuchs, 1987; Marston, 1989; Jitendra & Kameenui, 1993). For example, one teacher stressed problem solving in his science class, whereas the standardized achievement test given in his district stressed the memorization of facts. Therefore, he had to give his own tests to determine whether students were learning the material. The reading achievement test used at another teacher's school had the students identify words in lists. The teacher found that the words tested were quite different from the words in her literature-based program, which stressed reading in context using syntactically predictable books. She decided to develop her own test to place students into appropriate books as well as to monitor progress in her program.

7. Because it is not possible to administer standardized tests frequently, their utility as a tool for evaluating day-to-day instruction is limited (Bursuck & Lessen, 1987; Deno, 1985). For example, James was mainstreamed into a second-grade class for math. After one month, the teachers wanted to check his progress. Since the standardized tests were not to be given for another three months, James's teacher gave him her own informal test based on what she taught in class. In another instance, Clark was not allowed into Algebra 1 because of his poor performance on a standardized achievement test in math. After one month, Clark's teacher felt he was ready for Algebra 1. Because the achievement test could not be given again until May, the algebra and basic math teachers developed their own test of skills prerequisite for Algebra 1 and gave it to Clark.

Group-administered standardized achievement tests can be useful in some circumstances. One such situation involves making administrative and policy decisions on a school-district or even national level. For example, a district found that their students were below the national average on the problem-solving portion of a math achievement test and decided to spend more time on math problem solving at all levels in the district. However, the validity of group-administered achievement tests for making decisions about individual students at the classroom level is limited. These tests should be used with great caution and only in conjunction with informal, classroom-based measures.

In the past, school districts have not always included students with disabilities in their testing programs. Goals 2000 and IDEA-97 require that all students be included in school district assessments of progress toward goals and that appropriate accommodations for students with disabilities be used during these assessments. Common accommodations include changing the setting of the test (for example, allowing students to take tests in special education classrooms), changing the timing of the test (for example, providing extended time or more frequent breaks), changing the response format (for example, allowing students to mark responses in test books rather than on scantron sheets), and changing the presentation format (for example, using a braille edition of a test or giving directions in sign language) (Thurlow, Ysseldyke, & Silverstein, 1995).

Individually administered tests. A special education teacher or the school psychologist usually gives **individually administered diagnostic tests** as part of a student's case-study evaluation. Although these tests may screen student performance in several curricular areas, they tend to be more diagnostic in nature. For example, an individually administered diagnostic reading test may include subtests in the areas of letter identification, word recognition, oral reading, comprehension, and phonetic skills; a diagnostic test in math might include math computation, fractions, geometry, word problems, measurement, and time. Because individually administered diagnostic tests provide information on a range of specific skills, they can be useful as an information source in making educational decisions. For example, Tamara scored 2 years below grade level on the comprehension subtest of an individually administered diagnostic test in reading. Yet in an oral reading sample taken from her fourth-grade reader, she read both fluently and accurately. On the basis of these two findings, her teacher placed her into a literature-based reading program that stressed skills in reading comprehension.

Do It!

Ask an administrator at your local school district which students with disabilities take the district's standardized achievement tests and what accommodations they are allowed (for example, an oral test for students with learning disabilities). Also ask whether the scores for students with disabilities are counted in the district's overall test results.

WWW Resources

For more information on the topic of state and national testing policies, call up the web page for The National Center on Educational Outcomes (NCEO) on the Internet: <http://www.coled.umn.edu/nceo>.

What are some advantages of individually administered diagnostic tests? What are other sources of assessment information used in educational decision making for students with special needs?

Although individually administered diagnostic tests may be more helpful than group-administered achievement tests, they are still subject to many of the same problems. Again, you should always verify findings from these tests using more informal measures based on what you teach.

Psychological Tests

F Y I

Psychological tests may not be reliable or valid and may not have appropriate norms. Check the test manual or ask your school psychologist about the technical adequacy of tests used in your school.

Psychological tests are used as part of the process of evaluating students with special needs, particularly to determine whether a student has cognitive or learning disabilities. Reports of the results of these tests are often written by school psychologists and consist of a summary of the findings and the implications for instruction. **Psychological tests** can include intelligence tests and tests related to learning disabilities (Overton, 1996; Salvia & Ysseldyke, 1995).

The overall purpose of psychological tests is to measure abilities that affect how efficiently students learn in an instructional situation. These abilities are inferred based upon student responses to items that the test author believes represent that particular ability. For example, comprehension, an important learning ability, is often assessed on psychological tests (Salvia & Ysseldyke, 1995). To test their comprehension, students may be asked to read and answer questions about a series of directions or other printed material. Student scores are then compared to a norm group of other same-aged students, with an average score being equal to 100. Other abilities commonly assessed by psychological tests include generalization (the ability to recognize similarities across objects, events, or vocabulary), general or background information, vocabulary, induction (the ability to figure out a rule or principle based on a series of situations), abstract reasoning, and memory (Salvia & Ysseldyke, 1995).

Psychological tests can be helpful if they clarify why students may not be learning in class and lead to effective changes in instruction. For example, the results of Amanda's test showed that she had difficulty with visual memory. Her teacher, Ms. Fasbacher, felt that this was related to her poor performance in spelling. As a result, Ms. Fasbacher provided Amanda with extra practice on her weekly spelling lists. Interpreting the results of psychological reports will seem less daunting if you follow the general guidelines suggested here. First, do not be scared off by the sometimes generous amounts of technical terms and/or jargon. You have the right to expect that reports be translated into instructionally relevant language. Second, the results of psychological tests are most valid when corroborated by classroom experience. Further, in the event of discrepancies between psychological reports and your experience, do not automatically discount your experience. Keep in mind that your impressions are the result of many more hours of observation than are psychological evaluations, which are based on fewer samples of student behavior that take place outside the classroom. Third, be sure to check the technical adequacy of the psychological tests included in your report. You will be surprised to find that many of these tests may not be acceptable. Fourth, psychological tests may discriminate against students from culturally different or disadvantaged backgrounds. The various ways in which psychological and other tests can be biased, along with suggestions for making them more fair, are presented in the Professional Edge on page 268. Finally, the primary purpose of psychological tests is to establish possible explanations for particular learning, behavioral, or social and emotional problems. Keep in mind that such explanations should be springboards for helping students overcome these problems, not excuses for a student's lack of achievement.

The Professional Edge on page 269 contains lists of standardized tests commonly used in special education decision making. These include standardized group and individual achievement tests and psychological tests used to assess intelligence or cognitive functioning.

Environmental Inventory Process

Traditional formal and informal testing practices may be inappropriate for students with moderate to severe disabilities. These students often lack the critical language and motor skills that are necessary to respond to such tests. In addition, the abstract nature of the test items has little relation to the functional living skills that are so important to assess for these students. The **environmental inventory** is an alternative assessment process for students with moderate to severe disabilities. The purpose of this type of assessment is to find out what adaptations or supports are needed to increase the participation of these students in classroom as well as community environments (Vandercook, York, & Forest, 1989). The environmental inventory process involves asking yourself three questions:

1. What does a person who does not have a disability do in this environment?
2. What does a person who has a disability do in this environment? What is the discrepancy?
3. What types of supports and/or adaptations can be put in place in order to increase the participation level or independence of the person who has a disability label?

Cultural Awareness

Psychological tests can be biased against students from diverse backgrounds. Use them only in conjunction with other formal and informal measures.

Do It!

Examine sample copies of some of the standardized tests described in this chapter. What questions would you ask to ensure your correct interpretation and appropriate use of information from these sources?

Professional Edge

Strategies for Fair Assessment of Diverse Students

Grossman (1995) reports that while today's teachers are much more knowledgeable about the presence of bias in assessing poor students and students from culturally diverse backgrounds, bias and discrimination continue to exist. Here are some areas that can be problematic when assessing diverse students, along with some strategies for assessing and interpreting their performance more accurately.

Problem	Recommendation
1. Students exhibit test anxiety due to lack of familiarity with assessment process.	1. Give practice tests. Teach test-taking skills.
2. Students lack motivation to perform well on tests due to differing cultural expectations.	2. Qualify test performance with class performance.
3. Students do not respond to traditional motivators.	3. Individualize use of reinforcers; use individualistic, competitive, and cooperative goal structures.
4. Students' test scores are depressed when assessor not familiar or speaks different language.	4. Allow more time to establish rapport and gain trust.
5. Students have different communication styles; for example, they may not feel comfortable asking for help with directions or may respond using fewer words.	5. Check for understanding of directions; avoid automatically penalizing students for not saying enough or not giving details.
6. Students are unwilling to take risks; for example, they are reluctant to guess on a test even though it is to their benefit.	6. Teach when it is okay to guess on a test.
7. Students are accustomed to working at a slower pace.	7. Give extended time.
8. Students lack exposure to test content.	8. Eliminate content or don't give test.
9. Students are not proficient in language used on a test.	9. Assess in both English and students' native language.
10. Students speak using a different dialect.	10. Do not count dialectical differences as errors; examine your attitudes about nonstandard dialects for potential bias.

Check Your Learning

Why are standardized achievement tests and psychological tests not useful for students with moderate to severe cognitive disabilities?

An example of how this process is used in a classroom environment is shown in Figure 8.1 (Vandercook, York, & Forest, 1989) on page 270. This example involves Roberto, the student with moderate to severe disabilities whom you met at the beginning of the chapter, who is included in Ms. Benis's sixth-grade social studies class. The class is working in small groups on depicting the steps in the recycling process for paper, metal, and plastic. Each group is studying a different recycled material. Roberto lacks the motor and cognitive skills necessary to participate like everyone else. Ms. Benis has decided to assign Roberto to the group that his friend Seth is in. She also decides to use different materials for Roberto. Ms. Benis will have a para-

Professional Edge

Standardized Tests Commonly Used in Special Education Decision Making

You have many standardized tests to choose from to help you in making decisions for special education. When selecting an instrument, make sure it is appropriate for the student being tested. If you have questions about the suitability of a particular test, consult your school psychologist or special education teacher. The following lists provide the names and sources of commonly used standardized tests for special education decision making.

Standardized Achievement and Diagnostic Tests

Woodcock-Johnson—Revised Tests of Achievement
   Chicago: Riverside

Peabody Individual Achievement Test—Revised
   Circle Pines, MN: American Guidance Service

Kaufman Test of Educational Achievement:
Comprehension Form
   Circle Pines, MN: American Guidance Service

KeyMath Diagnostic Arithmetic Test—Revised
   Circle Pines, MN: American Guidance Service

Woodcock Reading Mastery Tests—Revised
   Circle Pines, MN: American Guidance Service

Test of Written Language—3
   Austin, TX: Pro-Ed

Test of Written Spelling—3
   Austin, TX: Pro-Ed

Test of Reading Comprehension—3
   Austin, TX: Pro-Ed

Gray Oral Reading Test—3
   Austin, TX: Pro-Ed

Intelligence Tests and Tests of Cognitive Functioning

Wechsler Intelligence Scale for Children—III
   San Antonio, TX: Psychological Corporation

Woodcock-Johnson—Revised Tests of Cognitive Abilities
   Chicago: Riverside

Stanford-Binet IV
   Chicago: Riverside

Kaufman Assessment Battery for Children
   Los Angeles: Western Psychological Services

---

professional help Roberto find pictures of sample recycled products; Seth will help Roberto paste these pictures onto the group's diagram. Mr. Howard, Roberto's special education teacher, will help Roberto identify recycled products in grocery stores and restaurants. Roberto's parents will help him sort the recycling at home.

Curriculum-Based Assessments

Because of the limited utility of standard achievement tests and psychological reports for day-to-day instructional decisions, you need other tools to be a partner in the evaluation process. **Curriculum-based assessment (CBA)** is an effective option, and in many instances can be an alternative to standardized tests. CBA has been defined as a method of measuring the level of achievement of students in terms of what they are taught in the classroom (for example, Bursuck & Lessen, 1987;

Figure 8.1   Environmental Inventory Process

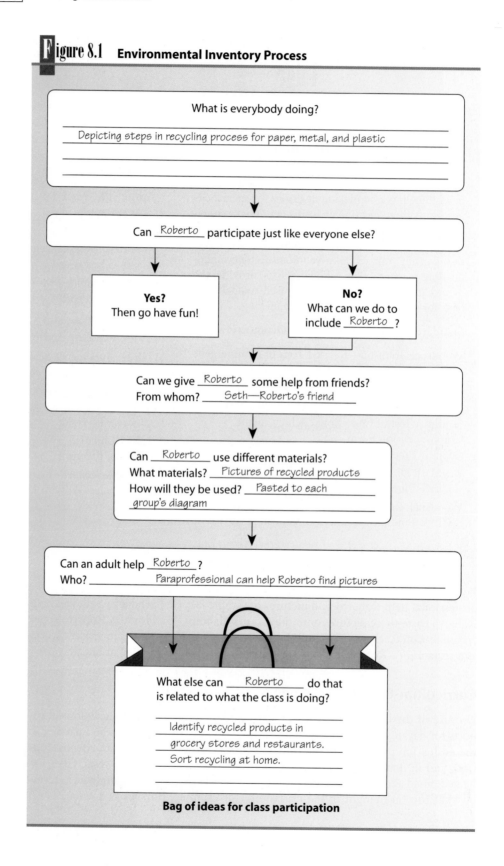

What is everybody doing?

Depicting steps in recycling process for paper, metal, and plastic

Can __Roberto__ participate just like everyone else?

Yes?
Then go have fun!

No?
What can we do to
include __Roberto__?

Can we give __Roberto__ some help from friends?
From whom? ____Seth—Roberto's friend____

Can __Roberto__ use different materials?
What materials? __Pictures of recycled products__
How will they be used? __Pasted to each
group's diagram__

Can an adult help __Roberto__?
Who? ____Paraprofessional can help Roberto find pictures____

What else can ____Roberto____ do that
is related to what the class is doing?

Identify recycled products in
grocery stores and restaurants.
Sort recycling at home.

Bag of ideas for class participation

Choate, Enright, Miller, Poteet & Rakes, 1995; Tucker, 1985). CBA has a number of attractive features. When using CBA, you select the skills that are assessed based on what you teach in class, thus ensuring a match between what is taught and what is tested. CBA compares students within a class, school, or district to show learning differences, not national norms (Marston, Tindal, & Deno, 1984), thus ensuring that a student referred for special education services is significantly different from his or her peers (Bursuck & Lessen, 1987). For example, in the vignettes at the beginning of this chapter, Ms. Lyons, before referring Rob to special education, gave him some curriculum-based assessments in math to determine the specific kinds of problems he was having. She then implemented a peer tutoring program and used these same tests to measure its effectiveness. Mr. Blount used an informal reading assessment based on his American history textbook to see how well his students were able to read this text. Finally, research shows that when teachers use CBA to evaluate student progress, and adjust their instruction accordingly, student achievement increases significantly (Fuchs, Fuchs, Hamlett, & Stecker, 1991; Shinn et al., 1997). The Case in Practice on pages 272–273 illustrates a scenario in which both standardized and curriculum-based assessments are used to help make a special education decision.

Before we describe the specifics of how to use curriculum-based assessments, we must point out that curriculum-based assessments are not without drawbacks. First, test items that accurately measure student performance may be hard to construct. Second, because curriculum-based assessments test what is taught, they may fail to measure other important information or skills that may not be taught directly. Third, because curriculum-based assessments relate to student performance at the individual classroom level, their use for evaluating student performance on a national or even statewide basis is limited. Finally, curriculum-based assessments are most appropriate for assessing academic skills covered in school. As such, they are not as effective when assessing problem-solving skills in real-world contexts.

What Kinds of Curriculum-Based Assessments Can You Create for Your Students?

Two major kinds of curriculum-based assessments are commonly used: probes of basic academic skills (for example, reading, math, and writing) and content-area strategy assessments (for example, probes of prerequisite skills, textbook reading, and note-taking). Although probes of basic academic skills relate more directly to elementary school teachers and content-area strategy assessments to middle and high school teachers, each of these measures is relevant for both groups. For example, high school students need to perform basic skills fluently if they are to have ready access to curriculum content; elementary school students need early training in learning strategies to make the difficult transition to high school instruction easier.

Probes of Basic Academic Skills

Probes are quick and easy measures of student performance in the basic skill areas of reading, math, and written expression. They consist of timed samples of academic behaviors and are designed to assess skill accuracy and fluency.

Case in Practice

Assessments in Special Education Decision Making

Darnell is 9 years old. He was referred for testing for a learning disability by his fourth-grade teacher, Ms. Davis. Ms. Davis was particularly concerned about Darnell's lack of progress in written language (for example, paragraph writing and spelling). Following an evaluation, a meeting was held to discuss Darnell's eligibility for special education. Present at the meeting were the school psychologist, Mr. Earl; the learning disabilities teacher, Mr. Bryant; Darnell's fourth-grade teacher, Ms. Davis; and Darnell's mother, Mrs. Lewis. The following information was presented after introductions were made.

Mr. Earl: We're all here today to take a careful look at some of the problems Darnell has been having with his writing to see if he may have a learning disability and be eligible for some extra help. I'll start by sharing the results of the intelligence testing I did with Darnell. Then, Mr. Bryant will discuss the results of a standardized achievement test in writing that he gave Darnell. Ms. Davis will share the results of some informal testing she has been doing in her class. Finally, Mrs. Lewis will tell us about Darnell's use of language at home.

I gave Darnell the Wechsler Intelligence Test for Children—III, a commonly used intelligence test for children. His overall score was 105, well within the average range. I think it's also important to point out that Darnell's verbal IQ of 103 was also in the normal range; he may be having trouble with his written language, but his oral language seems okay. Darnell seems to have the ability to be successful in writing.

Mr. Bryant: I gave Darnell the Woodcock-Johnson—Revised Tests of Achievement. His scores in all areas of written expression were well below what we might predict based on the IQ scores presented by Mr. Earl. His overall grade equivalence score in written expression is grade 2, month 3. Darnell scored particularly low in writing mechanics such as spelling, proofing, capitalization, punctuation, and fluency. His score in this area was grade 1, month 8.

Ms. Davis: At the end of last month, I was teaching my class to write "how to" papers, such as

Probes can sample a range of skills in a particular area, such as a mixed probe of fifth-grade math computation problems in addition, subtraction, multiplication, and division; or they can sample one skill area, such as letter identification or writing lowercase manuscript letters.

Typically, students work on probe sheets for one minute. The teacher then records the rate of correct and incorrect responses as well as any error patterns. Student performance rates have been shown to be useful for making many of the important evaluation decisions described earlier in the chapter, such as screening, diagnosis, program placement, curriculum placement, instructional evaluation, and program evaluation (Bursuck & Lessen, 1987; Deno & Fuchs, 1987; Shinn et al., 1997; Tindal & Marston, 1990). The Professional Edge on page 274 describes the importance of considering both student accuracy and student fluency when assessing basic academic skills.

Probes are classified according to how students take in task information (seeing, hearing) and how they respond (writing, speaking). They include four major types: see–say, see–write, hear–write, and think–write (Bursuck & Lessen, 1987). For ex-

Check Your Learning

What are the four major types of probes? Give an example of each.

"how to make a peanut butter and jelly sandwich." After about a week, I noticed that Darnell was having problems with this kind of writing. I wasn't surprised, since he was also having problems with other kinds of writing. I decided to do some extra things to help Darnell. First, I gave him a visual grid to help him organize his paper. For example, there was a specially marked spot for the introduction and conclusion, as well as for the steps for whatever was being described. I also went over to Darnell's desk as he was writing to give him some extra help. I did this for another week but saw no improvement. I think Darnell lacks more basic skills, such as how to write a complete sentence.

Let me show you what I mean. Yesterday, I had all my students do a written language probe in class.

I asked them to write a paragraph about how they wash their hair. I gave the students five minutes to write their paragraphs. This is what Darnell wrote:

First, I wanted to see whether Darnell wrote as much as the rest of the class. As you can see, Darnell wrote eight words, which is less than two words per minute. The average for the rest of the class was 30 words, or about six words per minute. I also judged Darnell's paragraph for quality; his paragraph lacked such features as a title, topic sentence, closing sentence, and the use of signal words, like "*First* you do this, and *next* you do that." The papers of all the other students in class except one had these features.

Mrs. Lewis: This sounds a lot like Darnell is at home. He has never had trouble following oral directions, but his handwriting and spelling have always been a problem. Getting him to write a letter to his grandmother is like pulling teeth.

REFLECTIONS

What different kinds of assessment were used here? What other measures might have been used? What instructional changes did Ms. Davis try before referring Darnell? Can you think of some other interventions that she could have tried? Do you think Darnell should be declared eligible for receiving special education services for learning disabilities on the basis of this information? Why or why not?

ample, when reading orally from a textbook, students *see* the text and *say* the words. Hence, oral reading is referred to as a see–say probe. Similarly, in a spelling probe, students *hear* the teacher dictate words and *write* the words as they are dictated. This is a hear–write probe.

As you develop curriculum-based assessments, keep in mind the following suggestions:

1. Identify academic skills that are essential in your particular room or grade. In the elementary grades, include skills in handwriting, spelling, written expression, reading (for example, letter identification, letter sounds, oral reading accuracy, comprehension), and math (for example, number identification, computation, problem solving, time, and money).

2. Select skills representing a *sample* of skills that are taught, not necessarily every skill. Performance on these skills then acts as a checkpoint for identifying students in trouble or measuring student progress. For example, in assessing reading performance, having students read a passage aloud from their reading or

Connections

Probes of academic skills will help you evaluate the instructional progress of students with special needs, an application of the *E* step of the INCLUDE strategy, as discussed in Chapter 4.

Professional Edge

Assessing Student Rates on Basic Academic Skills

When basic skills or other academic content are assessed informally in the classroom, **student accuracy** is usually stressed. For example, we say that Jill formed 85 percent of her cursive letters correctly, John was 90 percent accurate on his addition facts, or Al identified key pieces of lab equipment with 100 percent accuracy. Although accuracy is important because it tells us whether a student has acquired a skill or section of content, accuracy is not the only useful index of pupil performance. **Student fluency,** or how quickly a student is able to perform a skill or recall academic material, is also relevant. Before you consider the reasons for assessing student fluency provided here, consider this: If your car needed service and you had your choice between two mechanics, both of whom did accurate work and charged $35 an hour, but one of whom worked twice as fast as the other, which mechanic would you choose?

The Rate Rationale

1. Students who are proficient in a skill are more likely to remember the skill, even if they do not need to use it very often. If they forget the skill, they need less time to relearn it.

2. Students who are proficient in a basic skill are better able to master more advanced skills. For example, students who can perform addition problems fluently often acquire advanced multiplication skills more easily.

3. Performance of basic skills at an "automatic" level frees students to perform higher-level skills more readily. For example, students who can read fluently with understanding are more likely to be successful in high school classes that require reading lengthy textbook assignments in little time. Students who know their math facts without counting on their fingers can solve word problems more efficiently.

4. Students with special needs are often so labeled because they work more slowly than their peers. Fluency scores allow teachers to compare these students directly with their classmates on this important dimension of speed; they also provide a useful index of student progress, including, for some students, readiness for inclusion in general education classes.

---

literature books and answer comprehension questions may not represent all reading skills you have taught (for example, words in isolation), but it does include a representative sample of many of these skills.

Probes of reading skills.   The critical reading skills in the elementary years include letter identification, letter sounds, word recognition, and comprehension. Student ability to identify letter names and sounds can be assessed using a see-say probe. Word recognition and comprehension can be assessed using a see-say oral passage reading probe such as the one in Figure 8.2.

Although the easiest method for assessing comprehension is to use the questions that accompany most classroom reading series, if you are using a literature-based reading program, you may need to design your own questions, which can be a difficult task. Carnine, Silbert, and Kameenui (1997) have suggested one practical

✱ 491

Figure 8.2   See–Say: Oral Passage Reading

Time	1 minute
Materials	*Student*—Stimulus passage
	Examiner—Duplicate copy of stimulus passage, pencil, timer
Directions to Student	"When I say 'Please begin,' read this story out loud to me. Start here [examiner points] and read as quickly and carefully as you can. Try to say each word. Ready? Please begin."

Scoring

Place a slash (/) on your copy of the materials where the student started reading. As the student reads, place a mark (X) on your copy over any errors (mispronunciations, words skipped, and words given). (If student hesitates for 2–3 seconds, give him or her the word and mark it as an error.) If student inserts words, self-corrects, sounds out, or repeats, do not count as errors. When the student has read for 1 minute, place a slash (/) on your copy to indicate how far the student read in 1 minute. (It is usually good practice to let students finish the paragraph or page they are reading rather than stopping them immediately when 1 minute is over.) Count the total number of words read during the 1 minute (the total number of words between the two slashes). Tally the total number of errors (words mispronounced, words skipped, and words given) made during the 1-minute sample. Subtract the total number of errors from the total words covered to get number correct (total words – errors = correct words).

If students complete the passage before the minute is up, compute student rate using this formula:

$$\frac{\text{\# Correct Words}}{\text{Seconds}} \times \frac{60}{1} = \text{Correct Words Per Minute}$$

Note   Probe administered individually.

Billy decided to go down by the river and	(9)
demonstrate his fishing ability. He always could deceive	(17)
the fish with his special secret lure. He had his best	(28)
luck in his own place, a wooded shady spot downstream	(38)
that no one knew about. Today he was going to try	(49)
to catch a catfish all the boys called Old Gray. Old Gray	(61)
was a legend in this town, because even though many boys	(72)
had hooked him, he always managed to get away.	(81)
This time Billy knew that if he sat long enough, he could	(93)
catch his dream fish!	(97)

1. Who is the main character in this story?
2. Where does the story take place?
3. What problem is Billy trying to solve?
4. How is Billy going to try to solve the problem?
5. What do you think is going to happen?

S O U R C E : From *Curriculum-Based Assessment and Instructional Design* by E. Lessen, M. Sommers, and W. D. Bursuck, 1987, DeKalb, IL: DeKalb County Special Education Association. Used with permission.

Case in Practice

Using Story Grammars

Ms. Padilla's second-grade students have just read the story *The Funny Farola* by Ann Miranda and Maria Guerrero. The story is about a girl and her family who are participating in an ethnic festival in their city. The girl, Dora, makes a farola, which is a type of lantern people carry while marching in a parade. Dora's family laughed at her farola because it was in the shape of a frog. However, her unusual farola saves the day when it helps Dora and her parents find Dora's lost brother and sister.

Ms. Padilla is assessing Chantille's comprehension of the story using the story grammar retelling format.

Ms. Padilla: Chantille, you have just read *The Funny Farola*. Would you tell me in your own words what the story is about?

Chantille: The story is about a girl named Dora who made this funny frog that she carried in a parade. You see, her brother and sister got lost at the parade 'cause they were having such a good time, but they got found again 'cause they could see Dora's frog.

Ms. Padilla: Chantille, where does this story take place?

Chantille: It took place in a city and the people were having a big festi-

val. That's why they were having the parade.

Ms. Padilla: Chantille, what was the problem with Dora's frog?

Chantille: Well, it was called a farola, which is a kind of lantern. Everyone was making them for the parade. Dora's family laughed at her farola 'cause they had never seen a frog farola before.

Ms. Padilla: You said that Dora's sister and brother got lost. What did they do to solve that problem?

Chantille: Well, they saw Dora's frog so they knew where to find them.

Ms. Padilla: How did you feel at the end of the story?

Chantille: I felt happy.

Ms. Padilla: Why did you feel happy?

Chantille: Well, 'cause Dora's brother and sister found their mom and dad.

Ms. Padilla: Chantille, what lesson do you think this story teaches us?

Chantille: Not to get lost from your mom and dad.

A score sheet that Ms. Padilla completed for Chantille is shown in Figure 8.3. A plus (+) means that Chantille responded accurately to that element without any prompting or questioning; a checkmark (✓) means that Chantille mentioned the element after she was questioned or prompted; a minus (–) means that she failed to refer to the element even after questioning or prompts.

Look at Chantille's scores. As you can see, she had a good idea of who the main characters were and received a plus for this component ("Characters"). Chantille named two problems in the story: Dora making a farola that her family laughed at, and Dora's brother and sister getting lost. Chantille identified the problem of the lost kids without being prompted, and the problem of the funny farola with prompts; thus, a + and a ✓ were scored for "Goal/Problem." It was unclear from Chantille's response exactly how the characters tried to solve their problem, so she received a – for "Attempts." Chantille did say the problem was solved when Dora's brother and sister saw the frog; she received a + for this element of "Resolution." However, she did not say

model for designing comprehension questions based on story grammar. A **story grammar** is simply the description of the typical elements found frequently in stories. These include theme, setting, character, initiating events, attempts at resolution, resolution, and reactions. These elements of story grammar can be used to create comprehension questions that may be more appropriate than traditional

how this resolved the problem of her family laughing at the farola so she received a –. Chantille's reaction to the story was appropriate, so a + was scored. For "Setting," Chantille received a ✓; she identified the setting after Ms. Padilla prompted her. Finally, Chantille received a – for "Theme." This response was lacking, even after prompting.

Notice that Ms. Padilla's prompts included explicit references to the various story grammar components. For example, she asked, "You said that Dora's sister and brother got lost. What did they do to solve that problem?" as opposed to a more general question, such as, "What happened to Dora's sister and brother?" This use of specific language makes the story grammar components more clear, a necessary structure for younger, more naive learners.

REFLECTIONS

How could story retellings be incorporated into a classroom literature-based program? How do you think these results will be helpful to Ms. Padilla?

Figure 8.3 Story Retelling Checklist

Student Name	Story Grammars Evaluated												
	Theme		Setting		Characters		Goal/Problem		Attempts		Resolution		Reactions
Chantille	–		✓		+		+	✓	–		+	–	+

+ Responded correctly without prompting
✓ Responded correctly after prompting
– Did not identify relevant story grammar component

main-idea and detail questions, because story grammar describes the organization of most stories that elementary school students are likely to read. The Case in Practice shows how a teacher uses a story grammar with one of her second-grade students.

At times, you might not wish to ask questions about a story. Specific questions can give students clues to the answers, and they especially help students identify the

Professional Edge

Using Probes to Identify Children At Risk for Reading Problems

Over 20 years of research show that two early language skills are highly predictive of reading success in school: letter-naming fluency and phonemic segmentation (Kaminski & Good, 1996). Assessing both of these skills from the middle of kindergarten to the end of first grade can help you identify children who are at risk for having reading problems later on.

Letter naming fluency can be measured by giving a one-minute see–say letter naming probe using guidelines discussed in this chapter. While clear-cut national norms are not available, students who identify fewer than 15 correct letters per minute at the end of kindergarten, and fewer than 30 letters per minute by the end of first grade, may be at risk for having reading problems.

Phonemic segmentation involves the understanding that speech is composed of individual sounds (Snider, 1995). Phonemic segmentation involves the ability to say the individual sounds in words presented orally. For example, the teacher says, "sad," and the students says, "*ssss…aaaa…dd*." To get a rough estimate of student skill in phonemic segmentation, dictate 10 one-syllable words and have students say the individual sounds in each word. Note that this task is completely oral; no written words are presented to

students. If students are not able to say *all* of the individual sounds in *most* words, they may be at risk for reading problems and in need of segmentation instruction. Students who do poorly on both letter naming fluency and phonemic segmentation are even more likely to have trouble learning to read.

Research shows that while teaching your students to identify letters more quickly does not necessarily improve their chances of being better readers, teaching them phonological awareness skills does (Nation & Hulme, 1997; Smith, Simmons, & Kameenui, 1995). Snider (1995) suggests teaching sound segmentation and blending as follows:

Use a "Say it and move it" activity to model how to say the sounds in a word. For example, "Watch me. Every time I say a sound, I'm going to move one of these chips down. Fffffaaaaatt."

Model how to blend sounds into words. For example, "I'm going to say a word the slow way and then I'll say it fast. Mmmmmaaaaannnnn. Man. Now you try. If you can say the word fast, I'll show you a picture." (p. 448)

For more information on how to teach phonemic segmentation see Carnine el al. (1997) and Snider (1995).

kind of information you think is important to remember or the way you organize this information. One way to solve this problem is to have students retell stories after they read them. Students then must organize the information they think is important. You can then evaluate the completeness of their recall. Such a situation has two requirements in order for effective evaluation to occur: a standard set of criteria to evaluate the completeness of the retelling, and the opportunity to evaluate each student's retelling individually. The Professional Edge offers additional means of assessing students' reading skills.

Probes of written expression.   Written expression can be assessed using a think-write probe. In this probe, the teacher reads the students a story starter. The students then have 1 minute to plan a story and 3 minutes to write it. This probe is scored according to the number of "intelligible" words the student is able to write per minute. Intelligible words are those that make sense in the story. This way of scoring is useful for screening students for serious writing difficulty (Shinn & Hubbard, 1992). If you are interested in more diagnostic information, such as grammar usage, spelling, handwriting, punctuation, vocabulary, or ideas, you can score this probe differently or give another probe designed to measure these areas specifically (see Choate et al., 1995; Evans, Evans, & Mercer, 1986; and Howell & Morehead, 1993, for sample informal assessments in these areas).

Probes of math skills.   Teachers in the primary grades need to measure student identification of numbers, coins, and geometric figures. This assessment can be done as a see–say probe using numbers and symbols. Math computation and math problem solving can be assessed using see–write probes such as the one shown in Figure 8.4.

Content-Area Assessments

Content-area teachers may need to take a somewhat different approach to student assessment. Content-area classrooms are characterized by increased curricular demands with fewer opportunities for individualization; students are expected to learn more material and to take responsibility for learning much of it on their own.

> ■ **Do It!**
>
> Give an academic skill probe in an elementary school class. Summarize the results and share them with the teacher.

Figure 8.4 **See–Write: Math Computation**

Time	1 minute
Materials	*Student*—Response sheet, two pencils *Examiner*—Timer
Directions to Student	"When I say 'Please begin,' write the answers to these math problems as quickly and carefully as you can. Go across the page [examiner demonstrates]. If you have trouble with a problem, try it, write something, and then move on. Do not erase. Ready? Please begin." After 1 minute elapses, say "Please stop. Put your pencils down. Thank you."
Scoring	Count the number of correct digits (not answers) written. For example, here is a student's work for the problem 43 + 49:

$$\begin{array}{r} 1 \\ 43 \\ +\,49 \\ \hline 92 \end{array}$$

Score this as three correct digits: The answer has two correct digits (92) and the number carried represents one correct digit. Digits correct is often used because it is more sensitive to changes in student performance (see Tindal & Marston, 1990, for a more complete explanation).

S O U R C E : From *Curriculum-Based Assessment and Instructional Design* by E. Lessen, M. Sommers, and W. Bursuck, 1987, DeKalb, IL: DeKalb County Special Education Association. Used with permission.

Students who enter a class significantly behind their classmates either in background knowledge or independent learning skills are likely to struggle. Thus, it is important to identify these students early so that they can be better prepared when they enter a content class. For example, at the beginning of this chapter, Mr. Blount assessed his history students' ability to read the class textbook independently since students in his class were expected to read much of the material on their own.

Connections

Using probes of prerequisite skills is a good way to identify classroom demands as part of the INCLUDE strategy.

Probes of prerequisite skills. The decision whether or not to place a particular student in a given middle school or high school class depends on identifying which skills or content are prerequisite. For example, the English department at a high school developed a test of prerequisite skills for freshman English. Clarise, a student with a learning disability, was given this test at the end of eighth grade to find out whether this class was appropriate for her to take. For skill-oriented classes such as math and English, prerequisite skills would be those covered in elementary school or previously taught courses, such as computation skills for algebra and sentence writing for English. For classes that stress content rather than basic skills (for example, science), having the necessary background information to understand the material currently being presented is also vital.

Unfortunately, the process of determining whether students have necessary prerequisite skills can be problematic. A key problem involves identifying these skills. Teachers' choices of prerequisite skills often include skills that a student can bypass and still have access to course content, such as reading in a history class (which can be bypassed by using an oral text) or written expression in a science class (which can be bypassed by using oral tests and reports). When testing for prerequisite skills, you must be careful that you do not inadvertently exclude students with special needs, many of whom are capable of passing content classes despite their problems in certain basic-skills areas.

This and other problems suggest the need for a fair way of making placement decisions for students with special needs at the high school level. A potentially useful method is for teachers to develop probes to evaluate student performance on critical prerequisite skills. The probe-development process, which is similar to the process of developing curriculum-based assessments described earlier in the chapter, consists of the following steps:

1. Identify critical content learning or skills for your class.

2. Identify entry-level content or skills needed. Be certain these are not skills for which a bypass strategy would be possible.

3. Develop a probe to measure the identified skills.

4. Administer the probe to current classes to make sure that students passing the class are able to pass the probe test.

5. Set a minimum score necessary for student course entry based on the results of the preceding step. You may want to use an acceptable range rather than a single score, particularly during the initial stages of this process.

6. As with all educational decisions, no one score should be the sole basis for a decision. Other factors, such as student motivation and level of supportive assistance, will need to be considered.

What curriculum goals might a physical education teacher observing this class be assessing?

Measures of independent learning skills.   When students enter high school, they find an environment often not as supportive as the smaller elementary and junior high or middle school environments they left. The student body is often larger and more diverse. Daily routines change and curriculum is more difficult (Schumaker & Deshler, 1988). High schools also demand a much higher level of student independence through the application of a range of **independent learning skills.** These skills, often referred to as *learning strategies* or *study skills*, include note-taking, textbook reading, test-taking, written expression, and time management. Student ability to perform these various skills independently can make the difference between passing or failing a class. For example, at the beginning of the chapter, Mr. Blount decided to assess textbook reading skills since these were important for success in his class. A sample instrument to measure textbook reading skills, which was originally developed by Voix (1968) and later adapted by Lessen, Sommers, and Bursuck (1987), is shown in Figure 8.5 on pages 282–283. Notice that the reading tasks for this measure are taken directly from the students' history and science textbooks. Doing so ensures that the results are relevant for the particular classroom situation. Note also that this textbook reading assessment can be given to the entire classroom at once; this will be helpful since many students may have trouble reading their textbooks, not just students with special needs.

As with the basic and prerequisite skills mentioned earlier, probes can be developed to assess independent learning. A key consideration is that the tasks used for assessment should parallel the tasks students are faced with in your classroom: If you are evaluating textbook reading, the reading task should come from the textbook you are using in class; if you are measuring a student's ability to take lecture notes, the task should involve elements similar to a typical lecture delivered in your class.

Once the task has been selected, decide what kind of measure to use. Three possible choices are direct-observation checklists, analysis of student products, and student self-evaluation. With direct-observation checklists, a list of observable steps necessary to perform a given strategy is developed. Next, the teacher has a student perform a classroom task that requires him or her to use the strategy and records on the checklist which behaviors the student did or did not perform.

Although direct observation of student behavior can provide much useful information, it is time-consuming, particularly when you are a high school teacher who teaches many students each day. For most students, you can use either analysis of student products or student self-evaluations. Nonetheless, if you should have the luxury of a free moment with an individual student, such as before or after school or during a study hall, the time spent directly observing a student perform a task is very worthwhile.

Analysis of student products involves looking at student notebooks, tests, papers, and other assignments or written activities to find evidence of effective or ineffective strategy performance. In most cases, you can evaluate your whole classroom at once, and you do not have to score the products while you are teaching.

In **student self-evaluations,** students perform a task such as taking a test, are given a checklist of strategy steps, and are then asked to tell which of these steps they did or did not use (Bursuck & Jayanthi, 1993). Student self-reports are useful for several reasons. They can provide information about strategy behaviors that cannot be directly observed. Student evaluations also stimulate student self-monitoring, a

Connections

Sample direct-observation checklists can be found in Chapter 11.

Cultural Awareness

Student-centered assessment strategies such as self-evaluation are an important part of empowering students through multicultural education.

Figure 8.5   Evaluating Content-Area Textbook Reading Skills

Suggestions for specific types of questions are included here. The information in parentheses explains or offers additional information about a particular item.

Using Parts of the Book

1. On what page would you find the chapter called _____ ? (Tests ability to use table of contents.)

2. Of what value to you are the questions listed at the end of each chapter? (Tests understanding of a specific study aid.)

3. How are the chapters arranged or grouped? (Tests knowledge of text organization.)

4. What part of the book would you use to find the page reference for the topic _____ ? (Tests knowledge of index.)

5. On what page would you find the answer to each of the following questions? (Tests ability to use index.)

Using Source Materials (examples)

1. What library aid will tell you the library number of a book so that you would be able to find the book on the shelves? (Tests knowledge of functions of card catalog and computerized cataloging systems.)

2. What is a biography? (Tests knowledge of a type of reference book.)

3. Explain the difference between science fiction and factual science materials. (Tests knowledge of important types of science materials.)

Comprehension

The following questions would be based on a three- or four-page selection from the textbook.

Vocabulary

1. Turn to page _____ . How does the author define the word _____ ? (Tests ability to use context clues and the aids the author uses to convey the meaning of the word.)

2. Define _____ .

3. What is a _____ ?

4. *Vocabulary in context:* From the paragraph on page 584 beginning "In Poland, the Soviet Union . . . ," write an appropriate and brief definition of each of the following words: _____ , _____ , and _____ .

Noting Main Ideas

These questions would ask for main points of information, such as main ideas of longer, important paragraphs of the chapter or summary of an experiment. (*Examples:* What are atoms composed of? What reason was given for the conservation of human resources? What is the result of the photosynthetic process?)

Noting Details

These questions would ask for specific bits of information, such as an aspect of a process, the application of a law, the principal steps in an experiment, a life cycle, or incidents

(continued)

Figure 8.5 *(continued)*

in the life of a scientist. (*Examples:* Describe the photosynthetic process. What are the different stages in the cycle of precipitation and evaporation? List the major incidents in the life of Mme. Marie Curie.)

Drawing Conclusions
Ask questions about the significance or value of a finding, the implication of a description of some species or natural phenomenon, causes and effect, or a comparison of two or more types of organisms. The questions should call for answers that are not stated in the text. (*Examples:* Illustrate the term *balance of life*. What conclusion can you draw from the importance of the photosynthetic process? What is the principle difference between mitosis and meiosis?)

Applying Theoretical Information
These questions would ask for examples of practical uses of scientific law and principles. (*Examples:* Explain the relationship of photosynthesis to the conservation of plant life. Explain the idea that air confined in a small area exerts pressure in all directions, in relation to the action of air in a football.)

Following Directions
These questions would ask learners to show the sequence of steps or ideas for solving a problem or performing an experiment or the sequence of a chain of events. (*Examples:* What is the second step of the experiment? What should you do after you have placed the flask over the burner?)

Understanding Formulas and Symbols
These questions test student understanding of how symbols and formulas are used with scientific data. (*Examples:* What does the "H" refer to in the symbol H_2O? What does 40# mean?)

Maps and Graphs
Use questions that require knowledge of map and graph symbols and how to use them. (*Examples:* Use the graph on page 602 to answer these questions: By 1925, how many millions of people inhabited Earth? How many times will the world population have increased from 1900 to 2000? Use the map on page 174 to answer these questions: Who ruled Gascony in the 12th century? Who governed the major portion of Flanders after 1550?)

Study Reading
Directions: Read pages 584–586. Take notes. Then, close your book and keep it closed. However, you may use the notes you made to help you answer the following questions. (Have questions on a separate sheet for distribution after notes have been made.) *Note:* Ask detail, main idea, and inference questions.

S O U R C E : Adapted from *Evaluating Reading and Study Skills in the Secondary Classroom: A Guide for Content Teachers* by R. G. Voix, 1968, Newark, DE: International Reading Association.

Do It!

Develop and give a textbook reading probe like the one shown in Figure 8.5 in a high school class. Share the results with the teacher.

behavior critical for independent learning. Self-report measures can also include interview questions that further clarify strategy usage. For example, one teacher asked, "What was the first thing you did when you received your test?" As with all measures, student self-evaluations will need to be corroborated by information from other sources (for example, direct-observation checklists and student products).

Such corroboration may be particularly important for students with special needs, many of whom have difficulty evaluating their own behavior.

How Are Learning Probes Used to Make Special Education Decisions?

Academic probes can help teachers make many of the assessment decisions discussed earlier in this chapter. Several examples are discussed in the following sections.

Peer Comparison in Screening

The key question involved in screening is whether the student is different enough from his or her peers on important skills in a given academic area (or areas) to indicate that some form of classroom accommodation is necessary. If the difference between a student and his or her peers continues or worsens despite repeated attempts in the classroom to remediate, a referral to special education and a more comprehensive assessment *may* be called for.

FYI

Peer comparison and other classroom assessment procedures developed by Deno and colleagues are referred to as *curriculum-based measurement*.

The method of **peer comparison** suggested here was originally developed by Deno and his colleagues at the University of Minnesota (Deno, 1985, 1989; Deno & Fuchs, 1987; Marston, Tindal, & Deno, 1984). First, probes are selected in the area(s) of suspected difficulty. Next, the probes are given to the entire class or a representative subsample of the class (for example, five "average" performers).

Figure 8.6 shows probe results for oral reading in context. The scores are ranked from high to low, and then the class median is determined. The median, or middlemost score, is used to summarize the scores because it is affected less by extreme scores than the mean, or average, which could over- or underestimate the performance of the group as a whole.

FYI

See Hasbrouck and Tindal (1992) for curriculum-based norms in oral reading fluency for grades 2–5.

Figure 8.6 also gives a score equal to one-half of the median ("Median/2"). This score can be used as a cutoff for identifying students in trouble on that particular skill (Shinn & Hubbard, 1992). Such a cutoff point typically identifies 6 to 12 percent of a class or grade level who may be experiencing difficulty on a particular skill (Bursuck & Lessen, 1987; Marston et al., 1984). Some probes may identify more students in trouble. For example, we would expect a higher percentage of third graders to be discrepant on basic multiplication facts in the fall than in the spring, since these facts have not yet been covered in class. Similarly, many first graders score low on probes given during the first half of the year since many of these skills are being presented for the first time.

To see how these scores are used to make decisions about screening, look again at Figure 8.6. Oral reading in context represents the number of correct words read orally from a grade-level passage from a basal reader or books used in a classroom literature-based reading program. As shown, the class scores range from a high of 190 words read correctly per minute to a low of 50 words read correctly per minute. The median, or middlemost, score for the class is 123 words read correctly per minute. A score of 61.5 words read correctly per minute is half of the median. One student is below this point. Although this student may be in need of a classroom

Figure 8.6   **Classroom Performance on Academic Skill Probe in Reading**

Reading Orally in Context
Number of correct words per minute read orally

190	136	103
189	128	99
172	125	97
160	123	96
159	120	94
151	119	90
139	119	*50
136	117	

Median	123
Median/2	61.5

*Denotes score of Median/2 or lower

accommodation or a referral to special education, other factors should also be considered, including the student's performance across other academic skills assessed and whether or not other students in the class are having similar problems.

The Technology Notes feature on pages 286–287 illustrates a way you can use software to help you assess your students.

Fluency and Accuracy in Diagnosis

Curriculum-based assessment probes also can help teachers diagnose specific skills deficits. For example, a student who performs poorly on a math facts probe may not know the math facts or may simply be unable to write numbers fast enough. You could figure out which situation exists by examining the student's rates, or **fluency,** on think-write number writing. Likewise, keeping track of the number of errors per minute, or **accuracy,** in oral reading can help you detect a particular student's reading problem. Figure 8.9 on page 288 shows the results of an oral reading probe for two third-grade students. The correct reading rate for both students was 53. However, Student 1 was more accurate in her reading than Student 2. Student 1 seems to have a problem with reading rate. What she reads, she reads accurately; the problem is that 53 words correct per minute is slow for a third-grade student. Student 2, on the other hand, is making many word-identification errors as well and will need to be assessed further to find out if these errors are part of a pattern or whether they are due to carelessness.

The fact that curriculum-based assessment probes measure rate as well as accuracy adds an important diagnostic dimension. For example, if the reading

Check Your Learning

What kinds of diagnostic information can you learn by checking student rates of performing academic skills?

Technology Notes

Computerized Curriculum-Based Measurement

You may be wondering how you are going to assess your students systematically and still have time to prepare and teach your lessons. Researchers have developed a product that may help you (Fuchs, Fuchs, Hamlett, Philips, & Bentz, 1994). They have developed software that makes scoring and interpreting curriculum-based measures in math much easier. In the Fuchs et al. system, students take a weekly probe test that measures required math operations for a given grade level. Students then are taught to enter their own data into a computer program that scores their test and summarizes the results.

The software program summarizes student performance using a display like the one shown in Figure 8.7. The top chart shows the student's rate and accuracy on weekly math tests over time. This student (Sheila Hemmer) went from a score of 10 digits correct per minute at the beginning of October to a score of over 30 digits correct per minute in March. The skills profile at the bottom shows which skills (A1 = first skill in addition; S2 = second skill in subtraction) have been mastered and which may require more instruction.

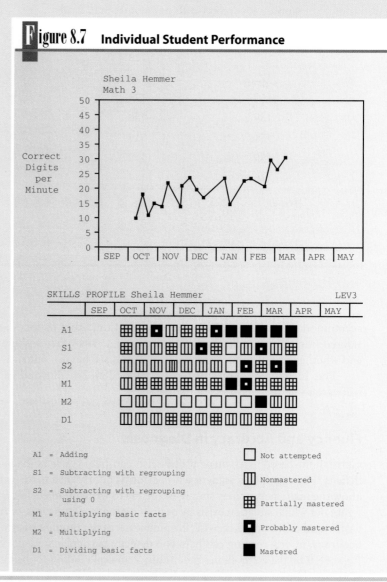

Figure 8.7 Individual Student Performance

performance of the two students just discussed had been reported solely as a percentage, the results would have looked like those shown in Figure 8.10 on page 288. Using percentages alone, Student 1 does not appear to have a problem at all. However, as previously shown, she is reading much more slowly than Student 2.

Teachers also receive a display like the one in Figure 8.8. The graph at the top shows the teacher, Mr. Martin, the progress of his students from October through March. The top line indicates scores at the 75th percentile; the middle line, scores at the 50th percentile; and the bottom line, scores at the 25th percentile. The lists below the graph provide information about which students should be watched, or monitored; areas in which the class has improved or not changed; and recommendations for skills that could be covered in whole-group instruction (most of the class needed instruction) or small-group instruction (only one or two students).

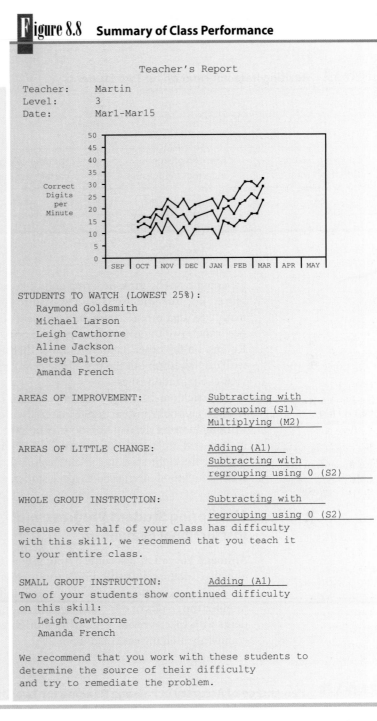

Figure 8.8 Summary of Class Performance

Teacher's Report

Teacher: Martin
Level: 3
Date: Mar1-Mar15

STUDENTS TO WATCH (LOWEST 25%):
  Raymond Goldsmith
  Michael Larson
  Leigh Cawthorne
  Aline Jackson
  Betsy Dalton
  Amanda French

AREAS OF IMPROVEMENT: Subtracting with
                               regrouping (S1)
                               Multiplying (M2)

AREAS OF LITTLE CHANGE: Adding (A1)
                               Subtracting with
                               regrouping using 0 (S2)

WHOLE GROUP INSTRUCTION: Subtracting with
                               regrouping using 0 (S2)
Because over half of your class has difficulty with this skill, we recommend that you teach it to your entire class.

SMALL GROUP INSTRUCTION: Adding (A1)
Two of your students show continued difficulty on this skill:
    Leigh Cawthorne
    Amanda French

We recommend that you work with these students to determine the source of their difficulty and try to remediate the problem.

Skill Mastery and Curriculum Placement

As we have already discussed, inclusive education involves the use of a variety of instructional grouping arrangements: same-skill groups, mixed-skill groups, and individualized instruction. Students with special needs benefit from all three of these arrangements. You can use curriculum-based assessment probes to form all of these

Figure 8.9   **Reading Rate Information for Two Students**

Student 1		Student 2	
Number of words correct per minute	Number of words incorrect per minute	Number of words correct per minute	Number of words incorrect per minute
53	2	53	16

grouping types by rank-ordering and then visually inspecting your students' probe scores. For example, Mr. Glass wanted to form mixed-skill cooperative groups in math. He used probe scores on a problem-solving task form by picking one lower performer, two middle performers, and one higher performer for each group. Ms. Robins, on the other hand, found that three of her students were having difficulty with capitalization but the rest of the class was not. She formed a small group to review capitalization rules.

Curriculum-based probes can also be used to place students appropriately within classroom instructional materials. Because students who are consistently working in materials that are too easy or hard for them are more likely to be off task in class and are at risk for eventually becoming discipline problems, placing students at the right spot in the curriculum is essential. The Professional Edge describes a method often used to place students in a reading curriculum.

Check Your Learning

How can curriculum-based assessment probes be used to place students in reading books?

Monitoring Student Progress and Instructional Evaluation

Although education has come a long way in terms of researching what constitutes effective teaching, it is still difficult to predict whether a given technique will work for a given student in a particular situation. It is thus important that we carefully monitor the results of our teaching. This monitoring is particularly relevant for students with special needs who, by definition, are less likely to respond favorably to commonly used instructional methods.

Figure 8.10   **Percentage of Accuracy in Passage Reading for Two Students**

Student 1	Student 2
Percentage of Accuracy	Percentage of Accuracy
96	70

Professional Edge

Using Curriculum-Based Assessment for Reading Placement

Finding books on topics your students are interested in is important in motivating them to read. But just as important is ensuring that students are able to read their books accurately and fluently. The following method has been used for years to place students in reading material that is at their reading level. As you will see, this method can be used for both basal and literature-based reading programs.

1. For basal readers, select three 300-word passages—one from the beginning, one from the middle, and one from the end—of each level book in a given series. For first and second grades, select briefer passages of between 100 and 200 words. For literature-based programs, first group books into levels of difficulty using one of the many available readability formulas. Beginning books can also be arranged according to predictability. Then proceed as noted for basals.

2. Select passages that contain few proper names, are related to topics familiar to most students, and are primarily flowing narratives rather than dialogue or poetry.

3. For each passage, construct a teacher score sheet similar to the one shown in Figure 8.3 on page 277.

4. Give the probes starting at a level at which you feel the student will be reasonably successful. (See Figure 8.2 on page 275 for oral reading probe directions.)

5. Find the median of the students' correct and error rates for the three passages and then compare them to the following placement figures. If the median scores fall at the instructional level or greater, continue to go up a level. *Stop at the highest level at which the student scores at the instructional level.* (The rate guidelines specified below were derived from Shinn & Hubbard, 1992.) If the student's median scores are below the instructional level, sample student reading behavior at lower levels. Thus, if any of a student's scores are at the frustration level, drop down a level or two and sample from three 300-word passages at that level. *Remember, these placement figures are to be used as general guidelines, not exact predictors of future student performance.* Therefore, we strongly suggest that you continue to monitor student performance and make placement changes as necessary.

Instructional Placement Standards

2nd Grade and Lower

  40–60 correct words/minute

  4 or fewer errors per minute

3rd Grade and Higher

  70–100 correct words/minute

  7 or fewer errors per minute

Curriculum-based assessment probes, because they are time-efficient, easy to give, and match what is taught in the classroom, are ideal for monitoring student progress in class. For example, Mr. Harris was interested in whether Maria, a student with learning disabilities, was retaining any of the words included on weekly spelling lists. She had scored 90 and above on her weekly tests, but Mr. Harris was still unsure whether she was remembering the words from one week to the next. He developed a spelling probe using words from previous spelling lists. He gave the probe to his entire class and found that Maria and 10 other students were retaining only 20 percent of the words. As a result, he started a peer tutoring

Check Your Learning

How can probes be used to monitor student progress?

program to help students review their words. Mr. Harris also set up group competitions and had awards for groups scoring the highest on the review probes. With these two activities implemented, Maria's and the other students' retention improved significantly.

A final example is worthy of mention. Mr. Rock recently switched his reading program from a basal series to a literature-based program. He wanted to make sure that several of the lower-performing students in his class were adding new words to their sight vocabularies. He randomly selected three 300-word passages from a literature book that all of these students had recently completed. He found that two of the students read the passages at mastery levels, but one student was reading at the frustration level. Mr. Rock decided to drop the student to an easier level of book and provide some high-frequency word drills with the student using a peer tutor. Again, teaching approaches, no matter how promising, may not work for all students. By monitoring his students' progress using CBA probes, Mr. Rock was able to make a helpful adaptation in a student's instructional program.

Summary

The assessments general education teachers make can contribute to six special education decisions: screening, diagnosis, program placement, curriculum placement, instructional evaluation, and program evaluation. Screening involves whether or not a student's performance is different enough from that of his or her peers to merit further, more in-depth assessments to see whether the student has a disability. Diagnosis relates to eligibility for special education services; namely, does the student meet federal guidelines for being classified as having a disability? If so, what is the nature and extent of the student's disability? The major program-placement decision involves determining the instructional setting where a student's special learning needs can be met. Curriculum-placement decisions concern where to begin instruction for students. Decisions in instructional evaluation involve whether to continue or change instructional procedures that have been initiated with students. The purpose of program-evaluation decisions is to determine whether a student's special education program should be terminated, continued as is, or modified.

General education teachers can go to a number of information sources to help them program for students with special needs. Group-administered standardized achievement tests can be used to screen students in difficulty, but they have serious drawbacks for making other types of decisions. Individually administered diagnostic tests provide more specific information but are susceptible to many of the same problems as group-administered tests. Psychological tests, such as tests of intelligence and tests related to learning disabilities, measure abilities that affect how efficiently students learn in an instructional situation. These tests can clarify why students may not be learning in class, but they are most helpful when corroborated by classroom experience. Be aware that psychological tests may discriminate against students from culturally diverse or disadvantaged environments. The purpose of an environmental inventory is to find out what adaptations or supports students with moderate to severe disabilities need to increase their participation in the classroom and the community. Curriculum-based assessments measure student achievement in terms of what they are taught in the classroom. As such, they are helpful in making a range of special education decisions, particularly those involving day-to-day instruction.

There are two major kinds of curriculum-based assessments: probes of basic academic skills and content-area strategy assessments. Probes of basic academic skills consist of timed samples of academic behaviors and are designed to assess skill accuracy and fluency. Probes can be developed for all basic skill areas, including reading, written expression, and math. Content-area assessments include probes of prerequisite skills and measures of independent learning skills. Probes of prerequisite skills help teachers make decisions about whether or not to place students in particular high school classes. Measures of independent learning skills, often referred to as learning strategies or study skills, include note-taking, textbook reading, test-taking, written expression, and time management. Three ways to measure skills in these areas include direct-observation checklists, analysis of student products, and student self-evaluations.

Curriculum-based assessment probes can be used to help make special education decisions. A peer comparison method can help screen students who are in academic difficulty. Probes can also be used to help teachers diagnose specific skill deficits by determining whether academic problems involve accuracy, fluency, or both. In addition, academic assessment probes can be used to help form instructional groups, as well as to place students into the appropriate reading materials. Finally, curriculum-based probes can help teachers monitor the progress of students in class by measuring student performance over time.

Applications in Teaching Practice

Collecting and Using Assessment Information

It is November 1, and you are concerned about two students in your literature-based reading program. The students' parents have commented that they have not seen improvement in their children's reading at home. You have also noticed that both of these students seem to pick trade books that are too hard for them. In addition, you have concerns about what progress they have made in their word identification and comprehension skills. You wonder whether you should make some changes in their reading program.

Questions

1. What areas of reading would you want to assess here? Why?
2. How would you assess each area using the curriculum-based assessment procedures described in this chapter? What probes would you give? What would your probes look like? How would you score them?

3. What additional assessment information (for example, standardized tests, psychological tests) would you collect?

4. How would you use the information you obtained in (2) and (3)? Under what circumstances would you decide to adapt the current program? Use an alternative program? Advocate for intensive instruction from a special education teacher?

5. What would you do to evaluate the changes suggested in (4)? What measures would you give? How often? What kinds of decisions would you be making?

Yolanda is a student with a learning disability in your class who has been receiving indirect support in the area of (pick one: reading, math, written expression). You are interested in knowing how she is doing in relation to the rest of the class. Select a subject area in which Yolanda has been receiving indirect support. Then, select a particular skill in that subject-matter area that you have been working on in your class (for example, in reading—sight-word reading, passage reading, comprehension, letter or letter-sound identification; in math—any math computation skill, word problems, money, geometry; in written expression—writing mechanics, writing productivity, quality of ideas). Next, describe a curriculum-based assessment strategy you would use to judge how well Yolanda is doing on that skill as compared with her classmates. Respond to the following questions in your description.

Questions

1. How would you use peer comparisons to measure the extent of Yolanda's problem?

2. What additional information would you collect to clarify Yolanda's problem?

3. How would you use probe information to measure the effectiveness of classroom supports for Yolanda?

4. How would you use probe information to help you instruct the rest of the class?

The high school resource room teacher has suggested that Antoine, who has a learning disability, be included in your second semester _____ (pick whatever area you will eventually be teaching) class. He has asked you to help collect some information to assist him in deciding what support service (if any) Antoine should receive. If you are a math teacher, describe a strategy for determining whether Antoine has the prerequisite skills for your class. Your strategy should respond to the following questions.

Questions

1. What skills would you include on your probe and why?

2. Are all of these skills essential, or could some of them be bypassed?

3. How will you design, administer, and score your probe?

4. How will you determine whether Antoine is in academic difficulty?

5. How would you use the information collected to determine needed support services for Antoine?

6. How might the information collected help you in teaching the rest of the class?

If you are teaching a class for which the ability to read the textbook is an important skill, select a sample textbook from your content area. Then, develop a probe of content-area reading skills using the model shown in Figure 8.5 on page 282.

Questions

1. How did you select the skills to be included on your measures?
2. How would you use the information collected to determine the nature and extent of classroom support needed for students with disabilities? For the rest of the class?

chapter **9**

Instructional
Adaptations

■ Ms. Diaz was teaching her fourth-grade class how to write percents for fractions using this example from her math book:

Write a percent for $\frac{7}{8}$.

$\frac{7}{8}$ means $7 \div 8$.

$$0.87\tfrac{4}{8} = 0.87\tfrac{1}{2} = 87\tfrac{1}{2}\%$$

$$8\overline{)7.00}$$

Divide until the answer is in hundredths. Give the remainder as a fraction.

$$\frac{64}{60}$$
$$\frac{56}{4}$$

$\frac{7}{8} = 87\tfrac{1}{2}\%$, or 87.5%

Ms. Diaz showed her students how to do this problem by writing the sample on the board and then pointing out that the fraction $\frac{7}{8}$ means 7 divided by 8 and that they have to divide until the answer is in hundredths and to give the remainder as a fraction. Following this instruction, Ms. Diaz assigned the students 15 similar problems to do independently. Abdul is a student with a learning disability in this class. Abdul has difficulty learning new skills unless he is given many opportunities for instruction and practice. Abdul answered none of the 15 problems correctly. He missed converting the fractions to percents because he forgot that $\frac{7}{8}$ means 7 divided by 8; Abdul divided 8 by 7 instead. How could this lesson have been taught to Abdul to prevent this misunderstanding?

■ Cecily is a student with a hearing impairment who is in Ms. Boyd's American history class. Cecily is failing history because the tests are based mainly on the textbook and she has trouble picking out main ideas in the text and understanding important vocabulary words. Cecily can read most of the words in the text but she reads very slowly, word by word. Last week, she was assigned a chapter to read for homework; it took her almost 2 hours to read 15 pages, and when she was done, she couldn't remember what she had read. The key words are highlighted, but Cecily can't figure them out from the context and doesn't know how to use the glossary. What can Ms. Boyd do to help Cecily read and remember key ideas in her textbook? What can she do to help Cecily understand new vocabulary words?

■ Albert has ADHD and is included in Ms. Olivieri's second-grade class. Albert has trouble following written

Learner Objectives

After you read this chapter, you will be able to

1. Adapt lessons when students do not have the preskills necessary to learn new skills.

2. Select and sequence instructional examples to help students acquire basic skills.

3. Adapt instruction by providing the direct instruction, practice, and review needed to help students acquire basic skills.

4. Describe adaptations you can make in providing background knowledge, organizing content, and teaching terms and concepts to help students acquire academic content.

5. Implement strategies for improving the clarity of your written and verbal communication with students.

6. Adapt independent practice activities for students.

directions and doing independent practice assignments that have more than one part. He also complains that his seatwork assignments are too hard for him. During seatwork, Albert is frequently out of his chair, either getting help from or bothering other students in the class. Ms. Olivieri feels that she is already spending too much time helping Albert. What should she do to make seatwork a more successful experience for Albert and give herself more time to work with other students?

FYI

This chapter presents guidelines for Steps 5 and 6 of the INCLUDE model presented in Chapter 4:

Step 5. Use information from Steps 1–4 to brainstorm instructional adaptations.

Step 6. Decide which adaptations to use.

As you have already learned, the curriculum methods and materials teachers use have a strong influence on how readily students learn in the classroom. In fact, the better the materials and teaching, the fewer the adaptations required for students with special needs. However, for a variety of reasons, you may not have control over the materials used in your school. Further, despite your best teaching efforts, some students will still need **instructional adaptations** if they are to master important skills and content. For example, in the vignettes above, merely showing Abdul how one problem is done is not enough. He needs guidance through a number of examples before he is ready to do problems independently. You could help Cecily pick out important information in her textbook by giving her a study guide that has questions pertaining to the most important content in each chapter. You could also have Cecily identify words she does not know and ask a classmate to help her with the meanings before she reads. For Albert, you could make sure all directions are clearly written using words Albert can decode; you could also give the directions orally and guide students through several practice examples before they are required to work independently. Of course, you also want to be sure that Albert has the necessary academic skills to complete assignments independently.

The purpose of this chapter is to provide you with strategies for adapting curriculum materials, teacher instruction, and student practice activities that are reasonable to carry out and that increase the likelihood of success for students with special needs. Remember, reasonable accommodations are those adaptations that can help a student without taking so much time and effort that they interfere with the teacher's responsibilities to other students. Further, these accommodations may be helpful for other students in class without formally identified special needs.

How Can You Adapt Basic-Skills Instruction for Students with Special Needs?

Basic-skills instruction primarily means instruction in the academic skills of reading, writing, and math. However, you may also apply effective principles for adapting basic-skills instruction to content areas such as science. Four aspects of basic-skills instruction that may need to be adapted for students with special needs are preskills, selection and sequencing of examples, rate of introduction of new skills, and direct instruction, practice, and review.

Teaching Preskills

Darrell is included in Ms. Rayburn's second-grade class. In language arts, he is experiencing a problem common to many students with special needs. On Tuesday, Darrell was at his desk reading a book on his favorite topic: magic. However, when Ms. Rayburn asked Darrell specific questions about the book, he was unable to answer them. It turned out that Darrell was unable to decode most of the words in the book and was just pretending to read.

Preskills are basic skills necessary for performing more complex skills. Prior to teaching a skill, you should assess students on the relevant preskills and, if necessary, teach these skills. Darrell was unable to comprehend the magic book because he lacked the word-identification skills needed to read the words. He may need instruction in word-attack skills; he may also need to be encouraged to read trade books at his reading level. Since commercially produced materials do not generally list preskills, you need to ask yourself continually what preskills are required and be on the lookout for students who lack them. This may mean informally assessing such skills. For example, before Mrs. Tompkins taught her kindergartners to tell time, she checked to see whether they could identify the numbers 1–12 and count by fives to 60. Before teaching students to look up words in a dictionary, Mr. Thurman checked to see whether his students could say the alphabet, could alphabetize words to the third letter, and knew whether to turn to the front, middle, or end of the dictionary when looking up a certain word.

If you are teaching a skill and find that most of your students lack the necessary preskills, teach these preskills directly before teaching the actual skill. If only one or two students lack preskills, you can provide these students with extra practice and instruction through a peer or parent volunteer, or with the help of a special service provider. For example, Ms. Cooper is preparing a lesson on how to find the area of a rectangle. Before beginning the lesson, she gave her students a multiplication probe and found that almost half the class was still having problems with their multiplication facts. Ms. Cooper set up a peer tutoring program in which students who knew their facts were paired with students who did not; they practiced facts for 10 minutes each day for a week. Ms. Cooper still introduced finding areas as scheduled, but she allowed students to use calculators until they had mastered their facts in the peer tutoring sessions.

Selecting and Sequencing Examples

The way you select and sequence instructional examples can affect how easily your students learn. For example, Alex's practice activities for the week in Mr. Huang's third-grade math class are shown in Figure 9.1 on page 298. Mr. Huang has been covering two-digit subtraction with regrouping. On Monday through Thursday, Alex was given five of these problems and got them all right. On Friday, he was asked to do a mixture of problems, some requiring regrouping and some not. Alex got only three of the problems correct because he was unable to discriminate between subtraction problems that required regrouping and those that did not. He was unable to differentiate these two types of problems in part because his daily practice pages had included only one problem type.

You can help students make key discriminations between current and previous problem types by at first using examples that require only the application of that

Cultural Awareness

Children learn many basic preskills both directly and vicariously before they reach school age. Children's cultural backgrounds and life conditions greatly affect what they know and can do.

FYI

Assessing student preskills does not always have to be done using paper-and-pencil tasks. Simply questioning your students orally takes less time and can give you relevant information immediately.

Figure 9.1   **Alex's Math Work**

Monday's Seatwork

$$
\begin{array}{r} {}^{2\,1}\!\!\not{3}5 \\ -17 \\ \hline 18 \end{array}
\qquad
\begin{array}{r} {}^{3\,1}\!\!\not{4}2 \\ -15 \\ \hline 27 \end{array}
\qquad
\begin{array}{r} {}^{2\,1}\!\!\not{3}8 \\ -19 \\ \hline 19 \end{array}
\qquad
\begin{array}{r} {}^{3\,1}\!\!\not{4}1 \\ -22 \\ \hline 19 \end{array}
\qquad
\begin{array}{r} {}^{6\,1}\!\!\not{7}4 \\ -49 \\ \hline 25 \end{array}
$$

Tuesday's Seatwork

$$
\begin{array}{r} {}^{5\,1}\!\!\not{6}4 \\ -38 \\ \hline 26 \end{array}
\qquad
\begin{array}{r} {}^{6\,1}\!\!\not{7}0 \\ -32 \\ \hline 38 \end{array}
\qquad
\begin{array}{r} {}^{8\,1}\!\!\not{9}1 \\ -58 \\ \hline 33 \end{array}
\qquad
\begin{array}{r} {}^{5\,1}\!\!\not{6}8 \\ -39 \\ \hline 29 \end{array}
\qquad
\begin{array}{r} {}^{7\,1}\!\!\not{8}2 \\ -28 \\ \hline 54 \end{array}
$$

Wednesday's Seatwork

$$
\begin{array}{r} {}^{8\,1}\!\!\not{9}4 \\ -57 \\ \hline 37 \end{array}
\qquad
\begin{array}{r} {}^{5\,1}\!\!\not{6}1 \\ -45 \\ \hline 16 \end{array}
\qquad
\begin{array}{r} {}^{2\,1}\!\!\not{3}3 \\ -19 \\ \hline 14 \end{array}
\qquad
\begin{array}{r} {}^{6\,1}\!\!\not{7}6 \\ -38 \\ \hline 38 \end{array}
\qquad
\begin{array}{r} {}^{7\,1}\!\!\not{8}1 \\ -47 \\ \hline 34 \end{array}
$$

Thursday's Seatwork

$$
\begin{array}{r} {}^{4\,1}\!\!\not{5}5 \\ -29 \\ \hline 26 \end{array}
\qquad
\begin{array}{r} {}^{2\,1}\!\!\not{3}0 \\ -18 \\ \hline 12 \end{array}
\qquad
\begin{array}{r} {}^{6\,1}\!\!\not{7}2 \\ -28 \\ \hline 44 \end{array}
\qquad
\begin{array}{r} {}^{8\,1}\!\!\not{9}6 \\ -59 \\ \hline 37 \end{array}
\qquad
\begin{array}{r} {}^{7\,1}\!\!\not{8}3 \\ -38 \\ \hline 45 \end{array}
$$

Friday's Seatwork

$$
\begin{array}{r} {}^{8\,1}\!\!\not{9}6 \\ -53 \\ \hline 313 \end{array}
\qquad
\begin{array}{r} {}^{3\,1}\!\!\not{4}3 \\ -18 \\ \hline 25 \end{array}
\qquad
\begin{array}{r} {}^{7\,1}\!\!\not{8}9 \\ -33 \\ \hline 416 \end{array}
\qquad
\begin{array}{r} {}^{5\,1}\!\!\not{6}7 \\ -28 \\ \hline 39 \end{array}
\qquad
\begin{array}{r} {}^{6\,1}\!\!\not{7}5 \\ -57 \\ \hline 18 \end{array}
$$

particular skill (Carnine, Silbert, & Kameenui, 1997). When students can perform these problems without error, add examples of skills previously taught to help students discriminate between the different problem types. Doing this also provides students with needed review. An easy adaptation for Alex would have been to add several problems that did not require regrouping to each daily practice session once he had shown that he could compute the regrouping problems accurately when presented alone.

Ms. Owens ran into another example-related problem when teaching her students word problems in math. In her examples, if a word problem included the word *more*, getting the correct answer always involved subtracting, such as in the following problem:

> Alicia had 22 pennies. Juanita had 13. How many more pennies does Alicia have than Juanita?

However, on her test, Ms. Owens included the following problem:

Mark read 3 books in March. He read 4 more books in April. How many books did Mark read?

Several students with special needs in Ms. Owens's class subtracted 3 from 4 because they thought the presence of the word *more* signaled to subtract. Ms. Owens needed to include problems of this latter type in her teaching to prevent such misconceptions. Consider this example: When Mr. Yoshida taught his students how to add *ed* to a word ending in *y*, he demonstrated on the board as follows:

carry + ed = carried   hurry + ed = hurried

Next, Mr. Yoshida had his students add *ed* to five words ending in *y*. Finally, he assigned students 10 practice problems in their English books that looked like this:

Write the past tense of *marry*.

A number of students were unable to answer the questions in the book, even though they knew how to add *ed* to words ending in *y*, because the practice examples in the book required students to know the meaning of "past tense" and how to form the past tense by adding *ed*. The book's practice activity was very different from the instructional examples Mr. Yoshida used, which only required students to add *ed* to words ending in *y*. Both these examples demonstrate an important part of selecting instructional examples: The range of your instructional examples should match the range of the problem types used when you assess student learning. Ms. Owens could have prevented problems in her class by expanding her range of examples to include word problems that contained the word *more* but that were not solved by subtracting. Mr. Yoshida could have better prepared his students for the practice activities in the English book by using examples that referred directly to forming the past tense by adding *ed*.

The following example shows a different example-selection problem. Tawana's class was covering several high-frequency sight words that appeared in trade books they used in their literature-based reading program. On Wednesday, Tawana learned the word *man*, but on Tuesday, after the word *men* was presented, she was unable to read *man* correctly. Tawana's word-identification problem illustrates an example-selection problem that concerns sequencing. The visual and auditory similarities of *man* and *men* will make learning these words difficult for many at-risk students and students with learning disabilities, who may have trouble differentiating words that look and/or sound the same. One way to prevent this problem is to separate the introduction of *man* and *men* with other, dissimilar high-frequency words, such as *dog, house,* and *cat*.

This same sequencing idea can be applied to teaching letter sounds. For example, when deciding on the order in which to teach the sounds, consider separating letters that look and sound the same, such as *b* and *d*, *m* and *n*, and *p* and *b*. The careful sequencing of instruction can also be applied to teaching higher-level content. For example, when Mr. Roosevelt, a high school chemistry teacher, taught the chemical elements, he separated those symbols that looked and/or sounded similar, such as bromine (Br) and rubidium (Rb), and silicon (Si) and strontium (Sr).

Deciding the Rate of Introduction of New Skills

Students sometimes have difficulty learning skills when they are introduced at too fast a rate. For example, Mr. Henry is teaching his sixth-grade students how to proof

FYI

Student errors and misconceptions also stem from the over- or undergeneralization of concepts. Careful selection and sequencing of a range of examples can help prevent these kinds of errors.

rough drafts of their writing for errors in using capital letters and punctuation marks. He reviews the rules for using capital letters, periods, commas, question marks, and exclamation points. Next, he has students take out their most recent writing sample from their portfolios to look for capitalization and punctuation errors. Carmen found that he had left out capital letters at the beginning of two sentences, but he did not find any of the punctuation errors he had made. He missed them because Mr. Henry taught his students to proof their papers for capital letters and punctuation marks simultaneously. A better pace would have been first to work on proofing for capitalization errors and then to add one punctuation mark at a time (first periods, then commas, followed by question marks, and then exclamation points).

In another example of the **rate of introduction** of new skills, Ms. Stevens is working on reading comprehension with her students. She introduces three new comprehension strategies at once: detecting the sequence, determining cause and effect, and making predictions. Carlos is a student who has a mild cognitive disability; he learns best when he is taught one strategy at a time. Ms. Stevens adapted Carlos's instruction by forming a group with three other students who, like Carlos, will benefit from learning these comprehension strategies one by one. She also deleted cause-and-effect and prediction questions from these students' written comprehension exercises until they had been taught these strategies directly in their small group. When Mr. Wallace, the special education teacher, came to co-teach, he worked with these students on detecting the story sequence.

These examples demonstrate an important principle about introducing new skills to students with special needs: New skills should be introduced in small steps and at a rate slow enough to ensure mastery prior to the introduction of more new skills. Further, you may want to prioritize skills and even delete some, as Ms. Stevens did. Many commercially produced materials introduce skills at a rate that is too fast for students with special needs. As just illustrated, a common adaptation is to slow down the rate of skill introduction and provide more practice. Other students in the class, including those with no formally identified special needs, often benefit from such adaptations as well. If a student happens to be the only one having a problem, you can seek additional support from special needs staff, paraprofessionals, peers, and/or parent volunteers. Slowing down the rate of skills introduced is an adaptation in the way curriculum is presented, but it is not the same as reducing the amount of curriculum to be learned. For some students, though, you may need to decrease the amount of curriculum. For example, Ms. Evers reduced Robin's curriculum by shortening her spelling lists from 15 to 5 words and selecting only words that Robin used frequently in her writing.

Providing Direct Instruction and Opportunities for Practice and Review

Students with special needs may require more direct instruction and review if they are to acquire basic academic skills. Consider this example: Lashonda is included in Ms. Howard's spelling class. On Monday, Ms. Howard gave students a pretest on the 15 new words for the week. On Tuesday, the students were required to use each word in a sentence. On Wednesday, the teacher scrambled up the letters in all the words and had the students put them in the correct order. On Thursday, students answered 15 fill-in-the-blank questions, each of which required one of the new spelling words. On Friday, Lashonda failed her spelling test even though she had successfully completed all the spelling activities for that week. She did poorly on her spelling test because the daily spelling activities did not provide her with enough direct instruction and practice on the spelling words. Although activities such as using spelling words in sentences are valuable in the right context, they do not provide practice on the more primary objective of this particular lesson, which is spelling all 15 words correctly from dictation. One way to help Lashonda would be to have a peer tutor give her a daily dictation test on all 15 words, have Lashonda write each missed word three times, and then retest her on all 15 words again.

These examples demonstrate another problem that students with special needs have when learning basic skills: **retention.** Melissa had mastered addition facts to 10 as measured by a probe test in October, but when she was given the same test in January, she got only half of the facts correct. Thomas could state the major causes of the Civil War in November, but he could not remember them when asked to compare them to the causes of World War I in February. A common adaptation you can use for these students is to schedule more skill review for them. This review should be more frequent following your initial presentation of the skill, and then can become less frequent as the skill is established. For example, instead of waiting until January to review addition facts, Melissa's teacher could provide review first weekly, then every other week, and then every month. Thomas's teacher could periodically review key concepts and information that he will need to apply later, either as homework, an instructional game or contest, or an activity in a co-taught class.

A related concern is that nondirect instructional approaches may be appropriate for some students but may need to be supplemented for others. For example, Felix and Bill are learning to read in Ms. Farrell's class. Neither boy has mastered the *ch* sound (as in *chin*). On Monday, Felix came to the word *chair* in his trade book. His teacher pronounced the word and stated, "When *c* and *h* are together in a word, they usually say *ch*." The next day, Felix came to the word *chip* in his book, and he

Connections

Direct instruction could help Abdul, whom you met at the beginning of the chapter. His teacher could teach the skill directly by listing the steps in solving these problems on the board; having students say all the steps; solving several sample problems for the students by following the listed steps; leading the students through solving similar problems using the steps until they are able to do them independently; and assigning problems for the students to do independently, reminding them to follow the steps listed on the board.

Some students need additional direct instruction and guided practice when they are learning new skills. What prerequisite concepts and skills might you teach for this assignment on essay writing?

FYI

Research shows that many students with learning disabilities need direct instruction in letter sounds in order to learn to identify words systematically.

figured it out, remembering what Ms. Farrell had told him the day before. For Felix, one example in his book and a brief teacher explanation was enough for learning to occur. On Monday, Bill also came across a *ch* word, and he, too, was told what the word was and what sound *c* and *h* make when they come together in a word. Unlike Felix, however, when Bill came across another *ch* word the next day, he could not remember the sound of these letters. Having the teacher tell him once the sound *ch* made was not enough. Bill will require more direct instruction and practice than Felix, such as that provided in the activity shown in Table 9.1.

This discussion of Felix and Bill raises an important issue: General education teachers need to know more than one approach to meet the needs of individual students. Felix can learn his sounds with minimal instruction, while reading books; Bill cannot. Bill's teacher may need to supplement the literature-based program with some direct instruction on letter-sound correspondences.

Table 9.1   Direct Instruction of *ch* Sound

Teacher	Students
1. Teach directly *ch* sound in isolation.	
Teacher writes on the board: *ch, or, ee, ch, th, sh, ch,* and *ing*.	
1. Teacher models by saying the sound of the new letter combination and tests by having the students pronounce it. Teacher points to *ch*. "These letters usually say *ch*. What sound?"	"ch"
2. Teacher alternates between the new combination and other combinations. Teacher points to a letter combination, pauses 2 seconds, and asks, "What sound?"	Say the most common sound.
3. Teacher calls on several individual students to identify one or more letter combinations.	
2. Teach directly *ch* sound in words.	
Teacher writes on the board: *chin, chair, chip, boot, beam, chomp, stain, chum, moon, chat*.	
1. a. Students identify the sound of the letter combination, then read the word. Teacher points under the underlined letters and asks, "What sound?"	"ch"
b. Teacher points to left of word. "What word?"	"chin"
c. Teacher repeats step 1(a–b) with remaining words.	
2. a. Students reread the list without first identifying the sound of the letter combination. Teacher points to *chin*, pauses 2 seconds, and asks, "What word?"	"chin"
b. Teacher repeats step 2(a) with remaining words.	
3. Teacher calls on individual students to read one or more words.	

SOURCE: Reprinted with the permission of Prentice-Hall, Inc., from *Direct Instruction Reading* (3rd ed.) by Douglas Carnine, Jerry Silbert, and Edward J. Kameenui. Copyright © 1997 by Macmillan College Publishing Company.

Another example reinforces the idea that some of your students with special needs may need more direct instruction and practice. Mr. Thomas is teaching his sixth-grade students the format for writing a letter to a friend, including where to put the date and inside address and how to write a salutation and closing using correct punctuation. First, he reviewed the various circumstances in which people write letters to friends. Next, he showed a sample letter using the overhead projector and wrote a letter with the class. Finally, he asked the students to write a letter for homework. Brenda handed in her letter the next day; although her ideas were good, she had the inside address in the wrong place, left out commas in the salutation, and forgot to include a closing. Brenda needed more instruction and guided practice on how to format a letter than Mr. Thomas had provided. He had shown the students one letter and had written one letter with them before assigning them to write a letter on their own for homework. Mr. Thomas could have continued to write letters with the class until even the lower performers seemed comfortable performing the task. He could also have had the students write a letter independently in class so that he could monitor their performance and provide corrective feedback if necessary.

Finally, it is important to remember that practice is most effective when it follows direct instruction; practice is never an adequate substitute for direct instruction. For example, Mr. Hanesworth designs a board game in which students get to move ahead if they can answer a division fact problem. The problem is that five students in his class still do not understand the concept of division. For them, this practice activity is likely to result in failure. Mr. Hanesworth can solve this problem by providing additional instruction on division for those students who need it while allowing the rest of the class to play the board game independently. Of course later on Mr. Hanesworth can reward the hard work of the small group by allowing them to practice a skill they know using a game-like format.

Clearly, you may need to adapt instruction to enable students with special needs to acquire basic skills. These adaptations include teaching preskills, selecting and sequencing examples, adjusting the rate of introduction of new skills, and providing additional direct instruction, practice, and review. Students may also need adaptations in the presentation of subject-matter content, the primary teaching focus as students move into the upper grades.

Cultural Awareness

Models repeated prior to task performance help Native American students who may be reluctant to try a new task too soon for fear of making a mistake in public (Longstreet, 1978).

Check Your Learning

How can basic-skills instruction be adapted for students with special needs through attention to preskills, example selection and sequencing, rate of introduction of new skills, and direct instruction with opportunities for practice and review?

How Can You Adapt the Instruction of Subject-Area Content for Students with Special Needs?

The instruction of academic content includes areas such as history and science. This instruction mainly involves the use of textbooks and lecture-discussion formats, but also can include other activities, such as videos, films, and cooperative learning. Computers also can play a significant role in content-area instruction, as discussed in the Technology Notes feature on page 304. Although content-area instruction generally is associated with instruction in secondary schools, the information presented here is relevant for elementary teachers as well. In this section, you will learn how you can adapt your teaching and materials to help students with special needs learn subject-area content. Strategies for making adaptations are stressed for the areas of activating background knowledge, organizing information, and teaching terms and concepts.

Technology Notes

Using Computers with Students At Risk

Although computers are not an educational panacea, they have the potential to be powerful learning tools for students at risk. Computers enable students who live in rural areas to access information they otherwise might not experience through Internet coursework, and they prove a strong motivational force for students in urban areas who often live in worlds in which poverty, violence, and substance abuse are common. Here are some examples of computer uses with students at risk:

Interactive multimedia programs can be powerful learning tools for students at risk.

- In San Francisco, Chinese-speaking inner-city middle school students are communicating with the rest of the world in Chinese with the help of translation software. The students even publish an on-line newsletter. The teacher reports that as a result of the project, students are enthusiastic and their achievement scores on standardized tests have improved dramatically.

- In Bellingham, Washington, the public schools have created "virtual museums," collections of student-created virtual artifacts related to major topics covered in their district's curriculum. Teachers and students at any school can access the museums since the district's schools are networked.

- In Norfork, Virginia, high school students are being mentored (or "telementored") by working scientists. The scientists are recruited from among professors, graduate and postdoctoral students, and professionals in the field. This system enables students to make choices in their studies, and it pro-

vides them with a close working relationship with someone committed to a science career.

- In two California school districts, students are using computers to learn in an integrated, literature-based language arts program. Teachers report that students are more productive in their written work and experiment with computer illustrations. The students are more willing to revise their work because of the ease of doing so on the computer.

Students and their teachers are also using computers to join international relief and support efforts, to form partnerships with student in other countries, to access sophisticated software such as imaging software for science, and to use simulations aimed at better international understanding.

SOURCE: Adapted from *Educational Leadership*, *53*(2), 1995–1996 (Special section on how technology is transforming teaching), 6–72; and *Educational Leadership*, *54*(3), 1996–1997 (Special section on networking), 6–50.

Activating Background Knowledge

The amount of background knowledge students have can greatly influence whether or not they can read subject matter with understanding. To illustrate, read this list of words:

are	making	between
only	consists	often
continuously	vary	corresponding
one	curve	points
draws	relation	variation
set	graph	table
if	values	isolated
variables	known	

Were you able to read all of them? Do you know the meanings of all these words? Now read the following passage:

> If the known relation between the variables consists of a table of corresponding values, the graph consists only of the corresponding set of isolated points. If the variables are known to vary continuously, one often draws a curve to show the variation. (From Michaelson, 1945, cited in Lavoie, 1991)

Chances are, if you were asked to summarize what you just read, you would be unable to do so despite the fact that you probably answered "Yes" when asked whether you could read and understand all of the words individually. You may lack the background knowledge necessary to understand this very technical paragraph. The knowledge students bring to a content-area lesson is often as important for understanding as the quality of the textbook or instructional presentation (Langer, 1984). For students to understand content material, they need to relate it to information they already know. Unfortunately, teachers often fail to consider background information. Students with disabilities and students who are at risk may have two problems with background knowledge: They may simply lack the necessary knowledge, or they may know the information but be unable to recall it and relate it to the new information being presented.

Using the PReP strategy. A teaching strategy for determining how much knowledge students already have about a topic so that you can decide how much background information to present in class before a reading assignment is called the **PReP** (*PreReading Plan*) **strategy** (Langer, 1984). The Professional Edge on page 306 describes how to use the PReP strategy. As you can see, it has three major steps:

1. **Preview the text or lesson and choose two to three important concepts.** In the example in the Professional Edge, the teacher has chosen the concept of photosynthesis and the key words *cycle* and *oxygen*.

2. **Conduct a brainstorming session with students.** This process involves three phases. In Phase 1, students tell you what comes to mind when they hear the concept. This gives you a first glance at how much they already know about the topic. In Phase 2, students tell you what made them think of their responses in Phase 1. This information can help you judge the depth and/or basis for their responses, and it also provides a springboard for students to refine their responses in Phase 3. In the Professional Edge example, two of the students mistakenly think that photosynthesis has to do with photography because of the presence of *photo* in the word. This error could be an opportunity to build on students' knowledge—you could explain that *photo* means *light* and that in photography, a camera takes in light and combines it with certain chemicals on film to make pictures. You could then say that plants take

Professional Edge

How to Use PReP

You can use the PReP (PreReading Plan) strategy to help you figure out what background information your students have about a particular concept or topic and what gaps, if any, exist in their knowledge of it. The following example shows how one teacher used the PReP procedure to find out what the students in his science class already knew about photosynthesis.

Step 1: Preview the text or lesson and choose two to three important concepts.

Before an eighth-grade science class reads about photosynthesis in their texts, the teacher conducts a PReP activity to help students recall and organize their knowledge of this concept and to determine which students are ready to read the material. The following dialogue focuses on the concept of photosynthesis. Other key words selected are *cycle* and *oxygen*.

Step 2: Conduct a brainstorming activity with students that includes the following three phases.

Phase 1: Initial association of concept

> *Teacher:* We're going to be reading in our texts about a process called photosynthesis. I'd like you to tell me anything that comes to mind when you hear the word *photosynthesis*. I'll write what you say on the board. Anyone?

During this phase, it becomes apparent that none of the students has much knowledge of the concept. The following responses are typical:

> *Student 1:* Sun shining on a plant.
> *Student 2:* Photograph.
> *Student 3:* Pictures.

Phase 2: Reflections on initial associations

> *Teacher:* Now I'd like each of you to think about what you said and to try to tell us what made you think of that response.
> *Student 2:* Photosynthesis sounds like a *photograph*. The first part of it anyway.

> *Student 3:* Yeah, I thought at first you said *photograph* and that made me think of pictures.
> *Student 1:* I remembered reading in a book about photosynthesis. There was this picture that showed rays coming out of the sun and going down to a plant. I just remembered the picture when I heard that word.

During this activity, the teacher helps the group see that they do know something about the concept. A discussion grows out of the meaning of the morpheme (word part) *photo* and how *photo* could be related to the sun and plants. This helps all of the students refine their responses in the third phase and helps some of them raise the level of their responses.

Phase 3: Reformulation of knowledge

> *Teacher:* Now that we've been thinking about this for a while, do any of you want to change or add to your previous responses, before we read about photosynthesis?
> *Student 1:* It is when the sun shines on plants and that helps the plants give oxygen.
> *Student 2:* Light like in photographs.
> *Student 3:* Like taking pictures.

Step 3: Evaluate student responses to determine the depth of their prior knowledge of the topic.

The teacher concludes that although Student 1 could successfully read the text, the others need help building the concept from what they know before reading about it. Students 2 and 3 receive help to ensure that they understand the morpheme *photo* and the role of light in the process of photography. They then can extend this knowledge to the role of light in the process of photosynthesis. Of course, concept teaching takes place, but it always begins with the knowledge students display.

SOURCE: Adapted from "Examining Background Knowledge and Text Comprehension" by J. Langer, 1984, *Reading Research Quarterly, 19*, pp. 468–481. Used by permission of International Reading Association.

in light, too, and when the light combines with chemicals in the plant, carbohydrates and oxygen are made. This process is called photosynthesis. In this way, you are using what the students already know to teach them a concept they do not know. In Phase 3, students can add to their responses based on the discussion in Phase 2.

3. Evaluate student responses to determine the depth of their prior knowledge of the topic. During this step, you will decide whether students are ready to read the text and/or listen to a lecture on photosynthesis or whether they first need more information. As shown in the Professional Edge example, Students 2 and 3 still do not seem to understand that photosynthesis is something plants do with light to make carbohydrates and oxygen. They need more information before they are ready to read the chapter. They might benefit from an illustration using concrete examples or a basic video on the topic.

Preparing anticipation guides. Anticipation guides can help you activate student knowledge about a particular topic and construct bridges to new information by encouraging students to make predictions (Moore, Readance, & Rickleman, 1989; Vacca & Vacca, 1986). **Anticipation guides** consist of a series of statements, some of which may *not* be true, related to the material that the student is about to read (Burns, Roe, & Ross, 1992). Before teaching, students read these statements that either challenge or support ideas they may already have about the subject. This process catches their interest and gives them a reason for listening and reading. Providing questions or statements prior to reading also aids comprehension for all students, including those with special needs.

You can make anticipation guides for your students by following the steps suggested in the Professional Edge on page 308.

Providing planning think sheets. Activating background information and building bridges to current knowledge is also of concern to teachers when asking students to write. Some researchers recommend a **planning think sheet** to help writers focus on background information as well as the audience and purpose of a paper (Englert et al., 1988). For audience, students are asked to consider who will read the paper. For purpose, students clarify why they are writing the paper (for example, to tell a story, to convey information, or to persuade someone). Finally, students activate background knowledge and organize that knowledge by asking themselves questions such as, "What do I know about the topic? How can I group/label my facts?" (Englert et al., 1988, pp. 107–108). A planning think sheet for a paper assignment might contain write-in lines on which students answer the following questions:

- What is my topic?
- Why do I want to write on this topic?
- What are two things I already know that will make it easy to write this paper?
- Who will read my paper?
- Why will the reader be interested in this topic? (Raphael, Kirschner, & Englert, 1986)

Organizing Content

Research shows that many students, including students with special needs, have difficulty understanding important ideas and their interrelationships in content areas

▌ D o I t !

Design an anticipation guide and a planning think sheet for a particular activity or assignment in a subject area you plan to teach.

Professional Edge

How to Make Anticipation Guides

You can use anticipation guides to prompt your students to think about a particular concept or topic and to help them use what they know to make predictions about the new material. The following steps describe how you can prepare these helpful tools for your students.

Procedure

1. **Step 1.** Identify the major concepts and details in the reading. (What information or ideas should be the focus of the students' attention?)

2. **Step 2.** Consider student experiences or beliefs that the reading will challenge or support. (What do students already know or believe about the selection they will be reading?)

3. **Step 3.** Create three to five statements that may challenge or modify your students' prereading understanding of the material. Include some statements that will elicit agreement between the students and the information in the text.

4. **Step 4.** Present the guide on the board, on an overhead projector, or on paper. Leave space on the left for individual or small-group responses. As each statement is discussed, students must justify their opinions. You may wish to have students first fill out the guide individually and then defend their responses to others in small groups or within a class discussion.

5. **Step 5.** After reading, return to the anticipation guide to determine whether students changed their minds about any of the statements. Have students locate sections in the reading that support their decisions.

6. **Step 6.** Another option for responding is to include a column for predictions of the author's beliefs. This can be completed after students have read the selection and can lead into your discussion of the reading.

SOURCE: Adapted from *Content Area Reading* (2nd ed.) by R. T. Vacca and J. L. Vacca, 1986, Boston: Little, Brown.

---

such as social studies (Lawton, 1995) and science (Scruggs & Mastropieri, 1994). These students can benefit from the use of supports or scaffolds that help them identify and understand important information (Carnine et al., 1997). As we discussed in Chapter 4, one form of support is to organize the curriculum according to "big ideas" rather than facts in isolation. Another form of support is to make these "big ideas" more evident to students through the use of **advance organizers, cue words for organizational patterns, study guides,** and **graphic organizers.**

FYI

Advance organizers help activate prior learning, keep students on task, and provide reference points for remembering tasks that need to be completed.

Using advance organizers. Advance organizers include information that makes content more understandable by putting it within a more general framework. They are particularly effective for students with special needs who may have limited background knowledge and reading and listening comprehension skills. Examples of advance organizers include the following:

- Identifying major topics and activities

- Presenting an outline of content

- Providing background information

- Stating concepts and ideas to be learned in the lesson
- Motivating students to learn by showing the relevance of the activity
- Stating the objectives or outcomes of the lesson (Lenz, 1983)

Employing cue words for organizational patterns.   "Big ideas" are often the central focus of a pattern of information. The most common patterns of information include the descriptive list and the sequence of events in time, comparison/contrast, cause/effect, and problem/solution (Ellis, 1996). Each of these patterns of information can be made more conspicuous for students through the use of cue words. For example, cue words for a list, description, or sequence might include *first, second,* or *third;* cue words for comparison/contrast would be *similar, different, on the other hand;* cause/effect might be signalled by *causes, effects, because, so that;* and cue words for problem/solution would be *problem, solution,* and *resolve.* Cue words are important for students with special needs, many of whom have difficulty telling the difference between important and unimportant information (Kinder & Bursuck, 1991).

Consider the following two passages, about the formation of the two-party system, that come from two different social studies texts.

Text 1

Ordinary People Formed a Political Party

The problem. You have learned how the policies of the Federalist party of the wealthy business people did not directly help the ordinary people. Small farmers had to pay the Whiskey Tax, but wealthy farmers who grew other crops did not. Ordinary people had lost a great deal of money when they sold their bonds to speculators. Government money was being paid primarily to wealthy people. The Alien and Sedition Acts were passed to keep ordinary people from gaining political power. A serious problem for the first few years in our country's history was that the party of the wealthy business people ignored the **viewpoint** of ordinary people.

What was a serious problem during the first few years of our country's history?

The solution. Although Thomas Jefferson didn't like the idea of political parties, Jefferson felt that ordinary people needed to be brought together and organized to get the political power that would result in the government doing things to help the ordinary person. Thomas Jefferson was a popular leader who gathered up the support of a great number of skilled workers, such as carpenters, blacksmiths, and other craftsmen, as well as shopkeepers and small farmers.

Jefferson began to organize a political party before the Presidential election of 1800. He felt confident that a political party of ordinary people could win elections because there were many more common people than wealthy business people. The political party of the ordinary people wanted to elect enough representatives to control Congress and to elect Thomas Jefferson to be President in the next Presidential election in 1800. That new political party was called by several names; the Democratic-Republicans, the Republicans, and also the Jeffersonian party. During the election campaign, the political party of the ordinary people made an issue of the unpopular Whiskey Tax and also the unpopular Alien and Sedition Acts. In the election of 1800, the party of the ordinary people won, and **Thomas Jefferson,** who also wrote the Declaration of Independence, became the third President of the United States. Also, enough legislators from the party of the ordinary people were elected to make those legislators the new majority in charge of Congress.

Why was Thomas Jefferson important to the development of political parties in the United States? (Carnine, Crawford, Harniss, & Hollenbeck, 1995, p. 207)

Text 2

The Constitution said nothing about the political parties that Washington had warned against. As early as the presidential election of 1792, however, something resembling two major parties appeared in American politics. These parties centered around Alexander Hamilton and Thomas Jefferson.

Rise of the two-party system.   In the election of 1792, Washington was re-elected by unanimous vote. Vice-President John Adams was also re-elected but against strong opposition. He was opposed by George Clinton of New York, a candidate backed by Thomas Jefferson and his followers.

Hamilton's followers came to be called Federalists. The Federalist Party was strongest in New England and along the Atlantic seaboard. It included many wealthy merchants, manufacturers, lawyers, and church leaders. John Adams, himself a Federalist, said that Federalists represented "the rich, the well-born, and the able."

The opposition party was led by Thomas Jefferson. Its members called themselves Republicans. Although some wealthy people were Republicans, most of Jefferson's supporters were the owners of small farms or wage earners in the growing towns. (Todd & Curti, 1982, p. 212)

Which passage is easier to understand? Most teachers would say the first one. The major heading is specific. The relationship between Federalist legislation and the formation of the Republican party is clear. This relationship is cast in the form of a problem/solution framework; the formation of the Republican party was the solution to a problem involving the Federalists trying to grab power from the ordinary people. This problem/solution structure is clearly signaled by boldface headings. Notice, too, that each section in the first passage is followed by a question that helps students sort out the main idea.

The second passage contains no explicit signals of the relationship between Federalist policies and the formation of the Republican party. It is also unclear why ordinary people so hated these policies. Students reading this passage will be required to make a number of inferences, inferences that may be difficult for students with special needs to make. Although rewriting the book is obviously not a reasonable adaptation here, you can help make the key concepts more explicit. A strategy for teaching students to recognize patterns of information is described in the Professional Edge. Two additional options for assisting students in organizing content material are study guides and graphic organizers.

Constructing study guides.   The general term **study guide** refers to outlines, abstracts, or questions that emphasize important information in texts (Lovitt & Horton, 1987). Study guides are helpful in improving comprehension for students with special needs in content-area classrooms (Lovitt, Rudsit, Jenkins, Pious, & Benedetti, 1985). For example, at the beginning of this chapter, Cecily was having trouble picking out key ideas in her American history text, a common problem for students at all educational levels. She might benefit from study guides that cue students to important information by asking them questions about it. Procedures for constructing study guides are shown in the Professional Edge on page 312. A sample study guide for a section of a social studies text on Truman's Fair Deal is shown in Figure 9.2 on page 313.

Horton (1987) has suggested the following additional modifications you might want to try:

1. Allow 2 or 3 inches of margin space in which students can take notes. Draw a vertical line to indicate the margin clearly. For example, in the study guide in

Professional Edge

Teaching Organizational Patterns

You can improve the ability of your students to comprehend subject-matter content by teaching them to recognize "big ideas" that are organized according to certain patterns. Teaching your students to recognize key patterns of information can be done by: (a) defining the patterns, (b) providing examples and nonexamples, (c) modeling how a reader thinks when reading a pattern, (d) providing students with practice recognizing cues that signal the pattern, (e) providing practice picking out key information, and (f) providing practice writing paragraphs using the patterns (Ellis, 1996; p. 103). An example of how to teach the list and describe strategy developed by Ellis (1996; pp. 103–104) is shown below.

1. Describe the list-and-description pattern to students.
   a. Explain the pattern.
   b. Show students examples of various texts that use this pattern (e.g., social studies textbook, encyclopedia, *Time* magazine).
   c. Discuss the advantages of recognizing the pattern (e.g., increases comprehension, helps you focus on what's important).

2. Present examples and nonexamples.
   a. Show students example phrases indicating list-and-describe formats (e.g., "There are many parts to...," "Three reasons why...").
   b. Show students examples and nonexamples of cue words for list-and-describe formats (example: "Three unfortunate events led to General 'Stonewall' Jackson being shot by his own men" versus nonexample: "General 'Stonewall' Jackson was shot late that night by his own men"). Cue students to discriminate between them.

3. Describe order in which list-and-describe formats may occur (general-to-specific, specific-to-general) and provide examples.

4. Practice identifying list-and-describe cue words, general topics, and specific details from text passages; indicate on a graphic organizer.
   a. Provide students with copies of the same text passage containing multiple paragraphs. Use think-aloud techniques as you read the first paragraph, looking for cue words that signal a list-and-describe format. Model the process of constructing a graphic that depicts the organizational pattern.
   b. Guide students as the whole class reads the second paragraph; collaborate with them to identify cue words, general topic, and details. Repeat with new paragraphs as necessary, gradually decreasing cues as students perform task.
   c. Have students form pairs. Have each pair analyze text passages to identify cue words, general topic, and details.

5. Write short essays using list-and-describe cue words.
   a. Provide a short list of general topics for each pair of students.
   b. Model the process of selecting a topic, identifying specifics, and writing a short essay.
   c. Have students write short essays and share them with other pairs of students. The other pair must identify the cue words used, general topic, and specifics.

Figure 9.2, the answer to the first vocabulary question is *Consumables are products that cannot be used over again.* You may want to have students write the word along with its complete definition in the margin. Some students with special needs will find new words easier to understand if you first use the overhead to go over the definition along with a series of positive and negative examples.

Professional Edge

How to Develop Study Guides

Study guides will help improve the comprehension of all your students, especially those with special needs who are included in content-area classrooms. The following steps show you how to develop a study guide from a content-area textbook.

1. Go through the entire book and mark the chapters you will cover throughout the term and those you will not.

2. Indicate the sequence in which you will assign the chapters; that is, note the one that comes first, second, and so forth.

3. Read the material in the first chapter carefully. Mark the important vocabulary, facts, and concepts that you expect students to learn. Cross out any material you do not intend to cover.

4. Divide the chapter into logical sections of 1000- to 1500-word passages. (The length will depend, of course, on how detailed the material is and how much of it you deem important.)

5. Write brief sentences that explain the main ideas or emphasize the vocabulary, facts, or concepts from the passage. Write 15 sentences per passage.

6. Place those sentences in order so that the material in one leads to the next, and so forth.

7. To create questions, either leave out a few words in each sentence or change each sentence into a question. For example, one important statement identified in a chapter on natural disasters was:

A 2 percent sales tax was passed to pay for relief efforts after the massive floods of 1993.

This statement could be turned into a question by leaving out several words:

_____ was passed to pay for relief efforts after the massive floods of 1993.

You could also change the statement into a question:

How did the people pay for the relief efforts after the massive floods of 1993?

8. Make a transparency of sentences and/or questions using large type.

9. Prepare sheets for the students, using regular type.

10. Prepare an answer sheet for the teacher.

11. Develop a multiple choice test to cover the material in the study guide. The test should have 10–15 items, with four possible choices for each question.

S O U R C E : From *Study Guides: A Paper on Curriculum Modification* by S. V. Horton, 1987, University of Washington.

Specific strategies for presenting new vocabulary are presented later in the chapter.

2. Print page numbers alongside the sentences in the study guide to show where to find the missing word in the textbook.

3. Print the missing words on the bottom of the page to serve as cues.

4. Leave out several words for more advanced students and fewer for students with special needs. For example, the **effect** part of the big idea could be simplified as, "The **effect** of strikes such as the railroad strike was that the stability of the American economy was threatened, and _____."

5. Arrange for peer teaching situations; pair students and have them take turns being the teacher and the student.

6. Use the study guide for homework assignments. Assign students a passage in the text and give them accompanying study guides (either with or without the pages marked for easy reference). Have them complete the guides and study the material for homework.

7. Ask students to keep and organize their study guides from a number of passages and to study them as they review for unit or end-of-semester tests.

8. Place reading passages, study guides, and tests on a computer.

9. Whenever possible, write the study guide at a reading level that fits most of your students. Students with reading and writing problems may need to have the study guide read to them or to respond to the questions orally.

10. Include only key information on the guide. When necessary, reduce the content load by having students answer fewer items. For example, Ms. Hall required that Al, a student with a mild cognitive disability in her fourth-grade class, answer only 4 of 10 questions on a study guide. When the students were tested on the content covered in the guide, Al was held responsible for answering only questions related to the four items he had answered.

Of course, study guides are not a substitute for direct instruction. The amount of direct instruction necessary will vary with the difficulty of the material. In general, students need more help completing study guides for texts that assume high levels of student background knowledge and in which key information needs to be

Do It!

Design a study guide for a chapter in a textbook that you plan to teach.

Figure 9.2   **Sample Study Guide for Truman's Fair Deal**

VOCABULARY

Consumables are products that _____

_____. Some examples of consumables are _____,

_____, and _____. A nonexample of a consumable is _____.

BIG IDEAS

The **problem** was that after World War II, price controls were lifted and the cost of

_____, _____, and other consumer goods went _____.

The **solution** was for workers to _____.

The **effect** was that _____ and _____.

Professional Edge

How to Use Study Guides

Once you have prepared study guides, you will need to teach your students how to use them. As with any adaptation, you will want to explain study guides clearly and specifically, making sure that your students with and without disabilities understand them. The following suggestions offer a systematic way to present these useful tools for understanding content.

1. Require your students to read the material before they use the study guides.

2. Pass out study guide sheets to students *after* they have read the material.

3. Place the transparency on the overhead projector. Expose only the first sentence or question.

4. Encourage students who can read and answer the question to raise their hands.

5. Call on a student to read and answer the question.

6. Distribute requests for answers to all students. From time to time, call on students who do not raise their hands.

7. Have students fill in the answers on their sheets, as they are identified.

8. Repeat the same process with the remaining questions. Cover those items on the transparency that have not yet been answered.

9. Ask related questions from time to time. The study guide sentences should serve as an outline for discussion.

10. Amplify on the sentences. Occasionally, give additional examples and illustrations.

11. Allow the students a few minutes to study their finished study guides after they have been completed and discussed.

12. Administer a test on the material.

13. Score the tests as soon as possible and inform students about their performance.

14. Show students the class average and discuss items that a number of students missed.

15. Show students how to keep a progress chart of their scores from the various tests.

SOURCE: From *Study Guides: A Paper on Curriculum Modification* by S. V. Horton, 1987, University of Washington.

inferred as opposed to being explicitly presented. Guidelines for using study guides are presented in the Professional Edge.

Creating graphic organizers. Another way teachers can help students organize content is to use **graphic organizers.** This strategy gives students a visual format to organize their thoughts while looking for main ideas. Archer and Gleason (1997) suggest the following guidelines for constructing graphic organizers:

1. Determine the critical content (for example, vocabulary, concepts, ideas, generalizations, events, details, facts) that you wish to teach your students. Helping students focus on the most critical information is important for several reasons. First, students with special needs may have trouble identifying the most important information in an oral lesson or textbook chapter. Second, it is easier for students to remember several main ideas than many isolated details. Third, trying to put too much information on a graphic organizer can make it so visually complex that students may have trouble interpreting it.

FYI

Teachers successfully use graphic organizers at all phases of instruction, from advance organizers to review. Graphic organizers, which are sometimes called concept maps or semantic webs, help make your lessons multisensory and are helpful for students with special needs.

Figure 9.3   **Compare–Contrast Graphic Organizer**

Attribute	Native Americans	Colonists
Land	Shared Lived close to it without changing it Respected it	Owned Cleared it Used it

Summarize

The Indians and colonists had different ideas about land. Indians shared the land while the colonists owned individual pieces of it. Indians lived close to the land; they respected it and did not change it. Colonists used the land for their own gain.

2. Organize the concepts in a visual representation that reflects the structure of the content, such as stories, hierarchies (top-down and bottom-up), feature analysis, diagrams, compare–contrast, timelines. Since the purpose of a graphic organizer is to clarify interrelationships among ideas and information, you should keep the visual display as simple as possible. Figure 9.3 shows a completed compare–contrast graphic organizer.

3. Design a completed **concept map.** Completing the map before you teach with it ensures that the information is clear and accurate and can be presented to your students in a timely manner. Figure 9.4 on page 316 shows a filled-in concept map.

4. Create a partially completed concept map (to be completed by students during instruction). Having students fill out the map as you present your lesson is an excellent way to keep them on task. Also, many students with special needs benefit from a multisensory approach; seeing the information on the graphic, hearing it from the teacher, and writing it on the map helps them better retain the information presented.

5. Create a blank concept map for students to use as a postreading or review exercise. This structure for review will be easy for students to use.

Once you have constructed graphic organizers, you can use them as follows:

1. Distribute partially completed concept maps to your students.

2. Place a transparency of the completed map on an overhead projector. Place a piece of paper under the transparency so that you will expose only those portions you wish students to attend to. This limiting of the amount of information you present at one time helps students with attention problems, who have trouble focusing on more than one piece of information at a time.

3. Introduce the information on the concept map, proceeding in a logical order; stress the relationships between the vocabulary, concepts, events, details, facts, and so on.

Figure 9.4   Sample Concept Map for a Science Selection on Hawks

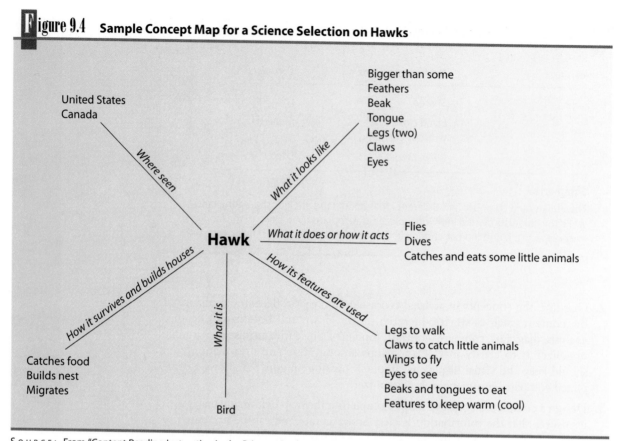

SOURCE: From "Content Reading Instruction in the Primary Grades: Perceptions and Strategies" by M. W. Olson and T. C. Gee, 1991, *The Reading Teacher, 45*(4), 298–307. Used by permission of International Reading Association.

4. At natural junctures, review concepts you have introduced. You can do this by placing the blank map on the overhead and asking students questions about the content. This review is essential for students with special needs, who often have difficulty learning large amounts of information at one time.

5. At the end of the lesson, review the critical content again using the blank concept map. You can also have students complete the blank maps for homework. These maps will help your students organize their studying and also help you find out what they have learned. (Carnine et al., 1997)

The Case in Practice illustrates how one teacher uses a graphic organizer called a story map to help her students better comprehend a particular story.

Teaching Terms and Concepts

Content-area instruction is often characterized by a large number of new and/or technical vocabulary words and concepts. Students who have special needs or who

Case in Practice

Teaching with Story Maps

Story maps are graphic organizers that provide students with a visual guide to understanding and retelling stories. They have been shown to help students with special needs read with better comprehension (Bos & Vaughn, 1994). In the account that follows, Ms. Barrows, a second-grade teacher, is using the story map in Figure 9.5 to teach her students the story "The Funny Farola" (Miranda & Guerrero, 1986). She has demonstrated using the maps for a week now, so her students are familiar with the for-mat. Today, she is providing guided practice for her students on how to use the maps.

Ms. Barrows: Boys and girls, today we're going to read a story entitled "The Funny Farola." A farola is a lantern used to give light. What do you think the story is going to be about?

(continued)

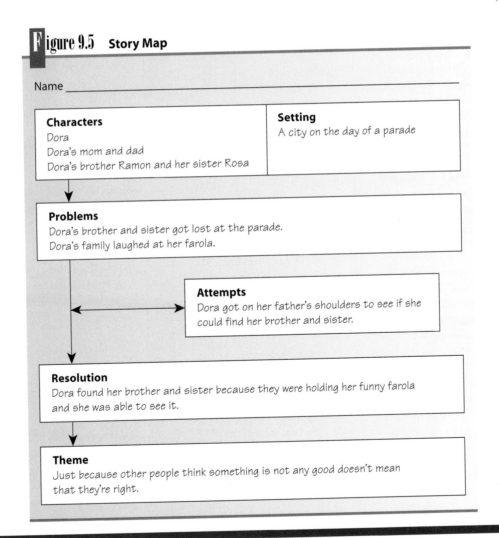

Figure 9.5 Story Map

Name _____

Characters	Setting
Dora	A city on the day of a parade
Dora's mom and dad	
Dora's brother Ramon and her sister Rosa	

Problems
Dora's brother and sister got lost at the parade.
Dora's family laughed at her farola.

Attempts
Dora got on her father's shoulders to see if she could find her brother and sister.

Resolution
Dora found her brother and sister because they were holding her funny farola and she was able to see it.

Theme
Just because other people think something is not any good doesn't mean that they're right.

Case in Practice (continued)

Juliane: Maybe it's going to be about a lantern that looks funny.

Lee: Maybe it's about something funny happening to someone who has a farola.

Ms. Barrows: Well, before we read and find out, who can tell me what a story map is?

Darwain: Well, it's a map that guides us through a story kind of like a regular map tells us where we're going when we're driving a car.

Ms. Barrows: That's right, Darwain. Now let's read the first page and find out who the main characters in this story are and where the story takes place. When you find out, we'll fill them in on our story maps. [She distributes a blank story map to each student.]

Harley: I know, the story is about Dora Rivers, her sister Rosa, her brother Ramon, and her mom and dad. I think Dora is the main character.

Ms. Barrows: That's right, Harley. Let's all fill in the main characters on our maps.

Ms. Barrows: Where do you think the story takes place? It's hard to tell because they don't come right out and say it.

Lovell: I think it takes place in a city.

Ms. Barrows: Why do you think so, Lovell?

Lovell: Because it sounds like it's a big parade, and cities have big parades.

Ms. Barrows: Good thinking, Lovell. When stories don't come out and say things, we have to figure it out by thinking hard, and that's what you did. Let's all fill in the setting on our maps. [They do.] Remember, we said last week that all stories have a problem that needs to be solved.

Read the next four pages and find out what the problem is here. [The students read the passage.] What's the problem?

Harley: Well, Dora's little brother and sister got lost at the parade.

Ms. Barrows: Right. That's one problem. Write it on your maps. Now, does anyone see another problem?

Eliseo: I know. Dora made a farola that looked like a frog and everybody laughed at her.

Ms. Barrows: Eliseo, what's wrong with a farola that looks like a frog? I thought it looked cute.

Eliseo: Well, I think it was because Dora's was different from everyone else's. In the pictures in the story, there were no farolas that looked like animals.

Ms. Barrows: That's right, Eliseo. Let's all put this problem on our maps. [They do.] Let's read the next page and find out what Dora and her mom and dad attempted to do to try to find her brother and sister.

Lovell: Dora got up on her father's shoulders to see if she could see her brother and sister.

Ms. Barrows: Do you think this will help Dora find her brother and sister?

Lesa: I don't think so. There are so many people there.

Ms. Barrows: Well, let's all finish the story and find out. [They finish reading the story.] So, did Dora find her brother and sister?

Juliane: Yes. She found them because they were carrying her funny farola and it really made them stand out in the crowd.

Ms. Barrows: That's right. Let's fill in how Dora solved the problem on

our story maps. [They do.] What about Dora's other problem? Was it solved, too?

Juliane: Yes. They didn't think Dora's farola was so funny anymore because it helped them find Dora's brother and sister.

Ms. Barrows: That's right. How do you think Dora felt at the end?

Lovell: I think she felt happy.

Ms. Barrows: Why do you think that, Lovell?

Lovell: Well, because she found her brother and sister and no one thought her farola was stupid anymore.

Ms. Barrows: Good thinking, Lovell. I'd like the rest of you to put how *you* think Dora felt, and why, on your maps. Remember, we said a part of stories is a lesson that they teach us. What lesson do you think this story teaches?

Harley: Well, just because something is different doesn't mean it's no good.

Ms. Barrows: Good thinking, Harley. Let's all put down the lesson of this story on our maps.

REFLECTIONS

How did Ms. Barrows use the story map to help her students comprehend the story? Which students do you think would benefit most from this approach? What should Ms. Barrows do to get her students ready for completing story maps on their own? How could you incorporate the use of story maps into a literature-based classroom reading program?

are at risk are likely to have difficulty with the vocabulary and concept demands of many content-area texts and presentations. For example, consider the following passage from a general science text:

> Thousands of years ago, Scandinavia was covered by a thick ice sheet. The mass of the ice forced the crust deeper into the denser mantle. Then the ice melted. The mantle has been slowly pushing the land upward since then. This motion will continue until a state of balance between the crust and mantle is reached again. This state of balance is called *isostasy* (ie-soss-tuh-see). (Ramsey, Gabriel, McGuirk, Phillips, & Watenpaugh, 1983)

Although the term *isostasy* is the one highlighted, other technical terms and concepts, such as *crust* and *mass*, also may pose a problem for students. These words may be particularly difficult because students are likely to be familiar with their nonscientific meanings, which are quite different from their technical meanings (for example, *mass* as in church; *crust* as in bread). You will need to check student understanding and teach the vocabulary directly if necessary, using one of the strategies covered in the next section.

Modeling examples, synonyms, and definitions. An approach to teaching terms and concepts has been proposed by Carnine and colleagues (1997). They suggest three related ways of teaching new vocabulary to students: modeling examples, synonyms, and definitions. Although there is some variation across these three methods, all of them use the following steps:

1. Pick a range of both positive and negative examples to teach your new word. Example selection is most important. A range of positive examples is used to make sure students can apply the word to a variety of contexts or forms. For example, if you are teaching your students to identify a *rectangle*, you want them to identify a rectangle whether it is big, small, empty, or shaded. Therefore, when showing students examples of rectangles, show them big rectangles, small rectangles, empty rectangles, and shaded rectangles. If you are teaching your students what a *vehicle* is, you want them to recognize a vehicle whether it is a car, boat, or bicycle. Whereas positive examples help students learn the range of a word, nonexamples help them discriminate the new word from other words that may be similar. For example, in teaching *rectangle*, use figures such as triangles, circles, and trapezoids as nonexamples. In teaching *vehicle*, use chair, house, or even an exercise bike as nonexamples. Generally, you should use at least six examples to teach a new word and include at least two nonexamples.

2. If you are teaching your word using a synonym, the student must already know the synonym. For example, when teaching the word *gigantic* using the synonym *huge*, make sure the students know what *huge* means. If you are teaching your word using a definition, the definition should be stated simply and clearly and should contain only words for which students know the meaning. Here is a definition of *vehicle* for third grade:

> *Vehicle:* A method of transportation that takes a person from one location to another.

This definition uses a number of words that third graders might not know. Here is a simpler definition that younger students might understand:

> *Vehicle:* An object that takes you from place to place.

This teacher is modeling positive and negative examples to clarify the meaning of a new concept. How can using both examples and nonexamples help make the meaning of new terms and concepts clear?

3. Tell students the meaning of the words either through modeling positive and negative examples or by presenting positive and negative examples using a synonym or a definition. For example, if you are teaching *rectangle* by modeling positive and negative examples, you would say the following as you pointed to your examples:

> This is a rectangle . . . This is a rectangle . . . This is *not* a rectangle . . . This is a rectangle.

If you were teaching *vehicle* using a definition, you might say:

> A vehicle is an object that takes you from place to place. What is a vehicle? [point to car] This is a car. It is an object that takes you from place to place. It is a vehicle. . . . This is a boat. It is an object that takes you from place to place. A boat is a vehicle. . . . This is a chair. A chair is an object but it doesn't take you from place to place. It is *not* a vehicle.

Finally, if you were teaching the word *gigantic* using the synonym *huge*, you might say this:

> Today we're going to learn the meaning of the word *gigantic*. What's the word? Gigantic means huge. [point to elephant] An elephant is a gigantic animal. It is huge. [point to a picture of a redwood tree] This is a redwood tree. It is gigantic. It is huge. [point to a smallish dog] This is a dog. The dog is not gigantic. The dog is not huge.

4. Ask students a series of yes or no questions to see whether they can discriminate examples from nonexamples. For example, "Is this a rectangle?" If students have been taught a word using a definition or synonym, follow your question with, "How do you know?" Their reasons for answering "yes" or "no" will tell you whether the students are correctly using the definition or just guessing. For example, to test whether students know what a vehicle is, you might say:

> What is this? (a car) Is a car a vehicle? (yes) Why do you say that? (because it is an object that takes you from place to place). What is this? (a chair). Is a chair a vehicle? (no). Why do you say that? (because it doesn't take you from place to place).

5. The purpose of this step is to find out whether students can discriminate the new word from words they have learned previously. This step is carried out through a series of open-ended questions. For example, in teaching *rectangle*, the teacher points to a rectangle along with other figures already taught and asks, "What is this?"

Teaching vocabulary by modeling examples or using synonyms and definitions can benefit all of your students. Use modeling examples when students do not understand words that could explain the meaning of the new word (for example, teaching students what a herringbone design is). Use teaching synonyms when students already know a word with a meaning similar to the new word; for example, the word *bow* could be taught by using the synonym *front*. Use definitions when a longer explanation is needed to define a word and students already understand the words that make up the explanation.

> **Cultural Awareness**
>
> Teaching vocabulary by modeling examples or using synonyms and definitions is especially helpful for students with limited English proficiency.

Making concept diagrams. Constructing **concept diagrams** is a method that combines graphic organizers with the definition, examples, and nonexamples approach just described (Bulgren, Schumaker, & Deshler, 1988). A sample concept diagram for the concept of nonviolent resistance is shown in Figure 9.6. First, the teacher selects key words from a story or lecture. Next, he or she constructs a diagram that features the word's definition; characteristics that are always present, sometimes present, and never present; and examples and nonexamples. Finally, the concept diagram is presented to students as follows:

1. Present the word and its definition.

2. Discuss the always, sometimes, and never characteristics.

3. Discuss one of the examples and one of the nonexamples in relation to the characteristics.

4. Check other examples and nonexamples to see whether they match the characteristics. (Carnine et al., 1997)

Figure 9.6   Concept Diagram

Concept Name:	Nonviolent resistance	
Definition:	Protesting in a peaceful way	

Always	Sometimes	Never
Peaceful	Done in a group Done individually	Violent

Examples	Nonexamples
Picketing	Shouting match
Boycott	Physical attack
Sit-in	Revolutionary war
Hunger strike	Riot

Check Your Learning

What are the major areas for making adaptations in subject-area instruction?

How Can You Improve Clarity in Written and Oral Communication?

In effective instruction, if ideas are clearly tied together, they are easier for students to understand. The need for instructional clarity applies to written communication, which in many school situations involves the use of textbooks, and oral communication, which includes instructional behaviors such as giving directions, asking questions, and delivering lectures. When a textbook is not written clearly or a lecture is not presented clearly, students have to make critical connections between ideas on their own, a skill that many at-risk students may not have. Students with special needs may not be able to recognize when they do not understand the material, or they may not be aware of strategies to try when instruction is difficult to understand. For example, when reading a text, they may not know how to use key words and headings or to look at the end-of-chapter questions to get main ideas. During oral presentations, students may not feel comfortable asking questions to clarify the information presented because they often are not sure what to ask and are afraid of looking stupid. Finally, students with special needs may lack the background knowledge necessary to construct meaning on their own. The implication here is that if you communicate clearly and use materials that do so as well, your students with special needs will be more successful.

Clarity in Written Communication

The importance of clear written communication is shown in these two textbook passages about western migration in the United States:

> Many of the farmers who moved in from New England were independent farmers. Land cost about a dollar an acre. Most men could afford to set up their own farms. Livestock farming was quite common on the frontier. Hogs could be fed in the forests. The cost of raising hogs was low. (Senesh, 1973, cited in Armbruster, 1984)

> Most of the farmers who moved in from New England were independent farmers. Being an independent farmer means that the farmer can afford to own his own farm. Around 1815, most men could afford their own farms because lands were cheap—it cost only about a dollar an acre. Many of these independent farms were livestock farms. For example, many frontier farmers raised hogs. Hog farming was common because hogs were inexpensive to keep. The cost of raising hogs was low because the farmer did not have to buy special feed for the hogs. The hogs did not need special feed because they could eat plants that grew in the surrounding forests. (Armbruster, 1984)

The second paragraph is much easier to understand; it requires fewer inferences by the reader and will require less adaptation by the teacher. The second passage defines "independent farmer" for the reader. If students were reading the first passage, you might have to provide this definition—which you could do orally or in a study guide. The reason farmers turned to raising livestock can be inferred from the first paragraph but is stated directly in the second. Students reading the first paragraph may need questions posed prior to reading in order to understand this relationship: for example, "Why did the farmers turn to raising livestock?" Obviously, having to adapt every paragraph like this would not be feasible. But this example underscores the need for adopting structurally and organizationally coherent textbooks. Then, if adaptations are still needed, you should do them only for sections containing the most important information.

Problems with textbook organization and clarity also can occur in explanations, especially when a sequence of events is being described. The ease with which students can understand the sequence depends on a number of factors, including the number of steps, the format used (list or paragraph form), and the presence of distracting information or material that is not related to the sequence.

Here is a passage about how baby alligators are hatched that students with special needs may struggle to understand:

> Adult female alligators make large cone-shaped nests from mud and compost. The female lays from 15 to 100 eggs with leathery shells in the nest and then covers it. The heat from both the sun and the decaying compost keeps the eggs warm. The eggs hatch in about 9 weeks. Unlike other reptiles that hatch from eggs, baby alligators make sounds while they are still in the shell. The mother then bites off the nest so the baby alligators can get out. When first hatched, baby alligators are about 15 to 25 cm long. (Berger, Berkheimer, Lewis, & Neuberger, 1979, p. 55, cited in Armbruster, 1984)

As you can see, the passage states a sequence of events leading up to the hatching of a baby alligator. It is written in paragraph format rather than a list, which makes it harder to decipher. Although the events are written in the correct order, the presence of a distractor, the sentence "Unlike other reptiles that hatch from eggs, baby alligators make sounds while they are still in the shell," breaks up the sequence and makes it harder for students to comprehend. A relatively easy adaptation would be to highlight the sentences in the sequence, or have the students put numbers next to each key sentence in the sequence. Of course, if a number of students in your class are having trouble with distracting information, you could provide direct instruction on how to identify and/or ignore distracting or irrelevant information.

Another aspect of written language that can make comprehension more difficult is the use of pronoun referents. A general rule of thumb is that the closer the pronoun is to its referent, the easier it is to translate. Consider this section of text.

> Now life began to change. The Eskimo hunters could see that these tools were useful. So they became traders, too. They trapped more furs than their families needed.
>
> Then they brought the furs to the trading posts. There they could trade the furs for supplies they had never had before. Because the new tools helped Eskimo hunters get along better, they became part of the Eskimo environment. (Brandwein & Bauer, 1980)

Many readers may have trouble figuring out who *they* refers to in this passage. Although the placement of most pronouns is not this problematic, understanding pronouns can be difficult for students with special needs. However, students can be taught to make sense of pronouns (Carnine et al., 1997). Before students read, identify unclear pronouns. Have students underline the pronouns in a passage. Then show them how to find the pronouns' referents by asking questions. For example:

Passage
Curtis and Dorva skipped school. They were grounded for a week. He was sorry. She got mad.

W W W   R e s o u r c e s

Get practical ideas about specific teaching problems from actual teachers in the field from Teachers Helping Teachers <http://www. pacificnet.net/~mandel/>.

Student Questioning

Teacher: Curtis and Dorva skipped school. Who skipped school?

Students: Curtis and Dorva.

Teacher: They were grounded for a week. Was Curtis grounded?

Students: Yes.

Teacher: Was Dorva grounded?

Students: Yes.

Teacher: He was sorry. Was Curtis sorry?

Students: Yes.

Teacher: Was Dorva sorry?

Students: No.

Teacher: She got mad. Did Dorva get mad?

Students: Yes.

Clarity in Oral Communication

Just as the quality of textbook writing affects student learning, so, too, does the quality of teachers' oral language. Three particularly important areas of oral language include giving directions, asking questions, and presenting subject matter (such as in a lecture).

Giving oral directions.   Giving oral directions is the most common way that teachers tell their students what they want them to do. When directions are not clear, valuable instructional time is wasted having to clarify them repeatedly. Consider this set of directions given by a middle school teacher at the beginning of a social studies lesson:

Unclear Instruction

All right, everyone, let's settle down and get quiet. I want you all to get ready for social studies. Shh. . . . Let's get ready. Alice and Tim, I want you to put those worksheets away. We need our books and notebooks. (Evertson et al., 1983, p. 143)

How clear is the teacher about what she wants her students to do? Now read this alternative set of directions:

Clearer Instruction

All right, everyone, I want all of you in your seats facing me for social studies. Now, I want you to get out three things: your social studies book, your spiral notebook, and a pencil. Put everything else away so that you just have those three things—the social studies book, the spiral notebook, and the pencil—out on your desk. [As students get out their materials, the teacher writes "Social Studies, page 55, Chapter 7 on Italy" on the chalkboard. She waits until students have their supplies ready and are listening before she begins talking.] (Evertson et al., 1983, p. 143)

In the first example, the teacher does not get the students' attention before giving them directions, a major problem. She is also unclear about what she wants her students to do. For example, words like "settle down" and "get ready" are not defined for the students. In the second example, the teacher first gets her students' attention, and then very specifically states all the things they need to do. Lavoie (1989) has suggested a number of guidelines for giving directions that are helpful for students with special needs:

1. State commands specifically, using concrete terms. In the Clearer Instruction example, the teacher was very specific about what the students needed to do to get ready for social studies. They had to get out three things: their book, notebook, and pencil. The first teacher told them only to "get ready."

2. Give "bite-size" directions; avoid a long series of directions. The second teacher first had her students sit down and face her; then she had them take out their materials; finally, she had them turn to the chapter they were going to read that day.

3. Whenever possible, accompany explanations with a demonstration. For example, Mr. Gaswami asked his students to take out their science books, turn to the beginning of the chapter, identify five key words, and define them using the glossary. Mr. Gaswami showed his students what he wanted them to do by opening his book to the chapter, pointing out that the key words were the ones that were italicized, and then demonstrating how to find and paraphrase the meanings using the glossary in the back of the book by doing several examples. He also wrote these directions on the board to help students remember all the steps.

4. Use cueing words such as "Look up here" and "Listen, please" before giving directions. Gestures such as a raised hand are also effective in getting students' attention.

Asking questions.   Asking students questions is a vital part of instructional clarity. The way you question your students is important for several reasons. Questioning is a quick way of assessing what your students have learned. In addition, questioning through the use of follow-up probes can help you analyze your students' errors. For example, Ms. Dilworth's third-grade class was given the following math problem:

> Three-fourths of the crayons in Bob's box of a dozen crayons are broken. How many unbroken crayons are there?

Ms. Dilworth asked Kareem what the answer was, and Kareem answered that there are four unbroken crayons left. Ms. Dilworth asked Kareem to explain how he got that answer. Kareem said, "Because three-fourths means three groups of four and since there is only one group left that group has four in it." By asking a question, Ms. Dilworth found out that Kareem did not know the concept of three-fourths. Questions can also be used to redirect students to the correct answer when they make mistakes. For example, Ms. Dilworth might have asked Kareem a number of follow-up questions:

> How many crayons did you start with? How many is a dozen? What fraction of the crayons were broken? What does three-fourths mean? What would one-fourth of twelve be?

Last, and perhaps most important, it is through effective questioning that your students can learn thinking skills. Well-constructed questions provide students with a model for effective thinking; in time, students learn to ask themselves these same questions as they solve problems. A reading comprehension strategy that uses

FYI

Another use of cueing is to let a student know that he or she can expect to be called on to respond orally only when you present a particular cue that only the student will know. This way the student can attend to a lesson with less anxiety about speaking in class.

Cultural Awareness

Strategies for questioning students with limited English proficiency are covered in Chapter 7.

Figure 9.7 **Questions Students Can Ask As They Read**

To Get the General Idea
- What is the story about?
  —What is the problem?
  —What is the solution?
- What makes me think so?

To Predict–Verify–Decide
- What's going to happen next?
  —Is my prediction still good?
  —Do I need to change my prediction?
- What makes me think so?

To Visualize–Verify–Decide
- What does this (person, place, thing) look like?
  —Is the picture in my mind still good?
  —Do I need to change my picture?
- What makes me think so?

To Summarize
- What's happened so far?
- What makes me think so?

To Think Aloud
- What am I thinking?
- Why?

To Solve Problems or Help When I Don't Understand
- Shall I
  —Guess?
  —Ignore and read on?
  —Reread or look back?
- Why?

S O U R C E : From "SAIL: A Way to Success and Independence for Low-Achieving Readers" by J. L. Bergman, 1992, *Reading Teacher, 49*(8), pp. 598–602. Used by permission of International Reading Association, T. Schuder, and J. Bergman.

Connections

Students with special needs benefit from being taught to think because efficient thinking may not come naturally to them and/or they may not have been exposed to good models of thinking. Strategies for teaching students thinking skills are described further in Chapter 10.

questions to teach students how to think while they are reading is shown in Figure 9.7. First, the teacher asks the students the questions in Figure 9.7 as they read stories. Over time, students are taught to ask themselves these questions as they read independently.

Although asking questions can be a very potent teaching strategy, to achieve maximum benefit, questioning needs to be carried out correctly. Kindsvatter, Wilen, and Ishler (1988) have suggested the following guidelines for using questioning in your classroom:

1. Phrase questions clearly to ensure that students know how to respond. For example, a vague question, such as "What about the Great Depression?" forces students to guess rather than to consider carefully a direct response to the question. A better wording would be, "What were the two primary causes of the Great Depression?"

2. Provide a balance between higher- and lower-level questions. The important point to keep in mind is that both kinds of questions are important. Lower-level, or convergent, questions help you find out whether students have the basic understanding necessary for higher-level thought. Further, critical and creative thinking can be developed by using convergent and evaluative questions. Although the current emphasis on incorporating more higher-level skills into the curriculum is positive, it is important to realize that lower-level knowledge is still important, particularly for students with special needs. Students with special needs may not readily

acquire lower-level knowledge. Failing to help them acquire these understandings can prevent them from ever developing higher-level understandings. Also, lower-level questions can give students an opportunity to succeed in class. Finally, research suggests that lower-level questions may be most appropriate in teaching basic skills to students who are at risk (Emmer, Evertson, Sanford, Clements, & Worsham, 1983; Rosenshine, 1979).

3. Adapt questions to the language and skill level of the class, including individual students in the class. Your questions should accommodate a range of needs, from lower-performing students to gifted students. For example, a question for a lower-performing student might be, "From what you have just read, how does the demand for a product affect its supply?" For students with more skills, the question might become, "Going beyond the article a little, how does price affect supply and demand and at what point is market equilibrium reached?"

4. Vary the "wait time" you give your students to answer questions. **Wait time** is the amount of time you give students to respond to questions in class.

5. Involve all of your students in classroom questioning by calling on nonvolunteers as well as volunteers. Calling on all of your students also allows you to monitor student learning efficiently. In addition, calling on nonvolunteers (who frequently are your students with special needs) demonstrates that you hold them accountable for listening and leads to higher levels of on-task behavior. However, as mentioned before, you should match questions with student ability to maximize the likelihood of student success. Finally, for lower-level questions, consider using **unison responding,** or having all students respond at once, together. Unison responding allows more student opportunities for practice and recitation and can lead to higher levels of correct responses and on-task behavior (Carnine, 1981).

Presenting content orally. Communicating clearly to your students when you are presenting subject-matter content orally, such as in a lecture, also is important. This section of a lecture was delivered during a geography lesson about Italy:

> **Teacher 1**
> Italy is in southern Europe, down by France and the Mediterranean Sea. It's a peninsula in the Mediterranean. There are a lot of beautiful islands in the Mediterranean off of Italy and Greece as well. Sardinia and Sicily are islands that are part of Italy. Corsica, Capri, and some other islands like Crete and Cyprus are in the same part of the world, but they don't belong to, although they may be close to, Italy. You could turn to the map of Europe that's in your text to see where Italy is. (Evertson et al., 1983, pp. 143–144)

The language used by this teacher lacks clarity. For example, he presents information about a number of islands but is unclear how these islands relate to the main topic, which appears to be the location of Italy. The teacher is also vague when he says, "[the islands] don't belong to, although they may be close to, Italy." In addition, the teacher uses the word *peninsula* but does not define it. Finally, this explanation needs the visual display of a map to bring clarity to it, but the teacher refers to a map at the end almost as an afterthought and makes use of the map voluntary. The only students who will know where Italy is after this lecture will be those who already knew in the first place. Many students with special needs could be left behind. Here is another lecture on the same topic that is much clearer:

Teacher 2

Now, I want all eyes on me. [The teacher then gestures to the world map next to her.] Raise your hand if you can show the class where Italy is. [Several students raise their hands. The teacher then has Maria read the names and show the class where France, Switzerland, Austria, and Yugoslavia and the Mediterranean Sea border on Italy.] Italy is in Europe. It is a large peninsula shaped like a boot that extends into the Mediterranean

Table 9.2   Instructional Clarity

Poor Clarity	Being Clear
Not telling students what they are expected to learn or the purposes of the activity.	Stating lesson goals; listing major objectives on the board.
Using verbal mazes; that is, starting a sentence and stopping to start again, pausing and repeating words to buy time, and halting in midsentence.	Using complete sentences in a straightforward way; focusing on the expression of one thought, point, direction, and so on at a time.
Presenting information or directions out of sequence; starting and stopping in the middle of a lesson.	Presenting information in the appropriate sequence; emphasizing important points; working from an outline with complex content and providing it to the students visually (for example, on a transparency or the board) as well as orally.
Moving from a major topic or skill to another without signaling the change.	Beginning and ending activities clearly; preparing students for transitions by giving them warnings; telling students what to expect and why the activity has changed.
Inserting extraneous information into the lesson; interrupting the lesson's flow with irrelevant comments or questions.	Sticking to the topic; making certain that the main concept is understood before adding complexity.
Presenting concepts without ample concrete examples; teaching skills without sufficient demonstration and practice time.	Having many, varied examples; planning adequate demonstrations and practice time.
Introducing complexity before the students are ready for it.	Teaching basic skills to an overlearned (highly developed) level before presenting refinements.
Using phrasing and vocabulary that is overly complex for the age or grade level.	Using words the students understand; repeating and restating major points and key ideas; checking frequently to see that students are with you.
Overusing negative adjectives and adverbs, such as "not all rocks," "not many countries," or "not very happy."	Being specific and direct: "the igneous rocks," "one-fourth of the countries," or "upset" or "annoyed."
Using ambiguous phrases and pronouns with vague or unidentifiable referents: "these," "them," "things," "etc.," "maybe," "more or less," "this thing," "all of this," "and so forth," "you know."	Referring to the concrete object whenever possible; using the noun along with the pronoun: "these bacteria," "this sum," "those problems," "all of the spelling words on page 20."
Being vague and approximate about *amount*—"a bunch," "a few," "a couple," "some"; *likelihood*—"may," "might," "chances are," "could be," "probably," "sometimes"; *nature*—"aspects," "sorts," "kinds."	Being as precise as possible. Specific information is more interesting and easier to remember than vague facts.

SOURCE: From *Organizing and Managing the Elementary School Classroom* by C. M. Evertson et al., 1983, Austin: Research and Development Center for Teacher Education, University of Texas.

Sea. [She writes *peninsula* on the board, sounding the syllables as she writes. Since students have studied the word once before, she calls on a student to define it.] Agnes, what is a *peninsula*?

Additional guidelines for presenting instructions clearly are shown in Table 9.2.

What Adaptations Can You Make to Help Students Succeed in Independent Practice?

As discussed in Chapter 4, the main purpose of practice activities is to provide students with opportunities for refining their skills while at the same time allowing you to monitor their performance. To achieve these purposes, students should be able to complete practice activities such as seatwork and homework independently.

Even under ideal circumstances and with the best intentions, it is difficult to design practice activities that meet the needs of all the students in your class. Problems arise because of individual characteristics, and adaptations need to be made. For example, students with severe reading problems may have difficulty reading directions that may be quite clear to everyone else. Students with attention problems may have trouble with questions that have multiple steps. Students with physical disabilities may be unable to perform the writing requirements of their assignments. In the case of students with severe cognitive disabilities, practice activities may need to be revamped totally so that they are consistent with the students' skill levels and the goals and objectives on their IEPs.

Adapting Seatwork Assignments

One problem with seatwork is that the practice activities may not contain enough items. This limitation is important since students with disabilities often require more practice to master skills or content. For example, Ms. Jennings has just taught her students to solve two-step story problems in math that require adding first and then subtracting. She first demonstrated three problems in front of the class and then guided her students through three more. Ms. Jennings then had her students complete independently five problems in the math book. She found that only half the students answered all of the problems correctly and that the rest of the class needed more practice. Many math books have extra problems for students who need more practice, but some do not. You may need either to make up your own items or to find similar items from other books.

Another common problem with seatwork is that the directions are too difficult. Complicated or confusing directions can prevent students from completing their seatwork successfully. For example, some directions are excessively wordy: "Use the words letters stand for and the sense of the other words to find out what the new word in heavy black print is" (Center for the Study of Reading, 1988, p. 14). This is just a convoluted way of saying, "Read." Other directions have too many steps: "Read the first sentence, and fill in the missing word. Read the second sentence. Find the word from the first sentence that makes sense in the second sentence and print it where it belongs. Then, do what the last sentence says. Repeat for all the other sentences" (Center for the Study of Reading, 1988, p. 14).

Affleck, Lowenbraun, and Archer (1980) have suggested a number of adaptations you can make for students with special needs when they encounter directions that are too difficult:

1. Verbally present the tasks. This adaptation can be done with the whole class, particularly when many students are having problems with the directions. You can accommodate the needs of individual students by pairing a worksheet with an auditory tape that explains the directions.
2. Add practice examples that you can do with the whole class or a small group of students who are having particular difficulty.
3. Write alternative sets of directions. You can project these onto a screen using an overhead projector or distribute individual copies to students.
4. Highlight the important words in the directions.
5. Have students help each other when the directions are difficult.

F Y I

Before starting independent practice, complete sample items for the students. Talk through each step, modeling your thought process and decision making. Use questioning to check that students understand directions. What other strategies will you use for adapting seatwork and homework?

Students may also have trouble when single pages of seatwork contain a number of different tasks. This combination of tasks can cause problems for students with special needs, who often have difficulty making the transition from one task to another. Consider the example shown in Figure 9.8. This worksheet has three different tasks. Students need to make a number of transitions within one worksheet to complete the activity successfully. Also, students are required to use words circled in part A as answers to Part C. Using answers from one part of a worksheet as answers to questions on another part is confusing and assumes that students answered the first part correctly. You could adapt this worksheet by visually cueing the change of task on the page (for example, draw a line between tasks), and correcting Part A before the students do Part C.

Finally, seatwork should provide opportunities for students to practice functional skills. When seatwork tasks are nonfunctional, much valuable practice time is wasted. For example, in Part A of the seatwork activity shown in Figure 9.8, students are required to circle the words that contain the same vowel sound as in the word *bit*. This task is nonfunctional because students must already be able to read the words to tell whether they have the short *i* sound. The exercise does not teach students to read the words; students can be successful only if they already can perform the skill. A more direct way to have students practice reading words that have the short *i* sound would be to have them read words orally to you in passages and/or lists and provide them with corrective feedback on missed words. Before you give a seatwork assignment to your students, ask yourself what the objective is and whether this task meets the objective. If you have a hard time answering either question, consider using a different worksheet.

Providing Feedback on Independent Practice Activities

You can also adapt student practice by the feedback you provide on students' performance. It makes good sense to correct and return students' work as soon as possible. Timely feedback allows you to find out right away where your students are making mistakes so you can reteach material if necessary. Providing feedback as quickly as possible is particularly important for students with special needs, who are less likely to learn material the first time it is presented. Returning papers soon after they are handed in also helps students know what they are doing correctly or incorrectly, and it gives them the opportunity to make corrections when the material is

Figure 9.8   Seatwork Activity

Name _____

The Sound of Short *i*

A. Say each word. Circle the words that have the vowel sound you hear in "hit."

lick	milk	cane	time
might	away	drink	gone
rabbit	house	sing	girl
this	come	five	fish

B. Make new words by changing the first letter or letters.

pick   _____   _____   _____

wing   _____   _____   _____

slip   _____   _____   _____

C. Fill in each blank with one of the words that you circled above to complete the sentences.

1. The boys and girls will _____ a song in school.

2. My father and I went to the river and caught a big _____.

3. _____ is not the book I want to read.

4. The fluffy little _____ ran across the road.

5. My mother gave me a glass of _____.

---

still fresh in their minds. In addition, regular feedback makes students feel more accountable for what they put on their papers.

Although providing timely feedback to students is a good practice, as a professional teacher and as an individual with a personal life as well, you may have limited time during and after school. Therefore, in grading your students' papers, efficiency is imperative. Here are some suggestions designed to help you save time:

1. Correct papers as you circulate. You can correct some papers as you circulate throughout the room during the seatwork period. First, carry a pen with different color ink than those used by students when they correct their own papers. Begin circulating and correcting the papers of your students with special needs first. This will ensure that those who are most likely to need your help receive it. Each time you stop at a student's desk, correct at least two items. Correct answers can be marked with a C, star, happy face, or whatever you prefer. Mark errors with a dot. When you find an error, try to determine whether the student simply made a careless mistake or did not know how to do the item correctly. If the student does not know how to do the item, show him or her how to do it, assign several similar problems, and say that you will be back to check the work in several minutes (Paine, Radicchi, Rosellini, Deutchman, and Darch, 1983, pp. 122–123).

2. Use spot checking. Reading 3 of the 10 comprehension answers assigned will give you a fairly good idea of whether students understand the material (Lavoie, 1989).

3. Use shared checking. Allow the first two students finished with an assignment to go to a corner and compare their answers. When they reach agreement on the answers, they design a "key." They can then check the other students' answers. If you have students exchange papers, have the corrector sign the paper at the bottom. This strategy helps ensure that students correct fairly and accurately (Lavoie, 1989).

4. Use easy checking. Design assignments in a way that makes them easy to correct. For example, put problems or questions in neat, orderly rows. When checking assignments from consumable workbooks, cut off the corners of the pages you have checked or corrected. This helps you (and the student) find the next page quickly (Lavoie, 1989).

5. Use self-checking. Dictate or show answers using an overhead projector while students correct their own papers. Require that pencil assignments be corrected in pen and vice versa. Making corrections in a different shade or color enables you to monitor the number of mistakes students make before completion of their final corrected copy. Having students color over each answer with a yellow crayon before the correction activity serves the same purpose, since their original answers are impossible to erase. After collecting papers, spot check them for accuracy and provide consequences accordingly (Lavoie, 1989).

Adapting Homework Assignments

Homework is on the rise in the United States, largely because of societal pressures to boost student achievement (Cooper & Nye, 1994). Unfortunately, as with in-class independent practice activities, students with special needs may have difficulty completing traditional homework assignments. The problems of students with special needs involve two factors: students' lack of time management and academic skills to complete these assignments independently, and the failure to establish a clear line of communication between home and school. Patton (1994) has reviewed the research literature on effective homework practices for students with special needs and come up with these strategies for adapting homework, which apply especially to students in secondary schools:

1. Involve parents from the outset. Establish an effective home–school communication system and let parents know the role they should play in the homework process. General education teachers are often confused about whose responsibility it is to communicate with the parents of students with special needs—the general education teacher or the special education teacher (Jayanthi, Nelson, Sawyer, Bursuck, & Epstein, 1995). Usually, whoever assigns the homework should communicate with the parents.

2. Assign homework from the beginning of the school year. This strategy gets students accustomed to the routine of having homework.

3. Schedule time and establish a routine for assigning, collecting, and evaluating homework. You need to be sure that you allow enough time to explain as-

Do It!

Select a commercially prepared student workbook page in the subject area and grade level you plan to teach. Critique a worksheet in light of the guidelines for adapting seatwork. How might you adapt this worksheet for a student with special needs?

All students can benefit from homework and other independent practice activities. What are some strategies you can use to adapt homework and other assignments for students with special needs?

signments to students with special needs. A quick explanation immediately before or after the bell is often not enough and results in homework either not done or done incorrectly. According to Patton (1994), a thorough explanation of a homework assignment should include the following components: state the purpose, give directions for completing the assignment, provide an estimate of how long the assignment should take, note in writing when the assignment is due, clarify the format to be used, identify the materials needed to complete the assignment successfully, indicate how the assignment should be evaluated, and always give both oral and written instructions.

4. Coordinate with other teachers. Students may have several different teachers. Students could conceivably be assigned homework in most or all of their classes on a given night, which could lead to a difficult situation for them. You should coordinate your planning with your fellow teachers, if only for the students in your classes who you feel are at risk for not completing homework.

5. Verify the clarity of your assignments. Do this by asking students to tell you what they are supposed to do, responding either as a group or individually. For example, you might take a student aside after class or after school and ask him what his homework is.

6. Whenever possible, allow students to start their assignments in class. This strategy allows you to see if any problems arise, *before* students take their assignments home.

7. Use assignment books and/or folders. Many students with special needs lack critical organizational and memory skills. Having places to write down due dates and keep their papers can be helpful. Assignment books can provide a valuable communication link with parents. Teachers can initial the book after class, indicating the assignment has been properly recorded. Parents can initial the book as well, confirming that they have seen the assignment. For more ideas on building student independence in completing assignments, see Chapter 10.

8. Implement classroom-based incentive programs. Students who are rewarded for completing their homework accurately will be more likely to do their homework regularly. Incentives may be particularly important for students with special needs, for whom homework is often a struggle with no obvious benefit.

9. Have parents sign and date homework. This adaptation is particularly powerful. Research shows that students whose parents are required to sign off on their homework spend more time doing their homework.

10. Evaluate assignments. As with independent practice in class, homework that is collected, evaluated, and graded is more meaningful to students. Many of the correcting strategies recommended for in-class activities can be applied to homework as well.

11. Establish relevance. Show students how a particular assignment relates to their lives in and out of school.

12. Give homework on skills students already can perform. Homework is a good way to help students build skill fluency, maintain their skills, or apply their skills to new settings or situations. Homework should not, however, require skills that the students have not yet acquired.

Even with the best homework assignments, students with special needs will still need adaptations. For example, students with reading problems may need extra assistance with homework directions. Students with physical disabilities may need assignments shortened, or they may need to respond orally rather than in writing. Remember to use the INCLUDE strategy introduced in Chapter 4 in coming up with adaptations that fit your assignments and the individual characteristics of your students with special needs. A survey of general education teachers (Polloway, Epstein, Bursuck, Jayanthi, & Cumblad, 1994) showed that teachers favored these homework adaptations: adjust length of assignment; provide extra teacher help; provide a peer tutor for assistance; set up student study groups; provide auxiliary learning aids, such as computers and calculators; check more frequently with students about assignments, such as when they are due and what is required; and allow alternative response formats, such as oral or written.

Of course, successful homework also depends on individual student skills. Not only do students need to be proficient in basic academic skills, but they also need to be able to learn independently. For example, they need to recognize their homework problems and seek help when necessary. They also need to manage their time effectively. Strategies for teaching these and other independent learning skills will be covered in more depth in Chapter 10.

FYI

Sometimes, homework is not a viable option, as in the case of students who work so hard during the day that they need a break or students whose life circumstances make homework irrelevant.

Adapting Materials for Students with Moderate to Severe Disabilities

Students with moderate to severe disabilities often cannot perform some or all of the steps in tasks performed every day by students without disabilities. In the past, this inability to perform tasks in the same way as other students was interpreted to mean that students with moderate to severe disabilities could not benefit from these activities. Today, the emphasis is on making adaptations and providing support for these students so that they can increase their participation level or level of independence in performing classroom activities (Lowell-York, Doyle, & Kronberg, 1995). You can use this five-step self-questioning process to make sure that students with moderate to severe disabilities are maximally included in your class:

1. **Can the student perform the same task, using the same materials?** Answering yes to this question means that goals and objectives from the student's IEP can be addressed within the general education curriculum. For example, Meg is in a fifth-grade class involved in a unit on nutrition. During math, they will be measuring ingredients for making fat-free blueberry muffins. In this case, Meg participates in the measurement activity under the same expectations for performance as her peers. No adaptations are required.

2. **Can the student perform the same task but with an easier step?** At this level, the student participates in the general education curriculum at a more basic level relative to his or her peers. This means that the activity is the same but the objectives are different. For example, in the nutrition example, Meg only measures out ingredients that do not involve fractions (for example, 1 cup, 1 teaspoon). Or, Meg identifies the words *cup* and *teaspoon* in the recipe.

3. **Can the student perform the same task but with different materials?** At this point in the process, the objectives continue to be the same but the materials are changed to make sure the student is an equal partner in the lesson. For example, Meg uses an adapted recipe with visual symbols to depict the ingredients and measurements. Meg also uses measuring spoons and cups that have enlarged handles that enable her to use them.

4. **Does the student need to perform a different task having the same theme as the classroom lesson?** In this option, the student participates in activities drawn from the general education curriculum that are thematically linked to what his or her peers are doing. The focus for the student with moderate to severe disabilities is on core IEP goals that are embedded in general education classroom activities. For example, Meg practices filling measuring cups and spoons; Meg tells another student in the class what her favorite breakfast foods are.

5. **Does the student require a different theme and a different task?** This option focuses on functional tasks that have a direct bearing on the day-to-day life of the student. The student's IEP goals and objectives are not dependent on the general education curriculum and are addressed independent of classroom routines and activities. For example, Meg leaves the classroom to work on toileting, dressing, and handwashing; she leaves school to learn cleaning skills at a local fast food restaurant; and she hands back papers to other students, with the teacher or a peer reading her the names on each paper. (Lowell-York et al., 1995)

Check Your Learning

What adaptations can you make in your practice activities to help all students succeed?

Connections

Other information on including students with moderate to severe disabilities is included in Chapters 5 and 8.

Do It!

Observe a student with moderate to severe disabilities included in a general education classroom. Observe how the teacher has used the five-step process of adapting instruction and materials.

Summary

Teachers who communicate clearly through the curriculum materials they use or the information they present orally in class will meet the needs of a broad range of their students without having to make adaptations. Nonetheless, despite your best efforts, you will still need to make some adaptations for students who are at risk or have other special needs.

In teaching basic skills, you may need to make adaptations in the areas of preskills, selecting and sequencing examples, rate of introduction of new skills, and the amount of direct instruction, practice, and review. Preskills are basic skills necessary for performing more complex skills. Before teaching a skill, you should assess the relevant preskills, and, if necessary, teach them. The range of examples you present should correspond directly with the types of problems you want students to solve, in and out of class. Examples can also be sequenced to make learning easier for students. Students sometimes have difficulty learning skills when they are introduced at too fast a rate. Introduce skills in small steps and at a slow enough rate to ensure mastery before you present more new skills. Finally, in learning basic skills, students at risk or with special needs may need more direct instruction, practice, and review.

In teaching subject-matter content to students with special needs, adaptations may need to be made in the areas of activating background knowledge, organizing content, and teaching terms and concepts. Students who have disabilities may lack background knowledge necessary for learning a content area, or they may know the information but be unable to recall it and relate it to the new information being presented. The PReP strategy, anticipation guides, and planning think sheets can help activate students' background knowledge. When content is well organized, students' understanding of important ideas and their interrelationships is enhanced. Student understanding also increases when study guides and graphic organizers are used. Students may also need help comprehending the large number of new and/or technical vocabulary words and concepts in content-area instruction. Strategies for teaching vocabulary that are effective for students with special needs include modeling examples, synonyms and definitions; and concept diagrams.

Your oral and written communication with students must be clear. Clear written communication requires fewer inferences by the reader, a help for students with special needs, who may lack the background knowledge and reasoning skills to make such inferences. Effective written communication also explains sequences of events logically and uses obvious pronoun referents. Clear oral communication involves the effective use of directions, questions, and lectures.

You may also need to make adaptations in student independent-practice activities. Seatwork can be adapted by increasing the number of practice items, clarifying the directions, and reducing the number of different activities on a page. Providing feedback on independent practice activities can be facilitated by correcting papers as you circulate and using spot checking, shared checking, easy checking, and self-checking. Effective homework adaptations for students with special needs include adjusting assignment length; providing extra teacher help; providing a peer tutor; setting up student study groups; providing auxiliary learning aids, such as calculators and computers; and allowing alternative response formats, such as oral or written responses.

Students with moderate to severe disabilities often cannot perform some or all of the steps in tasks. You can use a five-step questioning process to adapt your classroom activities for these students.

Applications in Teaching Practice

Developing a Repertoire of Instructional Adaptations

You want to teach a group of at-risk students to spell the following contractions: *can't, aren't, couldn't, shouldn't, wouldn't, don't, won't,* and *isn't.*

Questions

1. How will you evaluate whether your students have learned the contractions?
2. What preskills should you be concerned with, how will you assess them, and what will you do with students who do not know them?
3. How would you sequence your instruction? Why did you choose this particular sequence?
4. How will you provide direct instruction, practice, and review for your students?
5. At what rate will you introduce the contractions?

Design a study guide for a section of Chapter 2 of this text.

Questions

1. What steps did you go through in constructing your study guide?
2. How did you select the vocabulary and concepts that you included?
3. How would you use the study guide to teach at-risk students or other students with special needs?

Develop a graphic organizer for a major concept in Chapter 1 of this text.

Questions

1. How did you select the concept? Is it a "big idea?"
2. How would you use the graphic organizer to teach at-risk students or other students with special needs?

Design a lesson to teach the concept of "reasonable accommodations" using a definition.

Questions

1. Is your definition stated clearly, simply, and concisely?
2. What examples and nonexamples did you use?
3. How will you find out whether your students know the meaning of the concept?
4. How will you find out whether your students can discriminate this concept from other concepts presented in the text?
5. How would you teach the concept using a concept diagram format?

Strategies for Independent Learning

After you read this chapter, you will be able to

1. State ways that teachers can encourage student self-awareness and self-advocacy.

2. Describe ways that learning strategies can be developed and taught.

3. List and describe successful learning strategies in the areas of reading comprehension, note-taking, written expression, math problem solving, and time management.

4. Describe ways that students can learn to use learning strategies independently.

Gerald is a student with learning disabilities in Mr. McCrae's ninth-grade English class. Gerald has had problems in the area of written expression throughout his school years. It is not that he does not have good ideas. When Gerald talks about what he is going to write, it sounds great. However, when he tries to get his ideas on paper, writing becomes a very frustrating experience for him. First of all, Gerald's papers lack organization. They rarely have a good introduction and conclusion, and the body is usually out of sequence. Gerald also makes a lot of mechanical errors; his papers are full of misspellings, and he frequently leaves out punctuation marks and capital letters. When asked by Mr. McCrae why he does not proofread his papers, Gerald responded that he does. What can Mr. McCrae do to help Gerald learn to organize his papers better? What can be done to help Gerald proofread his papers better for mechanical errors?

Traci is a student in Ms. McCord's third-grade class. Although Traci was referred for special education services last year, she was not determined eligible for them. Traci has trouble solving story problems in math because she does not have a systematic way of working on them. When Traci starts a problem, she looks for the numbers right away rather than reading the problem carefully first. For example, one day she saw the numbers 23 and 46 in a problem and automatically added them to get an answer of 69. The problem called for subtraction, but Traci did not know that because she had not read the problem. What can Ms. McCord do to help Traci solve math word problems more successfully? How can Ms. McCord help Traci become a more independent problem solver?

Ronald is a student with a moderate cognitive disability who has problems with organization. He is often late for school because, according to his parents, he rarely plans ahead and is always getting his materials ready for school at the last minute. Ronald is usually late for class as well. He says that he cannot keep track of what he needs to bring to each class so he is constantly going back to his locker, which makes him late. His locker is a complete mess. Afternoons, Ronald has a part-time job bagging groceries as part of a work-study program. His supervisor has expressed concern that Ronald has been late for work several times, frequently forgets his uniform, and several times has missed his bus and has had to be driven home by one of the clerks. What can Ronald's teachers do to help him become better organized?

All of these students share a common problem: They are unable to meet the academic and organizational demands of school independently. Being able to work independently is a skill that becomes increasingly important as students move through the grades. Gerald needs to be able to organize his papers better, not just in English, but in all areas—teachers often judge quality on the basis of organization, neatness, or the number of spelling or punctuation errors. Traci needs to solve problems more systematically, not just in math, but in her other classes and out of school as well. Ronald will need a strategy for managing his time: Being punctual and having the necessary supplies or materials are essential in school as well as in the world of work. The fact is, as students move through the grades and on to careers or postsecondary education, more and more independence is expected by teachers and is necessary for student success.

Students need to perform independently in five key areas: gaining information, storing and retrieving information, expressing information, self-advocating, and managing time (Ellis & Lenz, 1996). Gaining information involves skills in listening to directions during lessons and on the job, or in reading and interpreting textbooks, source books, or other media. Storing information consists of strategies for taking notes and preparing for tests or other evaluations. Students also need to retrieve information when needed. For example, they need to remember how to carry out a job task such as cleaning and clearing a table, or safety procedures to follow during science lab. Expressing information includes the school tasks of taking tests and writing papers. It also involves tasks such as developing a menu for a fast-food restaurant. Self-advocacy skills help students set realistic school or life goals and develop and carry out a plan to meet those goals. Finally, students need to have the time management skills to organize their time and effort toward meeting their goals.

Although all of these skills become more important as students progress through school, independence should be stressed at all levels of instruction. Unfortunately, many students, including those who are at risk or have other special needs, lack basic independent learning skills. Traditionally, when students needed learning-strategy instruction, they were referred to special education classes, remedial reading or math programs, or special study-skills courses. In inclusive classrooms, learning strategies can be taught to students with special needs in several ways. Most often, learning strategies can be covered in class so that all students can benefit. For example, when Mr. Cooper discovered that many of his students in American history were having trouble taking notes, he presented a note-taking strategy to his whole class. Similarly, Ms. Carpenter taught her biology class a strategy for taking multiple choice tests because her students were scoring low as a group on these kinds of questions.

Occasionally, because of extraordinary student needs, strategy instruction might take place outside the classroom. For example, some students with special needs may need to have a strategy broken down into small steps, view multiple demonstrations of a strategy, and practice the strategy many times before they learn it. If the collaborative support of other education professionals is lacking, this level of instruction may be difficult to deliver within the time and curricular constraints of the general education classroom. Ronald, the student you met at the beginning of this chapter, has such extraordinary needs. Ronald needed a strategy designed specifically for his organizational problems; a plan for getting to his afternoon job on time would not be relevant for the rest of his classmates. In cases such as these—where a special educator teaches strategies to individual students—your job will be to encourage and monitor student use of the strategy in your class and to provide stu-

Connections

How does this chapter relate to the INCLUDE model presented in Chapter 4?

Cultural Awareness

The value placed on student independence may differ depending on a student's culture. For example, compared to European American students, many Hispanic, Native American, Filipino, and Southeast Asian students are more interested in obtaining teacher direction and feedback than working on their own (Grossman, 1995). Since being independent and taking direction are both important for students to do, teach your students to function in both manners.

Connections

Strategies for independence that are relevant for students with moderate to severe cognitive disabilities are discussed in Chapters 5 and 9.

dents with feedback on their performance. However, in most cases, you can teach many of these skills in your class while still covering the required academic content. In fact, teaching learning strategies to students will allow you to cover more material because your students will be able to learn on their own.

You should do all you can to encourage and teach independent learning strategies to your students. This chapter will focus on three major ways you can build student independence in learning: (1) encouraging student self-awareness and self-advocacy skills; (2) developing and teaching learning strategies directly in class; and (3) teaching students to use specific strategies on their own. Keep in mind that the strategies discussed apply most directly to students with high-incidence or sensory disabilities or to students who are at risk.

How Can You Encourage Student Self-Awareness and Self-Advocacy?

As students move through elementary, middle, and high school and on to postsecondary education or the world of work, the level of independence expected by those around them increases. Teachers expect students to come to class on time, master content through reading and lectures, keep track of assignments, organize study and homework time, set realistic career goals, and participate in curricular and extracurricular activities to meet these career goals. Students also are expected to recognize when they have a problem and to know where to go for help. Clearly, students need to look out for themselves, to become self-advocates.

In effective student **self-advocacy,** students need to be aware of their strengths and weaknesses, the potential impact of these strengths and weaknesses on their performance, the support they need to succeed, and the skills required to communicate their needs positively and assertively. A checklist of self-awareness and self-advocacy skills is shown in Figure 10.1 on page 342.

Adjusting to these changing expectations can be difficult for all students, but especially for students with disabilities. Many students with special needs are not aware of their strengths and weaknesses (Aune, 1991; Brinckerhoff, 1994) and lack self-advocacy skills (Durlak, Rose, & Bursuck, 1994). They will need to learn these skills while still in school.

Generally speaking, special educators have much of the responsibility for teaching self-advocacy directly. However, you are in a good position to teach all students about the opportunities and expectations of the adult world related to self-awareness and self-advocacy. For example, Meredith is a student in Ms. Gay's second-grade class. When Meredith does not understand how to do her seatwork, she is afraid to ask Ms. Gay for help. As a result, she often gets it wrong. Ms. Gay decided to spend 5 minutes with the whole class talking about knowing when and how to ask for help. She felt this discussion would help Meredith and other students in the class be more assertive when they have a problem. Cecil is a student with a vision impairment who is included in Mr. Jordan's algebra class. Even though Cecil sits in the front row, he is still unable to see the problems on the board because Mr. Jordan forms his numbers too small. However, Cecil does not feel comfortable asking Mr. Jordan to write larger. Cecil practiced asking Mr. Jordan for help with his special education teacher. Cecil then asked Mr. Jordan directly, who responded that it would be no problem to

Cultural Awareness

Self-advocacy relates to social and cultural factors that affect a student's self-concept and self-esteem. Strategies for independence can help students at risk or with special needs overcome learned helplessness and develop a stronger sense of self-efficacy.

Check Your Learning

Why might guiding students in establishing or choosing their own learning goals be an effective approach for introducing self-advocacy skills?

Figure 10.1 Self-Advocacy Checklist

Student's Name _____

Date _____

Rater _____

Instructions

This evaluation asks you to examine the student's skills in the area of self-advocacy (assertiveness and interpersonal skills). Please read each statement and indicate how you think this student compares to other students his or her age in these specific areas.

5 = Very high	2 = Below average
4 = Above average	1 = Very low
3 = Average	N/O = Not observed

1. ____ Recognizes he or she needs help.

2. ____ Knows when and how to request help.

3. ____ Participates verbally in class (appropriately).

4. ____ Makes eye contact with person to whom speaking.

5. ____ Is aware of kinds of accommodations available for testing and other needs and understands which are appropriate for his or her characteristics (for example, oral exams, extended time for tests, books on tape).

6. ____ Asks for appropriate help from peers.

7. ____ Actively participates in setting, establishing, and discussing IEP goals.

8. ____ Speaks in appropriate voice tone for situation.

9. ____ Cooperates when asked.

10. ____ Persists when necessary.

11. ____ Asks questions if does not understand.

12. ____ Works independently.

13. ____ Indicates confidence in academic abilities.

14. ____ Initiates work, participation, and questions.

15. ____ Volunteers answers in class.

16. ____ Indicates confidence in social abilities.

Other Comments/Concerns

_____
_____
_____
_____

S O U R C E : From *Preparing High School Students with Learning Disabilities for the Transition to Post-Secondary Education: Training for Self-Determination* by C. M. Durlak, 1992, unpublished doctoral dissertation, Northern Illinois University, DeKalb. Used by permission.

write bigger. Mr. Jordan also gave Cecil some additional pointers on how to describe his disability and ask his teachers for accommodations. Suggested practices that you can follow to help your students increase their level of self-awareness and self-advocacy are presented in the Professional Edge.

Professional Edge

Supporting Self-Advocacy Skills

Learning to be a self-advocate can be a challenge for students, and especially for students with special needs. You can help all your students learn to be more self-aware and to look out for themselves by fostering the skills and strategies they will need to become more sure of themselves. Following the suggestions described here will help you create a safe environment in which students can practice self-advocacy skills.

1. Support a schoolwide self-advocacy system. Some common classroom situations that require students to self-advocate or assert themselves are asking for clarification of lecture material; telling a teacher that they have a disability or other learning problem; making an appointment with the teacher to discuss needs or accommodations, such as extended time on tests; asking the teacher if they may tape class lectures; and obtaining teacher approval for having another student take notes or for them to copy another student's notes.

2. Establish a classroom climate in which students are comfortable enough to assert themselves. To foster such an atmosphere, you should provide students with constructive feedback on their self-advocacy skills. For example, part of being a good self-advocate is being able to assert oneself firmly but positively. Tom, a student with a physical disability, told his science teacher, Mr. Collins, that he was legally required to let him use a tape recorder in class. Mr. Collins explained to Tom that he could have been more positive, and, as a result, more effective in his request if he had explained carefully his disability and asked for permission to use the tape recorder rather than demanding it.

3. Emphasize students' strengths. Many students with special needs have low self-esteem, often because much of the attention they receive focuses on their weaknesses rather than their strengths. You can help students acquire a more balanced perception of themselves by giving them opportunities to use their strengths. For example, John has very poor reading skills but has a good memory for material that he has heard. His teacher often calls on John to summarize material that has been presented and praises him for having such a good memory. John's teacher also has John remind him when announcements need to be made at the end of the day since his teacher tends to forget.

4. Continually demonstrate in class that all of us are better at some things than others. Students are more accepting of their own problems when they realize that they are not the only ones who experience difficulty. For example, Melissa is a straight-A fifth grader but is not good in sports. Alexis is just the opposite. She has a severe reading disability but is the best athlete in the class. Their teacher set up a peer tutoring program whereby Melissa drilled Alexis on common reading words and Alexis helped Melissa learn to throw a softball during recess. Students also benefit from seeing that even teachers are not proficient at everything, and that the trick is to figure out ways to adjust to your problems. For example, Mr. Edgar has trouble printing a sentence on the chalkboard in a straight line. He showed the class that he has to put dots on either side of the chalkboard to help him line up his sentences. Ms. Edwards explains that certain words still give her spelling trouble and that she keeps a card in her purse with the correct spelling of these words that she can refer to as needed.

5. Help your students take charge of their lives by teaching them to set goals for themselves. An important first step is helping students understand their strengths and weaknesses. Having an understanding of their strengths and weaknesses helps ensure that their goals will be realistic. Next, show your students examples of both short- and long-term goals. Short-term goals could involve passing the next algebra test, doing all the math homework for the week, or

(continued)

Professional Edge *(continued)*

making sure that they have written down all their assignments. Long-term goals could include graduating from high school with a C average or better, becoming a computer programmer, or joining the Coast Guard.

When they are setting their goals, students should keep in mind these questions: Does my goal state what I want to achieve? Do I believe I can reach my goal? Can I really achieve my goal? How will I know when I have achieved my goal?

How Can You Effectively Teach Independent Learning Strategies in Class?

FYI

Collaboration with a school counselor or special educator can help you design effective self-advocacy skills for your students with special needs.

Another way you can help your students become more independent is to teach them strategies for learning how to learn (Dickson, Collins, Simmons, & Kameenui, in press). These methods are collectively referred to as learning strategies. **Learning strategies** are techniques, principles, or rules that enable a student to learn to solve problems and complete tasks independently (Lenz, Ellis, & Scanlon, 1996; Schumaker, Deshler, & Denton, 1984). Learning strategies, which are similar to study skills, not only emphasize the steps needed to perform a strategy (for example, steps to follow in reading a textbook), but they also stress why and when to use that strategy as well as how to monitor its usage. For example, when Ms. Blankenship taught her students a strategy for reading their textbook, she pointed out that the strategy would save them time yet improve their test scores. She also taught them how to judge how well they are using the strategy by filling out a simple checklist as they read.

An important component of teaching learning strategies effectively is to present well-designed strategies. As you recall from the discussions of effective materials in Chapters 4 and 9, the better your materials are designed, the greater the chance that they will work for your students with special needs, without requiring you to make major adaptations. Some effective guidelines for designing learning strategies are presented in the Professional Edge.

For students to utilize learning strategies independently, they must first learn to perform them accurately and fluently. The following teaching steps have proven effective for teaching learning strategies (Schumaker et al., 1984). These steps include many of the effective teaching practices described in Chapters 4 and 9.

Assessing Current Strategy Use

Students often are receptive to instruction when they can clearly see problems they are having and how the strategy you are teaching will help them overcome these problems. Therefore, learning-strategy instruction begins with an assessment of how well your students can currently perform a skill. As you learned in Chapter 8,

Professional Edge

Developing Your Own Learning Strategies

You can use the guidelines here either to create your own learning strategies or to evaluate ones that are commercially produced. By following these suggestions, you will not always need to depend on commercial publishers for your learning materials. Rather, you can develop learning strategies to fit the students in your class.

1. Identify skill areas that are problematic for most of your students, such as taking multiple choice tests or lecture notes.

2. For each skill area, specify student outcomes, such as scoring at least 10 percent higher on multiple choice tests or writing down key main ideas and details from a lecture.

3. List a set of specific steps students need to follow to reach the identified outcomes. You may want to ask other students who have good test-taking and note-taking skills what they do. Shown here is a sample reading comprehension strategy called **RAP**:

R *Read* a paragraph.
A *Ask* yourself what were the main idea and two details.
P *Put* main idea and details in your own words. (Ellis & Lenz, 1987)

4. Your strategy should contain no more than eight steps. Having more steps will make the strategy difficult to remember.

5. Your steps should be brief; each should begin with a verb that directly relates to the strategy.

6. To help students remember the steps, encase the strategy in a mnemonic device (for example, the acronym RAP for the reading strategy above).

7. The strategy should cue students to perform thinking (remember), doing (read), and self-evaluative (survey or check your work) behaviors.

8. Here is a textbook-reading strategy that was developed by teachers (Bartelt, Marchio, & Reynolds, 1994) and that meets the guidelines for developing an effective learning strategy:

R *Review* headings and subheadings.
E *Examine* boldface words.
A *Ask*, "What do I expect to learn?"
D *Do* it—Read!
S *Summarize* in your own words.

SOURCE: Adapted from "Generalization and Adaptation of Learning Strategies to Natural Environments: Part 2. Research into Practice" by E. Ellis, K. Lenz, and E. Sabornie, 1987, *Remedial and Special Education*, *8*(2), 6–23.

specific learning strategies can be assessed using direct-observation checklists, analyses of student products, and student self-evaluations.

You also need to assess whether your students have the preskills necessary to perform the strategy. For example, students who can discriminate between main ideas and details in a lecture are ideal candidates for learning a note-taking strategy; students who can read all the words on a test and understand the class content will benefit most from a test-taking strategy. On the other hand, students who cannot identify most of the words in their texts would not be logical candidates for learning a textbook-reading strategy; students whose seatwork activities are too hard for them will not benefit from a strategy to help them organize their independent practice activities. As you have learned, students with special needs often lack critical

Connections

The assessment strategies described in Chapter 8 apply to this discussion. Also recall the information in Chapter 9 on teaching preskills and providing direct instruction.

preskills. Before you decide to teach a particular strategy, you should identify its preskills and assess them separately. If most students lack the preskills, they can be taught as part of your everyday instruction. If only a few have problems with preskills, these students need to receive additional instruction in class, with a peer or adult tutor, through co-taught lessons, or in a learning center or special education setting.

Clarifying Expectations

Connections

Applying the INCLUDE strategy is an effective way to identify strategies that students need to succeed in your class.

Learning strategies have the potential of empowering your students because they enable students to learn and succeed in and out of school on their own, without undue help from others. When you introduce learning strategies to students, you need to point out their potential benefits clearly and specifically. Carefully explained expected outcomes can be motivating, particularly as students get older and teacher encouragement alone may not be enough to keep them interested. The first step in getting and keeping students motivated to learn is to give a strong rationale for why learning the strategy is important. This rationale should be directly tied to current student performance as well as to the demands of your class. For example, when introducing a new note-taking strategy, Mr. Washington pointed out that the class was able to identify on average only half of the main ideas presented on a note-taking pretest. He also told his class that half of the material on his tests would come from information presented during his lectures. Finally, Mr. Washington explained that taking good notes can help students out of school as well; in many job situations, employers give directions that need to be written down.

The next step in clarifying expectations is to explain specifically what students will be able to accomplish when they have learned the skill. For example, Ms. Thompson told her class that after learning a textbook-reading strategy, they would be able to do their homework faster. Also, give students an idea of how long it will take them to learn the strategy. For example, you could make a chart showing the instructional activities to be covered each day and the approximate number of days it will take to learn the strategy. The advantage of presenting the information on a chart is that steps can be crossed out or checked as completed. The act of checking off completed activities can be very motivating for students. It is also a way of demonstrating self-monitoring, an effective independent learning skill that we will discuss later in this chapter.

Demonstrating Strategy Use

In demonstrating strategies, keep in mind three important points. First, remember that the process one goes through in performing a task or solving a problem should be carefully explained. For example, demonstrate both thinking and doing behaviors. Talking aloud to yourself while performing the skill is particularly important for many students with special needs, who often do not develop spontaneously organized thinking patterns. Second, present both examples and nonexamples of appropriate strategy use, carefully explaining why they are examples or nonexamples. This explanation can help students tell the difference between doing a strategy the right way and doing it incorrectly, a distinction that can be difficult for students with special needs to make without direct instruction. For example, Mr. Washington demonstrated

Demonstrating the use of a learning strategy involves explaining both the thinking and the doing parts of a process, showing examples and nonexamples of effective strategy use, and checking learners' understanding. How do these steps help students with special needs acquire learning strategies?

effective and ineffective note-taking strategies using the overhead projector. As a student listened to a short lecture, he took notes systematically, writing down key ideas and details. Next, using the same lecture, he demonstrated ineffective note-taking by trying to write down every word. Finally, after you demonstrate, ask frequent questions to test student understanding. Frequent questioning can help you monitor student understanding and determine whether more demonstration is needed. Keep in mind that for many students, including those with disabilities, one demonstration may not be enough. See the Case in Practice on pages 348–349 for a sample script for demonstrating the **KWL** (**K** = what you already know; **W** = what you want to know; **L** = what you learned) **Plus** textbook-reading strategy (Ogle, 1986).

Encouraging Students to Memorize Strategy Steps

The purpose of having students memorize the steps in the strategy is to make it easier for them to recall the strategy when they need to use it. To help students learn the steps, you can post them prominently in your classroom at first so that you and your students can refer to them throughout the class or day. Students may also need to be drilled on saying the strategy steps. To practice, students could pair off and quiz each other; or you could ask students the strategy steps before and after class. For example, each day during the last several minutes of class, Ms. Henry quizzed four of her social studies students on the steps of the KWL reading strategy.

Even though memorizing a strategy can help students recall it, you may not want to spend too much time on this step, particularly for some of your students with special needs, who may have memory problems. For these students, you might include the steps to all the strategies they are learning in a special section of their assignment notebooks. For strategies used most often, cue cards listing strategy steps can be made to tape to the inside cover of textbooks or notebooks.

Connections

Strategies for memorizing information are also covered in Chapter 11 as part of study strategies.

Case in Practice

Teaching Script for Demonstrating KWL Plus

An important component of teaching a learning strategy effectively is to demonstrate its appropriate use. The following script shows how one teacher uses modeling to present a textbook-reading strategy to her eighth-grade class.

Teacher: Let's review the text-book reading strategy we talked about yesterday. Please take out the cue cards you made in class yesterday.

The teacher has students read each step individually and asks them what each step involves. Questions such as, "What are the steps? What might you do with the information you think of when brainstorming? What do you do after you read the passage?" are used.

Teacher: Now that we've reviewed each step, we need to learn how to use the whole strategy effectively. Before we move on, though, let's

read aloud all of the steps together as a group. When I point to the letter, say the letter, and when I point to the meaning, you read its meaning.

The students read the steps aloud: "*K* means 'what you already know,' *W* means 'what you want to know,' and *L* is 'what you learned.'"

Teacher: Good. Now I'm going to demonstrate how to use the strategy with a story I found about crayons. I'll put the passage on the overhead, as well as give each of you a copy so you can follow along at your desk. I'll work through each step of the strategy orally and write the information obtained at each step on the board. Use your cue

cards to help you see what step of the strategy I'm on.

The teacher then goes through the story, demonstrating correct usage of the steps and asking for feedback. The teacher also goes back over each step asking the students to verify that all of the steps to the strategy were followed and to explain how they were followed.

Teacher: What do we do now that we have a passage assigned to read? First, I brainstorm, which means I try to think of anything I already know about the topic and write it down.

The teacher writes on the board or overhead known qualities of crayons, such as "made of wax," "come in many colors," "can be sharpened," "several different brands."

Teacher: I then take this information I already know and put it into

Providing Guided and Independent Practice

Connections

Providing support for students when they first learn a skill is discussed in Chapter 4 as part of scaffolding.

As we have already stated, students must learn how to perform strategies accurately and fluently before they can attempt them independently. Such proficiency requires considerable practice. Five ways of providing practice on learning strategies are suggested. One way is to have students practice in controlled materials when they are first learning a strategy. **Controlled materials** are generally at the student's reading level, of high interest, and relatively free of complex vocabulary and concepts. Because controlled materials remove many content demands on the learner, they allow students to focus all their energy on learning the strategy. Controlled materials also allow for initial success, which is important for motivation. For example, Mr. Bernard was teaching his students a strategy for taking essay tests in current events. At first, he had his students practice this strategy on simply worded, one-part essay questions about material familiar to the students, such as people and events in the areas of rock music, movies, television, and sports. As students became better at using the strategy, Mr. Bernard gradually introduced more complex questions on categories, like "what crayons are made of" and "crayon colors." Next, I write down any questions I would like to have answered during my reading, such as "Who invented crayons? When were they invented? How are crayons made? Where are they made?" At this point, I'm ready to read, so I read the passage on crayons. Now I must write down what I learned from the passage. I must include any information that answers the questions I wrote down before I read and any additional information. For example, I learned that colored crayons were first made in the United States in 1903 by Edwin Binney and E. Harold Smith. I also learned that the Crayola Company owns the company that made the original magic markers. Last, I must organize this information into a map so I can see

the different main points and any supporting points.

At this point, the teacher draws a map on the chalkboard or overhead.
Teacher: Let's talk about the steps I used and what I did before and after I read the passage.

A class discussion follows.
Teacher: Now I'm going to read the passage again, and I want you to evaluate my textbook reading skills based on the KWL Plus strategy we've learned.

The teacher then proceeds to demonstrate the strategy incorrectly.
Teacher: The passage is about crayons. Well, how much can there really be to know about crayons besides there are hundreds of colors and they always seem to break in the middle? Crayons are for little

kids, and I'm in junior high so I don't need to know that much about them. I'll just skim the passage and go ahead and answer the question. Okay, how well did I use the strategy steps?

The class discusses the teacher's inappropriate use of the strategy.
Teacher: We've looked at the correct use of the strategy and we've seen how mistakes can be made. Are there any questions about what we did today? Tomorrow we will begin to memorize the strategy steps so that you won't have to rely on your cue cards.

S O U R C E : From *A Script for How to Teach the KWL Strategy* by S. Butson, K. Shea, K. Pankratz, and M. Lamb, 1992, unpublished manuscript. DeKalb: Northern Illinois University. Used with permission.

less familiar topics, such as the AIDS epidemic in Africa and the economic conditions in Mexico. Finally, he simply used sample test questions.

A second way to provide students with practice is first to guide them and then to allow them to perform independently. By guided practice, we mean giving students verbal cues when they are first attempting a skill. For example, before and while her students were practicing a strategy, Ms. Waters asked them questions such as, "What will you do first?" "Why did you do that?" "What should you do after you are done with the strategy steps?" "Which key words are you going to look for in the questions?" "How will you know which are the main ideas?" "Was the sentence I just read a main idea? Why?" Once most students seem able to answer your reminder questions, you can gradually stop asking them so that the students are eventually performing independently. Some students may need little guided practice or none at all. These students can be allowed to work independently right away.

A third practice technique is to give feedback that is specific and encourages students to evaluate themselves (Lenz et al., 1996). For example, Dominique has just performed the steps of a proofreading strategy in front of the class. Her teacher

Connections

Students who are gifted can benefit from learning strategies, but, as discussed in Chapter 7, may not need as much practice learning them. An advantage of co-teaching (Chapter 3) is that one of you can give students more strategy practice while the other works on another activity with students who do not need more practice.

says, "Good job, Dominique! I knew you could do it." Denise performed the same strategy in front of her class and her teacher asked, "How do you think you did? What do you need to focus on most the next time?" The feedback Dominique received does not clearly tell her what she did right; nor does it encourage self-evaluation. The feedback given to Denise encourages self-evaluation, a critical part of independent learning. Of course, if Denise cannot evaluate her own performance at first, the key parts of good performance will have to be pointed out to her and practice on self-evaluation provided.

Connections

Additional strategies for changing students' attributions were discussed in Chapter 6.

A fourth aspect of practicing learning strategies is to praise students only when they have produced work that is praiseworthy. Praise that is not tied to student performance, or is exaggerated, often for the purpose of enhancing student self-image, may only reinforce student inadequacy. For example, because of a history of failure in learning situations, students with special needs often see little relationship between their efforts and classroom success. When you give nonspecific praise to these students, it is easier for them to attribute your praise to something other than competence, such as sympathy ("I'm so bad at this, she has to pretend I did well").

Finally, encourage students to reinforce themselves and take responsibility for both their successes and failures. For example, after doing well on a note-taking strategy, Alicia was encouraged by her teacher to say, "I did a good job. This time I paid attention and wrote down all the main ideas. I need to do the same the next time." Alicia's teacher was showing her how to attribute her success to factors under her control. This approach can help her become a more active, independent learner.

Administering Posttests

FYI

Knowing which strategies to teach your students is an important outcome of using the INCLUDE strategy.

When it appears from your practice sessions that most students have acquired the strategy, give them the pretest again to test their mastery. If according to your posttest students have not acquired the strategy, identify where the breakdown occurred and then provide additional instruction and/or practice. If more than 20 percent of the students need extra practice or instruction, they can receive additional help in a large or small group. If less than 20 percent of the students require more assistance, those needing more individualized practice can be provided with peer tutors or support staff.

What Are Some Examples of Successful Learning Strategies?

There is a growing research base of learning strategies that work for students who are at risk or who have special needs. These strategies cover many areas, including reading comprehension, written expression, math problem solving, and time and resource management. An array of strategies that incorporate many of these effective practices are summarized in the following sections.

Reading-Comprehension Strategies

Reading-comprehension strategies are intended to help students meet the independent reading demands of content-area classes successfully, particularly in the middle and upper grades. Although reading primarily involves textbooks, students must be able to read and understand a variety of source books as well.

One example of a reading-comprehension strategy is SCROL (Grant, 1993). The **SCROL** strategy teaches students to use text headings to aid their comprehension and help them find and remember important information. The SCROL strategy has five steps. Advise students to do steps 3–5 every time they encounter a heading in the text they are reading.

1. *Survey* **the headings.** In the assigned text selection, read each heading and sub-heading. For each heading and subheading, try to answer the following questions: What do I already know about this topic? What information might the writer present?

2. *Connect.* Ask yourself, How do the headings relate to one another? Write down key words from the headings that might provide connections between them.

3. *Read* **the text.** As you read, look for words and phrases that express important information about the headings. Mark the text to point out important ideas and details. Stop to make sure that you understand the major ideas and supporting details. If you do not understand, reread.

4. *Outline.* Using indentations to reflect structure, outline the major ideas and supporting details in the heading segment. Write the heading and then try to outline each heading segment without looking back at the text.

5. *Look* **back.** Now, look back at the text and check the accuracy of the major ideas and details you wrote. Correct any inaccurate information in your outline. If you marked the text as you read, use this information to help you verify the accuracy of your outline.

PARS is a simplified textbook-reading strategy that is good for younger students or students without much experience using textbook-reading strategies (Cheek & Cheek, 1983). The four steps of PARS follow:

1. *Preview* **the material.** In this step, students scan the chapter to identify main ideas by surveying the introductory statement, headings, graphic aids, and chapter summary.

2. *Ask* **questions** that relate to the main ideas discovered when surveying the chapter.

3. *Read* **the chapter** in order to answer the questions developed.

4. *Summarize* the main ideas in the chapter.

CAPS is a self-questioning strategy that can be used to help students find answers to questions about what is important in a story (Leinhardt & Zigmond, 1988). Here are the steps:

C   Who are the *characters*?
A   What is the *aim* of the story?
P   What *problem* happens?
S   How is the problem *solved*?

Another reading-comprehension strategy is **POSSE** (Englert & Mariage, 1991). This strategy includes many reading practices that have been shown to aid reading comprehension, such as graphic organizers, text structures, stimulation of student background knowledge, and self-monitoring. The steps in this strategy are as follows:

P *Predict* ideas.
O *Organize* the ideas.
S *Search* for the structure.
S *Summarize* the main ideas.
E *Evaluate* your understanding.

Connections

Strategies for developing and using graphic organizers were covered in more depth in Chapter 9.

When students are *predicting*, they can be given a sentence starter such as, "I predict that . . . ." For this step, students are taught to use signals from a variety of sources, including the title, headings in bold, pictures, key words, and so on. Brainstorming is very important in this step. For example, look at the completed POSSE strategy sheet in Figure 10.2 for a section of text on the Bermuda Triangle. Before they read, students studied pictures, headings, and boldfaced vocabulary words in the text. On the basis of this information, as well as their background knowledge, they predicted that the story would be about ideas such as people disappearing, airplane instruments not working, and fighter planes disappearing. Students also had questions they wanted answered, such as, "What does it look like?" "Why do things disappear?" and "Who discovered it?"

When *organizing* their ideas, students are instructed to look back at their brainstormed ideas and see if a pattern or grouping exists ("Do any of these ideas go together? I think one category might be . . . "). For example, in Figure 10.2, students organized the background knowledge gathered in the first step into the categories of "What happened?" "What it looks like" "Where it is" and "Stories about it."

In the *search* and *summarize* steps, students organize short reading segments by searching for and identifying text structures and then summarizing the entire section (for example, "I think the main idea is . . . " and "My question about the main idea is . . . "). In the example in Figure 10.2, the major text structure identified involved using main ideas and then presenting supporting details. The students first identified topic sentences such as "Strange things happen" and "Where it [the Bermuda Triangle] is." They then generated questions for each topic sentence, such as, "What strange things happened in the Bermuda Triangle?" and "Where is the Bermuda Triangle?" Last, they answered these questions by finding supporting details: "What strange things happened in the Bermuda Triangle?" "Strange fog reported," "Compass goes wild," and "sky yellow."

When students *evaluate*, they perform three reading strategies to guide the group's discussion and comprehension of the passage: compare, clarify, and predict. For example, "I think we did [did not] predict this main idea" (compare); "Are there any clarifications?" (clarify); and "I predict the next part will be about . . . " (predict). Using the compare strategy, the students found that the Bermuda Triangle was not caused by a magnetic force but might be the result of tidal waves, currents, or earthquakes. The students also wanted to clarify terms such as *tidal wave:* What is a tidal wave? What causes one? Finally, the class predicted what the next section would be about; they thought it might talk about eyewitness accounts of people who had flown through the Bermuda Triangle and survived.

A technique used for teaching the POSSE strategy steps is a process called reciprocal teaching. **Reciprocal teaching** is a way to teach students to comprehend

Figure 10.2 **Partially Completed POSSE Strategy Sheet**

P redict what ideas are in the story.

People disappear
Ships and planes disappear near Florida
In a different country
Stories about it not all true
Not exactly a triangle
Instruments don't work
Five fighter planes disappeared
Stories on TV about it
Rescue planes used

Some ships and planes make it through
Magnetic force

Student Questions
What does it look like?
Why do things disappear?
Who discovered it?

O rganize your thoughts.

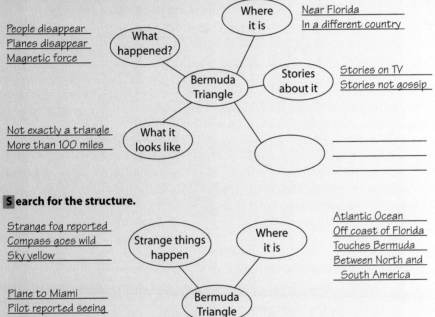

People disappear
Planes disappear
Magnetic force

Not exactly a triangle
More than 100 miles

What happened?

Where it is — Near Florida / In a different country

Bermuda Triangle

Stories about it — Stories on TV / Stories not gossip

What it looks like

S earch for the structure.

Strange fog reported
Compass goes wild
Sky yellow

Plane to Miami
Pilot reported seeing
  lights
Plane disappeared
Rescuers found
  nothing

Strange things happen

Where it is — Atlantic Ocean / Off coast of Florida / Touches Bermuda / Between North and South America

Bermuda Triangle

Incidents

Natural explanations — Tidal waves / Currents / Earthquakes

S ummarize. Summarize the main idea in your own words. Ask a "teacher" question about the main idea.

E valuate. Compare. Clarify. Predict.

S O U R C E : From "Making Students Partners in the Comprehension Process: Organizing the Reading 'POSSE' " by C. Englert and T. Mariage, 1991, *Learning Disability Quarterly*, 14, 123–138. Used by permission of Council for Learning Disabilities.

These students are engaged in a structured dialogue about the newspaper they are reading, a peer-modeled comprehension strategy called reciprocal teaching. What four strategies must students be taught before they can practice reciprocal teaching?

Check Your Learning

What makes reciprocal teaching a powerful technique for teaching reading comprehension to students who are at risk or have special needs? In what other areas could reciprocal teaching be used?

reading material by providing them with teacher and peer models of thinking behavior and then allowing them to practice these thinking behaviors with their peers (Palincsar & Brown, 1988). At first, the teacher leads the dialogue, demonstrating how the strategies can be used during reading. As instruction goes on, the teacher gives the students more and more responsibility for maintaining the dialogue. Eventually, students are largely responsible for the dialogue, though the teacher still provides help as necessary. Research shows that the most important part of the technique is the teacher releasing control and turning the dialogue over to the students (Englert & Mariage, 1991).

A sample dialogue for reciprocal teaching is presented in the Case in Practice. After reading the Case in Practice, think of the reasons that reciprocal teaching is such a powerful technique for teaching reading comprehension to students who are at risk or who have special needs. In what other areas could reciprocal teaching be used?

Note-Taking Strategies

Because lecturing is a common way for teachers to present information to students, particularly in middle school, junior high, and high school, students need strategies for recording key information in lectures so they can study it later. Suggested note-taking tips are listed in Figure 10.3 on page 356. These tips will help no matter which note-taking strategy is used.

The **five *R*'s of note-taking** (Pauk, 1989) is a helpful strategy for note-taking. The steps are listed here:

R *Record* main ideas and important details.
R *Reduce* to concise phrases.
R *Recite* key information using your concise phrases as cues.

Case in Practice

Reciprocal Teaching

The students in this class have just read a section of text that focuses on Loch Ness. They are now applying the search, summarize, and evaluate steps of POSSE.

Teacher: What is the main topic the text is talking about?

Peg: The Loch Ness monster.

Teacher: What was this section about? What was the main idea?

Peg: Oh, the lake. I have two questions: "What is a lake?" and "What lives in it?"

Teacher: Do you mean this particular lake or any lake?

Peg: This lake. Joe?

Joe: It's foggy, it's deep, and it's long and narrow.

Peg: Don?

Don: The land beside the lake, you don't know if it is real soft and you could fall through it.

Teacher: So it could be soft and swampy.

Ann: I think the Loch Ness monster lives there.

Teacher: Is Ann answering your question, Peg?

Peg: No.

Teacher: What was your question?

Peg: I had two: "What is a lake?" and "What lives in the lake?"

Joe: But they never answered that. I have a question about the main idea. Aren't we supposed to do a question about the main idea?

Teacher: Just about what we read.

Joe: Yes, but she asked us, "What lives in the lake?" but it doesn't really mention that in the book.

Teacher: That's true. The major idea has to do with Loch Ness and what it looks like. A minor idea that we really inferred rather than directly read in the article was that the Loch Ness monster lives in the lake.

Peg: Are there any clarifications?

Students: [No response.]

Teacher: I have a clarification. You had trouble reading some of these words and I wondered if you knew what some of them mean? What does ancestors mean?

[The teacher continues discussing vocabulary.]

S O U R C E : From "Making Students Partners in the Comprehension Process: Organizing the Reading 'POSSE' " by C. S. Englert and T. V. Mariage, 1991, *Learning Disability Quarterly, 14,* 133–134.

R *Reflect* on your notes by adding your own ideas.

R *Review* all the key information in your notes.

An important preskill for this strategy is identifying main ideas and details. Students may need direct instruction on this skill. This strategy can be enhanced by combining it with a column note-taking format. Students can have a 5-inch column for *recording*, a 2-inch column for *reducing*, and a 1-inch column for *reflecting*.

A prelistening strategy that helps students prepare themselves for lectures is called the **3R strategy** (Alley & Deshler, 1979). It involves three steps:

R *Review* notes and materials from the previous class.

R *Read* materials related to today's class.

R *Relate* lecture topic to other topic.

A note-taking strategy that incorporates some of the suggestions in Figure 10.3 is called **PASSING.** This strategy includes the following steps:

P *Prepare* for class.

A *Attend* to the teacher.

S *State* the topic.
S *State* the source.
I *Identify* key words and ideas.
N *Note* their meaning.
G *Give* the meaning in your own words.

Using the PASSING strategy, students can record information on a note-taking sheet like the one shown in Figure 10.4, which Inez kept. For example, Inez's science teacher lectured on koala bears. For the *P* step, Inez read the section on koala bears in her science book. For the *A* step, she attended to the lecture by keeping her eyes on the teacher and her notes and by trying to think about what her teacher was saying. For the two *S* steps, Inez stated the topic of the lecture (koala bears) as well as the source (science class). She then identified key words (the *I* step) *marsupials* and

Figure 10.3   Tips for Note-Taking

1. Take notes using either a two- or three-column system.

2. Take notes on only one side of the paper.

3. Date and label the topic of the notes.

4. Generally use a modified outline format, indenting subordinate ideas and numbering ideas when possible.

5. Skip lines to note changes in ideas.

6. Write ideas or key phrases, not complete sentences.

7. Use pictures and diagrams to relate ideas.

8. Use consistent abbreviations (e.g., w/ = with, & = and).

9. Underline or asterisk information the lecturer stresses as important.

10. Write down information the lecturer writes on the board or transparency.

11. If you miss an idea you want to include, draw a blank line so that you can go back and fill it in.

12. If you cannot automatically remember how to spell a word, spell it the way it sounds or the way you think it looks.

13. If possible, review the previous session's notes right before the lecture.

14. If the lecture is about an assigned reading topic, read the information before listening to the lecture.

15. As soon as possible after the lecture, go over your notes, filling in the key concept column and listing any questions you still have.

16. After going over your notes, try to summarize the major points presented during the lecture.

17. Listen actively! In other words, think about what you already know about the topic being presented and how new information is related to old information.

18. Review your notes before a test.

SOURCE: From *Strategies for Teaching Students with Learning and Behavior Problems* (3rd ed.) by C. S. Bos and S. Vaughn, 1994. Copyright © 1994 by Allyn and Bacon. Reprinted by permission.

Figure 10.4   PASSING Note-Taking Form

Name ___Inez___

Class ___Science___

Date ___3/13/98___

Topic ___Koala bears___   Source ___Lecture___

Identify key words	Note their meaning	Give the meaning in your own words
Marsupials	Like kangaroos—have pouch to carry young	Koala bears are marsupials. Marsupials are animals that carry their young in a pouch like kangaroos do.
Herbaceous	Live on eucalyptus leaves	Koalas are herbaceous animals. They eat eucalyptus leaves almost entirely.
	Never drink water—suck water from leaves	

herbaceous. In the *N* step, she noted their meaning. After the lecture, Inez gave the meanings of key words and ideas in her own words (the *G* step).

To learn this or other note-taking strategies, students need the preskill of being able to tell the difference between main ideas and details. For example, Inez chose key words that represented main ideas. Some students attempt to write down everything and need to be taught directly how to differentiate main ideas and details. For example, Mr. Abeles discovered that many students in his history class were unable to identify main ideas from his lectures. First, he gave his students rules to follow: main ideas are what a whole section or passage is about; details are what just one part of a section or passage is about. For several weeks, he stopped after presenting a section of material and put three pieces of information on the board—one main idea and two details. He asked the students which was the main idea and why. When his students were doing well at these tasks, Mr. Abeles had them write their own main ideas after a section of lecture; these then were shared with the class and corrective feedback was provided as necessary. Students also must be able to summarize material in their own words. One effective strategy for writing summaries involves the following steps: (1) skim the passage (or listen to a section of lecture); (2) list the key points; (3) combine related points into single statements; (4) cross out the least important points; (5) reread the list; (6) combine and cross out to condense points; (7) number the remaining points in logical order; and (8) write points into a paragraph in numbered order (Sheinker & Sheinker, 1989, p. 135). Finally, students should learn strategies for studying their notes, such as covering up one column and trying to say what is in the column, and then uncovering the column and comparing their responses to the actual information. Although some students can master this study strategy with only a verbal explanation, others may need more support in the form of a demonstration and guided practice.

Writing Strategies

Another area that requires student independence is writing and proofreading papers. One strategy that helps students organize themselves to carry out all the steps in the writing process is called **POWER** (Englert et al., 1988). The process involves the use of self-questioning, graphic organizers, and peer editing using the following steps:

P *Planning*
O *Organizing*
W *Writing*
E *Editing*
R *Revising*

The POWER strategy teaches students four different organizational structures for writing papers: stories, compare/contrast, explanations, and problem/solution (Englert et al., 1988). When writing stories, students use key story elements—Who? When? Where? What happened? How did it end?—to organize their papers. A compare/contrast structure includes information about what is being compared (for example, Native Americans and settlers), on what characteristic they are being compared (views about land), and on how they are alike and/or different (Native Americans shared land; settlers owned land). Explanations involve telling how to do something, such as explaining the steps in changing a tire. Finally, in a problem/solution structure, a problem is identified (for example, it took too long to travel from East to West in the early 1800s in America), the cause of the problem is explained (the only way to go East to West was by stagecoach), and the solution is stated (the transcontinental railroad was built).

For the *planning* stage, students focus on the audience for the paper, the purpose, and the background knowledge that will be necessary to write the paper. In the *organizing* step, students decide which organizational pattern fits their paper (for example, story, compare–contrast) and then complete a pattern guide to help them organize their ideas. A **pattern guide** is a graphic designed to help students organize their papers. A sample pattern guide for a compare–contrast paper is shown in Figure 10.5. Notice that the words that are not in boxes—"both same," "in contrast to," "similarly," and "however"—are key words that are used frequently when making comparisons. These words help students make the transition to writing sentences. For example, in Figure 10.5, two kinds of pizza are being compared and contrasted. The student might write, "The crusts of deep dish and regular pizza are *both the same* in that they both are made of white flour. This is *in contrast to* their thickness; deep dish pizza crust is much thicker."

In the *writing* stage, the teacher demonstrates and thinks aloud to show students how to take the information gathered in the planning and organizing steps and produce a first draft. For example, you can compose an essay comparing two kinds of pizza using the overhead projector, thinking out loud as you write. You can

Figure 10.5 **Pattern Guide for Compare–Contrast**

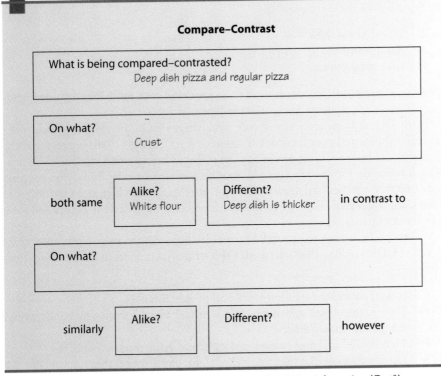

SOURCE: From "A Case for Writing Intervention: Strategies for Writing Informational Text" by C. S. Englert, T. E. Raphael, L. M. Anderson, H. M. Anthony, K. L. Fear, and S. L. Gregg, 1988, *Learning Disability Quarterly, 3*(2), p. 108. Used by permission of Council for Learning Disabilities.

involve students by asking questions such as, "What would a good topic sentence be?" "Is this a good example?" "How do you think I should end this?" "Why?" You could also have students write the paper along with you.

The *editing* step teaches students to critique their own writing and to identify areas in which they need clarification or assistance, an important self-evaluation skill. Editing is a two-step process involving student self-evaluation and peer editing. For self-evaluation, students reread and evaluate their draft, starring sections of the paper they like best and putting question marks in the margins by parts they think may be unclear. Finally, students think of two questions to ask their peer editors. For example, Jorge asked his peer editor whether he had used capital letters and punctuation correctly. He was also concerned about whether his paper was long enough and asked for suggestions on how to add information.

For **peer editing,** several steps are followed. First, writers read their papers to a peer editor while the editor listens. The peer editors then summarize the paper. Next, the editor evaluates the paper, giving an analysis of salient features of the writing that might guide a revision or lead to improvement. For example, the peer editor might suggest that the writer add key words to or reorganize the paper for clarity. These suggestions are shared with the writer. Then the peer editor and the writer brainstorm ways to improve the paper.

WWW Resources

Your students can research their papers more independently by accessing **Kid's Web,** a World Wide Web digital library specifically designed for children, at <http://www.npac.syr.edu/textbook/kidsweb>.

A research-based strategy called TAG can also help students with the peer editing process (Carlson & Henning, 1993; MacArthur & Stoddard, 1990). The **TAG** strategy involves three simple steps:

T *Tell* what you like.
A *Ask* questions.
G *Give* suggestions.

As discussed previously, students need to be provided with models and guided practice on these steps prior to doing them independently.

In the *revise* step, students decide on changes to be made using their self-evaluation sheets and peer feedback. Englert and colleagues (1988) suggest that the teacher model how to insert or change the order of information, all the while providing a rationale for any changes. All modifications are made directly on the first draft. Last, the teacher and student have a conference, and changes in writing mechanics are suggested. Following this conference, a final draft is composed on a clean sheet of paper.

When students have to proof their papers independently, they might use a strategy called COPS (Alley, 1988). In the **COPS** strategy, students question themselves as follows:

C Have I *capitalized* the first word and proper nouns?
O How is the *overall appearance* of my paper? Have I made any handwriting, margin, or messy errors?
P Have I used end *punctuation*, commas, and semicolons carefully?
S Do words look like they are *spelled* right; can I sound them out or use the dictionary?

Check Your Learning

In what ways might the COPS strategy be helpful to Gerald, whom you met at the beginning of this chapter?

Although COPS has been shown to be effective, students need preskills to perform this strategy adequately. Before teaching COPS, consider the following questions: Can the students recognize misspelled words? Do the students know rules for using capital letters and punctuation? Can they apply these rules? Can the students use a dictionary? If the answer to any of these questions is "no," teach these skills directly before teaching students the COPS strategy.

Several additional strategies can be used to help students with the various aspects of written expression. **SLOW CaPS** (Levy & Rosenberg, 1990, p. 27) is a strategy for writing four kinds of paragraphs: list or describe, show sequence, compare and contrast, and demonstrate cause/effect. Here are the steps:

S *Show* the type of paragraph in the first sentence.
L *List* the details you want to write about.
O *Order* the details.
W *Write* details in complete sentences and **CaP** off the paragraph with a **C** (concluding), **P** (passing/transition), or **S** (summary) sentence.

(Notice that the *a* in CaPS is not used and so is lowercased.)

A composition strategy called **DEFENDS** (Ellis & Lenz, 1987) is designed to help students write a paper defending a position.

D *Decide* on an exact position.
E *Examine* the reasons for the positions.

Cultural Awareness

Israel, Cohen, and Riel (1989) conducted a study to explore the effects of writing for authentic audiences of peers from different cultural backgrounds using the Internet. They found that essays written for distant peers were superior to essays written to be graded by their teachers; essays for authentic peers were more explicit and detailed.

F   *Form* a list of points that explain each reason.

E   *Expose* the position in the first sentence.

N   *Note* each reason and supporting points.

D   *Drive* home the position in the last sentence.

S   *Search* for errors and correct.

The following strategy is for revising essays using a word processor (Graham & Harris, 1987). Students instruct themselves using these steps:

1. Read your essay.

2. Find the sentence that tells you what you believe—is it clear?

3. Add two reasons why you believe it.

4. **SCAN** each sentence:
     Does it make *sense?*
     Is it *connected* to my belief?
     Can I *add* more?
     Note errors.

5. Make changes on the computer.

6. Reread your essay and make final changes.

The five-step study strategy here will help students learn unknown spelling words (Graham & Freeman, 1986). Students are required to carry out six steps:

1. Say the word.

2. Write and say the word.

3. Check the word.

4. Trace and say the word.

5. Write the word from memory and check your spelling.

6. Repeat the first five steps if you misspell the word in step 5.

Computer technology such as word processing software can also help students with special needs become independent writers. The Technology Notes feature on pages 362–363 describes available computer technology along with comments about its effectiveness in helping students with special needs to write.

Strategies for Problem Solving in Math

Increasingly, teachers are focusing on problem solving as a major component of the math curriculum. This concentration is consistent with the math standards developed by the National Council of Teachers of Mathematics (1990), which also stress the importance of teaching problem solving. However, research indicates that if students with special needs are to become good problem solvers, they must be taught *how* to problem solve directly. A common (but by no means the only) way to introduce problem solving to students in a classroom context is through story or word problems. A technique for teaching word problems that is effective for students with special needs is presented in the Professional Edge on pages 364–365.

Connections

The NCTM standards also stress the use of manipulatives, covered in Chapter 4, and performance-based tests, examined in Chapter 11.

Technology Notes

Using Computers to Enhance the Writing of Students with Special Needs

The capabilities of computer technology hold great promise in helping students with special needs become more independent writers. Although promising, however, computer technology is by no means a panacea. In deciding which technology to use, you will want to keep in mind what technology can and cannot do. Descriptions of computer technology used for writing, including its potential effectiveness for students with special needs, are presented below. The descriptions, adapted from MacArthur (1996), encompass four key areas: word processing, sentence generation and transcription, planning, and collaborative writing and publishing.

Computers can help students become more independent writers.

Word Processing

1. Word processing can make the process of revising easier. For example, it eliminates the physical act of recopying and reduces the feeling that revisions are punishment. However, word processing leads to higher quality writing only when it is presented to students in combination with direct instruction in revising strategies.

2. Word processors allow students to produce neat, printed work, and to make corrections without messy erasures. These features can be motivating for students who have messy handwriting or have trouble with other writing mechanics.

3. The visibility of text on the screen as well as the use of typing rather than handwriting facilitates collaborative writing with peers and instructional support for writing from teachers. For example, peer partners can work on written products together; both partners can see the text and typing does not recognize separate contributions. Teachers can observe students' writing processes and provide feedback and instruction when necessary.

4. Typing can be easier for some students than handwriting, but students need typing instruction if they are going to use word processing regularly.

5. Word processing is most effective for students with special needs when it is combined with effective writing instruction.

Sentence Generation and Transcription

1. **Spelling checkers** can help students identify misspelled words and spell them correctly, but they have definite limitations. Studies indicate that spellcheckers miss from 25 to 40 percent of student misspellings, including proper nouns, special terms, and misspelled words that are other words spelled correctly such as homonyms (for example, way for weigh, sail for sale).

2. Spelling checkers fail to suggest correct spellings for many words, especially words that are severely misspelled. The use of synthesized speech and word banks, described later, can help students overcome this problem.

3. Students with special needs may have trouble identifying the correct spelling from a list of words supplied by the spelling checker program, particularly when the list includes many possible choices. Providing direct instruction on how to locate and circle misspelled words may be helpful.

4. Speech synthesizers translate text into speech; this enables students to hear what they have written and read what others have written. Speech synthesizers can allow students with writing problems to use their general language sense to determine whether their writing is clear. The quality of speech synthesizers varies widely and should be checked prior to purchasing.

5. Voice-input technology (Wetzel, 1996) allows students to speak into a microphone and have their words appear on a screen in a word processing format, ready for revision and editing. Research suggests that this technology, while promising, needs to be made more user friendly before it is helpful for students with special needs (Wetzel, 1996).

6. Word prediction programs can help students with serious problems in spelling, punctuation, and syntax. In this program, the student types in a window on top of the word processor, and the software offers a list of possible words that would come next, the length of which is adjustable. If the appropriate word is on the list, the student can click on the word and it is automatically inserted into the text. Predictions are based on spelling, syntax, and words previously used by the student. Word prediction programs are available with speech synthesizers to read word lists as well as completed text.

7. With **word banks,** all words typed in the word processor are collected in an alphabetized list of words at the side of the screen. As a student types, the list automatically scrolls to find words beginning with the letters typed. For example, if the student typed *r,* the list would automatically go to the first word starting with *r.* You can individualize lists for your students by adding words that meet specific writing demands. Word banks also come equipped with speech synthesizers.

8. Research shows that **grammar and style checkers** are of limited use for elementary school students

or poor writers. While technology is always undergoing improvements, be sure to try these out carefully if you are considering using them with students.

Planning Processes

1. Many word processors have **prompting** programs; these programs remind students to engage in planning processes by asking them a series of questions or presenting reminders. Most commonly, prompts are provided prior to writing, such as asking students a series of "who, where, why, and when" questions prior to their writing an article for the school newspaper.

2. Programs are available that allow teachers to create **semantic webs** on the screen. Students can complete the webs, which are then automatically converted to a written outline.

3. Multimedia software includes programs that integrate drawing tools with writing as well as programs that include video and sound. Multimedia programs have the potential to promote the generation of ideas and provide students with background information for planning. For young students, multimedia software can provide a series of pictures on which to write a story. For older students, videos can be used to provide background information on a particular topic as the basis for a writing activity.

Collaborative Writing and Publishing with Networks

1. Electronic networks can offer expanded opportunities for collaborative writing and communication with diverse audiences. Collaborative writing experiences using local and national networks can be motivating for students with special needs by giving them a meaningful purpose for writing. These experiences can teach the important idea that writing is much more than just communicating with your teacher.

See MacArthur (1996) for specific references for technology referred to in this Technology Notes feature.

Professional Edge

The "Key Word" Strategy for Solving Math Story Problems: Is There a Better Way?

The "key word" strategy is an example of an ineffective strategy that many students with special needs use or are taught to use in solving math story problems (Kelly & Carnine, 1996). In this approach, students associate key words such as *more, in all, gave away,* and *left over* with certain mathematical operations. The "key word" strategy is attractive to teachers and students because sometimes it works. For example, the word *more* is commonly associated with subtraction, as in the problem, "Jose has 15 cents. Carmen has 10 cents. How much *more* money does Jose have?" Unfortunately, there are many times when *more* appears in a word problem that calls for addition, as in the problem, "Charmaine had 15 cents. Her mother gave her 10 *more* cents. How many cents does she have now?"

Kelly and Carnine (1996) suggest teaching students with special needs a more effective strategy for solving math word problems using problem maps and math fact families. Their strategy for teaching single operation addition and subtraction problems follows.

For any addition/subtraction situation, there are two "small" numbers and a "big" number (the sum).

An addition/subtraction number family is mapped this way:

The family above represents the following addition/subtraction facts:

$$7 + 9 = 16 \qquad 16 - 9 = 7$$
$$9 + 7 = 16 \qquad 16 - 7 = 9$$

A missing *big* number implies addition:

$$8 + 22 = \square$$

A missing *small* number implies subtraction:

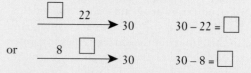

$$30 - 22 = \square$$

or

$$30 - 8 = \square$$

These maps can then be applied to a variety of addition and subtraction word problems. Kelly and Carnine (1996, p. 6) gave the following example involving comparison problems.

DRAW is a strategy for teaching students with special needs to solve multiplication facts that are not yet committed to memory (Harris, Miller, & Mercer, 1995). The DRAW strategy has the following steps:

D *Discover* the sign. (The student looks at the sign to figure out what operation to perform.)

R *Read* the problem. (The student says the problem aloud or to himself or herself.)

A *Answer*, or draw, and check. (The student thinks of the answer or draws lines to figure out the answer. The student checks his or her drawing and counting.)

W *Write* the answer. (The student writes the answer in the answer space.)

You can help students make the transition from pictures to abstract numbers by teaching them the **FAST DRAW** strategy. The FAST part of the strategy has these steps.

In comparison problems, the difference between two values being compared may be information given in a problem (e.g., Marco sold 57 fewer subscriptions than Lui) or the unknown in a problem (e.g., How much heavier was Mary?). Because of the words "sold fewer" in the following problem, many students with LD will subtract.

Marco sold 57 fewer magazine subscriptions than Lui. Marco sold 112 subscriptions. How many subscriptions did Lui sell?

Students can use number families to avoid this confusion. The first step is to represent the problem using a number family; students must determine whether each of the two numbers given in the problem is a small number or the big number. The students are shown a simple way to do this:

They find the sentence that tells about the comparison and read it without the difference number. For example, students are taught to read the first sentence without the 57: "Marco sold fewer subscriptions than Lui." Because Marco sold fewer subscriptions, Marco is represented by a small number. By default, Lui is the big number. The students write M for Marco and L for Lui:

The word problem also gives a number for the difference between Marco and Lui. That number always has to be a small number. Marco sold 57 fewer, so 57 is the other small number:

Next the students read the rest of the problem. The problem asks about Lui and gives a number for Marco, so the students draw a box around L and replace the M with 112:

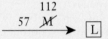

Because the problem gives both small numbers, the students write an addition problem.

$$\begin{array}{r} 57 \\ + 112 \end{array}$$

The answer tells how many magazine subscriptions Lui sold.

See Stein, Silbert, and Carnine (1997) for similar word problem strategies as applied to multiplication, division, and multistep story problems.

F *Find* what you're solving for. (Students look for the question in the problem.)

A *Ask* yourself, "What are the parts of the problem?" (Students identify the number of groups and the number of objects in each group.)

S *Set* up the numbers. (Students write the two numbers in the problem in a vertical format.)

T *Tie* down the sign. (Students add the multiplication sign to the problem.) (Harris et al., 1995, p. 6)

The **LAMPS** strategy (Reetz & Rasmussen, 1988) can be used as an aid to remember the steps in regrouping or carrying in addition. Here are the steps:

L *Line* up the numbers according to their decimal points.

A *Add* the right column of numbers and ask . . .

M *"More* than 9?" If so, continue to the next step.

P   *Put* the 1s below the column.
S   *Send* the 10s to the top of the next column.

To help with borrowing in subtraction, teach students to follow the **SLOBS** strategy (Reetz & Rasmussen, 1988). The steps are as follows:

S   *Smaller.* Follow steps.
L   *Larger.* Leap to subtract.
O   *Cross* off the number in the next column.
B   *Borrow* by taking one 10 and adding to the next column.
S   *Subtract.*

For the problem

$$\begin{array}{r} 72 \\ -\,46 \\ \hline \end{array}$$

Connections

More information on how to use self-instruction is included later in this chapter and in Chapter 12.

students would look at the top number on the right to see if it is smaller or larger than the bottom-right number. If it is smaller, the students must follow the rest of the steps. They would cross off the number in the next column to the left and borrow one unit from that column (reducing that number by one) and add it to the other column. For example, in $72 - 46$, borrow 10 from the left column. Then subtract. If the number is larger, students proceed directly to the subtract step. Repeat the steps if more digits are to be subtracted.

The **FOIL** strategy (Crawford, 1980) helps prevent algebra students from missing one of the four products needed to calculate multiplication of a binomial by another binomial. Four steps are followed:

F   Multiply *first* terms.
O   Multiply *outermost* terms.
I   Multiply *innermost* terms.
L   Multiply *last* terms.

For example, apply the FOIL strategy to this problem:

$$(x + 4)\,(x + 3)$$
$$A \quad B \quad C \quad D$$

In the *F* step, the student multiplies the first two factors in each binomial, $(x)\,(x) = x^2$, or using the letters, *AC*. Next, in the *O* step, the student multiplies the first factor in the first binomial and the second factor in the second binomial, $x \times 3 = 3x$, or *AD*. Then in the *I* step, the student multiplies the second factor of the first binomial and the first factor of the second binomial, $4 \times x = 4x$, or *BC*. Finally, in the *L* step, the second factors of both binomials are multiplied: $4 \times 3 = 12$, or *BD*. This strategy applies *only* to the special case of multiplying two binomials.

Strategies for Managing Time and Resources

In the early 1980s, an informal survey was done about the kinds of problems that lead to a student being referred for special education (Lessen & Bursuck, 1983). Interestingly, the problem behavior mentioned most often was not an academic one, nor was it a discipline problem, such as talking out or fighting. The problem mentioned most often was a lack of organization, a common characteristic of students with disabilities (C. Smith, 1994; S. Smith, 1980). Ronald, one of the students introduced at the beginning of the chapter, has trouble organizing.

Organizing study materials involves having the appropriate school supplies, making sure these supplies are brought to class when they are needed, and having an organized notebook to ensure easy access to information. First, you can make sure that your students obtain the appropriate school supplies by requiring that they tell their parents what materials they need, because you will not be able to call each of their parents individually each day to remind them what to bring. In many cases, teachers tell their students what to bring and assume that the students will do the rest on their own. However, this method may not be structured enough for some students, who, like Ronald, are likely to forget what you said, are not organized enough to write it down, or, even when they write it down, cannot find it when they get home. Second, you can encourage students to write the information down rather than trying to remember it. Having the information on the board or overhead will ensure that their lists are accurate. You may also want to duplicate the list and distribute it to your students. Finally, encourage your students to ask themselves these or similar questions, which can help them remember school supplies as well as assignments throughout the school year:

- What is due tomorrow in school?
- What do I need to do to get it done tonight?
- What materials or other things do I need to get the job done?
- Whom can I ask for help in doing this?

These questions can be posted on the board at first to help students remember them and to prompt their use. You can help motivate students to bring needed materials by providing positive recognition for those who do bring their supplies to school. For example, Mr. Gutierrez gave school pencils to students who had all their supplies in school. Ms. Habner put the names of her students on a "responsible students" list from which she chose people for classroom jobs. You may need to make adaptations for students with special needs. For example, students with physical disabilities may need a classmate or parent to bring their supplies into school. Students

Cultural Awareness

Teachers with a multicultural perspective take into account that students from different cultural backgrounds might have different routines as well as different resources for addressing, structuring, and completing projects.

Strategies for managing time and organizing materials help provide the structured routines that many students need to succeed in school. What are the three steps in teaching students how to use weekly assignment calendars?

who live in poverty might be unable to afford supplies other than materials the school or teacher provides.

Besides having to organize their materials, students also need to organize their time, particularly as they get older and the demands made on their time increase. More schools are now teaching their students to use schedule books to help them arrange their time (Bryan & Sullivan-Burstein, 1997; Jenson, Sheridan, Olympia, & Andrews, 1994; Patton, 1994). You can teach your students to use a weekly schedule book in the following ways:

1. Teach students to differentiate between short- and long-term assignments. Short-term assignments are those that can be completed in one or two days and that take one or two steps to get done, such as reading a chapter in history and answering the questions at the end of the chapter. Long-term assignments take more than two days to complete and take more than two steps to get done. Writing a five-page report on a current event is an example of a long-term assignment. The difference between short- and long-term assignments can be taught readily to the whole class at once by giving them the definitions and teaching them to apply these definitions to a series of examples.

2. Teach students to task analyze long-term tasks by breaking them into component tasks, estimating the amount of time it will take to perform each subtask, and then scheduling time to complete the subtasks in their schedule books. Start by modeling the task-analysis process. You can do this by distributing an already completed task analysis and timeline for your first several long-term assignments. Then, have students begin to develop their own task analyses, first under your guidance, and eventually, independently. The steps for performing a **task analysis** are explained in the Professional Edge.

3. Show students how to record information in their schedule books by entering fixed activities or activities you do every week; entering occasional activities, or activities that will be different from week to week; entering the due dates for assignments; prioritizing assignments; scheduling time to work on assignments; and monitoring assignment completion, including rescheduling or adding time to work on assignments.

Many schools have had success with schoolwide programs with a single system of keeping track of assignments in a schedule book used in every class. The consistency and repetition that are naturally a part of such a system seem to benefit students, including those with disabilities, many of whom are more successful when teachers stick to a daily routine. Students with special needs may need additional adaptations, however, such as having the classroom teacher check and/or initial their schedule book before they leave class. This step is particularly important when students are first learning to use a schedule book.

How Can Students Learn to Use Strategies Independently?

Some students may have trouble using a learning strategy independently, even after they have learned how to do it. Their problem could be that they may not know when to use a strategy, or if they are using it, how to keep track of how well they are doing and change their behavior if necessary.

Professional Edge

Teaching Students Task Analysis

An important part of time management is knowing how to analyze assignment tasks. Students who can judge the difficulty of their assignments and break them into manageable steps are better able to budget time for completing their work. Unfortunately, task analysis is a skill that is problematic for students, including those with special needs. Strategies for teaching students to analyze their assignments are described here.

Write the Assignment

Write a two-page paper comparing the baseball strike of 1994 to the baseball strike of 1981.

Before you begin a task analysis of your assignment, review the following steps:

Step 1: Decide exactly what you must do.
Step 2: Decide how many steps are needed to complete the task.
Step 3: Decide how much time each step will take.
Step 4: Set up a schedule.
Step 5: Get started.
Step 6: Finish the task.

Now you are ready to begin a task analysis of your assignment. Check off steps as they are completed in the boxes (❐).

Step 1: Decide exactly what you must do.

❐ Notice the key words in the directions. Look at the exact wording. List key words for this project.

1. _____*Two-page paper*_____
2. _____*Compare 1994 baseball strike to 1981 strike*_____

❐ Tell yourself aloud what you must do.
❐ Go over the directions *again*.

Step 2: Decide how many steps are needed to complete the task.

❐ List all the steps needed to do the task.
❐ Number the steps in the order of their importance.

Steps	*Order*
Find source information for both strikes in library	1
Write first draft	4
Edit	5
Write final draft	6
Make outline of paper	3
Read sources and take notes	2

(continued)

Professional Edge *(continued)*

Step 3: Decide how much time each step will take.

❐ Rewrite your steps in the order in which you numbered them.
❐ Now, consider the amount of time you would need to complete each step.
❐ Record the amount of time in the appropriate space.

Steps (List in sequence beginning with priorities)	Time
Find source information for both strikes in library	1 hour
Read sources and take notes	$2\frac{1}{2}$ hours
Make outline of paper	1 hour
Write first draft	3 hours
Edit	$\frac{1}{2}$ hour
Write final draft	$\frac{1}{2}$ hour

Step 4: Set up a schedule.

❐ Count the number of days you have to do the task. How many days?
❐ Look at a calendar.
❐ Plan a time for every step. Look back to where you estimated how much time each step would take.
❐ Make changes in your time plan. Some things will take less time. Some things will take more time.

Step 5: Get started.

❐ Stay on schedule. Check your calendar each day to see if you are proceeding on schedule.
❐ Make changes if needed. You can make changes in the time plan. You can make changes in the materials.
❐ Stop and look at your progress after each step is finished. Are you still on schedule?
❐ Get help if you find a problem you cannot solve. Whom did you ask for help?

Step 6: Finish the task.

❐ Complete your project on time.
❐ Evaluate the finished product. How do you think you did?
❐ Give yourself a reward. What is your reward?

S O U R C E : From *Blueprint for Study Strategies* by Montgomery County Public Schools, 1985, Rockville, MD: Board of Education of Montgomery County.

Four strategies that can help students perform tasks more independently are self-instruction, self-monitoring, self-questioning, and self-reinforcement. Like all learning strategies, these "self" strategies may need to be carefully taught using the teaching practices described in this chapter.

Self-Instruction

In **self-instruction,** learners are taught to use language to guide their performance. In essence, students are taught to talk themselves through a task. The idea is, if they can talk themselves through a task, they will not need help from anyone else. The first step needed to teach students self-instruction techniques is to explain that self-instruction involves giving yourself instructions on how to do a task. For example, self-instruction can be used to help get seatwork done or remember to use a strategy for a multiple choice test. Then ask the students to identify a situation that requires the use of a specific skill, such as getting their seatwork done in reading or taking a 10-minute science quiz on Friday. Demonstrate how to write down the steps needed to perform that task. For example, to get seatwork done, the student first decides how much effort to put into this task. Next, he or she decides what is supposed to be done. Finally, the student decides what the first step in completing the task should be, what the next step should be, and so forth, until the seatwork is done. When students are finished, they praise themselves for a job well done. Ask students to rehearse the steps through self-talk or peer review, going over all the steps involved in completing a seatwork task from beginning to end.

After you have demonstrated how to apply self-instruction, have the students practice in a role-play situation and give them feedback. In the seatwork task, for example, you could put a sample reading task on the screen using the overhead projector and demonstrate the steps by thinking out loud. The students could then practice in pairs and give each other feedback, with you monitoring and also giving feedback. Students could keep a chart or index card listing the task steps, which they should be encouraged to glance at periodically while performing the task.

Self-Monitoring

In **self-monitoring,** students watch and check themselves to make sure they have performed targeted behaviors. Self-monitoring is a critical aspect of independent learning, since being independent often requires students to check their performance to see whether it is effective and make a change when a particular strategy is not working (Reid, 1996). Self-monitoring can also be a strong motivator for students by providing them concrete evidence of their progress. In teaching self-monitoring to your students, first explain to them that self-monitoring is a way that they can check their own behavior to make sure they are doing the right thing. Ask the students to identify a behavior or a learning strategy that they need to do in class. For example, students may select a behavior such as being on task or on time for classes, or they may choose a strategy such as the COPS proofing strategy described earlier in the chapter.

The next step is to select a practical and expedient way for students to measure the behavior. One possibility is to have them count on a card or pocket counter the number of times the behavior occurs. For example, Yashika recorded on an index card the number of her talkouts in reading class. Another possibility is to use a checklist to keep track of behaviors as they occur. The checklist shown in Figure 10.6

Connections

The "self" strategies covered in this chapter apply to academic learning. These same strategies are sometimes referred to as *cognitive behavior management,* which is discussed in Chapter 12.

Figure 10.6 Self-Monitoring Checklist for Handwriting

	Monday	Tuesday	Wednesday	Thursday	Friday
Preparing to Write					
How is my posture; am I sitting up straight?	+				
Is the paper aligned correctly? Is it straight?	+				
Am I holding my pen correctly?	+				
Checking Mechanics					
Are the words written on the line?	+				
Are the capitals touching or nearly touching the top line?	O				
Are the lowercase letters filling one-half the space of the line?	O				
Checking Spacing					
Is there enough space between words but not too much?	+				

+ = Done
O = Not done

was developed to help students monitor their use of a self-questioning program in handwriting.

Teach students to use the measurement system through demonstration, practice, and feedback, and continue to encourage and reinforce the use of self-monitoring in your class. Self-monitoring can be applied to any learning strategy. To help students self-monitor the time-management skill of using a schedule book, for example, develop a checklist such as the one in Figure 10.7.

Self-Questioning

Self-questioning is a form of self-instruction in which students guide their performance by asking themselves questions. The idea behind self-questioning is that if students can guide their own behavior by asking themselves questions, then they will not always need a teacher or other adult present in order to perform. In teaching your students self-questioning, have the students first identify the behaviors, duties, or tasks that is required in class. For example, the students could identify steps needed to proof a writing paper, such as checking the correct use of capital letters, punctuation, spelling, and appearance. Have the students write these tasks in question form, for example, "Have I capitalized all words correctly? Have I used the right punctuation marks in the right places? Have I spelled all the words correctly? Is my paper neat?"

Figure 10.7   **Self-Monitoring Form for Time Management**

Student's Name _____

Class _____

Date _____

Directions: Answer the checklist every day after reviewing your schedule book at the end of the day. If you completed an activity, put a + in the box; if you did not complete the activity, put a – in the box.

Did you cross out completed activities?   ☐

Did you circle activities not completed?   ☐

Did you reschedule activities not completed?   ☐

Did you enter due dates for assignments?   ☐

Did you schedule study time?   ☐

S O U R C E : From "Programming for Independent Study Skill Usage" by W. D. Bursuck and M. Jayanthi, 1993, in S. Vogel and P. Adelman (Eds.), *Programming for Success for College Students with Learning Disabilities,* New York: Springer-Verlag.

As in self-monitoring, the next step is to select a practical and expedient way for students to measure the behavior, such as recording behaviors as they occur using a checklist. Students might practice self-questioning in pairs for feedback. Other practical measures include keeping task questions on index cards and putting them in a convenient place. For example, students might put the proofing questions on an index card and tape it to the inside cover of their notebooks.

Self-Reinforcement

As the term implies, **self-reinforcement** occurs when students reward themselves for behaving appropriately or achieving success in learning tasks. An important part of being an independent learner is recognizing when you have done a good job. As discussed before, students with special needs often attribute their success to factors other than their own efforts, such as luck. Teaching self-reinforcement is an effective way of helping students replace negative attributions with more positive ones. Students need to be coached to use self-reinforcement by praising or rewarding themselves explicitly for doing something right or being successful academically. The first step is to have students set a particular goal for themselves, such as getting all their homework in on time, getting all their seatwork done, being on time for class, taking accurate and complete notes during a lecture, studying for a test, or reading a book. Allow students to decide when and how they can reinforce themselves. For example, younger students might give themselves a star or sticker each time they beat their highest score on a math facts timed test. Older students might give themselves a point for each day they completed their homework. If they have four points by the end of the week, they could go out to lunch with a friend. Self-praise is also a good way of rewarding progress toward personal goals.

Connections

Reinforcement and related behavioral principles are explored further in Chapter 12.

Check Your Learning

How can students learn to initiate the use of strategies on their own?

Practice setting goals, acknowledging when a goal has been attained, and using different kinds of self-reinforcement. You will want to model for students how self-reinforcement works by demonstrating how you set goals for yourself, knowing when you have reached a goal, and reinforcing yourself for reaching the goal. For example, Mr. Hughes explained to his class that he needs to work on getting his lawn cut on time. Each time he cuts the lawn and has to rake up only one bag of grass clippings or less (his measure of lawn length is the longer the lawn, the more grass to rake), he treats himself to a milkshake at the local ice cream shop. Mr. Hughes also praises himself for saving time and effort each time he cuts the lawn and has little grass to rake up.

As students get older, they are expected to learn at home, school, and in the workplace with less support. They are also expected to set goals for themselves and take independent actions to meet those goals. For some students, being an independent learner does not come naturally. These students need to be taught directly independent learning and self-advocacy skills. They also need to be taught how to apply those skills in school and real-world settings with minimal support.

Summary

General education teachers can help all their students, including students with special needs, become independent learners. One way teachers can build student independence is to encourage student self-awareness and self-advocacy.

Another way to help your students become more independent is to design and teach effective learning strategies in class. Effective learning strategies can be developed by identifying skills that are problematic for most of your students, specifying relevant student outcomes, and listing a set of specific steps students need to follow to reach the identified outcomes; these steps should be brief (no more than eight) and encased in a mnemonic device. They should also cue students to perform thinking, doing, and self-evaluating behaviors. Methods of teaching learning strategies to students include assessing current strategy use, clarifying expectations, demonstrating and modeling strategy use, encouraging students to memorize strategy steps, providing guided and independent practice, and administering posttests.

Many strategies that can help students become independent learners are available. Reading-comprehension strategies include SCROL, PARS, CAPS, and POSSE. The reciprocal teaching technique provides teacher and peer models of effective thinking behaviors and then allows students to practice these behaviors with their peers. Some note-taking strategies are the five *R*'s of note-taking (record, reduce, recite, reflect, and review), the 3 *R*'s (review, read, relate; a prelistening strategy), and PASSING (prepare, attend to the teacher, state the topic and the source, identify key words and ideas, note their meaning, and give the meaning in their own words). POWER (planning, organizing, writing, editing, and revising) is a writing strategy that helps students organize themselves to carry out all the steps in the writing process through the use of self-questioning, graphic organizers, and peer editing.

Other strategies for written expression include TAG, COPS, SLOW CaPS, and DEFENDS. Strategies for problem solving in math are FASTDRAW, LAMPS, SLOBS, and FOIL. Students also need to learn strategies for managing their time and resources.

Four strategies that can help students learn to use strategies independently are self-instruction, self-monitoring, self-questioning, and self-reinforcement. In self-instruction, students are taught to use language to guide their performance. In self-monitoring, students watch and check themselves to make sure that they have performed targeted behaviors. Self-questioning is a form of instruction in which students guide their performance by asking themselves questions. Self-reinforcement occurs when students reward themselves for behaving appropriately or making progress in learning.

Applications in Teaching Practice

Designing Strategies for Independence

Latasha is a student who has a moderate hearing loss. Although her hearing aid helps, she still has to depend a lot on speech reading to communicate. She also speaks slowly and has trouble saying high-frequency sounds such as *sh* and *t*. Latasha has a poor self-image and is reluctant to interact with her peers and teachers. Design a self-advocacy program for Latasha.

Questions

1. What skills would you teach Latasha to use for self-advocacy?
2. How would you get Latasha to use these skills in your class and in other school and out-of-school situations?

Cal is a student with organizational problems; he is chronically late for class and rarely finishes his homework. Design an organizational strategy for Cal using the guidelines for developing strategies covered in this chapter.

Questions

1. How would you teach the organizational strategy you have designed using the guidelines for effectively teaching a learning strategy covered in this chapter?
2. How would you teach Cal to use the strategy independently using self-instruction? Self-monitoring? Self-questioning? And self-reinforcement?

Evaluate the design of any one of the learning strategies in this chapter using the guidelines in the Professional Edge on pages 369–370.

Questions

1. Is there anything you would change about the strategy? How would you teach the strategy using the six steps described in this chapter?
2. How would you help students apply the strategy independently using the four "self" strategies discussed in this chapter?

chapter 11

Evaluating Student Learning

Learner Objectives

After you read this chapter, you will be able to

1. Identify and describe adaptations that can be made before, during, and after testing students with special needs.

2. Describe ways to adapt report card grades.

3. Explain how performance-based and portfolio assessments can be used with students with disabilities.

Mr. Stevens is a high school earth science teacher. One of his students, Stan, has a learning disability that causes him to have trouble reading textbooks. Stan also has difficulty figuring out multiple choice test questions, the kind that Mr. Stevens uses on his exams and quizzes. Stan says that he knows the material but just needs more time to take the tests because he reads slowly. During the past marking period, Mr. Stevens gave four multiple choice tests, each worth 20 percent of the final grade. Scores on homework assignments counted for the remaining 20 percent. Stan earned a grade of B on his homework, but he had two D's, one C, and one F on the tests. Mr. Stevens assigned him a grade of D for the marking period. Mr. Stevens felt this was a fair grade since most of Stan's peers scored much higher on the tests. Mr. Stevens is also committed to keeping his reputation as a teacher with high standards. When Stan received his grade for the marking period, he asked his parents why he should work so hard when he couldn't seem to get good grades anyway. Stan's parents felt that he had improved last mark...... grade did not show it. They .... stop trying and eventually drop .... issues here? What could Mr.

.........obinson's third-grade class. She ....d has some trouble in reading ....nson's literature-based reading ....eased with her progress and has .... the first two grading periods. ....came very upset when they ....ing only at the first-grade level ....zed tests. They wondered how .... on the standardized tests ....me A's on her report card. ....parents if she were in your class? How could you change your grading procedures to prevent communication problems like this from occurring?

Lucille is a student with a mild cognitive disability who is in Ms. Henry's fourth-grade math class. On the basis of her current performance in math, which is at the first-grade level, Lucille's IEP team set math goals for her in the areas of basic addition and subtraction. The rest of the class is working on more difficult material based on the fourth-grade math curriculum. Lucille's IEP objective for the second marking period was to compute in writing 20 two-digit by two-digit addition problems with regrouping with 80 percent accuracy within 20 minutes. She received direct instruction on these problems from Mr. Brook, her special education teacher, who was co-teaching with Ms. Henry. As a result, she met her goal for the marking period. How should Ms. Henry grade Lucille? School policy mandates letter grades.

One of a teacher's major jobs is to evaluate the educational progress of students. The information collected during evaluation activities can indicate if teaching has been effective and can allow teachers to alter instruction as needed. Classroom evaluations are also helpful in giving students (and their parents) an idea of how well they are performing in school, and they can be used by principals and school boards to evaluate the effectiveness of their schools.

Even though evaluation activities are very important, the ways in which students are evaluated most frequently—testing and grading—can be problematic for students with disabilities, their teachers, and parents. For example, Stan and his earth science teacher have a problem because Stan's test scores are more a reflection of his learning disability than his knowledge of earth science. Jennifer's teacher has a problem in communicating the meaning of Jennifer's grades to her parents. She graded Jennifer based on her progress and her effort in class. Jennifer's parents, however, thought she was being graded in comparison with her peers and therefore expected their daughter to be performing at or above grade level, not below. Lucille's teacher needs to give Lucille a grade even though she has different curricular goals than the other students in the class. As you work with students who are included in your classroom, you will experience these and other challenges in evaluating the learning of students with disabilities and other students with special needs. In this chapter, you will learn a number of ways to solve these problems.

How Can Classroom Tests Be Adapted for Students with Special Needs?

Connections

How do the topics in this chapter fit into the IN-CLUDE framework presented in Chapter 4?

Although testing has always been a major part of U.S. education, the recent emphasis on school reform, with its dominant theme of raising educational standards, promises to make educators rely even more on tests in the future (Thurlow, Ysseldyke, & Silverstein, 1995). With this increasing emphasis on test performance have come concerns about the performance of students with disabilities on tests. As shown in the vignette about Stan at the beginning of this chapter, testing can be a very trying experience for many of these students and their families.

Most important in testing students with disabilities is making sure that test results reflect their knowledge and skills, not their disabilities. Fortunately, classroom tests can be adapted in ways that can help you test students with disabilities fairly and with a reasonable amount of accuracy. As shown in Table 11.1, adaptations can

Table 11.1 Examples of Testing Adaptations

Before the Test	During the Test	After the Test
Study guides	Alternative forms of response	Change letter or number grades
Practice test	Alternative means of response	Change grading criteria
Teaching test-taking skills	Alternative sites	Use alternatives to number and letter grades
Modified test construction	Direct assistance	
Individual tutoring	Extra time	

be made in three contexts: before the test; during test administration; and after the test, in grading procedures. Many of these adaptations will also benefit your students who do not have disabilities.

Adaptations before the Test

You can do a number of things before the test to help students with disabilities. First, you can prepare a study guide that tells students what to study for the test. A study guide can help students who waste valuable time studying everything indiscriminately instead of concentrating on the most important information. Study guides can also assist students with memory problems by focusing their efforts on only the most critical material. Second, you can give a practice test. This test can clarify your test expectations and also benefits the class by familiarizing students with the test format. Practice tests are also helpful to students who have trouble following directions or for those who are anxious about taking tests and often fail to cope immediately with an unfamiliar test format. Finally, many students with disabilities also benefit from tutoring before tests. This help can be offered before or after school by peer tutors or paraprofessionals. Tutors can provide guidelines for what to study or help directly with particularly difficult content.

Teaching test-taking skills.   Another option is to teach students **test-taking skills.** Students may need a number of test-taking skills, including ones for studying for tests, for taking objective tests, and for writing essay tests. At first, you might start working with students on test-taking strategies by helping them analyze the kinds of mistakes they usually make on tests. They can then use a test-taking strategy that fits their particular problem. For example, Bill and his teacher looked over his history tests for the last grading period and noticed that most of the questions he missed were taken from class lectures rather than the textbook. Bill begins to check his notes after class with one of his classmates, a kind of "study buddy," to make sure he does not miss any main ideas. He also decides to spend more time studying his notes before the test. Eric, on the other hand, notices that he tends to choose the first response (a) on multiple choice tests and that he is not reading the other answer choices carefully. His teacher suggests that he read each choice carefully before responding and put a check next to each answer as a way of making sure he has read each choice. At the secondary level, students might use a mistake analysis form such

FYI

Planning your tests and test adaptations at the beginning of instruction helps you clarify what is essential to teach and achieve a good match between your tests and instruction.

Connections

Strategies for developing and using study guides appear in Chapter 9.

Figure 11.1   Form for Analyzing Test-Taking Mistakes

Check (✓) any of the following mistakes you made when you took tests for three of your courses. Write DNA (does not apply) for a statement that does not apply to a test. For example, if a test has no true–false or multiple choice questions, write DNA for mistake 4 and mistake 5.

Test-Taking Mistakes	English	Social Studies	Health
1. Directions not followed.	✓		✓
2. Not all questions answered in allotted time	✓	✓	
3. Answers not checked carefully.	✓	✓	
4. True–false or multiple choice questions left unanswered.		DNA	
5. Correct true–false or multiple choice answers changed to incorrect ones.		DNA	
6. Wrong answer about information in notes and text.		✓	
7. Wrong answer about information in notes but *not* in text.	✓	✓	✓
8. Wrong answer for information written on the chalkboard.	✓	✓	✓
9. Wrong answer for information the teacher said to learn.	✓		
10. Wrong answer about a topic stated in a textbook heading.			
11. Wrong answer for a term printed in special type in the text.		✓	
12. Wrong answer about information in a numbered list.			

as the one shown in Figure 11.1 to help them focus on these and other types of test-taking problems. The teacher should first show students how to use the form by providing a number of examples in class.

When studying for tests, students often are required to remember a lot of material. This can be difficult for students with learning or cognitive disabilities, who may have memory problems. Students can benefit from strategies that help them remember important content for tests. For example, Greg uses a memorization technique called **chunking.** After he studies a chapter in his text, he tries to recall five to seven key ideas. These key thoughts help trigger his recall of more significant details. After reading a chapter about the life of Harriet Tubman, for example, he remembers information in chunks—her *early years*, her experiences with the *underground railroad*, and so on. These general ideas help him remember details such as when she was born and how many slaves she helped to freedom. Mnemonic devices can also help students remember information for tests. **Mnemonics** impose an order on information to be remembered using poems, rhymes, jingles, or images to aid memory. For example, Mr. Charles wants his class to remember the six methods of scientific investigation. He tells the students to think of the word *chrome* (Cermak, 1976). Here are the six steps of the **CHROME** strategy:

C *Categorization*
H *Hypothesis*
R *Reasoning*
O *Observation*
M *Measurement*
E *Experimentation*

Another mnemonic device that can help students remember definitions and factual information is called the keyword method (Mastropieri, 1988). The **keyword method** uses visual imagery to make material more meaningful to students and hence easier to remember. First, a vocabulary word or fact is changed into a word that sounds similar and is easy to picture. For example, to help remember that the explorer Hernando de Soto came from Spain, students were shown the picture in Figure 11.2 on page 382, a bull (to symbolize Spain) sipping a soda (the keyword for de Soto) at a counter (Carney, Levin, & Levin, 1993). When students are asked to name an explorer who came from Spain, they are told to think of the keyword for de Soto. Next, they are told to think back to the picture the keyword was in and remember what was happening in the picture. Finally, they are told to answer the question. (So who was an explorer from Spain?)

FYI

The keyword method recommended here for learning vocabulary is not to be confused with the "key word" strategy for teaching students to solve math story problems referred to in the Professional Edge in Chapter 10.

Students can help each other prepare effectively for tests using directly taught study strategies. What strategies might these students be using to prepare for an upcoming test?

Figure 11.2   Keyword for De Soto

SOURCE: From "Mnemonic Strategies: Instructional Techniques Worth Remembering" by R. N. Carney, M. E. Levin, and J. R. Levin, 1993, *Teaching Exceptional Children, 25*(4), 27. Reprinted by permission of the Council for Exceptional Children.

Cultural Awareness

Research shows that improving students' test-taking skills, including those of African American, Hispanic, and Native American students, and students who are poor, improves their scores on tests. From 5 to 14 hours of instruction spread over five to seven weeks appears to be the range of time to improve students' "test wiseness" (Grossman, 1995). Strategies for teaching "test wiseness" and other independent learning skills are covered later in this chapter.

Many students do poorly on tests because they do not study for tests systematically. Teach your students to organize their materials so that they avoid wasting time searching for such items as notes for a particular class or the answers to textbook exercises. Making random checks of your students' notebooks is one way to find out how well organized they are. For example, Ms. Barber stresses note-taking in her fifth-grade social studies class. Every Friday afternoon, she checks the notebooks of five students in her class. She gives students bonus points if they have notes for each day and if their notes are legible and include key information. Also, teach your students strategies for how to process material when they are studying. For example, Ms. Treacher shows her third graders a verbal **rehearsal strategy** for learning their spelling words. She demonstrates how she says the word, spells it out loud three times, covers the word, writes the word, and then compares her spelling to the correct spelling. Mr. Jacobs shows his class how they can summarize text and class material on the topic of nonviolent resistance using a concept map such as the one shown in Figure 11.3. Another effective rehearsal strategy is for students to ask themselves questions about the most important information to be learned.

Teaching test-taking strategies.   Many students, including those with special needs, do not test well because they lack strategies for taking the actual tests. For

Figure 11.3   **Concept Map: Studying for Tests**

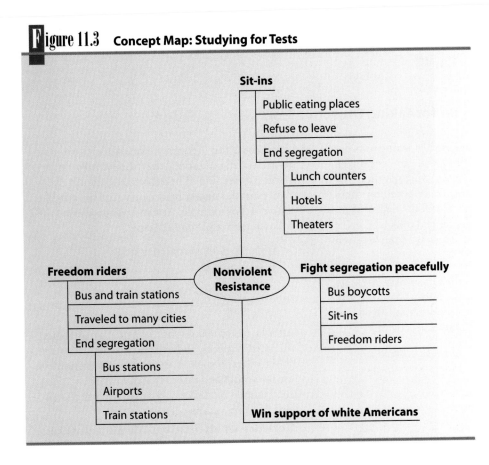

example, Sal rarely finishes tests in science because he spends too much time on questions that he finds difficult. Laura has trouble with true–false questions because she does not pay attention to key words such as *always, never, usually,* and *sometimes.* Lewis's answers to essay questions contain much irrelevant information and do not focus on what the questions are asking. The Professional Edge on pages 384–385 offers suggestions for teaching students strategies for taking objective tests.

Students also need strategies for taking essay tests. Performing well on essay tests requires that students know the content covered; can follow directions, including identifying and understanding key words; and can organize their ideas. All these areas can be problematic for students with disabilities. The following suggestions from Langan (1982) might prove helpful to students taking essay tests:

1. Read over the entire exam before you begin. If you have memorized information related to specific questions, jot it down before you write your answer.

2. Look for key instructional words in the questions to help you determine how to structure your answer and determine what information to include. For example,

Connections

You can design your own test-taking strategies using the guidelines for learning strategies presented in Chapter 10.

Professional Edge

Teaching Strategies for Taking Objective Tests

Many students flounder when taking tests because they do not approach tests in any organized way. You can help your students approach their objective tests more systematically by teaching them the strategies described here. The following six rules for responding to multiple choice and true–false items are based on a comprehensive review of the research literature.

1. **Respond to the test maker's intention.** Answers to test questions should take into account the way material is treated in class. For example, Rob had this item on his social studies test:

   > During the occupation of Boston, the British received their most severe losses at Bunker Hill.
   >   True
   >   False

   Even though Rob learned at a recent trip to the museum that the Battle of Bunker Hill was actually fought on Breed's Hill, his teacher had not brought up this point in class. Therefore, Rob responded by circling "True."

2. **Anticipate the answer.** Before students attempt to answer the question, they should fully understand its meaning. Therefore, they should try to figure out the answer before they read the possible answers. For example, Armand was answering the following multiple choice item:

   > What does an astronomer study?
   >   a. plants
   >   b. music
   >   c. history
   >   d. stars

   After he read the question, Armand thought about the word *astronomy* and what his teacher had talked about in class, such as the fact that astronomers use telescopes and that they look at stars and planets. He then read all the possible choices and circled "d. stars" as the correct answer.

3. **Consider all alternatives.** Many students with special needs, such as students with learning disabilities, tend to answer too quickly, choosing the first available choice. Students should be encouraged to read all the choices before responding. Students can monitor their behavior by

---

Do It!

Rewrite or adapt the strategies for taking essay tests as an illustrated handout for younger students who are expected to write one or two complete paragraphs in response to a question. Which key words would you teach younger students to help them answer appropriately?

you would include different information and use a different structure if you were asked to *list* the reasons for the American Revolution versus *discuss* them. Key words often used in essay tests are listed and defined in Table 11.2 on page 386.

3. Organize your answers. A rule of thumb in answering essay questions is that you should spend at least one-fourth of your time planning what you are going to write.

4. Leave time to proofread your answers for clarity, legibility, spelling, and grammar.

5. When writing an answer, leave margins and do not write on the back of the paper. If your writing is large, write on every other line. Leaving some extra space makes the exam easier for the teacher to grade.

putting a checkmark next to each choice after they have read it.

4. **Use logical reasoning strategies to eliminate unlikely answers.** Even if students do not know the answer to a question, they can improve their chances of getting it right by using what knowledge they do have to eliminate unlikely choices. For example, Dolores read the following item:

In which country would it be impossible to use a sled in the winter?
  a. Guatemala
  b. Canada
  c. Zimbabwe
  d. Norway

Dolores did not know the geographical locations of Guatemala or Zimbabwe, but she did know that Canada and Norway were countries where it snowed often. She then took a guess between *a* and *c*, and chose *a*, the correct answer. By eliminating two of the items, she improved her chance of getting the question right by 25 percent.

5. **Use time wisely.** As already mentioned, a frequent test-taking problem is failing to budget time. Some students spend so much time on some items that they have little time left for others.

While taking tests, students should check the time periodically to make sure they have enough time left to answer the remaining questions. You can assist students by writing the time remaining on the chalkboard several times during the testing period. Students also can be taught to estimate the amount of time they should spend on each question. For example, if students are taking a 100-item test in a 50-minute period, they should figure on spending no more than one-half minute per question. After 25 minutes, they can then check to see that they have completed at least 50 items. Finally, teach students to spend more time on items on which they have at least partial knowledge and less time on questions for which they have no knowledge.

6. **Guess, if all else fails.** Most tests do not have a penalty for guessing. On standardized tests especially, tell your students that if they do not answer a question, they have no chance of getting it right, but if they guess they have a 50 percent chance of getting true–false questions right and a 25 percent chance of getting most multiple choice questions right.

SOURCE: From "Are Learning Disabled Students 'Test-Wise'? A Review of Recent Research" by T. Scruggs & M. Mastropieri, 1988, *Learning Disabilities Focus*, 3(2), 87–97.

6. If you do not have time to write an answer, write your outline for the answer. Often, teachers will give you a substantial amount of credit if they can see that you knew the information and simply did not have time to write the answer.

Adaptations in Test Construction

All students benefit from tests that are written clearly and assess pertinent knowledge or skills. Thus, everything that you have learned about writing good tests in your teacher education program applies here. Still, test items can be well written but constructed in a way that results in problems for students with special needs. For example, Carmen has difficulty reading tests that are visually cluttered. She might benefit from triple spacing between test items and extra space between lines. Juan scores poorly on tests because he is unable to read many of the words used in the

Cultural Awareness

Strategies to prevent cultural bias on classroom and standardized tests are covered in Chapter 8.

Table 11.2   Key Words in Essay Questions

Key Word	Definition
Apply	Take the principles and discuss how they would apply to the novel situation.
Compare	Look for differences and similarities.
Contrast	Look for differences and similarities, stressing the differences.
Define	Provide a clear, concise statement that explains the concept.
Diagram	Provide a drawing.
Discuss	Provide an in-depth explanation. Be analytical.
Explain	Give the reasons or the causes. Present a logical development that discusses the reasons.
Illustrate	Use examples or, when appropriate, provide a diagram or picture.
Interpret	Explain and share your own judgment about it.
Justify	Provide reasons for your statements or conclusions.
List	Provide a numbered list of items.
Outline	Organize your answer into main points and supporting details. If appropriate, use outline form.
Prove	Provide factual evidence to support your logical argument.
Relate	Show the connectedness between the ideas.
Review	Provide a critical summary in which you not only summarize but also present your comments about it.
Summarize	Provide a synopsis without providing your comments.
Trace	Describe the development or progress of it.

S O U R C E : From *Strategies for Teaching Students with Learning and Behavior Problems* (3rd ed.) by C. Bos & S. Vaughn, 1994, p. 303. Boston: Allyn & Bacon. Reprinted by Permission.

items; the items contain complex sentences with many words that are above his reading level and that his teacher did not use while teaching. Consider, for example, the following item taken from a social studies test:

Circle the answer that best fits in the blank.

A country in southern Europe, which is on the Mediterranean Sea, _____ has a capital city by the name of Athens.

    a. Greece
    b. Italy
    c. Poland
    d. Croatia

This item could be written much more simply and still test the same information.

Circle the answer that best fits in the blank.

The southern European country whose capital is Athens is ⎯⎯⎯⎯⎯.

    a. Greece
    b. Italy
    c. Poland
    d. Croatia

A student with a reading problem could answer the first question incorrectly because of its awkward wording, not because he or she did not know the answer.

In essay-test construction, several adaptations might benefit students with problems in reading and written expression. For students with reading problems, highlight key words such as *analyze, compare–contrast, describe,* and *list.* You can also give students a form to complete to help them organize their responses. For example, this question was used on a science test:

Compare and contrast plant and animal cells by describing three ways they are alike and three ways they are different.

The following **response format** might aid students in writing an answer:

Ways that plant and animal cells are alike

    1. ⎯⎯⎯⎯⎯⎯⎯⎯⎯⎯⎯⎯⎯⎯⎯⎯⎯⎯⎯⎯
    2. ⎯⎯⎯⎯⎯⎯⎯⎯⎯⎯⎯⎯⎯⎯⎯⎯⎯⎯⎯⎯
    3. ⎯⎯⎯⎯⎯⎯⎯⎯⎯⎯⎯⎯⎯⎯⎯⎯⎯⎯⎯⎯

Ways that plant and animal cells are different

    1. ⎯⎯⎯⎯⎯⎯⎯⎯⎯⎯⎯⎯⎯⎯⎯⎯⎯⎯⎯⎯
    2. ⎯⎯⎯⎯⎯⎯⎯⎯⎯⎯⎯⎯⎯⎯⎯⎯⎯⎯⎯⎯
    3. ⎯⎯⎯⎯⎯⎯⎯⎯⎯⎯⎯⎯⎯⎯⎯⎯⎯⎯⎯⎯

Other practical ways of constructing both objective and essay tests that will allow you to measure student knowledge more accurately are shown in the Professional Edge on pages 388–389. Note that if changes in test construction are intended for the whole class, they can be incorporated into the original master before duplicating. When changes are intended only for one or two students, you can make them as students take the test. For example, Ms. Minter's co-teacher, Ms. James, blackened two of the four choices on Barry's multiple choice items and changed a matching question from having 12 items to three groups of four items each. For another student, she underlined key words in each question and changed several completion questions into true–false items.

Adaptations Involving Test Administration

The ways that tests are given to students with disabilities can also affect the accuracy of the results. Students who, like Stan, have reading comprehension problems might do better on tests if given more time to finish them or if permitted to take them orally. Students with written expression problems might benefit from a dictionary or a handheld spell checker, or by dictating their answers. Seating students with attention problems near you when they take a test might help them stay on task longer. The test administration adaptations shown in the Professional Edge on pages 390–391 are grouped according to students' areas of difficulty.

Do It!

Construct a test for a lesson you might teach containing objective items and essay or short-answer questions. Then create a modified version of this test for your students with special needs.

FYI

Another consideration in constructing tests is to arrange test items in chronological order to match the sequence of instruction.

Connections

Issues of fairness and other topics concerning student relations are taken up in more detail in Chapter 13.

Professional Edge

Modifications in Test Construction for Students with Disabilities

All of your students will do better on clearly written tests that ask questions pertaining specifically to the material covered in class and in the textbook. But your students with disabilities especially require well-phrased and visually accessible tests if they are to succeed at test taking. The following modifications, although beneficial to all your students, can be crucial for your students with special needs.

1. Tests should be typewritten and photocopied.

2. Make tests visually uncluttered by leaving sufficient space between items (triple space) and between lines of items ($1\frac{1}{2}$ spaces). Do not crowd pages with items; keep wide margins.

3. Use symmetrical spacing. For multiple choice tests, align possible responses vertically rather than horizontally, and type the question and possible responses on the same page. Permit students to circle the letter of the correct answer rather than write it in front of the item.

4. Provide additional spacing between different types of test questions. Provide separate directions and a sample item for each type of test question.

5. For completion, short-answer, and essay questions, leave sufficient space to write the answer. Students do not do as well when they must carry over their answers to the back of the page or onto the next page.

6. Leave space for students to answer on the test rather than using machine scoring or answer sheets. Some students have difficulty transferring answers from one page to another.

7. For students who have difficulty with multiple choice questions, reduce the number of possible answers. Students might choose the correct answer from three, for example, rather than from four or five possible responses.

8. For students who read slowly and for students who have organizational problems, avoid the following constructions in matching items: long matching lists—keep lists to five or six items and group by concepts; lengthy items; and having students draw lines to the correct answer, which can be confusing for students with visual–motor problems (Wood, Miederhoff, & Ulschmid, 1989). Lists with 10 to 15 entries in the

Cultural Awareness

Some African American, Brazilian American, Filipino American, and Hawaiian American students are accustomed to working at a slower pace. These students may benefit from extended time when taking tests (Grossman, 1995).

As the Professional Edge on pages 390–391 shows, students might also benefit from the use of an alternative **test site** such as a resource room. For example, testing in the resource room might help students with attention problems (by allowing them to take their tests in a setting with fewer distractions) and students with written language problems (by permitting them to answer test questions orally). Changing the test site also protects students who are taking the test in a different way from being embarrassed. However, before sending a student out of class to take a test, you should first try other options. For example, Ms. Edwards lets her students choose whether to have a test read to them. She allows those who do not want the test read aloud to work independently while she reads the test to the rest of the students. She also gives the students to whom she reads the test more help with directions and the meaning of key vocabulary or difficult questions. Mr. Collins and Ms. Klein are co-first column can be simplified by preselecting three to four choices from the second column for each item in the first column. Record the selected choices beside the item in the first column and have the student select the correct answer from the smaller pool. Consider this example:

Match the definition on the left with the word on the right by writing the letter for the word in the blank next to the definition.

1. in a sudden way ____   a. brightness
2. not able ____   b. visitor
3. to make bright ____   c. suddenly
4. one who visits ____   d. happiness
5. in a happy way ____   e. rearrange
6. to tell again ____   f. brighten
7. to arrange beforehand ____ g. retell
8. state of being happy ____   h. prearrange
9. to arrange again ____   i. unable
10. state of being bright ____ j. happily

These questions will be less confusing for your students with disabilities if you modify them using the guidelines just described:

1. in a sudden way ____   a. brightness
                            b. visitor
                            c. suddenly
                            d. retell

2. to make bright ____   a. happily
                            b. unable
                            c. brighten

9. Change fill-in-the-blank items to a multiple choice format, providing three or four choices for the blank. Students select the correct answer only from the choices given. This modification changes the task from one of recall (memory) to one of recognition.

10. For essay questions, review the questions, key words, and tasks with students individually and help students develop answer outlines. Permit dictated or taped responses when appropriate.

11. Consider color coding, underlining, enlarging, or highlighting key words and mathematical symbols.

SOURCE: Adapted from *Accommodations for Secondary Learning Disabled/Mainstreamed Students on Teacher-Made Tests* by J. N. Williams, 1986. Unpublished manuscript. Wheaton, MD: Wheaton High School.

teaching. Mr. Collins supervises the students taking the test silently while Ms. Klein reads the test to a group of students. If you do find it necessary to send a student out to take a test, be sure to coordinate your plans in advance with the special education teacher to avoid scheduling problems.

Alternative Test-Grading Procedures

You may also need to adapt the ways you grade student tests. For example, Matt has a learning disability. Because of his disability, he has trouble remembering large amounts of information for tests. This memory problem has affected Matt's test scores, which so far include two F's and one D. Matt's teacher, in collaboration with the special education teacher and Matt's parents, identifies the most important

Connections

The IEP team (see Chapter 2) provides guidelines for making test adaptations for individual students.

Professional Edge

Adaptations in Administering Classroom Tests

Even a well-constructed test will fail to measure the knowledge of students with disabilities accurately if it is inappropriately administered. The adaptations you will make in administering tests to your students who have special needs will depend on the students' area of difficulty. Use the following chart to help you decide which modifications to try with students with disabilities included in your class.

	AREA OF DIFFICULTY				
Adaptation	**Reading**	**Writing**	**Listening**	**Speaking**	**Organizing; Paying Attention**
Oral explanations of directions	X				X
Repetition of directions; student repetition of directions	X		X		X
Oral, taped, or dictated test; oral clarification of written answers by student	X	X			X
Written versus oral test; written versus oral directions			X	X	
Extra time	X	X		X	
Time checks during test					X
Segmented test with separate directions for each section	X		X		X
Peer or other assistance:					
to read directions	X				
to check comprehension	X				
to check spelling		X			

information in the chapter and tells Matt to study that for the test. When Matt takes the test, he answers only the 15 questions that his teacher marked with an asterisk, which test the key information he was told to study. The rest of the class answers 30 questions, the 15 that Matt answers plus 15 more covering other material contained in the chapter. Out of his 15 questions, Matt gets 13 correct. In deciding how to grade Matt, the teacher considers three grading options: changing student grades, changing the grading criteria, and using alternatives to traditional letters and numbers.

Adaptation	**AREA OF DIFFICULTY**				
	Reading	**Writing**	**Listening**	**Speaking**	**Organizing; Paying Attention**
Technological aids:					
placemarks or markers	X				X
word processor		X			
tape recorder	X	X		X	
Visual aids and cues; verbal and visual prompts for word retrieval			X	X	
Use of outlines, diagrams, charts, tables, and webs to organize or answer	X	X			X
Permitted use of noncursive writing		X			
Use of previously prepared notes or rehearsed answers				X	
Alternative sites:					
to minimize noise/distraction			X		X
for alternative testing	X	X			
Seating proximity to teacher			X		X
Teacher paraphrase or summary of student answers in complete thoughts				X	
Checklist for materials needed and preparation					X
Allowing answering directly on test rather than answer sheet		X			

S O U R C E :   Adapted from *Accommodations for Secondary Learning Disabled/Mainstreamed Students on Teacher-Made Tests* by J. N. Williams, 1986. Unpublished manuscript. Wheaton, MD: Wheaton High School.

You can change student grades with written comments or symbols, or by giving multiple grades. These options can help clarify what a grade means. In Matt's case, his teacher could give him a B on the test, but with an asterisk meaning that the test was on a different amount of content than that of the rest of the class. Giving multiple grades can be helpful on tests that require written responses. For example, on an English test, Jacinto is required to write an essay on the character of Boo Radley in the novel *To Kill a Mockingbird*. When his teacher grades his essay, she assigns him one grade based on the quality of his analysis of the character and another grade for writing mechanics.

A second option is to change the **grading criteria,** or the standard upon which the grade is based. For example, Matt's teacher could give him a grade of B by basing his grade on a different standard: 15 questions rather than 30. You may also want to base a student's "percentage correct" on items tried instead of on the total number of questions. This alteration may help students who work accurately but slowly. Giving partial credit is another possible option. For example, when Ms. Jordan grades student answers to math story problems, she gives students points for underlining key words in the question and setting up the equation correctly. These extra points can motivate students who are improving but do not increase their test scores significantly. Students can also be allowed to retake tests. They can then be graded by using their score on the retake or averaging their original score with their retake score.

A third grading option you may want to try is using alternatives to letter and number grades, such as pass/fail grades and checklists of skill competencies. For example, Matt could be given a grade of P (Pass), because he has mastered 7 of 10 key concepts in the chapter, or rated on a **competency checklist** showing which key concepts in the chapter he had learned.

What do general education teachers think of the testing adaptations described in this chapter? In a recent study, a national sample of over 300 general education teachers were asked if they found certain adaptations helpful and easy to use. The results of this survey are shown in Table 11.3.

Table 11.3 Testing Adaptations General Education Teachers Find Helpful and Easy to Use

Adaptation	Description
Test preparation	Give practice questions or the actual test as a study guide.
Test construction	Provide extra space on test for answering.
	Simplify wording of test questions.
	Highlight key words in questions.
	Use tests with enlarged print.
Test administration	Read test questions to students.
	Give frequent quizzes rather than exams only.
	Give open-book or open-notes tests.
	Give extended time to finish tests.
	Allow use of technological learning aids during test.
	Give individual help with directions during test.
	Allow students to answer fewer questions.
	Give feedback to individual students during test.

SOURCE: From "A National Survey of General Education Teachers' Perceptions of Testing Adaptations" by M. Jayanthi, M. Epstein, M. Polloway, & W. D. Bursuck (1996), *Journal of Special Education, 30*(1), 99–115.

How Can Report Card Grades Be Adapted for Students with Special Needs?

Report card grading is perhaps the most prevalent and controversial evaluation option used in schools. The practice of grading by letters and percentages began in the early 20th century (Cohen, 1983), a time of great faith in the ability of educational measures to assess students' current levels of learning accurately and also predict future levels of learning. High grades were seen as a sign of accomplishment, intended to spur students on to greater achievements. Those who received low grades were either placed in basic-level or special classes or were encouraged to join the workforce.

Times certainly have changed. Laws have been passed guaranteeing that our evaluations not discriminate on the basis of disability, race, or ethnicity. These laws also guarantee an appropriate education for all students, not just those who can succeed with minimal intervention. Further, our ability to compete in the emerging global economy will depend on better educational outcomes for *all* our citizens, not just a privileged few. These changes have led to new demands that go beyond the relatively simple matter of identifying "good" and "poor" students. For example, how can evaluations be modified to assure that they do not discriminate against students with disabilities? How can they be used to motivate students to stay in school, communicate educational competence and progress to parents and students, and guide our teaching as we move to meet the needs of an increasingly diverse student body? Although answers to these questions are beginning to emerge, in large part we continue to use a grading system that was intended to fulfill a purpose much more narrow in scope.

The use of traditional letter and number grades has caused problems for teachers, who must communicate with many audiences, including parents, students, administrators, and legislators. These audiences often are looking for information that is not readily communicated using a single number or letter (Carpenter, Grantham, & Hardister, 1983). For example, students may be interested in how much progress they have made, whereas their parents want to know how their children compare to their classmates as well as to children nationwide. Principals, on the other hand, may need to provide college admissions offices with indicators of student potential to do college work. Teachers also are increasingly left with many conflicting concerns about grading, including upholding the school's standards, maintaining integrity with other teachers, being honest with students, justifying grades with other students, motivating students for better future performance, communicating accurately to the students' next teacher, and avoiding the reputation of being an "easy" teacher (Rojewski, Pollard, & Meers, 1992; Vasa, 1981).

Increased inclusion in schools has put even more burdens on grading systems. As shown in the vignettes at the beginning of the chapter, grading can present serious challenges for students with disabilities and their teachers. Stan was not a good test taker, yet 80 percent of his report card grade in earth science was based on his test performance. He was concerned that his grade did not accurately reflect his effort or progress in class. Jennifer's parents were surprised to find that their daughter had received A's in reading all year but was reading below grade level on a recent standardized achievement test. Lucille was working on math skills that were more basic than those the rest of the class covered, and her teacher was unsure how to grade her performance.

Cultural Awareness

What do grades mean in the United States? How are grades used and to what ends? How do values about grades in the national culture affect students with special needs?

Modifications of report card grades for students with disabilities and other students with special needs must be carefully explained to prevent misunderstandings. What grading modifications might these people be discussing?

Cultural Awareness

In what ways might grading systems be unfair? Which student groups would be affected the most? What provisions do school districts make for evaluating students who are culturally different or whose first language is not English?

Despite these problems, a number of reasons support the continued use of grades. First, many parents want to see how their children compare to other students, and they demand grades. In addition, grades are efficient and can make decision making easier, particularly for schools making decisions about promotion to the next grade level and for colleges and universities making admissions decisions (Vasa, 1981). In spite of their many limitations, therefore, grades are likely to be used by teachers and schools for many years to come. Teachers need to recognize the limitations of certain types of grades, however, and adapt grading systems to ensure they are fair to all students. As summarized in Table 11.4, grades can be adapted by changing grading criteria, making changes to letter and number grades, and using alternatives to letter and number grades.

Changes in Grading Criteria

One way to adapt report card grades is to change the criteria on which they are based. Teachers often consider a number of factors when assigning student grades, including in-class work or seatwork, homework, ability, attendance, class participation, effort, attitude, reports or papers, extracurricular work, preparedness, organization, notebooks, and progress (Bursuck et al., 1996). One common adaptation is to vary the grading weights of requirements in terms of how much each one counts toward the final grade. In the case of Stan, for example, his teacher counted tests as 80 percent of the grade and homework as 20 percent. Mr. Stevens could help Stan by reducing the amount tests count from 80 percent to 60 percent and giving Stan more credit for other things he does well, such as being prepared, attempting all class activities, and participating in class. Grading students in areas such as effort should be based on the same objective standards that you use to measure the learning of academic content. In Stan's case, Mr. Stevens could define effort as the percentage

Table 11.4 **Examples of Grading Adaptations**

Adaptation	Description	Example
Change Grading Criteria		
A. Vary grading weights	**A.** Vary how much certain criteria (activities or products) count toward a grade.	**A.** Increase credit for participation in in-class group activities and decrease credit for essay exams.
B. Modify curricular expectations	**B.** Identify individualized curriculum on which to base grade.	**B.** Write on student's IEP that she will be graded on work on addition while rest of class works on fractions.
C. Use contracts and modified course syllabi	**C.** Teacher and student agree on quality, quantity, and timelines for specified work.	**C.** Written contract states that student will receive an "A" for completing all assignments at 80% accuracy, attending all classes, and completing one extra-credit report.
D. Grade on the basis of improvement	**D.** Assign extra points for improvement over previous performance.	**D.** Change a "C" to a "B" if student's total points were significantly higher than previous marking period.
Changes to Letter and Number Grades		
E. Add written comments	**E.** Add comments to clarify details on criteria used to determine the letter grade.	**E.** Write on report card that student's grade reflects performance on a modified program and not on regular classroom curriculum.
F. Add information from student activity log	**F.** Keep written anecdotal notes indicating student performance in specific areas over time.	**F.** State on student's report card that while student's grade was the same this quarter, daily records indicate student completed math assignments with less teacher assistance.
G. Add information from portfolios and/or performance-based assessment.	**G.** Collect student work that measures effort, progress, and achievement.	**G.** State on student's report card that student's written language showed an increase in word variety, sentence length, and quality of ideas.
Use Alternatives to Letter and Number Grades		
H. Use pass/fail grades	**H.** Give student a "pass" if he or she meets the minimum requirements for the class.	**H.** Give student a pass for completing 80% of daily work with at least 65% accuracy, and attending at least 90% of classes.
I. Use competency checklists	**I.** Construct a list of goals and objectives for the quarter.	**I.** Attach a checklist to report card indicating that during last quarter, student mastered addition facts, 2-digit addition with regrouping, and counting change to $1.00.

S O U R C E : From "Report Card Grading Adaptations for Students with Disabilities: Types and Acceptability" by D. Munk & W. D. Bursuck, 1998, *Intervention in School and Clinic, 33*(5), 306–308.

of school days on which Stan has his materials for class, completes his homework, and asks at least one question in class.

Another way to adapt grading criteria is to base student performance on **modified curricular expectations.** Expectations such as these are reflected in IEP goals and objectives, behavioral contracts, or course syllabi. For example, in the vignette

FYI

Changing grading criteria for a student with special needs often requires collaborating with the IEP team to make decisions about the student's IEP goals.

at the beginning of this chapter, Lucille's IEP stated that she had a modified curriculum in math. While the rest of the class was working on decimals, she was working on two-digit by two-digit addition problems with regrouping. Because her IEP objective was to score 80 percent or better when given 20 of these problems, her fourth-grade teacher and special education teacher agreed to give her an A if she met her objective, a B if she scored between 70 and 80 percent, a C if she scored between 60 and 70 percent, and so forth. To ensure that Lucille's parents had an accurate picture of her standing in relation to her peers, Lucille's teacher included a written comment on Lucille's report card indicating that her grade was based on different curricular expectations.

Grading criteria can also be adapted through the use of **grading contracts** or **modified course syllabi.** Both of these adaptations help ensure that grading modifications are clearly defined, based on objective criteria, and explained to the student and his or her parents. A grading contract is an agreement between the classroom teacher and the student about the quality, quantity, and timelines required to obtain a specific grade (Hess, 1987). An example of a grading contract follows:

Cultural Awareness

Cultural expectations and standards strongly influence the way families interpret and react to their children's grades. Teachers cannot take for granted that all parents will respond appropriately to their children's grades. Communication is the key.

- If (student) comes to class regularly, turns in all the required work that is completed with _____ percent accuracy, and does one extra credit assignment/project, he or she will receive an A.
- If (student) comes to class regularly and turns in all the required work with _____ percent accuracy, he or she will receive a B.
- If (student) comes to class regularly and turns in all the required work, he or she will receive a C.
- If (student) comes to class regularly and turns in 80 percent of the required work, he or she will receive a D.
- If (student) does not come to class regularly and turns in less than 80 percent of the required work, he or she will receive an F. (Hess, 1987)

In a modified course syllabus, you and the IEP team state the specific course requirements, expectations, grading criteria, and any other changes required because of the student's disability. Figure 11.4 shows an example of an adapted syllabus for an Introduction to Foods course in home economics (Hess, 1987).

Teachers can also base grades on the amount of improvement students make. **Improvement grades** can be incorporated into a traditional grading system by assigning extra points for improvement or by moving students up a grade on the scale if they improve, particularly if they are on the border between grades. A high C, for example, could be changed to a B if the student's test average or total points for the marking period were much higher than those of the previous marking period. Consider the case of Aretha, whose average on spelling tests for the last marking period is 77 percent, an improvement of over 40 percentage points over the preceding marking period. Although her true grade for spelling is a C, her teacher raises her grade to a B– because she has improved so much. Another student, Roberto, read five trade books this marking period as compared with one book the period before. Although most students in the class have read more books at more difficult levels, Roberto still receives a grade of O (outstanding) in reading because he read so many more books than before. His teacher will note on his report card that the books Roberto read were 1 to 2 years below grade level.

Connections

How might the strategy of grading on the basis of improvement help Stan and his parents, whom you met at the beginning of the chapter?

Figure 11.4   Adapted Course Requirements for Home Economics

1. Types of work to be completed by students:
   a. Read tests and pamphlets
      - Recipes with abbreviations and equivalents
      - Tables
      - Menus
   b. Demonstrate ability to:
      - Measure ingredients
      - Use and care for large and small appliances
      - Follow kitchen safety rules
      - Practice good nutrition and weight control
      - Recognize four basic food groups
      - Write menus
      - Prepare meals
   c. Successfully complete written, oral, and performance competency tests

2. The quantity of work to be completed by student:
   a. Read Chapters 1–10, 12, and 16 of the text
   b. Participate in two group projects
   c. Prepare a meal for four people independently
   d. Take weekly quizzes, 10 unit tests, and one final examination

3. The grade for the course will be determined as follows:

Weekly quizzes—10 points each	=	180 points
Unit tests—25 points each	=	250 points
Group projects—50 points each	=	100 points
Meal preparation	=	300 points
		830 points

747–830 points	=	A	498–580 points	=	D
664–746 points	=	B	0–497 points	=	F
581–663 points	=	C			

4. The quality of work will be determined by the home economics instructor based on objective test data and direct observation of the students.

5. Timelines for completion of work are:
   a. Complete assigned readings weekly.
   b. Complete group projects within two weeks after assignment.
   c. Complete individual meal preparation prior to end of semester.

This course was reviewed on _____

Signatures

Student _____

Special Education Teacher _____

Parent _____

Home Economics Teacher _____

Guidance Counselor _____

Principal _____

SOURCE: From *Grading-Credit-Diploma: Accommodation Practices for Students with Mild Disabilities* by R. Hess, 1987, Des Moines: Iowa State Department of Education.

Changes to Letter and Number Grades

Number and letter grades can be clarified by supplementing them with other ways of evaluating and reporting student progress, such as written or verbal comments, logs of student activities, and portfolios. Written or verbal comments can be used to clarify areas such as student ability levels as compared with peers and the extent of student effort. For example, Roberto's teacher gave him an "Outstanding" in reading but commented on his report card that the books he read were below grade level. Such comments about student ability levels can prevent misunderstandings. In the case of Jennifer in the chapter opening vignette, Jennifer's mother thought her daughter's high grade in reading meant that she was reading at grade level. An explanation on Jennifer's report card would have put her grade in context. But keep in mind a word of caution as you make report card comments denoting student ability levels. Students sometimes compare report cards with their classmates and might be embarrassed by comments that indicate they are working below grade level. To prevent this situation, you might use an alternative procedure, such as talking to the parents or sending them a separate note of clarification. In addition, report card comments should never state that the student is receiving special services; this would be a violation of student confidentiality. Finally, when a number or letter grade is given on a report card, the basis for arriving at that grade is often not clear. For example, does the grade represent student performance in comparison with his or her classmates, or is it based on the student's progress toward meeting objectives on his or her IEP? Failure to clarify the bases for grades can lead to communication problems with parents, as shown in the Case in Practice.

Because report card grades are primarily summaries of student performance, they provide little information about student performance over a period of time. You can use **daily activity logs** of student activities and achievement to provide ongoing information for students and their parents. Daily observations of students can be recorded in a notebook or journal, or directly on a calendar. One system uses self-sticking notes to record daily observations of students (Einhorn, Hagen, Johnson, Wujek, & Hoffman, 1991). Whatever the type of daily activity log used, entries should at least include the date, student's name, classroom activity, and a brief description of the observation. For example, Ms. Parks was concerned about the progress of one of her students, Carrie, in the area of word identification skills. Each day during an hour-long literature class, Ms. Parks observed how Carrie approached the trade books she was reading. One day she recorded that Carrie spontaneously used the beginning letter sound *r* to sound out the word "rabbit." Entries can be collected and summarized periodically for evaluations.

Information taken from the logs can be summarized periodically. These summaries can then be shared with parents as often as necessary to clarify student grades. For example, Leroy receives a D in math for the marking period. His parents call Leroy's teacher to set up a conference to discuss the grade and find out how Leroy can improve. Leroy's teacher shares a log summary indicating that Leroy did not follow along while she was demonstrating solutions to math problems on the chalkboard. Leroy's teacher and parents set up a contract for Leroy that encourages him to attend to such demonstrations.

Adding written comments to report card grades also enables you to communicate clearly to your students exactly what they need to do to improve in your class. This is important for students with special needs, who are less likely to be able to evaluate

Case in Practice

Explaining Grades

Jose is a student in Ms. Wittrup's fourth-grade class. When Ms. Diaz, Jose's grandmother, received Jose's most recent report card, she had some questions and made an appointment to see Ms. Wittrup and Ms. Talbot, Jose's special education teacher.

Ms. Wittrup: Ms. Diaz and Jose, I'm so glad you came in today. Ms. Diaz, I understand you have some questions about Jose's report card.

Ms. Diaz: Thank you for taking the time to see me. Yes, I do have some questions about Jose's report card. First of all, I noticed that Jose got a B in reading. This is an area where he's getting help in special education. Does this mean he doesn't need any more help?

Ms. Talbot: Jose's IEP objective for the first grading period was to read fluently and comprehend literature books that are at the second-grade reading level. His word-identification skills in that material are good, but he is still having some trouble with comprehension. Sometimes he has trouble summarizing what he has just read; other times he has a hard time answering questions that I ask him. That is why he received a B rather than an A. I think Jose has

a good chance of meeting this objective by the end of this marking period. Still, he is pretty far behind his fourth-grade classmates, so I think he needs to keep getting help from me.

Ms. Diaz: I think I understand better what his reading grade means, but I don't understand how Jose got only a C in math. He has always done better in math than in reading. Has he been fooling around in class and not paying attention?

Ms. Wittrup: No, Jose has been working hard in math. Jose doesn't have any special needs in math so he is in the regular program. As you can see from looking at my grade book, Jose scored an average of 75 percent on his math tests. His average for homework and in-class work was 80 percent. His overall average for the marking period was 78 percent, which is a C.

Ms. Diaz: Is there something I can do to help Jose with his math so that maybe he can get a B next time?

Ms. Wittrup: One thing that hurts Jose on his tests is that he is still making careless mistakes on basic math facts, particularly the multiplication facts. If you could help him with these at home, I think Jose might be able to pull his grade up to a B.

Ms. Talbot: We're very proud of Jose for getting an A in social studies. Remember we had all agreed that because Jose had reading problems we would let him use a taped text and take his tests orally. Well, Ms. Wittrup told me that Jose had an average of 95 percent on the two tests, which is an A. Good for Jose!

R E F L E C T I O N S

Ms. Diaz had a difficult time understanding what Jose's grades meant. What could Jose's teachers have done to prevent this confusion from occurring? Jose received a grade of A in social studies because he was allowed to use a taped textbook and to take the tests orally. How would you explain this adaptation to a concerned student who took the test without any of these supports and received only a C?

their performance and set goals for themselves based on grades alone (Gersten, Vaughn, & Brengelman, 1996). One large school district in Canada uses computer-generated report card "templates" and a large database of teacher comments to personalize their report cards by providing more prescriptive information for their students (Bailey & McTighe, 1996). An adaptation of a progress report from this district is shown in Figure 11.5 on page 400.

Note the presence of two key pieces of information: a clear statement of what the student needs to do to improve his English grade and specification of the important

Figure 11.5 **Personalized Grade Report**

In English 10, the class has just completed a unit on poetry that focused on developing an appreciation and understanding of this literary form. Students continue to use exploratory writing to respond to literature read in class. Mander failed to complete two assignments worth 25% collectively this term. This has significantly affected his overall mark. Mander can improve his performance by ensuring assignments are completed and handed in on time.

Mark to Date	70
Previous Mark	80
Effort	
excellent	
satisfactory	✓
needs improvement	
Periods Absent Since Beginning of Course	4
Periods Late Since Beginning of Course	6

This term Mander has studied the basic skills of algebra. In particular, he has studied units on the operations of polynomials, equation solving, and factoring polynomials. Class time is used wisely. He organizes work effectively. He aims for excellence. Keep up the good work, Mander!

Mark to Date	90
Previous Mark	75
Effort	
excellent	✓
satisfactory	
needs improvement	
Periods Absent Since Beginning of Course	None
Periods Late Since Beginning of Course	None

S O U R C E : Adapted from "Reporting Achievement at the Secondary Level: What and How." By J. Bailey & J. McTighe. In T. Guskey (ed.), *ASCD Year Book: 1996, Communicating Student Learning* (pp. 199–140). Alexandria, Virginia: Association for Supervision and Curriculum Development.

Check Your Learning

What are the three options for adapting report card grades for students with special needs? What are some specific strategies for each option? What are the advantages and disadvantages of each strategy?

content and/or requirements for each class. Note also that the student's level of effort is evaluated. While giving students credit for trying can be helpful for students with special needs (Bursuck et al., 1996), effort is much more difficult to assess than academic progress (Gersten et al., 1996). We suggest that great care be taken in assessing measures of effort. For example, Ms. Mosely defined excellent effort in her class as not having any unexcused absences from class, completing all homework and in-class assignments on time, and answering a question in class at least three days per week.

Alternatives to Letter and Number Grades

The most common alternatives to letter or number grades are pass/fail, credit/no credit grades, and checklists of competencies and skills. In **pass/fail** or **credit/no credit systems,** a list of minimum understandings or skills for a class is determined by the general education teacher in consultation with the special education teacher. These minimums may or may not relate specifically to a student's IEP. A grade of "Pass" or "Credit" is assigned if the identified understandings and skills are successfully mastered. No letter grades are given.

The major advantage of this alternative is that it relieves the teacher of the responsibility of grading students based on peer comparisons. Grades based on peer comparisons can be discouraging for students who try hard but do not have the ability to compete on an equal basis. Another advantage of pass/fail and credit/no credit systems is that the student knows what is expected and works toward a goal. A disadvantage of pass/fail grades is that their "all or nothing" nature puts a lot of pressure on the teacher, particularly in situations where minimum standards are not well defined. It is important, therefore, to be as specific as possible in setting your minimum standards. Here is an example of pass/fail requirements developed for an American history course that has the necessary specificity:

1. Be in attendance and on time for 90 percent of all class periods each semester.

2. Complete 75 percent of the daily work with at least 60 percent accuracy.

3. Complete a class project (with peer assistance if necessary), earning at least 60 percent of the available points.

4. Participate in class discussions at least once per week and attend all small-group project meetings held in class.

5. Score 60 percent or better on all weekly and semester tests. (Hess, 1987)

WWW Resources

Find out about testing and grading policies being used around the country by visiting the website of the Council of Chief State School Officers (CCSSO) at <http://www.ccsso.org>.

In using **competency checklists,** the general education teacher lists the goals and objectives of a given course and then checks off the objectives as they are achieved or mastered by the student (Hess, 1987). A key advantage of checklists is that they give more detailed information about student performance than grades, which makes them potentially more valuable to students, parents, and future employers. Checklists have several disadvantages, however. They may be time-consuming for teachers to keep up to date, the tasks and objectives may not be understood by parents, and they tend to focus on student weaknesses unless care is taken to state objectives in positive terms. Figure 11.6 on page 402 presents a sample checklist for calculator use.

How Can Performance-Based Assessment Benefit Students with Special Needs?

Ms. Johnson has just completed a unit on persuasive writing and has her students write letters to the editor of a local newspaper, trying to persuade readers to support the building of a new county facility for elderly people. Mr. Repp has been teaching drawing to scale as part of a map-reading unit and has his students make a map of the neighborhood that could be used by visitors from Japan. Ms. Overton's class is

Figure 11.6 **Calculator Use Checklist**

	Successfully Completed	Needs Further Work	Not Attempted
1. Identify the following hand calculator keys: on, off, C, CE			
2. Identify the following hand calculator keys: +, −, =, ×, ÷			
3. Compute written addition problems using a hand calculator			
4. Compute written subtraction problems using a hand calculator			
5. Compute written multiplication problems using a hand calculator			
6. Compute written division problems using a hand calculator			
7. Use a calculator in a functional manner when shopping			

S O U R C E : From *Grading-Credit-Diploma: Accommodation Practices for Students with Mild Disabilities* by R. Hess, 1987, Des Moines: Iowa State Department of Education.

working on basic bookkeeping skills and she has her students plan a budget for a fund-raiser to earn money to build a new jungle gym for the playground.

All of these teachers are checking their students' progress by using a method of evaluation called performance-based assessment. **Performance-based assessment** measures what students "can do with knowledge, rather than with the isolated specific bits of knowledge the student possesses" (Poteet, Choate, & Stewart, 1993, p. 5). Performance-based assessments measure learning processes rather than focusing only on learning products. They frequently involve using **authentic learning tasks,** or tasks that are presented within real-world contexts and lead to real-world outcomes. Mr. Repp could have asked his students to compute the mileage between several cities using a mileage key, a more traditional map-reading assignment. Instead, he has them create their own maps, within a real context, because he wants to see how well they can apply what they have learned to an actual problem. Not only does he evaluate their maps, but Mr. Repp also evaluates parts of the learning process, such as how well his students select and implement learning strategies and collaborate with their classmates during problem solving.

Using performance-based assessments can be very helpful for students with disabilities or other special needs who may be included in your classroom. Performance-based assessments can offer students options for demonstrating their knowledge that do not rely exclusively on reading and writing, areas that often impede the successful testing performance of students with disabilities. For example, Calvin, a student with reading problems in Mr. Repp's class, completed the map activity successfully but would have had trouble with a traditional paper-and-pencil test of the same material. Performance-based tests also are not subject to the same time constraints as traditional tests. Time flexibility can benefit students who may need more time, such as students with reading fluency problems, or students who need to work for shorter time periods, such as students with ADHD. Again, using the example of Mr. Repp's map-drawing activity, students had some time limits (they had to finish in 1 week) but did not have to do the entire project in one sitting. Students with disabilities may also have particular difficulty making the connection between school tasks and tasks in the real world. Performance-based assessments can help them understand this connection, particularly if the assessment is followed up with instruction directly geared to skill applications. For example, Ms. Johnson, whose students were required to write letters to the editor, discovered that many of her students were unable to support their arguments directly with specific examples. She therefore spent some class time demonstrating to students how they could support their arguments and guiding them through several practice activities.

Developing and Evaluating Tasks for Performance-Based Assessment

Performance-based assessments, like standardized tests and curriculum-based assessments, must be carefully designed and scored so that they can provide information that is helpful for instruction and that is viewed with credibility by parents, students, and administrators. A summary of a number of considerations in designing, administering, and scoring performance-based assessments (Wiggins, 1992) follows.

1. Choose learning outcomes that are not covered by your current classroom and standardized testing program. Traditional standardized and classroom tests are likely to assess student knowledge but to underassess the application of that knowledge. Therefore, choose **learning outcomes** for your performance-based tests that stress how well students apply, analyze, or synthesize information. In choosing your learning outcomes, try to think of the knowledge you cover as a tool for helping your students perform an important real-world function. For example, reading comprehension can be seen as a tool for reading an auto mechanics manual. Learning the steps in the scientific method can be seen as a tool for designing science experiments to test your own hypotheses. Identifying and using coins can be seen as a tool for making change at a supermarket checkout.

2. Design tasks within contexts that are meaningful for students. The tasks you pick should provoke student thought and interest. Wiggins (1992) suggests that a well-designed task will engage students so much that they will forget they are being evaluated. Tasks can be made more engaging by embedding them within a meaningful, motivating context. For example, Mr. Barnes wants to see how well his students apply the steps in the scientific method. He has one group of students interested in pop music design and carry out an experiment to see which of the four top radio stations plays the most music by female artists. Mr. Barnes also requires his students to summarize the results of their study and submit them to the editor of the school newspaper.

3. Clarify task expectations by giving students scoring standards and models of excellent performance during teaching. Although coming up with a specific solution to a performance-based task is always the student's responsibility, the goal of the task, as well as the standards on which it is based, should be clearly presented by the teacher. For example, in the music experiment in Mr. Barnes's class, the students were responsible for creating an experiment to see which station played the most music by female artists. However, the students were already familiar with characteristics of effective research design because Mr. Barnes discussed these in class and showed the students model research projects done by previous students.

4. Make testing conditions as authentic as possible. Standardized and traditional classroom tests require many constraints, such as time limits and limited access to references. In real life we have deadlines, but these deadlines rarely involve brief artificial periods of time, such as having to perform within 45-minute periods. Instead, timelines for performance-based tests should be based on performance of similar tasks in the real world. For example, individuals training to be auto mechanics will need to perform tasks based on time limits established by professional mechanics. Access to resources during performance-based tests is also generally not prohibited; in fact, it is encouraged. Imagine denying a lawyer access to case law books while he or she is constructing a defense for an upcoming case! Of course, students must be skillful enough to be able to absorb and apply these resource materials in a timely fashion.

5. Identify standards based on what is most important for doing an effective job. You must take great care in selecting the standards for judging performance-based assessments; a scoring system based on qualities that are widely agreed upon can assure that the results of your performance-based assessments will be useful. Identify key areas of performance by consulting the research literature, colleagues, administrators, and parents. These areas can involve both the products of performance-based tests and the processes students perform in constructing these products. For example, effective performance in math problem solving might include understanding the problem, solving the problem, and answering the problem (Szetela & Nicol, 1992). Areas of importance in evaluating written expression might be story idea, organization–cohesion, and conventions–mechanics (Tindal & Marston, 1990).

6. Develop an accurate scoring system. For each performance area identified, establish well-defined levels of quality. For example, *solving the problem* in the preceding math problem-solving example could be defined as consisting of the following five levels:

0   No attempt
1   Totally inappropriate plan
2   Partially correct procedure but with major fault
3   Substantially correct procedure with minor omission or procedural error
4   A plan that could lead to a correct solution with no arithmetic errors (Szetela & Nicol, 1992, p. 14)

In written expression, the area of *organization* could be defined as follows:

1   The writer has no paragraph structure. The main points are clearly separated from one another, and they come in a random order, as though the writer had not given any thought to what he or she intended to say before starting to write.

2 Paragraphs are present but lack a topic sentence; sentences within a paragraph are marginally related to each other.

3 Paragraphs are present and have some structure but are not well connected. The organization of this paper is standard and conventional. There is usually a one-paragraph introduction; three main points, each treated in one paragraph; and a conclusion that often seems tacked on or forced.

4 Paragraphs are present, topical structure and supporting detail are well developed, and concluding sentences are used.

5 The writer uses paragraphs that are intact not only in terms of sentences within them, but also in terms of the flow from one paragraph to the next. Structure is well developed; ideas are expressed systematically. This paper starts at a good point, has a sense of movement, gets somewhere, and then stops. (Tindal & Marston, 1990, p. 220)

For each level of quality identified, establish benchmarks or pieces of student work that exemplify each area of quality. For example, Figure 11.7 shows an example of level 2, partially correct procedure but with major fault. In attempting to solve this math problem involving money, the student was partially correct in that she added the $20 present from Samantha's grandparents to the $49 that Samantha originally had. However, a major fault of the student's problem solving is that she misunderstood that the $15 for Samantha's brother's birthday present was not an additional amount of money but a part of the total amount Samantha already had. Therefore, the student's performance was rated as level 2, partially correct procedure but with major fault.

Since the evaluation of performance-based assessments can be quite subjective, try giving another person your level criteria and examples and having him or her score a sample of your products and then check for agreement. Also, prior to testing, make sure students "know the objective of the test (what is to be done), the conditions under which the task is to be performed (use of dictionaries, timed or untimed), and the criteria to evaluate the performance" (Poteet et al., 1993, p. 11).

Cultural Awareness

Since teachers' evaluations of lower-income and non-European students can be prejudiced, performance-based assessments can be subject to bias. However, anecdotal evidence shows that when teachers follow specific scoring procedures, performance-based assessments provide much useful information about non-European students and students with limited English proficiency (Heath, 1993).

Figure 11.7 Exemplar for Partially Correct Procedure with Major Fault

Problem
Samantha had $49. She got $20 more from her grandparents for her birthday. Samantha wants to buy a pair of used in-line skates, but she needs to keep $15 to pay for her brother's birthday present. How much can Samantha pay for the in-line skates?

Strategy
To find the answer to the problem, you must first find out how much money she has by adding $49, $20, and $15. That is how much money she can pay for the in-line skates.

$49 ← Money Samantha first had
+ $20 ← Present from grandparents
+ $15 ← Money set aside for brother's birthday
$84 ← Money Samantha can pay for in-line skates

Adapting Performance-Based Assessments for Students with Disabilities

As we have discussed, using performance-based assessments has many potential benefits for students with special needs. Nonetheless, you may still need to adapt performance-based tests for students with disabilities. For example, Gregory is a student with cerebral palsy in Mr. Repp's social studies class. Gregory has very little control over fine motor movements in his hands. As a result, he is unable to write or draw. Gregory will obviously need to have the drawing-to-scale map task adapted. One possible adaptation would be to have Gregory make an audiotape to accompany the map that would provide the Japanese visitors with a self-guided tour. Or consider Rhonda, a student with a learning disability who has difficulty expressing herself in writing. Rhonda is included in Ms. Johnson's class, which is writing letters to the editor as a way of practicing persuasive writing skills. As an adaptation, Ms. Johnson has Rhonda develop an oral editorial that is sent to the local public radio channel. In some cases, then, adaptations for performance-based tests can be made just as readily as adaptations for traditional tests.

Some students with special needs may have problems with performance-based tests that are more difficult to accommodate. For instance, students might have difficulty making the connection between school tasks and real-world tasks. You will need to teach these students directly how to make those connections. For example, Ms. Riley's class is learning to compute subtraction problems. As a performance-based test, Ms. Riley has her class compare the prices of various brands of the same products in the grocery store and compute the price differences using subtraction. Cleo, a student in the class with a mild cognitive disability, is unable to perform the task because he had never used subtraction as it applies to money or products in the grocery store. The next day in class, Ms. Riley includes examples of subtracting amounts of money in her daily instruction. She also includes story problems dealing with the subtraction of money, some of which involve grocery store products. This adaptation helps Cleo make the connection between money and the supermarket.

Students with special needs also lack important preskills that are necessary for problem solving. You need either to teach them these preskills or to allow them to bypass the preskills altogether in order to carry out your performance-based tasks. For example, Sam has a learning disability in math; he does not know basic math facts and as a result cannot get Ms. Riley's product comparisons correct. Ms. Riley allows him to perform the task with a calculator. She also requires that he spend 5 minutes per day using a computer-based math fact program until he learns basic math facts. Anna has visual disabilities; she has another student read her the prices of the brands and she writes them down.

For students with more severe disabilities, you may need to modify or scale down performance-based tasks by using the curriculum adaptation process described in Chapter 9. For example, Derek has severe cognitive disabilities and lacks basic math skills other than simple number identification. Ms. Riley has Derek participate in the same task as the other students but has him perform an easier step. She has Derek pick groups of products that students are to compare. This task is more consistent with Derek's IEP goal of being able to classify "like" objects, such as three kinds of cola or two types of bread.

Finally, students with special needs may have trouble meeting the problem-solving demands of performance-based tests. For example, Peter has attention deficits and approaches problems impulsively; he rushes to find an answer and fails

Do It!

Develop a performance-based assessment for the area of instruction in which you plan to teach. Design a scoring system and examples for levels of performance.

Connections

Review Chapters 8 and 9 for information on testing and teaching preskills.

Connections

Scaffolding (see Chapter 4) and learning strategies instruction (see Chapter 10) are good ways to support students as they learn to carry out performance-based tasks.

As an alternative to pencil-and-paper tests, performance-based assessments allow students to demonstrate their knowledge and skills through application in real-world contexts. What are some ways to adapt performance-based assessments for students with special needs?

to consider all the options. For Peter, performance-based tests are important because they give him the opportunity to learn critical problem-solving skills. Nonetheless, for students like Peter to succeed, performance-based tasks need to be modified and problem-solving skills need to be taught directly. For example, Mr. Kelsey's class is applying work they have done in computing areas and perimeters to the task of planning a garden. Before having students design their own gardens, Mr. Kelsey carefully demonstrates how he would design his. This demonstration is very helpful for students in the class, such as Peter, who are not natural problem solvers and need a model to guide them. Mr. Kelsey also scales down Peter's assignment, asking him to design only one section of a smaller garden.

As you can see, the use of performance-based tests with students with disabilities can be helpful, but it can also be problematic. For this reason, use performance-based tests in conjunction with other classroom-based and standardized tests.

How Can Portfolio Assessment Benefit Students with Special Needs?

Another promising type of evaluation currently in use is **portfolio assessment**. A portfolio is "a purposeful collection of student work that exhibits the student's efforts, progress, and achievement in one or more areas. The collection must include

Table 11.5 Examples of Portfolio Contents

Type of Portfolio	Sample Contents
Reading	Audiotape of oral reading of selected passages
	Original story grammar map
	Transcript of story telling
	Log of books read with personal reactions, summaries, vocabulary
	Representative assignments; responses to pre- and postreading questions
	Favorite performance
	Journal entries including self-evaluation
Writing	Scrapbook of representative writing samples
	Selected prewriting activities
	Illustrations/diagrams for one piece
	Log or journal of writing ideas, vocabulary, semantic maps, compositions, evaluations
	Conference notes, observation narratives
	Student-selected best performance
	Self-evaluation checklists

Cultural Awareness

Student-centered evaluation, a key component of portfolio assessment, is an important part of effective multicultural education. Student-centered evaluation strategies include self-evaluation questionnaires, interviews, student entries in journals and learning logs, and think alouds (Dean, Salend, & Taylor, 1994, p. 41).

Connections

The strategies discussed for scoring performance-based assessments also apply to evaluating student portfolios.

student participation in selecting contents, the criteria for selection, the criteria for judging merit, and evidence of student self-reflection" (Paulson, Paulson, & Meyer, 1991, p. 60).

A portfolio collection typically contains the observable evidence or products of performance assessment, evidence that may or may not reflect authentic tasks (Poteet et al., 1993). Portfolios include many different sources of information, including anecdotal records, interviews, work samples, and scored samples such as curriculum-based assessment probes. As an example, sources of information for language arts that can be placed into a portfolio are shown in Table 11.5.

Using Portfolios to Maximum Advantage

To use portfolios to maximum advantage, consider the following guidelines:

1. Developing a portfolio offers the student an opportunity to learn about learning. Therefore, the end product must contain information that shows that a student has engaged in self-reflection.

2. The portfolio is something that is done *by* the student, not *to* the student. Portfolio assessment offers a concrete way for students to learn to value their own work and, by extension, to value themselves as learners. Therefore, the student must be involved in selecting the pieces to be included.

3. The portfolio is separate and different from the student's cumulative folder. Scores and other cumulative folder information that are held in central depositories should be included in a portfolio only if they take on new meaning within the context of the other exhibits found there.

4. The portfolio must convey explicitly or implicitly the student's activities, for example, the rationale (purpose for forming the portfolio), intents (its goals), contents (the actual displays), standards (what is good and not-so-good performance), and judgments (what the contents reveal).

5. The portfolio may serve a different purpose during the year from the purpose it serves at the end of the year. Some material may be kept because it is instructional, such as partially finished work on problem areas. At the end of the year, however, the portfolio should contain only material that the student is willing to make public.

6. A portfolio may have multiple purposes, but these must not conflict. A student's personal goals and interests are reflected in his or her selection of materials, but information included may also reflect the interests of teachers, parents, or the district. One almost universal purpose of student portfolios is to show progress on the goals represented in the instructional program.

7. The portfolio should contain information that illustrates growth. There are many ways to demonstrate growth. The most obvious is by including a series of examples of actual school performance or other real-world performance-based activities that show how the student's skills have improved. Changes observed on interest inventories, on records of outside activities such as reading, or on attitude measures are other ways to illustrate a student's growth.

8. Finally, many of the skills and techniques that are involved in producing effective portfolios do not just happen by themselves. By way of support, students need models of portfolios as well as examples of how others develop and reflect upon portfolios. (Paulson et al., 1991, pp. 61–62)

Using Portfolios with Students with Special Needs

Portfolios can be very helpful for teachers working with students with disabilities. Portfolios can assist teachers in evaluating student progress and guiding instruction. For example, Ms. Pohl is interested in finding out whether the extra math practice sheets she is sending home with Robert are improving his scores on weekly math computation tests. She consults Robert's portfolio and finds that his performance has improved quite a bit over the last 2 months. Ms. Pohl tells Robert's parents of his progress. They agree to continue the extra practice for at least another month.

Portfolios also emphasize student products rather than tests and test scores. This emphasis benefits students with special needs, many of whom are poor test takers. It may also highlight student strengths better than traditional tests, which tend to have a narrow academic focus. For example, Leshonn's teacher uses portfolios to evaluate her social studies students. Leshonn has problems in reading and writing but has good artistic ability and excellent oral language skills. During the last marking period, his class studied the growth of suburban areas after World War II. Leshonn designed a scale model of Levittown, one of the first planned communities. He also developed a tape-recorded explanation to go with the model that explained the key features of the community. His performance on these projects was excellent and enabled him to raise his overall grade for the class, as his scores on the two tests given during the marking period were low.

Finally, a key component of portfolio assessments is student self-evaluation. Students with special needs, who are often described as not being involved in their own learning, can benefit greatly from self-evaluations. For example, students might

Technology Notes

Computer-Based Portfolios

As we have discussed in this chapter, portfolios can be an effective means of evaluating the performance of your students. Traditionally, the contents of students' portfolios have been confined mainly to pencil-and-paper products. However, organizing and accessing these products can be overwhelming, even for the most organized teachers. Grady (1996) has developed a computer-based portfolio program that makes portfolios more efficient and accessible. The program is called the *Grady Profile Portfolio Assessment* (Aurbach & Associates, 1991). The Grady Profile allows the user to build portfolios using "stacks" of electronic cards that hold a variety of information. For example, separate cards store sound, graphic, and video exhibits. The Grady Profile also allows users to tailor their own evaluation criteria and create and print reports (Grady, 1996, p. 247).

An example display of a card designed to catalog oral information is shown above. Notice that this particular card presents information on student performance in oral reading. Using this card, a teacher, parent, or student can listen to an oral reading sample, examine an evaluation of the sample based on a

complete a self-assessment after they have finished a unit of instruction. This evaluation can then become a part of the student's portfolio (Einhorn et al., 1991).

The capabilities of portfolio assessment can be greatly expanded through the use of technology. A number of different ways that you can incorporate technology into your portfolio-assessment program are shown in the Technology Notes feature.

You may have to make adaptations when using portfolios with students with special needs, particularly in selecting and evaluating portfolio pieces. For example, Jerome was asked to select an example of his "best" work in written expression for his portfolio. However, he was uncertain what "best" work meant: Was it a paper that he tried his hardest on? Was it a paper that was the hardest to write? Or was it one that he or his teacher liked best? Because he did not know, Jerome simply selected one paper at random. Similarly, when LaShonda was asked to evaluate her efforts to solve a word problem in math, all she could come up with was whether or not she had the correct answer. You need to teach students such as Jerome and LaShonda how to select and evaluate portfolio pieces.

Cole, Struyk, Kinder, Sheehan, and Kish (1997) suggest teaching students the **RICE** strategy to help them become meaningfully involved in the portfolio process.

teacher-designed rubric, and then read teacher and/or student reflections on the performance. Student progress can be readily appraised by accessing samples of oral reading behavior taken over a period of time.

An example of a card designed to store student writing performance is shown next. In this card, a graphic exhibit of the student's writing was created by scanning a writing sample using a scanner that plugs into the computer. As with the oral reading sample, a teacher evaluation of the sample is presented using a writing rubric. Stories written throughout the year can be accessed easily and compared to measure progress.

The Grady Profile is also capable of storing and displaying videotapes of students' work. For example, as part of an ecology unit, students could videorecord an interview with a local recycling company executive and then transfer the video to a video card. Students could record future interviews to see how their interviewing techniques had improved. Finally, electronic portfolios such as the one shown here can facilitate parent–teacher and teacher–student communication. You can show parents multimedia displays of their child's performance in class during parent conferences. In addition, electronic portfolios can motivate students who say they cannot do something by showing them tapes that illustrate how much they have improved.

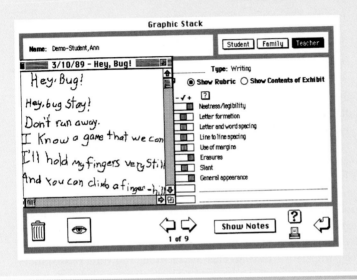

R—RATIONALE

Why are you keeping this portfolio? What do you want to chronicle? What is the purpose of the portfolio?

I—IDENTIFY GOALS

What are the specific things that you want to work on?
Standards: How will you know when you have reached your goal? What will you look for in the samples in your portfolio? Are there any standards that are currently being used that you might apply or adapt?

C—CONTENTS

What will you include in your portfolio to show your progress toward your goal (work samples, tests, etc.)? Will you include works in progress or only your best work? Will you include only specific class assignments or will you include "authentic" samples? Will you include self-evaluations of your samples? Will you note conditions in which the sample was collected—cooperative group, independent, paired project, etc.? Will you include evaluations by others—peers, teacher? Will you graph your own progress toward your goal?

E—EVALUATION

How frequently will you evaluate your portfolio? With whom will you evaluate your portfolio—pair, cooperative group, teacher? How will you show the relationship of the materials in your portfolio? (p. 267).

Finally, although portfolios are potentially valuable evaluation tools, they are also relatively new tools; in many cases, clear guidelines for selecting and scoring portfolio contents have yet to be developed (Salvia & Ysseldyke, 1995). Therefore, if you are using portfolios to evaluate the progress of students with special needs, such as whether they are meeting their IEP objectives, use them as a supplement, not as an alternative, to other assessment and evaluation procedures such as testing, grading, and curriculum-based assessments.

Summary

As a teacher, you have a number of tools at your disposal for evaluating your students' progress, including tests, report card grades, performance-based assessments, and portfolios. Although each of these evaluation methods can also help you measure the progress of students with special needs included in your class, they may need to be adapted to ensure that the evaluation information measures the students' skill levels or content knowledge, not their disabilities or other special needs.

Testing adaptations can be made before testing, during testing, and after testing, when tests are graded. Adaptations before the test include study guides, practice tests, tutoring, teaching test-taking skills and strategies, and modifying test construction. During the test, you can allow alternative forms of response, alternative means of response, alternative testing sites, extra time, and direct assistance. Adaptations after the test involve grading tests and include changing letter or number grades, using alternatives to letter and number grades, and changing the criteria upon which grades are based.

Adaptations in report card grades involve changing the grading criteria, making changes to letter and number grades, and using alternatives to letter and number grades. Ways of changing grading criteria include varying grading weights, modifying curricular expectations, using grading contracts and modified course syllabi, and grading on the basis of improvement. Letter and number grades can be changed by supplementing them with other ways of evaluating and reporting student progress, such as written comments, daily activity logs, and recording daily observations. Alternatives to letter and number grades include pass/fail grades, credit/no credit systems, and competency checklists.

Performance-based assessments measure learning processes rather than focusing exclusively on learning products and they frequently involve authentic, or real-world, tasks. They can be helpful in evaluating the performance of students with special needs because they do not rely exclusively on formats that create problems for students with disabilities. These assessments are not subject to the same time constraints as traditional tests, often a problem for students with special needs, and they also help students see the connection between school work and real-world tasks. Performance-based assessments can be developed, administered, and scored according to several guidelines, such as choosing learning outcomes not covered by your current testing programs, designing tasks within meaningful contexts, clarifying task expectations by providing scoring standards and models of excellence, making testing conditions authentic, and designing a scoring system based on what is most important for effective performance. Performance-based tests may need to be adapted for students with special needs by scaling down the task, allowing students to bypass preskills, and teaching problem solving directly using performance-based tasks.

Portfolio assessment can also benefit students with special needs. Portfolios are collections of student work that exhibit student efforts and achievements. Portfolios typically contain the observable evidence or products of performance assessment, such as anecdotal records, interviews, work samples, and scored samples. Necessary features of portfolios include student participation in collecting the contents, criteria for judging merit, and evidence of student self-reflection. Portfolios can benefit students with special needs because they de-emphasize traditional tests and teach students critical self-evaluation skills. However, students with special needs may need to be taught how to select and evaluate their portfolio pieces.

Applications in Teaching Practice

Adapting Evaluations for Students with Special Needs

Eugene, Tara, and Jamie are students in your fourth-grade class. Eugene has been identified as having a specific learning disability. He has good study skills, but his problems in reading and written expression place him at a disadvantage when he takes tests. Failure on tests has increased his test anxiety; he often misses items he knows because when he is anxious during a test he tends to get careless.

Tara has a learning disability and receives intensive reading instruction in the resource room. Her short-term objectives for this marking period include reading a first-grade literature book at a rate of 20 words correct per minute with four or fewer errors per minute and discerning who the main character of the story is, what the main problem in the story is, and how the problem is solved.

Jamie is a student with mild cognitive disabilities. You are about to start a unit on adding and subtracting fractions. The IEP objective for Jamie is to identify the fractions $\frac{1}{4}$, $\frac{1}{3}$, and $\frac{1}{2}$.

Questions

1. What tests will you be giving in this class?
2. For one of these tests, what adaptations might you need to make for Eugene before testing? In constructing the test? In administering the test? In grading the test?
3. At the end of the marking period, should you give Tara a grade in reading? Why or why not? Assuming that Tara met her short-term objectives in reading, what do you think her grade for the marking period should be? Should her grade be adapted in any way?
4. Describe a performance-based test that you could use to measure Jamie's knowledge of her target fractions. How would you score this test? How could you use portfolio assessment to measure Jamie's progress on this unit?

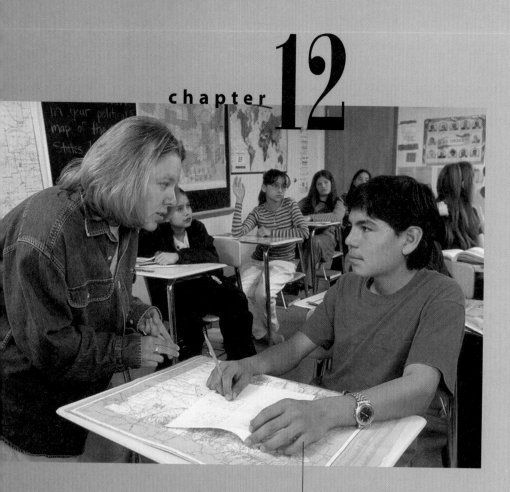

chapter 12

Responding to Student Behavior

1. Outline strategies for promoting positive behavior and preventing misbehavior with groups of students, including students with special needs.

2. Explain simple techniques for responding to individual student misbehavior.

3. Outline systematic approaches for increasing students' positive behaviors and decreasing their negative behaviors when simple techniques are not enough.

4. Identify how to help students manage their own behavior.

5. Describe a problem-solving approach for deciding how to respond to chronic, inappropriate individual student behavior.

Joseph, a junior with a learning disability, comes late to his applied algebra class at least twice each week. He seldom participates in class discussions, and he does not ask questions. Unless Mrs. Akers asks him not to, Joseph sits with his head down on his desk. When discussing Joseph with the special education teacher, Mrs. Akers describes his demeanor as sullen. Mrs. Akers has been teaching high school math for many years, and she believes that students have the responsibility to be interested in the subject, to attend class, and to participate. She knows that Joseph is heading toward a failing grade for this grading period, even though she thinks he could do the work with a little more effort. What is Joseph's responsibility for his learning? What is Mrs. Akers's responsibility for making instruction appealing to students like Joseph? What strategies could help Joseph meet Mrs. Akers's class expectations for him?

Darryl has a moderate cognitive disability. Every time he enters the classroom he says loudly, "I'm ba-ack," even if he has only been gone for a moment. Although he is in sixth grade, he frequently sucks his thumb and rocks in his chair. When he needs help, he calls out, "Teacher, Teacher," regardless of what is happening in the classroom at that moment. If assistance is not immediate, he continues to call out—with increasing volume. Darryl's language arts teacher, Mr. Lowell, is losing patience with these "babyish" behaviors. He believes that Darryl is learning many social skills through the small-group work the class does, and he knows Darryl's paraprofessional is ensuring that he is learning basic prereading skills. Mr. Lowell is most concerned about the impact of Darryl's behaviors on the class. Despite class discussions about how best to respond to Darryl's outbursts, several students continue to snicker when Darryl calls out, which often leads to other behavior problems. How could Mr. Lowell address both Darryl's inappropriate classroom behaviors and the class' response to them?

Marysha is extremely shy. Although her hearing impairment is moderate and she is an excellent speech reader, she rarely volunteers information in class. If she has a question about an assignment, she sits quietly until Mr. Davis notices her and asks what she needs. She usually stands alone on the playground, and in groups she agrees with anything classmates wish to do. Her acquiescence sometimes causes problems, as it did when she and two other students decided to sneak back to their classroom during recess without adult supervision. The incident was a minor one, but Mr. Davis is concerned about Marysha's gullibility; he worries that in the future she might be easily enticed by others to try alcohol or drugs or to join a gang. Why might Marysha be so reluctant to participate in interactions with her teachers and peers? What skills could Marysha learn to help her make decisions about her activities with her peers?

All teachers spend a portion of their time and energy monitoring student behavior and addressing inappropriate behavior. Whether you teach 5-year-olds in a kindergarten class or 17-year-olds in junior English, how you respond to student behavior will significantly affect students' learning. Further, the public has a high degree of interest in and continuing concern about discipline in U.S. classrooms. For example, in the 1996 Gallup poll of the public's attitudes toward schools, discipline was the concern cited second most often (after drug use).

To begin this discussion about classroom discipline, we present some basic understandings that will provide a context in which you should consider managing student behavior. First, it is essential to recognize that the word **discipline** has as its root the word *disciple*, or the follower of a teacher. Even though in current use discipline is often associated with obedience, discipline is really mostly about learning. It is a means to ensure that students have maximum opportunity to learn from their teachers. Discipline is never an end in and of itself. As you learn about approaches for increasing classroom discipline in this chapter, you will be finding ways to enhance your students' learning.

Second, some professionals view discipline and classroom management as negative, implying that these subjects are about teacher control and power. That view fails to take into account the very real dilemma teachers face in attempting to keep a class full of students interested in learning in a way that is safe and respectful of all students. If you are effective in classroom management, you will be providing conditions that enable your students to succeed (Smith & Mirsa, 1992). Rather than managing student behavior for your convenience or to command compliance, you will be guiding students in ways that contribute to their own best interests.

Third, teacher beliefs about discipline are strongly culturally based, and some evidence suggests that teachers are far more likely to refer students for discipline problems when they are from a culture other than the teacher's (Bullara, 1993). All teachers have an obligation to monitor their behavior to ensure that their responses are not based on racial bias or cultural ignorance. Further, they have a responsibility to recognize when their expectations are inconsistent with a student's culture. For example, a teacher recently described a dilemma his school faced in working with students from Somalia. The students were spitting, a clear violation of school rules. However, school professionals soon learned that the students were not misbehaving. Part of their religious custom called for complete fasting, including not swallowing their own saliva. Spitting, acceptable in their homeland, was perceived as misbehavior in a U.S. school.

Teachers who actively, carefully, and creatively apply approaches for classroom management and who monitor the success of their strategies, adapting them as needed, can have a positive influence on student learning (Bauer & Sapona, 1991; Walker & Shea, 1995). Many issues are beyond a teacher's control—you do not have the power to increase the financial support available to schools, nor can you remove the public pressures that surround many curriculum and school reform initiatives. However, you can affect and are ultimately accountable for the learning of your students. Using effective classroom management strategies will increase their learning by creating a positive classroom environment. Further, teachers who use effective management strategies will have far less need to change inappropriate student behavior.

In the sections that follow, you will learn procedures for group behavior management, strategies for responding to individual student behaviors, and a problem-solving approach for changing student behavior. Together, these techniques will provide you with a foundation for effective classroom management.

How Can You Prevent Discipline Problems?

Strategies for responding to disruptive student behavior and promoting positive academic and social behavior are discussed later in this chapter. The best topic with which to begin a discussion of discipline issues is prevention (Carpenter & McKee-Higgins, 1996; Doyle, 1990). In many cases, you will make the difference between having a classroom in which the stress level is high and "keeping control" is a constant struggle or having a classroom in which student learning is supported by the environment and behavior problems are rare. You can make this difference by creating an instructional environment conducive to learning and using effective communication to foster a positive classroom climate.

Instructional Environments Conducive to Learning

In Chapter 4, you learned that many factors contribute to creating an instructional environment that fosters student learning. Many of these same factors also promote appropriate classroom behavior. For example, you found out that teachers need to set clear expectations in their classroom through rules that students understand and follow (Bullara, 1993). You need only a few rules, but they should be specific, worded positively, posted and discussed with students early in the school year, and rehearsed while students learn them. Rules should also be monitored and changed as needed. Figure 12.1 on page 418 contains sample rules for students at the elementary level.

Another key factor related to the instructional environment and discipline is establishing clear classroom routines. These routines include those for beginning the school day or class period, those for transitioning from one activity to another, those for moving about in the classroom, and those for ending the school day or class period. Students who have routines are less likely to misbehave because they can meet classroom expectations for behavior.

Effective Classroom Communication

Teachers who treat their students with respect and trust are more successful in creating positive classroom environments in which fewer behavior problems occur (Jones, 1996). Communication between teacher and students is integral to fostering this trust and respect. However, teacher–student communication is a complex matter, and problems often arise. Sometimes, teachers provide students with too much

Do It!

Refer to Chapters 4, 9, and 10. Make a list of six key principles of effective instruction that also help reduce classroom behavior problems.

Figure 12.1 **Examples of Classroom Rules and Routines**

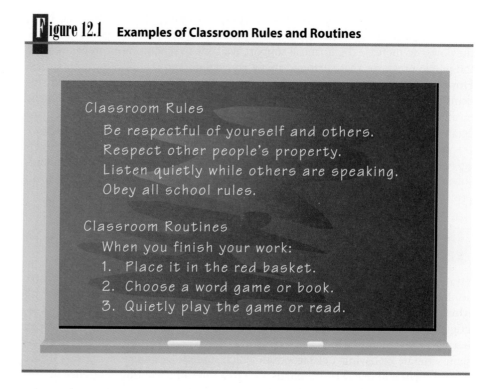

Classroom Rules
  Be respectful of yourself and others.
  Respect other people's property.
  Listen quietly while others are speaking.
  Obey all school rules.

Classroom Routines
  When you finish your work:
  1. Place it in the red basket.
  2. Choose a word game or book.
  3. Quietly play the game or read.

Cultural Awareness

Students who have limited English proficiency can be inadvertently overlooked in teacher–student communication because of their language difficulties and possible reluctance to interact. Misunderstandings are also more likely. You have the responsibility of fostering positive communication with this group of students.

information or information that is not clear. Students become confused when information is not relevant to the instruction being delivered. And sometimes, teachers give one message with words but convey another message with their tone of voice or nonverbal behaviors. The following communication factors affect classroom management (Bauer & Sapona, 1991):

1. The complexity and level of abstraction of the message
2. Students' background knowledge and experience to understand the content of the message
3. Students' understanding of classroom interactions and routines
4. Teacher and student awareness of nonverbal communication
5. Cognitive organization teachers provide before launching into specific content
6. The expectation that teachers and students listen to one another

Teacher–pupil interactions that affect learning and behavior include both formal interactions that are part of instruction and informal interactions in the classroom. One way to gain a sense of students' perceptions of your communication in class is to ask them.

The overall quality of your communication with your students is built in numerous small ways. For example, finding time each week to speak privately with students lets them know that you care about them as individuals. Asking older students sincere questions about their friends, out-of-school activities, or part-time jobs also conveys that you care. Taking the time to write positive comments on papers shows students that you appreciate their strengths and are not focusing only on their needs. When you encourage each student to achieve his or her own potential without continually comparing students to one another, you are communicating the idea that each class member has a valuable contribution to make. Teachers who fail to take these small steps toward positive communication with students, or who publicly embarrass a student or punish a group for the behavior of a few, soon create a negative instructional environment that thwarts appropriate behavior and effective learning.

Effective Teaching Methods

One other critical strategy for preventing behavior problems is to provide instruction that is relevant, interesting, and active. Recall from Chapters 9 and 10, for example, how learning is enhanced through the use of clear and systematic instructional approaches and learning strategies that actively engage students in their learning. We remind you of this information because effective instruction plays a critical role in classroom behavior management. Students who are given boring or outdated materials, who are asked to complete dozens of worksheets with little instructional value, and who have few opportunities to create their own learning through projects or activities are likely to resort to misbehavior.

Not all behavior problems can be prevented. Some will occur despite your best efforts to prevent them. Before you decide that the student is the one who has to change to resolve the behavior problem, remember to examine how your expectations, communication, teaching behavior, and other factors you control might be part of the problem.

How Can You Promote Positive Group Behavior?

In effective classrooms, teachers and students respect each other and students are busily engaged in learning. Students attend to their work, they interact with each other politely and without verbal or physical fighting, and they ignore the occasional misbehavior of classmates instead of encouraging it. In many classrooms, you can promote positive behaviors such as these by using behavior management strategies that are designed specifically for the whole class (Nelson, 1996). For example, all students might participate in earning privileges or rewards, as individuals or as members of cooperative learning groups. The following sections describe effective whole-group strategies such as the Good Behavior Game, other peer-mediated approaches to behavior management, and token economies.

The Good Behavior Game

The **Good Behavior Game** has long been regarded as a powerful strategy for reducing disruptive behaviors in classrooms (Barrish, Saunders, & Wolf, 1969). Even though it was first described nearly three decades ago, it still has value for today's classrooms. These are the procedures used in the game:

1. Explain to students that they will be divided into two teams, one seated on each side of the classroom. These teams will compete with each other to have the least number of negative behaviors during a class period or school day. The game can also be played so that students compete to have the greatest number of positive behaviors, and more than two teams can be used.

Cultural Awareness

Another type of diversity to monitor in your interactions with students is gender. You need to ensure that you interact with boys and girls equitably and that you respond to their behavior needs without bias.

FYI

The Good Behavior Game is a group behavior management technique in which student teams compete to display appropriate classroom behavior.

2. Describe the target behaviors for students. These behaviors should be specific. For example, out-of-seat behavior might be included, along with talking out during large-group instruction or making disruptive noises (for example, loud burps, audible sighs). Examples of positive behaviors might include promptly putting away materials when requested and remembering to place completed work in the teacher's "IN" basket. Examples and nonexamples of the behaviors should be given to ensure that all students understand expectations. Many minor misbehaviors could be targeted for this game, but you should select only two or three that are particularly relevant to your classroom. If you select too many behaviors, the game is less likely to be effective because students will have difficulty remembering the targeted behaviors and you will have difficulty monitoring them. Similarly, select only a limited number of positive behaviors that you are encouraging students to display.

3. Set a time period each day in which the game will be played. You might schedule it during language arts instruction or during the first half of the class period in a secondary setting.

4. Let students know that each time you notice one of the targeted behaviors being displayed, you will tell the person who has misbehaved and also tally a point against that person's team. In the positive version, appropriate behaviors noted are tallied.

5. At the end of each day, tally the points and announce which team won (least number of points or most number of points, depending on the variation of the game used).

WWW Resources

At <http://www.us.nizkor.org/~axis/inbehrec.html> you can access information about behavior issues related to inclusive education.

6. You might also wish to set an "all win" condition. For example, if both teams have fewer than 5 points or, positively, more than 10 points, a tie might be declared.

7. The winning team (or both teams) receives a reward. The reward should be based on a list of student preferences, keeping in mind feasibility. As explained later in this chapter, the amount of the reward and the type of reward should be based on student needs.

To maintain student interest in the Good Behavior Game, you could vary the rewards earned, change the instructional activity or time of day during which the game is played, or permit students to select their own teams. You might also find that it is most effective to save this approach for periods of the school year that are stressful for students, such as the late November through late December holiday time with its many classroom interruptions, or the 3 weeks prior to spring break or the close of the school year. This type of game approach could be very effective for Darryl, the student with a moderate cognitive disability you met at the beginning of the chapter. Darryl's teacher could identify ignoring Darryl's occasional talking out as a positive behavior for the class. By doing this, the class would be learning that it is not helpful to encourage Darryl's talking out and Darryl would not be inadvertently rewarded for this inappropriate classroom behavior. Of course, this program would need to be accompanied by additional instruction in how to interact appropriately.

One problem that can occur with the Good Behavior Game is when one student deliberately misbehaves, causing his or her team to lose repeatedly. If this happens, it might be preferable to exclude the student from the game and/or to create an individual behavior management plan of the sort described later in this chapter. Part of the plan could include allowing the student to earn the privilege of playing the game with the rest of the class.

What group strategies can be used for managing student behavior? What student behaviors might have preceded this teacher's use of card game privileges as a reward?

Other Peer-Mediated Approaches

How you group students for instruction can also serve as a group behavior management technique. For example, if you have students work with a learning buddy or peer tutor, you can probably reduce the amount of misbehavior because students will be more actively engaged in their learning and will have the added responsibility of serving as a "teacher." Similarly, if you have students work in small instructional groups so that no one can earn a reward unless the group completes their work, students have a natural incentive for focusing on their learning activities and are less likely to misbehave. For a shy student like Marysha, introduced at the beginning of this chapter, peer-mediated instructional approaches can foster appropriate social interactions because they create the need to interact positively within a small-group, structured instructional environment. Peer-mediated instruction is also highly recommended as a strategy for promoting positive behavior for students from racially and culturally diverse backgrounds (Adams & Hamm, 1991; Haynes & Gebreyesus, 1992).

Connections

Chapter 13 provides more detailed information on peers teaching each other.

Token Economy

Another long-respected group behavior management procedure that might be effective in your classroom is a **token economy** (Kazdin, 1977). This strategy creates a system in which students earn "money" that they exchange for rewards. As in any economy, certain tasks have more or less value than others, and rewards have more or less cost. One form of token economy has students receive imaginary money that they record in checkbooks. When they purchase a privilege, the cost of it is subtracted from the balance.

Use the following steps to create a classroom token economy:

1. Identify the behaviors for which students will earn credit. You might select completing and turning in work, keeping hands to self, talking in a classroom voice, bringing to class all needed (and specified) learning supplies, returning homework, or exhibiting other behavior that can be clearly observed. A number of behaviors can be specified and posted in the classroom. Students can be involved in deciding what behaviors to include.

2. Decide on the classroom "currency." You could use points, punches on a card, X's on a recording sheet, poker chips or other tokens, play money, or any other system. In choosing a currency, keep in mind that you will need to award it and monitor its use. In large classrooms, efficiency in issuing and exchanging the currency can become critical.

Check Your Learning

What versions of a token economy would be most effective for elementary school students? For middle school or junior high students? For high school students?

3. Assign a value to each target behavior. Simple behaviors would have a lower value. More difficult behaviors would have a higher value. In a very simple system, you would assign the same value (for example, one point) for each target behavior on a daily basis.

4. Decide on the privileges or rewards students will earn. Having variety in the possible "purchases" students can make will help maintain interest in the system. For older students, the list of options might include a "make your own homework assignment" privilege; for younger students, tokens might be redeemed for lunch with the teacher. It is important to include on the reward list at least one item that costs the minimum amount of currency a student might earn (for example, one point). This ensures that all students will have the opportunity to participate in the economy.

5. Assign purchase "prices" to the privileges and rewards. In general, if a reward is readily available and not limited in quantity, its purchase price should be lower. Items that are tangible (and perhaps literally cost more), limited in supply, or time-consuming should have a higher cost. One teacher had access to hundreds of sets of plastic beads; the beads became quite the rage in the classroom, but they were not very costly. However, lunch alone with the teacher was a high-priced privilege.

6. Explain the economy to students. As you have probably discerned, you can make an economy as simple or complex as you have the creativity to develop and your students have the ability to understand. It is often beneficial to demonstrate the economy with several examples to ensure that students understand it. When the economy is new, student participation should be carefully monitored to avoid a problem such as the one that occurred in Mr. Elliott's class when he used poker chips with young students. Mr. Elliott realized that he was running low on chips, and students had not purchased rewards. When he questioned the students, he learned that they thought the poker chips themselves were the reward!

7. Establish a systematic way for students to exchange their currency for privileges or rewards. In most classrooms, it is effective to allow students to use their currency once a week or once every 2 weeks on a particular day. By having a consistent time and a system for the exchange, you avoid a constant stream of student requests for privileges or rewards and the aggravation of the constant monitoring this would require.

How you establish your token economy will depend partly on the age of your students (Kaplan & Carter, 1995). For younger students, you may need to use tangible currency (for example, tokens, beads, play money). Older students are more capable of using points or other symbolic currencies. Likewise, younger students will need more opportunities to exchange their currency, whereas older students are more able to save their currency to earn more expensive privileges or rewards over a longer period of time.

Figure 12.2   Token Economy Reward Menu

Reward List*

Item	Points Needed
1. Five minutes of computer time	10
2. Five stickers	50
3. A cartoon pencil	75
4. Lunch in classroom with a friend	100
5. A book	125
6. Helping first graders in art for a specified time	150
7. Discount movie pass	150
8. Lunch at a restaurant with a teacher, principal, or other adult, and a friend	300

*Ten points can be earned each day.

Teachers are tremendously creative in adapting token economies to their students' needs and their own teaching styles (Anderson & Katsiyannis, 1997). The sample list of rewards from a token economy included in Figure 12.2 just begins to describe how many options exist. One teacher held an auction in her classroom every 2 weeks, offering items donated by local businesses or obtained at garage sales. Students bid on items using the currency they had earned. Another teacher wanted to encourage students to learn about real economies. She permitted students to borrow tokens from one another and to purchase items from one another using their currency. One student "sold" his designer pencils to classmates, with tokens as the currency of exchange.

To work effectively, a token economy should be carefully planned with flexibility for adjustment as the need arises. For example, you might need to change the reward list or the amount of currency required to obtain particular rewards. You should also keep in mind that token economies are best used when most or all of a class group need support for appropriate behaviors. Thus, you might use a token economy early in the school year, again right after the holiday break, and not again until the last month of school. During other periods, less comprehensive strategies may be adequate.

Do It!

With a classmate, create a token economy for a class of students at the level you plan to teach. What will you use for tokens? What will the rewards be? How many tokens will it take to obtain each reward? How will rewards be distributed?

What Are Some Simple and Effective Responses to Individual Behavior?

For some students, including students with special needs, the steps you take to create a positive and productive learning environment will not be sufficient to eliminate behavior problems, nor will group behavior management strategies always work. For some individuals, more specialized approaches are needed, and you will find it helpful to follow the steps of the INCLUDE model outlined in Chapter 4. However, before you decide to use specialized approaches in responding to a student's behavior, you can try a number of simpler strategies first. Teachers have long relied on this "principle of least intervention" in addressing student behavior needs. In this section, the strategies described include minimum interventions, such as "catch 'em being good," and techniques for managing students' surface behaviors.

Minimum Interventions

Teachers sometimes contribute unintentionally but significantly to student misbehavior. They do this by inadvertently bringing out negative student behaviors and by responding too strongly to minor misbehaviors, actions that sometimes cause the student to misbehave more. For example, when asked directly to begin work, a student might refuse. However, when given choices among which assignment to do first, the student might comply. Similarly, when reprimanded for using foul language in the classroom, some students will use the reprimand as a signal to continue the language to get further attention. Ignoring occasional inappropriate language might lessen the problem.

When working with students with special needs, it is essential to stay alert to how you might be contributing to a student's behaviors, either through your own responses to the behavior or through your classroom structure and lesson format. Here are four examples of very simple strategies teachers use to address minor student misbehavior.

Catch 'em being good.   A versatile and long-recognized strategy for reducing inappropriate student behavior and increasing appropriate behavior is called **"catch 'em being good."** When a student is behaving according to expectations, you acknowledge and reward the behavior. For example, if third grader Jeff enters the room and immediately begins his work, you might say to him, "I like the way you went right to your desk, Jeff. That's exactly what you're supposed to do!" This comment has the effect of rewarding Jeff's behavior. At the same time, it clearly lets other students know that going directly to one's seat is a behavior they should do, too. In a middle school social studies class, a teacher might privately say to a student who is chronically late, "I noticed you were at your seat with materials ready when the bell rang. Nice going." Although the privacy of the comment eliminates its potential positive impact on other students, it has the benefit of preventing student embarrassment.

Make low-demand requests first.   Sprague and Horner (1990) described a successful strategy for helping students with significant cognitive disabilities who have difficulty transitioning between activities such as coming in from recess or moving from one activity to another within the classroom. With this approach, make several low-demand and unrelated requests of the student prior to expecting the targeted request. For example, if it is time for Angel to put away his crayons to join a group reading a story, first get Angel's attention by saying something like, "Angel, give me five." Follow this with asking Angel to tell you his address (or another appropriate piece of personal information that he is learning). Next ask him to shake hands. Finally, request that Angel leave his coloring and join the reading group. Each of the requests is followed by verbal praise (for example, "Right," or "Good job").

Respond to apparent intent.   Another strategy for designing minimum interventions is based on the apparent **intent** of the behavior (Foster-Johnson & Dunlap, 1993). For example, a student begins pinching others every morning at around 11:00. Hypothesizing that the student is hungry, the teacher provides a snack for the student. Many other examples of this approach to using behavior intent to identify and change factors surrounding the student can be generated. For example, a student who becomes belligerent when an assignment is given may be signaling that he does not want to do the work or that the work is too difficult. Breaking the task into smaller parts or giving an assignment that begins with easier questions may decrease or eliminate the behavior. Likewise, a student who makes outrageously untrue statements in class (for example, "My father is going to marry Miss America"; "My job [at a fast-food restaurant] pays $50 an hour") may have the intent of getting adult attention. Chatting with the student for a moment before school or class, or creating individual time with an adult at school, may eliminate the need for further intervention. In all these cases, the teacher, acting as a sort of behavior detective, found that a simple modification effectively changed the behavior.

Use grouping strategies.   In many schools, students with disruptive behaviors tend to seek out others who misbehave as seatmates or groupmates. One group of researchers documented that a very simple strategy may significantly reduce misbehavior in such situations (Stainback, Stainback, Etscheidt, & Doud, 1986). They arranged for a highly disruptive student to be partnered in science class with students who were not disruptive. When this was done, the student's disruptive behaviors declined dramatically. When the student sat with disruptive peers, disruptive behaviors were far more frequent. The authors argue convincingly that grouping strategies are easily managed and should be part of any plan for addressing disruptive behavior. This strategy also has potential for a student like Marysha, one of the students described at the beginning of the chapter. Because she is extremely quiet, a teacher might decide to place her with a group of students who model positive social skills and who are unlikely to take advantage of her tendency to go along with whatever the group decides.

Managing Students' Surface Behaviors

Another relatively simple strategy for responding to student behaviors is the concept of managing their **surface behaviors.** Long and Newman (1971) long ago proposed that a teacher's initial response to student behavior often determines whether a problem situation will develop. If a teacher treats a minor misbehavior as a major infraction, the result might be a strong negative student response followed by a stronger teacher response until a serious behavior problem comes to exist. For example, if a student mutters something negative about an assignment under her breath and the teacher responds by stating in a stern voice, "What did you say?" the incident will escalate. The student might reply, "Nothing"; the teacher repeats the request, and the student eventually says something that gets her in trouble. Such interactions can be avoided if teachers are prepared to shift the focus of the interaction. Suggestions for heading off such problems include purposefully ignoring minor incidents and using humor to defuse tense classroom situations. Examples of initial response techniques are outlined in the Professional Edge on page 426.

These initial response techniques are most suited to minor misbehaviors and are unlikely to resolve serious discipline issues. Also, responding to students' surface behaviors can have the effect of increasing those behaviors. For example, if you use humor with a student and the student responds by talking back, then your humor may be increasing rather than defusing the inappropriate behavior. If this happens, switch to another approach or try a more systematic response to the behavior, such as the ones described in the next section.

Check Your Learning

What does it mean to respond to a student's apparent intent? How does this approach differ from traditional responses to student behavior?

Connections

Grouping strategies were introduced in Chapter 4. Their use to promote student social interactions is described in Chapter 13.

FYI

Surface behaviors are student reactions to classroom situations or events that might signal the beginning of a more serious discipline problem.

Strategies for Managing Students' Surface Behaviors

Knowing how to manage students' surface behaviors effectively can often head off a potentially tense classroom situation. The following strategies, most suited for responding to minor misbehaviors, can help you deal with problem behaviors as soon as they occur.

1. **Planned ignoring.** If a student's behavior is not likely to harm others or to spread to others, you might decide to ignore it, especially if the behavior signals another problem. For example, a student who repeatedly sighs loudly could be signaling a loss of interest; instead of responding to the sighing, recognize that student's need to change activities soon.

2. **Signal interference.** Communicate with students about surface behaviors by using nonverbal signals such as eye contact or gestures (for example, finger to lips to request silence).

3. **Proximity control.** Sometimes, simply moving closer to a misbehaving student resolves the problem.

4. **Interest boosting.** If a student appears to be losing interest in a task or activity, refocus attention by asking a specific question about the student's progress or by otherwise paying specific attention to the student's work.

5. **Tension reduction through humor.** For some minor misbehavior, your best response might be humor. For example, a student frustrated with an assignment tossed a textbook into the trashcan. Instead of scolding or lecturing, the teacher ex-claimed, "Two points!" and then went to the student to assist with the assignment.

6. **Hurdle help.** For some students, beginning an assignment can be overwhelming. As a result, they refuse to start working or they misbehave to avoid the work. You can help them begin and avoid a behavior issue by assisting with the first example, asking questions to facilitate their thinking, or prompting them to follow steps.

7. **Support from routine.** Creating more structure in the classroom can avert discipline problems. For example, having Rhonda begin each day by hanging up her coat, going to her seat, and coloring the picture you have placed on her desk might help her avoid being disruptive.

8. **Removing seductive objects.** When students bring radios, toys, or other distracting items to school, including dangerous objects, teachers should usually hold them for "safe-keeping." Other objects in the classroom environment can also become a focus for misbehavior and should be hidden. For example, if you have costumes at school for the class play, keep them in a closet; if you set up an intriguing science experiment, cover the materials until it is time to use them.

SOURCE: Adapted from "Managing Surface Behavior of Children in School" by N. J. Long & R. G. Newman, 1971, in N. J. Long, W. C. Morse, & R. G. Newman (Eds.), *Conflict in the Classroom: The Education of Children with Problems* (2nd ed.), 442–452. Belmont, CA: Wadsworth.

How Can You Respond to Individual Student Behavior When Simple Approaches Are Not Enough?

In many instances, students' behavior problems may need a more long-term and systematic intervention; that is, you may need to increase the desirable behavior a student displays or decrease the undesirable behavior, and a single conversation with the student or your casual or sporadic attention to the problem is not enough to address it. Although the principles for responding to student behavior are the same whether you are using simple or more systematic interventions, the latter responses are usually carried out across time in a consistent manner as part of a behavior intervention plan resulting from problem solving (Tobin, Sugai, & Colvin, 1996). The former, simple interventions, are used informally and occasionally.

Increasing Desirable Behaviors

All students, even the most challenging, have some appropriate behaviors you would like to increase. The primary strategy for increasing appropriate behavior is called **reinforcement.** Reinforcement is any response or consequence that increases a behavior (Walker & Shea, 1995). It is important for you to realize that reinforcement can increase negative as well as positive behaviors. For example, when a teacher puts a sticker on a student chart because the student completed his assignment without calling out for unneeded help, the student is more likely in the future to continue to work independently. However, when a teacher says to a student who is wandering around the classroom, "Sit down!" the student is also more likely in the future to wander again. In both instances, reinforcement was applied. In the first case, it rewarded a desirable behavior; in the second, it rewarded an undesirable behavior.

Positive and negative reinforcement.   Any time you respond to a behavior with a consequence that makes it more likely for the behavior to occur again, you are using **positive reinforcement** (Gardner et al., 1994). When you reward a student for appropriate behavior and that behavior increases, it is an example of positive reinforcement. Specifically, if you tell a student that after she completes five math problems she may use the classroom computer and she completes all of the problems, you are reinforcing math problem completion through the computer rewards.

Negative reinforcement operates somewhat differently. Suppose you set up a system with your freshman English students whereby they must have their homework signed each night by their parents until they have brought it back to school on time at least 9 out of 10 times. Because students see having homework signed by parents as an undesirable consequence, they will increase their promptness in turning in homework to avoid the consequence. Any increase in behavior to avoid a consequence is the result of **negative reinforcement** (Cipani, 1995). Although negative reinforcement can be effective, positive reinforcement should usually be tried first since it is preferable to have students working toward a positive outcome rather than under the threat or perception of a negative consequence.

Some professionals object to using positive reinforcement with students because they fear it teaches students that they are entitled to a payoff for appropriate behavior. They contend that students should complete their schoolwork and behave appropriately because these are the right things to do. This discussion is often addressed as one of external versus internal motivation (Cameron & Pierce, 1994). Although it certainly would be preferable for all students to learn and behave appropriately because of internal motivation and without the need for external rewards, some students who struggle to learn and behave as expected are simply not likely to do so. These students may respond in school because of internal motivation only when they are extremely interested in a subject or topic, or when they experience repeated success over an extended period of time.

Types of reinforcers.   For positive reinforcers to be used for students with special needs, keep these considerations in mind. First, recognize that many different types of reinforcers can be used.

WWW Resources

At <http://www.hood.edu/ seri/serihome.html>, the homepage for Special Education Resources on the Internet, you can access a wealth of information about disabilities, including information on specific behavior disorders such as depression and conduct disorders.

1. **Social reinforcers** are various types of positive interactions that a teacher, parent, or peer can give students for appropriate behavior and that increase the behavior. These reinforcers might include a positive phone call home to parents, a pat on the back or a hug, verbal praise, or selection as Citizen of the Month. Social reinforcers, especially clear and specific verbal praise, should always be tried before other positive reinforcers since they are the most natural type of reward in a school environment. If you find it necessary to employ other types of rewards, they should be used only in conjunction with social reinforcers since your long-term goal should always be to have students respond to rewards that occur naturally in their classroom environment.

2. **Activity reinforcers** involve activities such as playing games, having extra recess, helping a teacher in another class, and participating in other coveted individual or group pastimes. Generally, activities that directly relate to a student's educational goals (for example, practicing math skills on the computer) are preferable to those that are solely recreational (for example, playing a noneducational computer game).

3. **Tangible reinforcers** are prizes or other objects students can earn as symbols of achievement and that students want to obtain. A student who is earning baseball cards for completing assignments is receiving a tangible reinforcer. Stickers on papers is another example of this type of reinforcer. Tangible rewards can often be naturally integrated into classroom activities. For example, a student can earn the rocket pieces and household chemicals needed to create a highly interesting science experiment not offered to other students. However, make sure that the amount of the tangible reinforcer is appropriate for the amount of positive behavior required. Students earning the science materials just mentioned are expected to display appropriate behaviors over a lengthy period of time, not just for an afternoon. Conversely, if the tangible reinforcer is a scented sticker, perhaps an afternoon of appropriate behavior is the right amount for the reward being given.

Check Your Learning

What are the four different types of reinforcers? What is an example of each? How should you decide which type of reinforcer to use?

4. **Primary reinforcers** are food or other items related to human needs that a student finds rewarding. They are much more basic than secondary reinforcers, which include social reinforcers, activity reinforcers, and tangible reinforcers. Primary reinforcers used in schools often are edible and might include a piece of candy, a soft drink, or a piece of fruit. Although you might occasionally employ primary reinforcers as a special treat, generally they should be used only if a student is incapable of understanding more natural rewards, or if other types of rewards are not effective. This is important for two reasons. First, the potential negative impact of food reinforcers on student health is a concern. Second, food reinforcers are not a natural part of the school learning process. In school, students are expected to work to learn; to prepare for adulthood; or more immediately for some, to earn teacher praise or a grade; candy is not a routine part of the learning environment. If you plan to use primary reinforcers such as food, check with a school administrator to find out about local policies governing their use. Also check with parents, both for permission and about a student's possible food allergies. You should also keep in mind nutritional issues.

Effective use of positive reinforcers.   In addition to understanding that there are different types of positive reinforcers, you need to know some principles for using them effectively (McIntyre, 1992). These include the following:

1. **Make sure that the positive reinforcers are clear and specific and that students understand the relationship between their behavior and rewards.** The re-

wards students earn need to be specific and not otherwise available. For example, time working on the computer is not precise enough. If it is a reward, the amount of computer time for the specific behavior displayed should be clarified. Clarity and specificity are especially important when you use verbal praise. Saying to a student, "Good job!" is far less effective than saying, "Good job! You asked three other students for help before you asked me." The former praise is vague; the latter praise explicitly states what behavior is being rewarded.

2. **Vary how much and how often you reward students.** If a student has very little positive behavior, you may reward it heavily at first just to increase it. As the student learns to use the appropriate behavior more readily, you should decrease the amount of reward and the intensity of it. For example, if you were first rewarding a student with free-choice computer time for every two assignments completed, you might gradually change the reward so that the student must complete four assignments—and get at least 90 percent on each—in order to use the computer to practice math skills. Another way to vary rewards is to enlist parent assistance. For example, Donna's mother might agree to provide a special treat when the teacher sends a note home indicating that Donna completed her independent work within a specified time. The only caution in asking parents for their help is to be sure that the parents will provide the reward agreed upon, and that they will withhold it if their child has not behaved according to expectations.

3. **Make sure the student desires the rewards selected.** If you propose to make a positive phone call home when a student participates in group work but the student does not care what his or her parent thinks, your reward is unlikely to work. Instead, the student may be far more motivated by getting to choose three homework problems *not* to do. A sample list of rewards favored by some students is included in Figure 12.3 on page 430. You can determine your students' preferences by asking them what types of rewards they like or having them rank their preferences from a list of rewards you provide.

Related to the concept of reward desirability is that of **satiation.** Simply stated, a student who receives the same reward over a period of time may no longer find it rewarding (Schloss & Smith, 1994). If 5 minutes of free time is given repeatedly, after a while the student may come to expect the free time and not work to receive it. When this happens, it is important to change the reward. You can often avoid the problem of satiation by using a **reinforcement menu.** A reinforcement menu is a list of rewards from which students may choose. The menu can be posted in the classroom, or students can keep individual lists. The list could be similar to the reward list included in Figure 12.3 but it would probably have fewer items at one time, and some of the rewards might be reserved for extraordinary performance.

Decreasing Undesirable Behaviors

Most teachers find that students with special needs have some inappropriate classroom behaviors that need to be decreased. These might include aggressive behaviors such as calling classmates names or poking, pinching, or hitting others; verbal outbursts such as calling out answers, swearing, or making nonsense statements during large-group instruction; or other behaviors such as fleeing the classroom when feeling stressed, copying others' work, or refusing to work. Just as there are strategies to increase desirable behaviors, there are specific strategies you can use to decrease undesirable behaviors.

What individual strategies can you use in responding to individual behavior? How can teacher feedback strengthen positive behavior? How will you find out what types of rewards your students will respond to?

Do It!

Ask experienced teachers about their views on using rewards with students. What do they believe? Do the teachers' beliefs about using rewards differ?

Figure 12.3 Sample Rewards Suggested by Students

- Working with a friend in the hall
- Collecting the lunch money
- Taking attendance
- Taking the attendance cards to the office
- Duplicating and collating papers
- Early dismissal
- Writing something and photo-copying it
- Sitting at the teacher's desk to work
- Viewing videotapes on Friday afternoon
- Extra shop or P.E. time
- Special picnic lunches or food treats
- More assemblies
- Working on games or puzzles
- Typing on a typewriter

- Extra library time
- Helping the class line up at the door
- Reading a magazine
- Listening to a tape with head-phones
- Working on the computer
- Feeding the class animals
- Sitting next to a friend
- Obtaining legal hall passes
- Running errands for the teacher
- Taking notes to other teachers
- Taking good work to the principal or counselor
- Free time for special projects
- Extra recess
- Sticker on a behavioral report card

- Lunchtime basketball games, with the teacher serving as referee
- Popcorn during educational films
- Special parties
- Field trips
- Special art projects
- Listening to the radio
- Decorating the bulletin board
- Being a group leader
- Leading the class to the library
- Lunch with the teacher
- Note home to parents
- Watering the plants
- No-homework pass for one night
- Going to another classroom as a cross-age tutor

SOURCE: From *Effective Discipline* (2nd ed.) by D. D. Smith & D. M. Rivera, 1993, 77, Austin, TX: Pro-Ed. Copyright © 1993 by PRO-ED, Inc. Reprinted by permission.

Decreasing behavior is generally accomplished through one of these four sets of strategies: (1) differentially reinforcing behaviors that are incompatible with the undesirable behavior; (2) extinction, or ignoring the behavior until the student stops it; (3) removing something desirable from the student; and (4) presenting a negative or aversive consequence (Alberto & Troutman, 1994). The latter two sets of strategies, removing something desirable and presenting a negative or aversive consequence, are considered **punishment.** Punishment occurs when a consequence applied has the effect of decreasing a behavior. Each of the four sets of strategies is explained in the following sections.

Differential reinforcement of incompatible behaviors. Reinforcers can be used to decrease inappropriate behavior by increasing related appropriate behavior. Perhaps in your classroom you have a student like Patrick. Patrick has a severe learning disability. He tends to be very dependent on you for affirmation that he is doing his work correctly; he seems to be constantly at your elbow asking, "Is this right?" To change this behavior, you might want to try praising Patrick when you can catch him working independently at his desk. This technique is called **differential reinforcement of incompatible behaviors.** You are reinforcing a positive behavior—working at his desk—that is incompatible with the negative behavior—being at your desk asking for affirmation (Schloss & Smith, 1994). Your goal in this case is to get

WWW Resources

Many strategies that foster positive classroom behavior for typical students also help students with special needs. You can find some useful behavior management ideas at <http://www.cet.fsu.edu/tree/VE/BEES7C.HTML> and <http://www.csus.edu/ctl/f91troub.html>.

Professional Edge

Rewarding Positive Behavior to Reduce Negative Behavior

The following examples show how you can help students be more successful in your classroom by responding to positive behaviors that are incompatible with negative behaviors and rewarding the positive behaviors when you see them occurring.

Undesired Behavior	Positive Alternative Student Behavior That the Teacher Rewards
Talking back	Responding to positive responses such as "Yes, sir" or "Okay" or "I understand"; or to acceptable questions such as "May I ask you a question about that?" or "May I tell you my side?"
Cursing	Using acceptable exclamations such as "Darn" or "Shucks"
Being off task	Pursuing any on-task behavior: looking at book, writing, looking at the teacher, and so on
Being out of seat	Sitting in seat (bottom on chair, with body in upright position)
Noncompliance	Following directions within seconds (time limit will depend on student's age); following directions by the second time a direction is given
Talking out	Raising hand and waiting to be called on
Turning in messy papers	Making no marks other than answers; no more than a few erasures (depending on student needs and abilities); no more than three folds or creases
Hitting, pinching, kicking, pushing/shoving	Using verbal expression of anger; pounding fist into hand; sitting or standing next to other students without touching them
Tardiness	Being in seat when bell rings (or by the desired time)
Self-injurious or self-stimulatory behaviors	Sitting with hands on desk or in lap; hands not touching any part of body; head up and not touching anything (for example, desk, shoulder)
Inappropriate use of materials	Holding/using materials appropriately (for example, writing only on appropriate paper)

SOURCE: From "Accentuate the Positive . . . Eliminate the Negative!" by J. Webber & B. Scheuermann, 1991, *Teaching Exceptional Children, 24*(1), 13–19. Used by permission of the Council for Exceptional Children.

Patrick to come to your desk less by systematically rewarding him for appropriate behaviors that prevent him from being at your desk. Other examples of how to use this strategy are included in the Professional Edge.

Extinction.   Another approach to decreasing negative behavior is **extinction.** To extinguish a behavior, you stop reinforcing it; eventually the behavior will decrease. This strategy is often appropriate when a student has a minor but annoying undesirable behavior, such as tapping a pencil or rocking a chair, and when you have

Check Your Learning

What is extinction? What are the risks of using extinction to decrease students' undesirable behavior?

been reinforcing the behavior by calling attention to it or otherwise responding to it. However, extinction is appropriate only when the behavior is minor and does not threaten student well-being. Also, before an ignored behavior decreases, it is likely to increase; that is, at first the student might tap the pencil more loudly or rock more rapidly before stopping. If you respond to the behavior at this higher level (by telling the student to stop the noise or to keep still), you inadvertently reward the student for the exaggerated behavior through your response. If you think you cannot ignore a behavior while it increases, extinction is not the strategy to use.

Removing reinforcers. In some instances, you will decrease inappropriate behavior by taking away from the student something desired, a strategy called **removal punishment.** One example of removal punishment is **response cost,** which involves taking away a privilege, points, or some other reward (Schloss & Smith, 1994). An informal use of response cost occurs when teachers take away recess or an assembly because of misbehavior. More systematically, a student may lose a certain amount of free time each time he or she swears in class. Similarly, the student may lose the privilege of helping in another classroom because he or she refuses to begin assigned tasks.

If you are considering using response cost, keep in mind that it is effective only if the student currently has reinforcers that you can remove. For example, denying a student access to a special school program will decrease negative behavior only if the student wants to attend the program. Also, response cost sometimes fails because the negative behavior is being reinforced so strongly that the response cost is not effective. In the example just described, if the student receives a lot of peer attention from acting out in class, the response cost of not attending the school program might be too weak to counteract the strong appeal of peer attention. Finally, because response cost teaches a student only what not to do, it is essential that you simultaneously teach the student desired behaviors.

Another widely used removal punishment strategy is **time-out.** Time-out involves removing a student from opportunities for reward (Costenbader & Reading-Brown, 1995). Many elementary school teachers use a simple form of time-out when they require students misbehaving on the playground to spend a few minutes in a "penalty box." The reward from which students are removed is playtime with classmates. Time-out can be used in a number of ways, depending on the age of the student, the nature of the inappropriate behaviors, and the student's response to isolation. For example, it may be sufficient in a kindergarten or first-grade classroom to have a time-out chair in a quiet corner of the classroom. When Heather pushes another child, she is told to sit in time-out where she can observe other students in the reading circle and yet cannot interact with them. If this is not effective, placing a carrel on the student's desk or using a screen (possibly made from a large box) around a chair might be the next step. For older students and those with more challenging behaviors, time-out may need to be in a location totally removed from the student's class. For example, when Louis swears at his teacher, he is sent to the time-out room, a small, undecorated room with just a desk and chair that adjoins the counselor's office. However, for Cherri, time-out means going to Mrs. Eich's room across the hall, where she doesn't know the students.

If you use time-out, keep in mind the following considerations:

1. The length of the time-out should vary depending on the student's age, the type of challenging behavior, and the amount of time it takes for the time-out to achieve the result of decreasing an undesirable behavior. Younger students and those with limited cognitive ability often require shorter time-out periods than older students with learning and behavior problems.

2. When using time-out, students should be given a warning, should know why they are given a time-out, and should not have access to attractive activities during time-out. The warning provides students an opportunity to correct the behavior; the explanation ensures that students understand the reason for time-out; and the absence of attractions guarantees that time-out does not become a reward for the student. The last point is especially important. In one school, a student with autism was being "timed-out" from his inclusive classroom for running around the room. He was being sent to a special education classroom where he was using colored chalk on the chalkboard to entertain himself for long periods of time. Not surprisingly, his running behavior began increasing!

3. Giving a student attention as part of a time-out process sabotages its effectiveness. Sometimes, teachers who are using time-out accompany a student to the time-out area, explaining the student's behavior on the way, arguing with the student about the time-out procedure, or otherwise providing the student with a great deal of attention. This attention may reinforce the student's behavior and, in effect, negate the effect of using time-out. The student may increase the behavior because of the few minutes of undivided teacher attention that results from it.

4. If a student refuses to go to a time-out location, you may need to ask for assistance in enforcing your decision. However, you should also keep in mind that if time-out becomes a power struggle between you and a student, it might not be the appropriate strategy to use.

5. Be aware that for some students, isolation is in itself rewarding. For time-out to be effective, the environment from which the student is removed must be rewarding. Some students are happy to be left completely alone for as long as possible. For students who prefer isolation, time-out is clearly not an appropriate strategy for reducing misbehavior.

6. Attend to the safety needs of students in time-out settings. It is highly unethical to send an upset student to an unsupervised time-out location. If time-out is employed, it must include adult supervision, a safe location for the student, and monitoring for student comfort and safety. Your school district probably has written policies about the use of time-out. If not, it is especially important to work closely with a special educator, counselor, or administrator to be certain you use it appropriately.

> **Cultural Awareness**
>
> Punishments vary from culture to culture. Your students may come from families that use punishments such as shame, ostracizing, or severe physical punishment. Your knowledge of how students are punished at home should help you understand how they respond to punishment in school.

Presenting negative consequences.   The final set of strategies for decreasing undesirable student behavior is the least preferable because it involves presenting negative consequences to students (Gardner et al., 1994). It is referred to as **presentation punishment.** For example, when a teacher verbally reprimands a student, the reprimand is a negative consequence intended to decrease student misbehavior. It is a mild punisher, one of the most common used in schools (Johns & Carr, 1995).

Another type of presentation punishment is **overcorrection,** in which a student is directed to restore a situation to its original condition or a better condition than existed before the misbehavior. This strategy is useful when a student has damaged classroom property or otherwise created a mess. For example, a student who scribbles on a chalkboard might be assigned to erase and wash all the boards in the room. A student who writes on a desktop might be required to stay after school to clean all the desktops in the class. A student who throws trash on the floor might be given the task of sweeping the classroom and adjoining hallway. This strategy can make clear the undesirable consequences of negative behaviors, but it is not without problems. First, the student must be willing to complete the overcorrection activity; it might be extremely difficult to compel this behavior. If a student refuses to complete the task, a confrontation might occur. In addition, the overcorrection requires close teacher supervision. A student should not be left alone to complete the assigned task, which translates into a significant time commitment from the teacher.

Physical punishment is another traditional presentation punishment. Although corporal punishment, carried out within specific guidelines, is still permitted in schools in some states, most educators strongly oppose its use. Physical and other types of punishment have many potential negative effects, including the following (Morris, 1985):

1. Punishment often suppresses a student's undesirable behavior but does not change it. Once a student realizes or observes that physical punishment will no longer follow a behavior, that behavior is likely to recur. Thus, a student who is physically punished for stealing is likely to steal again if he or she is relatively sure that no one will discover the theft.

2. Although punishment might reduce or eliminate a particular behavior, other undesirable behaviors might be substituted. For example, a student strongly scolded for talking out might at the first opportunity deface a bulletin board as a way of "getting even."

3. Punishment often produces strong emotional responses in the student, such as anxiety and fear. These responses can interfere with the student's new learning in the classroom or in social situations. In one unfortunate middle school cafeteria incident, a student with a learning disability was threatened with a paddling when she threw food, a clear and serious violation of school rules. The student was so frightened that she left school and walked home along a busy highway, causing much consternation on the part of teachers and administrators who could not find her.

4. A student who is punished might respond with aggression and hostility toward the person who administers the punishment. This side effect would also influence the relationship between that person and the student. In a classroom in which the teacher uses punishment, the student might withdraw or lash out at the teacher in anticipation of the punishment about to be delivered.

5. When punishment is used, students might begin to avoid participating in a wide range of activities. Thus, when an art teacher repeatedly punishes a student for using materials carelessly, the student might become reluctant to use the materials at all, and this reluctance might extend to instruments in a music class or to equipment in a physical education class. The student might misbehave to avoid having to go to art, music, or gym.

6. Punishment sometimes has an opposite effect on behavior, increasing instead of decreasing it. This is especially true when the student craves adult attention. For example, if you verbally correct a student for using foul language, the student may enjoy your attention and increase the use of foul language in order to obtain your attention. In this case, the intended punisher clearly has not served its purpose.

WWW Resources

You can learn about legal issues related to discipline and students with special needs at this website: <http://www.ecs.org/ecs/23aa.html>.

FYI

School districts that allow corporal punishment usually have clear guidelines, including having advance parent permission, specifying how punishment is administered, and requiring the presence of a witness.

7. Through the teacher's modeling, students might learn that they, too, can control people by using punishment. For example, a student might imitate a teacher's scolding when tutoring a younger student. Likewise, the student might hit a classmate perceived as weaker if physical punishment is part of the school's discipline procedures. Similarly, students who are corporally punished at home might use hitting at school with peers.

In general, then, the message for you as a teacher responding to student behaviors in class is this: Increasing positive behaviors through the use of reinforcers, especially when these desirable behaviors can substitute for student undesirable behaviors, is the preferred approach to behavior management. If you find it necessary to decrease undesirable behaviors, the preferred strategies are reinforcing the positive incompatible behaviors and extinction. The use of removal or presentation punishment should be a last resort, only as part of an ongoing behavior intervention plan, and should involve a team decision. If you do use punishment, keep in mind all the potential problems with it and monitor its use closely.

How Can You Help Students Manage Their Own Behavior?

The strategies just outlined for increasing positive and decreasing negative student behavior rely on the teacher providing rewards or consequences to the student. Another set of strategies, far less teacher-directed, involves having students take an active role in managing their own behavior (Coleman, Wheeler, & Webber, 1993). These strategies are preferred because they promote student independence by giving students skills they can use in many school settings and outside of school as well.

Cognitive Behavior Management Strategies

In **cognitive behavior management (CBM),** students are taught to monitor their own behavior, to make judgments about its appropriateness, and to change it as needed (for example, see Meichenbaum, 1977). Many elements of CBM have already been introduced in Chapter 10 as a means of increasing student independence in academic learning and organization. Here they are applied to helping students manage their own classroom conduct and social behavior in a variety of situations. For example, Joseph, the student with a learning disability introduced at the beginning of this chapter, might be able to use CBM to manage his own classroom behavior.

Two types of CBM are commonly used to teach students how to manage their own behavior (Kaplan & Carter, 1995). These are self-monitoring and self-reinforcement.

Self-monitoring. Students learn to monitor and record their own behavior in **self-monitoring.** For example, a student might keep a daily tally of the number of assignments completed or the number of times he or she waited until the teacher was between instructional groups to ask a question. Students with more advanced skills could even wear headphones to listen to an audiotape with prerecorded signals and record whether or not they were on task at the sound of each tone. Students can also self-record their social behaviors. They could tally the number of times they left

Connections

CBM strategies are presented in an instructional context in Chapter 10.

Figure 12.4 Countoons: Sample Self-Recording Forms

1	2	3	4	5	6	7	8	9	10
11	12	13	14	15	16	17	18	19	20
21	22	23	24	25	26	27	28	29	30
31	32	33	34	35	36	37	38	39	40
41	42	43	44	45	46	47	48	49	50

Count your hand raising

1	2	3	4	5	6	7	8	9	10
11	12	13	14	15	16	17	18	19	20
21	22	23	24	25	26	27	28	29	30
31	32	33	34	35	36	37	38	39	40
41	42	43	44	45	46	47	48	49	50

Count your talk outs

SOURCE: From *Comprehensive Classroom Management* (4th edition) by V. Jones & L. Jones, 1995. Copyright © 1995 by Allyn and Bacon. Reprinted by permission.

their seat without permission or asked permission before leaving the classroom. An example of a student self-recording form is a *countoon*, illustrated in Figure 12.4.

Self-reinforcement. Another type of CBM, **self-reinforcement,** is often used in conjunction with self-evaluation. In this approach, students self-evaluate and then judge whether they have earned a reward. For example, Eric might award himself three points for a high score, two points for an average score, and no points for a low score. When he accumulates 20 points, he chooses a reward from his personal reinforcement menu. His favorite reward might be working with the kindergartners during their physical education period. The teacher periodically checks the accuracy of Eric's self-evaluation and self-reinforcement. He earns a bonus point for being accurate in his assessment of himself, even if that assessment is occasionally negative. If Eric has to give himself no points for a low score, and his teacher checks his accuracy that day, he will receive a bonus point because he accurately assessed his work.

Teaching CBM Strategies

Generally, teaching CBM strategies to a student with special needs has three main steps:

1. **Discuss the strategy with the student and present a rationale for its use.** If you cannot clarify for the student what the strategy is or how it works, the student might not be a good candidate for CBM. To check student understanding, ask the student to explain the approach back to you.

2. **Model for the student what you expect.** For example, you might use an old sample of the student's work and walk through the strategy you plan to use. Alternatively, you might use a brief role-play to demonstrate to the student how to self-monitor behavior and record it.

3. **Provide practice and feedback.** For this step, the teacher rewards the student for correctly using the approach until the student is confident enough to use the approach without such support. If you are teaching a student to use CBM, use reinforcers with the student until he or she has mastered the strategy. Even after mastery, it is helpful to reward the student periodically for successfully self-managing behavior. This step can be enhanced by helping the student develop a personal reinforcement menu so rewards are meaningful. Parents and colleagues can sometimes assist in implementing this step.

Although CBM is not appropriate for every student behavior problem, it has the advantage of teaching a student to monitor and take responsibility for his or her own behavior. Because of increased student responsibility, cognitive behavior management is a far more effective strategy for some students than are more traditional classroom rewards. Students can transfer self-management strategies to other classrooms and teachers and even into adult life.

How Can a Problem-Solving Approach Help You Respond to Student Behavior?

In this chapter, you have learned many approaches for responding to individual student behavior. However, we have not yet addressed one key issue: How do you know how serious a student behavior problem is, and which type of approach should you use in responding to it? The answer is to think of responding to student behavior as a problem-solving process, much like the interpersonal problem-solving process introduced in Chapter 3. By thinking systematically about student behavior problems, including using information you gather through the INCLUDE strategy, you and your colleagues will make sound decisions about how to intervene and will be better able to determine whether the strategy you select is effective (Ayres & Hedeen, 1996).

The steps for applying a problem-solving approach to change a student's behavior include: (1) identifying the problem by increasing your understanding of the behavior, (2) confirming your understanding of the behavior by observing it and recording your observations, (3) creating a plan for responding to the behavior by using rewards or consequences, (4) implementing your plan, and (5) monitoring the plan for effectiveness.

Identifying the Behavior Problem

When a student displays behaviors that are especially aggravating or seem directed at purposely causing a classroom disruption, it is tempting to respond by trying to stop the behavior in order to get back to the business of educating the student. First, however, you need to identify the problem, which involves understanding why the student is displaying a particular behavior. Inappropriate behaviors can be viewed as clues for diagnosing the student's goal or intent, and intent helps you understand the problem the student is displaying (Neel & Cessna, 1993). Students with inappropriate behaviors often have the same goals as students who display appropriate

Connections

Student intent was introduced earlier in this chapter. Do you remember how intent affects student behavior?

Table 12.1   Possible Student Intents

Intent	Goal	Example of Behavior
Power/Control	Control an event or a situation	Acts to stay in the situation and keep control: "You can't make me!"
Protection/ Escape	Avoid a task or activity; escape a consequence; stop or leave a situation	Has a tantrum at the start of every math lesson; skips social studies class
Attention	Become the center of attention; focus attention on self	Puts self in the forefront of a situation or distinguishes self from others; for example, burps loudly during class instruction
Acceptance/ Affiliation	Become wanted or chosen by others for mutual benefit	Hangs out with troublemakers; joins a clique or gang
Self-expression	Express feelings, needs, or preoccupations; demonstrate knowledge or skill	Produces drawings, for example, of aerial bombings, body parts, occult symbols
Gratification	Feel good; have a pleasurable experience; reward oneself	Acts to get or maintain a self-detemined reward, for example, hoards an object; indulges in self-gratifying behavior at others' expense
Justice/Revenge	Settle a score; get or give restitution, apology, or punishment	Destroys another's work; meets after school to fight; commits an act of vandalism

S O U R C E : Adapted from "Behavioral Intent: Instructional Content for Students with Behavior Disorders" by R. S. Neel & K. K. Cessna, 1993, in Colorado Department of Education Special Education Services Unit, *Instructionally Differentiated Programming: A Needs-Based Approach for Students with Behavior Disorders.* Used by permission.

behaviors, but are unskilled in expressing their intent in an acceptable way. If you understand intent, you can better plan interventions. Table 12.1 describes some common student behavior intents. Put simply, this conceptualization of student behaviors suggests that before responding you should ask, "Why is the student doing this?"

The following example might help to clarify the idea of identifying students' intents. Daniel is in the sixth grade. When the sixth-grade teaching team meets to discuss student problems, Mr. Adams expresses concern that Daniel sometimes swears in class. Ms. Jefferson adds that he sometimes picks fights with other students in class. Dr. Hogue agrees that Daniel is having problems and recounts a recent incident in which Daniel was sent to the office. As the teachers talk, they begin to look past Daniel's specific behaviors and focus instead on his intent. They realize that in one class, Daniel was disruptive when a difficult assignment was being given; in another, the problem was occurring as quizzes were being returned; and in the other, the incident was immediately prior to Daniel's turn to give an oral book report. The teachers agree that Daniel's intent has been to escape situations in which he might fail.

Once you identify the probable intent of a student's behavior, it becomes important to assist the student in changing the behavior to a more acceptable form, while still enabling the student to achieve the original intent. In Daniel's case, it would be easy for the teachers to decide on a reward system to get Daniel to swear less in Mr. Adams's class. However, this has more to do with the teachers' intent of having well-mannered students than it does with Daniel's intent to avoid the possibility of failing. An alternative approach would be to permit Daniel to receive his quizzes before the start of class, or perhaps to participate in the after-school homework club that includes a group that studies for the quiz. Another behavior to teach Daniel might be for him

Do It!

For common student intents, generate at least three additional appropriate ways in which the student could accomplish the intent.

to ask to give oral reports to one peer or to audiotape them beforehand. The question of intervening to address Daniel's behavior has shifted from "How can we get Daniel to be less disruptive in the classroom?" to "How can we help Daniel use more appropriate strategies to avoid situations in which he fears he will fail?"

This approach to understanding student behavior is more complex than looking at the surface behavior the student displays. However, if you carefully analyze the student's intent, you greatly increase the likelihood that you will be able to assist the student in displaying more appropriate behaviors. In the sections that follow, specific procedures for measuring student behavior and intervening to change it are recommended. All the strategies assume that you have completed the critical first step of clearly understanding the intent of the student's words or actions.

Observing and Recording Student Behavior to Understand the Problem Better

One component of understanding student behavior is creating a systematic way to measure its occurrence. By doing this, teachers are better able to judge if the behavior follows a particular pattern (for example, it occurs during certain types of activities or at certain times of day). Patterns assist in understanding the intent and the seriousness of the behavior in relation to teachers' classroom expectations. At the same time, by accurately measuring the behavior when it becomes a concern and continuing to do so after a plan for addressing it is implemented, teachers can see if their efforts to change the behavior have been successful. Sometimes you will observe and record student behavior yourself. However, if you find that it is not feasible to collect observational information about your students, a school psychologist, a special education teacher, or an administrator can probably help you in this task. Likewise, a parent volunteer, teaching assistant, or student teacher can gather information by observing. The key is to create a support system for yourself rather than to decide against the strategy. The Technology Notes feature on page 440 includes several strategies for efficiently gathering data about students.

Anecdotal recording. One useful strategy for measuring student behavior is to record specific incidents, including what happened immediately before the behavior (antecedents) and what happened as a result of the behavior (consequences). This approach is called an **ABC** (antecedents–behaviors–consequences) **analysis.** For example, Ms. Carlisle is observing Carlos. When the class is directed to form cooperative groups (antecedent), Carlos gets up from his seat and heads for the pencil sharpener (behavior). Ms. Carlisle tells Carlos to join his group (consequence). By keeping an ongoing ABC log of Carlos's behaviors in the classroom, Ms. Carlisle found out that whenever the class is transitioning from one activity to another, Carlos is likely to be off task. A sample ABC analysis is shown in Figure 12.5 on page 441.

Event recording. One easy way to measure a behavior is to count how many times the behavior occurs in a given period of time. This approach is most useful when the behavior is discrete, that is, has a clear starting and stopping point. For example, it might be appropriate to use **event recording** to count the number of times John is late to class during a week or the number of times David blurts out an answer during a 30-minute large-group social studies lesson. On the other hand, event recording probably would not be helpful in measuring Jane's tantrum or Jesse's delay in

Technology Notes

Technological Aids for Recording Behaviors

Several simple forms of technology can assist you in recording student behavior. Here are a few suggestions.

Anecdotal Recording

The computer is a powerful tool for keeping anecdotal records about a student. If you create a file and record your ABC analyses or other anecdotal information in chronological order, you will have a clear and accurate record that can be shared with others or used as a basis for deciding how to intervene to help a student and whether a particular intervention is successful.

Event Recording

Any of the counters available for golf or other sports can be used to keep track of classroom events. For example, if you want to count how many times Yvonne appropriately calls out an answer during a 20-minute lesson, you could wear a wrist counter and simply "click" it each time Yvonne calls out. At the end of the lesson, you could then transfer your tally to a computer or paper record.

Permanent Products

If part of your problem concerns the amount of work a student begins, finishes, or completes accurately, a computer record might be a preferred strategy. For example, if a student begins to write a story on the computer but does not complete it, this record can be saved for future reference. Another alternative is to have students use a tape recorder for assignments that can be completed out loud. This specific evidence of the student's work can give a sense of how much of an assignment the student completed.

These teachers are evaluating a program for behavioral observation and record keeping.

Duration Recording

If a student's behavior is audible (for example, a tantrum), you can create an accurate record of duration. When the behavior begins, you simply start tape-recording and stop when it ceases. You can then later time the behavior.

Interval and Time Sampling

A tape-recorded signal to remind you to observe for a behavior, or a watch that will emit a tone at specified intervals, can help you systematically gather information about student behavior. In addition, you could record the behavior using a printing calculator. For example, if you plan to indicate with a "+" or "–" whether a student is working appropriately with peers at the end of each 5-minute segment, you could simply strike either of those keys on a calculator. After the recording period, you would have a printed record of your observations.

Source: From "Recording Behavior with Ease" by M. A. Koorland, L. E. Monda, & C. O. Vail, 1988, *Teaching Exceptional Children, 21*(1), 59–61. Used by permission of the Council for Exceptional Children.

starting his assignment, because these behaviors have more to do with how long they last than the number of times they occur.

Event recording is relatively easy. You could keep a tally on an index card taped to your desk or planbook or kept as a bookmark in one of your textbooks. Some

Figure 12.5   ABC Analysis

Student Name   Denton R.   Date   2/26

Location   Science—Mr. B   Observer   Mr. D

Start Time   1:02   Stop Time   1:15

Antecedents	Behaviors	Consequences
1:03 Students getting books out and open to begin class.	Denton pulls out his cap and puts it on.	Students around D. start laughing and saying "hey."
1:05 Teacher notices D. and tells him to remove cap.	D. stands, slowly removes cap, and bows.	Students applaud.
1:14 Teacher asks D. a question.	D. says, "Man, I don't know."	Student says, "Yeah, you're stupid." Others laugh.

teachers use a "beads-in-a-pocket" strategy, transferring any small object from one pocket to another when a count is observed. The key to this type of recording is to have an accurate total of the number of times a behavior occurred.

Permanent product recording.   If your concern about student behavior relates to academics, it may be simplest to keep samples of work as a means of measuring behavior, a strategy called **permanent product recording.** For example, if students in American history class regularly have to respond to 10 discussion questions during a single class session, you might keep Sam's completed work to document the percentage of questions he is attempting or the percentage of his responses that are correct.

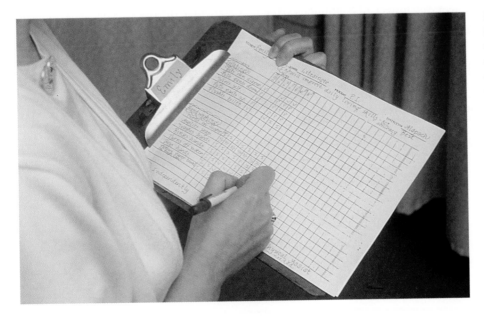

How might a behavior chart help you collaborate with others to develop a plan for responding to a student's behavior? What other methods of recording behavior might you use to determine if your behavior management plan is working?

Check Your Learning

For what behaviors besides tantrums might you want to record the duration of a student's behavior?

Duration recording.   For some behaviors, your concern is the length of time the behavior lasts. The strategy of **duration recording** might apply to a young student who cries each morning at the start of the school day, a middle school student who takes an extraordinary amount of time to locate all her learning materials, or a high school student who delays beginning assignments. Often, accurately recording duration requires that you have a stopwatch and are able to notice the moment the behavior begins and the moment it ends. However, duration recording can also measure how long students take to complete assignments by asking them to write on their papers the time when they began and finished their work. A sample duration recording form is included in Figure 12.6.

Interval recording.   Sometimes, you have concerns about a student's behavior not addressed by any of the systems just described. For example, you might be concerned about how well a student is staying on task during an independent assignment or the extent to which a student plays with others during free-choice time. In these cases, **interval recording** may be the best measuring strategy. To use this approach, you specify a length of time for the observation and then divide the time into smaller intervals. For example, you might observe a 10-minute work or play period divided into 20-second intervals. As you observe the student for each 20-second interval, you indicate whether the behavior has been present for that entire interval or not by marking a + or – on the recording form.

Check Your Learning

What is the difference between interval and time sampling as strategies for observing and recording student behavior?

Time sampling.   Whereas interval recording requires that you observe a student continuously, **time sampling** uses a similar strategy but involves only periodic observations of the student. For example, if you wanted to observe whether Patricia played alone or with others during a 30-minute recess, you could divide the time period into ten 3-minute observations. At the end of each 3-minute interval, you would glance to see whether Patricia was playing with others or alone *at that moment* and record your observation accordingly. In the completed form in Figure 12.7, you can see that Patricia was on task for approximately 40 percent of the intervals. Time sampling is less demanding than interval recording because you observe only momentarily instead of continuously, but it does include the risk that the behaviors you observe at each sampling are not typical of what has occurred until that moment. This system can also be expedient when your goal is to observe several students at one time; by glancing at three different students and immediately recording the be-

Figure 12.6   **Sample Duration Recording**

Student Name _____	Observer _____

Target Behavior   _Refusal to begin assigned work_

Date	Location	Start Time	Stop Time	Comments
10/13/98	Classroom	10:15 a.m.	10:24 a.m.	Writing assignment
10/14/98	Classroom	10:37 a.m.	10:55 a.m.	Peer edits; P.E.–11 a.m.
10/17/98	Music	11:15 a.m.	11:22 a.m.	Group singing; kept head down and ears covered

Figure 12.7 Time Sampling

Student Name ___Patricia___   Date ___11/21/98___

Location ___Classroom___   Observer ___K. Powers___

Behavior ___On-task___   Start Time __1:10__ Stop time __1:40__

Interval Length: 3 minutes

+ = Behavior occurred at end of interval   − = Behavior did not occur at end of interval

Minute:

1		2		3		4		5		6		7		8		9		10	
+	+	−	−	−	−	+	−	−	+	+	+	+	−	−	−	−	+	−	−

On-task = 40% (eight intervals out of 20)

havior of each one, you can look at the behavior patterns of each student during a single observational period.

Other considerations. Teachers sometimes say that measuring behavior with the precision implied by these approaches is not realistic. It is certainly true that you will not routinely have the time to use these strategies with many students. However, when you are faced with a student whose behavior is particularly persistent and puzzling, the time you take to record it systematically will give you a clearer picture of how to address the problem. Further, if you work with colleagues in a co-taught class and streamline data collection by using generic, multipurpose recording forms, you may find that recording observations is not as burdensome as you might imagine. Finally, do not forget to talk to students about their behavior; their perspective can add important information to other data you gather (Thorson, 1996).

Developing a Plan

The result of observing and recording behavior is a profile of the student's behavior. This profile gives you a sense of the seriousness of the behavior and can help you develop a plan that is either relatively unobtrusive (for minor misbehavior) or extremely systematic (for chronic, serious behavior problems). It can also alert you as to whether you might also be contributing to the problems and help you decide how to change your own teaching behavior. For example, you might realize through your observations that the student begins to misbehave only when you have asked students to sit listening to you for extended periods of time. Instead of considering a student-change plan, the first strategy might be to consider a teacher-change plan!

If you decide that you need a systematic response to student behavior, review the options presented in this chapter to select an approach. Specifically, first consider whether you can prevent the behavior by changing your classroom arrangement or instructional practices. Next, decide if a group behavior management

Case in Practice

Analyzing a Behavior Plan

Misty is a student who has many charming characteristics, but she can also create major disturbances in her classroom. Misty is categorized as having a mild cognitive disability, but her teachers agree that her disability also has an emotional component. In her second-grade classroom, Misty craves teacher attention and often brings flowers or other small gifts to her teacher. However, when Misty is asked to complete a challenging assignment, she is likely either to have a loud and lengthy tantrum or to cross her arms, put her head down, and say again and again, "I can't, I can't, I can't."

Mr. Kennedy has worked with the special education teacher and school psychologist to devise a plan to address this negative behavior. When Mr. Kennedy is about to assign Misty work to do, he alerts her that he is about to give it, and then presents only half the assignment at one time. Misty has learned to say "I know I can, I know I can" before she ever sees the assignment. When Misty looks at the first item, she is to raise her hand for help if she does not know how to complete it. If she does her steps—saying "I know I can," accepting the assignment, and raising her hand if stuck—she earns 10 points toward her favorite activity in school: helping the art teacher clean up at the end of the day. It takes 50 points to get to help. Although Mr. Kennedy does not want Misty to work only to get to help the art teacher and has concerns about whether helping the art teacher is instructionally appropriate for Misty, he sees that she is making progress. He will gradually remove the reward system after she has more self-confidence.

REFLECTIONS

How is Mr. Kennedy implementing the behavior plan for Misty? Why do you suppose he and his colleagues decided on this set of procedures? How did they discover what type of reward Misty would work for? What does Mr. Kennedy mean when he says he is worried about the art-helping activity being "instructionally appropriate"? What do you think? How would you deal with this concern? If this plan does not work for Misty, what alternative plan could be tried? How could the reinforcers and the frequency of reinforcement be altered?

technique is indicated so you do not single out one student. If these options do not seem appropriate, you might employ simple strategies directed at a single student that do not require ongoing attention. The final set of approaches is reserved for persistent and serious behavior problems. This set includes all the options for increasing positive and decreasing negative behaviors. If appropriate, you might also use a cognitive behavior management strategy. The Case in Practice models the development of a behavior plan.

Implementing the Plan

Once you have identified how to change the student's behavior, you are faced with the task of implementing your plan. It is important to have a clear structure for implementation because the key to managing student behavior effectively is a systematic response.

Contracts.   One straightforward way to use one or combine several of the strategies for increasing or decreasing behavior is through **behavior contracts.** A behavior contract is an agreement between the teacher and student that clearly specifies the expectations for the student, the rewards for meeting expectations, the consequences of not meeting expectations, and the timeframe for which the agreement is valid (Kaplan & Carter, 1995). Contracts are best used with students like Joseph and perhaps Donna and Marysha, who are old enough to understand their content and whose disabilities either do not affect their cognitive functioning or affect it only marginally. However, simple contracts can be used with almost any student (Walker & Shea, 1995). As you review the sample contract in Figure 12.8, notice that it has more detail than some very simple student contracts you may have seen.

Figure 12.8   Sample Student Contract

For _____ Marta _____
                        (Student name)

I agree to do these things (what, how much, how well, how often, how measured):

In the lunchroom, eat my lunch quietly and without causing a disruption to children around me for 10 minutes of the 20-minute lunch period. Ms. Longleiter will tell me if I'm doing ok.

For doing them I will receive (what, how much, how often, when):

I will leave the lunchroom with Ms. Longleiter for an extra 10 minutes of recess.

Outstanding performance will be if I

Keep my contract 3 days in a row

My bonus for outstanding performance is

15 extra minutes of reading game time with one of my friends (in the afternoon of the same day the bonus is earned).

If I don't meet the terms of my contract, this is the consequence:

I will have time-out until recess begins and I will not be allowed to choose an activity during Friday morning "Choices" time

This contract will be renegotiated on

April 3, 1998

Marta   _Ms. Kornick_
Student signature   **Teacher signature**

March 17, 1998   _March 17, 1998_
Date   **Date**

For students with special needs who have behavior challenges, simple contracts are often ineffective in changing behavior. The added components of the contract in Figure 12.8 significantly increase its impact on the student.

The original and still most comprehensive information on how to write student behavior contracts comes from Homme (1970). He stresses these points:

1. The reward that goes with the contract should be immediate, that is, as close in time as possible to the performance of the desired behavior.

2. Initial contracts should call for and reward small amounts of the desired behavior. For example, requiring a student to read an entire book in order to earn a reward would probably be too frustrating a task for a student with a reading problem. Instead, the student could be rewarded for each chapter (or even each chapter section or page) completed.

3. Reward frequently with small amounts. This approach has been proven a more effective method than fewer, larger rewards.

4. A contract should call for and reward accomplishments rather than obedience; that is, reward the completion of assigned work or appropriate behavior rather than "teacher pleasing" behaviors such as staying in seat.

5. Reward the performance only after it occurs. This rule seems obvious, but it is often overlooked. Students who are allowed privileges or rewards before or during work performance are far less likely to complete the performance successfully than those rewarded after it.

6. The contract must be fair. The amount of work required of the student and the payoff for completing the work must be balanced.

7. The terms of the contract should be clear to the student. The contract should be put in writing and discussed with the student. Each component of the contract should be expressed in language the student understands. If the student is not able to understand a contract, this strategy is probably not the best one. The student and teacher should sign the contract.

8. The contract must be honest. The teacher should be willing to carry out the contract as written and to do so immediately. In practice, this means that you should be sure you can deliver on the promises you make.

9. The contract should be positive. It should specify student accomplishments and rewards rather than restrictions and punishments.

10. Contracts should be used systematically. If the contract is enforced only occasionally, the result may be worse (or at least very confusing) for the student than not using one at all.

Other implementation strategies. For young students or students with limited cognitive abilities, contracts might be too complex. In such cases, you can use simpler strategies. For example, you might note in your planbook that you need to check student work at the end of each 15-minute segment. Alternatively, you might set an egg timer at the beginning of the independent work period to remind yourself to reward a student after 5 minutes of sustained work. If you are using a group strategy, you can announce to the class that the strategy is in effect for the class period or a certain period of time. There is no single right way to implement a behavior response plan. As long as you have clearly identified the behavior of concern, have a specific approach for addressing it, and create a systematic strategy for responding to it, your plan will probably succeed.

Monitoring the Plan

You began gathering information about the student's behavior prior to thinking about how to respond to it. You should continue to keep behavior records as you implement your plan so you can determine if it is working. To do this, use the same recording strategies presented earlier in this chapter. Remember that some students' behavior will not change rapidly; you should be committed to following your plan for a minimum of 2 or 3 weeks before deciding it is not effective.

As you monitor your plan, any of these situations might occur: First, the inappropriate behavior may cease completely, or the desired behavior may be displayed consistently. If this happens, you may decide to withdraw gradually the rewards and consequences you have implemented. For example, if you are using a contract with a student to eliminate his use of profane language in class and no profane language is occurring, you can make it gradually more difficult for the student to earn a reward, and then stop using a contract altogether. This is called **fading out** the reward system.

Second, the plan you are implementing may have value but need modification. Perhaps it takes too much time to implement, or the rewards need adjustment. Such alterations are not unusual; simply modify the plan and continue to monitor its effectiveness. For example, if you created a point system for your sophomore keyboarding class that includes points for being seated when the bell rings, points for turning homework in at the beginning of class, and points for having an assignment notebook and pen in class, you might discover that the system is too difficult to monitor. You might eliminate the points for everything except homework for all but the two students who chronically fail to come to class on time with supplies in hand.

Third, the plan may not be working. As you track the number and duration of tantrums for one of your students, you might learn that time-out seems to be causing more tantrums that last longer. If a situation like this occurs, try to analyze what happened. A special education teacher, psychologist, or counselor might be able to assist you in this analysis and to suggest an alternative plan. In fact, in instances in which problem solving about a student fails to achieve the results you had hoped for, shared problem solving with colleagues as outlined in Chapter 3 is highly recommended as your next course of action. Special educators often have had extensive preparation in behavior modification and considerable experience in designing effective behavior management systems. In some schools, the school counselor or school psychologist might also be available as a resource. Of course, school administrators might also assist you on behavior topics, especially if you have students who are particularly disruptive. A shared problem-solving session involving all or at least some of these individuals can be very helpful for both you and the student.

Finally, it is imperative that you work closely with parents to resolve student behavior problems. Parents can sometimes clarify why a student is behaving in a particular way (for example, a death in the family or a divorce, a weekend trip, a cultural response to a school activity). In addition, they can reinforce school messages at home, and they can help provide tangible or activity rewards at home earned by appropriate behavior during the school day. By creating partnerships with parents, you increase options for responding to student behavior.

Do It!

Obtain permission to attend a meeting at which professional educators problem solve about a student's behavior. What procedure do they use? What role does a parent play? What types of strategies are proposed? How will the plan they develop be monitored?

Summary

Responding to student behavior begins with prevention: By setting clear expectations and fostering respect and communication, teachers can create a classroom learning environment that encourages appropriate behavior and discourages inappropriate behavior. Such basic techniques will meet the needs of many students with disabilities. In addition, you can use simple group techniques such as the Good Behavior Game and token economies to promote positive student behavior.

Some students, however, will need additional behavior supports. By using low-intrusion strategies such as grouping students and managing surface behaviors, small behavior problems can be prevented from becoming serious ones. However, if such strategies are inadequate, systematic use of strategies for increasing behavior (e.g., reinforcement) and decreasing behavior (e.g., extinction, overcorrection, punishment) may be needed. For some students, self-management strategies such as self-monitoring and self-reinforcement also can be employed.

A problem-solving approach, often completed with colleagues and parents, can help you decide how serious a student behavior is and which set of alternatives might be needed to address it. The approach includes identifying the problem behavior, clarifying it by observing and recording it, developing a plan to address the behavior, implementing the plan, and monitoring the plan's effectiveness.

Applications in Teaching Practice

Developing Strategies for Responding to Individual Student Behavior

Ms. Bind teaches freshman English. One of her students is Russell, a student with learning and behavior problems. Russell tends to be a class clown. He makes flippant remarks that border on being disrespectful of other students and Ms. Bind. He often is reprimanded for chatting with other students instead of listening, and then he will complain that he doesn't know how to do an assignment that was just explained. The other students generally like Russell, and they sometimes urge him to further classroom antics. Ms. Bind is not alone in her concern about Russell's behavior. His other teachers report a similar pattern. All are concerned about his slipping grades and worry that in high school it will be difficult for him to get the adult supervision that helped him be more successful in middle school. Ms. Bind's tally of classroom incidents from the last week suggests that Russell is reprimanded at least three times per class period. The reprimands tend to occur when the class is transitioning from one activity to another, for example, from a large-group lecture to an individual assignment.

Ms. Bind, special education teacher Mr. Clark, and counselor Ms. Lassaux have been meeting about Russell. Their first step was to think about Russell's intent. They decided that the behaviors he is displaying probably have to do with seeking attention, from both peers and teachers. They spend a considerable time discussing what type of attention is available to Russell through more appropriate sources, and they weigh the pros and cons of various alternatives for responding to Russell's behavior. They also drift into a conversation about the impact the other students are having on maintaining Russell's behavior. Ms. Bind is convinced that if Russell's audience were not so attentive, many of his problems might take care of themselves.

Questions

1. What strategies could Ms. Bind and the other teachers use to address the group response to Russell's behavior? What cautions would you have for them in trying these strategies?
2. What simple strategies could Ms. Bind use to help Russell behave more appropriately in class? For each strategy, identify potential positive outcomes that could occur but also outline potential problems that could arise.
3. What types of reinforcement might work for Russell? How could Ms. Bind ascertain what reinforcers to use if reinforcement is the strategy decided on? Which types of reinforcers would you avoid in this case?
4. How do you think Russell would respond to strategies designed to decrease his negative behavior? For example, how might Russell react if he received a detention each time he disrupted class? What type of negative consequence is detention?
5. Is Russell likely to be able to use cognitive behavior management? Why or why not? If you decided to try a CBM strategy, how would you go about it?
6. How should Russell be involved in this discussion about his behavior? What contributions could he make?
7. What are the next steps Ms. Bind and her colleagues should take? For each problem-solving step, outline what you think might occur.

Approaches for Building Social Relationships

After you read this chapter, you will be able to

1. Describe how children with and without disabilities interact with one another and how to promote positive interactions among them.

2. Use a variety of strategies to promote friendship and social support between students with and without disabilities or other special needs.

3. Outline how to establish peer tutoring programs in inclusive schools and describe the characteristics of those programs.

4. Explain how to use cooperative learning strategies as a means of facilitating inclusive education.

5. Describe social-skills needs of students with disabilities and explain how students can learn these skills.

■ Lucy is a fifth-grade student in Ms. Englert's class at Miller Elementary School. She has a moderate cognitive disability. Three times each week for approximately 1 hour in the afternoon, Lucy has the responsibility of going to Mr. Allen's first-grade class as a teaching assistant. Lucy helps the first graders with their written work, helps Mr. Allen supervise them when they work at learning stations, and reads with them as a tutor. The younger children respect Lucy and look forward to her time in their class. Lucy wouldn't dream of missing her teaching assistant time; it makes her feel important and useful. Both Ms. Englert and Mr. Allen also know that the experience provides Lucy with opportunities to practice her learning. What is this approach and why did Ms. Englert and Mr. Allen decide to try it for Lucy? What are the potential benefits and drawbacks of this program for both Lucy and the first-grade students she helps to teach?

■ Kathleen's eighth-grade social studies class is studying the impact of civil wars in developing countries on the citizens and economies of those countries. Mr. Geib announces at the beginning of class that the students should move into their teams for a cooperative assignment that will take the entire class period. The 32 students shove desks into groups and gather their own materials. After a little reminder that this is not visiting time, the students settle into groups of five or six. Kathleen's group has five members of varying abilities and skills. Behavior stemming from Kathleen's emotional disability is usually not evident in this group. Her peers do not respond to her teasing and inappropriate comments. They help her be a constructive group member to help the team get extra points and a possible "free pass" on a future assignment. The two other students in the class who have identified disabilities are in two other groups. Mr. Geib distributes materials to the students and gives directions. When everyone is working, he goes from group to group, answering questions and helping students stay focused on their assignment. What is the impact of this type of grouping arrangement in a diverse classroom? Is it more or less effective than traditional instruction? How can Mr. Geib avoid the problem of some students doing all the work for their groups while other students contribute little? What is the social benefit of this classroom grouping arrangement?

■ Twice each week, Mark is excused from his advisory period to attend a 30-minute FOCUS group. The group, which includes six students and is led by Ms. Kosleski, the school social worker, is designed to enable students to talk about how they respond to other people in different types of situations and how they might improve their social skills. For example, today the group is discussing how to talk to a teacher a student is angry with. They discuss what might have prompted the anger, what they might want to say to the teacher, and what might be best to say. They role-play a situation in which Ms. Kosleski is the teacher. The students provide feedback to each other on their responses, and Ms. Kosleski monitors to make sure the students are following the group rule of "no put-downs." This group has been meeting for six weeks. It will end in approximately three more. What will the students gain by participating? Why are schools focusing on providing social-skills training to students? How might training groups function as support groups for students?

One of the most important reasons given for the trend toward inclusive education for students with special needs is the social benefit (Bear & Minke, 1996; Farmer & Farmer, 1996; Sale & Carey, 1995). Many educators believe that students with disabilities and other exceptional needs learn appropriate social behaviors and develop friendships only when they have opportunities to interact with their nondisabled peers. At the same time, students without special needs learn that individuals with disabilities are people very much like other people, and they develop sensitivity to people who are not exactly like them and a sense of social responsibility to include individuals with special needs in the classroom community.

Connections

You can use the INCLUDE strategy presented in Chapter 4 to guide you through a problem-solving process to meet students' social-skills needs.

How do the social benefits of inclusive education occur? Is it sufficient to integrate students with disabilities into a classroom? Does integration alone help other students become more sensitive and responsive? If not, what does nurture a positive classroom social environment for all students? What if some students continue to have difficulty in their social interactions with peers, teachers, and other adults in school? What if classmates complain that adaptations for students with special needs are not fair? These are the topics we will explore in this chapter on approaches for building positive social relationships.

As you begin to think about this aspect of inclusive education, you need to keep in mind a few ideas. First, although much of the emphasis on teaching and learning in teacher preparation, including much of the emphasis in this book, concerns academics, your responsibilities as a teacher also include helping all students, whether or not they have special needs, to learn social skills. Attention to social skills should begin at a very early age and continue throughout students' school years. Second, you do not need to teach social skills to students apart from your regular class time. As you read this chapter, you will realize that many skills related to developing positive social relationships can be incorporated into your daily instruction, as Mr. Geib was doing in Kathleen's class. When you think about inclusive education, the issue of social relationships becomes part of your classroom expectations; that is, for some students the social component of their education is the primary classroom goal, whereas for others it is just a part. For example, Lucy's purpose in being in her fifth-grade classroom might have as much to do with learning important life social skills, such as talking to peers and participating in group activities, as it does with learning arithmetic skills. She has further opportunities to refine her social skills working as a teacher's assistant. Kathleen is learning how to be a member of a group without being disruptive. For Mark, however, academic expectations and social expectations are equally important. One of your responsibilities as a teacher in an inclusive class-room is to clarify these expectations with special educators.

What Is the Teacher's Role in Promoting Positive Social Interactions among Students with and without Disabilities?

A beginning point for creating a classroom in which students understand, appreci-ate, support, and interact respectfully with each other is to look at what we know about children's interactions. This knowledge provides a basis for thinking about how you can then group students and supervise their interactions to accomplish the social goals of inclusion.

Research on social relationships and interactions among students with and without disabilities has been ongoing almost since special education programs began in public schools (Bennett, 1932). During the 1950s and 1960s, researchers studied the social adjustment and acceptance by peers of students with cognitive disabilities. Sometimes, they found that students in special education classes had better social adjustment than similar students in general education classes (Cassidy & Stanton, 1959). At other times, there seemed to be few differences (Blatt, 1958). More consistent were the findings on students' peer acceptance: Researchers found that students with cognitive disabilities were less accepted and more rejected by their peers than students without disabilities (Johnson & Kirk, 1950; Miller, 1956).

When mainstreaming became an important issue during the 1970s, additional studies were completed to help educators understand the social needs of students with disabilities in general education settings. What became clear was that placing students with disabilities, especially those with cognitive disabilities, in classrooms with nondisabled peers did not alone ensure that positive social relationships would develop. In fact, the opposite was true. Students in classes with mainstreamed peers generally disliked peers with disabilities, or did not accept them (Goodman, Gott-lieb, & Harrison, 1972; Iano, Ayers, Heller, McGettigan, & Walker, 1974). In at-tempting to identify why these consistent negative findings occurred, many different characteristics of students with disabilities were examined, including aca-demic potential, label, age, gender, behavior, and physical appearance. Also studied were the ways in which students received special education services, teachers' be-haviors, the amount of time students spent in mainstream classrooms, and the types of interactions among students with and without disabilities. The picture that emerged was not clear. Many characteristics and other factors seemed to contribute to student social problems, but none was singularly important.

Connections

This research is part of the efficacy studies that were mentioned in Chapter 1 in the section on the develop-ment of special education services.

With the trend toward inclusion, attention has focused once again on the interactions of students with disabilities with their nondisabled peers. Two recent studies (Conderman, 1995; Sale & Carey, 1995) have confirmed earlier research: Even when traditional special education labels were eliminated and all services were delivered in general education, students with disabilities and other special needs were less likely to be favorably nominated by their peers and more likely to be unfavorably nominated than other students. In contrast, however, other studies suggest a more positive outlook. Evans, Salisbury, Palombaro, Berryman, and Hollowood (1992) found that students' social status among peers had more to do with other students' general standards and values than with disability. Farmer and Farmer (1996) reported that students with disabilities were well integrated into their classroom's social structure and were not "outcasts." This complex picture of students' social relationships suggests that unless teachers and other adults in schools monitor and in some cases intervene, simply mixing students with and without disabilities in single classrooms may not result in an integrated social system for them (McIntosh, Vaughn, Schumm, Haager, & Lee, 1993; Siperstein, Leffert, & Widaman, 1996; Stainback, Stainback, & Wilkinson, 1992).

At the same time, the fact that student social relationships might not occur spontaneously does not mean that inclusion has failed. What it does mean is that as a teacher, you have a significant responsibility to ensure that peer relationships develop. Many professionals have been working to develop strategies to help you accomplish this. Generally, these strategies can be grouped into three categories: (1) creating opportunities for students with and without disabilities to have face-to-face interactions, (2) nurturing support and friendship between students with and without disabilities, and (3) providing positive role models. Figure 13.1 illustrates these strategies.

Creating Opportunities for Social Interactions

The first component for promoting positive interactions among students with and without disabilities is providing opportunities for them to interact. In both elementary and secondary classrooms, this means structuring activities and assigning students to groups so that interactions become part of classroom instruction, as was accomplished in Kathleen's classroom, described at the beginning of the chapter. Eichinger (1990) demonstrated how important heterogeneous grouping is. She reported a study in which pairs of elementary students, one nondisabled and one with a severe disability, were assigned to work on one of two types of activities during a 30-minute, twice-per-week recess period. Some pairs were given a single set of play materials, such as art supplies, and were directed to share them to accomplish a goal. The other pairs were given duplicate sets of materials and directions to work alone on a project or activity. Not surprisingly, in the pairs sharing materials, the students with disabilities interacted with their peers more, engaged in more cooperative play, and showed more positive affect. Cooper and McEvoy (1996) found that by arranging friendship groups for the explicit purpose of teaching students interaction skills, positive peer interactions could be nurtured.

The implications of these and similar studies are clear: Teachers begin the process of developing positive peer interactions by maximizing students' opportunities for interactions. In what other ways could you apply this concept to the class setting in which you will teach?

WWW Resources

The Hamilton and District Extend-a-Family website at <http://www.networx.on.ca/~eaf/index.htm> can provide you with information about friendships for students with disabilities. The organization has as its goal providing children with disabilities a greater range of social experiences and friendship and supporting their families.

Do It!

With a classmate, brainstorm a list of ways you could create classroom opportunities for students to interact with each other. How would your ideas fit into your classroom instruction?

Figure 13.1 **Creating Positive Peer Relationships**

Providing opportunities for social interactions

Nurturing supportive
behavior and friendships

Serving as a role model and providing access
to other positive models

Nurturing Support and Friendship

Having students interact is a start, but it is not enough. The second component in building social relationships is to nurture mutual support and friendship between students with and without disabilities. One program that has been demonstrated to be effective in promoting friendships is **Special Friends** (Voeltz et al., 1983). In this program, students without disabilities learn about students with disabilities, including how to play and communicate with them. The basis for the program is friendship, not peer teaching. In one study in which this program was evaluated for its impact on students' interactions (Cole, Vandercook, & Rynders, 1988), it was found that Special Friends students develop reciprocal relationships; that is, the students with disabilities contributed to play, communicated, and expressed positive affect in approximately equal amounts with nondisabled students.

Another strategy for promoting student support is **Circle of Friends** (Snow & Forest, 1987, cited in Villa & Thousand, 1992). When a new student, especially one with many special needs, joins a class group, the students learn to build a circle of friends around that student. As part of this process, they review their own circle of friends by drawing four concentric circles around a figure representing themselves. The first circle contains closest friends, such as family members. The second circle contains others close to the student, such as neighbors and family friends. The third circle contains acquaintances, such as members of the student's soccer team. The outer circle contains people paid to help, such as teachers and camp counselors. The purpose of the activity is to help students understand how many people are part of their lives and to encourage them to become part of the circle of friends for the student with a disability.

The Special Friends and Circle of Friends programs are only two of many strategies for promoting friendship and support. Other strategies include pairing students on the basis of shared interests so that they have a natural basis for becoming friends (Fox, 1989) and having students brainstorm ideas for welcoming and making friends with a new class member with a disability (Stainback et al., 1992). In addition, teachers can nurture supportive interactions by rewarding students when they offer to assist a student with a disability or when they include such students in their games and conversations (Collins, Nall, & Branson, 1997). Teachers of elementary students might also consider incorporating friendship skills into their instruction. By teaching students how to greet one another, how to express friendship, and how to resolve conflicts, teachers can foster positive peer relationships and provide students with a strong basis for lifelong interaction skills (Cooper & McEvoy, 1996).

Sometimes you will have to address problems related to student support and friendship. Some students (and some teachers, too) express concern about the fairness of making many exceptions for students with special needs, such as changing the consequences for misbehavior, altering the amount or type of work expected, grading on a more generous scale, or using rewards to which other students may not have access. The Professional Edge offers advice about responding to issues of fairness.

Providing Positive Role Models

A third component of promoting positive peer relationships is offering positive role models (Kloomok & Cosden, 1994). There are several ways to do this. First, as a teacher in an inclusive school, you might be the most influential model for students learning how to interact with a peer with a disability. If you are positive in your interactions and avoid responding to a student with a disability as a "guest" instead of a full classroom member, students will respond in a similar way. For example, if you talk to a student with a severe disability as though he or she is a very young child even though you are teaching an eighth-grade class, other students will probably treat the student as a young child. However, if you speak in an age-appropriate voice, so will your students. Similarly, if you expect a student with a learning disability to behave at the same level as other students instead of making exceptions (provided that this expectation is appropriate), peers in the class will have the same expectations. Interacting with students with disabilities in the same way as you would interact with anyone else provides the modeling that will help shape all student interactions.

Cultural Awareness

Students' interactions with others are determined partly by cultural expectations. Be sure to consider this fact as you work to have a positive influence on how your students treat one another.

FYI

A colleague or community member who has a disability might be a great resource as a positive role model for students.

Professional Edge

Responding to Issues of Fairness

A problem that seems to exist in schools is confusion between fairness and equality. As Richard LaVoie, in his videotape *How Difficult Can This Be?*, points out, responding to every student in the same way demonstrates equality. However, responding to each student based on need is the meaning of fairness. He contends that schools should try to be places of fairness, not equality. Here are some suggestions for addressing fairness:

1. Be clear about your own beliefs and values concerning the appropriateness and justice of making exceptions for students with special needs.

2. Discuss issues related to fairness openly with students. This openness includes alerting them to accommodations students with disabilities in class might receive, discussing their own special needs, and role-playing situations that could occur in class that might not be perceived as "fair" and how to respond to them.

3. Prevent students from basing their perception of themselves and their achievement on other students. It is your responsibility to avoid discouraging conversations in which students compare themselves with classmates, either positively or negatively.

4. If a student says something like, "Yeah, but Stanley yelled in the room and *he* didn't get his name on the board. That's not fair!" the best way for you to respond is to say, "Let's just talk about you. What was it that made you yell?" The worst response is to engage in a conversation about Stanley's special needs.

5. If parents attempt to compare their child with another, politely but firmly explain that it is ethically and legally inappropriate for you to discuss other students. Then ask them to clarify their concerns about their child. If they are dissatisfied with your response, enlist the support and assistance of your building administrator.

Students without disabilities also need to see that students with disabilities and other special needs have many *abilities*. Pointing out contributions made by a student with a disability, giving students with disabilities standard classroom responsibilities, and recognizing a student's best effort—whether or not it fits within traditional curriculum standards—all these actions lead peers to recognize that the student is a valuable classroom community member (Stainback, Stainback, & Jackson, 1992). Family and community or national support groups also can be resources for providing positive role models. Parents or siblings might gladly talk about a student's abilities as part of school awareness activities (Rothman & Cosden, 1995). The Professional Edge on page 458 presents additional ideas on positive role models for fostering social relationships among students with and without disabilities.

Promoting positive peer relationships needs to be part of your automatic teaching behaviors throughout the course of the school year. Evidence suggests that a long-term approach for fostering peer interactions is most effective, and that when teachers stop attending to students' social relationships, these relationships tend to deteriorate (Fox, 1989).

> **Do It!**
>
> Identify and contact local and national support groups for people with disabilities. Ask a representative of each about the availability of speakers and other resource materials.

Professional Edge

Social Success from Social Support

One of the major goals of current trends toward inclusive practices is to foster in students with disabilities social skills that can help them throughout their lives, in jobs, with family, in recreational settings, in post-secondary school environments, and so on. One way to accomplish this goal is to provide the social support that students need. Here are some research results that can help you understand your role in social support:

1. Students with mental retardation tend to have social networks that are similar in size to those of students without disabilities, but they rely largely on adult family members and adults outside the home for general support instead of peers as do other students (Wenz-Gross & Siperstein, 1996).

2. Students with learning disabilities who believe that their disabilities are modifiable and not a stigma report that they feel more support from their families and peers, regardless of their actual level of academic achievement. The sense of social support is clearly important to these students (Rothman & Cosden, 1995).

3. Students with learning disabilities who perceive themselves to be doing well in their academics based their perceptions largely on feedback they received in their classroom. Positive teacher feedback is viewed as a critical component of maintaining positive perceptions of student self-worth (Bear & Minke, 1996).

4. Students with mild cognitive disabilities and learning disabilities do not use their families for support to problem solve, and they do not use peers as do other students as a source of emotional support (Wenz-Gross & Siperstein, 1997).

These studies suggest that, as a teacher, you can help foster social support by directly teaching students how to create a social network of friends, helping students to understand the nature of their disabilities, providing supportive feedback to students on a frequent basis, and teaching students to ask friends, adults, and family members for assistance when needed.

How Can Teachers Provide Education about Individuals with Disabilities?

Check Your Learning

Why should your instructional program include information about individuals with disabilities? What strategies can you use to ensure that your instructional program educates your students about people with disabilities?

Besides promoting positive social interactions between students with and without disabilities, teachers play an important role in educating their students about all types of differences among individuals, including disabilities (Stainback, Stainback, East, & Sapon-Shevin, 1994). Even during years in which you have few or no students with disabilities in your class, you can positively affect student understanding and attitude toward individuals with disabilities by building information about them into your curriculum. In this section, these strategies are described: informing students through direct instruction, using video and print media, demonstrating and using adaptive technology, and arranging simulation activities. The Case in Practice suggests why there is a strong need for school-based disability awareness and sensitivity training.

Case in Practice

Intervening to Promote Positive Social Interactions

Mrs. Haynes is in a quandary. This afternoon during her last-period eighth-grade science class, she discovered that four girls who share a lab station had taped a sign to their lab table that said, "Only really cool and cute people are allowed to sit here." The girls had told a less popular student with a mild cognitive disability and mild cerebral palsy that she couldn't join them for the lab because she wasn't cool and certainly wasn't cute. The girl, Shana, had quietly sat at the end of the lab station for the entire period, fighting back tears. The other girls had been giggling the entire time. With many student questions and an interruption from the office, Mrs. Haynes had not realized what was happening until near the end of the period. She had felt like strangling

the four girls, and her heart was broken for Shana. She had decided that Shana needed attention more immediately than the other girls and had spent nearly a half hour after school with her. She would call the girls' parents tonight, as she had told them she would, but she was still extremely disappointed that four of her students could be so cruel. The incident also made her wonder what else went on that she was unaware of. She resolved to spend the evening deciding how to take proactive steps to influence the thinking of these and her other students.

REFLECTIONS

Why might girls in middle school be so insensitive to peers' feelings? How might elementary school students or high school students convey the same message? If you were Mrs. Haynes, what would you have said to Shana after school? Why? How would you talk to the other girls' parents? What consequence would you impose for the girls' cruel prank? How would you go about educating these students about individuals with disabilities and the diversity that exists among all people? What activities could be incorporated into this science class? What similar activities could be used in an elementary school or high school classroom?

Informing through Direct Instruction

One of the most straightforward strategies for teaching students about individuals with disabilities is to provide them with relevant information. For example, you might invite guest speakers to your class to discuss what it is like to have a disability and how people with disabilities lead successful lives. Alternatively, you might arrange to have professionals who provide services to individuals with disabilities talk about their careers. You can also find individuals to speak to your students through local disability advocacy groups or parent groups. A local college or university might also be a valuable resource.

You also can educate students about disabilities by incorporating relevant topics into the curriculum. As you teach, you can mention famous individuals with disabilities who contributed to various fields. For example, when studying the presidents, you can raise the fact that Franklin D. Roosevelt had polio and used a wheelchair. In science, you can explain Thomas Edison's hearing loss and Albert Einstein's alleged learning disability. In the fine arts, examples of individuals with disabilities include actress Marlee Matlin, singer Stevie Wonder, and composer Ludwig von Beethoven. Students' understanding and respect for individuals with disabilities are better fostered through an ongoing education program rather than occasional "special events" that highlight this topic. For example, if your school participates in an

How do students without disabilities learn about their peers with disabilities? How can teachers promote friendships between students with and without exceptionalities?

ongoing program to increase students' understanding of racial, cultural, religious, and other types of diversity, disability awareness is appropriately included as another type of diversity.

A third source of direct information about disabilities is special awareness programs. An example of a program for use in inclusive classrooms is *Kids on the Block*, a set of puppets and supporting materials and books about disabilities. The puppets "talk" to students about having disabilities and interacting with classmates and others who have them. This program, typically staffed by volunteers, is available in many communities. Your community might have another similar program with the same purpose. For example, the *Mad Hatters*, a drama troupe, performs skits about people with and without disabilities and then leads discussions with students about what each character might be feeling (McGookey, 1992). The goal is to promote awareness that people with disabilities are individuals and to make nondisabled students more comfortable interacting with them. The special educators in your school should know what programs are available in your area and how you can access them.

Using Video and Print Media

Individuals with disabilities have gained a greater voice in all aspects of our society, and their visibility also has increased in the media. A trip to your local library or video store or a casual reading of television program guides or your newspaper can lead you to a wealth of information. You could identify how the information relates to your instructional goals, find ways to incorporate it into your lessons, and arrange discussions so that your students feel free to ask questions and share their insights.

Your school or district might have educational videos about students with disabilities. Many award-winning movies also address disability and are appropriate for older students. These films include *My Left Foot, Rainman, Gaby—A True Story, Born on the Fourth of July, The Miracle Worker, If You Could See What I Hear, The Other Side of the Mountain, Children of a Lesser God* (McGookey, 1992), and *Forrest Gump.* Television shows and made-for-TV movies also address disability topics.

Books written by and for children exist about virtually every type of disability and other special need (McCarty & Chalmers, 1997; Orr et al., 1997). Reading or assigning an appropriate book to your class can be an excellent strategy for introducing a new student and his or her special needs. A reading assignment can also help open a discussion about interacting and treating a classmate respectfully.

Newspapers carry stories about individuals with disabilities, requirements of the Americans with Disabilities Act, and trends toward inclusive education. National newspapers such as *USA Today* and *The Wall Street Journal* are a source of this type of information, but your local paper also carries stories you can use. For example, when a major league baseball player had a seizure during a ball game, the local newspaper ran a story on what to do if you see someone having a seizure. The high-interest article became a valuable teaching tool for sports-minded middle school students.

Demonstrating and Using Adaptive Technology

Another means of educating students about individuals with disabilities is by exploring technology resources (Male, 1997). For example, you can teach students about the powerful tools available to facilitate communication, including touch screens, talking word processors, customized computer keyboards, computer voice input, and word prediction programs. You can demonstrate for students the capabilities of talking computers, calculators, and watches. Some specific ideas for using technology to enhance communication between students with disabilities and other classmates are included in the Technology Notes feature on pages 462–463.

Arranging Simulation Activities

In addition to teaching students about disabilities directly, through the use of films, books, other media, and demonstrations of adaptive technology, you can help students understand what it is like to have a disability by arranging simulations (Anderson & Milliren, 1983; Hallenbeck & McMaster, 1991). A **simulation** is an activity in which students experience what it might be like to have a disability as they carry out typical school, home, or community activities. An important component is providing opportunities for students to discuss what they learn from simulation experiences and how they could be more sensitive and respectful to their classmates with disabilities. In one school district, all secondary students attended an assembly at which class members who had participated in simulation activities shared their experiences (Hallenbeck & McMaster, 1991). The following sections describe effective simulations for specific types of disabilities. Keep in mind, however, that students also need to understand that simulating a disability is not exactly like having the disability. Classroom discussions based on simulations should address this fact.

D o I t !

Create a resource list of videos, television programs, and books about people with disabilities.

Technology Notes

Using Technology to Build Positive Peer Relationships

Technology can be a powerful tool for building positive social peer relationships in your classroom. Here are two examples of how to use technology with students with and without disabilities.

Dialogue Journals

Most teachers have learned that computers are important tools for motivating reluctant writers to share their thoughts and ideas. Computers can also facilitate communication between students with and without disabilities by using them to create dialogue journals. A dialogue journal is a realistic writing situation in which students are encouraged to share their thoughts and feelings with an agemate, while teachers simply manage and monitor the process. Dialogue journals focus on meanings rather than formality, and they provide a nonthreatening climate for students' writing activities. Students are matched either with a known peer or a "mystery" peer from another class, and they write to each other approximately once

Students with disabilities sometimes communicate with peers and others by using adaptive technology.

each week. Computer disks make transferring journals from class to class a relatively simple task. At some point, teachers should probably arrange for students to meet each other and discuss the journals face-to-face, but this is not as essential as the writing process itself.

By pairing students with and without disabilities, students can gain greater understanding of each

Simulations for physical disabilities. Physical disabilities can be safely simulated in a number of ways using simple materials. For example, to show students what it is like to have limited dexterity, ask them to perform fine motor tasks such as picking up a paper clip, sorting papers, and writing while wearing a bulky glove. Another way of demonstrating limited motor control is to have students keep their dominant hand in their pocket and complete schoolwork or eat lunch using only their nondominant hand. Painting by holding a paintbrush between their teeth sensitizes students to individuals who do not have the use of their arms.

Students might also experience what it is like to use a wheelchair, which you could borrow from your special services office or rent from a health supply store. In one activity, students are paired for a schoolwide scavenger hunt, with one student in a wheelchair and the other as a companion. Students perform simple tasks that they normally take for granted, such as getting a drink from a drinking fountain, using the bathroom, making a phone call from a public phone, and getting to a second-floor classroom or out to a sidewalk.

other's perceptions. In a project in which hearing and deaf students participated (Kluwin, 1996), students responded very positively to the experience. However, teachers commented that some problems occurred when students were mismatched with regard to maturity or developmental levels, or when students in general did not have skills for personal writing. To maximize the effectiveness of dialogue journals, teachers should encourage students to use a conversational style in their journals; students without disabilities should not be overprepared for the experience, or else prejudice may occur; teachers should suggest topics as needed; students should be matched; and teachers should monitor the writing, paying attention to issues of privacy.

Problem-Solving Videos

Teachers can use videotapes of popular television shows, movies, or other instructional video materials to work with students on social skills and problem solving. Using the Improving Social Awareness–Social Problem Solving Project (Elias & Clabby, 1989), teachers can guide students to use these steps in real-life interactions by applying them as they view a video:

1. Look for signs of different feelings.
2. Tell yourself what the problem is.

3. Decide on your goal.
4. Stop and think of as many solutions to the problem as you can.
5. For each solution, picture all the things that might happen.
6. Choose your best solution.
7. Plan it and make a final check.
8. Try it and rethink it.

This approach to addressing social skills and problem-solving appears to have great value because it draws on television as a means of focusing student attention, enables even nonreaders to participate, promotes discussion, and presents opportunities for later role-playing. Younger students and those with attentional problems can be shown shorter videotapes, perhaps 15 minutes or less; older students and those with better attentional skills can view longer tapes. Teachers, of course, play a critical role in guiding student thinking and facilitating student discussion.

S O U R C E : Adapted from Elias, M. J., & Taylor, M. E. (1995). "Building social and academic skills via problem solving videos." *Teaching Exceptional Children*, 27(3), 14–17; and Kluwin, T. N. (1996). "Getting hearing and deaf students to write to each other through dialogue journals." *Teaching Exceptional Children*, 28(2), 50–53.

Simulations for sensory disabilities. Swimmer's earplugs can be used to simulate a hearing impairment. Activities that students might try while "hearing impaired" include eating lunch with friends in a noisy cafeteria, watching a television show or video with classmates with the sound unamplified, and talking on the phone. Students could discuss visual clues they used to tell what others were saying and how they felt when they missed important messages. For vision impairments, a blindfold or eye patch can be an effective simulation. Partial sight can be simulated by using waxed paper or crumpled plastic wrap inserted into glasses frames. Activities while "vision impaired" might include eating lunch, completing a written assignment, reading from the board, or locating a book on a shelf. Discussion topics might include the difference between not being able to see at all and not being able to see well, and how others were and were not helpful to the student experiencing impaired vision.

Simulations for learning and cognitive disabilities. Students can learn what it is like to have a learning or cognitive disability by experiencing some of the inherent

Cultural Awareness

According to the U.S. Census Bureau, the overall rate of disability among all Americans is 19.4 percent. However, the rate is highest for Native Americans at 21.9 percent followed closely by African Americans at 20 percent. For Asian Americans, the rate of disability is only 9.9 percent. Of what significance is this information when thinking about the social relationships of students with and without disabilities?

frustrations of these disabilities. For example, students using their nondominant hand to write their names on a card as they hold the card to their foreheads will discover how difficult it can be to make your hand do what you want it to do. Having students write or trace a pattern by watching their hands in a small mirror is also effective. Another simulation is the game Simon Says, but played in reverse such that students do the opposite of the command given (Anderson & Milliren, 1983). For example, when the leader says, "Jump on your right foot," students must jump on the left foot. They discover the difficulty of reversing operations. One other strategy is to give students a reading assignment far above their reading level and then ask complex questions about it. Discussion based on these simulations can highlight the frustration of knowing that one is not "dumb" but not being able to complete certain activities successfully, of wanting to give up when tasks are difficult, and of worrying about what others will think when one cannot do as well as they can.

Simulation activities can be divided among classroom teams, with each team reporting their experiences to the whole class. Older students might extend their experience by preparing simulation activities for younger students, leading them through the activities, and conducting follow-up discussions.

How Can You Develop and Support Peer Tutoring?

Students also learn about disabilities and other special needs through direct experience and interaction with classmates. **Peer tutoring** is a system of instruction in which pairs of students help one another and learn by teaching (Jenkins & Jenkins, 1988). The tutor role is most often held by a peer in the same class, school, or school district. Tutees are the students who receive the instruction from peer tutors. When peer tutoring is used with students with disabilities, the goal is often twofold: (1) fostering social interactions and (2) enhancing academic achievement (Yasutake, Bryan, & Dohrn, 1996).

Recent studies of peer tutoring have demonstrated its impact on students' peer interactions. For example, peer tutoring has been found to increase the number of interactions between students with disabilities and their nondisabled tutors (Fulton, LeRoy, Pinchney, & Weekley, 1994). It also helps students who are not liked by classmates to become more socially accepted (Garcia-Vasquez & Ehly, 1992). However, peer tutoring generally does not seem to influence student self-concept either positively or negatively (Cohen, Kulik, & Kulik, 1982).

In the area of academic achievement, peer tutoring has been demonstrated to improve the achievement of tutees. For example, in a study in which sixth-grade students taught math concepts to younger students with moderate cognitive disabilities, the younger students' knowledge of beginning mathematics improved (Vacc & Cannon, 1991). Similar results have been found when the tutees are students who have high-incidence disabilities or are at risk for school failure and when the subject matter is either reading or mathematics (Fantuzzo, King, & Heller, 1992; Mathes & Fuchs, 1994). For example, students at risk for school failure have been found to increase the amount of time they spend on school tasks and their achievement in a peer tutoring program (Greenwood, 1991).

Peer tutoring also has a positive impact on tutors, particularly when older tutors with marginal skills work with younger students. Students who serve as tutors learn their academic content better, and they have more positive attitudes toward school

WWW Resources

Thousands of websites related to peer tutoring can be found on the Internet. If you type the phrase *peer tutoring* in one of the major search engines (e.g., Internet Sleuth, Webcrawler, Yahoo!), you'll find many resources to help you establish a successful program.

Professional Edge

Tips for Successful Peer Tutoring

Peer tutoring outcomes are influenced by many factors, including the type of material being practiced, the age and sex of the students involved, and the level of achievement and amount of training the tutors and tutees have. Keep in mind the following tips for fostering successful peer tutoring.

1. Many aspects of the school curriculum are amenable to instruction and practice via peer and cross-age tutoring.

2. A student of any age may be either the tutor or tutee; the older student does not necessarily have to be the tutor.

3. Peer and cross-age tutors are often high achievers, but an achiever at any level might serve equally well as a tutor. More important than actual ability is the tutor's ability to teach without making value judgments about the tutee.

4. Same-sex partners work best in both cross-age and peer tutoring, especially for older students.

5. Tutors should be trained both in how to interact with their tutees and in how to present content to them and record their learning.

6. Tutoring can influence both cognitive and affective objectives for students.

SOURCE: Adapted from "Peer and Cross-Age Tutoring: The Lessons of Research" by M. D. Rekrut, 1994, *Journal of Reading, 37*(5), 356–362. Used by permission of International Reading Association.

and learning (Cohen et al., 1982). Not surprisingly, these results are most pronounced when the tutor has not already mastered the academic content used in tutoring (Jenkins, & Jenkins, 1981).

Research on peer tutoring programs has addressed factors such as the age of the tutor and the tutee, the amount of time allocated for tutoring, the content selected for peer tutoring, and the amount of program structure. All these factors influence peer tutoring outcomes. The Professional Edge summarizes advice about all types of peer tutoring based on such research (Rekrut, 1994).

Developing Peer Tutoring Programs

Developing a **peer tutoring program** can be as simple or complex as you want it to be. You can create your own system within your classroom, partner some or all of your students with another group of students, or help coordinate a schoolwide tutoring program. Established and researched programs also exist, such as the *Classwide Peer Tutoring Program* (Greenwood, Delquadri, & Hall, 1989) described in Figure 13.2 on page 466. Steps for setting up a peer tutoring program of your own are described in the following sections.

Selecting tutors.   To create a **same-age tutoring** program in your classroom, consider pairing students who are high achievers rather than pairing high achievers with low achievers. Then assign other students based on their being fairly similar in their understanding of the topic. This arrangement reduces the problem of high

FYI

Give all your students, not just those who are high-achieving, a chance to be tutors. Lower-achieving students can benefit socially and academically from tutoring younger students.

Figure 13.2   Steps in *Classwide Peer Tutoring*

1. Assign all students to tutoring pairs that are changed weekly.
2. Assign each tutoring pair to one of two classroom teams.
3. Teach all students a specific series of steps for presenting and practicing content.
4. Teach all students specific strategies for correcting tutees and rewarding correct responses.
5. Provide tutoring pairs with daily assignments.
6. Instruct tutors to keep score: When a tutee answers a question correctly, a point is scored for the team.
7. Announce the winning team and post points.
8. Reward the winning team with a privilege or class applause.
9. Reverse the tutor/tutee arrangement each session or have both students take the tutor role within each session.

FYI

Use more than one tutoring arrangement in your classroom to avoid the problem of tutees feeling stigmatized because they are receiving assistance.

Cultural Awareness

Arrange tutoring groups so that students from differing cultural, racial, ethnic, and socioeconomic backgrounds have opportunities to interact. Giving students a chance to socialize and learn with students from different backgrounds helps reduce stereotyping and prejudice.

achievers becoming impatient with other students and the concern about high-achieving students missing their own opportunities for learning. However, same-age tutoring has two drawbacks: High-achieving students do not learn patience for students with special learning needs, and lower-achieving students lose learning role models. Another approach is to pair students randomly and use a **reciprocal tutoring** approach in which both students alternate between the tutor and tutee roles (Greenwood et al., 1989).

In a **cross-age tutoring** approach, older students tutor younger ones. For example, if you teach in the primary grades, you might ask the fifth-grade teachers to provide tutors for your students. Teachers could collaborate to partner entire classes and institute a regularly scheduled cross-class tutoring. If a middle school, junior high, or high school is located nearby, these students could also serve as tutors. In a middle school or high school, you might establish a peer tutoring program for the school a level below yours so that high school students tutor in the middle school and middle school students tutor in the elementary school. At the secondary level, older students might serve as tutors and mentors for younger ones. Seniors might be paired with freshmen in this way.

As you decide how to establish a tutoring program, keep in mind students with disabilities and other special needs. Sometimes, students with disabilities can serve as tutors to their classmates. An older student without a disability can be an ideal tutor for a younger student who has a disability. Also, an older student who has a learning or cognitive disability or who is at risk for school failure can be an effective tutor for a younger student with or without a disability. In other words, you can structure a tutoring program in many ways. What is important is making deliberate decisions about how to structure it, basing decisions on the strengths and needs of the students.

Depending on your goals, you might turn to adult tutors. In some school districts, the best available pool of tutors are college students or adult volunteers such as students' parents or grandparents or recently retired teaching staff (Scruggs & Mastropieri, 1992). Adults can make better judgments about the content being taught and learned. Tutees often look up to older tutors, who provide a special type of individual attention. Adults also have the maturity that eliminates potential behavior problems that sometimes occur with peer partners. Of course, if your goals include helping students improve peer relations, some form of *peer* tutoring is your best option.

Deciding how much tutoring should occur.   The specific time allocation for peer tutoring depends on the needs of the students and the structure of the program. Although research has not provided clear guidelines, in many cases tutoring in elementary schools occurs two to four times each week for 20 or 30 minutes and up to daily for one class period in high schools (Jenkins & Jenkins, 1985; Maheady, Mallette, & Harper, 1991). This amount of tutoring ensures continuity yet does not detract significantly from the rest of students' educational programs.

Providing time for peer tutoring.   Peer tutoring can occur as part of independent work time or as a periodic activity in which an entire class participates. Cross-age tutoring needs to occur on a schedule that accommodates both the tutor and the tutee. Optimal times can include the beginning of the school day as students arrive, the middle of the afternoon when both the tutor and the tutee need a change-of-pace activity, near the end of the school day, or after school. As much as possible, tutoring in a content area should occur within the content-area classes.

Selecting content and format for tutoring.   Effective peer tutoring programs provide practice on skills already taught by the teacher and use standard formats that help tutors know how to do their job (Jenkins & Jenkins, 1985; Maheady et al., 1991). For example, many studies of peer tutoring have tutors and tutees working on basic math facts, spelling or vocabulary words, or comprehension questions on social studies or science materials already taught in class.

How can peer tutoring programs benefit students in your classroom? What combinations of tutors and tutees might work best for the grade level you plan to teach?

Check Your Learning

What are the various types of peer tutoring? In what situations might you choose to use each type?

Highly structured formats for tutoring sessions are best. For example, tutors might be instructed to begin the session by reviewing all eight words from last time and then showing each new word, waiting for a response, and marking the response as correct or incorrect. The tutor praises correct responses, corrects errors, and asks the tutee to repeat corrected responses. If the students finish their list, they review it until the end of the tutoring session. This example illustrates the need for a clear set of procedures for tutors to follow, whatever format you use. Clear procedures help keep participants in tutoring sessions on task.

Training tutors. Many authors distinguish between effective and less effective peer tutoring programs on the basis of the preparation tutors receive for their teaching roles. Evidence suggests that intensive tutor training results in better tutoring outcomes (Barron & Foot, 1991). Tutor training should accomplish five main purposes:

1. It should provide tutors with the structures and procedures for tutoring as described above.

2. It should give tutors a systematic way of tracking the tutees' learning.

3. It should help tutors develop positive interaction skills, including ways to praise tutees and ways to correct their errors.

4. Training should prepare tutors in problem-solving skills so that they can generate ideas about how to proceed when the procedures are not working, or when the tutee gets confused or misbehaves.

5. Tutor training adds perceived value and credibility to the program and its participants.

Sample topics for a peer tutor training program are outlined in Figure 13.3.

Supporting Peer Tutoring Programs

Part of a tutor training program includes follow-up and assessment. For example, in a cross-age tutoring program, it is important to bring tutors together periodically to discuss how they are doing and how they have resolved problems and to thank them for their work. When tutoring extends beyond your own class group, it is a nice touch to provide tutor appreciation certificates or other tokens of appreciation.

Several other factors go into the supports needed for a successful peer tutoring program. These factors are discussed in the sections that follow.

Management and supervision. Once your peer tutoring program is established, you should continue to supervise it. This ongoing supervision enables you to praise tutor pairs having constructive work sessions, identify potential problems when they are small and easily resolved, and monitor student learning. If you have the assistance of a paraprofessional in your classroom, this person can help with day-to-day supervision responsibilities. As your tutoring program progresses, you might find it necessary to revise the format, regroup students, introduce "graduates," and devise new ways to thank the tutors for their work.

Staff and administrative support. Unless you plan a peer tutoring program that stays within the confines of your classroom, you will need the support of your colleagues and administrators. Other teachers might have ideas on how to pair stu-

Figure 13.3   Topics for Training Peer Tutors

1. Sensitivity to others' feelings, needs for acceptance, and fears of rejection.

2. Ways to develop positive relationships with tutees, including using respectful language, giving positive reinforcement, showing personal interest, and offering constructive feedback.

3. Effective communication and interaction skills
   - Giving clear directions
   - Making teaching interesting to the tutee
   - Acting interested—and being interested
   - Explaining things in another way
   - Correcting the tutee without criticism
   - Praising correct responses
   - Admitting mistakes

4. Tutoring procedures and guidelines
   - Having all needed materials prepared
   - Beginning a session without teacher assistance
   - Breaking big steps into smaller ones
   - Showing how to do something if the tutee does not understand
   - Giving the tutee time to think before responding
   - Helping but not doing the work for the tutee
   - Monitoring time to finish on schedule
   - Reviewing what has been taught

5. Procedures for gathering data on the tutee's learning, such as using a checklist or helping the tutee chart progress.

6. Problem solving about issues that could come up during peer tutoring.

7. The tutoring schedule and the need for commitment.

dents and arrange formats and opportunities for tutoring, and the special services staff might have creative ways of including students with special needs in the tutoring program. Administrators can provide support and assistance in arranging schedules, communicating with parents, and finding a small budget for the incidental supplies you might need.

Assistance from volunteers.   In addition to helping with tutoring, volunteers might also be willing to manage a peer tutoring program, thus relieving you of many of the details of operation. For example, volunteers could establish the procedures for recruiting peer tutors or could offer the tutor training, match tutors with tutees, monitor the tutoring sessions, assess student learning, problem solve with tutors, and arrange a thank-you event for them. Education majors or other teacher trainees

■ Do It!

Volunteer to help set up a peer tutoring program in a local school. What are the program's objectives? What difficulties did you encounter? What were the most rewarding aspects of the project?

■ Connections

Chapters 2 and 3 included strategies for parent communication. These strategies could be part of your approach to communicating with parents about peer tutoring.

in local colleges or universities could assist in these tasks, as could members of a parent or community organization familiar with peer tutoring.

Communication about peer tutoring. Support for peer tutoring programs often depends on communication with parents and other community members. If you plan a peer tutoring program for your students, you will want to alert the parents and explain your instructional approach and rationale. If you participate in a tutoring program that includes several classes, you might want to write a letter to parents announcing the availability of the program and providing its rationale. Although most parents will readily agree to permit their children to participate as tutors or tutees, a few might have questions about tutors losing instructional time teaching others and about the effectiveness of tutoring for students who have difficulty learning. Being prepared for questions such as these will help you answer them readily. Also, your administrator can provide support in this area. As your tutoring program progresses, you can keep parents apprised of student activities through periodic notes or class newsletters, or through updates provided by your home–school hotline or district newsletter.

How Can You Use Cooperative Learning Strategies to Facilitate Social Inclusion?

Peer tutoring offers one structured alternative for promoting positive peer relationships. Another option for accomplishing this goal is cooperative learning. Cooperative learning has its roots in the U.S. civil rights and school desegregation movements. Very soon after the *Brown v. Board of Education* Supreme Court decision established that separate schools cannot be equal, Gordon Allport (1954) wrote that simply putting students of different races in the same schools would not accomplish integration. He went on to clarify that integration would require opportunities for students to interact with one another in situations in which they had equal status. Further, he stated that school administrators would have to endorse the students' interactions strongly. In practice, this meant that students needed opportunities to interact with one another in structured social situations not controlled by teachers but strongly sanctioned by school authorities, situations free of unreasonable academic pressures that might put some students in a lower "status." Cooperative learning was developed as a means of creating these conditions during traditional classroom instruction (Sharan et al., 1984). For nearly three decades, cooperative learning has been proposed as a strategy for promoting positive student interactions in diverse classrooms. It has been used as a strategy for achieving racial and cultural integration, for assisting socially isolated learners, for fostering inclusive education for students with disabilities and other special needs, and for accommodating culture-based learning styles.

Understanding the Rationale for Cooperative Learning

As you can see from the history of cooperative learning, its primary purpose was to increase students' ability to interact with each other in appropriate ways. Many studies over the past 20 years have addressed this topic. For example, Solomon and his colleagues (1990) have found that students in classrooms stressing cooperative learning spontaneously express more concern for other students and help each other more than do students in comparable classes in which cooperative learning is not emphasized. Students in cooperative classrooms also are more likely to show affection toward other class members, invite others to join a group activity, and thank or praise each other. Although fewer studies are available on secondary students, the same trend exists. For example, in a study of cooperative learning in a tenth-grade biology class, students experienced a higher level of self-esteem than did students in a comparison class; they felt their class was treated more fairly, and they displayed more cohesiveness and less competitiveness as a group (Lazarowitz & Karsenty, 1990).

For students with disabilities, the social benefits of cooperative learning appear to accrue in the same way that they do for other students. In one review of nearly 100 studies of cooperative learning (Johnson, Johnson, & Maruyama, 1983), the positive social impact existed for students with disabilities as well as for students with other special needs, especially so when these students were given specific instruction in collaborative skills (Putnam, Rynders, Johnson, & Johnson, 1989). In fact, cooperative learning is often recommended as a fundamental component of inclusive classrooms (Putnam, 1993b). While the value of cooperative learning lies first in its potential for creating positive peer interactions, it also can enhance learning and achievement (Lou et al., 1996; Qin, Johnson, & Johnson, 1995). For students without disabilities, cooperative learning has strongly and repeatedly been demonstrated to be an effective instructional approach for student achievement in reading, math, science, and thinking skills (Lazarowitz & Karsenty, 1990; Slavin, 1994).

The academic outcomes in cooperative learning for students with disabilities vary and cannot always be assumed to be strong (Tateyama-Sniezek, 1990). However, some evidence does suggest that for students with high-incidence disabilities, cooperative learning is at least as effective as other instructional approaches (Cosden, Pearl, & Bryan, 1985; Mathes, Fuchs, & Fuchs, 1997). Even stronger results have been noted for other students with special needs, including students who are gifted and talented (Coleman, Gallagher, & Nelson, 1993) and those at risk for school failure (Slavin, Madden, Karweit, Livermon, & Dolan, 1989). For students with severe cognitive disabilities or multiple disabilities, the issue of academic achievement as traditionally measured is not usually a central concern.

Learning the Characteristics of Cooperative Learning Approaches

Cooperative learning generally has four fundamental and essential characteristics (Johnson & Johnson, 1992). First, the students in the groups have positive interdependence. They either reach their goal together, or no one is able to achieve it. For example, in Mr. Reilly's classroom, the students earn points if all the members in their cooperative group get at least 70 percent on their weekly spelling test. Group members work very hard to help all members learn spelling words. Second, cooperative learning requires face-to-face interactions. In Mr. Reilly's class, students have opportunities to work directly with their group members to accomplish their learning goals. Third, members of cooperative groups have individual accountability. On the weekly spelling test, students who have difficulty learning their words are not excused from taking the test, nor are high achievers permitted to answer for all

WWW Resources

At <http://www.nwrel.org/scpd/sirs/2/snap5.html> you can read about cooperative learning occurring in two secondary schools in the state of Washington.

Cultural Awareness

Research shows that students with limited English proficiency and minority students benefit both academically and socially from cooperative learning arrangements (Slavin et al., 1989).

group members. Each member is required to make a contribution. Finally, cooperative learning stresses student interpersonal skills, such as how to ask questions, how to praise classmates, and how to help another student learn.

These four characteristics of cooperative learning distinguish it from other approaches to learning common in schools. For example, much school learning is competitive, that is, based on winners and losers. Spelling matches or other instructional games in which only one student wins are competitive. Another example of school competition is found in many athletic programs. A second type of traditional learning approach is individualistic. In individualistic learning, student achievement is not dependent on how others achieve. For example, a teacher sets up a system in which all students who complete 90 percent of their homework are listed on the class "good work habits" honor roll. If all the students in the class meet the standard of 90 percent, all can be listed. If only one student meets the standard, only that student will be listed. All students can be winners; one student's winning does not affect other students' chances of success. An individualistic approach is also the basis for special education and most remedial programs.

All three approaches—cooperative, competitive, and individualistic—have a place in schools. However, the social and interactive components of cooperative learning are not possible in either of the other two approaches, and so this approach needs to be added deliberately to the school curriculum.

Developing Cooperative Learning Programs

Given the many positive effects of cooperative learning for all students, you will probably want to use it as an instructional approach in your classroom. You might decide to use cooperative groups three times each week for language arts activities, for instance, or once each week for test review. Regardless of how you incorporate cooperative learning into your classroom, you can achieve the best results by following some basic guidelines.

Check Your Learning

Compare the steps for creating a peer tutoring program with those for establishing a cooperative learning program. How are they alike? How do they differ? What accounts for the similarities and differences?

Form cooperative learning groups. One of your first considerations in creating a **cooperative learning program** is deciding on the size and makeup of the groups. Regardless of the specific cooperative learning approach you choose, the age, abilities, and needs of your students help determine group size. For example, if you teach second grade, you will probably use groups of three at the beginning of the school year and consider larger groups after students become accustomed to cooperative learning procedures. If you teach eighth grade, you might be able to begin the year with groups of five. Other factors besides age should be considered, too. In a class with mature students, larger groups are possible; in a class with immature students, groups of three might be best (or even teaming in pairs). Students with very limited abilities might need a smaller group; more able students can succeed in a larger group. Notice that the range of group size is from two to five or six. Larger groups become difficult for students to participate in and for teachers to manage.

You should assign students to cooperative groups to create heterogeneous groupings; that is, if your class group includes four students with disabilities, you should distribute them among the cooperative groups. Likewise, your students who are high achievers and low achievers should be assigned across groups. The success of cooperative learning is based on students learning to value and respect the con-

How can cooperative groups be used to teach both academic content and skills for working with peers? What skills do students need to work successfully?

tributions each makes. Deciding to place students together in groups according to ability undermines the entire purpose of this instructional approach.

Teachers sometimes ask how long cooperative groups should be kept intact. There is not a single right answer to that question. If you change groups too frequently, students will not have enough opportunity to learn about each other and to reach a high level of cooperative functioning. However, if you keep the same groups for too long, students do not have the chance to work with other classmates. A general guideline is to keep cooperative groups for at least a 2- or 3-week unit but to change them at least at the end of each grading period.

Prepare students for cooperative learning. A high school English teacher participated in a university class on cooperative learning and decided that she and the special educator could use this strategy in their inclusive class. They carefully planned a series of cooperative activities, assigned students to their groups, and waited for positive results. They quickly learned why *teaching* students to cooperate is such an important component in developing cooperative learning programs! The high school students bickered with each other and were impatient with students who did not immediately answer questions. Some decided to try to complete their work alone, even though it required input from others. Before students work together, it is essential to teach them cooperative skills.

The skills for cooperative group members have been categorized under the headings *forming, functioning, formulating,* and *fermenting* (Johnson, Johnson, Holubec, & Roy, 1984). These skills are summarized in Figure 13.4 on page 474. Forming skills are those students need to move into cooperative groups and carry out basic tasks with politeness and respect. Functioning skills are procedural, including monitoring time limits, asking for help, and clarifying other group members' statements.

Connections

Additional information on student grouping arrangements can be found in Chapter 4.

Figure 13.4 Student Cooperative Group Skills

Forming Skills

- Move into cooperative learning groups without making undue noise and without bothering others.
- Stay with the group during cooperative lessons; don't move around the room.
- Use quiet voices.
- Encourage everyone to participate.
- Use names.
- Look at the speaker.
- Avoid put-downs.
- Keep one's hands and feet to oneself.

Functioning Skills

- Give direction to the group's work by stating or restating the assignment's purpose, setting or calling attention to time limits, and offering ideas on how to complete the assignment.
- Express support and acceptance verbally and nonverbally (for example, praise, eye contact).
- Ask for help or clarification if you do not understand.
- Offer to explain or clarify if you do understand and someone else does not.
- Paraphrase others' contributions.
- Energize the group by being enthusiastic or suggesting new ideas.
- Describe one's feelings as appropriate.

Formulating Skills

- Summarize out loud what has just been read without referring to notes or other materials.
- Seek accuracy by correcting someone else's summary or adding important information to it.
- Seek elaboration by asking others to relate the information to other lessons and other things they know.
- Seek clever ways to remember important ideas.
- Ask others to explain their reasoning process.
- Ask others to plan out loud how they would teach the information to another student.

Fermenting Skills

- Criticize ideas, not people.
- Identify sources of disagreement within the learning group as the disagreement occurs.
- Integrate a number of different ideas into your point of view.
- Ask others to justify their conclusions or answers.
- Extend others' answers or conclusions by adding other information.
- Probe by asking questions that lead to deeper analysis.
- Go past the first answer to generate other plausible answers.
- Test reality by checking time and instructions.

S O U R C E: Adapted from *Circles of Learning* by D. W. Johnson, R. T. Johnson, E.J. Holubec, & P. Roy, 1984, Alexandria, VA: Association for Supervision and Curriculum Development. Copyright © 1984 by ASCD. Used with permission.

These skills help the group interact constructively and productively. Formulating skills are more advanced procedural skills and include asking other students to elaborate on their comments so that everyone understands them better, devising strategies for remembering important information, and relating new information to information previously learned. Fermenting skills are those students use to participate in their groups as critical thinkers and problem solvers. These skills include integrating members' ideas to form a new idea, questioning others about their ideas to analyze them further, attempting to provide multiple answers, and expressing or testing hypotheses.

Forming and functioning skills are usually introduced to students first and practiced in groups using games or simple instructional activities that have little academic demand. In addition to helping students learn how to get into their groups and how to speak to each other with respect, one clear example of a functioning skill concerns assigning student roles. All cooperative group members should have assigned **group roles** that help the group function effectively. In some classrooms, group-member assignments include the encourager, the monitor, the leader, and the recorder, as shown in Figure 13.5. The *encourager* has the responsibility of making positive comments to other group members. The *monitor* helps keep the group on task and watches the time. The *leader* gets the group started on its task and facilitates its work. The *recorder* writes down any information the group is responsible for producing. Depending on students' ages and skills, additional responsibilities can be added. In some classrooms, group roles rotate so each student has an opportunity to try all roles. If a student with a disability cannot carry out a role (for example, recorder), a classmate might help out, or that student is not assigned that role.

FYI

Encourager, monitor, leader, and recorder are group-member roles students might take on during cooperative learning. You can add other roles as needed or eliminate one of these roles for smaller groups.

Figure 13.5   Student Roles in Cooperative Groups

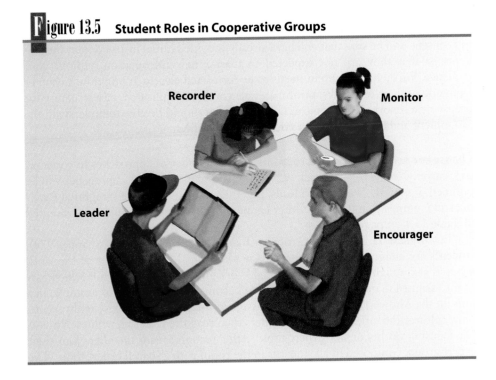

One other functioning skill is especially important: the ability to give feedback. Students can be taught that effective feedback has six key elements:

1. It focuses on the behavior of a person, not the individual's personality.
2. It describes what the person did, not what the other person wished the person had done.
3. It is nonjudgmental.
4. It is specific instead of general.
5. It is concise.
6. It occurs immediately after a group activity, not later. (Hill & Hill, 1990)

Here is an example of a student providing appropriate feedback to another student: "Cecily, today in the group you told Mel he was dumb because he didn't know the answer. That's against group rules." Notice how this very brief example meets all the characteristics of effective feedback. The student speaking did not tell Cecily that *she* was the dumb one, nor did the student tell Cecily what she should have said.

In general, preparing students for cooperative groups includes identifying the skills they need to learn, planning how you will teach them, teaching the skills and allowing students opportunities to practice them, and gradually increasing your expectations for students' cooperative behavior. Steps for preparing students for cooperative learning are outlined in the Professional Edge.

Select curricular content.   Almost any subject matter you teach can be adapted for cooperative learning. In elementary schools, cooperative learning is used in language arts for reading and writing activities as well as in math, science, and social studies. In secondary schools, cooperative learning works well in English, but also in math, science, social studies, fine arts, and other coursework. The key to selecting content is to be sure that you have already provided initial instruction to the students so that they are not expected to master new information without your guidance. Further, the content needs to be formatted clearly. It might be a chapter from one of their textbooks, print materials you have duplicated, or a structure for preparing a report on the topic at hand. Students should be able to understand the assignment and how to go about completing it readily.

Choose cooperative learning programs.   The number of approaches to cooperative learning seems to grow each year. For our discussion, three approaches will be outlined: Jigsaw II, Numbered Heads Together, and Cooperative Integrated Reading and Composition (CIRC). Other cooperative learning programs are presented in Table 13.1 on page 478.

In a **Jigsaw II** classroom (Aronson, Blaney, Stephen, Sikes, & Snapp, 1978), students are assigned to heterogeneous work groups. Each member of the work group is also assigned to an expert group. Work groups meet and decide which part of the assigned material each member is to become an expert on. For example, in a unit on the Midwest, experts might be assigned for these topics: geography, economy, culture, and cities. All team members then read the material, with each member focusing on his or her expert topic. After reading, team members join their expert group, composed of all students in the room with a shared expert topic. The expert groups review their portion of the instructional material, then return to teach it to their work-group members. Group members ask each "expert" questions to

Professional Edge

Steps for Teaching Cooperative Skills

For cooperative learning programs to be successful, it is critical that students learn social skills to guide their interactions with classmates. These are some suggestions for effectively teaching cooperative skills to your class.

1. Identify the skills students need to learn, based on your observations and other assessments of their skills and needs.

2. Clarify for students why they are being asked to learn cooperative skills and explain how they should interact. For example, you might use a playground or hallway altercation as a nonexample of cooperative interactions, or stage occasional role-plays in which you model positive or negative responses.

3. Identify the skills to students. For example, label one skill "Encouraging."

4. Demonstrate the skill for students. For encouraging, use phrases such as "Keep trying," "That's a good response," and " You really did a good job on that." Use a few examples of poor skills to teach students to discriminate between positive and negative examples.

5. Have students practice skills, first with a partner, then with a small group.

6. As students learn several skills, have them play an instructional game in their cooperative group, stressing practice on cooperative skills. Ask the groups to identify examples of positive skills used and examples of situations in which skills were not used well.

7. Praise examples of student skills that you observe. If a student consistently fails to use cooperative skills, talk with that student's group and, if necessary, work privately with the student.

---

help clarify the information being presented. After all group members have taught their segment of the information and the groups have had an opportunity to review their learning, a quiz or other evaluation procedure is used, and each group member is graded individually on this assessment.

In **Numbered Heads Together** (Kagan, 1990), students are assigned to cooperative groups and count off by numbers. The teacher then poses a question to the group and students are asked to put their heads together to be sure that all group members know the answer. After a brief time, the teacher brings the students back and calls out a number. All the students with that number stand and one student responds to the question, or they all write the answer on a slate and hold it up for the teacher to see. Students responding correctly score points for their teams.

Cooperative Integrated Reading and Composition (CIRC) is a cooperative learning program designed to help students in upper elementary grades work on reading, writing, and other language arts (Slavin, 1994). If reading groups are used, only two or three groups are formed within the class. In a literature-based language arts program, groups would not be needed. Within one of these structures, students work with one or two other students with similar reading ability, and two such groups form a team. For example, a classroom could have three reading groups, but within those groups, each student is assigned a partner. These partners are parts of teams that cross reading groups; one team might be composed of two students with low reading ability and two students with average reading ability.

Table 13.1 Cooperative Learning Approaches

Approach	Source	Description
Group Investigation	Shlomo Sharan and Rachel Hertz-Lazarowitz	Heterogeneous teams of two to six members plan how to complete an assigned project by identifying tasks to do and resources needed and deciding which group members will have which task responsibilities. Once tasks have been completed, group members develop a shared report that is presented to the class. The class provides feedback to the team.
Jigsaw	Elliott Aronson and colleagues	Each of the four members of the heterogeneous work groups is assigned as an expert on a specific part of the assigned materials. Experts from all class work groups meet and learn material on their specific topic as provided by the teacher. Experts then return to their work groups and teach the materials to work-group members. Work-group members have access only to the materials on which they are the expert. Individual quizzes are then given.
Learning Together	David Johnson and Roger Johnson	Heterogeneous groups of two to six members learn specific skills for interacting with one another. They then work together in various formal and informal group structures to learn material.
Student Teams–Achievement Divisions (STAD)	Robert Slavin and colleagues	Heterogeneous four-member teams learn materials together and take quizzes separately. Students earn points based on their own improvement over past quiz scores. These points are contributed to a team score.
Team Assisted Individualization (TAI)	Robert Slavin and colleagues	The four members of heterogeneous teams work at their own pace on individualized math materials. Members help each other and check each other's work, even though they might be on different units. Individual tests are taken to pass out of a unit. Teams earn points each week based on the number of units members have successfully completed.
Teams–Games–Tournaments (TGT)	David DeVries and Keith Edwards	Three-member teams help each other learn material. Team members are then assigned to tournament tables for competition with others from class with similar achievement levels. Quizzes are given or an instructional game based on the material learned is played. Members contribute points to their teams based on their performance at their tournament table.

SOURCE: Based on *Cooperative Learning* (2nd ed.) by R. E. Slavin, 1994, Boston: Allyn and Bacon; *Learning Together and Alone* (4th ed.) by D. W. Johnson & R. T. Johnson, 1994, Boston: Allyn and Bacon; and *Cooperative Learning and Strategies for Inclusion* by J. W. Putnam, 1993, Baltimore: Brookes.

Teachers introduce stories to the reading groups or the class and distribute story packets to students. Students then read silently and aloud with their partners; work on related writing, spelling, and vocabulary activities; and check each other on completing assigned tasks. At the end of three class periods, students take a comprehension test and complete other assessments of their learning. Other elements of this comprehensive program that require specialized materials include direct instruction in reading comprehension provided at least once each week, the use of writing activities designed to be integrated into the rest of the language arts program, and reporting about books read independently at home.

Monitor program effectiveness. Much of the work in developing a cooperative learning program is deciding which approach to use, preparing materials, and helping students learn cooperative skills. However, once students are established in cooperative groups, your role becomes one of monitoring and managing your class. For example, if you notice that a student is having difficulty in a group, you might decide to join that group briefly to see if students can resolve their own problem or need your assistance. If a student seems to be struggling because of the complexity of the lesson content, you can make an on-the-spot adaptation to help the student and the group. If a student is being disruptive, your proximity might be sufficient to settle that student. As you monitor, you can also observe students' use of cooperative skills and check the progress of their learning. For example, you might observe whether students are using the learning strategies described in Chapter 10 to help them succeed in the lesson. By observing, you can plan your next lessons and address any issues concerning cooperative skills.

Many of the teaching strategies presented in this text can be incorporated into cooperative learning experiences. For example, a student in a cooperative group could have adapted materials. The group could use a learning strategy to practice problem solving. You can use an entire array of instructional interventions and strategies for independence as part of your cooperative learning activities. Cooperative groups provide a constructive classroom structure, one that provides opportunities for adapting instruction for individual needs, building self-esteem and group spirit, addressing students' own goals, and promoting positive attitudes toward others. You have an almost limitless number of options for using this structure to accomplish your academic and social goals for students. One example of this approach in action is presented in the Case in Practice on page 480.

How Can You Help Students with Disabilities Improve Their Social Skills?

For many students with disabilities and other special needs, your efforts to create a classroom learning environment that fosters positive peer relationships will enable them to be class members who are liked and valued by their peers. For some students, though, you will need to go further. Research has shown that some students with disabilities have persistent problems in their social interactions (Kavale & Forness, 1996; O'Reilly & Glynn, 1995) and that these students benefit from specific instruction to help them learn needed social skills (Doren, Bullis, & Benz, 1996; Sugai & Lewis, 1996).

Social skills can be thought of as the behaviors that help students interact successfully with their peers, teachers, and others and that help students win social acceptance. They include accurately recognizing and responding to emotions expressed by others; identifying and effectively solving social problems, such as disagreements about who can play with a toy or decisions about sneaking out of school with a group of peers; expressing preferences in socially acceptable ways; and initiating kind or helpful acts. Social skills range from very simple to complex. For

Do It!

Create a lesson plan that you could use to teach social skills in your anticipated classroom. Try your lesson plan on a group of students in your field experiences.

Case in Practice

Cooperative Learning in Action

In Mrs. Robinson's third-grade classroom, students are preparing for today's lesson on ecology and the environment. The students move into their work groups and check to see that all group members remember their expert assignments. They also check to see that each group member has paper and pencil as directed by Mrs. Robinson. Once all are settled, the students move to their expert groups. Today's expert groups are reviewing the topics addressed during the past week: (1) information about littering and its impact, (2) recycling programs, (3) products made from recycled materials, and (4) landfills and why they are controversial. Greg's expert group is reviewing littering. Greg has a moderate cognitive disability and was deliberately assigned to this group by his teacher because the topic is immediately related to life skills Greg needs to learn. He joins his group with another member of his work group. In this way, Greg can participate in the review but is not totally responsible for all the information addressed. Greg's learning about littering is that it is

wrong. He also participated earlier in the week in the class litter pick-up on the school grounds. After 15 minutes, the students return to their work groups. For the next 30 minutes, they take turns leading the review on their part of the environment information. Greg tells his group, "Don't litter. Pick it up." He also shows the "before" and "after" photos of the schoolyard. The group's other littering "expert" eventually takes over, and Greg listens for awhile, but eventually he leaves the group and gets paper and crayons. He comes back to the group saying, "I make a picture about litter." A group member clears a space at the table for him and he begins to draw, showing his classmates his picture several times. The group asks him what several of the objects drawn are, and they continue their other expert reports. On the next day, the students complete their review test

on ecology and the environment. Greg answers simple questions about ecology out loud as they are asked by the student teacher. Mrs. Robinson monitors the larger group taking the written test.

REFLECTIONS

What approach to cooperative learning is being used in this classroom? What has Mrs. Robinson done to ensure that the lesson will run smoothly? How can you tell that Mrs. Robinson has taught students cooperative skills? Which skills do you think she might have emphasized? What did Mrs. Robinson do to ensure that Greg would be a valued class member while also taking into account that he could not learn much of the information presented during the unit? In what other way could she have addressed this issue? If you were Mrs. Robinson, what would you be particularly interested in observing as you monitored the students in this class working in their cooperative groups? How else could Greg's learning about the unit have been assessed?

example, for a young student or a student with a moderate cognitive disability, social skills might include learning how to greet others by saying "Hi" instead of hugging, to take turns during games or large-group activities, and to ask to join a group. For adolescents with learning or behavior problems—students like Kathleen and Mark, whom you met at the beginning of this chapter—social skills might include expressing emotions appropriately, disagreeing with others (especially adults) in acceptable ways, and avoiding situations in which confrontation is likely to occur. Although special educators will play an active role in teaching social skills to students with especially strong needs, you can also address them. Ways in which you can bring social-skills training to your classroom include informal instruction, behavioral interventions, and formal social skills training.

Using Informal Instruction

As illustrated throughout this chapter by examples of teachers actively nurturing the development of positive peer social relationships in their classrooms, you have many informal opportunities to help students develop social skills that will help them throughout their lives (McIntosh, Vaughn, & Bennerson, 1995; Yasutake & Bryan, 1995). For example, if you are showing students an instructional video and appropriate student interactions occur as part of it, you might want to point out in a class discussion what made the interactions so positive. Then students could practice the same skills. Similarly, classrooms could include social skills as part of class-wide or school themes. For example, in a middle school students illustrated stories that demonstrated how to respond when peers were pressuring them to make fun of other students. Finally, you can individually instruct students in social skills as appropriate situations occur. When Mr. Calles observed Charles, a sophomore with a moderate cognitive disability, stick his tongue out at another student when the student laughed at him, he made it a point to speak with both boys about other ways to interact.

Even though you may consider your primary responsibility to be teaching academic content to your students, your alertness to the need to develop student social skills and your willingness to incorporate informal social skills instruction into your instruction can contribute significantly to a sense of classroom community. Forming a positive classroom community is essential for inclusive schools.

Using Behavioral Interventions

Another strategy for teaching social skills to students is to use behavioral interventions such as the ones you learned about in Chapter 12. For example, you can reward your entire class for treating a new class member with respect and friendship. If you have a student whose social problems include teasing class members or talking out of turn, you can reward your class for not responding to the inappropriate behaviors. To use these types of behavioral interventions, you need to identify clearly the behaviors you want to foster and choose an appropriate reward structure, create a simple record-keeping system, explain the intervention to students, and systematically implement your plan. For example, in a first-grade classroom, a student with a mild cognitive disability joined the group. Ashi would periodically leave his seat or group and roam from desk to desk, sometimes leaving the classroom. At the beginning of the school year, the teacher explained to the other first graders that Ashi needed to move more than other students and that this behavior was acceptable for Ashi but not for the rest of the class. She then asked students not to stop working if Ashi came to their desks and not to make a commotion if he left the room. When she noticed that students were following her directions, she would reward the class with five extra minutes of recess or an extra story in the afternoon. As the school year progressed, she gradually quit this type of reward and transitioned to thanking students for understanding Ashi's needs.

Behavioral interventions can also be used to reinforce appropriate social skills. When teachers see a student with social-skills needs interacting appropriately, they should make a positive comment to the student. In secondary schools, these comments are usually offered in private to avoid embarrassing the student. For example, a student advisor overheard a conversation between a chemistry teacher and a student with an explosive temper. The teacher was chiding the student for failing to

Connections

Chapter 12 addressed strategies for increasing desirable student behavior. These strategies also can be applied in teaching social skills.

turn in assignments on time. The student replied, "Yeah, I know I haven't been doing too well on the homework." Later, the advisor congratulated the student for acknowledging the teacher's feedback without becoming defensive or making a comment that might have led to detention.

Using Social-Skills Training Programs

Check Your Learning

How could you apply what you have learned about social skills and student social relationships to the students introduced in the vignettes at the beginning of this chapter? If you were Lucy, Kathleen, or Mark's teacher, what strategies would you include to foster positive student interactions with each of them?

If you have several students who need social-skills instruction, you might find useful one of the many prepackaged **social-skills training programs** available to teachers. For example, *Think Aloud* (Camp & Bash, 1985) is a social problem-solving package designed for use with elementary school students. Students are taught to ask themselves a series of questions whenever they are faced with a problematic situation. The questions are, What is the problem? What should I do? What is my plan? and, Am I following the plan? Teachers rehearse these steps with students and provide opportunities for students to practice the steps in structured situations. Teachers also remind students to look for the steps when they observe students behaving appropriately.

An example of a social-skills package for adolescents is *Skillstreaming the Adolescent* (Goldstein, Sprafkin, Gershaw, & Klein, 1980). This package includes structured procedures for teaching nearly 50 different social skills using modeling, role-playing, and feedback. Teachers can select and use only the skill lessons most pertinent to their class groups. For example, if a high school class is having problems because several students are extremely aggressive, the module on that topic might be helpful.

However you decide to help students develop social skills, keep in mind that several other professionals are available in your school who may have advanced training in teaching social skills and who can assist you in this aspect of your curriculum. For example, if your school has a teacher for students with emotional disabilities, he or she might be able to co-teach social-skills lessons with you. Similarly, a school counselor or social worker could help you build social-skills lessons into your instructional program.

With your understanding of strategies and approaches for building student social relationships, you now have the final ingredient for making your classroom a place where students want to come and want to learn. You know about the foundations of special education and the procedures followed for identifying students with disabilities. You have a strategy—INCLUDE—for guiding your decisions about student needs and interventions. You know how important the support and assistance of colleagues and parents is, whether for planning an instructional program for a student, teaching with you in the classroom, or problem solving when concerns arise. You also understand some of the most important characteristics and needs of students with disabilities and other special needs. You have learned many strategies for helping students succeed in your classroom, including creating a positive instructional environment, assessing student needs, making instructional interventions, helping students to be independent, and evaluating their learning. You have learned, too, several approaches for responding to students' discipline and behavior needs and for fostering positive social relationships among students.

What is most important, however, is the statement that appeared in the first chapter of this text: Students with disabilities and other special needs are people first. If you keep that in mind and use the knowledge you have gained, you will positively touch the lives and learning of all the students who call you teacher.

Summary

In addition to fostering the academic growth of students in inclusive schools, teachers also work to ensure that their students with and without disabilities and other special needs build positive social relationships. Learning social skills is especially important since research over the past four decades has demonstrated that students with disabilities sometimes are more likely than other students to have a negative status in their classrooms.

Teachers can help students develop positive peer relationships in inclusive classrooms by creating ways for students to have face-to-face interactions, nurturing the development of friendship and support among students, and providing positive role models. Another aspect of addressing the social curriculum in general education classrooms is educating students without special needs about individuals who have disabilities or other special needs. Direct presentation of information, the use of print or video media or adaptive technology, and the use of simulation activities are approaches to introducing students to the characteristics and needs of students with disabilities.

One specific instructional approach that helps create positive student relationships is peer tutoring. Peer tutoring has a long history and has recently received renewed attention. It benefits both tutors and tutees, including students with disabilities. Teachers can create tutoring programs that are contained within their classrooms or that use several class groups or even an entire school. A second instructional approach recommended for inclusive classrooms is cooperative learning. In cooperative learning, students accrue both social and academic benefits. To set up a cooperative learning program, teachers need to decide on group issues, prepare students to work cooperatively, identify the instructional content to be used in the groups, and select a cooperative learning approach, such as Jigsaw II, Numbered Heads Together, or Cooperative Integrated Reading and Composition.

Sometimes, students with disabilities need additional intensive instruction to learn social skills. This instruction can involve informal social-skills instruction as part of the classroom curriculum, behavioral interventions, and formal social-skills training programs, often taught in partnership with special service providers such as special education teachers.

Applications in Teaching Practice

Planning for Promoting Positive Peer Relations

Mr. Barkley is reviewing his class roster and his plans for the upcoming school year. He knows that he will have four students with learning and behavior disabilities—Jay, Doug, Ray, and Jasmine—in his sixth-hour class. He also will have Theodore, a bright young man with cerebral palsy who uses a wheelchair and has a personal attendant. Theodore cannot write or type; he points to symbols on his communication board. Having talked to other teachers, Mr. Barkley is a little worried about this group because several of the other students in the class also have special needs, including Kusi, with ADHD, and Micki, who is gifted/talented. Right now, his planning list looks like this:

1. Talk to Ms. M. [special education teacher]. What are reasonable expectations for the students with disabilities? Does Theodore need any extraordinary assistance? What is he going to be like in class? Do I need to know anything special about having the personal attendant in my classroom? Does she know what to do for Theodore? Can she also work with other students if it doesn't negatively affect Theodore? Should Jay, Doug, Ray, or Jasmine sit near each other or be separated? What should they be able to do in class—everything? 80 percent? What are the social goals for these students? Could we review the students' IEPs to clarify what I should stress with them?

2. Talk to counselor. Can she teach some basic social-skills lessons with the class during the first 6-week grading period? Twice each week for 20 minutes?

3. Set up cooperative learning groups for first grading period and get all materials ready. Goal: Two cooperative learning activities per week, with first 2 weeks spent on teaching social skills in groups. Group size? Maybe three, given class composition, with a move to four for the second quarter.

4. Check on availability of after-school tutoring program at elementary school this year. Reward for some of the students? Other peer tutoring options?

5. Request more information on Jasmine—see note about her participation in a social work group on Thursdays during advisory period.

Mr. Barkley's planning list goes on along these lines for two more pages.

Questions

1. Why is Mr. Barkley concerned about the social interactions of his students? Why is this part of his responsibility as much as teaching his academic subject matter? How does having students with disabilities in his room increase needs in the social-skills area?

2. What could Mr. Barkley do to sensitize his students to Theodore's needs? What might he do if Jay, Doug, Ray, or Jasmine becomes the object of student complaints about fairness during the course of the school year?

3. What approach to peer tutoring is Mr. Barkley considering? What options might he try to arrange? Who in his class might be the best candidates for each of the peer tutoring approaches?

4. What questions might Mr. Barkley have concerning the social needs of Kusi and Micki?

5. Mr. Barkley notes that he needs to spend the first 2 weeks of cooperative learning sessions on social skills. What skills might he teach? How can he teach them? What academic content could be included in the lessons in which social skills are being taught?

6. It appears that Mr. Barkley has one student who will receive social-skills instruction in a separate group, and he is requesting that the counselor help him teach social skills during the first grading period. How could a special education teacher also help Mr. Barkley address the social needs of all his students?

Glossary

ABC analysis. Systematic recording of antecedents, behaviors, and consequences as a strategy for analyzing student behavior.

absence seizure. Seizure that is brief and often characterized by momentary lapses of attention. Also called a *petit mal seizure*.

academic learning time. The time students are meaningfully and successfully engaged in school.

academic survival skills. Skills needed to succeed in school, including regular and punctual attendance, organization, task completion, independence, motivation, and appropriate social skills.

acceleration. Approach for educating gifted and talented students based on allowing them to move through all or part of the curriculum at their own, accelerated pace.

accuracy. The extent to which a student's academic performance is without errors.

acquired immune deficiency syndrome (AIDS). Disease resulting from HIV, in which the body becomes unable to fight infection.

activity reinforcer. Positive activity that causes a behavior to increase. An example of an activity reinforcer is a student being rewarded with extra time to work on the computer.

ADA. *See* Americans with Disabilities Act.

adaptive physical educator. Specialist with expertise in assessing students' motor needs and designing and delivering physical education programs that accommodate those needs.

ADD. *See* attention deficit disorder.

ADHD. *See* attention deficit–hyperactive disorder.

administrator. Professional responsible for managing some aspect of schools; includes principals, assistant principals, department chairpersons, team leaders, special services coordinators, district administrators, and others.

advance organizer. Information, often presented as organizational signals, that makes content more understandable by putting it within a more general framework.

advocate. Individual who works to ensure that parents understand their rights and that school professionals provide an appropriate education for parents' children with disabilities.

AIDS. *See* acquired immune deficiency syndrome.

alternative teaching. Co-teaching option in which students are divided into one large and one small group. The large group receives the planned instruction. The small group receives reteaching, preteaching, enrichment, or other special instruction.

American Sign Language (ASL). A sign language not based on the grammmar or structures of English, used by some people with hearing impairments.

Americans with Disabilities Act. Civil rights law passed in 1990 that protects individuals with disabilities from discrimination and requires building and transportation accessibility and reasonable accommodations in the workplace.

anecdotal recording. Strategy for recording behavior in which incidents before and after a behavior are recorded along with a description of the behavior.

annual goal. Broad statement describing estimated yearly outcomes for a student with a disability. Annual goals address areas of identified needs.

annual review. Yearly process of convening a team that includes a parent, teacher, administrator, and others as needed to review and update a student's IEP.

anticipation guide. Series of statements, some of which may not be true, related to material that is about to be presented during instruction, given to students as a way of activating their knowledge by making predictions about the topic.

anxiety. Condition in which an individual experiences extraordinary worry in some situations or worries excessively about future situations.

articulation. Production of speech sounds.

Asperger's syndrome. Mild form of autism in which an individual develops speech but has chronic difficulty in forming and sustaining social relationships, gross motor problems, and intense interests in a narrow range of topics.

assessment. Process of gathering information to monitor progress and make educational decisions.

assistive technology. Any of a wide variety of technology applications designed to help students with disabilities learn, communicate, and otherwise function more independently by bypassing their disabilities.

asthma. Physical condition in which an individual experiences difficulty breathing, especially during physically or psychologically stressful activities.

at risk. Term used to describe students who have characteristics, live in conditions, or have experiences that make them more likely than others to experience failure in schools.

attention deficit disorder (ADD). Term sometimes used as a synonym for attention deficit–hyperactive disorder.

attention deficit–hyperactive disorder (ADHD). Medical condition in which students have significant inability to attend, excessive motor activity, and/or impulsivity.

attribution retraining. Teaching program that increases student task persistence and performance by convincing them that their failures are due to effort and can therefore be overcome.

augmentative communication. Alternative systems of communication, often using pictures, symbols, and/or words accessed through computer or other technology, sometimes used by students with disabilities.

authentic learning tasks. Tasks used in performance-based assessment that are based on real-world contexts and lead to real-world outcomes.

autism. Condition in which an individual lacks social responsiveness from a very early age, has a high need for structure and routines, and demonstrates significant language impairments. These characteristics interfere with learning.

basal textbook. A book used for instruction in basic-skills areas that contains all key components of the curriculum to be taught for that subject. Often called a *basal*.

basic-skills instruction. Instruction in the tool skills of reading, writing, and math.

behavior contract. Agreement between a teacher (or other adult) and student that clearly specifies student performance expectations, rewards for meeting expectations, consequences of not meeting expectations, and the time frame for which the agreement is valid.

big ideas. Important principles that help learners understand the connections among facts and concepts they learn.

bilingual education program. Education approach in which students with limited English skills learn core subjects in a separate setting in their native language and spend the remainder of their school day with English-speaking peers.

bilingual special education program. Special education approach in which students with disabilities with limited English skills learn core subjects in a separate setting in their native language.

bilingual special education teacher. Teacher who works with students with disabilities whose native language is not English.

bilingual teacher. Teacher who teaches students whose native language is not English.

blind. Condition in which an individual has little or no vision and relies on auditory and other input for learning.

braille. Writing system, used by individuals who have vision impairments, that uses various combinations of six raised dots punched on paper read with the fingertips.

brainstorming. Strategy for generating solutions to problems in which participants call out ideas, building on one another's responses, deferring all evaluation.

Brown v. Board of Education. Supreme Court decision in 1954 that established that it is unlawful and discriminatory to create separate schools for African American students. This "separate cannot be equal" concept was later applied to students with disabilities.

CAPS. Four-step learning strategy for helping a student decide what is important in a story: ask who the characters are; identify the aim of the story; decide what problem happens; and determine how the problem is solved.

catch 'em being good. Behavior management strategy in which a teacher notices appropriate student behavior and positively comments on it, either privately to the student or publicly to the class.

CBA. *See* curriculum-based assessment.

CBM. *See* cognitive behavior management.

cerebral palsy. Most common type of orthopedic impairment among public school students, caused by brain injury before or during birth and resulting in poor motor coordination and abnormal motor patterns.

child abuse. Situation in which a parent or other caregiver inflicts or allows others to inflict injury on a child, or permits a substantial risk of injury to exist.

child neglect. Situation in which a parent or other caregiver fails to provide the necessary supports for a child's well-being.

CHROME. Mnemonic for remembering the six methods of scientific investigation: categorization, hypothesis, reasoning, observation, measurement, and experimentation.

chunking. Memorization strategy in which students are taught to remember five to seven key ideas at one time.

CIRC. *See* Cooperative Integrated Reading and Composition.

Circle of Friends. Program designed to help students without disabilities understand how important it is to have friends with disabilities and to encourage them to form friendships with classmates with disabilities.

classroom climate. The overall atmosphere of a classroom, including whether it is friendly and pleasant, based on the expectations of teachers and their interactions with students.

classroom grouping. Various grouping arrangements, such as teaching the whole class at once or in small groups, that modify the classroom environment. Classroom grouping may be teacher centered or peer mediated.

classroom instruction. Strategies through which a teacher presents curriculum content to students.

classroom organization. Strategies through which a teacher establishes and maintains order in a classroom.

cluster programs. Special education service delivery system in which students with similar needs from several schools or an entire district attend a single school to receive special education services.

cognitive behavior management (CBM). Behavior management strategy in which students learn to monitor and change their own behavior.

cognitive disability. *See* mental retardation.

collaboration. A style of interaction professionals use in order to accomplish a goal they share, often stressed in inclusive schools.

community-based education. Approach to instruction in which what is learned in school is related to activities that occur in the community.

competency checklist. Evaluation technique in which student learning is checked against a listing of key concepts or ideas being taught.

comprehension. Reading skill involving understanding the meaning of what has been read.

concept diagram. Specific type of graphic organizer used to present vocabulary words that includes definitions and characteristics.

concept map. Graphic organizer showing relationships among concepts of instruction as well as essential characteristics of the concepts.

constructivistic teaching. Type of teaching based on the belief that students are capable of constructing meaning on their own, in most cases, without explicit instruction.

consultant. Specialist who provides particular expertise to teachers and others when an extraordinary student need arises.

consultation. Specialized problem-solving process in which one professional with particular expertise assists another professional or parent who needs the benefit of that expertise; used as an instructional approach for some students with disabilities.

consulting teacher. Special education teacher who meets with general education teachers to problem solve and monitor student progress but who typically has little or no direct contact with students.

content-area textbook. A book used for instruction in science, social studies, or other content areas.

controlled materials. Instructional materials at the student's reading level, of high interest and free of complex vocabulary and concepts, often used while teaching students a learning strategy.

Cooperative Integrated Reading and Composition (CIRC). Cooperative learning program for teaching reading, writing, and other language arts to students in upper elementary grades.

cooperative learning. Student-centered instructional approach in which students work in small, mixed-ability groups with a shared learning goal.

cooperative learning program. Program in which cooperative learning approaches are integral to instruction.

COPS. Learning strategy for proofreading papers with these steps: Have I capitalized the first word and proper nouns? How is the overall appearance of my paper; have I made any handwriting, margin, or messy errors? Have I used end punctuation, commas, and semicolons carefully? Do words look like they are spelled right; can I sound them out or use a dictionary?

co-teaching. Instructional approach in which two or more teachers or other certified staff share instruction for a single group of students within a single classroom setting.

counselor. Specialist with expertise in meeting students' social and affective needs.

credit/no credit grading system. *See* pass/fail grading system.

cross-age tutoring. Peer tutoring approach in which older students tutor younger ones.

cross-categorical approach. Instructional approach in which the cognitive, learning, affective, and social and emotional needs of students, not their disability labels, form the basis for planning and delivering instruction.

cue words. Words that make patterns of information more conspicuous for students, such as the words "similar" and "different" signalling the presence of a compare/contrast pattern.

curriculum-based assessment (CBA). Method of measuring the level of achievement of students in terms of what they are taught in the classroom.

curriculum placement. Type of assessment decision concerning where to begin instruction for students.

cystic fibrosis. Genetically transmitted disease in which the body produces excessive mucus that eventually damages the lungs and causes heart failure.

daily activity log. Strategy for providing ongoing information for students and their parents about learning by noting daily observations of student work, effort, and outcomes.

deaf. Hearing impairment in which the individual cannot process linguistic information through hearing with or without the use of hearing aids and relies on visual and other input for learning.

deaf–blind. Condition in which an individual has both significant visual and hearing impairments that interfere with learning.

decibel (dB). Unit for measuring the loudness of sounds.

decoding. Reading skill involving accurately identifying words and fluently pronouncing them.

DEFENDS. Learning strategy for writing a defense of a position with these steps: decide on an exact position; examine the reasons for the position; form a list of points to explain each reason; expose the position in the first sentence; note each reason and supporting points; drive home the position in the last sentence; and search for errors and correct.

depression. Condition in which an individual is persistently and seriously unhappy, with a loss of interest or pleasure in all or almost all usual activities. Symptoms of depression include changes in appetite or weight, sleep disturbances, loss of energy, feelings of worthlessness, and thoughts of death or suicide.

diabetes. Disease in which the body does not produce enough insulin to process the carbohydrates eaten.

diagnosis. Type of assessment decision concerning whether or not a student meets established federal guidelines for being classified as having a disability and, if so, the nature and extent of the disability.

diagnostic teaching. Sample lessons and other instructional activities carried out with students experiencing extreme academic or behavioral difficulty as part of screening.

differential reinforcement of incompatible behaviors. Reinforcing an appropriate behavior that is incompatible with another undesirable behavior in order to increase the positive behavior.

direct instruction. Research-based instructional approach in which the teacher presents subject matter using a review of previously taught information, presentation of new concepts or skills, guided practice, feedback and correction, independent student practice, and frequent review.

disability. Condition characterized by a physical, cognitive, psychological, or social difficulty so severe that it negatively affects student learning. In the Americans with Disabilities Act, a disability is defined as a condition that limits some major life activity.

discipline. Term to describe the set of classroom expectations, including rules for behavior, that serves as a means for facilitating student learning.

discovery learning. *See* inquiry learning.

Down syndrome. Most prevalent type of biologically caused cognitive disability, caused by the failure of one pair of chromosomes to separate at conception.

DRAW. Strategy for teaching multiplication facts that are not yet committed to memory, consisting of these steps: discover the sign; read the problem; answer, or draw and check; write the answer.

due process. Procedures outlined in IDEA for ensuring that parents' and children's rights are protected and for resolving disputes between parents and school district personnel concerning any aspect of special education.

duration recording. Strategy for recording behavior in which the length of time a behavior occurs is recorded.

echolalic speech. Occurs when an individual communicates by repeating what others have said instead of producing original speech.

ED. *See* emotional disturbance.

educable mentally handicapped (EMH). Somewhat outdated term still used occasionally to refer to persons with mild cognitive disabilities.

EHA. Education for the Handicapped Act. *See* P.L. 94-142.

emotional disturbance (ED). Condition in which an individual has significant difficulty in the social and emotional domain, so much so that it interferes with learning.

enrichment. Approach for educating gifted and talented students based on helping them elaborate on or extend concepts being presented to all students.

environmental inventory. Assessment procedure, often used for students with moderate or severe disabilities, designed to find out what adaptations or supports are needed to increase student participation in classroom and community environments.

epilepsy. Physical condition in which the brain experiences sudden but brief changes in its functioning leading to seizures.

evaluation. Procedures used to determine whether teaching is effective, to provide feedback to students and their parents about student learning, and to inform school boards and communities about school effectiveness.

event recording. Strategy for recording behavior in which each occurrence of the behavior is counted.

example selection. Teacher choice of examples during instruction. Example selection directly affects student understanding of instruction.

example sequence. Order of presentation of examples during instruction. Example sequence directly affects student understanding of instruction.

exemplar. A sample student performance designed to specify a level of achievement in authentic learning evaluation. For example, a writing sample of an "average" seventh grader is an exemplar against which other students' writing can be compared.

expressive language. An individual's ability to communicate meaning clearly through speech.

extinction. Strategy for decreasing negative behavior by no longer reinforcing it; most effective when the undesirable behavior has been inadvertently reinforced by the teacher.

facilitated communication. Method of assisting individuals with autism and other disabilities to communicate by gently supporting the wrist, arm, or shoulder on a typewriter or computer keyboard. This method is controversial.

fading out. Gradual process for decreasing the use of behavioral strategies to support appropriate student behavior.

FAE. *See* fetal alcohol effects.

FAS. *See* fetal alcohol syndrome.

FAST DRAW. Strategy for helping students make the transition from pictures to abstract numbers. The following steps are performed before beginning the DRAW strategy: find what you're solving for; ask yourself, "What are the parts of the problem?"; set up the numbers; tie down the sign.

fetal alcohol effects (FAE). Mild form of fetal alcohol syndrome (FAS), often without physical characteristics. Students with FAE often experience a variety of learning and behavior problems in school.

fetal alcohol syndrome (FAS). Medical condition caused by prenatal maternal abuse of alcohol, often resulting in slight physical abnormalities and learning, cognitive, or emotional disabilities.

finger spelling. Communication system in which each alphabet letter is assigned a specific hand position. Finger spelling is often used to communicate proper names or technical words for which no other sign language signs exist.

five R's of note-taking. Learning strategy for note-taking with these steps: record the main ideas and important details; reduce to concise phrases; recite key information using your concise phrases as cues; reflect on your notes by adding your own ideas; and review all the key information.

fluency. The rate at which a student performs an academic task such as calculating math problems or reading.

FOIL. Four-step learning strategy for multiplying binomials in algebra: multiply the first terms; multiply the outermost terms; multiply the innermost terms; and multiply the last terms.

functional curriculum. Instructional approach in which goals and objectives are based on real-life skills needed for adulthood. Examples of skills addressed in a functional curriculum include shopping and making purchases; reading common signs such as exit, stop, and sale; riding public transportation; and interacting with peers and adults.

general education teacher. Elementary, middle school, junior high, or high school teacher whose primary responsibility is teaching one or more class groups.

generalized tonic-clonic seizure. Seizure involving the entire body. Also called a *grand mal seizure.*

gifted or talented. Demonstrated ability far above average in one or several areas including overall intellectual ability, leadership, specific academic subjects, creativity, athletics, or the visual or performing arts.

Good Behavior Game. Strategy for reducing disruptive behavior and promoting positive behavior in the classroom in which students work on teams to earn points for appropriate behavior toward a reward.

grading contract. Agreement between a teacher and student that specifies the quantity, quality, and timeliness of work required to receive a specific grade.

grading criteria. The standard on which a student's academic performance is evaluated and graded.

grand mal seizure. *See* generalized tonic-clonic seizure.

graphic organizer. Visual format that helps students to organize their understanding of information being presented or read and the relationships between various parts of the information.

group-administered standardized achievement test. Standardized achievement test given to large groups of students at one time, usually administered by general education teachers, useful as a screening measure.

group investigation. Cooperative learning program in which teams of two to six members plan and carry out shared projects and develop a report that is presented to the class. Class members provide feedback to each team.

group roles. Assigned roles for students in cooperative groups that help the group function effectively. Roles commonly assigned include encourager, monitor, leader, and recorder.

handicap. Term, generally no longer preferred, to describe disabilities.

hard of hearing. Hearing impairment in which an individual has some hearing through which to process linguistic information, possibly with the assistance of hearing aids or other assistive devices.

hearing impairment. Condition in which an individual has the inability or limited ability to receive information auditorily such that it interferes with learning.

hemophilia. Genetically transmitted disease in which blood does not properly coagulate.

hertz (Hz). Unit for measuring the pitch or tone of sounds.

heterogeneous grouping. *See* mixed-skill grouping.

high-incidence disability. Any of the most common disabilities outlined in P.L. 105-17, including learning disabilities, speech or language impairments, mild mental retardation, and serious emotional disturbance.

HIV. *See* human immunodeficiency virus.

homework. The most common form of student practice.

homogeneous grouping. *See* same-skill grouping.

human immunodeficiency virus (HIV). Viral disease in which the body loses its ability to fight off infection. Individuals with HIV often become infected with AIDS.

hyperactive-impulsive disorder. Type of ADHD characterized by excessive movement and other motor activity including fidgeting, a need to move around a room even when others are seated, and rapid changes in activities.

IDEA. Individuals with Disabilities Education Act. *See* P.L. 101-476.

IDEA-97. Individuals with Disabilities Education Act of 1997. *See* P.L. 105-17.

IEP. *See* individual education program.

IFSP. *See* Individualized Family Service Plan.

improvement grade. Giving credit in evaluation of student performance for progress made, based on the student's level of learning prior to instruction.

impulsivity. The extent to which an individual acts before thinking, often a characteristic of students with high-incidence disabilities or ADHD.

INCLUDE. Strategy for accommodating students with special needs in the general education classroom.

inclusion. Term to describe a professional belief that students with disabilities should be integrated into general education classrooms whether or not they can meet traditional curricular standards and should be full members of those classrooms.

inclusion specialist. Special education teacher responsible for providing a wide variety of supports to students with disabilities and general education teachers who teach them. Inclusion specialists most often work with students with low-incidence disabilities. Sometimes called a *support facilitator.*

independent learning skills. Skills students need to manage their own learning, including note-taking, textbook reading, test-taking, written expression, and time management.

Individualized Education Program (IEP). Document prepared by the multidisciplinary team or annual review team that specifies a student's level of functioning and needs, the instructional goals and objectives for the student and how they will be evaluated, the nature and extent of special education and related services to be received, and the initiation date and duration of the services. Each student's IEP is updated annually.

Individualized Family Service Plan (IFSP). Education plan for children receiving services through P.L. 99-457. Similar to an IEP.

individualized instruction. Instruction designed to meet the specific needs of a student with a disability; a requirement of IDEA.

individually administered diagnostic test. Diagnostic achievement test given to one student at a time, often administered by a special education teacher or school psychologist, useful as a diagnostic measure. These tests provide more specific information than group-administered achievement tests do.

inquiry learning. The most common method of nondirect instruction. *See also* nondirect instruction.

instructional adaptation. Any strategy for adapting curriculum materials, teacher instruction, or student practice activities that increases the likelihood of success for students with special needs.

instructional assistance team. Team of teachers, specialists, and administrators that solves problems about students experiencing academic or behavior difficulty and decides whether students should be individually assessed for possible special education services.

instructional evaluation. Type of assessment decision concerning whether to continue or change instructional procedures that have been initiated with students.

instructional materials. The textbooks, manipulatives, models, and technology used as part of instruction.

intent. The purpose or goal of a student's behavior, not always clear from the behavior itself. An example of an intent occurs when a student repeatedly calls out in class to gain the teacher's attention; that is, the intent is teacher attention.

interval recording. Strategy for recording behavior in which observation occurs for brief segments of time and any occurrence of the behavior during the segment is noted.

itinerant teacher. Special education teacher who provides services to students with disabilities and reaches in two or more schools.

Jigsaw. Cooperative learning program in which work group team members are assigned to expert groups to master part of the assigned material to which no other group has access. In the work group, each team member has an opportunity to present his or her part of the material. Students are then assessed for mastery individually.

Jigsaw II. Cooperative learning program in which students interact in both work groups and expert groups to learn assigned materials. Students are then assessed separately.

job coach. A special education professional who accompanies students with disabilities to job sites and helps them master the skills needed to perform the job.

keyword method. Mnemonic for remembering definitions and factual information in which visual imagery is used to enhance recall.

KWL Plus. Three-step learning strategy for reading comprehension: what you already know; what you want to know; what you learned.

LAMPS. Learning strategy for remembering the steps for regrouping in addition with these steps: line up the numbers according to their decimal points; add the right column of numbers and ask . . . ; if more than nine continue to the next step; put the 1s below the column; and send the 10s to the top of the next column.

LD. *See* learning disability.

learned helplessness. Characteristic of some students with disabilities in which they see little relationship between their own efforts and school or social success, often resulting in a belief that they cannot perform challenging tasks.

learning and behavior disabilities. Term used to describe collectively learning disabilities, serious emotional disturbance, and mild cognitive disabilities.

learning disability (LED). Condition in which a student has dysfunction in processing information typically found in language-based activities, resulting in interference with learning. Students with learning disabilities have average or above average intelligence but experience significant problems in learning how to read, write, and/or use a computer.

learning outcomes. Specific goals or outcomes students are expected to accomplish as a result of a unit of instruction.

learning strategies. Techniques, principles, or rules that enable a student to solve problems and complete tasks independently.

Learning Together. Cooperative learning program in which groups of two to six members learn specific skills for interacting with one another and then work together in various formal and informal group structures to learn material.

least restrictive environment (LRE). The setting as similar as possible to that for students without disabilities in which a student with a disability can be educated, with appropriate supports provided. For most students, the LRE is a general education classroom.

legal blindness. Visual impairment in which an individual's best eye, with correction, has vision of 20/200 or less, or the visual field is 20 percent or less.

low demand request. Behavior management strategy in which the teacher helps a student transition from one activity to another by making a series of simple requests of the student that are unrelated to the targeted task.

low-incidence disability. Any of the less common disabilities outlined in P.L. 105-17, including multiple disabilities, hearing impairments, orthopedic impairments, other health impairments, visual impairments, deaf-blindness, autism, and traumatic brain injury.

LRE. *See* least restrictive environment.

mainstreaming. Term for placing students with disabilities in general education settings when they can meet traditional academic expectations with minimal assistance, or when those expectations are not relevant.

maintenance goal. Type of goal teams set that describes what the team wants to accomplish in terms of its own effectiveness.

manipulatives. Concrete objects or representational items used as part of instruction. Examples of commonly used manipulatives include blocks and counters.

MDT. *See* multidisciplinary team.

mediation. Process in which a neutral professional assists parents and school district personnel in resolving disputes concerning any aspect of a student's special education.

mental retardation. Condition in which an individual has significant limitations in cognitive ability and adaptive behaviors that interfere with learning. Also referred to as a *cognitive disability*.

minimum intervention. Strategy for promoting positive behavior that is nonintrusive and often spontaneous instead of systematic and long term. Examples of minimum interventions include noticing positive student behavior and commenting on it and moving students from one activity to another by making unrelated but easily accomplished requests first.

mixed-skill grouping. Classroom grouping arrangement in which students are clustered for instruction without focusing on specific skill needs. Also referred to as *heterogeneous grouping*.

mnemonic. A device or code used to assist memory by imposing an order on the information to be remembered.

mobility specialist. Specialist who helps students with visual impairments learn to be familiar with their environments and able to travel from place to place independently and safely.

model. Concrete representation that can help students make connections between abstractions and real-life physical objects or processes.

modified course syllabus. A document produced by the IEP team that states the specific course requirements, expectations, grading criteria, and other changes necessary because of a student's disability.

modified curricular expectations. Individualized expectations, different from those of other students, set for students with disabilities on the basis of the goals and objectives summarized in the IEP.

multicultural education. Approaches to education that reflect the diversity of society.

multidisciplinary team (MDT). Team including teachers, specialists, administrators, and parents who assess a student's individual needs, determine eligibility for special education, and develop the IEP.

multimedia software. Computer programs that combine written words, graphics, sound, and animation.

multiple disabilities. Condition in which individuals have two or more of the disabilities outlined in P.L. 101-476, although no one can be determined to be predominant.

multiple intelligences. Concept proposed by Howard Gardner (1993) that suggests there are seven types of intelligence, not just one.

multisensory approach. Instructional approach that emphasizes the use of more than one modality for teaching and learning. For example, having a student read a vocabulary word, spell it out loud, and then write it on paper is a multisensory approach to teaching vocabulary.

muscular dystrophy. Disease that weakens muscles, causing orthopedic impairments. This disease is progressive, often resulting in death during the late teenage years.

negative example. Instructional stimulus that does not illustrate the concept being taught, used with examples to ensure that students understand the instruction. Also called *nonexample*.

negative reinforcement. A potential negative consequence to a behavior that causes the behavior to increase.

nondirect instruction. Instructional approach often used for teaching higher-order thinking skills, including problem solving, in which the teacher guides learning by challenging students' thinking and helping them address problems.

novelty. Approach for educating gifted and talented students based on allowing students to learn traditional content using alternative or unusual strategies that might include working with an adult mentor, creating materials for other students to use, or using a problem-based learning approach.

Numbered Heads Together. Cooperative learning program in which students number off. The teacher poses a question; the students work together to ensure all members know the answer, and then the teacher calls a number. Students with the number stand, and one is called upon to respond to the question, with correct responses scoring points for the team.

nurse. Specialist who has expertise in understanding and responding to students' medical needs and who sometimes serves as a liaison between medical and school professionals.

occupational therapist. Specialist with expertise in meeting students' needs in the area of fine motor skills, including self-help skills such as feeding and dressing.

one-to-one instruction. Classroom grouping arrangement in which individual students work with either a teacher or computer in materials geared to their level and at their own pace.

orthopedic impairments. Physical conditions that seriously impair the ability to move about or to complete motor activities and interfere with learning.

other health impairments. Conditions in which an individual has a disease or disorder so significant that it affects his or her ability to learn. Examples could include sickle-cell anemia and AIDS.

overcorrection. Type of presentation punishment in which a student makes restitution for misbehavior. An example of overcorrection is a student cleaning all the desks in a room as a consequence for writing on one desk.

parallel teaching. Co-teaching option in which students are divided into small groups and each group receives the same instruction from one of the teachers in the room.

paraprofessional. Noncertified staff member employed to assist certified staff in carrying out education programs and otherwise help in the instruction of students with disabilities.

PARS. Learning strategy for reading textbooks with these steps: preview the material, ask questions, read the chapter, and summarize the main ideas.

partially sighted. Condition in which an individual has a significant visual impairment but is able to capitalize on residual sight using magnification devices and other adaptive materials.

pass/fail grading system. Evaluation procedure in which minimum competency levels established by the teacher are identified; students meeting or exceeding these are given a passing evaluation and those not meeting them are given a failing evaluation.

PASSING. Learning strategy for note-taking with these steps: Prepare for class, attend to the teacher, state the topic, state the source, identify key words and ideas, note their meaning, and give the meaning in your own words.

passive learner. Learner who does not believe in his or her own ability, has limited knowledge of problem-solving strategies, and is unable to determine when to use a strategy.

pattern guide. A graphic organizer designed to help students organize their written papers.

peer comparison. A component of curriculum-based assessment in which a student's performance is compared to that of classmates as a means of determining whether a learning problem exists.

peer editing. Component of student writing in which students review, evaluate, and provide feedback to each other about their written work.

peer tutoring. Student-centered instructional approach in which pairs of students help one another and learn by teaching.

peer tutoring program. Program emphasizing the use of peers as teachers.

performance-based assessment. Method of evaluation that measures what students can do with knowledge rather than measuring specific bits of knowledge the student possesses.

permanent product recording. Strategy for recording behavior in which samples of student work and other permanent evidence of student behavior are collected and evaluated.

personal assistant. Paraprofessional specially trained to monitor and assist a particular student with a disability.

personal role. One of the roles individuals bring to a team, consisting of characteristics, knowledge, skills, and perceptions based on life experiences broader than those in the professional area.

petit mal seizure. *See* absence seizure.

physical punishment. Type of presentation punishment, not recommended for use by teachers, that involves a negative physical consequence for misbehavior.

physical therapist. Specialist with expertise in meeting students' needs in the area of gross motor skills.

placement. Location in which education will occur for a student with a disability.

P.L. 94-142. Legislation, also called the *Education for the Handicapped Act (EHA)*, passed in 1975, which set federal guidelines for special education and related services and the procedures for establishing and monitoring them.

P.L. 99-457. Legislation passed in 1986 that extended the provisions of special education to very young children, those birth to 5 years of age.

P.L. 101-476. Individuals with Disabilities Education Act, legislation passed in 1990 that updated and extended P.L. 94-142. P.L. 101-476 is also called *IDEA.*

P.L. 105-17. Individuals with Disabilities Education Act, legislation passed in 1997 that updated and extended P.L. 101-476. P.L. 105-17 is also called *IDEA-97.*

planning think sheet. Set of questions to which students respond as a strategy for assisting them to activate background knowledge in preparation for writing.

portfolio assessment. Method of evaluation in which a purposeful collection of student work is used to determine student effort, progress, and achievement in one or more areas.

positive reinforcement. A consequence to a behavior that causes it to increase. Also called a *reward.*

POSSE. Learning strategy for reading comprehension with these steps: predict ideas, organize the ideas, search for the structure, summarize the main ideas, and evaluate your understanding.

POWER. Learning strategy for writing with these steps: planning, organizing, writing, editing, and revising.

PReP strategy. Strategy for determining how much background information students have about a topic.

prereferral assistance team. *See* instructional assistance team.

present level of functioning. Information about a student's current level of academic achievement, social skills, behavior, communication skills, and other areas that is included on an IEP.

presentation punishment. Presenting negative consequences as a strategy for decreasing behavior.

preskill. Basic skill necessary for performing a more complex skill.

primary reinforcer. Food or other items related to human needs that cause a behavior to increase, used only occasionally in schools. An example of a primary reinforcer is a piece of licorice earned for appropriate behavior.

probe. Quick and easy measure of student performance (accuracy and fluency) in the basic-skill areas of reading, math, and written expression consisting of timed samples of academic behaviors.

probe of basic academic skills. *See* probe.

probe of prerequisite skills. Specific type of probe designed to assess whether a student has the prerequisite skills needed to succeed in the planned instruction.

professional role. One of the roles individuals bring to a team, including knowledge, skills, and perceptions based on professional training and experience.

program evaluation. Type of assessment decision concerning whether a special education program should be terminated, continued as is, or modified.

program placement. Type of assessment decision concerning where a student's special education services will take place.

psychological test. Test designed to measure how efficiently students learn in an instructional situation; often used to assess intelligence and to determine whether learning disabilities exist.

psychologist. *See* school psychologist.

psychometrist. Specialist with expertise in assessment who in some states completes much of the individual assessment required to determine eligibility for special education services.

pullout model. Instructional approach in which students with disabilities leave the general education classroom once or more each day to receive special education services.

punishment. Any response of consequence that has the effect of decreasing a behavior.

rate of introduction. The pace at which new skills are introduced during instruction.

RAP. Note-taking strategy consisting of three steps: read the paragraph; ask yourself "What was the main idea and what were two details?"; put the main idea and details in your own words.

READS. Textbook-reading strategy consisting of five steps: review headings and subheadings; examine boldfaced words; ask, "What do I expect to learn?"; do it—read!; summarize in your own words.

reasoning. A range of important learning skills, including comprehension, generalization, induction, and sequencing.

rebound effect. Potential side effect of medication in which as medication wears off the individual displays symptoms worse than those that existed before medication was given. Rebound effects are a particular concern for medications prescribed for students with ADHD.

receptive language. An individual's ability to understanding what people mean when they speak.

reciprocal teaching. Teaching students to comprehend reading material by providing them with teacher and peer models of thinking behavior and then allowing them to practice these thinking behaviors with their peers.

reciprocal tutoring. Same-age tutoring approach in which students in the same class are randomly assigned and take turns teaching each other. *See also* reciprocal teaching.

regular class. One placement for students with disabilities. Also referred to as a *general education class*.

rehearsal strategy. Test-taking strategy that involves saying information out loud, repeating it, checking it for accuracy, and repeating it again as part of studying.

reinforcement. Any response or consequence that causes a behavior to increase.

reinforcement menu. List of rewards from which students may choose, often most effective if students participate in its development.

related services. Services students with disabilities need to benefit from their educational experience. Examples of related services include transportation, speech therapy, physical therapy, and counseling.

removal punishment. Taking away from a student something that is desired as a strategy for decreasing inappropriate behavior.

residential facility. Placement for students with disabilities when their needs cannot be met at a school. Students attend school and live at a residential facility.

resource room. Classroom to which students come for less than 50 percent of the school day to receive special education.

resource teacher. Special education teacher who provides direct services to students with disabilities either in a special education or general education classroom and who also meets to solve problems with teachers. Resource teachers most often work with students with high-incidence disabilities.

response cost. Type of removal punishment in which a student loses privileges or other rewards as a consequence of inappropriate behavior.

response format. The way in which a student is expected to respond to test items. Examples of response formats include writing true or false, circling a correct answer from a list of four, drawing a line to match items, or writing an essay.

retention. Ability to remember information after time has passed.

RICE. Strategy for involving students in the portfolio process. Steps include: rationale—why are you keeping a portfolio?; identify goals—what do you want to improve?; contents—what will you include in your portfolio?; evaluation—how, and when, will you assess your portfolio?

Ritalin. Psychostimulant medication commonly prescribed for individuals with ADHD.

same-age tutoring. Peer tutoring approach in which students in the same class or grade level tutor one another, typically with higher-achieving students assisting lower-achieving students.

same-skill grouping. Classroom grouping arrangement in which all students needing instruction on a particular skill are clustered for that instruction. Also referred to as *homogeneous grouping.*

satiation. Situation in which a positive reinforcer, used repeatedly, loses its effectiveness.

scaffolding. Instructional approach for teaching higher-order thinking skills in which the teacher supports student learning by reviewing the cognitive strategy to be addressed, regulating difficulty during practice, providing varying contexts for student practice, providing feedback, increasing student responsibility for learning, and creating opportunities for independent student practice.

school psychologist. Specialist with expertise to give individual assessments of students in cognitive, academic, social, emotional, and behavioral domains. This professional also designs strategies to address students' academic and social behavior problems.

SCORER. Test-taking strategy that includes these steps: schedule your time; clue words; omit difficult questions; read carefully; estimate your answers; review your work.

screening. Type of assessment decision concerning whether or not a student's academic or behavior performance is different enough from that of his or her peers to merit further, more in-depth assessment.

SCROL. Learning strategy for teaching students to use text headings to aid their comprehension with these steps: survey the headings, connect, read the text, outline, and look back.

Section 504. The section of the Vocational Rehabilitation Act of 1973 that prohibits discrimination against all individuals with disabilities in programs that receive federal funds.

self-advocacy. Extent to which a student can identify supports needed to succeed and communicate that information effectively to others, including teachers and employers.

self-awareness. Extent to which a student has an accurate perception of his or her learning strengths, learning needs, and ability to use strategies to learn independently.

self-control training. A strategy in which students who lack self-control are taught to redirect their actions by talking to themselves.

self-image. Individual's perception of his or her own abilities, appearance, and competence.

self-instruction. Strategy in which students are taught to talk themselves through tasks.

self-monitoring. Strategy in which students are taught to check whether they have performed targeted behaviors.

self-questioning. Strategy in which students are taught to guide their performance by asking themselves relevant questions.

self-reinforcement. Strategy in which students reward themselves for behaving appropriately or achieving success in learning tasks.

sensory impairment. Disability related to vision or hearing.

separate class. Classroom in which students with disabilities spend 50 percent or more of the school day.

separate school. School serving only students with disabilities.

shared problem solving. Process used by groups of professionals, sometimes including parents, for identifying problems, generating potential solutions, selecting and implementing solutions, and evaluating the effectiveness of solutions.

short-term objective. Description of a step followed in order to achieve an annual goal.

sickle-cell anemia. Inherited disorder occurring most often in African Americans in which red blood cells are abnormally shaped and weakened.

signed exact English (SEE). A form of sign language in which spoken English is converted word-for-word into signs.

sign language interpreter. Specialist who listens to instruction and other communication and relays it to students with hearing impairments through sign language.

simulation. Activity in which students experience what it might be like to have a disability; in a technology context, simulations are computer programs that teach problem solving, decision making, and risk taking by having students react to real-life and imaginary situations.

SLOBS. Learning strategy to help students with regrouping in subtraction with these steps: if smaller, follow the steps; if larger, leap to subtract; cross off the number in the next column; borrow by taking one 10 and adding to the next column; subtract.

SLOW CaPS. Learning strategy for writing four kinds of paragraphs with these steps: show the type of paragraph in the first sentence; list the details you want to write about, order the details; write details in complete sentences; CAP off the paragraph with a concluding, passing, or summary sentence.

slow learner. Student whose educational progress is below average, but not so severe as to be considered a cognitive disability, and is consistent with the students abilities.

social cues. Verbal or nonverbal signals people give that communicate a social message.

social reinforcer. Positive interpersonal interaction that causes a behavior to increase. An example of a social reinforcer is a teacher praising a student's appropriate behavior.

social skills. Behaviors that help students interact successfully with their peers, teachers, and others and that help them win social acceptance.

social-skills training program. Systematic instruction designed to help students acquire social skills.

social worker. Specialist with expertise in meeting students' social needs and fostering working relationships with families.

sophistication. Approach for educating gifted and talented students based on helping students learn complex principles about subject matter being presented to the entire class.

special education. Specially designed instruction provided by the school district or other local education agency that meets the unique needs of students identified as disabled.

special education teacher. Teacher whose primary responsibility is delivering and managing the delivery of special education services to students with disabilities.

Special Friends. Program designed to promote friendships between students with disabilities and those without disabilities.

special services coordinator. Administrator responsible for interpreting guidelines related to educating students with disabilities and assisting other school district personnel in carrying out those guidelines.

speech articulation. The ability to produce sounds correctly at the age where they would normally be expected to develop.

speech or language impairment. Condition in which student has extraordinary difficulties in communicating with others due to causes other than maturation and that interferes with learning.

speech reading. Strategy used by individuals with hearing impairments to gain information by watching a person's lips, mouth, and expression. Only a small proportion of a spoken message can typically be discerned through speech reading.

speech/language therapist. Specialist with expertise in meeting students' communication needs, including articulation and language development.

spina bifida. Birth defect in which there is an abnormal opening in the spinal column, often leading to partial paralysis.

spinal cord injury. Condition in which the spinal cord is damaged or severed because of accident or injury, leading to orthopedic impairments.

STAD. *See* Student Teams–Achievement Divisions.

standardized achievement test. Norm-referenced test designed to measure academic progress, or what students have retained in the curriculum.

station teaching. Co-teaching option in which students are divided into small groups and each group receives part of its instruction from each teacher.

stereotypic behavior. An action or motion repeated over and over again. Examples of stereotypic behaviors include spinning an object, rocking the body, and twirling.

story grammar. Description of the typical elements of stories, including theme, setting, character, initiating events, attempts at resolution, resolution, and reactions.

story map. Graphic organizer for narrative material.

student evaluation. Determination of the extent to which students have mastered academic skills or other instructional content, frequently communicated through grades.

student self-evaluation. Assessment approach in which students are asked to perform a task, are given a checklist of strategy steps for the task, and then are asked to tell which of these steps they did or did not use.

Student Teams–Achievement Divisions (STAD). Cooperative learning program in which groups of four members learn material together and take quizzes separately. Students earn points based on their own improvement over past quiz scores. These points are contributed to a team score.

study guide. General term for outlines, abstracts, or questions that emphasize important information in texts.

stuttering. Speech impairment in which an individual involuntarily repeats a sound or word, resulting in a loss of speech fluency.

support facilitator. *See* inclusion specialist.

surface behavior. Initial student behaviors that teachers could interpret as misbehavior. Responding appropriately to surface behaviors can prevent them from escalating into more serious discipline problems.

TAG. Learning strategy for peer editing with these steps: tell what you like, ask questions, and give suggestions.

TAI. *See* Team Assisted Individualization.

tangible reinforcer. Prizes or other objects students want and can earn through appropriate behavior and that cause that behavior to increase. An example of a tangible reinforcer is a school pencil earned for appropriate behavior.

task analysis. Six-step strategy for managing time: decide exactly what you must do; decide how many steps are needed to complete the task; decide how much time each step will take; set up a schedule; get started; finish the task.

task goal. Type of goal teams set that describes the business the team was formed to accomplish.

TBI. *See* traumatic brain injury.

teacher-centered instruction. Classroom instructional arrangement in which the pattern of interaction is between teacher and student, with the teacher as the central figure.

team. Formal work group that has clear goals, active and committed members, leaders, clear procedures followed in order to accomplish goals, and strategies for monitoring effectiveness.

Team Assisted Individualization (TAI). Cooperative learning program in which groups of four members work at their own pace on individualized math materials and seek assistance as needed from other team members. Individual tests are taken to pass out of a unit. Teams earn points each week based on the number of units members have successfully completed.

team role. One of the formal or informal roles individuals bring to a team, consisting of contributions made to help ensure effective team functioning. Examples of formal team roles include team facilitator, recorder, and timekeeper. Examples of informal team roles include compromiser, information seeker, and reality checker.

team teaching. Co-teaching option in which students remain in one large group and teachers share leadership in the instructional activity of the classroom.

Teams–Games–Tournaments (TGT). Cooperative learning program in which groups of three members help each other learn assigned material. Team members then compete at tournament tables with classmates at a similar achievement level. Quizzes are given or instructional games played based on the assigned material. Members contribute points to their teams based on their performance at their tournament table.

test administration. The conditions under which a test is given to students.

test construction. The way in which test items are worded, ordered on the test, and formatted.

test site. The location in which a test is given.

test-taking skills. Learning strategies taught to students to help them succeed in studying for and taking tests.

3R strategy. Three-step learning strategy to help students prepare for lectures: review notes and materials from the previous class; read materials related to today's class; relate lecture topic to other topics.

three-year reevaluation. Triannual process of reassessing the needs of a student with a disability, carried out by a multidisciplinary team.

time-out. Type of removal punishment in which a student is removed from opportunities for reward. An example of timeout is a "penalty box" for misbehavior on the playground.

time sampling. Strategy for recording behavior in which a behavior is periodically observed and measured during a specified time period.

token economy. Group behavior management procedure in which students earn a representative or token currency for appropriate behavior that can later be exchanged for rewards.

tracking. Educational practice of grouping students for instruction by their perceived ability level.

transition plan. Document for students with disabilities who are as young as 14 years old that describes strategies for assisting them prepare to leave school for adult life.

transition specialist. Special educator who helps prepare students with disabilities for postschool activities, including employment, vocational training, or higher education.

transition time. The time it takes a group of students to change from one classroom activity to another.

traumatic brain injury (TBI). Condition in which an individual experiences a significant trauma to the head from accident, illness, or injury and that affects learning.

tutorial. Computer program designed to present new material to students in small sequential steps and/or to review concepts.

unison responding. All students responding at once to teacher questions or other instruction.

visual impairment. Condition in which an individual has an inability or limited ability to receive information visually, so much so that it interferes with learning.

wait time. Amount of time a teacher gives a student to respond to a question.

written language difficulties. Problems that students with learning and behavior disabilities have with skills related to handwriting, spelling, and written expression.

References

Aber, M. E., Bachman, B., Campbell, P., & O'Malley, G. (1994). Improving instruction in elementary schools. *Teaching Exceptional Children, 26*(3), 42–50.

Abikoff, H. (1991). Cognitive training in ADHD children: Less to it than meets the eye. *Journal of Learning Disabilities, 24,* 205–209.

Abramowitz, A. J., & O'Leary, S. G. (1991). Behavioral interventions for the classroom: Implications for students with ADHD. *School Psychology Review, 20,* 220–234.

Adams, D., & Hamm, M. (1991). Diversity gives schools infinite learning possibilities: Learning cooperatively proves successful tool to highlight many cultural values. *School Administrator, 4*(48), 20–22.

Adams, L. (Ed.). (1994). *Attention deficit disorders: A handbook for Colorado educators.* Denver, CO: Colorado Department of Education.

Adams, L., Carl, C. A., Covino, M. E., Filibin, J., Knapp, J., Rich, J. P., Warfield, M. A., & Yenowine, W. (1991). *Guidelines paper: Traumatic brain injury.* Denver, CO: Special Education Services Unit, Colorado Department of Education.

Affleck, J. Q., Lowenbraun, S., & Archer, A. (1980). *Teaching the mildly handicapped in the regular classroom.* Columbus, OH: Merrill.

Algozzine, B., Ysseldyke, J. E., & Campbell, P. (1994). Strategies and tactics for effective instruction. *Teaching Exceptional Children, 26*(3), 34–36.

Alley, G., & Deshler, D. (1979). *Teaching the learning disabled adolescent: Strategies and methods.* Denver, CO: Love.

Alley, G. R. (1988). Effects of generalization instruction on the written language performance of adolescents with learning disabilities in the mainstream classroom. *Reading, Writing, and Learning Disabilities, 4,* 291–309.

Allport, G. (1954). *The nature of prejudice.* Cambridge, MA: Addison-Wesley.

Alper, S., & Ryndak, D. L. (1992). Educating students with severe handicaps in regular classes. *Elementary School Journal, 92,* 373–387.

American Academy of Pediatrics. (1976). Committee on nutrition: Megavitamin therapy for childhood psychoses and learning disabilities. *Pediatrics, 58,* 910–911.

American Psychiatric Association. (1994). *Diagnostic and statistical manual of mental disorders* (4th ed.). Washington, DC: Author.

American School Board Association. (1997). The new IDEA. *American School Board Journal, 184*(12), 20.

American Speech-Language-Hearing Association. (1982). Definitions: Communicative disorders and variations. *ASHA, 24,* 949–950.

Anderson, C., & Katsiyannis, A. (1997). By what token economy?: A classroom learning tool for inclusive settings. *Teaching Exceptional Children, 29*(4), 65–67.

Anderson, K., & Milliren, A. (1983). *Structured experiences for integration of handicapped children.* Rockville, MD: Aspen.

Archer, A. (1977). *Instructional materials for the mildly handicapped: Selection, utilization, and modification.* Eugene, OR: Northwest Learning Resource System, University of Oregon.

Archer, A. (1992). Promoting school success: Study skills and what we've learned from DI. *ADI News, 11*(4), 14–19.

Archer, A., & Gleason, M. (1997). Direct instruction in content area reading. In D. Carnine, J. Silbert, & E. Kameenui (Eds.), *Direct instruction reading* (3rd ed., pp. 339–393). Columbus, OH: Merrill.

Arends, R. I. (1991). *Learning to teach.* New York: McGraw-Hill.

Armbruster, B. B. (1984). The problem of "inconsiderate text". In G. G. Duffy, L. R. Roehler, & J. Mason (Eds.), *Comprehensive instruction: Perspectives and suggestions* (pp. 202–217). New York: Longman.

Armbruster, B. B., & Anderson, T. H. (1988). On selecting "considerate" content area textbooks. *Remedial and Special Education, 9*(1), 47–52.

Armstrong, R. (1996). ADD: Does it really exist? *Phi Delta Kappan, 77,* 424–428.

Armstrong, T. (1994). *Multiple intelligences in the classroom* (p. 6). Alexandria, VA: Association for Supervision and Curriculum Development.

Armstrong v. Kline, 476 F. Supp. 583 (E. D. Pa. 1979).

Aronson, E., Blaney, N., Stephen, C., Sikes, J., & Snapp, M. (1978). *The jigsaw classroom.* Beverly Hills, CA: Sage.

Atwood, A. (1993). Movement disorders and autism acquired in review of communication abound. *American Journal of Mental Retardation, 99,* 450–451.

Aune, E. (1991). A transition model for postsecondary-bound students with learning disabilities. *Learning disabilities Research and Practice, 6,* 177–187.

Aurback & Associates. (1991). *Grady profile: Portfolio assessment.* St. Louis, MO: Author.

Ayres, B. J., & Hedeen, D. L. (1996). Been there, done that, didn't work: Alternative solutions for behavior problems. *Educational Leadership, 53* (5), 48–50.

Babbitt, B. C. (1993). Hypermedia: Making the mathematics connection. *Intervention in School and Clinic, 28*(5), 294–302.

Babbitt, B. C., & Miller, S. P. (1996). Using hypermedia to improve the mathematics problem-solving skills of students with learning disabilities. *Journal of Learning Disabilities, 29*(4), 391–401, 412.

Bailey, D. B., Buysse, V., Edmondson, R., & Smith, T. M. (1992). Creating family-centered services in early intervention: Perceptions of professionals in four states. *Exceptional Children, 58,* 298–309.

Bailey, J., & McTighe, H. (1996). Reporting achievement at the secondary level: What and how. In T. Guskey (Ed.), *ASCD yearbook: 1996 communicating student learning* (pp. 199–240). Alexandria, VA: Association for Supervision and Curriculum Development.

Banks, J. A. (1993). Multicultural education: Development, dimensions, and challenges. *Phi Delta Kappan, 75,* 22–28.

Barad, D. (1985). *Adapting instruction in general education for students with communication disorders.* Unpublished manuscript, Northern Illinois University.

Bardak, J. (1995). Collaboration in schools : Meeting the needs of all students. *Developmental Disabilities Bulletin, 23*(1), 120–138.

Barkley, R. (1995). *Taking charge of ADHD: The complete authoritative guide for parents.* New York: Guilford Press.

Barkley, R. A. (1990). *Attention deficit hyperactivity disorder: A handbook for diagnosis and treatment.* New York: Guilford Press.

Baroody, A. J. (October, 1989). Manipulatiaves don't come with guarantees. *Arithmetic Teacher,* 4–5.

Barrish, H. H., Saunders, M., & Wolf, M. M. (1969). Good Behavior Game: Effects of individual contingencies for group consequences on disruptive behavior in a classroom. *Journal of Applied Behavior Analysis, 2,* 119–124.

Barron, A. M., & Foot, H. (1991). Peer tutoring and tutor training. *Educational Research, 33,* 174–185.

Barth, R. S. (1990). *Improving schools from within.* San Francisco: Jossey-Bass.

Bartelt, L., Marchio, T., & Reynolds, D. (1994). *The READS strategy.* Unpublished manuscript, Northern Illinois University.

Battle v. Commonwealth of Pennsylvania, 629 F.2d 269 (3d Cir. 1980).

Bauer, A. M., & Sapona, R. H. (1991). *Managing classrooms to facilitate learning.* Englewood Cliffs, NJ: Prentice-Hall.

Bauwens, J., & Hourcade, J. J. (1995). *Cooperative teaching: Rebuilding the schoolhouse for all students.* Austin, TX: PRO-ED.

Bay, M., & Bryan, T. (1992). Differentiating children who are at risk for referral from others on critical classroom factors. *Remedial and Special Education, 13*(4), 27–33.

Bear, G. G., & Minke, K. M. (1996). Positive bias in maintenance of self-worth among children with LD. *Learning Disability Quarterly, 19,* 23–32.

Bear, T., Schenk, S., & Buckner, L. (1992/1993). Supporting victims of child abuse. *Educational Leadership, 50*(4), 42–47.

Beiderman, G. B., Davey, V. A., Ryder, C., & Franchi, D. (1994). The negative effects of positive reinforcement in teaching children with developmental delay. *Exceptional Children, 60,* 458–465.

Beirne-Smith, M., Patton, J. R., & Ittenbach, R. (1994). *Mental retardation* (4th ed.). New York: Merrill.

Bennett, A. (1932). *Subnormal children in elementary grades.* New York: Teacher's College, Columbia University, Bureau of Publications.

Bennett, C. I. (1995). *Comprehensive multicultural education: Theory and practice* (3rd ed.). Boston: Allyn and Bacon.

Bergan, J. R., & Tombari, M. L. (1975). The analysis of verbal interactions occurring during consultation. *Journal of School Psychology, 13,* 209–226.

Berger, C. F., Berkheimer, G. D., Lewis, L. E., & Neuberger, H. J. (1979). *Houghton Mifflin Science* (p. 55). Boston: Houghton Mifflin.

Bergman, J. L. (1992). SAIL: A way to success and independence for low-achieving readers. *The Reading Teacher, 45*(8), 598–602.

Biklen, D. (1993). *Communication unbound.* New York: Teachers College Press.

Blankenship, C., & Lilly, M. S. (1981). *Mainstreaming students with learning and behavior problems: Techniques for the classroom teachers.* New York: Holt, Rinehart, & Winston.

Blatt, B. (1958). The physical, personality, and academic status of children who are mentally retarded attending special classes as compared with children who are mentally retarded attending regular class. *American Journal of Mental Deficiency, 62,* 810–818.

Blatt, B. (1987). *The conquest of mental retardation.* Austin, TX: PRO-ED.

Board of Education of Hendrick Hudson School District v. Rowley, 458 U.S. 176 (1982).

Bos, C. S., & Vaughn, S. (1994). *Strategies for teaching students with learning and behavior problems* (3rd ed.). Boston: Allyn and Bacon.

Bowman, B. T. (1994). The challenge of diversity. *Phi Delta Kappan, 76,* 218–224.

Brandel, D. (1992). Collaboration: Full steam ahead with no prior experience! *Language, Speech, and Hearing Services in Schools, 23,* 369–370.

Brandwein, P. F., & Bauer, N. W. (1980). *The United States, living in our world: Research, evaluation, and writing.* Barton R. Clark et al., consulting social scientists. San Francisco and New York: Center for the Study of Instruction/Harcourt, Brace, Jovanovich.

Brent, R., & Anderson, P. (1993). Developing children's listening strategies. *The Reading Teacher, 47*(2), 122–126.

Brinckerhoff, L. (1994). Developing effective self-advocacy skills in college-bound students with learning disabilities. *Intervention in School and Clinic, 29*(4), 229–237.

Brolin, D. E., & Schatzman, B. (1989). Lifelong career development. In D. E. Berkell & J. M. Brown (Eds.), *Transition from school to work for persons with disabilities* (pp. 22–41). New York: Longman.

Brown, G. (1994). Augmentative communication systems: Practical ideas for home and school programs. In F. LaRoy & J. Streng (Eds.), *A new dawn of awakening: Proceedings of the 1994 conference* (pp. 63–64). Arlington, TX: Future Education.

Brown, G. M., Kerr, M. M., Zigmond, N., & Haus, A. (1984). What's important for student success in high school? Successful and unsuccessful students discuss school survival skills. *High School Journal, 68,* 10–17.

Brown v. Board of Education, 347 U.S. 483 (1954).

Bryan, T. (1997). Assessing the personal and social status of students with learning disabilities. *Learning Disabilities Research & Practice, 12*(1), 63–76.

Bryan, T., & Sullivan-Burstein, K. (1997). Homework how-to's. *Teaching Exceptional Children, 29*(6), 32–37.

Bryan, T. H., & Bryan, J. H. (1986). *Understanding learning disabilities* (3rd ed.). Palo Alto, CA: Mayfield.

Bulgren, J. A., Schumaker, J. B., & Deshler, D. (1988). Effectiveness of a concept teaching routine in enhancing the performance of LD students in secondary-level mainstream classes. *Learning Disability Quarterly, 11,* 3–17.

Bullara, D. T. (1993). Classroom management strategies to reduce racially-biased treatment of students. *Journal of Educational and Psychological Consultation, 4*(4), 357–368.

Burgess, D. M., & Streissguth, A. P. (1992). Fetal alcohol syndrome and fetal alcohol effects: Principles for educators. *Phi Delta Kappan, 74,* 24–29.

Burke, W. W. (1988). Team building. In W. B. Reddy, & K. Jamison (Eds.), *Team building: Blueprints for productivity and satisfaction* (pp. 3–14). Alexandria, VA: NTL Institute for Applied Behavioral Science.

Burns, P. C., Roe, B. D., & Ross, E. P. (1992). *Teaching reading in today's elementary schools.* Boston: Houghton Mifflin.

Bursuck, W. D., & Jayanthi, M. (1993). Programming for independent study skill usage. In S. Vogel & P. Adelman (Eds.), *Programming for success for college students with learning disabilities* (pp. 177–205). New York: Springer-Verlag.

Bursuck, W. D., & Lessen, E. (1987). A classroom-based model for assessing students with learning disabilities. *Learning Disabilities Focus, 3*(1), 17–29.

Bursuck, W. D., Kinder, D., & Epstein, M. H. (1989). Teacher ratings of school survival skills in junior high school. In S. L. Braeten, R. B. Rutherford, T. F. Reilly, & S. A. Diagami: (Eds.). *Programming for adolescents with behavior disorders* (pp. 1–9). Reston, VA: Council for Children with Behavioral Disorders.

Bursuck, W. D., Polloway, E. A., Plante, L., Epstein, M. H., Jayanthi, M., & McConeghy, J. (1996). Report card grading and adaptations: A national survey of classroom practices. *Exceptional Children, 62*(4), 301–318.

Butson, S., Shea, K., Pankratz, K., & Lamb, M. (1992). *A script for how to teach the KWL strategy.* Unpublished manuscript, Northern Illinois University.

Cameron, J., & Pierce, W. D. (1994). Reinforcement, reward, and intrinsic motivation: A meta-analysis. *Review of Educational Research, 64,* 363–423.

Camp, B. W., & Bash, M. A. (1985). *Think aloud.* Champaign, IL: Research Press.

Carlberg, C., & Kavale, K. (1980). The efficacy of special versus regular class placement for exceptional children: A meta-analysis. *Journal of Special Education, 14,* 295–309.

Carlson, C., & Henning, M. (1993). *The TAG peer editing procedure.* Unpublished manuscript, Northern Illinois University.

Carman, R. A., & Adams, W. R. (1990). *Study skills: A student's guide for survival.* New York: Wiley.

Carney, R. N., Levin, M. E., & Levin, J. R. (1993). Mnemonic strategies: Instructional techniques worth remembering. *Teaching Exceptional Children, 25*(4), 24–30.

Carnine, D. W. (1981). High and low implementation of direct instruction teaching techniques. *Education and Treatment of Children, 4,* 42–51.

Carnine, D. W., Caros, J., Crawford, D., Hollenbeck, K., & Harniss, M. K. (1996). Designing effective United States history curricula for all students. In J. Brophy (Ed.), *Advances in research on teaching, Vol. 6, History teaching and learning* (pp. 207–256). Greenwich, CT: JAI Press.

Carnine, D., Crawford, D., Harniss, M., & Hollenbeck, K. (1995). *Understanding U.S. history: Volume 1—Through the Civil War.* Eugene, OR: Considerate Publishing.

Carnine, D. W., Silbert, J., & Kameenui, E. (1997). *Direct instruction reading* (3rd ed.). Columbus, OH: Merrill.

Carpenter, D., Grantham, L. B., & Hardister, M. P. (1983). Grading mainstreamed handicapped pupils: What are the issues? *Journal of Special Education, 17*(2), 183–188.

Carpenter, S. L., & McKee-Higgins, E. (1996). Behavior management in inclusive classrooms. *Remedial and Special Education, 17,* 195–203.

Carter, R. T., & Goodwin, A. L. (1994). Racial identity and education. In L. Darling-Hammond (Ed.), *Review of research in education* (vol. 20, pp. 291–336). Washington, DC: American Educational Research Association.

Cassidy, V. M., & Stanton, J. E. (1959) *An investigation of factors involved in the educational placement of mentally retarded children: A study of differences between children in special and regular classes in Ohio.* (U.S. Office of Education Cooperative Research Program, Project No. 43) Columbus: Ohio State University. (ERIC Document Reproduction Service No. ED 002 752)

Cawley, J. F., Fitzmaurice, A. M., Lepore, A. F., Sedlak, R., & Althaus, V. (1979). LD youth and mathematics: A review of characteristics. *Learning Disability Quarterly, 2*(1), 29–44.

Cawley, J. F., Miller, J., & School, B. (1987). A brief inquiry of arithmetic word problem solving among learning disabled secondary students. *Learning Disabilities Focus, 2*(2), 87–93.

Center for the Study of Reading. (1988). *A guide to selecting basal reading programs: Workbooks.* Cambridge, MA: Bolt, Beranck, and Newman.

Cermak, L. S. (1976). *Improving your memory.* New York: Norton.

Cesaroni, L., & Garber, M. (1991). Exploring the experience of autism through firsthand accounts. *Journal of Autism and Developmental Disorders, 21,* 303–313.

Chaffin, J. (1975). Will the real "mainstreaming" program please stand up! (Or . . . should Dunn have done it?). In E. L. Meyen, G. A. Vergason, & R. J. Whelan (Eds.), *Alternatives for teaching exceptional children.* Denver, CO: Love.

Chalmers, L., & Faliede, T. (1996). Successful inclusion of students with mild/moderate disabilities in rural school settings. *Teaching Exceptional Children, 29*(1), 22–25.

Cheek, Jr., E. H., & Cheek, M. C. (1983). *Reading instruction through content teaching.* Columbus, OH: Merrill.

Choate, J. S., Enright, B. E., Miller, L. J., Poteet, J. A., & Rakes, T. A. (1995). *Curriculum-based assessment and programming.* Boston: Allyn and Bacon.

Christenson, S., Ysseldyke, J., & Thurlow, M. (1989). Critical instructional factors for students with mild handicaps: An integrated review. *Remedial and Special Education, 10*(5), 21–31.

Christof, K. J., & Kane, S. R. (1991). Relationship building for students with autism. *Teaching Exceptional Children, 24*(2), 49–51.

Christopolos, F., & Renz, P. (1969). A critical examination of special education programs. *Journal of Special Education, 3,* 371–379.

Cipani, E. C. (1995). Be aware of negative reinforcement. *Teaching Exceptional Children, 27*(4), 36–40.

Clark, B. (1992). *Growing up gifted* (4th ed.). New York: Merrill.

Clark, E. (1996). Children and adolescents with traumatic brain injury: Reintegration challenges in education settings. *Journal of Learning Disabilities, 29,* 549–560.

Clements, D. H., & McMillen, S. (1996). Rethinking concrete manipulatives. *Teaching Children Mathematics, 2*(5), 270–279.

Cohen, M., & Riel, M. M. (1989). The effect of distant audiences on students' writing. *American Educational Research Journal, 26,* 143–159.

Cohen, P. A., Kulik, J. A., & Kulik, C. C. (1982). Educational outcomes of tutoring: A meta-analysis of findings. *American Educational Research Journal, 19,* 237–248.

Cohen, S. B. (1983). Assigning report card grades to the mainstreamed child. *Teaching Exceptional Children, 15,* 186–189.

Cole, C. M., & McLeskey, J. (1997). Secondary inclusion programs for students with mild disabilities. *Focus on Exceptional Children, 29*(6), 1–15.

Cole, D. A., Vandercook, T., & Rynders, J. (1988). Comparison of two peer interaction programs: Children with and without severe disabilities. *American Educational Research Journal, 25,* 415–439.

Cole, K. B., Struyk, L. R., Kinder, D., Sheehan, J. K., & Kish, C. K. (1997). Portfolio assessment: Challenges in secondary education. *The High School Journal, 80*(4), 261–272.

Coleman, M., Wheeler, L., & Webber, J. (1993). Research on interpersonal problem-solving training: A review. *Remedial and Special Education, 14*(2), 25–37.

Coleman, M. R., Gallagher, J. J., & Nelson, S. M. (1993). *Cooperative learning and gifted students: Report on five case studies.* Chapel Hill, NC: Gifted Education Policy Studies Program, Frank Porter Graham Child Development Center, University of North Carolina at Chapel Hill.

Collins, B. C., Ault, M. J., Hemmeter, M. L., & Doyle, P. M. (1996). Come play! Developing children's social skills in an inclusive preschool. *Teaching Exceptional Children, 29*(1), 16–21.

Comber, G., Zeiderman, H., & Maistrellis, N. (1989). The Touchstones Project: Discussion classes for students of all abilities. *Educational Leadership, 49*(6), 39–42.

Conderman, G. (1995). Social status of sixth- and seventh-grade students with learning disabilities. *Learning Disability Quarterly, 18,* 13–24.

Connor, F. (1990). Physical education for children with autism. *Teaching Exceptional Children, 23*(1), 30–33.

Connors, C. K., & Blouin, A. G. (1982/1983). Nutritional effects on the behavior of children. *Journal of Psychiatric Research, 17,* 193–201.

Cook, L., & Friend, M. (1993). Educational leadership for teacher collaboration. In B. Billingsley (Ed.), *Program leadership for serving students with disabilities* (pp. 421–444). Richmond, VA: Virginia Department of Education.

Cook, L., & Friend, M. (1995). Co-Teaching: Guidelines for effective practice. *Focus on Exceptional Children, 28*(2), 1–12.

Cooper, C. S., & McEvoy, M. A. (1996). Group friendship activities: An easy way to develop the social skills of young children. *Teaching Exceptional Children, 28*(3), 67–69.

Cooper, H. (1989). Synthesis of research on homework. *Educational Leadership, 47*(3), 85–91.

Cooper, H., & Nye, B. (1994). Homework for students with learning disabilities: The implications of research for policy and practice. *Journal of Learning Disabilities, 27*(8), 470–480.

Coppola, M. A. (1987). The "perfect" student: Being alert to autism. *Education Digest, 52,* 33–35.

Corman, L. & Gottlieb, J. (1978). Mainstreaming mentally retarded children: A review of research. In M. R. Ellis (Ed.), *International review of research in mental retardation* (Vol. 9, pp. 147–172). New York: Academic Press.

Cortes, C. E. (1978). Chicano culture, experience and learning. In L. Morris, G. Sather, & S. Scull (Eds.), *Extracting learning styles from social/cultural diversity: A study of five American minorities.* Norman, OK: Southwest Teacher Corps Network.

Cosden, M., Pearl, R., & Bryan, T. E. (1985). The effects of cooperative and individual goal structures on learning disabled and nondisabled students. *Exceptional Children, 52,* 103–114.

Costenbader, V., & Reading-Brown, M. (1995). Isolation timeout used with students with emotional disturbance. *Exceptional Children, 61,* 353–363.

Cott, A. (1977). *The orthomolecular approach to learning disabilities.* New York: Huxley Institute.

Cott, A. (1985). *Help for your learning disabled child: The orthomolecular treatment.* New York: Time Books.

Council for Exceptional Children. (1993). *CEC Statement on Inclusion.* Reston, VA: Author.

Cowen, E. L., Pederson, A., Babijian, H., Izzo, L. D., & Trost, M. A. (1973). Long-term follow-up of early detected vulnerable children. *Journal of Consulting and Clinical Psychology, 41,* 438–446.

Crawford, C. G. (1980). *Math without fear.* New York: New Viewpoints/Vision Books.

Cronin, M. E. (1996). Life skills curricula for students with learning disabilities: A review of the literature. *Journal of Learning Disabilities, 29,* 53–68.

Cullinan, D., & Epstein, M. H. (1994). Behavior disorders. In N. Haring, L. McCormick, & T. Haring (Eds.), *Exceptional children and youth.* Columbus, OH: Merrill.

Cullinan, D., Epstein, M. H., & Lloyd, J. (1983). *Behavior disorders of children and adolescents.* Englewood Cliffs, NJ: Prentice-Hall.

Culross, R. B. (1997). Concepts of inclusion in gifted education. *Teaching Exceptional Children, 29*(3), 24–26.

D'Alonzo, B. J., Giordano, G., & Cross, T. L. (1995). Inclusion: Seeking educational excellence for students with disabilities. *Teacher Educator, 31*(1), 82–95.

Dalrymple, N. (1990). *Some social behaviors that students with autism need help to learn and apply in everyday situations.* Bloomington, IN: Indiana Resource Center for Autism, Institute for the Study of Developmental Disabilities.

Daniel R. R. v. State Board of Education, 874 F.2d 1036, 53 Ed. Law Rep. 824 (5th Cir. 1989): 91, 107, 111.

Davis, G. A., & Rimm, S. B. (1994). *Education of the gifted and talented* (3rd ed.). Boston: Allyn and Bacon.

Dean, A. V., Salend, S. J., & Taylor, L. (1994). Multicultural education: A challenge for special educators. *Teaching Exceptional Children, 26*(1), 40–43.

DeBoer, A. (1995). *Working together.* Longmont, CO: Sopris West.

Deitz, D. E. D., & Ormsby, D. (1992). A comparison of verbal social behavior of adolescents with behavioral disorders and regular class peers. *Behavioral Modification, 16*(4), 504–524.

Deluke, S. V., & Knoblock, P. (1987). Teacher behavior as preventive discipline. *Teaching Exceptional Children, 19*(4), 18–24.

Dennis, R. E., & Giangreco, M. F. (1996). Creating conversation: Reflections on cultural sensitivity in family interviewing. *Exceptional Children, 63,* 103–116.

Deno, S., & Fuchs, L. (1987). Developing curriculum-based measurement systems for data-based special education problem solving. *Focus on Exceptional Children, 19*(8), 1–16.

Deno, S. L. (1985). Curriculum-based measurement: The emerging alternative. *Exceptional Children, 52,* 219–232.

Deno, S. L. (1989). Curriculum-based measurement and special education services: A fundamental and direct relationship. In M. Shinn (Ed.), *Curriculum-based measurement: Assessing special children* (pp. 1–17). New York: Guilford Press.

Deno, S., Maruyama, G., Espin, C., & Cohen, C. (1990). Educating students with mild disabilities in general education classrooms: Minnesota alternatives. *Exceptional Children, 57,* 150–161.

Deshler, D. D., Putnam, M. L., & Bulgren, J. A. (1985). Academic accommodations for adolescents with behavior and learning problems. In S. Braaten, R. B. Rutherford, & W. Evans (Eds.), *Programming for adolescents with behavioral disorders* (Vol. 2, pp. 20–30). Reston, VA: Council for Children with Behavior Disorders.

Diana v. State Board of Education, C. A. No. C-70–37 R. F. P. (N. D. Cal.) (1970).

Díaz-Rico, L. T., & Weed, K. Z. (1995). *The crosscultural, language, and academic development handbook: A complete K–12 reference guide.* Boston: Allyn and Bacon.

Dickson, S. V., Collins, V., Simmons, D. C., & Kameenui, E. J. (1998). *Metacognition: Curricular and instructional implications for diverse learners.* In D. C. Simmons & E. J. Kameenui (Eds.), *What reading research tells us about children with diverse learning needs* (pp. 361–380). Hillsdale, NJ: Lawrence Erlbaum.

Dixon, P. N., & Ishler, R. E. (1992). Professional development schools: Stages in collaboration. *Journal of Teacher Education, 43,* 28–34.

Doe v. Withers, 20 IDLER 422 (W. Va. Cir. 1993).

Doman, G., & Delacato, D. (1968). Doman–Delacato philosophy. *Human Potential, 1,* 113–116.

Doren, B., Bullis, M., & Benz, M. R. (1996). Predictors of victimization experiences of adolescents with disabilities in transition. *Exceptional Children, 63,* 7–18.

Doyle, W. (1986). Classroom organization and management. In M. Wittrock (Ed.), *Handbook of Research on Teaching* (pp. 392–431). New York: Macmillan.

Doyle, W. (1990). Classroom management techniques. In O. C. Moles (Ed.), *Student discipline strategies,* (pp. 83–105). Albany, NY: State University of New York Press.

Drew, C. J., Logan, D. R., & Hardman, M. L. (1992). *Mental retardation: A life cycle approach* (5th ed.). New York: Merrill.

Drugs & Drug Abuse Education. (1994). Prevalence of any illicit drug use 1979–1993. *Drugs & Drug Abuse Education, 25*(8), 56.

Dunn, L. M. (1968). Special education for the mildly handicapped—Is much of it justifiable? *Exceptional Children, 35,* 5–22.

DuPaul, G. J., Barkley, R. A., & McMurray, M. B. (1991). Therapeutic effects of medication on ADHD: Implications for school psychologists. *School Psychology Review, 20,* 203–219.

Durlak, C. M. (1992). *Preparing high school students with learning disabilities for the transition to postsecondary education: Training for self-determination.* Unpublished doctoral dissertation, Northern Illinois University.

Durlak, C. M., Rose, E., & Bursuck, W. D. (1994). Preparing high school students with learning disabilities for the transition to postsecondary education: Teaching the skills of self-determination. *Journal of Learning Disabilities, 27*(1), 51–59.

Dyson, L. L. (1996). The experiences of families of children with learning disabilities: Parental stress, family functioning, and sibling self-concept. *Journal of Learning Disabilities, 29,* 280–286.

Early, M., Cooper, E. K., & Saneusanio, N. (1983). *People and places: Reading skills 7.* New York: Harcourt Brace Jovanovich, Inc.

Edgar, E. (1987). Secondary programs in special education: Are many of them justifiable? *Exceptional Children, 53,* 555–561.

Edgington, R. (1968). But he spelled it right this morning. In J. I. Arena (Ed.), *Building spelling skills in dyslexic children* (pp. 23–24). San Rafael, CA: Academic Therapy Publications.

Education Daily. (1997, July 17). 1997 Individuals with Disabilities Education Act analysis (special supplement). *Education Daily, 30*(137), 1–28.

Eichinger, J. (1990). Goal structure effects on social interaction: Nondisabled and disabled elementary students. *Exceptional Children, 56,* 408–416.

Einhorn, R., Hagen, C., Johnson, J., Wujek, C., & Hoffman, L. (1991). *Authentic assessment: A collaborative approach.* Flossmoor, IL: SMA Communication Development Project.

Elam, S. M., Rose, L. C., & Gallup, A. M. (1996). The 28th annual Phi Delta Kappa/Gallup poll of the public's attitudes toward the public schools. *Phi Delta Kappan, 78,* 41–59.

Elias, M. J., & Taylor, M. E. (1995). Building social and academic skills via problem solving videos. *Teaching Exceptional Children, 27*(3), 14–21.

Elliott, S. N., & Sheridan, S. M. (1992). Consultation and teaming: Problem solving among educators, parents, and support personnel. *Elementary School Journal, 92,* 315–338.

Ellis, E. (1996). Reading strategy instruction. In D. Deshler, E. Ellis, & K. Lenz (Eds.), *Teaching adolescents with learning disabilities: Strategies and methods* (2nd ed., pp. 61–125). Denver, CO: Love.

Ellis, E., & Lenz, B. K. (1996). Perspectives on instruction in learning strategies. In D. Deshler, E. Ellis, & B. K. Lenz (Eds.), *Teaching adolescents with learning disabilities: Strategies and methods* (2nd ed., pp. 9–60). Denver, CO: Love.

Ellis, E., & Lenz, K. (1987). A component analysis of effective learning strategies for LD students. *Learning Disabilities Focus, 2,* 94–107.

Ellis, E., Lenz, K., & Sabornie, E. (1987). Generalization and adaptation of learning strategies to natural environments: Part 2: Research into practice. *Remedial and Special Education, 8*(2), 6–23.

Ellis, E. S., & Sabornie, E. S. (1990). Strategy-based adaptive instruction in content-area classes: Social validity of six options. *Teacher Education and Special Education, 13*(2), 133–144.

Emmer, E. T., Evertson, C. M., Sanford, J. P., Clements, B. S., & Worsham, M. E. (1983). *Organizing and managing the junior high classroom.* Austin: Research and Development Center for Teacher Education, University of Texas.

Englert, C., & Mariage, T. (1991). Making students partners in the comprehension process: Organizing the reading "POSSE." *Learning Disability Quarterly, 14,* 123–138.

Englert, C. S., Raphael, T. E., Anderson, L. M., Anthony, H. M., Fear, K. L., & Gregg, S. L. (1988). A case for writing intervention: Strategies for writing informational text. *Learning Disabilities Focus, 3*(2), 98–113.

Epilepsy Foundation of America. (1986). *Epilepsy: Questions and answers.* Landover, MD: Author.

Epstein, M. A., Shaywitz, S. E., Shaywitz, B. A., & Woolston, J. L. (1991). The boundaries of attention deficit disorder. *Journal of Learning Disabilities, 24,* 78–86.

Epstein, M. H., & Sharma, J. (1997). *Behavioral and emotional rating scale: A strength-based approach to assessment.* Austin, TX: PRO-ED.

Epstein, M. H., Kinder, D., & Bursuck, W. D. (1989). The academic status of adolescents with behavior disorders. *Behavioral Disorders, 4*(3), 157–165.

Epstein, M. H., Patton, J. R., Polloway, E. A., & Foley, R. (1992). Educational services for students with behavior disorders: A review of Individualized Education Programs. *Teacher Education and Special Education, 15,* 41–48.

Evans, D., & Carnine, D., (1990). Manipulatives—The effective way. *ADI News, 10*(1), 48–55.

Evans, D. W., Harris, D. M., Adeigbola, M., Houston, D., & Argott, L. (1993). Restructuring special education services. *Teacher Education and Special Education, 16,* 137–145.

Evans, I. M., Salisbury, C. L. Palombaro, M. M., Berryman, J., & Hollowood, T. M. (1992). Peer interactions and social acceptance of elementary-age children with severe disabilities in an inclusive school. *Journal of the Association for Persons with Severe Handicaps, 17,* 205–212.

Evans, S. S., Evans, W. H., & Mercer, C. (1986). *Assessment for instruction.* Boston: Allyn and Bacon.

Evertson, C. M., Emmer, E. T., Clements, B. S., Sanford, J. P., Worsham, M. E., & Williams, E. L. (1983). *Organizing and managing the elementary school classroom.* Austin, TX: Research and Development Center for Teacher Education, University of Texas.

Fang, F. (1996). Traveling the internet in Chinese. *Educational Leadership, 54*(3), 28–29.

Fantuzzo, J. W., King, J. A., & Heller, L. R. (1992). Effects of reciprocal peer tutoring on mathematics and school adjustment: A component analysis. *Journal of Educational Psychology, 84,* 331–339.

Farmer, T. W., & Farmer, E. M. Z. (1996). Social relationships of students with exceptionalities in mainstream classrooms: Social networks and homophily. *Exceptional Children, 62,* 431–450.

Feingold, B. F. (1975). *Why your child is hyperactive.* New York: Random House.

Feldhusen, J. F., Van Winkle, L., & Ehle, D. A. (1996). Is it acceleration or simply appropriate instruction for precocious youth? *Teaching Exceptional Children, 28*(3), 48–51.

Felton, R. H. (1993). Effects of instruction on the decoding skills of children with phonological-processing problems. *Journal of Learning Disabilities, 26*(9), 583–589.

Ferguson, D. L. (1995). The real challenge of inclusion: Confessions of a "rabid inclusionist." *Phi Delta Kappan, 77,* 281–287.

Figueroa, R. A. (1989). Psychological testing of linguistic-minority students: Knowledge gaps and regulations. *Exceptional Children, 56,* 145–153.

Filipek, P. A. (1995). Neurobiologic correlates of developmental dyslexia: How do dyslexics' brains differ from those of normal readers? *Journal of Child Neurology, 10*(Suppl. 1), 62–69.

Fisher, C. W., Berliner, D., Filby, N., Marliare, R., Cahan, L., & Dishaw, M. (1980). Teaching behavior, academic learning time, and student achievement: An overview. In C. Denham & A. Lieberman (Eds.), *Time to learn* (pp. 7–32). Washington, DC: National Institute of Education, Department of Education.

Fletcher, J., & Martinez, G. (1994). An eye-movement analysis of the effects of scotopic sensitivity correction on parsing and comprehension. *Journal of Learning Disabilities, 27,* 67–70.

Florence County School District No. 4 v. Carter (S. Ct. USLW 3040) (1993).

Flowers, D. L. (1993). Brain basis for dyslexia: A summary of work in progress. *Journal of Learning Disabilities, 26*(9), 575–582.

Ford, A., Davern, L., & Schnorr, R. (1990). Inclusive education: "Making sense" of the curriculum. In S. Stainback & S. Stainback (Eds.), *Curriculum considerations in inclusive classrooms: Facilitating learning for all students* (pp. 37–61). Baltimore, MD: Paul H. Brookes.

Ford, B. A. (1992). Multicultural education training for special educators working with African-American youth. *Exceptional Children, 59,* 107–114.

Forest, M., & Lusthaus, E. (1990). Everyone belongs with the MAPS action planning system. *Teaching Exceptional Children, 22*(2), 32–35.

Foster-Johnson, L., & Dunlap, G. (1993). Using functional assessment to develop effective, individualized interventions for challenging behaviors. *Teaching Exceptional Children, 25*(3), 44–50.

Fowler, M. (1994). *Attention deficit disorder: NICHCY briefing paper.* Washington, DC: National Information Center for Children and Youth with Disabilities.

Fox, C. L. (1989). Peer acceptance of learning disabled children in the regular classroom. *Exceptional Children, 56,* 50–59.

Freeman, B. J. (1994). Diagnosis of the syndrome of autism: Where we have been and where we are going. In F. LaRoy & J. Streng (Eds.), *A new dawn of awakening: Proceedings of the 1994 conference* (pp. 1–6). Arlington, TX: Future Education.

Friend, M., & Cook, L. (1992). The new mainstreaming: How it really works. *Instructor, 101*(7), 30–32, 34, 36.

Friend, M., & Cook, L. (1996). *Interactions: Collaboration skills for school professionals* (2nd ed.). White Plains, NY: Longman.

Friend, M., & Cook, L. (1997). Student-centered teams in schools: Still in search of an identity. *Journal of Educational and Psychological Consultation, 8,* 3–20.

Fuchs, D., & Fuchs, L. S. (1995). What's "special" about special education? *Phi Delta Kappan, 76,* 522–530.

Fuchs, L. S., Fuchs, D., Hamlett, C., Philips, N., & Bentz, J. (1994). Classwide curriculum-based measurement: Helping general educators meet the challenge of student diversity. *Exceptional Children, 60*(6), 518–537.

Fuchs, L. S., Fuchs, D., Hamlett, C. L., & Stecker, P. M. (1991). Effects of curriculum-based measurement and consultation on teacher planning and student achievement in mathematics operations. *American Educational Research Journal, 28,* 617–641.

Fulton, L., LeRoy, C., Pinchney, M. L., & Weekley, T. (1994). Peer Education Partners: A program for learning and working together. *Teaching Exceptional Children, 26*(4), 6–11.

Galbraith, J. (1985). The eight great gripes of gifted kids: Responding to special needs. *Roeper Review, 8*(1), 16.

Gallagher, J. J., & Gallagher, S. A. (1994). *Teaching the gifted child* (4th ed.). Boston: Allyn and Bacon.

Garcia, G. E., & Pearson, P. D. (1994). Assessment and diversity. In L. D. Hammond (Ed.), *Review of research in education.* Washington, DC: American Educational Research Association.

Garcia-Vasquez, E., & Ehly, S. W. (1992). Peer tutoring effects on students who are perceived as not socially accepted. *Psychology in the Schools, 29,* 256–266.

Gardner, H. (1993). *Multiple intelligences: The theory in practice.* New York: Basic Books.

Gardner, R., Sainato, D. M., Cooper, J. O., Heron, T. E., Heward, W. L., Eshelman, J. W., & Grossi, T. A. (1994). *Behavior analysis in education: Focus on measurably superior instruction.* Pacific Grove, CA: Brooks/Cole.

Gartner, A., & Lipsky, D. K. (1989). *The yoke of special education: How to break it.* New York: National Center on Education and the Economy.

Germinario, V., Cervalli, J., & Ogden, E. H. (1992). *All children successful: Real answers for helping at risk elementary students.* Lancaster, PA: Technomic.

Gerry, M. (1987). Procedural safeguards insuring that handicapped children receive a free appropriate public education. *National Information Center for Handicapped Children and Youth New Digest,* (Number 7). Washington, DC: National Information Center for Handicapped Children and Youth.

Gersten, R., Vaughn, S., & Brengelman, S. U. (1996). Grading and academic feedback for special education students and students with learning difficulties. In T. R. Guskey (Ed.), *ASCD yearbook 1996: Communicating student learning.* Alexandria, VA: Association for Supervision and Curriculum Development.

Giangreco, M. F., Dennis, R., Cloninger, C., & Schattman, R. (1993). "I've counted Jon": Transformational experiences of teachers educating students with disabilities. *Exceptional Children, 59,* 359–372.

Giangreco, M. F., Edelman, S. W., MacFarland, S., & Luiselli, T. E. (1997). Attitudes about educational and related service provision for students with deaf–blindness and multiple disabilities. *Exceptional Children, 63,* 329–342.

Goldberg, S. S., & Kuriloff, P. J. (1991). Evaluating the fairness of special education hearings. *Exceptional Children, 57,* 546–555.

Goldstein, A. P., Sprafkin, R. P., Gershaw, N. J., & Klein, P. (1980). *Skillstreaming the adolescent.* Champaign, IL: Research Press.

Goldstein, H., Moss, J. W., & Jordan, L. J. (1965). *The efficacy of special class training on the development of mentally retarded children* (U.S. Office of Education Cooperative Research Program Project Number 619). Urbana, IL: University of Illinois Institute for Research on Exceptional Children. (ERIC Document Reproduction Service No. ED 002-907)

Good, T. L. (1983). Classroom research: A decade of progress. *Educational Psychologist, 18*(3), 127–144.

Goodman, H., Gottlieb, J., & Harrison, R. H. (1972). Social acceptance of EMR children integrated into a non-graded elementary school. *American Journal of Mental Deficiency, 76,* 412–417.

Grady, E. (1996). The Grady profile. *Intervention in School and Clinic, 31*(4), 246–251.

Graham, S., & Freeman, S. (1986). Strategy training and teacher- vs. student-controlled study conditions: Effects on LD students' spelling performance. *Learning Disability Quarterly, 9,* 15–22.

Graham, S., & Harris, K. R. (1987). Improving composition skills of inefficient learners with self-instructional strategy training. *Topics in Language Disorders, 7*(4), 66–77.

Graham, S., & Miller, L. (1980). Handwriting research and practice: A unified approach. *Focus on Exceptional Children, 13*(2), 1–16.

Graley, J. (1994). A path to the mainstream of life: Facilitated communication/behavior/inclusion: Three interacting ingredients. In F. LaRoy & J. Streng (Eds.), *A new dawn of awakening: Proceedings of the 1994 conference* (pp. 67–68). Arlington, TX: Future Education.

Grandin, T. (1984). My experiences as an autistic child and review of selected literature. *Journal of Orthomolecular Psychiatry, 13,* 144–174.

Grant, R. (1993). Strategic training for using text headings to improve students' processing of content. *Journal of Reading, 36*(6), 482–488.

Greenwood, C. R. (1991). Longitudinal analysis of time, engagement, and achievement in at-risk versus non-risk students. *Exceptional Children, 57,* 521–535.

Greenwood, C. R., Delquadri, J. C., & Hall, R. V. (1989). Longitudinal effects of classwide peer tutoring. *Journal of Educational Psychology, 81,* 371–383.

Griffith, D. R. (1992). Prenatal exposure to cocaine and other drugs: Developmental and educational prognoses. *Phi Delta Kappan, 74,* 30–34.

Gritzmacher, H. L., & Gritzmacher, S. C. (1995). Referral, assessment, and placement practices used in rural school districts with Native American students in special education. *Rural Special Education Quarterly, 14*(1), 11–19.

Grossman, H. (1995). *Special education in a diverse society.* Boston: Allyn and Bacon.

Guild, P. (1994). The culture/learning style connection. *Educational Leadership, 51*(8), 16–21.

Guthrie, L. F., & Richardson, S. (1995). Turned on to language arts: Computer literacy in the primary grades. *Educational Leadership, 53*(2), 14–17.

Hahn, H. (1989). The politics of special education. In D. K. Lipsky & A. Gartner (Eds.), *Beyond separate education: Quality education for all* (pp. 225–241). Baltimore, MD: Paul H. Brookes.

Hallahan, D. P., & Kauffman, J. M. (1997). *Exceptional learners: Introduction to special education* (7th ed.). Boston: Allyn and Bacon.

Hallahan, D. P., Kauffman, J. M., & Lloyd, J. W. (1985). *Introduction to learning disabilities*. Englewood Cliffs, NJ: Prentice-Hall.

Hallahan, D. P., Kauffman, J. M., & Lloyd, J. W. (1996). *Introduction to learning disabilities*. Boston: Allyn and Bacon.

Hallenbeck, M. J., & McMaster, D. (1991). Disability simulation. *Teaching Exceptional Children, 23*(3), 12–15.

Hamre-Nietupski, S. H., McDonald, J., & Nietupski, J. (1992). Integrating elementary students with multiple disabilities into supported regular classes: Challenges and solutions. *Teaching Exceptional Children, 24*(3), 6–9.

Hardman, M. L., Drew, C. J., Egan, M. W., & Wolf, B. (1996). *Human exceptionality: Society, school, and family* (5th ed.). Boston: Allyn and Bacon.

Harniss, M. K. (1996). *Task requirements of content area textbooks: Effects on the academic achievement and engagement of middle-level students.* Unpublished manuscript, University of Oregon, Eugene.

Harris, C. A., Miller, S. P., & Mercer, C. D. (1995). Teaching initial multiplication skills to students with disabilities in general education classrooms. *Learning Disabilities Research & Practice, 10*(3), 180–195.

Harris, K. C. (1995). School-based bilingual special education teacher assistance teams. *Remedial and Special Education, 16,* 337–343.

Harris, K. R., & Graham, S. (1996). Memo to constructivists: Skills count, too. *Educational Leadership, 53*(5), 26–29.

Harry, B. (1992a). Making sense of disability: Low-income Puerto Rican parents' theories of the problem. *Exceptional Children, 59,* 27–40.

Harry, B. (1992b). Restructuring the participation of African-American parents in special education. *Exceptional Children, 59,* 123–131.

Harry, B., Torguson, C., Katkavich, J., & Guerrero, M. (1993). Crossing social class and cultural barriers in working with families. *Teaching Exceptional Children, 26*(1), 48–51.

Hasbrouck, J. E., & Tindal, G. (1992). Curriculum-based oral reading fluency norms for students in grades 2–5. *Teaching Exceptional Children, 24,* 41–44.

Haynes, N. M., & Gebreyesus, S. (1992). Cooperative learning: A case for African-American students. *School Psychology Review, 21,* 577–585.

Heath, D. (1993). Using portfolio assessment with secondary LED students yields a cross-cultural advantage for all. *BeOutreach, 4*(1), 27.

Hendrickson, J. M., Shokoohi-Yekta, M., Hamre-Nietupski, S., & Gable, R. A. (1996). Middle and high school students' perceptions on being friends with peers with severe disabilities. *Exceptional Children, 63,* 19–28.

Henry, B. (1992). Restructuring the participation of African-American parents in special education. *Exceptional Children, 59,* 123–131.

Hess, R. (1987). *Grading-credit-diploma: Accommodation practices for students with mild disabilities.* Des Moines, IA: Iowa State Department of Education.

Hill, S., & Hill, T. (1990). *The collaborative classroom: A guide to cooperative learning* (pp. 21–35). Portsmouth, NH: Heinemann.

Hobbs, N. (1975). *The futures of children.* San Francisco: Jossey-Bass.

Hoge, R. D., & Renzulli, J. S. (1993). Exploring the link between giftedness and self-concept. *Review of Educational Research, 63,* 449–465.

Holman, L. J. (1997). Working effectively with Hispanic immigrant families. *Phi Delta Kappan, 78,* 647–649.

Holmes v. Sobol, 1987–88, *EHRL* DEC. 559:463.

Homme, L. (1970). *How to use contingency contracting in the classroom.* Champaign, IL: Research Press.

Honig v. Doe, 108 S. Ct. 592 (1988).

Hoover, K. H., & Hollingsworth, P. M. (1982). *A handbook for elementary school teachers.* Boston: Allyn and Bacon.

Horton, S. V. (1987). *Study guides: A paper on curriculum modification.* Unpublished manuscript, University of Washington.

Howell, K. M., & Morehead, M. K. (1993). *Curriculum-based evaluation for special and remedial education* (2nd ed.). Columbus, OH: Merrill.

Howell, K. W., Evans, D., & Gardner, J. (1997). Medications in the classroom: A hard pill to swallow? *Teaching Exceptional Children, 29*(6), 58–61.

Hutchinson, N. L. (1993). Students with disabilities and mathematics education reform. *Remedial and Special Education, 14*(6), 20–23.

Hynd, G. W., Voeller, K. K., Hern, K. L., & Marshall, R. M. (1991). Neurobiological basis of attention-deficit hyperactivity disorder (ADHD). *School Psychology Review, 20,* 174–186.

Iano, R. P., Ayers, D., Heller, H. B., McGettigan, J. F., & Walker, V. S. (1974). Sociometric status of retarded children in an integrative program. *Exceptional Children, 40,* 267–271.

Idol-Maestas, L., & Ritter, S. (1986). Teaching middle school students to use a test-taking strategy. *Journal of Educational Research, 79*(6), 350–357.

Irlen, H. (1991). *Reading by the colors: Overcoming dyslexia and other reading disabilities through the Irlen method.* Garden City Park, NY: Avery.

Isaacson, S. L. (1987). Effective instruction in written language. *Focus on Exceptional Children, 19*(6), 1–12.

Janney, R. E., Snell, M. E., Beers, M. K., & Raynes, M. (1995). Integrating students with moderate and severe disabilities into general education classes. *Exceptional Children, 61,* 425–439.

Jarolimek, J., & Foster, C. D. (1993). *Teaching and learning in the elementary school.* New York: Macmillan.

Jayanthi, M., & Friend, M. (1992). Interpersonal problem solving: A selected literature review to guide practice. *Journal of Educational and Psychological Consultation, 3,* 147–152.

Jayanthi, M., Epstein, M., Polloway, E., & Bursuck, W. D. (1996). A national survey of general education teachers' perceptions of testing adaptations. *Journal of Special Education, 30*(1), 99–115.

Jayanthi, M., Nelson, J. S., Sawyer, V., Bursuck, W. D., & Epstein, M. H. (1995). Homework-communication problems among parents, general education, and special education teachers: An exploratory study. *Remedial and Special Education, 16*(2), 102–116.

Jenkins, J. R., & Jenkins, L. M. (1981). *Cross age and peer tutoring: Help for children with learning problems.* Reston, VA: Council for Exceptional Children.

Jenkins, J., & Jenkins, L. (1985). Peer tutoring in elementary and secondary programs. *Focus on Exceptional Children, 17*(6), 1–12.

Jenson, W. R., Sheridan, S. M., Olympia, D., & Andrews, D. (1994). Homework and students with learning disabilities and behavior disorders: A practical, parent-based approach. *Journal of Learning Disabilities, 27*(9), 538–549.

Jitendra, A. K., & Kameenui, E. J. (1993). Dynamic assessment as a compensatory assessment approach: A description and analysis. *Remedial and Special Education, 14*(5), 6–18.

Johns, B. (1997). Changes in IEP requirements based on the reauthorization of IDEA. *CCBD Newsletter, 11*(2), 1, 4.

Johns, B. H., & Carr, V. G. (1995). *Techniques for managing verbally and physically aggressive students* (pp. 17–22). Denver, CO: Love.

Johnson, D. W., & Johnson, R. T. (1994). *Learning together and alone* (4th ed.). Boston: Allyn and Bacon.

Johnson, D. W., & Johnson, R. T. (1992). *Learning together and alone: Cooperative, competitive, and individualistic learning* (3rd ed., pp. 1–21). Englewood Cliffs, NJ: Prentice-Hall.

Johnson, D. W., Johnson, R. T., Holubec, E. J., & Roy, P. (1984). *Circles of learning.* Alexandria, VA: Association for Supervision and Curriculum Development.

Johnson, D. W., Johnson, R. T., & Maruyama, G. (1983). Interdependence and interpersonal attraction among heterogeneous and homogeneous individuals: A theoretical formulation and a meta-analysis of the research. *Review of Educational Research, 53,* 5–54.

Johnson, G. O., & Kirk, S. A. (1950). Are mentally handicapped children segregated in the regular grades? *Exceptional Children, 17,* 65–68; 87–88.

Johnson, M. J., & Pajares, F. (1996). When shared decision making works: A 3-year longitudinal study. *American Educational Research Journal, 33,* 599–627.

Jones, B. E., Clark, G. M., & Soltz, D. F. (1997). Characteristics and practices of sign language interpreters in inclusive education programs. *Exceptional Children, 63,* 257–268.

Jones, K. H., & Bender, W. N. (1993). Utilization of paraprofessionals in special education: A review of the literature. *Remedial and Special Education, 14*(1), 7–14.

Jones, M. M., & Carlier, L. L. (1995). Creating inclusionary opportunities for learners with multiple disabilities: A team-teaching approach. *Teaching Exceptional Children, 27*(3), 23–27.

Jones, V. (1996). "In the face of predictable crises:" Developing a comprehensive treatment plan for students with emotional or behavioral disorders. *Teaching Exceptional Children, 29*(2), 54–59.

Jones, V., & Jones, L. (1995). *Comprehensive classroom management: Motivating and managing students at risk* (4th ed.). Boston: Allyn and Bacon.

Jones, V., & Jones, L. (1990). *Comprehensive classroom management.* Boston: Allyn and Bacon.

Kagan, S. (1990). A structural approach to cooperative learning. *Educational Leadership, 47*(4), 12–15.

Kameenui, E., & Simmons, D. (1991). *Designing instructional strategies: The prevention of academic learning problems.* Columbus, OH: Merrill.

Kaminski, R. A., & Good, R. H. (1996). Toward a technology for assessing basic early literacy skills. *School Psychology Review, 25*(2), 215–227.

Kanner, L. (1964). *A history of the care and study of the mentally retarded.* Springfield, IL: Charles C. Thomas.

Kaplan, J. S., & Carter, J. (1995). *Beyond behavior modification: A cognitive-behavioral approach to behavior management in the school* (3rd ed., pp. 133–183). Austin, TX: PRO-ED.

Katsiyannis, A. (1990). Extended school year policies: An established necessity. *Remedial and Special Education, 12*(1), 24–28.

Katsiyannis, A., & Conderman, G. (1994). Section 504 and procedures: An established necessity. *Remedial and Special Education, 15,* 311–318.

Kauffman, J. M. (1995). Why we must celebrate a diversity of restrictive environments. *Learning Disabilities Research & Practice, 10,* 225–232.

Kauffman, J. M. (1997). *Characteristics of emotional and behavioral disorders of children and youth* (6th ed.). Columbus, OH: Merrill.

Kauffman, J. M., Lloyd, J. W., Baker, J., & Reidel, T. (1995). Inclusion of all students with emotional or behavioral disorders? Let's think again. *Phi Delta Kappan, 76,* 542–546.

Kaufman, M. J., Gottlieb, J., Agard, J., & Kukic, M. (1975). Mainstreaming: Toward an explication of the construct. In E. L. Meyen, G. A. Vergason, & R. J. Whelan (Eds.), *Alternatives for teaching exceptional children* (pp. 35–54). Denver, CO: Love.

Kavale, K. A., & Forness, S. R. (1996). Social skills deficits and learning disabilities: A meta-analysis. *Journal of Learning Disabilities, 29,* 226–237.

Kazdin, A. E. (1977). *The token economy: A review and evaluation.* New York: Plenum.

Kehle, T. J., Clark, E., & Jenson, W. R. (1996). Interventions for students with traumatic brain injury: Managing behavioral disturbances. *Journal of Learning Disabilities, 29,* 633–642.

Kelly, B., & Carnine, D. (1996). Teaching problem-solving strategies for word problems to students with learning disabilities. *LD Forum, 21*(3), 5–9.

Kerschner, J. R. (1990). Self-concept and IQ as predictors of remedial success in children with learning disabilities. *Journal of Learning Disabilities, 23,* 368–374.

Kinder, D., & Bursuck, W. D. (1991). The search for a unified social studies curriculum: Does history really repeat itself? *Journal of Learning Disabilities, 24,* 270–275.

Kindsvatter, R., Wilen, W., & Ishler, M. (1988). *Dynamics of effective teaching.* New York: Longman.

King-Sears, M. E., & Cummings, C. S. (1996). Inclusive practices of classroom teachers. *Remedial and Special Education, 17,* 217–225.

Kirk, S. A., Gallagher, J. J., & Anastasiow, N. J. (1997). *Educating exceptional children* (8th ed., pp. 512–557). Boston: Houghton Mifflin.

Kirst, M. W. (1991). Improving children's services: Overcoming barriers, creating new opportunities. *Phi Delta Kappan, 72,* 615–618.

Kloomok, S., & Cosden, M. (1994). Self-concept in children with learning disabilities: The relationship between global self-concept, academic "discounting," nonacademic self-concept, and perceived social support. *Learning Disability Quarterly, 17,* 140–153.

Kluwin, T. N. (1996). Getting hearing and deaf students to write to each other through dialogue journals. *Teaching Exceptional Children, 28* (2), 50–53.

Knapp, M. S., Turnbull, B. J., & Shields, P. M. (1990). New directions for educating the children of poverty. *Educational Leadership, 48*(1), 4–8.

Kohn, A. (1996). *Beyond discipline* (pp. 22–36). Alexandria, VA: Association for Supervision and Curriculum Development.

Koorland, M. A., Monda, L. E., & Vail, C. O. (1988). Recording behavior with ease. *Teaching Exceptional Children, 21*(1), 59–61.

Koskinen, P. S., Wilson, R. M., Gambrell, L. B., & Neuman, S. B. (1993). Captioned video and vocabulary learning: An innovative practice in literacy instruction. *The Reading Teacher, 47*(1), 36–43.

Kruger, L. J., Struzziero, J., Watts, R., & Vacca, D. (1995). The relationship between organizational support and satisfaction with teacher assistance teams. *Remedial and Special Education, 16,* 203–211.

Landfried, S. E. (1989). "Enabling" undermines responsibility in students. *Educational Leadership, 47*(3), 79–83.

Langer, J. (1984). Examining background knowledge and text comprehension. *Reading Research Quarterly, 19,* 468–481.

Larry P. v. Riles, 793 F. 2d 969 (9th Cir. 1984).

LaVoie, R. (1991). *How difficult can this be? Understanding learning disabilities.* Portland, OR: Educational Productions.

LaVoie, R. D. (1989). *Mainstreaming: A collection of field-tested strategies to help make the mainstreaming classroom more successful for learning disabled children, their classmates . . . and their teachers.* Norwalk, CT: The Connecticut Association for Children with Learning Disabilities.

Lawton, M. (1995, Nov. 8). Students post dismal results on history test. *Education Week, 1,* 12.

Lazarowitz, R., & Karsenty, G. (1990). Cooperative learning and students' academic achievement, process skills, learning environment, and self-esteem in tenth-grade biology classrooms. In S. Sharan (Ed.), *Cooperative learning* (pp. 123–149). New York: Praeger.

Leinhardt, G., & Zigmond, N. (1988). The effects of self-questioning and story structure training on the reading comprehension of poor readers. *Learning Disabilities Research, 4*(1), 41–51.

Lenk, L. L. (1995). A sense of place: Inclusive educational settings for students with disabilities. *Journal for a Just and Caring Education, 1*, 311–319.

Lenz, B. K. (1983). Using the advance organizer. *Pointer, 27*, 11–13.

Lenz, B. K., & Alley, G. R. (1983). *The effects of advance organizers on the learning and retention of learning disabled adolescents within the context of a cooperative planning model.* Final research report submitted to the U.S. Department of Education, Office of Special Education, Washington, DC.

Lenz, B. K., Alley, G., & Schumaker, J. B. (1987). Activating the inactive learner: Advance organizers in the secondary content classroom. *Learning Disability Quarterly, 10*, 53–67.

Lenz, B. K., Ellis, E. S., & Scanlon, D. (1996). T*eaching learning strategies to adolescents and adults with learning disabilities.* Austin, TX: PRO-ED.

Lerner, J. (1997). *Learning disabilities: Theories, diagnosis, and teaching strategies* (7th ed.). Boston: Houghton Mifflin.

Lerner, J. W., Lowenthal, B., & Lerner, S. R. (1995). *Attention deficit disorders: Assessment and teaching* (p. 180). Pacific Grove, CA: Brooks/Cole.

Lessen, E., & Bursuck, W. D. (1983). *A preliminary analysis of special education referral forms for a rural school district.* Unpublished data collection, Northern Illinois University.

Lessen, E., Sommers, M., & Bursuck, W. (1987). *Curriculum-based assessment and instructional design.* DeKalb, IL: DeKalb County Special Education Association.

Levy, N. R., & Rosenberg, M. S. (1990). Strategies for improving the written expression of students with learning disabilities. *LD Forum, 16*(1), 23–30.

Licht, B. G., Kistner, J. A., Ozkaragoz, T., Shapiro, S., & Clausen, L. (1985). Causal attributions of learning disabled children: Individual difference of their implications for persistence. *Journal of Educational Psychology, 77*, 208–216.

Lilly, M. S. (1971). A training model for special education. *Exceptional Children, 37*, 740–749.

Lilly, M. S. (1979). *Children with exceptional needs.* New York: Holt, Rinehart, & Winston.

Lilly, M. S. (1992). Labeling: A tired, overworked, yet unresolved issue in special education. In W. Stainback & S. Stainback (Eds.), *Controversial issues confronting special education: divergent perspectives* (pp. 85–95). Boston: Allyn and Bacon.

Linehan, M. F. (1992). Children who are homeless: Educational strategies for school personnel. *Phi Delta Kappan, 74*, 61–66.

Lipsky, D. K., & Gartner, A. (1992). Achieving full inclusion: Placing the student at the center of educational reform. In W. Stainback & S. Stainback (Eds.), *Controversial issues confronting special education: Divergent perspectives* (pp. 1–12). Boston: Allyn and Bacon.

Little, J. W. (1982). Norms of collegiality and experimentation: Workplace conditions of school success. *American Educational Research Journal, 19*, 325–340.

Lombardi, T. P., Odell, K. S., & Novotny, D. E. (1990). Special education and students at risk: Findings from a national study. *Remedial and Special Education, 12*(1), 56–62.

Long, N. J., & Newman, R. G. (1971). Managing surface behavior of children in school. In N. J., Long, W. C. Morse, & R. G. Newman (Eds.), *Conflict in the classroom: The education of children with problems* (2nd ed., pp. 442–452). Belmont, CA: Wadsworth.

Longstreet, E. (1978). *Aspects of ethnicity.* New York: Teachers College Press.

Lord-Maes, J., & Obrzut, J. E. (1996). Neuropsychological consequences of traumatic brain injury in children and adolescents. *Journal of Learning Disabilities, 29*, 609–617.

Lortie, D. C. (1975). *Schoolteacher: A sociological study.* Chicago: University of Chicago Press.

Lou, Y., Abrami, P. C., Spence, J. C., Poulsen, C., Chambers, B., & d'Apollonia, S. (1996). Within-class grouping: A meta-analysis. *Review of Educational Research, 66*, 423–258.

Lovitt, T. C., & Horton, S. V. (1987). How to develop study guides. *Journal of Reading, Writing, and Learning Disabilites, 3*, 333–343.

Lovitt, T. C., Rudsit, J., Jenkins, J., Pious, C., & Beneditti, D. (1985). Two methods of adapting science materials for learning disabled and regular seventh graders. *Learning Disability Quarterly, 8*, 275–285.

Lowell-York, J., Doyle, M. E., & Kronberg, R. (1995). *Module 3. Curriculum as everything students learn in school: Individualizing learning opportunities.* Baltimore, MD: Brookes.

Lynch, E. W., Lewis, R. B., & Murphy, D. S. (1993a). Educational services for children with chronic illnesses: Perspectives of educators and families. *Exceptional Children, 59*, 210–220.

Lynch, E. W., Lewis, R. B., & Murphy, D. S. (1993b). Improving education for children with chronic illnesses. *Principal, 73*(2), 38–40.

Lynch, P. (1991). *Multimedia: Getting started.* Sunnyvale, CA: Publix Information Products.

Maag, J. W., & Reid, R. (1994). Attention-deficit hyperactivity disorder: A functional approach to assessment and treatment. *Behavioral Disorders, 20*, 5–23.

MacArthur, C. (1996). Using technology to enhance the writing processes of students with learning disabilities. *Journal of Learning Disabilities, 29*(4), 344–354.

MacArthur, C. A., & Stoddard, B. (1990, April). *Teaching learning disabled students to revise: A peer editor strategy.* Paper presented at the Annual Meeting of the American Education Research Association, Boston, MA.

Maheady, L., Mallette, B., & Harper, B. F. (1991). Accommodating cultural, linguistic, and academic diversity: Some peer-mediated instructional options. *Preventing School Failure, 36*(1), 28–31.

Maker, J. C. (1993). Gifted students in the regular classroom: What practices are defensible and feasible? In C. J. Maker (Ed.), *Critical issues in gifted education: Programs for the gifted in regular classrooms* (Vol. III, pp. 413–436). Austin, TX: PRO-ED.

Male, M. (1997). *Technology for inclusion: Meeting the special needs of all students* (3rd ed., pp. 153–168). Boston: Allyn and Bacon.

Mandlebaum, L. H., & Wilson, R. (1989). Teaching listening skills. *LD Forum, 15*(1), 7–9.

Marsh, L. G., & Cooke, N. L. (1996). The effects of using manipulatives in teaching math problem solving to students with learning disabilities. *Learning Disabilities Research & Practice, 11*(1), 58–65.

Marston, D. (1996). A comparison of inclusion only, pull-out only, and combined service models for students with mild disabilities. *The Journal of Special Education, 30*(2), 121–132.

Marston, D. B. (1989). A curriculum-based measurement approach to asessing academic performance: What it is and why do it. In M. R. Shinn (Ed.), *Curriculum-based measurement: Assessing special children* (pp. 18–78). New York: Guilford Press.

Marston, D., Tindal, G., & Deno, S. (1984). Eligibility for learning disability services: A direct and repeated measurement approach. *Exceptional Children, 50*, 554–556.

Marzola, E. S. (1987). Using manipulatives in math instruction. *Reading, Writing, and Learning Disabilities, 3*, 9–20.

Mastropieri, M. A. (1988). Using the keyboard method. *Teaching Exceptional Children, 20*(4), 4–8.

Mathes, P. G., & Fuchs, L. S. (1994). The efficacy of peer tutoring in reading for students with mild disabilities: A best-evidence synthesis. *School Psychology Review, 23*, 59–80.

Mathes, P. G., Fuchs, D., & Fuchs, L. S. (1997). Cooperative story mapping. *Remedial and Special Education, 18*, 20–27.

McCarty, H., & Chalmers, L. (1997). Bibliotherapy: Intervention and prevention. *Teaching Exceptional Children, 29*(6), 12–13, 16–17.

McGookey, K. (1992). Drama, disability, and your classroom. *Teaching Exceptional Children, 24*(2), 12–14.

McIntosh, R., Vaughn, S., & Bennerson, D. (1995). FAST social skills with a SLAM and a RAP. *Teaching Exceptional Children, 28*(1), 37–41.

McIntosh, R., Vaughn, S., Schumm, J. S., Haager, D., & Lee, O. (1993). Observations of students with learning disabilities in general education classrooms. *Exceptional Children, 60*, 249–261.

McIntyre, T. (1992). *The behavior management handbook: Setting up effective management systems.* Boston: Allyn and Bacon.

McIntyre, T., & Silva, P. (1992). Culturally diverse childrearing practices: Abusive or just different? *Beyond Behavior, 4*(1), 8–12.

McKenzie, J. (1996). Making WEB meaning. *Educational Leadership, 54*(3), 30–32.

McKeown, M. G., & Beck, J. L. (1990). The assessment and characterization of young learners' knowledge of a topic in history. *American Educational Research Journal, 27*(4), 688–726.

McKeown, M. G., Beck, J. L., Sinatra, G. M., & Loxterman, J. A. (1992). The contribution of prior knowledge and coherent text to comprehension. *Reading Research Quarterly, 27*, 78–93.

McLeskey, J., & Waldron, N. L. (1996). Responses to questions teachers and administrators frequently ask about inclusive school programs. *Phi Delta Kappan, 78*, 150–156.

McNulty, B. A., Connolly, T. R., Wilson, P. G., & Brewer, R. D. (1996). LRE policy: The leadership challenge. *Remedial and Special Education, 17*, 158–167.

Mead, J. F. (1995). Including students with disabilities in parental choice programs: The challenge of meaningful choice. *West's Education Law Quarterly, 4*, 570–603.

Meichenbaum, D. (1977). *Cognitive behavior modification: An integrative approach.* New York: Plenum.

Mendaglio, S., & Pyryt, M. C. (1995). Self-concept of gifted students: Assessment-based intervention. *Teaching Exceptional Children, 27*(3), 40–45.

Mercer, C. D. (1997). *Students with learning disabilities* (5th ed.). Columbus, OH: Merrill.

Mercer, C. D., Lane, H. B., Jordan, L., Allsopp, D. H., & Eisele, M. R. (1996). Empowering teachers and students with instructional choices in inclusive settings. *Remedial and Special Education, 17*, 226–236.

Mercure, C. M. (1993). Project Achievement: An after-school success story. *Principal, 73*(1), 48–50.

Mike, D. G. (1996). Internet in the schools: A literacy perspective. *Journal of Adolescent and Adult Literacy, 40*(1), 4–13.

Miller, R. V. (1956). Social status of socioempathic differences. *Exceptional Children, 23*, 114–119.

Mills v. Board of Education of District of Columbia, 348 F. Supp. 866 (D.D.C. 1972).

Miranda, A., & Guerrero, M. (1986). The funny farola. In *Adventures* (pp. 42–53). Boston: Houghton Mifflin.

Montgomery County Public Schools. (1985). *Blueprint for study strategies.* Rockville, MD: Board of Education of Montgomery County.

Moody, J. D., & Gifford, V. D. (1990). *The effect of grouping by formal reasoning ability, formal reasoning ability levels, group size, and gender on achievement in laboratory chemistry.* (ERIC Document Reproduction Service No. ED 326 443).

Moore, D. W., Readance, J. E., & Rickleman, R. (1989). *Prereading activities for content-area reading and learning* (2nd ed.). Newark, DE: International Reading Association.

Morehouse, J. A., & Albright, L. (1991). Training trends and needs of paraprofessionals in transition service delivery agencies. *Teacher Education and Special Education, 14*, 248–256.

Morgan, D. P. (1993). Substance use prevention and students with behavioral disorders: Guidelines for school professionals. *Journal of Emotional and Behavioral Disorders, 1*, 170–178.

Morris, R. J. (1985). *Behavior modification with exceptional children: Principles and practices.* Glenview, IL: Scott, Foresman.

Morse, W. C. (1987). Introduction to the special issue. *Teaching Exceptional Children, 19*(4), 4–6.

Mosteller, F., Light, R., & Sachs, J. (1996). Sustained inquiry in education: Lessons from skill grouping and class size. *Harvard Educational Review, 66*(4), 797–828.

Munk, D., & Bursuck, W. D. (1998). Report card grading adaptations for students with disabilities. *Intervention in School and Clinic, 33*(5), 306–308.

Nation, K., & Hulme, C. (1997). Phonemic segmentation, not onset-rime segmentation, predicts early reading and spelling skills. *Reading Research Quarterly, 32*(2), 154–167.

National Association of State Directors of Special Education. (1997). *Comparison of key issues: Current law and 1997 IDEA amendments.* Alexandria, VA: Author.

National Committee to Prevent Child Abuse. (1997, July). *Child abuse and neglect: Statistics.* <http://www.childabuse.org/rsch2/html>: Author.

National Council of Teachers of Mathematics. (1990). *Mathematics for the young child.* Reston, VA: Author.

National Information Center for Children and Youth with Disabilities. (1991). The education of children and youth with special needs: What do the laws say? *NICHCY News Digest, 1*(1), 1–15.

National Information Center for Children and Youth with Disabilities. (1993). Including special education in the school community. *NICHCY News Digest, 2*(2), 1–7.

Neel, R. S., & Cessna, K. K. (1993). Behavioral intent: Instructional content for students with behavior disorders. In K. K. Cessna (Ed.), *Instructionally differentiated programming: A needs-based approach for students with behavior disorders* (pp. 41–50). Denver, CO: Colorado Department of Education.

Nelson, J. R. (1996). Designing schools to meet the needs of students who exhibit disruptive behavior. *Journal of Emotional and Behavioral Disorders, 4*, 147–161.

Oakland, T. (1981). Nonbiased assessment of minority group children. *Exceptional Education Quarterly, 1*(3), 31–46.

Oberti v. Board of Education of the Borough of Clementon School District, 789 F. Supp. 1322, 75 Ed.Law Per. 259 (D. N. J. 1992), 801 F. Supp. 1393 (D. N. J. 1992), aff'd 995 F.2d 1204, 83 Ed.Law Rep. 1009 (3d Cir. 1993): 89, 111, 112, 134, 135, 236.

Ogle, D. M. (1986). K. W. L.: A teaching model that develops active reading of expository text. *The Reading Teacher, 39*, 565.

Okolo, C. M. (1993). Computers and individuals with mild disabilities. In J. Lindsey (Ed.), *Computers and exceptional individuals* (pp. 111–141). Austin, TX: PRO-ED.

Olson, M., & Gee, T. C. (1991). Content reading: Instruction in the primary grades: Perceptions and strategies. *The Reading Teacher, 45*(4), 298–307.

O'Neil, J. (1992). On tracking and individual differences: A conversation with Jeannie Oakes. *Educational Leadership, 50*(1), 18–21.

O'Neill, D. K., Wagner, R., & Gomez, L. M. (1996). Online mentors: Experimenting in science class. *Educational Leadership, 54*(3), 39–42.

O'Reilly, M. F., & Glynn, D. (1995). Using a process social skills training approach with adolescents with mild intellectual disabilities in a high school setting. *Education and Training in Mental Retardation and Developmental Disabilities, 31*, 187–198.

Ornstein, A. C. (1990). *Strategies for effective teaching.* New York: Harper and Row.

Orr, L. E., Craig, G. P., Best, J., Borland, A., Holland, D., Knode, H., Lehman, A., Mathewson, C., Miller, M., & Pequignot, M. (1997). Exploring developmental disabilities through literature: An annotated bibliography. *Teaching Exceptional Children, 29*(6), 14–15.

Osborne, A. G. (1996). *Legal issues in special education.* Boston: Allyn and Bacon.

Overton, T. (1996). *Assessment in special education* (2nd ed.). New York: Macmillan.

Paine, S. C., Radicchi, J., Rosellini, L. C., Deutchman, L., & Darch, C. B. (1983). *Structuring your classroom for academic success.* Champaign, IL: Research Press.

Palincsar, A., & Brown, A. (1988). Teaching and practicing thinking skills to promote comprehension in the context of group problem solving. *Remedial and Special Education, 9*(1), 53–59.

Palma, G. M. (1994). Toward a positive and effective teacher and paraprofessional relationship. *Rural Special Education Quarterly, 13*(4), 46–48.

Patton, J. R. (1994). Practical recommendations for using homework with students with disabilities. *Journal of Learning Disabilities, 27*(9), 570–578.

Patton, J. R., Payne, J. S., & Beirne-Smith, M. (1986). *Mental retardation* (2nd ed.). Columbus, OH: Merrill.

Patton, J. R., Payne, J. S., Kauffman, J. M., Brown, G. B., & Payne, R. A. (1991). *Exceptional children in focus* (5th ed.). Englewood Cliffs, NJ: Prentice-Hall.

Pauk, W. (1989). *How to study in college.* Boston: Houghton Mifflin.

Paulson, F., Paulson, P., & Meyer, C. (1991). What makes a portfolio a portfolio? *Educational Leadership, 48*(5), 60–63.

Pearson, P. D. (1996). Reclaiming the center. In M. F. Graves, P. van den Broek, & B. M. Taylor (Eds.), *The first R: Every child's right to read* (pp. 259–274). New York: Teachers College Press.

Pearson, S. (1996). Child abuse among children with disabilities: Implications for special educators. *Teaching Exceptional Children, 29*(1), 14–37.

Peckham, V. C. (1993). Children with cancer in the classroom. *Teaching Exceptional Children, 26*(1), 26–32.

Pennington, B. F. (1995). Genetics of learning disabilities. *Journal of Child Neurology, 10*(Suppl. 1), 69–77.

Pennsylvania Association for Retarded Children v. Commonwealth of Pennsylvania, 334 F. Supp. 1257 (E.D. Pa. 1971); 343 F. Supp. 279 (E.D. Pa. 1972).

Pertsch, C. F. (1936). *A comparative study of the progress of subnormal pupils in the grades and in special classes.* New York: Teacher's College, Columbia University, Bureau of Publications.

Peterson, R. L. & Ishii-Jordan, S. (1994). *Multicultural issues in the education of students with behavior disorders.* Cambridge, MA: Brookline Books.

Phillips, V., & McCullough, L. (1990). Consultation-based programming: Instituting the collaborative ethic in schools. *Exceptional Children, 56*, 291–304.

Polloway, E. A., Bursuck, W. D., Jayanthi, M., Epstein, M. H., & Nelson, J. S. (1996). Treatment acceptability: Determining appropriate interventions within inclusive classrooms. *Intervention in School and Clinic, 31*(3), 133–144.

Polloway, E. A., Epstein, M. H., Bursuck, W. D., Jayanthi, M., & Cumblad, C. (1994). Homework practices of general education teachers. *Journal of Learning Disabilities, 27*(8), 100–109.

Poplin, M. S. (1988). Holistic/constructive principles of the teaching/learning process: Implications for the field of learning disabilities. *Journal of Learning Disabilities, 21*, 401–416.

Poteet, J. A., Choate, J. S., & Stewart, S. C. (1993). Performance assessment and special education: Practices and prospects. *Focus on Exceptional Children, 26*(1), 1–20.

Pratt, C., & Moreno, S. J. (1994). Including students with autism in typical school settings. In F. LaRoy and J. Streng (Eds.), *A new dawn of awakening: Proceedings of the 1994 conference* (pp. 143–146). Arlington, TX: Future Education.

Prigatano, G. P. (1992). Personality disturbances associated with traumatic brain injury. *Journal of Consulting and Clinical Psychology, 60*, 360–368.

Pugach, M. C., & Johnson, L. J. (1995). *Collaborative practitioners, collaborative schools.* Denver, CO: Love.

Putnam, J. W. (1993a). *Cooperative learning and strategies for inclusion.* Baltimore, MD: Brookes.

Putnam, J. W. (1993b). The process of cooperative learning. In J. W. Putnam (Ed.), *Cooperative learning and strategies for inclusion: Celebrating diversity in the classroom* (pp.15–40). Baltimore, MD: Brookes.

Putnam, J. W., Rynders, J. E., Johnson, R. T., & Johnson, D. W. (1989). Collaborative skill instruction for promoting interactions between mentally handicapped and nonhandicapped children. *Exceptional Children, 55*, 550–557.

Putnam, L., & Wesson, C. (1990). The teacher's role in teaching content-area information. *LD Forum, 16*(1), 55–60.

Qin, Z., Johnson, D. W., & Johnson, R. T. (1995). Cooperative versus competitive efforts and problem solving. *Review of Educational Research, 65*, 129–143.

Ramirez-Smith, C. (1995). Stopping the cycle of failure: The Comer Model. *Educational Leadership, 52*(5), 14–15.

Ramsey, W. L., Gabriel, L. A., McGuirk, J. F., Phillips, C. R., & Watenpaugh, T. R. (1983). *General Science.* New York: Holt, Rinehart, & Winston.

Rankin, J. L., & Aksamit, D. L. (1994). Perceptions of elementary, junior high, and high school student assistant team coordinators, team members, and teachers. *Journal of Educational and Psychological Consultation, 5*, 229–256.

Raphael, T. E., Kirschner, B. W., & Englert, C. S. (1986). *Text structure instruction within process writing classrooms: A manual for instruction* (Occasional Paper No. 104). East Lansing, MI: Michigan State University, Institute for Research on Teaching.

Rappaport, J. (1982/1983). Effects of dietary substances in children. *Journal of Psychiatric Research, 17*, 187–191.

Ratey, J. J., Grandin, T., & Miller, A. (1992). Defense behavior and coping in an autistic savant: The story of Temple Grandin, Ph.D. *Psychiatry, 55*, 382–391.

Raynes, M., Snell, M., & Sailor, W. (1991). A fresh look at categorical programs for children with special needs. *Phi Delta Kappan, 73*, 326–331.

Raywid, M. A. (1993). Finding time for collaboration. *Educational Leadership, 51*(1), 30–34.

Reetz, L., & Rasmussen, T. (1988). Arithmetic mind joggers. *Academic Therapy, 24*(1), 79–82.

Reeve, R. E. (1990). ADHD: Facts and fallacies. *Intervention in School and Clinic, 26*(2), 70–78.

Reid, R. (1996). Research in self-monitoring with students with learning disabilities: The present, the prospects, the pitfalls. *Journal of Learning Disabilities, 29*(3), 317–331.

Reid, R., & Katsiyannis, A. (1995). Attention-deficit/hyperactivity disorder and Section 504. *Remedial and Special Education, 16*, 44–52.

Reid, R., Maag, J. W., & Vasa, S. F. (1994). Attention deficit hyperactivity disorder as a disability category: A critique. *Exceptional Children, 60*, 98–214.

Reinhiller, N. (1996). Coteaching : New variations on a not-so-new practice. *Teacher Education and Special Education, 19*, 34–38.

Rekrut, M. D. (1994). Peer and cross-age tutoring: The lessons of research. *Journal of Reading, 37*, 356–362.

Reyes, M. L., & Molner, L. A. (1991). Instructional strategies for second-language learners in the content areas. *Journal of Reading, 35*(2), 96–103.

Reynolds, M. C., & Heistad, D. (1997). 20/20 analysis: Estimating school effectiveness in serving students at the margin. *Exceptional Children, 63*, 439–449.

Riccio, C. A., Hynd, G. W., Cohen, M. J., & Gonzalez, J. J. (1993). Neurological basis of attention deficit hyperactivity disorder. *Exceptional Children, 60*, 118–124.

Roberts, R., & Mather, N. (1995a). Legal protections for individuals with learning disabilities: The IDEA, Section 504, and the ADA. *Learning Disabilities Research and Practice, 10*(3), 160–168.

Roberts, R., & Mather, N. (1995b). The return of students with learning disabilities to regular classrooms: A sellout? *Learning Disabilities Research & Practice, 10,* 46–58.

Robinson, S., & Smith, J. (1981). Listening skills: Teaching learning disabled students to be better listeners. *Focus on Exceptional Children, 13*(8), 1–15.

Roblyer, M. D., Edwards, J., & Havriluk, M. A. (1997). *Integrating educational technology into teaching.* Columbus, OH: Merrill.

Rodger, S. (1995). Individual education plans revisited: A review of the literature. *International Journal of Disability, Development, and Education, 42,* 221–239.

Rodgers-Rhyme, A., & Volpiansky, P. (1991). *PARTNERS in problem solving staff development program: Participant guide.* Madison, WI: Wisconsin Department of Public Instruction.

Rogers, K. (1986). Do the gifted think and learn differently?: A review of recent research and its implications. *Journal for the Education of the Gifted, 10,* 17–40.

Rojewski, J. W., Pollard, R. R., & Meers, G. D. (1992). Grading secondary vocational students with disabilities. *Exceptional Children, 59*(1), 68–76.

Rosenfield, S. A., & Gravois, T. A. (1996). *Instructional consultation teams: Collaborating for change.* New York: Guilford Press.

Rosenshine, B., & Meister, C. (1992). The use of scaffolds for teaching higher-level cognitive strategies. *Educational Leadership, 49,* 26–33.

Rosenshine, B., & Stevens, R. (1986). Teaching functions. In M. C. Wittrock (Ed.), *Handbook of research on teaching* (pp. 376–391). New York: Macmillan.

Ross, R., & Kurtz, R. (1993). Making manipulatives work: A strategy for success. *Arithmetic Teacher, 40*(5), 254–257.

Rothman, H. R., & Cosden, M. (1995). The relationship between self-perception of a learning disability and achievement, self-concept and social support. *Learning Disability Quarterly, 20,* 203–212.

Rothstein, LL. F. (1995). *Special education law* (2nd ed.). New York: Longman.

Runge, A., Walker, J., & Shea, T. M. (1975). A passport to positive parent–teacher communication. *Teaching Exceptional Children, 7*(3), 91–92.

Ryndak, D. L., Downing, J. E., Morrison, A. P., & Williams, L. J. (1996). Parents' perceptions of educational settings and services for children with moderate or severe disabilities. *Remedial and Special Education, 17,* 106–118.

Sadker, M., Sadker, D., & Klein, S. (1991). The issue of gender in elementary and secondary education. In G. Grant (Ed.), *Review of research in education* (pp. 269–334). Washington, DC: American Educational Research Association.

Safran, S. P., & Safran, J. S. (1996). Intervention assistance programs and prereferral teams: Directions for the twentieth-first century. *Remedial and Special Education, 17,* 363–369.

Sailor, W. (1991). Special education in the restructured school. *Remedial and Special Education, 12,* 8–22.

Sale, P., & Carey, D. M. (1995). The sociometric status of students with disabilities in a full-inclusion school. *Exceptional Children, 62,* 6–19.

Salend, S. J., & Taylor, L. (1993). Working with families: A cross-cultural perspective. *Remedial and Special Education, 14*(5), 25–32, 39.

Salend, S. J., Dorney, J. A., & Mazo, M. (1997). The roles of bilingual special educators in creating inclusive classrooms. *Remedial and Special Education, 18,* 54–64.

Salvia, J., & Ysseldyke, J. (1995). *Assessment in special and remedial education* (6th ed.). Boston: Houghton Mifflin.

Sapon-Shevin, M. (1994). Why gifted students belong in inclusive schools. *Educational Leadership, 52*(4), 64–68, 70.

Sapon-Shevin, M. (1996). Full inclusion as disclosing tablet: Revealing the flaws in our present system. *Theory into Practice, 35*(1), 35–41.

Sardo-Brown, D., & Hinson, S. (1995). Classroom teachers' perceptions of the implementation and effects of full inclusion. *ERS Spectrum, 13*(2), 18–24.

Savage, R. C., & Wolcott, G. F. (1994). *Educational dimensions of acquired brain injury* (pp. 3–12). Austin, TX: PRO-ED.

Savoie, J. M., & Hughes, A. S. (1994). Problem-based learning as classroom solution. *Educational Leadership, 52*(3), 54–57.

Sawyer, R. J., McLaughlin, M. J., & Winglee, M. (1994). Is integration of students with disabilities happening? *Remedial and Special Education, 15,* 204–215.

Schaps, E., & Solomon, D. (1990). Schools and classrooms as caring communities. *Educational Leadership, 48*(3), 38–42.

Scheerenberger, R. C. (1983). *A history of mental retardation.* Baltimore, MD: Brookes.

Schloss, P. J., & Smith, M. A. (1994). *Applied behavior analysis in the classroom.* Boston: Allyn and Bacon.

Schuller, C. F. (1982). Using instructional resources and technology. In D. E. Orlosky (Ed.), *Introduction to education* (pp. 400–429). Columbus, OH: Merrill.

Schumaker, J. B., & Deshler, D. D. (1988). Implementing the Regular Education Initiative in secondary schools: A different ball game. *Journal of Learning Disabilities, 21*(1), 36–42.

Schumaker, J. B., Deshler, D. D., & Denton, P. (1984). *The learning strategies curriculum: The paraphrasing strategy.* Lawrence, KS: University of Kansas.

Schunk, D. (1989). Self-efficacy and cognitive achievement. Implications for students with learning disabilities. *Journal of Learning Disabilities, 22*(1), 14–22.

Scott, P. B., & Raborn, D. T. (1996). Realizing the gifts of diversity among students with learning disabilities. *LD Forum, 21*(2), 10–18.

Scruggs, T., & Mastropieri, M. (1988). Are learning disabled students "test-wise"? A review of recent research. *Learning Disabilities Focus, 3*(2), 87–97.

Scruggs, T. E., & Mastropieri, M. A. (1992). Effective mainstreaming strategies for mildly handicapped students. *Elementary School Journal, 92,* 389–409.

Scruggs, T., & Mastropieri, M. (1994). The construction of scientific knowledge by students with mild disabilities. *Journal of Special Education, 28,* 307–321.

Senesh, L. (1973). *The American way of life* (p. 149). Chicago: Science Research Associates.

Sharan, S., Kussell, P., Hertz-Lazarowitz, R., Bejarano, Y., Raviv, S., & Sharan, Y. (1984). *Cooperative learning in the classroom: Research in desegregated schools.* Hillsdale, NJ: Erlbaum.

Shaywitz, S. E., Escobar, M. D., Shaywitz, B. A., Fletcher, J. M., & Makuch, R. (1992). Evidence that dyslexia may represent the lower tail of a normal distribution of reading ability. *New England Journal of Medicine, 326,* 145–150.

Shea, T. M., & Bauer, A. M. (1991). *Parents and teachers of children with exceptionalities: A handbook for collaboration* (2nd ed.). Boston: Allyn and Bacon.

Shea, T. M., & Bauer, A. M. (1994). *Learners with disabilities: A social systems perspective of special education.* Madison, WI: Brown & Benchmark.

Sheinker, J., & Sheinker, A. (1989). *Meta-cognitive approach to study strategies.* Rockville, MD: Aspen.

Sheridan, S. M., Welch, M., & Orme, S. F. (1996). Is consultation effective?: A review of outcome research. *Remedial and Special Education, 17,* 341–354.

Shinn, M. R., & Hubbard, D. D. (1992). Curriculum-based measurement and problem-solving assessment: Basic procedures and outcomes. *Focus on Exceptional Children, 5,* 1–20.

Shinn, M. R., Collins, V. L., & Gallagher, S. (1998). Curriculum-based measurement and problem solving assessment. In M. R.

Shinn (Ed.), *Advanced applications of curriculum-based measurement* (pp. 143–174). New York: Guilford Press.

Shriner, J. G., Ysseldyke, J. E., Gorney, D., & Franklin, M. J. (1993). Examining prevalence at the ends of the spectrum: Giftedness and disability. *Remedial and Special Education, 14*(5), 33–39.

Sileo, T. W., Sileo, A. P., & Prater, M. A. (1996). Parent and professional partnerships in special education: Multicultural considerations. *Intervention in School and Clinic, 31,* 145–153.

Silver, L. B. (1987). The magic cure: A review of the current controversial approaches for treating learning disabilities. *Journal of Learning Disabilities, 20*(8), 498–504.

Silver, L. (1995). Controversial therapies. *Journal of Child Neurology, 10*(Suppl. 1), 596–599.

Simich-Dudgeon, C., McCreedy, L., & Schleppegrell, M. (1988/1989). *Helping limited English proficient children communicate in the classroom: A handbook for teachers.* Washington, DC: National Clearinghouse for Bilingual Education.

Simpson, R. L. (1995). Children and youth with autism in an age of reform: A perspective on current issues. *Behavioral Disorders, 21,* 7–20.

Simpson, R. L., & Myles, B. S. (1990). The general education collaboration: A model for successful mainstreaming. *Focus on Exceptional Children, 23*(4), 1–10.

Siperstein, G. N., Leffert, J. S., & Widaman, K. (1996). Social behavior and the social acceptance and rejection of children with mental retardation. *Education and Training in Mental Retardation and Developmental Disabilities, 31,* 271–281.

Sirvis, B. (1988). Physical disabilities. In E. L. Meyen & T. M. Skrtic (Eds.), *Exceptional children and youth: An introduction* (3rd ed., pp. 387–411). Denver, CO: Love.

Skrtic, T. M., Sailor, W., & Gee, K. (1996). Voice, collaboration, and inclusion: Democratic themes in educational and social reform initiatives. *Remedial and Special Education, 17,* 142–157.

Slavin, R. E. (1994). *Cooperative learning* (2nd ed.). Boston: Allyn and Bacon.

Slavin, R. E., Madden, N. A., Karweit, N. L., Livermon, B. J., & Dolan, L. (1989). Can every child learn? An evaluation of "Success for All" in an urban elementary school. *Journal of Negro Education, 58,* 357–366.

Slavin, R. E., Madden, N. A., Dolan, L. J., Wasik, B. A., Ross, S. M., & Smith, L. J. (1994). "Whenever and wherever we choose:" the replication of "Success for All." *Phi Delta Kappan, 75,* 639–647.

Smith, C. R. (1994). *Learning disabilities: The interaction of learner, task, and setting.* Boston: Allyn and Bacon.

Smith, D. D., & Luckasson, R. (1995). *Introduction to special education: Teaching in an age of challenge* (2nd ed.). Boston: Allyn and Bacon.

Smith, D. D., & Rivera, D. M. (1993). *Effective discipline* (2nd edition). Austin, TX: PRO-ED.

Smith, M. A., & Mirsa, A. (1992). A comprehensive management system for students in regular classrooms. *Elementary School Journal, 92*(3), 354–371.

Smith, S. (1980). *No easy answers.* New York: Bantam Books.

Smith, S. B., Simmons, D. C., & Kameenui, F. (1995). *Phonological awareness: Curricular and instructional implications for diverse learners.* Technical Report No. 22. Eugene, OR: National Center to Improve the Tools of Educators.

Smith, S. W. (1990). Individualized education programs (IEPs) in special education—from intent to acquiescence. *Exceptional Children, 57,* 6–14.

Snider, V. E. (1995). A primer on phonemic awareness: What it is, why it's important, and how to teach it. *School Psychology Review, 24*(3), 443–455.

Snider, V. E. (1997). Transfer of decoding skills to a literature basal. *Learning Disabilities Research & Practice, 12*(1), 54–62.

Snow, J., & Forest, M. (1987). Circles. In M. Forest (Ed.), *More education integration* (pp. 169–176). Downsview, Ontario: G. Allan Roeher Institute.

Snyder, T. D. (1993). Trends in education. *Principal, 73*(1), 9–14.

Solomon, D., Watson, M., Schaps, E., Battistich, V., & Solomon, J. (1990). Cooperative learning as part of a comprehensive classroom program designed to promote prosocial development. In S. Sharan (Ed.), *Cooperative learning.* New York: Praeger.

Sontag, J. C., & Schacht, R. (1994). An ethnic comparison of parent participating and information needs in early intervention. *Exceptional Children, 60,* 422–433.

Sparks, D., & Sparks, G. M. (1984). *Effective teaching for higher achievement.* Alexandria, VA: Association for Supervision and Curriculum Development.

Sprague, J. R., & Horner, R. H. (1990). Easy does it: Preventing challenging behaviors. *Teaching Exceptional Children, 23*(1), 13–15.

Stainback, S., & Stainback, W. (1988). Educating students with severe disabilities in regular classes. *Teaching Exceptional Children, 21*(1), 16–19.

Stainback, S., & Stainback, W. (1992). Schools as inclusive communities. In W. Stainback & S. Stainback (Eds.), *Controversial issues confronting special education: Divergent perspectives* (pp. 29–44). Boston: Allyn and Bacon.

Stainback, S., Stainback, W., East, K., & Sapon-Shevin, M. (1994). A commentary on inclusion and the development of a positive self-identity by people with disabilities. *Exceptional Children, 60,* 486–490.

Stainback, S., Stainback, W., & Jackson, H. J. (1992). Toward inclusive classrooms. In S. Stainback & W. Stainback (Eds.), *Curriculum considerations in inclusive classrooms: Facilitating learning for all students* (pp. 3–17). Baltimore, MD: Brookes.

Stainback, W., Stainback, S., & Wilkinson, A. (1992). Encouraging peer supports and friendships. *Teaching Exceptional Children, 24*(2), 6–11.

Stainback, W., Stainback, S., & Stefanich, G. (1996). Learning together in inclusive classrooms: What about curriculum? *Teaching Exceptional Children, 28*(3), 14–19.

Stainback, W., Stainback, S., Etscheidt, S., & Doud, J. (1986). A nonintrusive intervention for acting-out behavior. *Teaching Exceptional Children, 19*(1), 38–41.

Stein, M., Silbert, J., & Carnine, D. (1997). *Designing effective mathematics instruction: A direct instruction approach* (3rd ed., pp. 216–254). Columbus, OH: Merrill.

Stephen, V. P., Varble, M. E., & Taitt, H. (1993). Instructional and organizational change to meet minority and at risk students' needs. *Journal of Staff Development, 14*(4), 40–43.

Stevens, L. J., & Price, M. (1992). Meeting the challenge of educating children at risk. *Phi Delta Kappan, 74,* 18–23.

Strang, J. D., & Rourke, B. P. (1985). Arithmetic disability subtypes: The neuropsychological significance of specific arithmetical impairment in childhood. In B. P. Rourke (Ed.), *Neuropsychology of learning disabilities* (pp. 167–182). New York: Guilford Press.

Stump, C. S., & Wilson, C. (1996). Collaboration: Making it happen. *Intervention in School and Clinic, 31,* 310–312.

Sugai, G., & Lewis, T. J. (1996). Preferred and promising practices for social skills instruction. *Focus on Exceptional Children, 29*(4), 1–24.

Swanson, J. M., Cantwell, D., Lerner, M., McBurnett, K., Pfiffner, L., & Kotkin, R. (1992). Treatment of ADHD: Beyond medication. *Beyond Behavior, 4*(1), 13–16, 18–22.

Szetela, W., & Nicol, C. (1992). Evaluating problem solving in mathematics. *Educational Leadership, 49*(8), 42–45.

Tateyama-Sniezek, K. (1990). Cooperative learning: Does it improve the academic achievement of students with handicaps? *Exceptional Children, 56,* 426–437.

Taylor, R. L. (1993). *Assessment of exceptional students* (3rd ed.). Boston: Allyn and Bacon.

Taylor, R. L., Richards, S. B., Goldstein, P. A., & Schilit, J. (1997). Teacher perceptions of inclusive settings. *Teaching Exceptional Children, 29*(3), 50–54.

Terman, L. (1925). *Genetic studies of genius (Vol. I): Mental and physical traits of 1000 gifted children.* Stanford, CA: Stanford University Press.

Thorson, S. (1996). The missing link: Students discuss school discipline. *Focus on Exceptional Children, 29*(3), 1–12.

Thousand, J. S., & Villa, R. A. (1990). Strategies for educating learners with severe disabilities within their local home schools and communities. *Focus on Exceptional Children, 23*(3), 1–24.

Thurlow, M. L., Ysseldyke, J. E., & Silverstein, B. (1995). Testing accommodations for students with disabilities. *Remedial and Special Education, 16*(5), 260–270.

Tindal, G. A., & Marston, D. B. (1990). *Classroom-based assessment: Evaluating instructional outcomes.* Columbus, OH: Merrill.

Tobin, T., Sugai, G., & Colvin, G. (1996). Patterns in middle school discipline records. *Journal of Emotional and Behavioral Disorders, 4*, 82–94.

Todd, L. P., & Curti, M. (1982). *Rise of the American nation.* Orlando, FL: Harcourt Brace Jovanovich.

Torgesen, J. (1991). Learning disabilities: Historical and conceptual issues. In B. Wong (Ed.), *Learning about learning disabilities* (pp. 3–39). San Diego, CA: Academic Press.

Trueba, H. T., Moll, L. C., & Diaz, S. (1982). *Improving the functional writing of bilingual secondary school students* (Final Report; NIE 400–81–0023). Washington, DC: National Institute of Education.

Tucker, B. F., & Colson, S. E. (1992). Traumatic brain injury: An overview of school re-entry. *Intervention in School and Clinic, 27*, 198–206.

Tucker, J. A. (1985). Curriculum-based assessment: An introduction. *Exceptional Children, 52*, 199–204.

U.S. Department of Education. (1991). *Thirteenth annual report to Congress on the implementation of the Individuals with Disabilities Education Act.* Washington, DC: Author.

U.S. Department of Education. (1996). *To assure the free appropriate public education of all children with disabilities: Eighteenth annual report to Congress on the implementation of The Individuals with Disabilities Education Act.* Washington, DC: Author.

U.S. Department of Justice, Civil Rights Division, Coordination and Review Section. (1990). *The American with Disabilities Act requirements: Fact sheet.* Washington, DC: Author.

Udvari-Solner, A., & Thousand, J. S. (1996). Creating a responsive curriculum for inclusive schools. *Remedial and Special Education, 17*, 182–192.

United Cerebral Palsy Associations. (n.d.). *Cerebral palsy: Facts and figures.* Washington, DC: Author.

Vacc, N. N., & Cannon, S. J. (1991). Cross-age tutoring in mathematics: Sixth graders helping students who are moderately handicapped. *Education and Training in Mental Retardation, 26*, 89–97.

Vacca, R. T., & Vacca, J. L. (1986). *Content area reading* (2nd ed.). Boston: Little, Brown.

Van Tassel-Baska, J., Patton, J. M., & Prillaman, D. (1991). *Gifted youth at risk: A report of a national study.* Reston, VA: Council for Exceptional Children.

Vandercook, T., York, J., & Forest, M. (1989). The McGill Action Planning System (MAPS): A strategy for building the vision. *Journal of the Association for Persons with Severe Handicaps, 14*(3), 205–218.

VanGundy, A. B. (1988). *Techniques of structured problem solving* (2nd edition). New York: Van Nostrand Reinhold.

VanRiper, C., & Emerick, L. (1984). *Speech correction: An introduction to speech pathology and audiology.* Englewood Cliffs, NJ: Prentice-Hall.

Vasa, F. (1981). Alternative procedures for grading handicapped students in the secondary schools. *Education Unlimited, 16*–23.

Vaughn, S., & Schumm, J. S. (1995). Responsible inclusion for students with learning disabilities. *Journal of Learning Disabilities, 28*, 264–270, 290.

Vaughn, S., Schumm, J. S., Jallad, B., Slusher, J., & Saumell, L. (1996). Teachers' views of inclusion. *Learning disabilities: Research & Practice, 11*, 96–106.

Vergason, G. A., & Anderegg, M. L. (1992). Preserving the least restrictive environment. In W. Stainback & S. Stainback (Eds.), *Controversial issues confronting special education: Divergent perspectives* (pp. 45–54). Boston: Allyn and Bacon.

Villa, R. A., Thousand, J. S., Meyers, H., & Nevin, A. (1996). Teacher and administrator perceptions of heterogeneous education. *Exceptional Children, 63*, 29–45.

Voeltz, L. J., Hemphill, N. J., Brown, S., Kishi, G., Klein, R., Fruehling, R., Collie, J., Levy, G., & Kube, C. (1983). *The special friends program: A trainer's manual for integrated school settings.* Honolulu, HI: University of Hawaii, Department of Special Education.

Voix, R. G. (1968). *Evaluating reading and study skills in the secondary classroom: A guide for content teachers* (pp. 46–48). Newark, DE: International Reading Association.

Voltz, D. L., & Elliott, R. N. (1990). Resource room teacher roles in promoting interaction with regular educators. *Teacher Education and Special Education, 13*, 160–166.

Wade, S. L., Taylor, H. G., Drotar, D., Stancin, T., & Yeates, K. O. (1996). Childhood traumatic brain injury: Initial impact on the family. *Journal of Learning Disabilities, 29*, 652–661.

Wadsworth, D. E., & Knight, D. (1996). Paraprofessionals: The bridge to successful full inclusion. *Intervention in School and Clinic, 31*, 166–171.

Walker, J. E., & Shea, T. M. (1995). *Behavior management: A practical approach for educators* (6th ed., pp. 80–115). Englewood Cliffs, NJ: Merrill.

Wallis, C. (1994, July 18). Life in overdrive. *Time*, pp. 42–50.

Wallis, S. (1993, September). Multicultural teaching: Meeting the challenges that arise in practice. *Curriculum Update*, pp. 1–8.

Walther-Thomas, C., Bryant, M., & Land, S. (1996). Planning for effective co-teaching: The key to successful inclusion. *Remedial and Special Education, 17*, 255–265.

Wang, M. C., & Reynolds, M. C. (1996). Progressive inclusion: Meeting new challenges in special education. *Theory into Practice, 35*(1), 20–25.

Wang, M. C., Reynolds, M. C., & Walberg, H. J. (1988). Integrating the children of the second system. *Phi Delta Kappan, 70*, 248–251.

Webber, J., & Scheuermann, B. (1991). Accentuate the positive . . . eliminate the negative! *Teaching Exceptional Children, 24*(1), 13–19.

Wenz-Gross, M., & Siperstein, G. N. (1996). The social world of preadolescents with mental retardation: Social support, family environment and adjustment. *Education and Training in Mental Retardation and Developmental Disabilities, 31*, 177–187.

Wenz-Gross, M., & Siperstein, G. N. (1997). Importance of social support in the adjustment of children with learning problems. *Exceptional Children, 63*, 183–195.

Wetzel, K. (1996). Speech-recognizing computers: A written communication tool for students with learning disabilities? *Journal of Learning Disabilities, 29*(4), 371–380.

Wheelock, A. (1992). The case for untracking. *Educational Leadership, 50*(2), 6–10.

Wiggins, G. (1992). Creating tests worth taking. *Educational Leadership, 49*(8), 26–33.

Wigle, S. E., & Wilcox, D. J. (1996). Inclusion: Criteria for the preparation of education personnel. *Remedial and Special Education, 17*, 323–328.

Williams, J. N. (1986). *Accommodations for secondary learning disabled/mainstreamed students on teacher-made tests.* Unpublished manuscript, Wheaton High School, Wheaton, MD.

Williams, W., & Fox, T. J. (1996). Planning for inclusion: A practical process. *Teaching Exceptional Children, 28*(3), 6–13.

Winebrenner, S. (1992). *Teaching gifted kids in the regular classroom: Strategies and techniques every teacher can use to meet the academic needs of the gifted and talented.* Minneapolis, MN: Free Spirit.

Wisniewski, L., & Alper, S. (1994). Including students with severe disabilities in general education settings. *Remedial and Special Education, 15*(1), 4–13.

Witt, J. C., Gresham, F. M., & Noell, G. H. (1996). What's behavioral about behavioral consultation? *Journal of Educational and Psychological Consultation, 7,* 327–344.

Wolery, M., Werts, M. G., Caldwell, N. K., Snyder, E. D., & Lisowski, L. (1995). Experienced teachers' perceptions of resources and supports for inclusion. *Education and Training in Mental Retardation and Developmental Disabilities, 30,* 15–26.

Wong, B. (1996). *The ABCs of learning disabilities.* San Diego, CA: Academic Press.

Wood, J. W., Miederhoff, J. W., & Ulschmid, B. (1989). Adapting test construction for mainstreamed social studies students. *Social Education, 53*(1), 46–49.

Wright-Strawderman, C., Lindsey, P., Navarette, L., & Flippo, J. R. (1996). Depression in students with disabilities: Recognition and intervention strategies. *Intervention in School and Clinic, 31*(5), 261–275.

Wyman, S. L. (1993). *How to respond to your culturally diverse student population.* Alexandria, VA: Association for Supervision and Curriculum Development.

Yasutake, D., & Bryan, T. (1995). The influence of induced positive affect on middle school children with and without learning disabilities. *Learning Disabilities: Research and Practice, 10,* 22–37.

Yasutake, D., Bryan, T., & Dohrn, E. (1996). The effects of combining peer tutoring and attribution training on students' perceived self-competence. *Remedial and Special Education, 17,* 83–91.

Yell, M., Clyde, K., & Puyallup, S. K. (1995). School district: The courts, inclusion, and students with behavioral disorders. *Behavioral Disorders, 20*(3), 179–189.

Yell, M. L. (1990). The use of corporal punishment, suspension, expulsion, and timeout with behaviorally disordered students in public schools: Legal considerations. *Behavioral Disorders, 15*(2), 100–109.

Yell, M. L. (1995). The least restrictive environment mandate and the courts: Judicial activism or judicial restraint? *Exceptional Children, 61,* 578–581.

Yell, M. L., & Shriner, J. G. (1997). The IDEA amendments of 1997: Implications for special and general education teachers, administrators, and teacher trainers. *Focus on Exceptional Children, 30*(1), 1–19.

York, J., Vandercook, T., MacDonald, C., Heise-Neff, C., & Caughey, E. (1992). Feedback about integrating middle-school students with severe disabilities in general education classes. *Exceptional Children, 58,* 244–258.

York-Barr, J., Schultz, T., Doyle, M. B., Kronberg, R., & Crossett, S. (1996). Inclusive school in St. Cloud: Perspectives on the process and people. *Remedial and Special Education, 17,* 92–105.

Ysseldyke, J., & Christensen, S. (1987). *TIES: The instructional environment scale.* Austin, TX: PRO-ED.

Ysseldyke, J. E., & Algozzine, B. (1995). *Special education: A practical approach for teachers* (3rd ed.). Geneva, IL: Houghton Mifflin.

Ysseldyke, J. E., Algozzine, B., & Thurlow, M. L. (1992). *Critical issues in special education* (2nd ed.). Boston: Houghton Mifflin.

Zentall, S. S. (1993). Research on the educational implications of attention deficit hyperactivity disorder. *Exceptional Children, 60,* 143–153.

Zetlin, A. G., Padron, M., & Wilson, S. (1996). The experience of five Latin American families with the special education system. *Education and Training in Mental Retardation and Developmental Disabilities, 31*(1), 22–28.

Zirkel, P. A. (1994). De jure: Costly lack of accommodations. *Phi Delta Kappan, 75,* 652–653.

Name Index

510

Subject Index

Text Credits

List on pp. 127 & 130 from "On Selecting 'Considerate' Content Area Textbooks" by B. B. Armbruster and T. H. Anderson, 1988, *Remedial and Special Education, 9*(1), pp. 47–52. Copyright © 1988 by PRO-ED, Inc. Reprinted by permission.

List on pp. 140–141 from "The Use of Scaffolds for Teaching Higher-Level Cognitive Strategies" by B. Rosenshine and C. Meister, 1992, *Educational Leadership, 49*(7), pp. 26–33. Copyright © 1985 by ASCD. All rights reserved.

Extract on p. 309 from *Understanding U.S. History, Vol. I,* by Douglas Carnine, Donald Crawford, Mark Harniss, and Keith Hollenbeck, 1995, p. 207, Eugene: Considerate Publishing/University of Oregon. Used by permission of Considerate Publishing.

Extract on pp. 404–405 reprinted with permission of Prentice Hall, Inc. from *Classroom-Based Assessment: Evaluating Instructional Outcomes* by George A. Tindal and Douglas Marston. Copyright © 1990 by Macmillan College Publishing Company.

Photography Credits

Will Faller: pp. xxii, 20, 31 (top left, top right), 32, 41, 49, 68, 85, 98, 106, 118, 136, 138, 146, 157, 166, 174, 195, 211, 213, 232, 258, 262, 280, 304, 333, 347, 354, 376, 381, 440, 441, 450, 462, 467, 473.

Will Hart: pp. 15. 17, 24, 28, 31 (top center, bottom left, bottom center), 36, 88, 134, 165, 186, 238, 294, 301, 320, 367, 407, 414, 421, 455 (all photos).

Brian Smith: pp. 31 (bottom right), 244, 338, 362, 394, 460.

Stephen Marks: pp. 266, 429.

Image courtesy of Scholastic Entertainment Inc. and the National Captioning Institute. Scholastic, The Magic School Bus® and associated designs and logos are trademarks of Scholastic Inc. © 1998 Scholastic Inc. Based on *The Magic School Bus* book series © Joanna Cole and Bruce Degen. All rights reserved: p. 37.

...n Kermani/Gamma Liaison: p. 111.

...rt Harbison: pp. 220, 252.